Macroeconomics after Kalecki and Keynes

Macroeconomics after Kalecki and Keynes

Post-Keynesian Foundations

Eckhard Hein

Professor of Economics, Institute for International Political Economy, Berlin School of Economics and Law, Germany

EE Edward Elgar
PUBLISHING

Cheltenham, UK • Northampton, MA, USA

Published by
Edward Elgar Publishing Limited
The Lypiatts
15 Lansdown Road
Cheltenham
Glos GL50 2JA
UK

Edward Elgar Publishing, Inc.
William Pratt House
9 Dewey Court
Northampton
Massachusetts 01060
USA

Paperback edition 2024

A catalogue record for this book
is available from the British Library

Library of Congress Control Number: 2022948546

This book is available electronically in the **Elgar**online
Economics subject collection
http://dx.doi.org/10.4337/9781803927282

ISBN 978 1 80392 727 5 (cased)
ISBN 978 1 80392 728 2 (eBook)
ISBN 978 1 0353 3904 4 (paperback)

Printed and bound by CPI Group (UK) Ltd, Croydon, CR0 4YY

Contents

Preface and acknowledgements

Why another book on post-Keynesian economics? Well, because this book tries to close a gap which I see in the post-Keynesian macroeconomics literature. On the one hand, as reviewed in detail in Chapter 2, there are now several books summarising the state of the art in post-Keynesian research. Most importantly, we have Marc Lavoie's (2014) *Post-Keynesian Economics: New Foundations*, of which a revised edition is currently forthcoming, which provides a comprehensive general overview of all the areas of post-Keynesian research. Then there are more specific research-oriented books in the area of distribution and growth, like Robert Blecker's and Mark Setterfield's (2019) *Heterodox Macroeconomics: Models of Demand, Distribution and Growth*. My own *Distribution and Growth after Keynes: A Post-Keynesian Guide* (Hein 2014a) also falls into this category. On the other hand, there are some introductory books, like John E. King's (2015) *Advanced Introduction to Post Keynesian Economics* or Marc Lavoie's (2006a) *Introduction to Post-Keynesian Economics*, together with a range of books with collected essays. All these books have their specific values and merits. However, none of them provides a comprehensive and teachable post-Keynesian macroeconomic model, which includes the main features of post-Keynesian macroeconomics and from which a full macroeconomic policy mix for monetary policy, fiscal policy and wage or incomes policies can be derived. To gradually develop such a model and to derive the related macroeconomic policy mix, for closed and open economies, is therefore the main purpose of this book.

I started the work on such a project when I was still based at the Macroeconomic Policy Institute (IMK) in the Hans Böckler Foundation, Duesseldorf, and spent some time as a visiting professor at the Vienna University of Economics and Business (WU) in 2007 and 2008, working together with Engelbert Stockhammer, then based at the WU. Together, we developed a post-Keynesian alternative model to the 'new consensus macroeconomic' (NCM) model for a closed economy. A comprehensive version of the model was finally published in the *Review of Political Economy* (Hein and Stockhammer 2010).[1] The model includes conflict inflation and an inflation barrier, endogenous income distribution among three classes (rentiers, manager/firm owners, workers), an income generation process built on a Kaleckian distribution and growth model, a discussion of the effectiveness of interest rate policies, several medium- to long-run endogeneity channels of the inflation barrier and the development of a full post-Keynesian macroeconomic policy mix to stabilise such an economy.

Based on this, we published two versions for teaching purposes. There is a simplified version, published in Giuseppe Fontana's and Marc Setterfield's (2009a) *Macroeconomic Theory and Macroeconomic Pedagogy*, which focusses on the inflation generation process and on the medium-run endogeneity of the inflation barrier, but only contains a simplified income generation process in levels with implicit functions and a brief outline of the post-Keynesian macroeconomic policy mix (Hein and Stockhammer 2009b). We thought that this could be used for undergraduate teaching. Then, we have a shortened version, which links the macroeconomic model with post-Keynesian endogenous money theory and focusses on the interaction of inflation generation and income generation as well as the resultant macroeconomic policy mix but omits a detailed presentation of the endogeneity channels of the inflation barrier (Hein and Stockhammer 2011b). This version was published in our jointly edited *Modern Guide to Keynesian Macroeconomics and Economic Policies* (Hein and Stockhammer 2011a), and we thought this version could serve for graduate teaching.

However, when I moved to the Berlin School of Economics and Law in 2009, I learned that the simplified Hein and Stockhammer (2009b) model was still too complicated for under-graduate teaching, because second year students had difficulties in understanding the interaction of inflation and income generation processes. A model with constant prices would have been a better starting point. The Hein and Stockhammer (2011b) model for graduate teaching was also far from perfect, because the students in our interdisciplinary Master International Economics programme only study Kaleckian distribution and growth models in their second semester and thus had difficulties in understanding the income generation process in the mac-roeconomics course of their first semester.

Therefore, in 2016, I started to reformulate the income generation process of the Hein and Stockhammer (2010, 2011b) model in levels, first producing a constant price version, and also extending this from the closed to the open economy. Then I introduced conflict inflation and discussed the interaction of inflation with income generation for closed and open econo-mies, including various policy options, as well as the endogeneity of the inflation barrier. The manuscript used in class grew year by year, and I received several comments from graduate students, junior and senior colleagues and visiting researchers, so that two years ago I felt confident to go for publication. However, the contents, in essence Chapters 4–6 of the current book, were too much for a paper and too little for a book. Therefore, I thought that embed-ding the macroeconomic models and the post-Keynesian macroeconomic policy mix into the broader post-Keynesian research programme and the historical-theoretical foundations of this school of thought in the works of Marx, Keynes and Kalecki, on which I had done some work in the past, was a good idea. The results can now be found in Chapters 2 and 3 of the book. Furthermore, I wanted to include a review of some applications of post-Keynesian approaches in currently vibrant areas of macroeconomic research, in which I have been partly involved myself. These include the work on macroeconomic regimes in finance-dominated capitalism, regime changes, growth drivers, stagnation tendencies and the role of macroeconomic policy regimes. In addition, the post-Keynesian contributions to the research on the macroeconomic implications of the ecological constraints to growth seem to be most interesting and relevant. Reviews on these research areas can be found in Chapters 8 and 9 of the book. In order to address these areas, however, the presentation of the underlying macroeconomic models had to go beyond the short run, and the different versions of the basic post-Keynesian distribu-tion and growth models, in comparison to their neoclassical and classical/orthodox Marxian competitors, had to be presented in Chapter 7.

For some sections, indicated in the respective chapters of the book, I could draw on and build on, to different degrees, some of my previously (co-)authored work, published in aca-demic journals and books, without reproducing any of them in full or in detail:

Chapter 2

Hein, E. (2017a), 'Post-Keynesian macroeconomics since the mid-1990s – main develop-ments', *European Journal of Economics and Economic Policies: Intervention*, **14**(2), 131–72.

Chapter 3

Hein, E. (2014a), *Distribution and Growth after Keynes: A Post-Keynesian Guide*, Cheltenham, UK: Edward Elgar Publishing, Chapter 5.

Chapter 4

Hein, E. and Prante, F.J. (2020), 'Functional distribution and wage inequality in recent Kaleckian growth models', in H. Bougrine and L.-P. Rochon (eds.), *Economic Growth and Macroeconomic Stabilization Policies in Post-Keynesian Economics: Essays in Honour of Marc Lavoie and Mario Seccareccia, Book Two*, Cheltenham, UK: Edward Elgar Publishing.

Hein, E. (2020), 'Gender issues in Kaleckian distribution and growth models: on the macroeconomics of the gender wage gap', *Review of Political Economy*, **32**(4), 640–64.

Chapters 5 and 6

Hein, E. and Stockhammer, E. (2010), 'Macroeconomic policy mix, employment and inflation in a post-Keynesian alternative to the new consensus model', *Review of Political Economy*, **22**(3), 317–54.

Hein, E. and Stockhammer, E. (2011b), 'A post-Keynesian macroeconomic model of inflation, distribution and employment', in E. Hein and E. Stockhammer (eds.), *A Modern Guide to Keynesian Macroeconomics and Economic Policies*, Cheltenham, UK: Edward Elgar Publishing.

Chapter 7

Hein, E. (2017b), 'The Bhaduri/Marglin post-Kaleckian model in the history of distribution and growth theories – an assessment by means of model closures', *Review of Keynesian Economics*, **5**(2), 218–38.

Chapter 8

Hein, E. (2018d), *Verteilung und Wachstum: Eine paradigmenorientierte Einführung unter besonderer Berücksichtigung der post-keynesianischen Theorie*, 2. grundlegend überarbeitete und stark erweiterte Auflage, Marburg: Metropolis, Chapter 13.

Hein, E. and Martschin, J. (2021), 'Demand and growth regimes in finance-dominated capitalism and the role of the macroeconomic policy regime: a post-Keynesian comparative study on France, Germany, Italy and Spain before and after the Great Financial Crisis and the Great Recession', *Review of Evolutionary Political Economy*, **2**(3), 493–527.

Chapter 9

Hein, E. and Jimenez, V. (2022), 'Zero growth and macroeconomic stability: a post-Keynesian approach', *European Journal of Economics and Economic Policies: Intervention*, **19**(1), 41–60.

Chapter 10

Hein, E. (2014b), 'State and perspectives of post-Keynesian economics – views of a non-methodologist', in S. Dullien, E. Hein and A. Truger (eds.), *Makroökonomie, Entwicklung und Wirtschaftspolitik/Macroeconomics, Development and Economic Policies: Festschrift für/for Jan Priewe*, Marburg: Metropolis.

I am most grateful to the referees, editors and publishers of these journals and books. Most of all, however, I would like to thank my co-authors, Valeria Jimenez, Judith Martschin, Franz Prante and Engelbert Stockhammer, for their collaboration. I am also indebted to those colleagues and friends who provided helpful comments on these papers and book chapters.

At different stages of development of the current book manuscript, I have received very helpful comments and recommendations, too, and I would like to thank Valeria Jimenez, Benjamin Jungmann, Won Jun Nah, Franz Prante, Ricardo Summa, Achim Truger and Ryan Woodgate for these. In particular, I am grateful to Marc Lavoie for comments on and discussions of Chapters 4 and 5, although some disagreements may remain. I would also like to thank Jan Priewe for our debates on the contents of Chapters 2 and 9 – I am sure these will continue. I have also benefitted from the discussions with Garmen Giovanazzi on gendered Kaleckian distribution and growth models, short-run versions of which can be found in Chapter 4, and with Giuseppe Fontana on the perspectives of post-Keynesian economics (after my presentation at the 2021 FMM event in Berlin), which can be found in Chapter 10. I am grateful to them, too.

For assistance in the editing of the previous manuscripts used in class, I am indebted to Sophie-Dorothee Rotermund. Christoph Häusler, Benjamin Jungmann and Ryan Woodgate have provided invaluable help in preparing the final manuscript for the publisher. Without their assistance, a timely submission would have been impossible, and I am most grateful to them. Many thanks also go to the staff of Edward Elgar for the support in the publication process and to the Berlin School of Economics and Law for providing the required resources, in particular a research sabbatical semester in the spring/summer 2021, which allowed me to draft a major part of the manuscript.

Last but not least, I would like to thank my previous and current students in the Master International Economics programme at the Berlin School of Economics and Law and the attendees of my invited lectures on post-Keynesian economics at other universities, and of my presentations at various events, including international summer and winter schools, in particular the summer schools of the Forum Macroeconomics and Macroeconomic Policies (FMM). Their interest in post-Keynesian macroeconomics has been a main driving force for writing this book.

Although I received a lot of help in preparing this book, it goes without saying that I am alone responsible for the final contents.

Eckhard Hein
Berlin, March 2022

NOTE

1. A shortened version of that paper without detailed discussion of endogeneity channels of the inflation barrier (Hein and Stockhammer 2009a) is included in an edited book by Philip Arestis and Malcolm Sawyer (2009) on *Unemployment: Past and Present*.

List of variables

If variables have more than one meaning, the first use in this book is mentioned first. Variables are explained in the respective chapters.

ROMAN LETTERS

A	productivity of human and physical capital
a	nominal exchange rate
a_r	real exchange rate
B	credit, debt
B_F	corporate debt
B_{FB}	corporate debt held/granted by banks
B_{FR}	corporate debt held/granted by rentiers
B_{FRoW}	corporate debt held/granted by the rest of the world
B_G	government debt
B_{GB}	government debt held/granted by banks
B_{GR}	government debt held/granted by rentiers
B_{RoWR}	foreign debt held/granted by domestic rentiers
B^S	short-term credit granted by banks
B^S_F	short-term credit granted by banks to firms
B^S_G	short-term credit granted by banks to the government
b	fraction of credit granted by banks and held by banks
b	net export-capital rate
C_a	autonomous consumption
C_G	public consumption
C_{HH}	private household consumption
C_Π	consumption out of profits
$C_{\Pi a}$	autonomous consumption out of profits
C_R	consumption out of rentiers' income
C_W	consumption out of wages
c	propensity to consume
c_a	autonomous consumption-capital rate
c_Π	propensity to consume out of profits
c_R	propensity to consume out of rentiers' income
c_{RW}	propensity to consume out of rentiers' wealth
D	aggregate demand function in Keynes (1936)
D	deposits
D	government deficit
D'	primary government deficit
D_c	value of constant capital used up in production (depreciation) in Marx's theory
D_R	deposits held by rentiers

E	emissions of CO_2/greenhouse gas
E_F	firms' accumulated retained earnings
E_R	equity held by rentiers
Ex	real exports
e	employment rate
e^{CB}	employment rate affected by central bank policies
e^{FP}	employment rate affected by fiscal policies
e^f	full employment rate
e^N	stable inflation rate of employment (SIRE)
FB_E	external sector financial balance
FB_F	firm sector financial balance
FB_G	government sector financial balance
FB_P	private sector financial balance
FB_R	rentiers' households financial balance
FB_W	workers' households financial balance
FI^{net}	net revenues from cross-border payments for wages, capital incomes and transfers
G	government expenditures for goods and services, government consumption
G_{r0}	government real expenditure level to reach the target employment rate
G_{r1}	reaction coefficient for government real expenditures function
g	rate of capital accumulation, GDP growth rate
g_f	foreign GDP growth rate
g_n	natural rate of growth, labour force growth plus labour producitivity growth
H	hours worked
h	profit share
h_F^T	target profit share of firms
h_W^T	target profit share of workers
h_0, h_2, h_3, h_4, h_5	constant and coefficients in the profit share function
I	real net investment
I_a	autonomous investment, animal spirits
I^g	real gross investment
Im	real imports
i	long-term nominal interest rate
i_B	interest rate on short-term bank credit
i_{CB}	base rate of interest in the money market set by central banks
i_f	foreign interest rate
i_r	long-term real interest rate
i_{r0}^e	central bank's estimation of the real interest rate at the SIRE
J	energy
j	energy intensity of real GDP
K	capital stock
K_B	broad capital stock including physical and human capital
k_i	institutional factors determining productivity growth
L	labour force
l	labour force participation rate
l_o	labour-output ratio

M	central bank money, reserves
M_B	central bank money held by banks
M_R	central bank money held by rentiers
m	mark-up in firms' pricing
m_B	mark-up in commercial banks' interest rate setting
MEC	marginal efficiency of capital
N	employment
N_F	female employment
N_M	male employment
NX	net exports
n	hours worked per person
P	population
p	price
p_i	output price in industry i
p_{Ex}	price for export goods in domestic currency
p_f	foreign price
p_{Im}	price for import goods in domestic currency
$\hat{p}$	inflation rate
$\hat{p}^e$	expected inflation rate
$\hat{p}^T$	inflation target
$\hat{p}^u$	unexpected inflation
Q	expected yields from capital asset
q	inverse of the product of labour productivity and the labour force,
q	CO_2 emissions-energy ratio (carbon footprint)
R	rentiers' income
R^{net}	rentiers' income net of taxes
R_{FR}	rentiers' income from firms
R_{GR}	rentiers' income from government
R_{FRoW}	interest income of the RoW from the domestic firm sector
R_{RoWR}	domestic rentiers' interest income from the RoW
r	rate of profit
r_n	normal rate of profit
S	saving
S_G	government saving
S_Π	saving out of profits
S_R	saving out of rentiers' income
S_W	saving out of wages
S_{WF}	saving out of female wages
S_{WM}	saving out of male wages
s	propensity to save
s_Π	propensity to save out of profits
s_R	propensity to save out of rentiers' income
s_W	propensity to save out of wages
s_{WF}	propensity to save out of female wages
s_{WM}	propensity to save out of male wages
T	taxes

T_F	taxes on retained earnings
T_{FR}	taxes on interst revenues of rentiers from firms
T_{GR}	taxes on interest revenues of rentiers from the government
T_Π	taxes on profits
T_R	taxes on rentiers' income
T_W	taxes on wages
t	tax rate
t_F	tax rate on retained earnings
t_Π	tax rate on profits
$t_{\Pi 0}$	tax rate to reach the SIRE
$t_{\Pi 1}$	reaction coefficient in tax rate function
t_R	tax rate on rentiers' income
t_W	tax rate on wages
U	unemployment
u	rate of capacity utilisation
u_f	foreign rate of capacity utilisation
u_n	normal or target rate of capacity utilisation
u^N	non accelerating inflation rate of unemployment (NAIRU)
udc	unit direct labour costs
ue	unemployment rate
uoc	unit overhead labour costs
utc	unit total costs
v	capital-potential output ratio
W	wages
W_d	wages of direct labour
W_F	female wages
W_M	male wages
W_o	wages of overhead labour
W^{net}	wages net of taxes
w	nominal wage rate
w_F	female nominal wage rate
w_M	male nominal wage rate
w_r	real wage rate
w_r^s	subsistence or conventional real wage rate
Y	real output/income
Y_F	female labour output
Y_f	foreign income
Y_M	male labour output
Y^n	nominal output/income
Y_p	real output/income in production
Y^p	potential output given by the capital stock
y	labour productivity
y_F	female labour productivity
y_M	male labour productivity
Z	aggregate supply function in Keynes (1936)
z	relationship between unit material costs and unit labour costs

GREEK LETTERS

α	animal spirits, expected trend growth rate
β	coefficient in the investment function
Γ	indicator for wage inequality
γ	growth rate of autonomous consumption
δ	government expenditure-capital rate and/or government deficit-capital rate
ε	gender wage equality parameter
η	effect of wage inequality on the average propensity to save out of wages
θ	coefficient in the investment function
ι	coefficient in interest rate reaction function
λ	government debt-capital rate
μ	unit raw material and semi-finished product inputs
ξ_1, ξ_2	coefficient in the open economy inflation function
o	currency premium
Π	profits
Π^{net}	profits net of taxes
Π_F	retained profits
Π_F^{net}	retained profits net of taxes
π	coefficient in the price Phillips curve
ρ	share of males in total employment
σ	saving rate
τ	tax-capital ratio
ϑ	pass-through factor for the increase in nominal unit labour cost growth to inflation
φ	coefficient in nominal wage growth function
ϕ	coefficient in net export function
ψ	coefficient in net export function
χ	coefficient in net export function
Ω	wage share
Ω_F	female wage share
Ω_M	male wage share
Ω^N	wage share associated with SIRE/NAIRU
Ω_W^T	target wage share of workers
Ω_F^T	target wage share of firms
$\Omega_0, \Omega_1, \Omega_2, \Omega_3, \Omega_4$	constant and coefficients in wage share function
ω	reaction coefficient in nominal wage growth function

GENERAL

∂x	partial change or derivative of x
dx	change or total differential of x
$\dot{x}$	time rate of change of x
$\hat{x}$	growth rate of x
$\bar{x}$	constant or exogenous value of x

x^S supply of x

x^D demand for x

x^{Dn} notional or potential demand for x

x^e expected or ex ante value of x

x^T target value of x

x_r real value of x

x^n nominal value of x

x_t x in period t

x^* short-run equilibrium value of x

x^{**} long-run equilibrium value of x

1. Introduction

The economic policy responses towards the Global Financial Crisis and the Great Recession 2007–2009, as well as to the COVID-19 crisis 2020, have shown the limits of monetary policies by central banks and have meant a comeback for active fiscal policy stabilisation on a massive scale, not seen for decades (Arestis 2017, Sawyer 2017). Also, the pressing and urgent socio-ecological transformation to deal with the challenges of climate change seems to require 'Big Government', as Minsky (1986a, p. 15) used to call it. The recent crises and the economic policy responses towards these crises have thus undermined the relevance and applicability of the mainstream 'new consensus models' (NCMs) (Clarida et al. 1999, Goodfriend and King 1997), which are based on new classical and new Keynesian economics and have dominated macroeconomic research, macroeconomic policy recommendations and macroeconomic teaching since the late 1990s.[1] In these NCMs, the short-run Phillips curve is upward sloping in inflation-output or inflation-employment space due to nominal and real rigidities, which are based on the 'microfoundations' of imperfectly competitive markets. In the long run, however, there is no effect of aggregate demand or economic policies on the 'non-accelerating inflation rate of unemployment' (NAIRU), as the core of these models, which is exclusively determined by structural characteristics of the labour market, the wage bargaining institutions and the social security system. The long-run Phillips curve is thus vertical. Inflation-targeting monetary policies applying the interest rate tool are supposed to stabilise output and employment in the short run around the NAIRU-level of output, but in the long run they are considered to be neutral with respect to real variables (i.e. equilibrium output and employment) and thus only affect inflation. Initially, the financial sector and the related potential instabilities were not modelled at all. Furthermore, fiscal policy has been downgraded by the NCMs and has been restricted to supporting monetary policies in achieving price stability by means of balancing the government budget over the cycle.

Of course, mainstream orthodox economics has acknowledged the limitations to the stabilising capacity of monetary policies in deep recessions and the relevance of fiscal policies in such situations, as well as the lack of the relevance of a financial sector in the NCM. Empirically, Blanchard and Leigh (2013, 2014), for example, have shown that fiscal multipliers are positive and particularly large during recessions. Blanchard (2019) has accepted that interest rates for the past decades have been below GDP growth rates, such that public debt stabilisation does not require primary surpluses in the government's financial balances. However, the emanating 'new fiscalism' (Lavoie and Seccareccia 2017) rather returned to the 'fiscalist' economic policy implications of the neoclassical synthesis of the 1950s and 1960s.[2] Short-run counter-cyclical fiscal policies are recommended, but in the long run, the government budget should be balanced again (Carlin and Soskice 2015, Chapter 14). Right after the 2007–09 crises, the missing financial sector in the NCM was acknowledged by Woodford (2010), the author of the celebrated monograph on the NCM (Woodford 2003). He proposes to integrate the financial sector as an intermediator between saving and investment

1

at the macroeconomic level. The focus should be on market-based intermediation and thus go beyond the new Keynesian 'bank-lending channel' and 'financial accelerator channel' of economic fluctuations, which had already been proposed in the 1990s (Bernanke and Gertler 1995, Bernanke et al. 1996, Kiyotaki and Moore 1997). However, these approaches just extend the long-run supply-side perspective of the NCM to banks and financial markets, which may then cause short-run problems and frictions. They do not take into account the principal endogeneity and demand determination of money and credit in a monetary production economy, which make saving endogenous to investment and other autonomous expenditures, both in the short and in the long run. They also ignore the medium- to long-run effects of aggregate demand on the supply side of the economy, which undermines concepts like the natural rate of unemployment, the NAIRU or the natural rate of growth, to which the economy is said to converge in the long run. Here is not the place to attempt a comprehensive review of the responses of mainstream macroeconomics towards the crisis. However, it is worth mentioning that Lavoie (2018) in his review also points out that several leading mainstream macroeconomists still adhere to strict microfoundations of macroeconomics. This means making use of utility maximising agents with rational expectations in dynamic stochastic general equilibrium (DSGE) models, although these models have been fundamentally challenged from several perspectives, even from critical orthodox authors.[3] Therefore, Palley's (2013a, p. 193) characterisation of mainstream economics after the crises as 'Gattopardo economics' does not seem to be completely out of touch with reality, because 'Gattopardo economics adopts ideas developed by critics of mainstream economics, but it does so in a way that ignores the thrust of the original critique and leaves mainstream analysis unchanged'.

Post-Keynesians have criticised the NCM from the very start, and thus well before the 2007–09 crises, and then, of course, during these crises, and have presented amendments and alternatives.[4] The post-Keynesian macroeconomic critique has been related to the assumption of a stable long-run NAIRU determined exclusively by supply-side factors, to which actual unemployment, determined by effective demand, can be adjusted by means of monetary policy interventions. The critique has focussed on the assumption of the independence of this NAIRU from the development of actual unemployment and hence from aggregate demand in the goods market and from monetary as well as fiscal policies. In short, what has been questioned is the assumed long-run neutrality of money, finance and credit in the NCM. Furthermore, post-Keynesians have been critical of the sole reliance on central bank interest rate policies as the only macroeconomic policy tool in the NCM, the absence of considerations of financial sector instabilities and the downgrading of fiscal policies as a stabilising tool.

Based on this post-Keynesian literature, several attempts have been made to amend the NCM or provide alternative post-Keynesian macroeconomic models and macroeconomic policies, some of them designed for teaching purposes in the classroom.[5] All these contributions have their specific merits, but usually they do not provide a comprehensive post-Keynesian alternative to the NCM, including most of the main features of post-Keynesian macroeconomics. Furthermore, they do not provide a full post-Keynesian macroeconomic policy mix for the areas of monetary, fiscal and incomes policies, as well as their interactions, taking also the international environment into account. Also the recent introductory (text)books to post-Keynesian economics by King (2015) and Lavoie (2006a), as well as the advanced (text)books by Lavoie (2014) on post-Keynesian economics in general and by Blecker and Setterfield (2019) and Hein (2014a) on distribution and growth do not contain full alternative post-Keynesian macroeconomic models with the respective post-Keynesian macroeconomic policy mix.

Therefore, the first objective of this book is to provide the foundations for post-Keynesian macroeconomics and a comprehensive post-Keynesian macroeconomic model with the respective macroeconomic policy mix, in order to achieve full employment and constant inflation and to avoid external imbalances. The second objective is to embed these post-Keynesian macroeconomics and macroeconomic policies into the post-Keynesian research programme more generally. Finally, the third objective is to present the application of some of these post-Keynesian macroeconomics in some recent areas of research.

The book is organised as follows. Chapters 2 and 3 provide the methodological and historical-theoretical context for modern post-Keynesian macroeconomics. In Chapter 2, the methods and the history of post-Keynesian economics are reviewed. First, heterodox economics in general, including post-Keynesian economics, is distinguished from orthodox economics from a methodological perspective, following Lavoie's (2014, Chapter 1) five presuppositions. Then the different strands in post-Keynesian economics are presented: The fundamentalist Keynesians, the Kaleckians, the Kaldorians, the Sraffians and the institutionalists. Their differences and, in particular, their commonalities are pointed out. It is argued that there are five major claims or features common to these strands, which make post-Keynesian economics a distinct school of thought in heterodox economics. Then, the stages of development of post-Keynesian economics since the foundation of this school with the works of Michal Kalecki (1932, 1933, 1935) and John Maynard Keynes (1933a, 1936, 1937) are presented. Finally, the current state of post-Keynesian economics as an alternative to mainstream orthodox economics is briefly assessed.

Chapter 3 addresses the roots of post-Keynesian macroeconomics in the works of Kalecki and Keynes in more detail, focussing on the principle of effective demand, money, credit and finance. Applying Schumpeter's (1954) distinction between 'monetary analysis' and 'real analysis', not only Kalecki's and Keynes's theories have to be considered as 'monetary analysis', but also Marx's. Furthermore, Kalecki was considerably influenced by Marx's (1885) approach towards effective demand and capital accumulation. That is the reason why also Marx's views on money, effective demand and capital accumulation are presented in this chapter. Finally, since there has been some confusion, partly also in post-Keynesian economics, about the relationship between endogenous credit, finance, investment and saving, the monetary circuit approach is presented in the last part of Chapter 3, in order to shed some clarifying light on these relationships.

Chapters 4–6 contain the core of the book and gradually develop a full post-Keynesian short-run macroeconomic model and the implications for a post-Keynesian macroeconomic policy mix in order to achieve full employment, inflation stability and a balanced current account. The basic structure of the model is inspired by the previous but incomplete works of Hein and Stockhammer (2009b, 2010, 2011b).[6] The model versions are built on a post-Keynesian view of a monetary production economy with creditor-debtor relationships and the endogeneity of the volume of credit and the stock of money. The short-term interest rate is an exogenous policy variable under control of the central bank, and the long-term interest rate is also affected by liquidity and risk assessments of banks and financial wealth holders. Since there are no systematic feedbacks of economic activity on these determinants, the long-term interest rate is also taken as an exogenous variable for the income generation process. In the models, there are three groups of private actors, rentiers (creditors), firms (debtors) and workers. Income distribution between these three groups is important and affects the level of output and employment. The models are short-run models in the sense that all the stocks (capital, financial assets and liabilities) are taken as given and exogenous, as results of past developments. The labour force and labour supply are also taken to be given and exogenous. Usually, neither the capital stock nor the labour force is fully utilised, which means that the model economies are characterised by the underutilisation of the capital stock and by unemployment. As indicated by Keynes (1936) and Kalecki (1935, 1954), such underutilisation is the normal state of affairs in capitalist or monetary production economies.

Chapter 4 starts with a detailed explanation of the post-Keynesian horizontalist approach towards interest, credit and money, which is used in the following macroeconomic models. Then several model versions with fixed prices are developed, starting with the basic model for a closed private economy without taxes and government expenditures. The effects of changes in model parameters, like firms' animal spirits, rentiers' propensity to save, the profit share and the rate of interest on equilibrium output and income are derived. It is shown that the model generates the paradox of thrift and a paradox of costs; aggregate demand is hence wage-led. Changes in the rate of interest or the stock of debt have no unique effects. In the next step, the government is explicitly introduced into the fix price model and the roles of taxes, government expenditures and government budget deficits are discussed. Then, some open economy features are included, introducing exports and imports of goods and services with the rest of the world and analysing the effects of exogenous changes in interest rates, income distribution and the nominal exchange rate. In the next step, wage inequality is integrated into a closed economy version of the model, and the macroeconomic effects of relative income concerns in the consumption function are discussed. Finally, the focus is shifted to the short-run macroeconomics of gender pay gaps, both for a closed and an open economy model.

Whereas distribution conflict only affects income shares in the model versions of Chapter 4, Chapter 5 introduces the post-Keynesian notion of conflict inflation. Distribution conflict between firms and workers thus determines the wage and profit shares and may generate conflict inflation if distributional claims are inconsistent. Distribution between rentiers (creditors) and firms (debtors) is mainly determined by interest rate policies of the central bank and is affected by (unexpected) inflation generated in the distribution conflict between workers and firms. Workers' bargaining power is determined by the institutional features of the labour market and the social benefit system in the medium to long run and by the rate of employment in the short run. The model generates a short-run 'inflation barrier', and thus a 'stable inflation rate of employment' (SIRE), and hence a kind of NAIRU. However, it is shown that this 'inflation barrier' is endogenous to demand-determined employment and macroeconomic policies in the medium to long run through various channels. Against this background, the interaction of the SIRE with the rate of employment determined by the goods market is analysed, and it is shown that the SIRE may be highly unstable. For central bank interest rate policies, the stabiliser suggested in the NCM, it is found that the effectiveness of these policies is asymmetric in the short run and may be detrimental in the medium to long run. Introducing the government into the model, it is shown that government expenditure policies do not suffer from these limitations. Then, an open economy version of a macroeconomic model with conflict inflation is presented, and the role of the real exchange rate for the stabilisation around the SIRE is examined. While the models presented in that chapter already include some endogeneity channels of the SIRE, via the interest rate, the tax rate or the real exchange rate, some further channels are finally presented: Persistence mechanisms in the labour market, wage aspirations based on conventional behaviour and long-run investment effects on the capital stock and on firms' pricing behaviour.

Based on the model results of Chapter 5, a comprehensive post-Keynesian macroeconomic policy mix as an alternative to the NCM is presented in Chapter 6. This post-Keynesian policy mix requires co-ordination amongst the economic policy actors of each of the areas. In this alternative policy package, monetary policy should be aiming at stable distribution of income by targeting a long-term nominal (real) interest rate, which should not exceed trend nominal (real) GDP growth. Furthermore, central banks, together with the legal regulation of financial institutions by governments, are responsible for the stability of the financial system, and the central bank has to act as a lender of last resort for the banking system and, in particular, as a guarantor of government debt. Nominal stabilisation, that is, stable inflation, should be tackled by income and wage policies, in particular through mediation of distributional conflicts via wage bargaining co-ordination at the macroeconomic level. This would also contribute to stable income distribution. Real stabilisation and aggregate demand management, both in the short and in the long run, should be the task of fiscal policy, making use of government expenditures and government deficits/surpluses, following a 'functional finance' (Lerner 1943) approach. Macroeconomic policies should be co-ordinated internationally, in order to avoid current account imbalances. Existing current account imbalances should be addressed symmetrically by deficit and surplus countries, and deficit countries should improve non-price competitiveness by means of industrial and regional policies.

While the main focus of this book is on short-run macroeconomics, in particular in the models in Chapters 4 and 5, Chapters 7–9 address rather medium- to long-run topics. In order to discuss the recent issues of demand and growth regimes before and after the 2007–09 crises or the macroeconomic implications of ecological constraints, some basic knowledge about distribution and growth theories is required. As recent books by Blecker and Setterfield (2019), Foley et al. (2019), Hein (2014a) and Lavoie (2014, Chapter 6) contain detailed and extensive presentations of orthodox and heterodox distribution and growth theories, Chapter 7 presents only the basic versions in a unified modelling framework. The chapter makes use of the method of model closures in order to distinguish between different approaches. Such approaches include the old and new neoclassical as well as the classical and orthodox Marxian distribution and growth theories, all driven by the supply side. As alternatives, this chapter focusses on several varieties of the demand-driven post-Keynesian distribution and growth models, including the Kaldor-Robinson model, the Kalecki-Steindl approach with the post- and the neo-Kaleckian models and finally the Sraffian supermultiplier model driven by non-capacity creating autonomous demand growth. In the context of the post-Kaleckian model, the important distinction between wage- and profit-led demand and growth is presented. Finally, also productivity growth and hence the growth of potential output are endogenised into a Kaleckian demand-led growth model.

Chapter 8 discusses macroeconomic demand and growth regimes in finance-dominated capitalism, recent stagnation tendencies and the role of macroeconomic policy regimes. In Chapters 4, 5 and 7, different regimes or cases are derived regarding the effects of changes in functional income distribution, interest rates or indebtedness as exogenous variables on endogenous equilibrium demand, output and growth. In Chapter 8, the perspective is changed such that the focus is on the sources, the financing and the drivers of demand and growth. First, based on the macroeconomic channels of influence of financialisation, that is, an increasing dominance of the financial sector, financial motives and financial instruments since the late 1970s/early 1980s in advanced capitalist economies, the concept of demand and growth regimes in finance-dominated capitalism is presented. Focussing on the sources of demand and the way the macroeconomic demand components are financed, the debt-led private demand boom regime, the domestic demand-led regime, the weakly export-led regime and the export-led mercantilist regime are distinguished. Second, some empirical results on demand and growth regimes before the 2007–09 Global Financial Crisis and Great Recession, the changes in regimes in the course of and after these crises and the emanating tendency towards stagnation are presented. Third, the identified regimes, the regime changes and the related tendencies towards stagnation are integrated into a stylised Kaleckian distribution and growth model, relying on and extending the framework introduced in Chapter 7. Finally, the most recent debate on growth drivers in post-Keynesian economics and comparative political economy is addressed. The concept of a macroeconomic policy regime, integrating the post-Keynesian notion of a desirable or functional macroeconomic policy mix developed in Chapter 6, is introduced and applied. From all this it is concluded that current stagnation tendencies can be viewed to a large extent as the result of 'stagnation policy' (Steindl 1976, 1979).

Chapter 9 deals with some of the recent debates in post-Keynesian and ecological economics addressing the macroeconomic implications of ecological constraints. First, the relationship between post-Keynesian and ecological economics is reviewed, and it is argued that these two heterodox schools of thought have some basic features in common, which should facilitate communication and an improved understanding of the issues at stake. Second, the immediately pressing problem of climate change and the required ecological transformation of modern economies is touched upon. Concepts of de-growth and green growth are reviewed, and their macroeconomic implications are pointed out. Finally, implications of low or even zero long-run growth imposed by ecological constraints for macroeconomic stability in a monetary production economy are addressed. The question of a growth imperative given by endogenous money and credit and positive interest rates and the requirement of positive profit rates is examined, in particular. It is shown that zero growth with endogenous credit, positive interest rates and positive profits is possible and can be stable under a set of restrictive assumptions regarding the behaviour of firms, households and the government, and specific conditions regarding model parameters, like the rate of interest and the propensities to consume out of income and out of wealth. Finally, the conditions for stable employment with zero growth and technological progress are explored. It is concluded that a socio-economic and -ecological transformation in order to respect the environmental constraints is a huge challenge and requires a significant transformation of capitalism as we know it. Green New Deal concepts for the socio-ecological transformation, as well as stabilising low or zero growth in the long run, would have to be more closely linked with the post-Keynesian macroeconomic policy mix derived in Chapter 6.

Based on the current challenges for macroeconomics and the elaborations in this book, Chapter 10 contains a short outlook on the perspectives for post-Keynesian economics. It is argued that, first, post-Keynesians should improve their research programme in those areas which are underdeveloped, without giving up their strengths in macroeconomics and macroeconomic policies. This also implies improving the cooperation with other heterodox schools, like ecological economics, institutional economics and Marxian economics, and with critical and comparative political economy and international political economy, in order to contribute to a pluralistic political economy research programme. Second, it is argued that post-Keynesians would have to focus and concentrate on defending and improving the heterodox academic infrastructure, regarding university positions, research funding, graduate programmes, journals and appropriate journal rankings, associations and networks, conferences and summer schools. Third, in order to have an impact on economic policies and to contribute to a more progressive social environment for academic research, post-Keynesians need to maintain and to improve their cooperation with trade unions, social movements and progressive political parties, as well as with research institutes and think tanks outside the university sector.

In this book, we will mainly make use of comparative static or comparative dynamic models based on linear equations. This means that we will derive equilibrium output/income, profits and investment/saving in the short-run models in Chapters 4 and 5, as well as equilibrium capital accumulation, output growth and capacity utilisation (and/or profit shares), as well as profit rates in the long-run growth models in Chapters 7–9. Changes in model parameters and in coefficients in the behavioural equations will generate a new static or dynamic equilibrium. With this method, we can check the existence and the stability of an equilibrium, but a detailed analysis of the transition from one equilibrium to another, that is, of the disequilibrium process, is beyond the scope of this method. We thus follow Dutt's (2011, p. 143) justification of the use of equilibrium analysis:

> [I]t should be pointed out that equilibrium should be thought of not as an actual state of rest, or a tranquil state, but rather as a theoretical tool of analysis . . . [T]he equilibrium in a model does not imply a position of rest for actual economies, since in the model many things which can actually change over time are held constant in order to abstract from their influences. If these things change erratically, they need not be modelled formally. But if they do change systematically, the equilibrium model can be the basis of examining the results of the endogenous dynamics of these state variables.

In our view, the method of comparative statics or dynamics is thus a useful first step in modelling macroeconomic issues. It allows us to organise our thoughts regarding causalities and interdependencies of macroeconomic variables, and it also provides a useful tool to compare and distinguish different theories and approaches. Further developments and refinements can then include the explicit considerations of out-of-equilibrium dynamics based on linear or non-linear equations.

We are thus using models as didactic tools in order to highlight and focus on certain relationships or interdependencies, abstracting from other developments by keeping the related variables constant. Equilibrium is thus a theoretical tool of analysis – and not an actual state of the economy or a point of rest towards which the economy will tend in 'historical time'. This also means that we will use 'periods' or 'runs' as theoretical and modelling concepts, which do not necessarily refer to historical episodes. A 'short-run' – or a 'short-period' – equilibrium is thus an equilibrium in which certain variables are held constant or are taken to be exogenous. These variables may then vary and are determined endogenously within the model when it comes to the 'medium-run' or 'long-run' equilibrium. For example, for the derivation of short-run equilibria in Chapter 4 we hold the capital stock, the stocks of financial assets and liabilities, the labour force and the technical conditions of production constant. Within the short run, output/income adjust to demand, and we can derive the equilibrium output/income and examine its stability. In Chapter 5, we then add the explicit consideration of inflation expectations and assume that these expectations adapt from short run to the next short run, that is, in the medium run, still holding the stocks of capital, assets, liabilities and labour, as well as the technical conditions of production constant. Only in Chapter 7, in the context of distribution and growth theories, do we then allow for the changes in the capital stock in the long run, and in Chapter 9, we will also present a model with long-run endogenous stocks of financial assets and liabilities. Further explanations are provided in the respective chapters.

NOTES

1. See Carlin and Soskice (2009, 2015, Chapter 3), Romer (2000), Walsh (2002) and Woodford (2003, 2009) for different presentations of NCMs. For textbook versions of new classical and new Keynesian economics, see Snowdon and Vane (2005, Chapters 5 and 7), for example.
2. For textbook presentations of the neoclassical synthesis, see Felderer and Homburg (1992, Chapters 5–6), Froyen (2002, Chapter 8) and Snowdon and Vane (2005, Chapter 3), for example.
3. For fundamental critique of DSGE models, see, for example, Bertocco (2017), Bertocco and Kalajzic (2019), Colander et al. (2009), Dullien (2011), Kirman (2010), Kurz (2010), Rogers (2014, 2018) and Storm (2021).
4. For post-Keynesian assessments of the NCM and its main elements, the NAIRU and an inflation-targeting central bank, before and in the course of the 2007–09 crises, see, for example, Arestis (2006, 2009), Arestis and Sawyer (2004a), Davidson (2006), Fontana (2009a), Fontana and Palacio-Vera (2002, 2004), Gnos and Rochon (2007), Hein (2006a), Kriesler and Lavoie (2007), Lavoie (2006b), Palley (2007a), Rochon and Rossi (2006a), Sawyer (2002), Setterfield (2006, 2009a), Smithin (2007), Stockhammer (2008) and Wray (2007), amongst several others.
5. See for example the contributions by Fontana and Setterfield (2009b), Howells (2009), Lavoie (2009a), Sawyer (2009a) and Smithin (2009) in Fontana and Setterfield (2009a), as well as the papers by Harvey (2018), Herr (2014b) and Lavoie (2010b), amongst others.
6. This refers in particular to the basic model in Chapter 5. However, the models in this book are different from Hein and Stockhammer (2009b) where the focus has been on the determination and the endogeneity of the NAIRU and where the demand generation process has been treated using only implicit functions for a closed economy. It is also different from Hein and Stockhammer (2010, 2011b), where the demand generating process has been built on a neo-Kaleckian closed economy distribution and growth model with interest and credit, which presupposes some basic knowledge of post-Keynesian distribution and growth theory and modelling. This is not required for Chapter 5 of this book, because the models are formulated in levels, and the basics are provided in the fixed price models in Chapter 4.

2. Introduction to post-Keynesian economics: methods, history and current state*

2.1 INTRODUCTION

In this chapter, we will briefly review the methods and the history of post-Keynesian economics. First, we will distinguish heterodox economics in general, including post-Keynesian economics, from orthodox economics from a methodological perspective. Next, we will review the different strands in post-Keynesian economics and try to point out their differences and, in particular, their commonalities, which make post-Keynesian economics a distinct school of thought in heterodox economics. Then, we will sketch the stages of development of post-Keynesian economics since the foundation of this school with the works of Michal Kalecki (1932, 1933, 1935) and John Maynard Keynes (1933a, 1936, 1937). Finally, we will assess the current state of post-Keynesian economics as an alternative to mainstream orthodox economics. This review will remain somewhat rudimentary, but the features of post-Keynesian macroeconomics will then be developed and presented in more depth in the following chapters of this book.

2.2 HETERODOX ECONOMICS VS. ORTHODOX ECONOMICS

Post-Keynesian economics is part of heterodox economics more generally, such as classical, Marxian, old institutional, evolutionary political economy, social, feminist and ecological economics, and so on, which provide alternatives to neoclassical or orthodox economics. In the area of macroeconomics, which this book focusses on, the post-Keynesian and Marxian schools of thought are the main heterodox opponents of the currently dominating orthodox mainstream new Keynesian and new classical schools,[1] and the new consensus macroeconomics (NCM) based on these schools, with a dominance of the new Keynesian input to this NCM (Figure 2.1).[2]

Following Lavoie (2011a, 2014, Chapter 1), several presuppositions can be singled out, which unite heterodox approaches against the orthodox/neoclassical mainstream and its modern macroeconomic incarnations, represented in the new Keynesian and the new classical schools, as well as the NCM.[3]

Regarding the epistemology and the ontology, that is, the science of learning and the basic categories of the scientific systems and their relationships, heterodox economics is based on 'realism'. The objective of economics is to tell relevant stories and to explain the actual working of the economy in the real world, starting from Kaldor-type 'stylised facts' (Kaldor 1957). Orthodox economics, by contrast, is founded on 'instrumentalism', which means that an economic assumption is considered sound, irrespective of observed data or facts, if it leads to the calculation of equilibrium positions and is conducive to accurate predictions, as pointed out by Friedman (1953). Therefore, from the orthodox perspective, it is always legitimate to

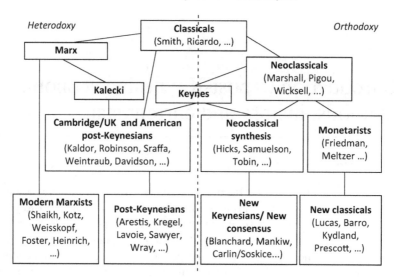

Source:　Based on Hein (2019b, p. 240).

Figure 2.1　Heterodox and orthodox schools in macroeconomics

start from unrealistic first principles, like given production technologies, given preferences and given initial endowments, as well as strictly profit and utility maximising behaviour of economic agents (the *homo economicus*) in perfectly competitive markets.

Regarding the concept of rationality, heterodox economics assumes 'environment-consistent rationality' and 'satisficing agents'. It is acknowledged that individuals face severe limitations in their ability to acquire and process information, in particular because the latter may simply be non-existent and because there is no 'true' model to process available information, not to mention the fact that current decisions may change the set of possible future states. Thus, expectations are based on irreducible or fundamental uncertainty, which is different from probabilistic risk. Following norms, conventions, customs, rules of thumb, as well as the establishment of institutions that reduce uncertainty are considered as rational or reasonable responses. Orthodox theory by contrast assumes 'model-consistent rationality' and 'optimising agents'. Individuals possess quasi-unlimited knowledge about present and future states of the economy, and they have the ability to calculate economic outcomes applying the 'true' model of the economy. In this sense, they are assumed to possess 'perfect information' and have 'rational expectations'.

With respect to the applied method, heterodox approaches favour 'organicism' and 'holism'. They consider individuals as social beings in the context of their environment, given by class, gender, culture, social norms, institutions and history. From this perspective, all sorts of micro-macro paradoxes can arise, which means that reasonable behaviour at the micro level may not generate the intended results at the macro level, when interrelationships between individual actions are taken into account ('paradox of thrift', 'paradox of costs', 'paradox of debt', 'paradox of liquidity', and so on). The orthodox method is based on 'methodological individualism' and 'atomicism', which means that the analysis has to start from the pre-social individual and his/her preferences. The behaviour of a representative agent as a utility and profit maximiser under constraints provides the microfoundation of orthodox macroeconomics (and of institutions). Macroeconomic results can be obtained by aggregating microeconomic behaviour. Therefore, micro-macro paradoxes are ruled out by design in orthodox economics.

With respect to the economic core, heterodox schools of thought focus on 'production' and 'growth'. Whereas the classical economists and Marx were preoccupied with the creation, distribution and extension of resources, by means of accumulation of (part of) the surplus and by technical progress, Kalecki and Keynes, starting in the early/mid-1930s, focussed on the utilisation of resources, because monetary production economies usually operate below full employment. In this context, prices in heterodox schools are considered as (re-)production prices and are affected by income distribution, which itself is determined by socio-institutional factors. On the contrary, the starting point and the focus of orthodox theory are 'exchange', 'allocation' and 'scarcity'. According to this perspective, economics is about the efficient allocation of scarce resources. Prices are assumed to reflect scarcity, exchange is the starting point of economic analysis, and production and growth are only extensions to this basic perspective. Income distribution is determined by production technologies.

Regarding the political core, heterodox schools at the minimum require 'regulated markets' and continuous state intervention into the economy. It is held that unfettered markets, irrespective of price flexibility or inflexibility, generate instabilities, unacceptable inequalities and inefficiencies. The notion of free markets is considered a myth, because there has always been an institutional framework for the market economy. Furthermore, it is argued that unrestricted competition tends towards market concentration and thus towards undermining itself. Therefore, permanent market regulation and aggregate demand management by the state are required. This contradicts the orthodox view that 'unfettered' and free markets are generally stable and generate an optimal allocation at full employment levels of activity, at least in the long run. State interventions are said to generate inefficiencies, and hence for orthodox economists these are only acceptable when there are externalities and/or monopoly abuses.

2.3 STRANDS OF POST-KEYNESIAN ECONOMICS AND BROAD COMMONALITIES

Based on the general presuppositions uniting heterodox economics, different strands of post-Keynesian economics can be distinguished in a 'big tent' approach, which, as will be seen below, focusses on the commonalities rather than the differences of these strands. In an early paper, Hamouda and Harcourt (1988) mentioned three strands, American post-Keynesians, neo-Ricardians and Kaleckians, but had difficulties in classifying outstanding individuals, like Kaldor, Goodwin, Pasinetti and Godley.[4] Therefore, Lavoie (2011a, 2014, Chapter 1) distinguishes five strands of post-Keynesian economics with the respective representatives, which are presented here in revised order:

- The first strand is represented by the fundamentalist Keynesians, directly inspired by John Maynard Keynes, the older Joan Robinson, as well as Hyman Minsky, G.L.S. Shackle and Sydney Weintraub. Major themes are fundamental uncertainty, the features of a monetary production economy, financial instability and methodological issues.
- The Kaleckians are the second strand, drawing on the works of Michal Kalecki, Josef Steindl and the younger Joan Robinson, with cost-plus pricing, class conflict, effective demand, income distribution and growth as major themes.

- The third strand consists of the Kaldorians, basing their works on the contributions by Nicholas Kaldor, Roy F. Harrod, Richard Goodwin, John Cornwall and Wynne Godley. The major themes are economic growth, productivity regimes, structural change, open economy constraints to growth and the nexus between the economic and the financial systems.
- The Sraffians or neo-Ricardians constitute the fourth strand, drawing on the works of Piero Sraffa and Pierangelo Garegnani, and focussing on issues like relative prices in multi-sectoral production systems, choice of techniques, capital theory, long-period equilibrium positions of the economy and recently also on autonomous demand-driven growth.
- The fifth strand are the institutionalists, relying on the works of Thorstein Veblen, Gardiner Means, P.W.S. Andrews, John Kenneth Galbraith, Abba Lerner and Alfred Eichner, and concentrating on themes like pricing, the theory of the firm, monetary institutions and behavioural and labour economics.

King (2015, Chapter 9) lists the Sraffians and the institutionalists (the latter together with evolutionary economics) as distinct heterodox schools, however with some links, commonalities and overlaps with the post-Keynesian research programme, and would thus only include the first three strands in post-Keynesian economics. This may be a matter of taste, but Sraffians and institutionalists should be included in post-Keynesian economics, if we apply a big tent approach, because these strands share the five characteristics of post-Keynesian economics to be sketched below.

Starting with Eichner and Kregel (1975) several attempts have been made to single out what the different strands of post-Keynesianism have in common and what distinguishes post-Keynesian economics from orthodox economics and other strands of heterodox economics. It can be argued that post-Keynesians adhere to the five presuppositions of heterodox economics in general, and that they can be distinguished from other schools of heterodox economics by the following five characteristics, which might apply to the different strands to different degrees, but on which all five strands would likely agree.

First, there is the focus on a monetary theory of production, in which money is non-neutral in the short and the long run, as Keynes (1933a) in his contribution to the Spiethoff festschrift has famously claimed. Money and monetary variables are important for short- and long-run economic processes, and the latter cannot be sensibly analysed without considering monetary and financial variables.

Second, based on the notion of a monetary production economy, there is the dominance of the principle of effective demand in the short and long run. This is true for both Keynes (1933a, 1936), as explained, in particular, in the drafts leading to the *General Theory* (Keynes 1979), as well as for Kalecki (1932, 1933, 1935, 1939). In a monetary production economy, investment creates its own saving, through changes in the level of economic activity and income or through changes in distribution, provided that the propensities to save out of different types of incomes differ. Post-Keynesians, starting with Kalecki (1943a, 1954), Kaldor (1957), Robinson (1956, 1962) and Steindl (1952), have moved this principle from short-run income and employment determination to long-run growth theory and have argued that growth and even productivity growth are largely demand-determined as well.

Third, there is the importance of the notion of fundamental uncertainty, which is different from probabilistic risk. Future events are not known, and there is hence no way to allocate probability values to them; or as Keynes (1937, p. 214) famously put it, fundamental uncertainty means that '(w)e simply do not know'. Expectations cannot be based on a true model of the economy, and will themselves feedback on the outcome of economic processes.

Fourth, based on the first three characteristics, post-Keynesians insist that economic processes take place in historical and irreversible time (Robinson 1962, p. 26) – and are thus largely path dependent. There is no pre-determined equilibrium towards which the economy will or can adjust in historical time. On the contrary, the long period is just a succession of short periods, according to Kalecki (1971, p. 165). This means that concepts such as an inflation barrier or a non-accelerating inflation rate of unemployment (NAIRU), or potential growth, are endogenous to the actual time path of the economy driven by effective demand – they have no independent existence and can thus not be seen as pre-existing long-run centres of gravity.

Fifth, there is the importance of distributional issues and distribution conflict for economic outcomes. This is true both with respect to the determination of income, employment and inflation, and as well to growth and technological progress. Different strands of post-Keynesian economics may focus on different aspects of distributional issues and may have different theories of distribution, but they all agree that distribution conflict and the institutions which moderate this conflict are important for the overall macroeconomic outcome, in the short run and in the long run.

Together with the five presuppositions, which post-Keynesian economics shares with other heterodox economics, the five core claims or characteristics provide the ten main features of post-Keynesian economics, as summarised in Table 2.1.

2.4 STAGES OF DEVELOPMENT OF POST-KEYNESIAN ECONOMICS

The development of what has become 'post-Keynesian economics' has gone through different stages since the 1930s, as for example described by Fontana (2009b, Chapter 2) and Lavoie (2014, Chapter 1).[5]

2.4.1 The 1930s and 1940s

In the 1930s and 1940s, the history of post-Keynesian economics started with Kalecki's (1932, 1933, 1935, 1939, 1943a) and Keynes's (1933a, 1936) revolution in macroeconomics, based on the introduction of the principle of effective demand in a monetary production economy. Tables 2.2 and 2.3 provide short biographies of the two founding fathers of post-Keynesian economics with their main book publications.[6] The focus in this period was clearly on the determination of output and employment, involuntary unemployment and the trade cycle, and on economic policies to overcome short- and long-run effective demand failures, recessions, stagnation and involuntary unemployment (Kalecki 1943b, 1944, Keynes 1943). Both Kalecki and Keynes also presented important contributions to international economics and the future of the international currency system after World War II (Kalecki and Schumacher 1943, Keynes 1942).

Table 2.1   Ten main features of post-Keynesian economics

Five presuppositions	Five core claims
1. Epistemology/ontology: Realism	6. Non-neutrality of money in the short and in the long run
2. Rationality: Environment-consistent rationality and satisficing agents	7. Principle of effective demand in the short and in the long run
3. Method: Holism and organicism	8. Fundamental uncertainty
4. Economic core: Production and growth	9. Historical and irreversible time, path dependence
5. Political core: Regulated markets	10. Distribution conflict

Table 2.2   Short biography of Michal Kalecki

- 22 June 1899: Born in Lodz, Poland
- 1917: Bachelor's degree in engineering
- 1921: Gdansk Polytechnic, studies in engineering, private studies on Tugan-Baranovsky and Luxemburg
- 1924: Left university without degree, work as a business journalist
- 1929: Research Institute of Business Cycles and Prices, Warsaw
- 1930: Marriage with Ada Szternfeld
- 1933: *Essay on the Business Cycle Theory* (in Polish)
- 1935: Publications in *Revue d'Economie Politique* and in *Econometrica*
- 1936: Scholarship to travel to Sweden and England
- 1937: Cambridge, first meeting with Keynes
- 1939: *Essays in the Theory of Economic Fluctuations*
- 1940: Researcher at the Oxford Institute of Statistics
- 1943: *Studies in Economic Dynamics*
- 1945: Paris, Montreal, New York: Economic Department of UN
- 1954: *Theory of Economic Dynamics*
- 1955: Return to Poland
- 1957: Chairman of the Committee for the Perspective Plan
- 1958: University professor and member of the Polish Academy of Sciences
- 1963: *Introduction to the Theory of Growth in a Socialist Economy* (English version 1969b)
- 1969a: *Studies in the Theory of Business Cycles*
- 4 April 1970: Death in Warsaw
- 1970: *Selected Essays on the Dynamics of the Capitalist Economy, 1933–1970*
- 1972: *Selected Essays on the Economic Growth of the Socialist and the Mixed Economy*

Source: Based on information in Toporowski (2013, 2018).

Starting from Keynes's short-run approach, Harrod (1939) and Domar (1946) made first attempts at moving beyond short-run macroeconomics, in which the capital stock is fixed, to consider the capacity effects of investment and their impact on the long-run stability of growth. In Kalecki's books (1939, 1943a, 1954), however, capacity effects of investment were already included in his theory of the trade cycle. Furthermore, we have seen some fundamental work on the role of government deficits for macroeconomic stability with Lerner's (1943)

Table 2.3   Short biography of John Maynard Keynes

- 5 June 1883: Born in Cambridge, UK
- 1897: School at Eton
- 1902: Student at King's College, Cambridge
- 1905: Degree in mathematics
- 1905: Student of Marshall's
- 1906: Indian Office
- 1909: Fellow of King's College
- 1911: Editor of the *Economic Journal*
- 1913: *Indian Currency and Finance*
- 1915: Treasury, member of the British delegation in Versailles
- 1919: *The Economic Consequences of the Peace*
- 1920: *A Treatise on Probability*
- 1922: *A Revision of the Treaty*
- 1923: *A Tract on Monetary Reform*
- 1925: Marriage with Lydia Lopokova
- 1930: Member of the Economic Council of the Prime Minister
- 1930: *A Treatise on Money, 2 volumes*
- 1931: *Essays in Persuasion*
- 1933: *Essays in Biography*
- 1936: *The General Theory of Employment, Interest and Money*
- 1939: Government advisor on war finance and currency issues, member of British delegation in Bretton Woods
- 21 April 1946: Death in Tilton, Sussex, UK

Source: Based on information in Skidelsky (2003).

approach towards functional finance, and Domar's (1944) work on the stability condition for government debt dynamics.

2.4.2   The 1950s and 1960s

The 1950s and 1960s saw further extensions of the principle of effective demand from the short to the long period. This led to the appearance of the post-Keynesian distribution and growth models of the first generation, associated with the works of Kaldor (1955/56, 1957), Pasinetti (1962, 1974) and Robinson (1956, 1962), in which saving adjusts to investment in the long-run growth equilibrium at normal capacity utilisation through changes in functional income distribution.[7] Kaldor (1966) also presented his more applied export-led growth approach focussing on sectoral and regional divergences, dynamic returns to scale, cumulative causation and path dependence in economic development. Furthermore, this was the period of the critique of aggregate neoclassical theory in the 'Cambridge controversies in the theory of capital', starting with Robinson (1953/54). In this debate the theoretical consistency of an aggregate neoclassical production function was fundamentally challenged, and it was shown that the results derived from the aggregate neoclassical production do not generally hold for a more-than-one-good economy (Harcourt 1969, 1972).[8] Sraffa (1960) provided the analytical foundations for this critique.

2.4.3   The 1970s

The 1970s were a promising 'romantic age' in the face of the problems of the then dominating mainstream neoclassical synthesis school, according to Fontana (2009b, Chapter 2). This period saw attempts at defining the contours of a 'post-Keynesian' paradigm in economics, most prominently by Davidson (1972), Eichner and Kregel (1975), Eichner (1978) and Kregel (1973). Robinson and Eatwell (1973) also published an introductory textbook along Sraffian/post-Keynesian lines. This was accompanied by the founding of two journals for post-Keynesians that are still important to this day, the *Cambridge Journal of Economics* in 1977 and the *Journal of Post Keynesian Economics* in 1978. This period also gave rise to important works on the theory of the firm and on pricing theory, by Eichner (1976), Harcourt and Kenyon (1976) and Wood (1975).[9] Furthermore, Kaldor's (1966, 1970a) export-led growth approach was further developed (Dixon and Thirlwall 1975), and the first version of Thirlwall's (1979) balance-of-payments constrained growth model was published (Thirlwall's law), which argues that the long-run growth rate of an economy is limited or even determined by foreign income growth and by the income elasticities of exports and imports.[10] In monetary and financial economics, Minsky (1975, 1977, 1986a) put forward his financial instability hypothesis, arguing that periods of tranquillity always carry the seeds of financial fragility because of endogenous changes in investors' appetite for risk. Rowthorn (1977) presented an important paper to understand conflict inflation, and Garegnani (1978, 1979) provided an attempt at linking the Sraffian long-period theory of prices of production with the Keynesian theory of effective demand, in order to liberate the latter from marginalist remnants.

2.4.4   The 1980s and 1990s

The period of the 1980s and 1990s, with the dominance of monetarism and new classical economics succeeding the neoclassical synthesis as the mainstream, was an 'age of uncertainty' (Fontana 2009b, Chapter 2) for post-Keynesians, with a strong focus on methodology, the history of economic thought and on 'what Keynes really meant'. However, it also saw further attempts at synthesising the essence of post-Keynesian economics (Arestis 1996a) and the publication of some textbook-like monographs on post-Keynesian economics, such as Arestis (1992), Bhaduri (1986), Carvalho (1992), Chick (1983), Davidson (1982, 1994/2011), Dutt and Amadeo (1990), Lavoie (1992), Lee (1998), Palley (1996a), Reynolds (1987) and Sawyer (1985). Also new journals widely open for post-Keynesians were founded, like the *International Review of Applied Economics* in 1987 and the *Review of Political Economy* in 1989.

During this period, important contributions to the theory of endogenous money were made (Kaldor 1982, 1985, Lavoie 1984, 1996a, Moore 1988a, 1988b, 1989a). However, this period also saw the beginning of the infamous 'horizontalist versus structuralist' debate on interest rates, money and credit, which mainly concerned the slope of money and credit supply curves (Lavoie 1996a, 1999, Moore 1989a, Palley 1994a, Pollin 1991, Wray 1990).[11] Furthermore, Wray (1998) published a monograph on the chartalist approach towards understanding money, which has since developed into what is now called 'modern money theory' (MMT).

In the 1980s, the second generation of post-Keynesian distribution and growth models, based on the works of Kalecki (1939, 1943a, 1954) and Steindl (1952), was put forward by Dutt (1984, 1987) and Rowthorn (1981). These models treat the rate of capacity utilisation as an endogenously adjusting variable also in the long run. The long-run adjustment of saving to investment thus does not rely on changes in functional income distribution, which is mainly determined by mark-up pricing in these models, but takes place via varying degrees of utilisation of growing productive capacities. These basic neo-Kaleckian distribution and growth models only generated wage-led regimes, with positive effects of a rising wage share on equilibrium aggregate demand, capital accumulation and growth. However, including a directly negative effect of the wage share into the investment function, as in Bhaduri and Marglin's (1990) and Kurz's (1990) post-Kaleckian models, or allowing for negative effects of a rising wage share on net exports, as in Blecker's (1989) neo-Kaleckian open economy model, have made profit-led regimes possible, too.[12]

2.4.5   Since the Early 2000s

In the current period, which started in the early 2000s and has been dominated by orthodox new Keynesian economics and the NCM, we have seen the following main developments in post-Keynesian economics.[13] We have observed a fuller integration of distribution issues and distributional conflict into short- and long-run post-Keynesian macroeconomics, both in theoretical and empirical/applied works. A prominent example has been the research on wage- vs. profit-led demand and growth (Blecker 2016a, Hein 2014a, Chapter 7, Lavoie 2017a, Lavoie and Stockhammer 2013a, 2013b, Stockhammer 2017a, Stockhammer and Onaran 2013).[14] Regarding theoretical controversies, the debate on the Kaleckian treatment of the rate of capacity utilisation as an endogenous variable beyond the short run and on the relevance of Harrodian instability in Kaleckian models has figured prominently (Hein et al. 2011, 2012a). Recently, this has led to the introduction of non-capacity creating autonomous demand growth, the so-called Sraffian supermultiplier process (Serrano 1995a, 1995b), into Kaleckian distribution and growth models. These models allow one to tame Harrodian instability in the face of a given firm's target rate of utilisation to be achieved in the long run (Allain 2015, Dutt 2019, Lavoie 2016a, Hein and Woodgate 2021).[15] Apart from functional income distribution, the roles of wage dispersion and of household income inequality for aggregate demand, growth and financial stability have been considered, focussing in particular on the relative income hypothesis and related household debt dynamics (Hein and Prante 2020, Kapeller and Schütz 2015, Kim et al. 2014, Prante 2018, Setterfield and Kim 2017). Gender and other types of segregation have also been included in post-Keynesian macroeconomics and distribution and growth models in this period (Blecker and Seguino 2002, Braunstein et al. 2020, Braunstein et al. 2011, Hein 2020, Onaran et al. 2019, Seguino 2019, 2020). Examples of the integration of wage dispersion and a gender pay gap into post-Keynesian short-run macroeconomic models will be shown in Chapter 4. With this focus on the role of several dimensions of distribution for macroeconomic outcomes, post-Keynesians have been doing for decades what, after the recent Global Financial Crisis and the Great Recession, has tended to become more relevant and fashionable in mainstream economics, too.

Furthermore, we have seen further developments in the integrated analysis of money, finance, distribution conflict, effective demand, capital accumulation and growth and its application to changing institutional and historical circumstances, in particular the process of financialisation (Hein 2012a, Palley 2013a). In this context, Minsky's (1986a) work on money manager capitalism, as the latest stage of the development of capitalism, has been re-discovered and further elaborated (Tymoigne and Wray 2014), and several (further) attempts have been made at modelling Minsky's financial instability hypothesis (Charles 2008a, 2008b, 2008c, 2016a, Dafermos 2018, Kapeller and Schütz 2014, Meirelles and Lima 2006, Lima and Meirelles 2007, Nikolaidi and Stockhammer 2017, Nishi 2012a, Ryoo 2013a, 2013b, 2016, Stockhammer and Michell 2017).[16]

For the integrated analysis of money, finance, distribution conflict, effective demand, capital accumulation and growth, it is by now standard to carry out the macroeconomic analysis of these developments in stock-flow consistent models (Godley and Lavoie 2007, Nikiforos and Zezza 2017, Zezza and Zezza 2019). This is true both for analytical small scale models (Hein 2008, 2012a, 2014a, Chapters 9–10) as well as for richer and more realistic large scale numerical simulation models (Belabed et al. 2018, Detzer 2018, Prante et al. 2022a). As will be presented in more detail in Chapter 8 of this book, in this research, different demand and growth regimes, both before and after the crisis, have been distinguished, that is, debt-led private demand boom, domestic demand-led (after the crisis stabilised by government deficits), weakly export-led and export-led mercantilist regimes. The sources and drivers of these regimes and the respective regime changes have been analysed and discussed, and they have been linked to the stagnation tendencies since the Global Financial Crisis and the Great Recession 2007–09 (Hein 2019a). In this context, post-Keynesians have started focussing on issues in critical comparative political economy and international political economy and linking with research in these disciplines (Hein et al. 2021, Hein and Martschin 2021, Kohler and Stockhammer 2021, Stockhammer 2022).

Recently, post-Keynesians have also turned to integrating the ecological constraints into macroeconomics and distribution and growth models and have started to examine the effects on macroeconomic stability (Cahen-Fourot and Lavoie 2016, Fontana and Sawyer 2013, 2016, 2022, Hein and Jimenez 2022), as will be reviewed in more detail in Chapter 9 of this book. Some authors have extended stock-flow consistent models to include an ecological dimension and have presented a stock-flow-fund ecological macroeconomic model in order to analyse the problems of a socio-economic and ecological transition (Dafermos and Nikolaidi 2019, Dafermos et al. 2017, 2018).[17]

In international and development economics, Thirlwall's (1979) balance-of-payments constrained growth model has been further developed, refined and applied (Blecker 2016b, 2021, McCombie 2011, 2019, Setterfield 2011, Thirlwall 2002, 2011, 2013, 2019).[18] Harvey (2007/8, 2009, 2019) has been one of the few working continuously on post-Keynesian international monetary and exchange rate theory. In monetary/financial development economics, the role of currency hierarchies, exchange rates and foreign debt has been highlighted and extensively been analysed (De Paula et al. 2017, Fritz et al. 2018, Herr and Priewe 2006, Priewe 2008, Priewe and Herr 2005).[19]

Further textbooks or textbook-like monographs and edited volumes on post-Keynesian economics have been published since the early 2000s. These include at a more general introductory level the books by King (2015) and Lavoie (2006a), as well as the collections of essays by Holt and Pressman (2001) and Rochon and Rossi (2016, 2017b). The late Łaski (2019) has published an introduction to the Kaleckian variant of post-Keynesian economics. Davidson (2002, 1994/2011, 2015) and Jespersen (2009) have provided introductions to the fundamentalist post-Keynesian stream, as do Hayes (2006) and Tily (2007) with a focus on reading Keynes. Mitchell et al. (2019) have supplied an introductory textbook focussing on MMT. Heine and Herr (2013) is an introductory textbook comparing a specific version of fundamentalist monetary post-Keynesianism with the neoclassical synthesis and neoclassical economics. Prante et al. (2020, 2022b) provide an introduction to macroeconomics focussing on a comparison of NCM and a post-Keynesian/Kaleckian alternative. At an advanced level, Lavoie (2014) has published a comprehensive account of post-Keynesian economics. Blecker and Setterfield (2019) and Hein (2014a) have released more advanced books focussing on post-Keynesian theories of distribution and growth, and Wray (2012) on MMT. The collected essays in Harcourt and Kriesler (2013), Hein and Stockhammer (2011a) and King (2012a) are also more advanced presentations of various fields of post-Keynesian economics.

Several intellectual biographies on the founding mother and fathers and the main contributors to post-Keynesian economics have also helped to consolidate and shape this school of thought: Lopez G. and Assous (2010) and Toporowski (2013, 2018) on Michal Kalecki, Davidson (2007), Dostaler (2007), Hayes (2019) and Skidelsky (1983, 1992, 2000, 2003) on John Maynard Keynes, Harcourt and Kerr (2009) on Joan Robinson, King (2008a) on Nicholas Kaldor, Neilson (2019) on Hyman Minsky, Perez Caldentey (2019) on Roy Harrod and Roncaglia (2009) on Piero Sraffa.[20] Furthermore, and most important for the identity of post-Keynesian economics as a distinctive school of thought, some highly readable books on the history of post-Keynesian economics by Harcourt (2006), King (2002) and Pasinetti (2007) have been published. Finally, some new post-Keynesian journals have entered the stage, like the *European Journal of Economics and Economic Policies: Intervention* (*EJEEP*) in 2004 (as *Intervention: Journal of Economics*) and the *Review of Keynesian Economics* in 2012. Since the beginning, *EJEEP* has contained interviews with heterodox economists, many of them post-Keynesians (see also Ederer et al. 2012).

2.5 THE CURRENT STATE OF POST-KEYNESIAN ECONOMICS

2.5.1 Macroeconomic Policy Relevance

We have seen that, based on the ten main features of post-Keynesian economics outlined above, over the last eight decades or so, there has emerged a solid body of post-Keynesian economics in the areas of macroeconomics, employment and unemployment, distribution and growth, money, credit and finance, international money and finance, financialisation, financial instability and financial crisis, the economics of European integration, as well as development and emerging market economics. Against the background of these developments, post-Keynesians have been well equipped to criticise the dominant mainstream macroeconomics, the NCM since the late 1990s/early 2000s,[21] and to provide economic policy alternatives, even well before the 2007–09 crises.[22] Comprehensive post-Keynesian macroeconomic models, to be presented in detail and further developed in Chapters 4 and 5 of this book, have provided alternatives to the mainstream NCM. This has allowed the derivation of a full post-Keynesian macroeconomic policy mix as an alternative to the one implied and proposed by the mainstream NCM, which failed so dramatically in the face of the 2007–09 crises. The main elements, drawing on Arestis (2013) and Hein and Stockhammer (2009b, 2010, 2011b), are summarised in Table 2.4, briefly outlined below, and are then fully explained in Chapter 6 of this book. This rather general post-Keynesian policy mix has also been specified for the special conditions of the Eurozone, for example (Arestis and Sawyer 2011, 2013, Hein 2018a, Hein and Detzer 2015a, 2015b, Hein and Martschin 2020, Hein et al. 2012b, Sawyer 2013). In the USA, a specific version of the post-Keynesian macroeconomic policy

Table 2.4   Macroeconomic policy recommendations: New consensus models (NCM) and post-Keynesian models (PKM) compared

	NCM	PKM
Monetary policy	Inflation targeting by means of interest rate policies, which affects unemployment in the short run, but only inflation in the long run	Target low interest rates which mainly affect distribution, and stabilise monetary, financial and real sectors by applying other instruments (lender of last resort, credit controls, etc.)
Fiscal policy	Supports monetary policy in achieving price stability by balancing the budget over the cycle	Real stabilisation in the short and in the long run with no autonomous deficit targets; reduction of inequality
Labour market and wage/incomes policy	Determines the NAIRU in the long run and the speed of adjustment in the short run; focus should be on flexible nominal and real wages	Affects price level/inflation and distribution; focus on stable nominal wage and nominal unit labour cost growth, as well as compressed wage structure
International economic policies	Free trade, free capital flows and flexible exchange rates	Regulated capital flows, managed exchange rates, infant industry protection, regional and industrial policies
Economic policy co-ordination	Clear assignment in the long run; co-ordination at best only in the short run	No clear assignment; economic policy co-ordination required in the short and the long run, both nationally and internationally

Source: Based on Hein (2017a, p. 154).

approach has become prominent recently and has been livelily discussed in a broader public framework, 'modern money (or monetary) theory' (MMT), which contains a special focus on the unconstrained role of government spending in sovereign money systems (Kelton 2020, Mitchell et al. 2019, Tcherneva 2006, Wray 1998, 2012).[23]

As shown in Table 2.4, in the orthodox NCM approach, put forward by, for example, Carlin and Soskice (2009, 2015, Chapters 1–3),[24] inflation-targeting monetary policies are recommended as the main stabilising economic policy tool. Central bank policies applying the interest rate tool have short-run real effects on unemployment, but in the long run only the inflation rate is affected. Fiscal policies are to support inflation-targeting monetary policies by balancing the public budget over the cycle. The labour market, together with the social security system, determines equilibrium unemployment, the NAIRU in the long run and the speed of adjustment towards this rate in the short run. Regarding international economic policies, mainstream economics would be in favour of free trade, free capital flows and flexible exchange rates, reaping the presumed stabilisation effects from flexible exchange rates and the benefits from comparative advantages and the related international division of labour. Since, at least in the long run, there is a clear division of labour between the different areas of economic policymaking, ex ante co-ordination is not required – each area of policymaking would have to follow its tasks as outlined.

The macroeconomic policy mix based on post-Keynesian models advocates the co-ordination of economic policies between the different areas, both in the short and the long run, because there is no clear-cut assignment of policymakers and their instruments to just one specific economic policy target, as full employment, stable inflation, equitable distribution of income and wealth or financial stability.

Generally, it is acknowledged that central bank interest rate policies have real effects, both in the short run and the long run. Central banks should thus target low long-term real interest rates using their short-term monetary interest rate tool and contribute to stabilising the monetary, financial and real sectors of the economy using other instruments than just the interest rate: Credit controls, asset-based reserve requirements, etc. Above all, central banks have to act as lender of last resort for the banking sector and as guarantor of government debt. The latter has been and still is an important lesson to learn in order to overcome the Eurozone crisis and the underlying design failures, that is, the lack of a convincing lender of last resort for the member countries' governments and a guarantee of public debt (Arestis and Sawyer 2011, Goodhart 1998, Hein 2013/14, Hein and Detzer 2015a, 2015b, Wray 2012, Chapter 5.7). The exact monetary policy strategy with respect to the interest rate, 'activist' or 'parking it', has been a matter of debate (Rochon and Setterfield 2007). Whereas some authors have been in favour of central banks using the interest rate tool for real stabilisation purposes (Fontana and Palacio-Vera 2007, Palley 2007a, Setterfield 2006), others have rejected any fine-tuning by means of interest rate policies and have instead been in favour of targeting a short-term or long-term interest rate that is conducive to growth and employment (Gnos and Rochon 2007, Hein and Stockhammer 2010, 2011b, Lavoie 1996b, Rochon and Setterfield 2007, Setterfield 2009a, Smithin 2007, Wray 2007). However, irrespective of the precise view on interest rate policies in general, there is broad agreement amongst post-Keynesians that lowering interest rates in a deep recession has little real effect. Therefore, also quantitative easing policies, as the responses towards the Global Financial Crisis and the Great Recession 2007–09 and the COVID-19 crisis 2020, have only limited effects. Only to the extent that long-term interest rates are reduced, capital gains are generated and balance sheets of commercial banks are improved, and that the domestic currency is depreciated, might we see positive effects on aggregate demand (Lavoie 2016b). However, these effects are considered to be way too small and thus ineffective in terms of overcoming the crisis and the stagnation tendencies, unless they are supported by active and expansionary fiscal policies.

In a post-Keynesian macroeconomic policy mix, fiscal policies have a major impact on economic activity and the distribution of disposable income, and should thus actively take care of real stabilisation of the economy in the short and the long run, using government expenditures as the main tool without any autonomous government deficit targets. The post-Keynesian macroeconomic policy mix thus follows a functional finance approach in the tradition of Lerner (1943) (Arestis and Sawyer 2003, 2004b, Setterfield 2009b). Potential limits to government debt in this kind of approach are a matter of controversy between those sympathetic to neo-chartalism, which is at the core of MMT (Wray 2012), and the critics of such an approach (Palley 2015a, 2015b). The relevance of government debt limits will depend on the precise institutional link between the government and the central bank, the international acceptance of the national currency, and whether private and public debt is denominated in the domestic currency (Lavoie 2013). In particular, if central banks act as a lender of last resort for the government and guarantee government debt, and private agents thus do not have to fear the illiquidity or insolvency of the government, the level of government debt or government debt-income ratios should be of minor concern, as has been pointed out by the proponents of MMT.

Wage and incomes policies should mainly focus on nominal stabilisation, which means on stable unit labour cost growth at the target rate of inflation (Arestis 1996a, 2013, Davidson

2006, Hein and Stockhammer 2010, 2011b, Setterfield 2006). To what extent wage policies can and should contribute to redistribution in favour of the labour income share, with an aim of stimulating aggregate demand and growth, is controversial amongst post-Keynesians. The effect of rising nominal wages and unit labour costs on functional income distribution and aggregate demand will depend on the concrete and specific circumstances in the country or region under consideration, in particular on the degree of international competition and the nature of the demand regime (Hein 2014a, Chapters 5–7). However, to the extent that wage and income policies manage to reduce wage dispersion and wage inequality, the demand effects seem to be favourable at any rate, as shown by Palley (2017).

Finally, regarding international economic policies, post-Keynesians hold that absolute advantage may be more important than comparative advantage due to the underutilisation of productive resources, static and dynamic economies of scale and endogenous potential growth. Following Kaldor's (1970a) export-led growth model, countries may enter into a virtuous (or a vicious) circle of export demand that drives output and productivity growth, which then feeds back on export growth. Moreover, Thirlwall's law (1979), which introduces a balance-of-payments constraint into the model, has shown that the growth rate consistent with a balanced current account is determined in the long run by the growth of external income and the income elasticities of demand for exports and imports. In order to improve the balance-of-payments constrained growth rate, countries would thus have to increase the income elasticity of demand for their exports and to reduce their income elasticity of demand for imports, hence improve their non-price competitiveness, by appropriate industrial and regional policies, including infant industry protection. For this purpose, regulated capital flows and thus capital controls are important. This also provides the conditions for international economic policy co-ordination and managed exchange rates, which should contribute to international financial stability. Several post-Keynesians would thus be in favour of a return to a cooperative world financial order and a system with fixed but adjustable exchange rates, symmetric adjustment obligations for current account deficit and surplus countries and regulated international capital flows in order to avoid the imbalances that have contributed to the 2007–09 financial and economic crises and to prevent export-led mercantilist policies by major economies. Keynes's (1942) proposal for an International Clearing Union is an obvious blueprint to be further developed for this purpose (Davidson 1982, 2009, 2011, Chapter 17). Few others, in particular the followers of MMT (Wray 2012, pp. 185–6), would not be willing to give up the presumed national sovereignty and policy space which, in their view, seems to be preserved by floating exchange rates. However, this seems to apply only to countries which are able to issue the key currency in the world economy, that is, the USA, and it ignores also negative feedback effects of currency depreciation on distribution, inflation and domestic demand, as we will show in Chapter 5.

2.5.2   On Micro and Macro

Our brief review of the stages of development of post-Keynesian economics and economic policy recommendations has mainly focussed on macroeconomics and macroeconomic policies. However, this does not imply that post-Keynesians have nothing to say about microeconomics. On the contrary, in Lavoie (2014) we find two chapters on micro, Chapter 2 on 'Theory of choice' and Chapter 3 on 'Theory of the firm'. Also in King (2015), Chapter 5 is devoted to 'Post Keynesian microeconomics'. Here, and fully in line with the ten features of post-Keynesian economics explained above, it is argued that post-Keynesian microeconomics is based on the following principles: First, in a capitalist economy, decisions of firms are the driving force. Second, markets are imperfect, dominated by oligopolistic or monopolistic competition, and firms are thus price setters and quantity takers. Third, fundamental uncertainty prevents precise maximisation strategies from being applied by firms or households; satisficing rather than maximising behaviour dominates the scene. King (2009, 2012b, 2015, Chapter 5) has also clarified, that, of course, post-Keynesians reject the orthodox/mainstream requirement of the 'micro-foundation of macroeconomics', because it is a micro-reduction strategy: Macroeconomics is reduced to the microeconomics of representative, utility maximising agents with rational expectations acting in efficient markets. There are no fallacies of composition, no downward causations such that individuals are affected by their environment and no emerging properties of the economic and social systems, which are external to individual choices. However, the rejection of the orthodox 'micro-foundations of macroeconomics' should not imply their replacement by some heterodox 'macro-foundations of microeconomics', as King (2015, p. 45) argues: '(M)acroeconomics and microeconomics should be thought of as existing side by side, closely related to and influencing each other but also relatively autonomous and neither constituting the foundations of the other'.

This review has already contained some examples of the inclusion of features and changes of the micro conditions and behaviours in post-Keynesian macroeconomic models. From the theory of the firm, post-Keynesian macroeconomic models of financialisation have included the shift from manager-dominated firms and a coalition of managers and workers against shareholders towards a shareholder-manager coalition against workers, or from 'retain and invest' towards 'downsize and distribute' strategies (Lazonick and O'Sullivan 2000). In the same context, several macroeconomic models of financialisation mentioned above in Section 2.4.5 have entertained the notion of an interest- and dividend-elastic mark-up and included the respective distributional effects at the aggregate level. Furthermore, with respect to the household and consumer theory, in the literature on financialisation referred to above, we have observed the revival of the relative income hypothesis and the inclusion of wealth and credit availability effects in the consumption functions of the macroeconomic models. In this context, post-Keynesians have drawn on the results of other schools of thought in economics, that is, old institutionalism, experimental and behavioural economics and critical political economy, as well as of other disciplines, that is, political science, sociology and psychology. Together with modern Marxian economics, post-Keynesian economics thus provides the macroeconomics of a broader political economy research programme, which would include other heterodox approaches in economics and benefit from the research in other social sciences.

2.5.3   Post-Keynesian Institutional Academic Infrastructure

Post-Keynesian economics since Kalecki and Keynes has developed and survived as a contested and embattled minority in economics. For this, an academic infrastructure – as part of heterodox economics in general – has been required.[25]

First, as has been reviewed above in this chapter, there are now available a range of updated textbooks or textbook-like monographs and edited volumes on post-Keynesian economics in general, as well as on macroeconomics, distribution and growth in particular, most of them for graduate programmes. Furthermore, and most importantly for the identity of post-Keynesian economics as a distinctive school of thought, there are the books on the history of post-Keynesian economics and the range of intellectual biographies on eminent post-Keynesians.

Second, as an outlet for academic research, post-Keynesians have access to a range of journals with an explicit post-Keynesian leaning, or which are at least widely open to this approach, several of them (co-)edited by leading current post-Keynesians: The *Cambridge Journal of Economics*, the *Journal of Post Keynesian Economics, Metroeconomica*, the *Review of Political Economy*, the *International Review of Applied Economics*, the *European Journal of Economics and Economic Policies*: *Intervention*, the *Review of Keynesian Economics*, the *Journal of Economic Issues*, the *International Journal of Political Economy*, the *Review of Radical Political Economics*, the *PSL Quarterly Review* (the former *Banca Nazionale del Lavoro Quarterly Review*), the *Brazilian Journal of Political Economy, Investigacion Economica*, the *Bulletin of Political Economy*, the *Contributions to Political Economy*, *Panoeconomicus* and the *Review of Evolutionary Political Economy*, amongst other journals with a more specific focus, like the *European Journal of the History of Economic Thought* or *Structural Change and Economic Dynamics*. Although currently a broad range of heterodox journals in general and post-Keynesian journals, in particular, exist, the inappropriately low ranking of these journals in the dominant journal lists is a major problem and obstacle for the future development of post-Keynesian economics, as analysed by Dobusch and Kapeller (2012) and Lee et al. (2010), for example.

Third, post-Keynesians have established or are part of a range of associations and networks, organising international conferences and workshops, as well as summer schools for graduate students on a regular basis. In North America, there is a network organised by the Levy Economics Institute in the USA, with annual conferences and Minsky summer seminars in Annandale-on-Hudson, NY. In South America, with the largest post-Keynesian academic community in Brazil, the Brazilian Keynes Association (AKB) has been running annual conferences for several years. In Argentina, an Argentinean Post-Keynesian Association (APKA) is in preparation, and the main proponents have already hosted some online seminars. In Australia, post-Keynesians are the main organisers of and contributors to the Australian Society of Heterodox Economics (SHE) conferences. In Asia, there is the Japanese Society for Post Keynesian Economics organising seminars and conferences, as well as a Keynes Society Japan with annual conferences. In Europe, we have the Post-Keynesian Economics Society (PKES) in the UK with annual workshops, PhD seminars and summer schools. In Denmark, a Nordic post-Keynesian network has been organising some conferences in Copenhagen and Aalborg. In France, there have been several post-Keynesian conferences at the University of Dijon, the University of Grenoble and the University of Lille, partly co-organised by the French Association pour le Développement des Etudes Keynésiennes (ADEK). French post-Keynesians are also involved in the Association Française d'Economie Politique (AFEP) and its conferences and other activities. In Italy, recently an Italian Post-Keynesian Network has been founded and several online seminars and workshops have been organised. In Spain, the University of the Basque Country, in cooperation with the Cambridge Centre for Economic and Public Policy, has been organising important and growing annual international conferences for two decades. In Germany, we have the German Keynes Society with small annual conferences for German speaking participants, and the Forum for Macroeconomics and Macroeconomic Policies (FMM) with large annual international conferences in Berlin for more than two decades, as well as biennial summer schools for graduate students and young researchers, which also take place in Berlin. Furthermore, post-Keynesians are actively involved in broader associations, as for example the Association for Heterodox Economics (AHE), the European Association for Evolutionary Political Economy (EAEPE) or the World Economics Association (WEA).

Fourth, post-Keynesians have so far been successful in defending or newly establishing graduate programmes containing major elements of post-Keynesian economics, amongst other heterodox approaches. There are several programmes at Brazilian universities, for example at the Federal University of Rio de Janeiro and the University of Campinas. In the USA, there are the master and PhD programmes at American University, Washington, DC, Colorado State University, the University of Massachusetts Amherst, the New School for Social Research, New York, the University of Missouri, Kansas City, and the University of Utah, Salt Lake City. Furthermore, there is a master programme at the Levy Economics Institute of Bard College, Annandale-on-Hudson, NY. In the UK there are the programmes at Leeds University Business School, the University of Greenwich, London, the University of the West of England, Bristol, and the School of Oriental and African Studies, London. In France there are programmes at the University Sorbonne Paris North, the University of Lille and the University of Grenoble, for example. In Spain, there is the programme at the University of the Basque Country, Bilbao, and in Italy there are programmes at the University of Rome 3 and at the University of Rome, La Sapienza, amongst others. In Germany, we have the master programmes at the Berlin School of Economics and Law and the HTW University of Applied Sciences Berlin. The Berlin School of Economics and Law is cooperating with the PhD programmes of the University Sorbonne Paris North in France and the University of the Basque Country, Bilbao, in Spain.

What was encouraging was a newly created joint Erasmus Mundus Master Programme on Economic Policies in the Age of Globalisation (EPOG), funded by the European Commission from 2013 to 2019, with the University Sorbonne Paris North (then University Paris 13), the University of Turin, the Berlin School of Economics and Law, Kingston University London and the University of Witwatersrand in Johannesburg as major partners, and Seoul National University, the Federal University of Rio de Janeiro and the University of Massachusetts Amherst cooperating. Also a follow-up Erasmus Mundus Master Programme on Economic Policies for the Global Transition (EPOG+) is funded by the European Commission from 2020 to 2025, with the Technical University Compiègne Paris, Sorbonne University Paris, the University of Turin, the University of Rome, the Berlin School of Economics and Law, Vienna University of Economics and Business and the University of Witwatersrand in Johannesburg as major partners, and a long list of international associated partners.

NOTES

*   This chapter partly draws on Hein (2017a). See also Hein (2014b) and Hein and Lavoie (2019). For more extensive discussion of some of the issues raised in this chapter, see, for example, Lavoie (2006d, 2011a, 2014, Chapter 1).

1.   Dequech (2012) defines 'orthodox economics' as an intellectual category referring to the dominant school of thought and its methods. 'Mainstream economics' as a sociological concept is referring to what is taught at the most important universities, what is published in the most important journals, what receives the research funds from the most important institutions and what wins the most important awards. Lavoie (2012) then distinguishes between the 'mainstream', referring to the dominant textbook approach, and the 'dissenters'. The latter group is composed of 'orthodox' and 'heterodox' dissenters.

2.   For a still relevant and highly readable textbook that distinguishes different schools of thought in macroeconomics, see Snowdon and Vane (2005).

3.   For the foundation of the 'new neoclassical synthesis' or the 'new consensus model' (NCM) see Clarida et al. (1999) and Goodfriend and King (1997). For a textbook version, which even allows for several links and comparisons with the post-Keynesian models developed in this book, see Carlin and Soskice (2006, 2009, 2015). For an attempt at presenting a unified framework, which contains the Carlin and Soskice NCM model but also, through changes in assumption, some features of the post-Keynesian model to be developed in this book, see Prante et al. (2020, 2022b).

4.   For further classifications, see also Arestis (1996a).

5.   See also the more comprehensive books on the history of post-Keynesian economics by Harcourt (2006), King (2002) and Pasinetti (2007).

6.   For extensive intellectual biographies, see Feiwel (1975), Lopez G. and Assous (2010), Sawyer (1985) and Toporowski (2013, 2018) on Michal Kalecki, as well as Davidson (2007), Dostaler (2007), Harrod (1951), Hayes (2019) and Skidelsky (1983, 1992, 2000, 2003) on John Maynard Keynes. On Kalecki, see also the book reviews by Hein (2011a, 2019c).

7.   For textbook presentations of the first generation post-Keynesian distribution and growth models by Kaldor, Pasinetti and Robinson, see Blecker and Setterfield (2019, Chapter 3), Hein (2014a, Chapter 4) and Lavoie (2014, Chapter 6). Basic versions of these models will be shown in Chapter 7 of this book.

8.   For a textbook presentation of the capital controversy, see Hein (2014a, Chapter 3), and for a broader elaboration in the context of the history of economic thought, see Lazzarini (2011).

9.   For a textbook presentation of the post-Keynesian theory of the firm, see Lavoie (2014a, Chapter 3).

10. For textbook presentations of Kaldor's export-led growth approach and Thirlwall's balance-of-payments constrained growth model, see Blecker and Setterfield (2019, Chapters 8–10), Hein (2014a, Chapter 4) and Lavoie (2014, Chapter 7).

11. See Rochon and Rossi (2017a) for recent contributions to this debate.

12. For textbook presentations of the second generation post-Keynesian distribution and growth models based on the works of Kalecki and Steindl, see Blecker and Setterfield (2019, Chapter 4), Hein (2014a, Chapters 5–7) and Lavoie (2014, Chapter 6). Basic versions of these models will be included in Chapter 7 of this book.

13. For a more detailed review of the development of post-Keynesian macroeconomics since the mid/late 1990s, see Hein (2017a).

14. See also the four special issues on the Bhaduri and Marglin (1990) model in the *Review of Keynesian Economics*, 2016, 4 (4) and 2017, 5 (1)–(3).

15. See also the recent special issues on autonomous demand-led growth in *Metroeconomica*, 2019, 70 (2), and in the *Review of Keynesian Economics*, 2020, 8 (3). A basic version of this model will be presented in Chapter 7 of this book.

16. For a broader assessment of Minsky's work, see recently Lavoie (2020b).

17. See also the special issue on 'De-growth, zero growth and/or green growth? Macroeconomic implications of ecological constraints' in the *European Journal of Economics and Economic Policies: Intervention*, 2022, 19 (1).

18. See also the recent special issue on Thirlwall's law in the *Review of Keynesian Economics*, 2019, 7 (4).

19. For a more extensive review of several areas in international economics from post-Keynesian perspectives, see Lavoie (2014, Chapter 7) and our brief review in Chapter 5 of this book.

20. See also the previous intellectual biographies by Feiwel (1975) on Michal Kalecki, by Harrod (1951) on John Maynard Keynes and by Targetti (1992) and Thirlwall (1987) on Nicholas Kaldor.

21. See, for example, Carlin and Soskice (2009, 2015, Chapter 3), Clarida et al. (1999), Goodfriend and King (1997), Romer (2000), Walsh (2002) and Woodford (2003, 2009).

22. See, for example, Arestis (2006, 2009, 2011a), Arestis and Sawyer (2004a), Davidson (2006), Dullien (2011), Fontana (2009a), Fontana and Palacio-Vera (2002, 2004), Gnos and Rochon (2007), Hein (2006a), Kriesler and Lavoie (2007), Lavoie (2006b, 2009a), Palley (2007a), Rochon and Rossi (2006a), Sawyer (2002, 2009a), Setterfield (2006, 2009a), Smithin (2007, 2009), Stockhammer (2008) and Wray (2007).

23. For a European version, see Ehnts (2017). For controversies on MMT see, for example, Epstein (2019a, 2019b, 2020), Febrero (2009), Fiebiger (2016a), Fiebiger et al. (2012), Lavoie (2013), Palley (2015a, 2015b, 2020), Prates (2020), Rochon and Vernengo (2003), Tymoigne and Wray (2015), Vernengo and Pérez Caldentey (2020) and the contributions in the special issue of the *Real World Economics Review*, 2019, (89), on 'modern monetary theory and its critics'.

24. The Carlin and Soskice (2009, 2015, Chapter 3) three equations model is different from those new Keynesian/ NCM models relying on rational expectations and utility maximisation of a single individual household, in which there is no firm sector and no role of aggregate demand, but fluctuations in unemployment reflect changes in equilibrium employment in the face of some real interest rate rigidities, as shown by Dullien (2011). The Carlin and Soskice three equations model contains investment by the firm sector, mark-up pricing and quantity adjustment by firms, an interest-elastic IS goods market equilibrium curve, a Phillips curve with

adaptive expectations and an interest rate rule applied by the central bank. It thus allows for a short-run role of money and effective demand. However, the long-run equilibrium is determined by the supply side only, like other new Keynesian/NCM models, as Lavoie (2015a) in his review of Carlin and Soskice (2015) also clearly points out. Prante et al. (2020, 2022b) present an attempt at changing some of the assumptions in the Carlin and Soskice (2015) model and generating some features of the post-Keynesian model to be developed in this book.

25. For details on the heterodox and post-Keynesian institutional academic infrastructure, regarding journals, associations and networks, as well as graduate programmes, see also the *Heterodox Economics Directory* (Kapeller and Springholz 2021), from which some of the information presented here has been taken.

3. The principle of effective demand, money, credit and finance: Marx, Kalecki, Keynes and the monetary circuit school

3.1   INTRODUCTION

The rejection of Say's law, and hence of the notion that there are no other long-run limits to output and growth than those given by productive capacities, unites several strands of heterodox macroeconomic theory. As Keynes (1979) masterfully described in the drafts leading to the *General Theory of Employment, Interest, and Money* (1936), Say's law cannot be assumed to hold in a monetary or entrepreneur economy, because there may be leakages from the circuit of income (i.e. saving) which are not exactly compensated for by injections (i.e. investment) of the same amount. Thus, aggregate demand may systematically deviate from aggregate supply, with no adjustment mechanism other than changes in output, income and employment. Therefore, output, income, employment and growth are determined by aggregate demand and thus adjust towards the latter, in the short and in the long run.

The principle of effective demand, and the claim that economic activity in a monetary production economy is demand determined in the short and in the long run, is therefore the core of post-Keynesian macroeconomics, currently found in all the different strands of post-Keynesian economics, as outlined in Chapter 2 of this book. The foundations of the principle of effective demand can draw not only on Keynes's contributions, but can already be found in Marx's and Kalecki's work, in particular, where they are closely linked with the notion of distributional conflict between classes or social groups.[1] Regarding modern Marxian economics, however, the long-run relevance of aggregate demand is only supported in the monopoly capitalism and underconsumptionist school (Foster 2014).

The rejections of Say's law and its replacement by the principle of effective demand in the works of Marx, Kalecki and Keynes are based on their respective views of capitalist economies as monetary production economies. Following Schumpeter's (1954, pp. 277–8) distinction, all three contributions can be classified as following 'monetary analysis':

> Monetary Analysis introduces the element of money on the very ground floor of our analytical structure and abandons the idea that all essential features of economic life can be represented by a barter-economy model. Money prices, money incomes, and saving and investment decisions bearing upon these money incomes, no longer appear as expressions – sometimes convenient, sometimes misleading, but always nonessential – of quantities of commodities and services and of exchange ratios between them: they acquire a life and an importance of their own, and it has to be recognized that essential features of the capitalist process may depend upon the 'veil' and that the 'face behind it' is incomplete without it.
>
> (Schumpeter 1954, p. 278)

In monetary analysis, money and monetary variables are thus essential for the determination of the real variables of the system, both in the short and in the long run. This is opposed to 'real analysis', where money is seen as a veil, which has no long-run effects on the real economy:

> Real Analysis proceeds from the principle that all essential phenomena of economic life are capable of being described in terms of goods and services, of decisions about them, and of relations between them. Money enters the picture only in the modest role of a technical device that has been adopted in order to facilitate transactions. This device can no doubt get out of order, and if it does it will indeed produce phenomena that are specifically attributable to its *modus operandi*. But so long as it functions normally, it does not affect the economic process, which behaves in the same way as it would in a barter economy: this is essentially what the concept of Neutral Money implies.
>
> (Schumpeter 1954, p. 277, italics in the original)

In this chapter, we will outline the foundations of the principle of effective demand and the relationships with the respective notions of a capitalist or a monetary production economy in the works of Marx, Kalecki and Keynes. Furthermore, in order to clarify the link between endogenous credit, finance, investment and saving, we will turn to the monetary circuit school in the final section of this chapter.

3.2   KARL MARX'S THEORY OF MONEY AND EFFECTIVE DEMAND

In *Capital, Vol. 1*, Karl Marx (1867, pp. 97–144) discusses three principal roles of money: Money as a standard of value, money as a means of circulation and 'money as money', including money as a store of value, as a means of payment and as universal money. Money as a medium of circulation means that the succession of sales (C-M) and purchases (M-C) in the circuit C-M-C (commodity – money – commodity) of simple commodity production is interrupted. This function of money provides Marx with the first argument to explicitly reject Ricardo's version of Say's law in his *Theories of Surplus Value*, and it constitutes Marx's 'possibility theory of crisis' (Marx 1861–63, pp. 499–508).[2] In the 'possibility theory of crisis' the existence and the use of money is the reason why a general crisis of overproduction *may* occur; it is not yet an explanation why an actual crisis *will* occur.[3] Since 'money as money' includes its potential to function as a store of value (hoarding), an increase in the willingness to hoard causes a lack of aggregate demand for the economy as a whole and may therefore trigger a general crisis of overproduction. Of course, this will only hold true if the demand for holding money does not constitute a demand for production and output. If money were a produced commodity, an increase in the demand for money would not generate a deficiency of aggregate demand, because it would mean an increase of demand for the reproducible money commodity. Therefore, money cannot be a reproducible commodity if Say's law is to be rejected – a conclusion Marx did not seem to be aware of, because he built his theory of money on the assumption of a money commodity, that is, gold, although with some ambiguities (Hein 2004, 2006b, 2019b, Heinrich 1991).

For Marx (1861–63, p. 511), a second argument against Say's law derives from the function of money as a means of payment. Money functions as a means of payment when the sale of a commodity and the realisation of its price are separated in time. The seller becomes a creditor, the buyer a debtor, and money is the standard and the subject of a creditor-debtor contract. In such a system, on the one hand, the demand for commodities is no longer limited by income created in production. On the other hand, money as a means of payment increases the vulnerability and fragility of the system. Capitalists do not only have to find appropriate demand for their produced commodities, but they have to find it within a certain period of time in order to be able to meet their payment obligations as debtors. If there are unanticipated changes in market prices for final products between the purchase of a commodity as an input for production financed by credit and the sale of the final product, capitalists may be unable to meet their payment commitments. Default of individual units of capital may interrupt credit chains and cause a general crisis.[4]

The rejection of Say's law and its necessary replacement by a theory of effective demand, as well as the need for endogenous money for the expansion of capitalist economies also become clear in Marx's (1885, pp. 396–527) discussion of simple and expanded reproduction in *Capital, Vol. 2*. In the schemes of reproduction, Marx analyses the conditions for capitalist reproduction in a two-sector model without foreign trade and economic activity by the state. Sector 1 produces means of production, and sector 2 produces means of consumption. The value of supply of each sector is given by constant capital costs expended in production (D_c), wage costs (W) and normal profits (Π). Normal profits are either determined by the rate of surplus value, if relative prices are determined by labour values, or by the general rate of profit for the economy as a whole, if relative prices are determined by prices of production. In the long run, changes in demand do not affect these values or prices of production. The demand for output of sector 1 consists of gross investment ($p_1 I^g$) in constant capital of both sectors while the demand for output of sector 2 consists of consumption demand out of profits ($p_2 C_\Pi$) and out of wages ($p_2 C_W$). For the values of aggregate demand and aggregate supply, we therefore have the following expression, where the indices denote the departments:

$$D_{c1} + W_1 + \Pi_1 + D_{c2} + W_2 + \Pi_2$$
$$= p_1 I_1^g + p_1 I_2^g + p_2 C_{W1} + p_2 C_{W2} + p_2 C_{\Pi1} + p_2 C_{\Pi2}. \tag{3.1}$$

Assuming that wages for the workers' class as a whole are completely spent on consumption goods, and hence $W_1 + W_2 = p_2 C_{W1} + p_2 C_{W2}$, we get:

$$\Pi_1 + \Pi_2 = p_1 I_1 + p_1 I_2 + p_2 C_{\Pi1} + p_2 C_{\Pi2}. \tag{3.2}$$

where $p_1 I_i = p_1 I_i^g - D_{ci}$, $i = 1,2$, denotes net investment. From this, Kalecki's (1968a) interpretation of Marx's schemes of reproduction arises: As capitalists cannot determine their sales and their profits, but can only decide on their investment and consumption expenditures, these expenditures have to ensure that *produced* profits will become *realised* profits. Therefore, net investment determines saving, which is only out of profits ($S = S_\Pi$), in Marx's schemes of reproduction:

$$S = S_{\Pi1} + S_{\Pi2} = \Pi_1 - p_2 C_{\Pi1} + \Pi_2 - p_2 C_{\Pi2} = p_1 I_1 + p_1 I_2 = p_1 I. \tag{3.3}$$

The capitalists' investment and consumption expenditures thus determine their aggregate profits – it is the capitalists who have to advance the required amount of money in order to realise their produced and expected profits.

So far as the entire capitalist class is concerned, the proposition that it must itself throw into circulation the money required for the realization of its surplus value (correspondingly also for the circulation of its capital, constant and variable) not only fails to appear paradoxical, but stands forth as a necessary condition of the entire mechanism. For there are only two classes: the working class disposing only of its labour-power, and the capitalist class, which has a monopoly of the social means of production and money.

(Marx 1885, pp. 424–5)

A realisation failure, the inability to sell commodities at predetermined prices, may occur if there is insufficient investment or consumption demand by capitalists. Aggregate supply will then exceed aggregate demand and the economy will suffer from unused productive capacity and higher unemployment and, hence, from a crisis.[5]

Whether Marx's principle of effective demand provides the conditions for an underemployment equilibrium, or a state of rest, is a matter of debate. Whereas Sardoni (2011) argues that Marx's microeconomics only allow for dynamic disequilibrium processes, Hein (2006b, 2019b) claims that Marx's contributions are, in principle, consistent with an underemployment equilibrium or state of rest of the Kalecki and Keynes type, which we will discuss below.

What is clear from Marx's (1885) analysis in *Capital, Vol. 2*, is that, with the values/prices of individual commodities given independently of demand, by labour values or prices of production, in a growing economy the money advanced by capitalists has to increase. As potential sources for additional money advances and hence for the endogeneity of money, Marx (1885, pp. 349–50) proposes the transfer of money from hoards and an increasing velocity of money in circulation (Sardoni 1997). However, these sources can only temporarily facilitate an ongoing process of economic expansion, because hoards have a finite amount and the velocity of circulation of money has an upper bound due to payment conventions and institutional factors. In the long run, therefore, the money stock has to increase; according to Marx (1885, pp. 350, 494–5) by means of increasing the production of the money commodity. Looking at Marx's (1894) views on interest and credit in the manuscripts on monetary and financial issues, included by Engels in *Capital, Vol. 3*, there is an alternative of the endogeneity of money, which is more consistent with Marx's rejection of Say's law. This rejection implies that hoarding and hence demanding money, and thus triggering a problem of aggregate demand, cannot be equivalent to demanding a reproducible money commodity. The more convincing alternative of endogenous money and endogenous means of finance is thus the endogenous creation of credit money 'out of nothing'. This is Marx's (1894, pp. 400–13) view in *Capital, Vol. 3*. There he does not suppose that the credit supply of commercial banks is limited by private saving but assumes that commercial banks, in principle, can create credit without limits, which will then circulate as credit money (De Brunhoff 1976, pp. 93–9, Reuten 1988):

The credit given by a banker may assume various forms, such as bills of exchange on other banks, cheques on them, credit accounts of the same kind, and finally, if the bank is entitled to issue notes – bank-notes of the bank itself. A bank-note is nothing but a draft upon the banker, payable at any time to the bearer, and given by the banker in place of private drafts. This last form of credit appears particularly important and striking to the layman, first because this form of credit money breaks out of the confines of mere commercial circulation into general circulation, and serves there as money; and because in most countries the principal banks issuing notes, being a particular mixture of national and private banks, actually have the national credit to back them, and their notes are more or less legal tender; because it is apparent here that the banker deals in credit itself, a bank-note being merely a circulating token of credit.

(Marx 1894, pp. 403–4)

The quantity of credit money is therefore endogenous for capitalist reproduction and is determined by the credit demand of capitalists. Analysing the medium of circulation in the credit system, Marx (1894, p. 524) then concludes that '[t]he quantity of circulation notes is regulated by the turnover requirements, and every superfluous note wends its way back immediately to the issuer'.

According to Marx, the rate of interest is determined in the market for money capital, where there is no 'natural rate' as a centre of gravity for actual rates (Marx 1894, pp. 358–69). Instead, the rate of interest is given by concrete historical, institutional and political factors, which reflect the relative powers of credit-granting money capital and credit-taking industrial capital. There is, however, a long-run upper bound for the rate of interest given by the rate of profit, assuming the rate of profit to be independent of the rate of interest. Only in the sense of setting a long-run maximum limit can the rate of profit be considered to determine the rate of interest (Marx 1894, p. 360). Therefore, the interest rate in Marx's system can be seen as a monetary category determined by the relative powers of industrial and money capital. With these power relations given, the rate of interest is an exogenous variable for income determination, accumulation and growth, whereas the quantities of credit and money are endogenous.[6]

However, as is broadly agreed, there is no theory of investment demand in Marx's models, taking into account these monetary considerations, hence no demand-side determination of the level of output or the rate of growth of the economy (Kalecki 1968a, Sebastiani 1991). Of course, there are other parts in Marx's work in which capital accumulation is assumed to be determined by the rate of profit. *Capital, Vol. 1*, Chapter XXV, 'The general law of capitalist accumulation', provides a theory of accumulation, which has become the foundation for the profit squeeze theory of economic crisis.[7] Furthermore, *Capital, Vol. 3*, Part III, 'The law of the tendency of the rate of profit to fall', contains a theory of accumulation leading to an over-accumulation crisis based on Marx's specific view on the type of technical change, that is, a tendency of the organic composition of capital to rise and the rate of profit to fall.[8] However, both approaches assume that capitalists' expenditures and thus capital accumulation are determined by profits, that is, that saving out of profits determines investment. Hence, they do not pay sufficient attention to Marx's views on aggregate demand, to profits determined by capitalist expenditures and to those monetary factors, as the rate of interest and credit availability, which could have an impact on these expenditures.

3.3   MICHAL KALECKI'S THEORY OF MONEY, DISTRIBUTION AND EFFECTIVE DEMAND[9]

Michal Kalecki did not elaborate on the monetary and financial system of a capitalist economy in a systematic way. Nevertheless, his 'laconic' (Sawyer 2001a, p. 487) writings on the subject are perfectly compatible with modern post-Keynesian endogenous money and credit theory, as Dymski (1996) and Sawyer (1985, pp. 88–107, 2001a, 2001b) have claimed. As will be explained in more detail below, in two early papers, Kalecki (1932, 1969a, Chapter 3) supposes that an economic expansion requires the simultaneous expansion of the volume of credit, as a precondition to allow for the financing of increasing production and investment, independently of prior saving. The volume of credit is determined by credit demand, and the banking sector is capable of supplying the required amount of credit at a given rate of interest.

Based on these monetary foundations, we can outline Kalecki's theory of income distribution and effective demand following the elaborations in Kalecki (1954, Chapters 1–5, 1971, Chapters 5–8). Assuming a closed economy without government activity, production takes place in three departments of the economy: Department 1 produces investment goods, department 2 consumption goods for capitalists and department 3 consumption goods for workers. For simplification and to avoid discussing the inter-sectoral provision of raw materials and intermediate products, we assume, with Kalecki (1954, Chapter 3, 1971, Chapter 7), that each department is vertically integrated, which means that it produces all required raw materials and intermediate products within the department. Total national income (pY) is divided between workers and capitalists. Workers receive wages (W), and capitalists receive profits (Π), including retained earnings, dividends, interest and rent.

Applying Kalecki's determination of functional income distribution by mark-up pricing to a simple case without intermediate products, we can derive the profit share including overhead costs, and thus also overhead labour costs, as well as the wage share for direct labour as follows. We have to bear in mind that Kalecki's (1954, Chapters 1–2, 1971, Chapters 5–6) theory of pricing and income distribution presented here applies to the industrial and service sectors of the economy, where, in principle, output can be expanded within the short run, assuming that firms usually hold excess capacity and there is unemployed labour. Changes in demand will therefore affect the volume of output and the rate of capacity utilisation, but not output prices. In the primary sector, as in agriculture, however, output cannot be expanded in the short run. Changes in demand will hence have a direct impact on prices and distribution. In what follows, we will abstract from the latter.

In oligopolistic or monopolistically competitive markets, firms have some constrained price setting power, with the constraints given by the oligopolistic or monopolistic competitors. Firms determine prices (p) in the goods markets by applying a mark-up (m) on unit direct labour costs (W/Y), with W for nominal wages and Y for real output. Unit direct labour costs are equivalent to the ratio of the nominal wage rate (w = W/N) and labour productivity (y = Y/N), with N representing employment. Unit material costs, also considered in Kalecki's pricing and distribution theory (1954, Chapters 1–2, 1971, Chapters 5–6), can be ignored here, because we are assuming vertically integrated sectors. The mark-up and unit direct labour costs are both assumed to be constant up to full capacity output. Starting from pricing of the individual firm, we obtain the weighted average price in each of our j departments mentioned above:

$$p_j = \left(1 + m_j\right)\frac{w_j}{y_j}, \quad m_j \geq 0, \quad j = 1, 2, 3. \tag{3.4}$$

Generally, the mark-up is affected by the degree of price competition in the respective goods markets, by non-price competition (i.e. by marketing and product differentiation), as well as workers' bargaining power in the labour market, which each constrain the price setting power of the individual firm. More specifically, according to Kalecki (1954, Chapter 1, 1971, Chapter 5), the 'degree of monopoly' and hence the mark-up have mainly four determinants.

First, the mark-up is positively related to the degree of concentration within the respective industry or department (Kalecki 1954, p. 17, 1971, pp. 49–50). A high degree of market concentration makes price leadership by the most important firms, tacit agreements or more or less formal cartels more likely. The degree of concentration has thus a positive impact on the degree of monopoly and the mark-up, ceteris paribus.

Second, the degree of monopoly and the mark-up are negatively related to the relevance of price competition relative to other forms of competition, such as, for example, product differentiation, marketing and so on (Kalecki 1954, p. 17, 1971, p. 50). If price competition is replaced by other types of competition, the mark-up will therefore have a tendency to rise. The first two determinants of the mark-up can be summarised as the 'degree of price competition among firms in the goods markets'.

Third, Kalecki (1954, pp. 17–18, 1971, pp. 50–51) argues that overhead costs may affect the degree of monopoly and hence the mark-up. Since a rise in overhead costs squeezes profits, 'there may arise a tacit agreement among the firms of an industry to "protect" profits, and consequently to increase prices in relation to unit prime costs' (Kalecki 1954, p. 17, 1971, p. 50). However, Kalecki (1954, p. 18, 1971, p. 51, emphasis in the original) adds that '[t]he degree of monopoly *may*, but need not necessarily, increase as a result of a rise in overheads in relation to prime costs'.

Fourth, Kalecki (1954, p. 18, 1971, p. 51) claims that the power of trade unions has an adverse effect on the degree of monopoly and the mark-up. In a kind of strategic game at the firm level, firms anticipate that strong trade unions will demand higher wages if the mark-up and hence profits exceed 'reasonable' levels, so that the mark-up can only be sustained at the expense of ever rising prices and finally a loss of competitiveness of the respective firm relative to other firms. This will induce the firm to constrain the mark-up in the first place. The same argument holds true for an industry or a department relative to other industries or departments. What is important for powerful trade unions to be successful in squeezing the mark-up is some heterogeneity amongst the firms, which limits their price setting power in the goods market.[10] If wage bargaining takes place at the firm or the industry level, this implies that the competing firms or the competing industries are not facing an equivalent rise in wages and nominal unit labour costs. Therefore, the ability of specific firms or industries facing wage hikes to shift the respective increase of unit labour costs to prices is constrained by the competition of other firms or industries. The same will hold true if firms face the same increase in nominal wages but show differences in productivity advances, so that only the most productive firm will be able to shift wage increases to prices, whereas less productive firms have to squeeze their mark-up in order to remain price competitive. The average mark-up of the industry, the department and the economy as a whole will thus fall. Therefore, with this heterogeneity, higher bargaining power of trade unions can lead to a lower mark-up and, as we will show below, a lower profit share and thus a higher wage share, associated, however, with rising prices and higher inflation, as Kalecki (1971, Chapter 14) in his 'Class struggle and the distribution of income' has pointed out.

Having explained the determinants of the mark-up, we can now see that this mark-up in the price equation (3.4) determines the share (h) of gross profits (Π) in income or the value added (pY) in each department and thus also the share of wages (W) for direct labour in each department ($\Omega = 1 - h$):

$$h_j = \frac{\Pi_j}{p_j Y_j} = \frac{\Pi_j}{W_j + \Pi_j} = \frac{m_j W_j}{W_j + m_j W_j} = \frac{m_j}{1 + m_j}, \quad j = 1, 2, 3, \tag{3.5}$$

$$\Omega_j = 1 - h_j = \frac{W_j}{p_j Y_j} = \frac{W_j}{W_j + \Pi_j} = \frac{W_j}{W_j + m_j W_j} = \frac{1}{1 + m_j}, \quad j = 1,2,3. \quad (3.6)$$

The aggregate profit and wage shares for the economy as a whole, that is, the shares of profits as well as wages in national income, can then be derived by taking the weighted average of the industry or department profit and wage shares, or the weighted average of the mark-ups determining these shares:

$$h = \frac{\Pi}{pY} = \frac{\Pi}{W + \Pi} = \frac{m}{1 + m}, \quad (3.7)$$

$$\Omega = 1 - h = \frac{W}{pY} = \frac{W}{W + \Pi} = \frac{1}{1 + m}. \quad (3.8)$$

Therefore, functional income distribution is determined by the mark-ups in firms' pricing and the respective determinants of the mark-up as outlined above and by the department or industry composition of the economy, because profit shares (and wage shares) amongst departments may differ.[11]

Since the national product has to be equal to the sum of investment expenditures ($p_1 I$), consumption out of profits ($p_2 C_\Pi$) and consumption out of wages ($p_3 C_W$) in the closed economy without a government, it follows that:

$$pY = W + \Pi = p_3 C_W + p_2 C_\Pi + p_1 I. \quad (3.9)$$

Subtracting wages from both sides of equation (3.9), we obtain:

$$\Pi = p_2 C_\Pi + p_1 I - S_W. \quad (3.10)$$

Profits are thus equal to consumption out of profits plus investment minus saving out of wages ($S_W = W - p_3 C_W$). If workers do not save and rather spend their income entirely on consumption goods ($W = p_3 C_W$), equation (3.10) becomes:

$$\Pi = p_2 C_\Pi + p_1 I. \quad (3.11)$$

Profits are thus equal to consumption out of profits plus investment in the capital stock. Kalecki (1954, p. 46) reads the causality of this equation from right to left:

> Now, it is clear that capitalists may decide to consume or to invest more in a given period than in the preceding one, but they cannot decide to earn more. It is, therefore, their investment and consumption decisions which determine profits, and not vice versa.

Therefore, Kaldor (1955/56, p. 96) has summarised Kalecki's approach famously as follows: 'Mr. Kalecki's theory of profits . . . can be paraphrased by saying that "capitalists earn what they spend, and workers spend what they earn"'.

With given prices, the expenditures of workers determine the output of department 3 producing consumption goods for workers, whereas the expenditures of the capitalists determine the outputs of departments 1 and 2, producing investment goods and consumption goods for capitalists, respectively. The value of the output of department 3 is equal to the sum of wages in the economy, and the value of the outputs of departments 1 and 2 is equal to total profits in the economy. It should not come as a surprise that Kalecki's results so far do not diverge from those of Marx, because Kalecki's considerations are based on Marx's (1885, pp. 396–527) schemes of reproduction in *Capital, Vol. 2*.

We can further elaborate on Kalecki's approach, following Kalecki (1954, Chapter 3) and assuming that capitalists' consumption expenditures are composed of an autonomous part $(p_2 C_{\Pi a})$ and a part which is proportional to profits, ignoring any time lags. Therefore, we obtain the following simple function for consumption out of profits, with c_Π representing the constant marginal propensity to consume out of profits:

$$p_2 C_\Pi = p_2 C_{\Pi a} + c_\Pi \Pi, \quad C_{\Pi a} \geq 0, \; 0 \leq c_\Pi < 1. \tag{3.12}$$

Inserting equation (3.12) into equation (3.11) yields the following determination of the equilibrium level of profits in the economy as a whole:

$$\Pi = \frac{p_2 C_{\Pi a} + p_1 I}{1 - c_\Pi} = \frac{p_2 C_{\Pi a} + p_1 I}{s_\Pi}, \quad 0 \leq c_\Pi < 1, \; 0 < s_\Pi \leq 1. \tag{3.13}$$

Profits are thus determined by capitalists' autonomous consumption, by their investment in capital stock and by the propensity to consume or the propensity to save out of profits $(s_\Pi = 1 - c_\Pi)$. As equation (3.13) shows, we arrive at a first Kaleckian multiplier, which contains the sum of profits realised by the firms as a multiple of their autonomous consumption and investment expenditures. Since income distribution and hence the share of profits in national income are mainly determined by the mark-up in firms' price setting, the change in profits takes place through a change of aggregate production, thus the degree of utilisation of the capital stock, and in national income. Of course, a change in the compositions of capitalists' expenditures will also affect income distribution through the changes in the weights of the industries or departments for the average profit and wage shares.

Taking into account that the share of gross profits in national income is defined as in equation (3.7), equation (3.13) becomes:

$$pY = \frac{p_2 C_{\Pi a} + p_1 I}{(1 - c_\Pi) h} = \frac{p_2 C_{\Pi a} + p_1 I}{s_\Pi h}, \quad 0 \leq c_\Pi < 1, \, 0 < s_\Pi \leq 1. \tag{3.14}$$

Equation (3.14) displays a second Kaleckian multiplier, linking capitalists' autonomous consumption and investment expenditures with value added and national income. An increase in investment expenditures (or in capitalists' autonomous consumption) will thus trigger an increase in aggregate output, and saving will adjust to investment through a multiplier process with respect to income and profits. Therefore, investment for the economy as a whole cannot be constrained by aggregate saving:

In the present conception investment, once carried out, automatically provides the savings necessary to finance it . . . If investment increases by a certain amount, savings out of profits are *pro tanto*
higher.

(Kalecki 1954, p. 50, 1971, p. 83, emphasis in the original)

Of course, this mechanism requires that capitalists can either draw on liquid reserves or have
access to bank credit, in order to finance their expenditures before profits are earnt. If an
increase in investment is financed by liquid reserves, profits in department 1, which produces
investment goods, will rise and the liquid reserves spent will flow to these capitalists. If the
increase in investment is financed by bank credit, the associated increase in profits in department 1 will be accumulated as bank deposits. These bank deposits can then be used to buy
bonds issued by the investing firms, which will allow them to repay the initial bank credit.

One important consequence of the above is that the rate of interest cannot be determined by the
demand for and supply of new capital because investment 'finances itself'.

(Kalecki 1954, p. 50, 1971, p. 84)

Kalecki has thus provided a brief outline of a monetary circuit approach, which is by now
prominent and widely accepted in post-Keynesian macroeconomics and which will be explicitly presented and discussed in Section 3.5 below. In this approach, money and credit are
endogenous variables and the interest rate is an exogenous variable with respect to the income
generation process.[12] Kalecki had already put forward such a view in *Mechanism of Business
Upswing*, originally published in Polish in 1935:[13]

The financing of additional investment is effected by the so called creation of purchasing power.
The demand for bank credit increases and these are granted by banks. The means used by the
entrepreneurs for construction of new establishments reach the industries of investment goods. This
additional demand makes for setting to work idle equipment and unemployed labour. The increased
employment is a source of additional demand for consumer goods and thus results in turning higher
employment in the respective industries. Finally the additional investment outlay finds its way
directly and through the workers' spending into the pockets of capitalists (we assume that workers
do not save). The additional profits flow back as deposits to the banks. Bank credits increase by the
amount additionally invested and deposits by the amount of additional profits. The entrepreneurs
who engage in additional investment are 'propelling' into the pockets of other capitalists profits
which are equal to their investment, and they are becoming indebted to these capitalists to the same
extent via banks . . .
    It should be pointed out that the increase in output will result in an increased demand for money
in circulation, and thus will call for a rise in credits of the Central Bank . . . Therefore the precondition for the upswing is that the rate of interest should not increase too much in response to an
increased demand for cash.

(Kalecki 1969a, pp. 28–9, 1971, pp. 29–30)

The multiplier effect of autonomous consumption and exogenous investment expenditures
by capitalists in equation (3.14) depends inversely on the propensity to save out of profits and
the profit share in national income. Therefore, the Kaleckian approach contains a paradox of
saving – that is, an increase in the propensity to save lowers profits and national income. It
also contains a paradox of costs – that is, a higher profit share and a lower wage share are detrimental to GDP and national income without, however, directly affecting the sum of profits,
as can be seen in equation (3.13). Increasing the propensity to save and/or reducing the wage

share, and thus lifting the profit share, in an economic recession with high unemployment will have contractive effects on aggregate demand, output and employment and will therefore make the economic situation worse.

Summing up, Kalecki's approach towards profits contains a 'dualism' regarding the determination of the share of profits in national income, which is mainly affected by active mark-up pricing of firms in incompletely competitive goods markets, and regarding the determination of the level of profits, which is mainly determined by capitalists' expenditures for investment and consumption purposes:

> There are two elements in Kalecki's analysis of profits, the share of gross profit in the product of industry is determined by the level of gross margin, while the total flow of profits per annum depends upon the total flow of capitalists' expenditure on investment and consumption.
> (Robinson 1977, pp. 13–14)

We have followed Kalecki's determination of profits and national income for a closed private economy. However, the argument can easily be extended to an open economy with government activity, following Kalecki (1954, Chapter 3, 1971, Chapter 7). Kalecki starts again with the accounting equation for the gross national product: The sum of profits net of taxes (Π^{net}), wages net of taxes (W^{net}) and direct and indirect taxes (T) has to be equal to the sum of investment ($p_1 I$), consumption out of profits ($p_2 C_\Pi$), consumption out of wages ($p_3 C_W$), government expenditures on goods and services (G) and the export surplus, which is given by exports (p_{Ex} Ex) minus imports (p_{Im} Im). The p_i's represent again the price indices for capital goods, consumption goods demanded by capitalists and by workers, export goods and import goods in domestic currency, respectively, which are each assumed to be inelastic with respect to changes in demand and output:

$$\Pi^{net} + W^{net} + T = p_1 I + p_2 C_\Pi + p_3 C_W + G + p_{Ex} Ex - p_{Im} Im. \tag{3.15}$$

Subtracting wages and taxes from both sides of equation (3.15), we obtain:

$$\Pi^{net} = p_1 I + p_2 C_\Pi + G - T + p_{Ex} Ex - p_{Im} Im - S_W. \tag{3.16}$$

Therefore, in an open economy, profits net of taxes are equal to investment plus consumption out of profits, plus the government's budget deficit (G − T), plus the export surplus (p_{Ex} Ex − p_{Im} Im), minus saving out of wages ($S_W = W^{net} - p_3 C_W$). An export surplus and a government budget deficit can thus increase the amount of profits above the level given by capitalists' expenditures for investment and consumption purposes (subtracting workers' saving if positive). Whereas the export surplus is associated with a deficit in the financial balances of foreign countries or the external sector for the country in consideration, government expenditures exceeding tax revenues means a deficit in the financial balances of the government sector of the considered country.

> The above shows clearly the significance of 'external' markets (including those created by the budget deficits) for a capitalist economy. Without such markets profits are conditioned by the ability of capitalists to consume or to undertake capital investment. It is the export surplus and the budget deficit which enable capitalists to make profits over and above their own purchases of goods and services.
> (Kalecki 1954, p. 52, 1971, pp. 85–6)

So far, we have treated investment in Kalecki's approach as exogenous. When it comes to a theory of investment, in his early works on the business cycle, Kalecki (1969a, Chapter 1, 1971, Chapter 1) distinguished three stages in the investment activity, with respective lags: (1) investment decision and orders, (2) production of investment goods and (3) delivery of finished equipment. Therefore, what is important for the purpose of our current section is to look at the first stage, the investment decisions and orders. Different investment functions can be found in Kalecki's work, and, in his last publications, he was still looking for an adequate modelling of firms' investment decisions. In the introduction to the *Selected Essays on the Dynamics of the Capitalist Economy 1933–1970*, only published posthumously, he writes:[14]

> It is interesting to notice that the theory of effective demand, already clearly formulated in the first papers, remains unchanged in all the relevant writings, as do my views on the distribution of national income. However, there is a continuous search for new solutions in the theory of investment decisions, where even the last paper represents – for better or for worse – a novel approach.
>
> (Kalecki 1971, p. viii)

In his early work published in 1933 in Poland, Kalecki (1969a, Chapter 1, 1971, Chapter 1) supposes that the rate of capital accumulation ($g=I/K$), relating investment to the capital stock, depends positively on the expected gross rate of profit ($r=\Pi/pK$) and negatively on the rate of interest (i).[15] Since he observes that the long-term rate of interest does not vary much over the cycle, the investment function is simplified and the rate of capital accumulation is supposed to depend positively on the rate of profit. Profits, under the conditions of a classical saving hypothesis when workers do not save, are determined by capitalists' consumption and investment expenditures, as we have shown above, with investment being the main force. And the rate of profit also depends on the capital stock (K) in the denominator. Therefore, present investment decisions are positively affected by past investment decisions leading to current investment and profits, and negatively by the volume of the present capital stock in existence:

$$g = \frac{I}{K} = g\left(\underset{+}{r}\right) = g\left(\underset{+}{I}, \underset{-}{K}\right). \tag{3.17}$$

The positive demand and profit effects of investment stimulate further investment, on the one hand, but the capital stock and capacity effects of investment dampen further investment, on the other hand. These contradicting effects of investment are then used by Kalecki in order to generate a model of the trade cycle around a stationary state with zero net investment in capital stock on average over the cycle.[16] We will not follow the derivation of the trade cycle in any detail. Let us just notice that what is important in trade cycle theory is the endogenous generation and determination of the turning points and the maxima and minima. In this model they are generated because the rising (falling) capital stock feeds back negatively (positively) on the rate of profit, and a low (high) rate of profit dampens (stimulates) investment and hence the growth of the capital stock. Kalecki (1939, pp. 148–9) summarised the problem in his follow-up model relying on a similar mechanism as follows:

> We see that the question, 'What causes periodical crises?' could be answered shortly: the fact that investment is not only produced but also producing. Investment considered as expenditure is the source of prosperity, and every increase of it improves business and stimulates a further rise of investment. But at the same time every investment is an addition to capital equipment, and right from birth it competes with the older generation of this equipment. The tragedy of investment is that

it causes crisis because it is useful. Doubtless many people will consider this theory paradoxical. But it is not the theory which is paradoxical, but its subject – the capitalist economy.

The analysis of the interaction of demand and capacity effects of investment is at the roots of many trade cycle theories starting with Harrod (1939) and the multiplier-accelerator model by Samuelson (1939). It is also the main concern of post-Keynesian growth theory, in the tradition of Kaldor (1955/56, 1957) and Robinson (1956, 1962), on the one hand, and of Kalecki (1943a, 1954) and Steindl (1952), on the other hand (Hein 2014a, Chapters 4–7), which we will outline in Chapter 7 of this book.

In Kalecki's later work then, in particular in Kalecki (1954, Chapter 9, 1971, Chapter 10), investment decisions are affected by firms' financial resources and by changes in profits and in the capital stock, which together determine the movement of the rate of profit. Following his 'principle of increasing risk' (Kalecki 1937), internal means of finance have an impact on investment under the condition of imperfect capital markets. Own means of finance restrict firms' access to external finance, because they indicate firms' creditworthiness to potential lenders. But they also affect firms' willingness to go into debt, because firms want to avoid the risk of insolvency and potential bankruptcy, which may be associated with fixed nominal payment obligations (Kalecki 1954, Chapter 8, 1971, Chapter 9). Therefore, retained profits have a positive effect on investment through the provision of financial means. Furthermore, retained earnings and own capital improve access to external finance in financial markets, because firms can offer more collateral.

> The access of a firm to the capital market, or in other words the amount of rentier capital it may hope to obtain, is determined to a large extent by the amount of its entrepreneurial capital. It would be impossible for a firm to borrow capital above a certain level determined by the amount of its entrepreneurial capital.
>
> (Kalecki 1954, p. 91, 1971, p. 105)

Accumulation of own capital also reduces the risk of illiquidity or insolvency the firm or the entrepreneur will have to take and will thus improve the willingness to invest.

Taking these arguments into consideration, in Kalecki (1954, Chapter 9, 1971, Chapter 10) an investment function is obtained in which investment decisions and thus, with a lag, the level of investment are affected positively by retained profits (Π_F) and by changes in current profits ($d\Pi$), and negatively by changes in the capital stock (dK).

$$I = I\left(\underset{+}{\Pi_F}, \underset{+}{d\Pi}, \underset{-}{dK} \right). \tag{3.18}$$

A direct impact of the rate of interest on investment is denied again, because Kalecki holds that the long-term rate of interest is rather stable in the course of the trade cycle and therefore cannot contribute to an explanation of cyclical fluctuations in investment, which he is interested in.

Finally, aiming at an explanation of the long-run process of economic development, Kalecki (1954, Chapter 14, 1968b, 1971, Chapter 15) in his further work adds another element to his investment function representing semi-autonomous '"development factors" such as innovations, which prevent the system from settling to a static position and which engender a long-run upward trend' (Kalecki 1954, p. 151). To reap the benefits from innovations they have to be embodied, at least partly, in the capital stock and thus have an impact on investment.

It should be mentioned here that, for Kalecki (1937), the amount of investment determined by the 'principle of increasing risk' does not necessarily generate a long-run macroeconomic equilibrium, but is rather derived at the microeconomic level: 'We examined the planning of the entrepreneur in a given situation which in general is *not* the position of long run equilibrium' (Kalecki 1937, p. 445, italics in the original). Going beyond the planning horizon of the entrepreneur in the single period and applying a period by period analysis, in which investment spending feeds back on profits and saving out of profits (retained earnings), he argues: 'This accumulation of savings causes a parallel shift of the curve of marginal risk to the right. For the entrepreneur can invest the new amount without reducing his safety or increasing illiquidity' (Kalecki 1937, p. 446). Therefore, applying the 'principle of increasing risk' to the investment function, the macroeconomic feedbacks need to be taken into account. We will do so in Chapter 4 of this book.

3.4   JOHN MAYNARD KEYNES'S THEORY OF MONEY AND EFFECTIVE DEMAND

John Maynard Keynes's research programme of a monetary theory of production provides the foundation for his principle of effective demand. In particular, the drafts preceding the *General Theory* (Keynes 1979), but less so the *General Theory* (Keynes 1936) itself, aim at providing a monetary theory of production, which Keynes (1933a, pp. 408–9; italics in the original) outlines as follows:

> In my opinion the main reason why the problem of crises is unsolved . . . is to be found in the lack of what might be termed a *monetary theory of production* . . . The theory which I desiderate would deal . . . with an economy in which money plays a part of its own and affects motives and decisions and is, in short, one of the operative factors in the situation, so that the course of events cannot be predicted, either in the long period or in the short, without a knowledge of the behaviour of money between the first state and the last.

In the drafts of the *General Theory*, Keynes (1979, pp. 76–101) distinguishes an entrepreneur or a monetary economy from a barter economy, a real-wage or cooperative economy and a neutral economy. In the barter economy, there cannot be any deviation of aggregate demand from aggregate supply, because in real exchange nobody can sell without buying simultaneously and aggregate demand is hence always equal to aggregate supply by definition. In the real-wage or cooperative economy, economic agents make use of money but only as means of exchange in order to facilitate trade and the allocation of the social product. Therefore, there are no leakages from the income circuit, and aggregate demand always equals aggregate supply, too. In the neutral economy, money may additionally be used as a store of value, and there may hence be leakages from the circuit. However, these leakages are exactly offset by injections of the same amount through an endogenous economic process, and aggregate demand therefore corresponds to aggregate supply.[17] In an entrepreneur or monetary economy, however, there may be leakages from the income circuit, which are not exactly compensated for by injections. Aggregate demand may therefore deviate from aggregate supply, and the latter will have to adjust to the former. Say's law will therefore not generally hold in such an economy and has to be replaced by the principle of effective demand. There are two reasons for this.

The first reason Keynes provides is that in a monetary economy income may be used by households for other purposes than direct spending on consumption goods. It is the specific nature of money, which may cause leakages from the circuit and, hence, may be responsible for insufficient aggregate demand. Money can neither be fully substituted by other goods or assets nor can it be reproduced by means of employing factors of production:

> Perhaps anything in terms of which the factors of production contract to be remunerated, which is not and cannot be a part of current output and is capable of being used otherwise than to purchase current output, is, in a sense, money. If so, but not otherwise, the use of money is a necessary condition for fluctuations in effective demand.
>
> (Keynes 1979, p. 86)

Already in the first chapter of his *Treatise on Money*, Keynes (1930a) had pointed out that, unlike the view in classical and neoclassical orthodoxy, money does not derive from exchange, facilitating barter by means of singling out a specific commodity, which serves as standard of value and means of exchange. He proposed an alternative theory of money:

> Money of account, namely that in which debts and price and general purchasing power are *expressed*, is the primary concept of a theory of money.
>
> A money of account comes into existence along with debts, which are contracts for deferred payment, and price lists, which are offers of contracts for sale or purchase. Such debts and price lists, whether they are recorded by word of mouth or by book entry on baked bricks or paper documents, can only be expressed in terms of a money of account.
>
> Money itself, namely that by delivery of which debt contracts and price contracts are *discharged*, and in the shape of which a store of general purchasing power is *held*, derives its character from its relationship to the money of account, since the debts and prices must first have been expressed in terms of the latter . . . Money proper in the full sense of the term can only exist in relation to money of account.
>
> (Keynes 1930a, p. 3, italics in the original)

What this money and this standard of value is, in which contracts of all types (credit contracts, wage contracts, etc.) are denominated, is defined by the state. Money is thus a creature of the state, as had already been pointed out by Knapp (1905), to whom Keynes (1930a, p. 4) favourably refers, when he argues that '(t)o-day, all civilised money, is, beyond the possibility of dispute, chartalist'. The state also provides the institutions to enforce contracts. The money defined by the state is thus also the means of payment for settling contracts and the means of circulation for commodity exchange, and it is the most liquid store of wealth. Since the major part of state money is fiat money, the holding of it causes the problem of aggregate demand failures, because

> 'money has, both in the long and the short period, a zero, or at any rate a very small, elasticity of production' and 'it has an elasticity of substitution equal, or nearly equal, to zero.'
>
> (Keynes 1936, pp. 230–1)

But why should there be a desire to hold money, as the most liquid store of wealth, and forego the interest which could be earned by holding a less liquid financial asset? 'Why should anyone outside a lunatic asylum wish to use money as a store of wealth?' (Keynes 1937, p. 216).

According to Keynes, the main reason for this is fundamental uncertainty, which is different from probabilistic risk:

> By 'uncertain' knowledge, let me explain, I do not mean merely to distinguish what is known for certain from what is only probable . . . The sense in which I am using the term is that in which the prospect of a European war is uncertain, or the price of copper and the rate of interest twenty years hence, or the obsolescence of a new invention, or the position of private wealth-owners in the social system in 1970. About these matters there is no scientific basis on which to form any calculable probability whatever. We simply do not know.
>
> (Keynes 1937, pp. 213–14)

This fundamental uncertainty generates liquidity preference to cope with uncertainty:

> Because, partly on reasonable and partly on instinctive grounds, our desire to hold money as a store of wealth is a barometer of the degree of our distrust of our own calculations and conventions concerning the future . . . The possession of actual money lulls our disquietude; and the premium which we require to make us part with money is the measure of the degree of our disquietude.
>
> (Keynes 1937, p. 216)

Liquidity preference, triggered by fundamental uncertainty, thus also provides an explanation for the rate of interest, as a monetary phenomenon, which is the price for parting with money and holding less liquid financial assets.

The second reason for the invalidity of Say's law in a monetary economy is that monetary injections may not automatically offset monetary leakages from the circuit of incomes. In a modern credit economy, monetary injections are independent of current income. They may hence be insufficient to make aggregate demand equal to aggregate supply at full employment. In particular, in a monetary or entrepreneur economy, firms' production and investment decisions are geared towards monetary profits, and firms' spending for investment purposes may therefore be insufficient for full employment:

> The distinction between a co-operative and an entrepreneur economy bears some relation to a pregnant observation made by Karl Marx, – though the subsequent use to which he put this observation was highly illogical. He pointed out that the nature of production in the actual world is not, as economists seem often to suppose, a case C-M-C', i.e. of exchanging commodity (or effort) for money in order to obtain another commodity (or effort). That may be the standpoint of the private consumer. But it is not the attitude of *business*, which is a case of M-C-M', i.e. of parting with money for commodity (or effort) in order to obtain more money . . . An entrepreneur is interested, not in the amount of product, but in the amount of *money* which will fall to his share.
>
> (Keynes 1979, pp. 81–2, italics in the original)

From these considerations it follows that the equilibrium level of output and employment in a monetary economy is not determined by available resources, but by effective demand. And an important part of effective demand, investment, is determined by monetary criteria: Entrepreneurs have to achieve a minimum rate of return on monetary advances. This rate of return is then affected by the monetary rate of interest, as we will see below. In a monetary production economy, Say's law is therefore replaced by the 'principle of effective demand'. Aggregate spending determines output and employment; investment determines saving and is determined by monetary criteria itself.

In Chapter 3 of the *General Theory*, Keynes (1936, pp. 23–34) explains his principle of effective demand distinguishing the aggregate supply function $[Z=Z(N)]$ and the aggregate demand function $[D=D(N)]$. The Z-function represents the 'aggregate supply price of output', that is, aggregate supply in nominal terms, as a function of employment (N). The supply price per unit of output (p) consists of unit production costs plus unit normal profits, and aggregate supply is then given by the level of employment and labour productivity $(y=Y/N)$, that is, real output (Y) per unit of labour employed, in the following way:

$$Z = Nyp. \tag{3.19}$$

The shape of the Z-function, therefore, will be affected by the technology of production determining the productivity of labour and by the price setting behaviour of firms affecting output prices. With constant marginal and hence average labour productivity and constant nominal wage rates, and thus constant nominal unit labour costs, as well as constant mark-ups, and therefore constant output prices, the Z-function will be linear, as in Figure 3.1.

The D-function presents the proceeds expected by the entrepreneurs, also as a function of employment. In an economy in which Say's law is to hold, Z- and D-functions coincide, and the level of employment can then be determined by the neoclassical full employment labour market equilibrium based on the utility maximising labour supply of households and the profit maximising labour demand of firms (Keynes 1936, p. 26). In a monetary production economy, however, aggregate demand may diverge from aggregate supply, as explained above, and the D-function will hence be different from the Z-function, and this will give rise to the principle of effective demand.

With Keynes (1936, pp. 28–32) we can distinguish two components of the D-function: A first, which is affected by income, that is, income-dependent consumption (pC), and a second, which is independent of income, that is, autonomous or exogenous investment (pI). For the first component, we can assume a constant marginal propensity to consume out of income for the economy (c) as a whole, which is positive but below unity. Total nominal income (pY) is given by employment, labour productivity and the price level $(pY=Nyp)$, and nominal aggregate demand is hence:

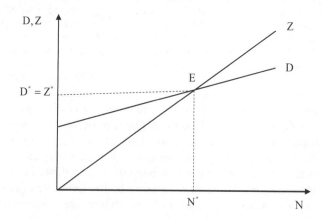

Figure 3.1   Keynes's (1936) 'principle of effective demand'

$$D = cpY + pI = c(Nyp) + pI, \quad 0 < c < 1. \tag{3.20}$$

The point of intersection (E) of the Z- and D-curves in Figure 3.1 is 'the effective demand' (Keynes 1936, p. 25). Aggregate demand at this level of employment is exactly equal to aggregate supply, and firms can sell the level of output associated with this level of employment at the expected or required prices. For this equilibrium level of employment (N*) we have:

$$Z(N^*) = D(N^*). \tag{3.21}$$

and hence:

$$N^* = \frac{pI}{(1-c)yp}. \tag{3.22}$$

An increase in investment (or any other autonomous demand component, like income-independent consumption, government expenditures or exports in a more complex model) will raise the equilibrium level of employment. The same is true for an increase in the propensity to consume out of income. Therefore, we have the paradox of saving again: A fall in the propensity to consume and hence a rise in the propensity to save $(s = 1 - c)$ will lead to a lower level of equilibrium demand, output and employment.

As can easily be seen, our derivation of equilibrium employment in the D-Z-model can be translated into equilibrium income from the well-known textbook 'Keynesian' income-expenditure model (Froyen 2002, Chapter 5), here in nominal terms, because from equation (3.22) we also get:[18]

$$pY^* = (Nyp)^* = \frac{pI}{(1-c)} = \frac{pI}{s}. \tag{3.23}$$

with pY^* as equilibrium income and $[1/(1-c) = 1/s]$ as the income multiplier of investment.

The volume of employment determined by the point of effective demand in Figure 3.1 and by equation (3.22) may well deviate from full employment in the labour market. However, any response in the labour market, that is, any change in nominal wages affecting output prices and/or real wages and income distribution, will only have an impact on employment through aggregate demand in the goods market.

With involuntary unemployment, that is, employment determined by the principle of effective demand falling short of full employment in the labour market, falling nominal wages would thus have to stimulate consumption or investment, or both, in order to reduce involuntary unemployment. As Keynes (1936, Chapter 19) explains, there is little to be expected for an increase in consumption. If wages fall and prices decrease in step, real wages and income distribution will remain constant and consumption out of wages will not increase, nor will consumption out of profits. If, more realistically, a fall in nominal wages is not accompanied by an equivalent fall in prices, real wages, wage shares and consumption out of wages will fall, with little, if any, compensation from consumption out of profits. In this case, the average propensity to consume is likely to fall, with further negative effects on aggregate demand, output and employment:

> It will, therefore, involve some redistribution of real income (a) from wage earners to other factors entering into marginal prime cost whose remuneration has not been reduced, and (b) from entre-preneurs to rentiers to whom a certain income fixed in terms has been guaranteed . . . The transfers from wage earners to other factors of production is likely to diminish the propensity to consume. The effect of the transfer from entrepreneurs to rentiers is more open to doubt. But if rentiers rep-resent on the whole the richer section of the community and those whose standard of life is least flexible, then the effect of this will be unfavourable.
>
> (Keynes 1936, p. 262)

For the discussion of the effects of a fall in nominal wages on investment, we briefly have to explain Keynes's theory of investment. According to Keynes (1936, Chapter 11), the induce-ment to invest depends positively on the marginal efficiency of capital (MEC) and negatively on the long-term rate of interest (i) in the financial markets:

$$I = I\left(\underset{-}{i}, \underset{+}{MEC}\right).$$
(3.24)

The marginal efficiency of capital relates expected future yields of a capital asset to the cur-rent supply price of that asset:

> I define the marginal efficiency of capital as being equal to the rate of discount which would make the present value of the series of annuities given by the returns expected from the capital asset dur-ing its life just equal to its supply price.
>
> (Keynes 1936, p. 135)

Therefore, the marginal efficiency of capital makes sure that the following condition holds, with Q_t denoting the expected yields or revenues derived from a capital asset in period $t = 0, \ldots, n$:

$$p_0 K_0 = Q_0 + \frac{Q_1}{1 + MEC} + \frac{Q_2}{(1 + MEC)^2} + \ldots + \frac{Q_n}{(1 + MEC)^n} = \sum_{t=0}^{n} \frac{Q_t}{(1 + MEC)^t}.$$
(3.25)

According to Keynes (1936, p. 136), the marginal efficiency of each real capital asset is falling with increasing investment in that capital asset for two reasons. First, in the short run, increasing investment means increasing demand for that capital good, which will then trigger a rising supply price because of rising marginal costs in producing that capital good. Second, in the long run, when investment will have caused an increase in the capital stock and hence in productive capacities, additional output can only be sold at lower prices, such that expected marginal revenues will fall. On the one hand, Keynes thus refers to neoclas-sical marginalist reasoning when it comes to explaining a falling schedule of the marginal efficiency of a specific capital asset.[19] On the other hand, however, Keynes (1936, pp. 137–44) clearly distinguishes his marginal efficiency of capital from the neoclassical marginal pro-ductivity of capital: The marginal efficiency of capital is concerned with expected future monetary revenues and not with current, technologically determined marginal physical products of the capital stock – which is assumed to determine the real rate of interest in neoclassical economics.[20]

Aggregating the schedules for individual capital assets to the capital stock of the economy as a whole, we arrive at the downward sloping curve in the marginal efficiency of capital investment space shown in Figure 3.2.

For a given monetary long-term rate of interest in financial markets, as an alternative rate of return, entrepreneurs will thus realise all those investment projects in the capital stock with a marginal efficiency of capital above that rate of interest. A rise in the rate of interest will thus lower the level of investment. An improvement in expected yields will shift the schedule of the marginal efficiency of capital to the right and thus increase the level of investment for a given rate of interest.

> It is important to understand the dependence of the marginal efficiency of a given stock of capital on changes in expectation, because it is chiefly this dependence which renders the marginal efficiency of capital subject to the somewhat violent fluctuations which are the explanations of the Trade Cycle.
>
> (Keynes 1936, pp. 143–4)

Kalecki (1936), in his review of Keynes's (1936) *General Theory*, was quite critical of Keynes's investment theory, based on the idea of a downward sloping schedule of the marginal efficiency of capital giving rise to an 'equilibrium' level of investment for the economy as a whole, as soon as the monetary rate of interest is given (Lopez G. 2002, Sardoni 2011, Chapter 6). Kalecki argued that an individual firm at a given moment in time may be faced with a downward sloping schedule of the marginal efficiency of capital. However, higher investment of the firm, contributing to higher aggregate investment, income, profits and thus profit expectation for the economy as a whole, will shift this schedule upward and thus cause a cumulative process and not an equilibrium position.

> Keynes's concept, which tells us only how high investment should be in order that a certain disequilibrium may turn into equilibrium, meets a serious difficulty along this path also. In fact, the growth of investment in no way results in a process leading the system toward equilibrium. Thus it

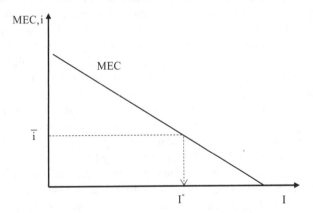

Figure 3.2   Interest rate, marginal efficiency of capital and investment

is difficult to consider Keynes's solution of the investment problem to be satisfactory. The reason for this failure lies in an approach which is basically static to a matter which is by its nature dynamic.

(Kalecki 1936, p. 231)

Coming back to Keynes's theory, a rise in expected output prices will improve the marginal efficiency of capital, that is, shifting the marginal efficiency of capital schedule in Figure 3.2 to the right, and raise investment for a given rate of interest. A fall in money wages and in expected output prices, triggered by involuntary unemployment in the labour market, will thus lower the marginal efficiency of capital, that is, shifting the marginal efficiency of capital schedule in Figure 3.2 to the left, and it will cause lower investment, aggregate demand, output and employment for a given rate of interest:

> The expectation of a fall in the value of money stimulates investment, and hence employment generally, because it raises the schedule of the marginal efficiency of capital, i.e. the investment demand schedule; and the expectation of a rise in the value of money is depressing, because it lowers the schedule of the marginal efficiency of capital.

(Keynes 1936, pp. 141–2)

Hence, also through the marginal efficiency of capital channel, falling money wages as a response to involuntary unemployment will not improve aggregate demand and employment but will rather make the economic situation worse.

Let us now turn to the rate of interest, as the second determinant of investment in the capital stock. As mentioned above, in Keynes's approach the rate of interest is a monetary category, which is mainly determined by liquidity preference, since it can be understood as the price to induce wealth holders to part with non-interest bearing liquidity and hold less liquid but interest-bearing assets instead. This is, in essence, what Keynes (1936) also explains in more detail in Chapter 17 of the *General Theory*, where the monetary rate of interest is explained by the liquidity premium of money.

In the *General Theory*, however, it is now also assumed that the stock of money is given (Keynes 1936, p. 247) and that financial wealth holders have the portfolio choice between non-interest bearing money and interest-bearing bonds. Based on this, Keynes (1936, pp. 165–74, pp. 194–209) in Chapters 13 and 15 provides a liquidity preference theory of the interest rate, as a theory of money demand with an inverse relationship between the nominal interest rate in the bonds market and money demand for speculative purposes, which has facilitated the re-integration of Keynes's approach into neoclassical orthodoxy. Following Chapters 13 and 15 of the *General Theory*, an increase in nominal money supply should cause a fall in the rate of interest in the bonds market, because part of this increase in money will be used by households to raise their demand for bonds, which increases bond prices and lowers the effective rate of interest on bonds. This should then stimulate investment, aggregate demand, output and employment. The same effect should be obtained if, with involuntary unemployment in the labour market, nominal wages and prices fall and thus real money supply rises. This real balance effect à la Keynes would then automatically bring the economy back to the neoclassical full employment equilibrium, unless there are rigidities in the system: Sticky nominal wages and prices, interest-inelastic investment ('investment trap') or a lower bound for the rate of interest given by long-term expectation ('liquidity trap'), so called Keynes cases. Starting with Hicks's (1937) IS-LM model, and its further developments by Modigliani (1944) and Patinkin (1949), appending a neoclassical labour market, a neoclassical production function and flexible prices, this has become the neoclassical synthesis interpretation of Keynes's theory in modern textbooks (Felderer and Homburg 1992, Chapter V, Froyen 2002, Chapter 8, Snowdon and Vane 2005, Chapter 3).

Indeed, Keynes's assumption of a given stock of money and his liquidity preference theory of the interest rate as a theory of money demand give rise to the real balance effect on the rate of interest, as Keynes (1936, pp. 262–4) acknowledges. However, he does not believe that the overall effect of falling money wages and prices on investment will be favourable, because of the negative effects on the marginal efficiency of capital mentioned above and in particular because it will increase the entrepreneurs' real burden of debt:

> Indeed if the fall of wages and prices goes far, the embarrassment of those entrepreneurs who are heavily indebted may soon reach the point of insolvency, – with severely adverse effects on investment.
>
> (Keynes 1936, p. 264)

Flexible money wages are thus not an instrument of stability but rather a source of instability in a monetary production economy. Rigid money wages are thus a prerequisite for macroeconomic stability.

Furthermore, focussing on the destabilising effects of falling money wages and prices on aggregate demand, via redistribution, expectations and the marginal efficiency of capital and, in particular, via the real debt effects, which were highlighted already by Fisher (1933), requires accepting that money is predominantly credit money generated endogenously by creditor-debtor-contracts in the economy. This is in contrast to the assumption of a given stock of money in the *General Theory*, as Keynes had to acknowledge in a debate with Ohlin, Hawtrey and Robertson in *The Economic Journal* in 1937/38.[21] In this debate, Keynes comes to the conclusion that investing firms have a finance demand for money. This finance demand has to be supplied by commercial banks, by means of creating credit 'out of nothing' at a given rate of interest before the income-generating process – based on investment and the multiplier – takes place. Endogenously generated credit is thus required at the beginning of each period to sustain demand at a given level of production and employment, since this level of demand usually requires positive investment. For a continuously expanding economy, commercial banks will have to increase credit at the beginning of each period, otherwise increasing interest rates will abort investment and economic expansion:

> This means that, in general, the banks hold the key position in the transition from a lower to a higher scale of activity. If they refuse to relax, the growing congestion of the short-term loan market or of the new issue market, as the case may be, will inhibit the improvement, no matter how thrifty the public purpose to be out of their future incomes. On the other hand, there will always be *exactly* enough *ex post* saving to take up the *ex post* investment and to release the finance which the latter had been previously employing. The investment market can become congested through shortage of cash. It can never become congested through shortage of saving. This is the most fundamental of my conclusions in this field.
>
> (Keynes 1973, p. 222)

Keynes has thus provided the basics of a monetary circuit approach, but he did not draw the full conclusions with regard to the endogeneity of money and credit and the exogeneity of the rate of interest. Therefore, we will explain in more detail in the following section the monetary circuit approach in order to clarify the relationship between endogenous credit and money, finance, investment and saving.

As should be clear at this stage, the required endogeneity of credit and money in Keynes's theory of effective demand undermines the validity of any real balance effect, à la Keynes or à la Pigou. It also undermines the endogeneity of the rate of interest and requires the rate of interest to be exogenous for the income-generating process, as famously claimed by Pasinetti (1974, p. 47, emphasis in the original):

> However important a role liquidity preference may play in Keynes' monetary theory, it is entirely immaterial to his theory of effective demand. What this theory requires, as far as the rate of interest is concerned, is not that the rate of interest is determined by liquidity preference, but that it is determined *exogenously* with respect to the income generation process. Whether, in particular, liquidity preference, or anything else determines it, is entirely immaterial.

We will come back to this in more detail in Chapter 4 of this book where we present some basic post-Keynesian macroeconomic models based on post-Keynesian monetary theory.

For these models, the choice of the investment function will be important. Finishing this section, let us thus briefly compare Keynes's and Kalecki's investment theories, each of which we have presented above. According to Lopez G. (2002, p. 613), there is an important distinction of Kalecki's view from Keynes's and thus a major difference between the investment theories proposed by the two founding fathers of the 'principle of effective demand':

> Although Kalecki recognized that psychological factors influence investment decisions, he insisted that capitalists do not react solely on expectations, but rather make their decisions on the basis of realized profits, which provide both the finance and the stimuli for investing.

However, we also find some common ground between Keynes and Kalecki, because Keynes (1936, Chapter 11) puts forward a second argument for a negative relationship between the rate of interest and investment in capital stock, which is associated with investment finance. For a firm operating with borrowed capital an increasing rate of interest means an increase in fixed payment obligations relative to uncertain yields from real investment. This implies an increase in borrower's and in lender's risk.[22] For the borrower, the risk of future insolvency and bankruptcy increases, and for the lender, the risk of credit default rises:

> Two types of risk affect the volume of investment which have not commonly been distinguished, but which it is important to distinguish. The first is the entrepreneur's or borrower's risk and arises out of doubts in his own mind as to the probability of his actually earning the prospective yield of which he hopes. If a man is venturing his own money, this is the only risk which is relevant.
>
> But where a system of borrowing and lending exists, by which I mean the granting of loans with a margin or real or personal security, a second type of risk is relevant which we may call lender's risk. This may be due either to moral hazard, i.e. voluntary default or other means of escape, possibly lawful, from the fulfilment of the obligation, or to the possible insufficiency of the margin of security, i.e. involuntary default due to the disappointment of expectations.
>
> (Keynes 1936, p. 144)

The effects of interest rate variations on investment will therefore not only depend on the relationship between the rate of interest and the expected rate of profit, but also on the degree of debt finance of the firms' capital stock. On the one hand, the investor's credit demand is affected by the amount of his own capital in order to minimise borrower's risk and hence future insolvency or bankruptcy. On the other hand, the commercial bank's willingness to supply credit will be affected by the collateral and hence the own capital the investor has to offer, or by the share of expected profits which is not yet earmarked for fixed interest payments, in order to minimise lender's risk. These arguments are quite similar to Kalecki's (1937) 'principle of increasing risk', which is an important factor in some of Kalecki's investment theories, as we have explained above.

Starting in Chapter 4, we will introduce these considerations into a full post-Keynesian macroeconomic model, including the feedbacks of investment on aggregate demand and profits, and we will analyse the macroeconomic implications. First, however, we turn to the monetary circuit school for a clearer understanding of the relationship between credit, finance, investment and saving.

3.5   ENDOGENOUS CREDIT, FINANCE, INVESTMENT AND SAVING IN THE MONETARY CIRCUIT SCHOOL

3.5.1   The Basics of the Monetary Circuit Theory

For the principle of effective demand to hold in the works of Marx, Kalecki and Keynes, it is required that firms or capitalists have access to means of finance, independently of any previous saving by any actor in the economy. More fundamentally, income-generating spending for production purposes requires access to finance before income is generated, out of which economic agents can then save. Finance has thus to be clearly distinguished from saving. This has been made clear, in particular, in the monetary circuit school, which we will refer to here in order to clarify this issue.[23] The starting point of the monetary circuit theory is the post-Keynesian conviction that economic processes should be analysed as taking place in historical time and that they can therefore be treated sequentially. Since production in a monetary economy requires monetary advances in order to obtain the required factors of production, monetary circuit models focus on the creation of money via the creation of short-term credit, the circulation of credit money and finally the dissolution of the credit relationship and the related effects on the quantity of credit money (Graziani 1994). Based on this framework, further assumptions about commercial banks' credit supply, about firms' credit demand deriving from their production and investment decisions, about functional income distribution and about consumption and portfolio decisions of private households then allow for the analysis of the effects of monetary policies on income shares, investment, aggregate demand and growth. This will be the focus of the following chapters of this book. In the current section, we will only focus on a simple monetary circuit approach for a given level of economic activity, determined by aggregate demand, with a given distribution of income.

Analysing a monetary circuit, we distinguish between the following sectors of the economy: The firm sector (F), the banking sector (Bank) and the private household sector (HH), which is divided into workers' households (HH$_w$) and rentiers' households (HH$_R$). The firm sector obtains short-term credit from the banking sector and pays wages to workers' households and financial income to the rentiers' households and maybe also to banks, which then forward this income to their owners, the rentiers' households. Firms produce investment and consumption goods with a given capital stock and labour hired from the workers' households. For the sake of simplicity, we assume that the capital stock does not depreciate, so that we can ignore depreciation and replacement investment. In addition, intermediate products are ignored for the sake of simplicity. Firms sell the investment goods produced to other firms and consumption goods to households. Furthermore, firms issue financial liabilities, that is, corporate bonds, in the financial market in order to finance their capital stock in the long run, or they obtain long-term loans from the banking sector for this purpose.

The banking sector only consists of private banks, and we ignore a central bank for reasons of simplicity. We focus on the endogenous credit generation in the interaction of the commercial banking sector with the firm sector, in particular. The focus will thus be on a 'pure credit economy' without central bank money. All payments are made by transferring money between the accounts the agents hold with the commercial banking sector, that is, only credit money is considered. Liquidity is held in terms of deposits with commercial banks.

Workers' households sell their labour power to firms, receive wages and spend these wages on consumption goods produced and supplied by the firm sector. Therefore, we assume that workers' households do not save. Rentiers' households receive capital income from their holdings of financial assets and also from their ownership of the commercial banks. Rentiers' income is partly consumed and partly saved. Rentiers can hold their saving either in terms of corporate bonds issued by the firm sector or in terms of deposits with the commercial banking sector. These deposits are the most liquid financial asset in the model economy and do not generate interest income. Payments are made by transfers of deposits. Corporate bonds are less liquid but provide the holders with an interest income.

The agents in our model economy interact in the following macroeconomic markets: The investment and consumption goods market, the labour market and the credit and financial markets. For the latter we distinguish between a market for short-term credit, which we will simply call the credit market, and a market for long-term credit and corporate bonds, which will be labelled the financial market. Long-term external finance of the firms' capital stock only consists of long-term debt and corporate bonds. For the sake of simplicity, we ignore the issuance of equity and a market for stocks and shares, which, however, could be treated in a similar way as the bonds and long-term credit market in our model. Internal finance of the capital stock consists of accumulated retained profits, as we will explain below. Short-term credit is created at the beginning of each monetary circuit and extinguished at the end. Long-term credit and corporate bonds have a maturity of several circuits. They are treated as stocks at the beginning of the circuit inherited from the past, which of course will change in the course of a circuit.

In the credit market, commercial banks grant short-term credit to those private agents who are willing to pay the rate of interest determined by commercial banks and who are considered to be creditworthy. For the simple circuit without a government, we shall assume that only firms will demand short-term credit in order to initiate production. Provided that firms are considered to be creditworthy, commercial banks are ready to supply firms' short-term credit demand at a given short-term rate of interest (i_B). In a credit economy, therefore, the main task of commercial banks is to collect and process information about creditworthiness, to supervise and control borrowers in order to make sure that interest is paid and finally credit is paid back, to avoid capital losses themselves.[24] Commercial banks also allow private agents, households and firms, to hold deposits with them. For the sake of simplicity, we shall assume that banks do not pay interest on deposits. The net income of the private banking sector derived from lending to firms is assumed to be distributed immediately and completely to those rentiers' households who own the private banks and will thus provide a part of rentiers' income.

In order to transform short-term credit granted by commercial banks into long-term finance of the capital stock, firms retain part of the profits. Part of the capital stock enlargement thus is not burdened with an increase in long-term debt. However, firms also have to make use of the financial market, issuing corporate bonds or obtaining long-term credit from banks, in order to long-term finance the increase in the capital stock. Whereas the credit market is characterised by the creation of credit money as a precondition for initiating a production and income-generating process, the financial market is characterised by the allocation of already existing income and wealth. We assume a uniform long-term interest rate (i) in the financial market which usually exceeds the rate of interest on short-term credit and is affected by the liquidity preference of rentiers' households and banks.

In our simple monetary circuit model, we have therefore two interest rates: the interest rate for short-term bank credit and the long-term interest rate in the financial market. As long as liquidity preference does not change, the spread between the two rates will remain constant.

For this model economy, we are now able to discuss the four phases of a monetary circuit.[25] These four phases are presented in a sequential and chronological order to clearly distinguish the different types of transactions and their roles in a monetary circuit. Of course, in the real world several monetary circuits take place simultaneously with transactions at different frequencies, so that different phases from different circuits will take place simultaneously. We may also have transactions for the same circuit taking place at different speeds and therefore different phases overlapping.

3.5.2 A Monetary Circuit without Interest on Short-Term Credit and without Rentiers Holding Deposits

For the simplest circuit in Figure 3.3, we assume that the rate of interest on short-term bank credit is zero and that households have no inclination to hold a stock of deposits, that is, liquidity preference is zero, too. We will relax these assumptions further below. In order to trace

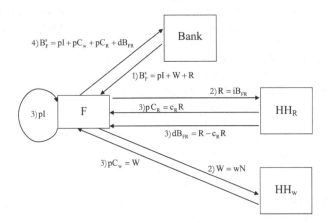

Figure 3.3   A monetary circuit without interest on short-term credit and without rentiers holding deposits

the monetary flows, we start with a given level of economic activity in which firms correctly anticipate the level of effective demand in the goods market.

In the first phase, the 'efflux-phase' (Seccareccia 2003), firms demand short-term credit in the credit market. We assume that at the start of the circuit neither firms nor households dispose of liquid funds, that is, deposits with the commercial banking sector. With a given capital stock, inherited from the past, initiating production requires the purchase of labour power as an input. We abstract from intermediate products. Wages have to be paid in advance for the whole period of production and circulation. Therefore, in order to initiate production, firms need short-term credit (B_F^s) for the wage bill (W) to be paid. The wage bill (W = wN) is determined by the nominal wage rate (w) set in the labour market and by the amount of labour (N) required for planned production, with the labour productivity (y = Y/N) given by the technical conditions of production. Furthermore, at the start of the circuit, firms need short-term credit in order to fulfil their payment commitments to rentiers (R), which are given from the past. These payment commitments to rentiers' households ($R = iB_{FR}$) are determined by the long-term rate of interest (i) on the stock of corporate bonds held by rentiers at the beginning of the circuit (B_{FR}). If firms intend to invest in the capital stock, they will also need purchasing power, that is, short-term credit, for the purchase of investment goods (pI = dpK) from other firms. Therefore, 'initial finance' (Graziani 1989, p. 7) to be supplied by commercial banks' credit has to cover the wage bill, payment commitments of firms to rentiers' households and intra-sectoral payments for investment goods in the firm sector:

$$B_F^s = pI + W + R = pI + wN + iB_{FR}. \tag{3.26}$$

The 'ex nihilo' creation of short-term credit implies that deposits with commercial banks and hence credit money equal to the amount of short-term credit are created.

There has been a debate amongst and between authors from the monetary circuit school and post-Keynesians about the necessary amount of credit creation at the start of a monetary circuit (Rochon 2005). In our view, this debate has two aspects, which are usually not treated separately.

First, there is the question for which purposes firms demand 'initial finance'. Graziani (1989) assumes that firms only need short-term credit for the wage bill. According to Lavoie (1992, pp. 152–7), 'initial finance' is not only required for the wage bill but also for payment commitments to rentiers' households. Parguez and Seccareccia (2000) and Seccareccia (1996, 2003), however, hold that 'initial finance' also has to cover firms' planned purchases of investment goods. We follow this approach, because in this view there is no problem of profit realisation, as will be seen below. For the other approaches, however, it remains unclear how produced profits are completely realised as money profits.

Second, the quantity of 'initial finance' has to be determined. This amount crucially depends on the velocity of circulation of credit money created by commercial banks. In a rejoinder to Renaud (2000), for instance, Nell (2002) in a two-sector framework shows that 'initial finance' only has to cover a fraction of value added, if each unit of credit money is used for several goods and financial market transactions within a circuit, before it is paid back to the issuing bank and hence destroyed. In order to avoid the associated complications, in what follows we will assume that each unit of credit money is only used for one goods or financial market transaction. This assumption is only made for convenience, and it does not change anything of substance in our analysis.

In the second phase of the circuit, firms use 'initial finance' in order to initiate production. They buy labour power, and workers' households receive wages (W), and firms pay capital income, that is, interest on the stock of corporate bonds, to rentiers' households (R). The flow of credit money created in the first phase has now partly been received as income by workers' and rentiers' households. Short-term credit bound for the purchase of investment goods is still held in the firm sector. At the end of the second phase of the circuit, firms are in a position to produce the planned amount of consumption and investment goods.

In the third phase, the 'reflux-phase' (Seccareccia 2003), workers' households make use of their wage income and purchase consumption goods ($pC_W = W$). This part of short-term credit created in the first phase, therefore, flows back to the firm sector and stands ready for repayment to the banking sector. Rentiers' households use a part of their capital income, according to their average propensity to consume ($c_R < 1$), for the purchase of consumption goods, too ($pC_R = c_R R$). Therefore, this part of 'initial finance' also flows back to the firm sector. Simultaneously, firms use short-term credit granted for investment purposes in order to purchase the produced investment goods (pI). Therefore, this part of credit money remains within the firm sector and is also available for repayment to the banking sector. The consumption expenditures of the household sector and the investment expenditures of the firm sector constitute effective demand in the goods market, and we have assumed above that firms' supply of goods exactly meets this effective demand. Consumption and investment expenditures also help to realise profits (Π), as the difference between sales revenues and wage costs. Since 'workers spend what they get', the sum of realised profits at the macroeconomic level is determined by firms' investment expenditures and rentiers' households' consumption expenditures, as shown for Kalecki's approach in Section 3.3 above:

$$\Pi = pI + pC_R + pC_W - W = pI + pC_R. \tag{3.27}$$

So far, the firm sector has received credit money flows amounting to $pI + W + c_R R$, which falls short of initial credit granted to firms equal to $pI + W + R$. Firms are therefore not yet able to repay the whole amount of short-term credit to the banking sector. Therefore, rentiers' saving $S_R = (1 - c_R)R$ has to be considered next. If rentiers use the whole amount of saving for the purchase of corporate bonds issued by firms in the financial market, rentiers' saving will also flow back to the firm sector and will be available for the repayment of short-term credit. Firms will transform short-term investment finance into long-term finance of their capital stock extensions. Of course, this will increase their payment commitments to rentiers' households at the start of the next circuit. It can also be seen that saving is not a precondition for the creation of credit and investment. It is an endogenously generated source of long-term investment finance, that is, 'final finance' (Graziani 1989, p. 7). 'Final finance' does not only draw on rentiers' saving but also on the difference between realised profits and capital income distributed to rentiers' households, the saving of the firm or the retained profits of enterprise (Π_F):

$$\Pi_F = \Pi - R = pI + pC_R - R. \tag{3.28}$$

As will become clear in the following chapters, we assume profits of enterprise to be positive in order for production to take place. This further implies that prices set by firms in the goods market do not only have to cover wage and capital costs but also retained profits of enterprise.

Since $S_R = R - pC_R$, equation (3.28) can be rearranged to generate the familiar goods market equilibrium condition of the equality of investment and saving, with the latter composed of firms' retained earnings, which are saved by definition, and saving out of rentiers' income:

$$pI = \Pi_F + R - pC_R = \Pi_F + S_R. \tag{3.29}$$

Coming back to the monetary circuit, retained profits are already in the hands of the firms and can thus be used to pay back short-term credit to the banking sector. If rentiers now use their saving completely for the purchase of bonds issued by firms ($S_R = dB_{FR}$), the missing funds for the repayment of short-term credit will flow back to the firms. This will enable the firms to pay back the whole amount of initial short-term credit to commercial banks, $B_F^s = pI + W + R$, in the fourth phase of the monetary circuit:

$$B_F^s = pI + pC_w + pC_R + dB_{FR}. \tag{3.30}$$

The monetary circuit will therefore be closed. Short-term credit will be repaid and liquidity created initially will be destroyed. Firms have realised their profits and increased their capital stock through investment, as well as their indebtedness through the increase in the stock of corporate bonds held by rentiers' households. Retained profits are equivalent to firms' ownership of this increase in the capital stock; the saved part of profits distributed to rentiers in terms of interest payments constitutes a financial claim on the increase in the capital stock, that is, future interest payments out of profits. If we had allowed for the emission of shares, it would also have constituted ownership of a part of the increase in the capital stock and an implicit future claim on distributed profits in terms of dividends.

Even if each circuit is closed and there are no disturbances by liquidity preference and hence deposit holdings, the 'initial finance' decisions by commercial banks, together with the production and investment decisions by firms, determine the level of economic activity and its increase over time. Whereas firms' production and investment decisions depend on sales and profit expectations, commercial banks' financing decisions will depend on expectations about firms' ability and willingness to service and pay back credit. This means that creditworthiness and the perspectives of the production and investment projects of firms will matter for 'initial finance'. Summing up, firms' production decisions and commercial banks' financing decisions will jointly determine the level of economic activity and hence employment.

3.5.3   A Monetary Circuit with Interest on Short-Term Credit and with Rentiers Holding Deposits

Let us now in a second, more complicated circuit assume that firms also have to pay interest on short-term credit granted by the commercial banks and that rentiers' households may have liquidity preference and hold part of their saving as deposits with commercial banks, as shown in Figure 3.4. Again, we assume that each unit of credit money is only used for one goods or financial market transaction and that there are no liquid funds in the model economy at the beginning of the circuit.

In the first phase, the 'efflux-phase', firms do not only need short-term credit in order to pay for investment expenditures, wages and interest on the stock of corporate debt held by

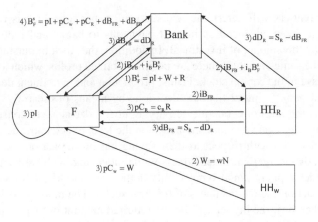

Figure 3.4   A monetary circuit with rentiers holding deposits and firms paying interest on short-term bank credit

rentiers, as well as on long-term credit granted by (iB_{FB}), but also for the interest payments on short-term credit $(i_B B_F^s)$:[26]

$$B_F^s = pI + W + iB_{FR} + iB_{FB} + i_B B_F^s = pI + W + R. \tag{3.31}$$

In the second phase, firms use this 'initial finance' in order to pay wages to workers' households and interest to rentiers' households, as well as to commercial banks. Interest payments to banks do not only contain interest on short-term credit, but also interest on long-term credit from banks, because firms also need long-term credit from banks in order to close the circuit and pay back short-term credit, when there is liquidity preference of rentiers' households, as will become clear below. We assume here that commercial banks transfer all the interest they receive as income to their owners, who are part of the rentiers' household sector. Rentiers' income is thus made up of three components: $R = iB_{FR} + iB_{FB} + i_B B_F^s$.

In the third phase, the 'reflux-phase', workers spend their wages on consumption goods and the respective amount of credit money flows back to the firm sector. Firms buy investment goods from each other, and the respective amount of credit money remains within the firm sector. Rentiers spend part of their income for consumption purposes, and part of the credit money used for interest payments flows back to the firm sector through this channel. If rentiers now have liquidity preference and only use part of their saving to buy corporate bonds but another part to increase their deposits with commercial banks $(dD_R = R - pC_R - dB_{FR})$, it means that the firm sector will only receive back the amount of $pI + W + pC_R + dB_{FR}$, whereas it needs $pI + W + R$ to pay back short-term credit.

Therefore, firms need long-term credit from the banking sector equal to the amount of deposits of rentiers $(dB_{FR} = dD_R)$ to be able to pay back short-term credit in the fourth phase:

$$B_F^s = pI + pC_w + pC_R + dB_{FR} + dB_{FB}. \tag{3.32}$$

Short-term credit will thus be destroyed at the end of the circuit. Similar to the simple circuit presented above, with workers not saving, investment expenditures of firms and consumption expenditures of rentiers will determine realised profits, part of which is retained whereas the other part has been advanced as interest payments to banks and rentiers. The capital stock increases by the amount of investment. In addition, the stock of outstanding debt rises, although not to the same amount if there are positive retained profits, which long-term finance part of the increase in the capital stock. Firms' production and investment decisions, together with commercial banks' 'initial finance' decisions by means of creating short-term credit money determine the level of economic activity. Rentiers' decisions to consume and to save have an impact on aggregate demand and hence on the level of economic activity and profits. Their portfolio decision with respect to their saving has an impact on the structure of the firms' liabilities, that is, on their indebtedness with rentiers and with banks, as we have seen. In a model in which rentiers can also buy equity in the stock market, their portfolio decisions will have an impact on the indebtedness of the firm sector. The more deposits they hold and the less equity they buy, the higher will be the required amount of long-term bank credit to close the circuit and the higher will be the indebtedness of the firm sector with the banks. Furthermore, rentiers' portfolio choice might affect the relative prices of debt and equity, which may then have an impact on the spending and investment decisions at the beginning of the next circuit.

3.5.4 A Monetary Circuit Including a Government – but without Interest on Initial Finance and without Rentiers Holding Deposits

We can finally also include the government (Gov) in the monetary circuit approach, as shown in Figure 3.5. In order to keep the model simple, we assume that banks do not charge interest on initial finance and that rentiers do not hold deposits. With these simplifications, initial finance is composed of short-term credit by banks (B^s) to firms (B_F^s) and to the government (B_G^s). For firms, this includes expenditures for wages and interest payments on the stock of debt inherited from the past, as well as firms' investment expenditures, as in the previous models. For the government, it contains expenditures for interest payments on the stock of

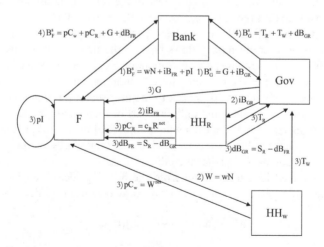

Figure 3.5   A monetary circuit including a government and without interest on initial finance and without rentiers holding deposits

government debt inherited from the past (iB_{GR}), as well as government demand for goods and services (G) produced by firms (government consumption):

$$B^s = B^s_F + B^s_G,\tag{3.33}$$

$$B^s_F = wN + iB_{FR} + pI,\tag{3.34}$$

$$B^s_G = iB_{GR} + G.\tag{3.35}$$

In the second phase, firms use this 'initial finance' in order to pay wages to workers' households and interest to rentiers' households, and governments pay interest on the stock of government debt to rentiers. Rentiers' income is thus composed of two components: $R = iB_{FR} + iB_{GR}$.

In the third phase, the 'reflux-phase', firms buy investment goods from each other, and the government executes its expenditures for goods and services. Workers pay taxes (T_W) to the government and use their net income $(W^{net} = W + T_W)$ for the purchase of consumption goods from the firm sector. Rentiers pay taxes (T_R) to the government and spend part of their net income $(R^{net} = R - T_R)$ according to their propensity to consume $(0 \le c_R < 1)$ for consumption purposes. Through these expenditures, firms recover the amount of $C_W + C_R + pI + G = W - T_W + R - T_R - S_R + pI + G$, whereas governments receive $T_W + T_R$.[27] Therefore, in order to allow the government and the firms to repay initial finance to banks, rentiers need to spend their saving $S_R = R - T_R - pC_R$ on purchasing additional bonds issued by firms and governments such that the respective gaps can be filled. For the government this is $dB_{GR} = G + iB_{GR} - T_W - T_R$ and for firms it is $dB_{FR} = W + iB_R + pI - pC_W - pC_R - pI - G$. We thus need $S_R = R - T_R - pC_R = dB_{FR} + dB_{GR}$. Under these conditions, initial finance will completely flow back to firms and governments, which enables them to pay back the short-term credit to the banks and to close the monetary circuit.

$$B^s_F = pI + pC_W + pC_R + G + dB_{FR},\tag{3.36}$$

$$B^s_G = T_W + T_R + dB_{GR}.\tag{3.37}$$

Short-term credit will thus be destroyed at the end of the circuit. In the course of the circuit, firms realise profits, net of tax payments of rentiers on their interest income received from firms, as already indicated by Kalecki's approach presented in Section 3.3 above. In order to show this, we can start from the income and expenditures identity of our model economy:

$$\Pi^{net}_F + T_\Pi + \left(iB_{FR}\right)^{net} + T_{FR} + W^{net} + T_W + \left(iB_{GR}\right)^{net} + T_{GR}$$
$$= pI + pC_R + pC_W + G + iB_G,\tag{3.38}$$

with pre-tax incomes on the left-hand side and expenditures on the right-hand side of the equation. Π^{net}_F represents retained profits net of taxes, T_Π taxes on retained profits, $\left(iB_{FR}\right)^{net}$ interest revenues of rentiers from firms net of taxes, T_{RF} taxes on interest revenues of rentiers from firms, W^{net} wages net of taxes, T_W taxes on wages, $\left(iB_{GR}\right)^{net}$ interest revenues of rentiers from the government net of taxes and T_{GR} taxes on interest revenues of rentiers from the government. Assuming that taxes on retained profits are zero and that workers spend their net wages, both in line with our monetary circuit model in this section, and considering that $\left(iB_{GR}\right)^{net} + T_{GR} = iB_{GR}$, equation (3.38) reduces to:

$$\Pi_F^{net} + \left(iB_{FR}\right)^{net} + T_{FR} + T_W = pI + pC_R + G. \tag{3.39}$$

This implies:

$$\Pi^{net} = \Pi_F^{net} + \left(iB_{FR}\right)^{net} = pI + pC_R + G - T_{FR} - T_W. \tag{3.40}$$

Total profits from production net of taxation (Π^{net}), splitting into retained profits and interest payments to rentiers, each net of taxes, are thus determined by investment expenditures, consumption expenditures of rentiers and government expenditures minus tax revenues from income generated in production.

   At the end of the circuit, we have a higher capital stock which has increased by the amount of investment, as well as a higher stock of outstanding debt of the firm sector and also higher own capital given by the retained earnings, which each contribute to the long-term finance or funding of the increase in the capital stock. Furthermore, if government expenditures for goods and services together with government interest payments exceed tax revenues, the stock of government debt will also increase. In this model, it is now the government's expenditure decisions, as well as, again, firms' production and investment decisions, together with commercial banks' 'initial finance' decisions, creating short-term credit money, which determine the level of economic activity. Rentiers' decisions to consume and to save have an impact on aggregate demand and hence on the level of economic activity and profits. Their portfolio decision with respect to their saving, buying additional corporate debt and/or additional government debt, might have an impact on the relative rates of interest on these two types of debt. If we allow for rentiers' holding liquidity in terms of deposits with banks, which implies that firms and the government also go into long-term debt with banks, rentiers' portfolio choice will also affect the structure of debt of those two sectors. Furthermore, if we allow the firm sector to issue equity as well, rentiers' portfolio decisions might impact the relative price of debt and equity, as well as the liability composition of the firms' balance sheets.[28] These effects may then have an impact on the spending and investment decisions at the beginning of the next circuit.

   Having so far outlined the basic characteristics of monetary circuit theory and explained the endogeneity of money and credit within this framework, in the analysis of the following chapters we will make some simplifying assumptions. We shall assume that the monetary circuit is closed in each period. Therefore, we can do without a distinction between short-term finance of production ('initial finance') and long-term finance of investment ('final finance') and only deal with the latter. Under these conditions, we do not have to distinguish between an interest rate for short-term bank credit and a long-term rate in the financial market. Instead, we will disaggregate the banking sector and introduce a central bank, which is in control of the short-term rate of interest in the money market where it interacts with commercial banks. And, of course, we will consider the long-term interest rate in the long-term credit or financial market for 'final finance' of the non-financial sector. Depending on the model variant, this will consist of government bonds, corporate bonds and long-term bank loans.

NOTES

1. For a short comparison of Marx, Kalecki and Keynes on effective demand and some implications for modern heterodox short- and long-run macroeconomics, see Hein (2018b).
2. Ricardo's version of Say's law differs from the neoclassical version, because it is neither associated with full employment of labour nor is there an economic mechanism equating saving and investment, like the real interest rate in the neoclassical capital market. It simply implies that saving and investment are identical, because capitalists save in order to invest (Garegnani 1978, 1979).
3. On Marx's rejection of Say's law and its comparison with Keynes's theory, see more extensively Hein (2004, 2006b), Kenway (1980) and Sardoni (2011, pp. 11–23). For a comparison of Marx's theory of value and distribution, money, effective demand and capital accumulation with Sraffa, Kalecki, Keynes and Minsky, see Hein (2019b).
4. The role of credit in economic crises is explored in more detail by Marx (1894, pp. 476–519) in *Capital, Vol. 3*. See Hein (2004, 2006b, 2008, Chapter 5, 2019b) for reviews. In this context, Arnon (1994), Crotty (1986, 1993), Hein (2019b) and Pollin (1994) have pointed out some similarities to Minsky's (1975, 1977, 1986a) theories of financial instability and crisis in his 'financial instability hypothesis', but also some important differences.
5. Note that in Marx's theory, as in the classical approaches, unemployment is a structural feature, even if the productive capacities given by the capital stock are fully utilised, in order to safeguard positive profits (Garegnani 1978, 1979).
6. For further elaborations, see Hein (2004, 2006b, 2019b). See also Argitis (2001), Panico (1980, 1988) and Pivetti (1987, 2015) for similar results with respect to Marx's theory of the rate of interest, and Sardoni (1997) for some ambiguities in Marx's reasoning.
7. For the short-run version of the profit-squeeze approach explaining business cycles see Goodwin (1967); for the long-run version explaining economic stagnation see Glyn and Sutcliffe (1972) and the work in the 'social-structure of accumulation' (SSA) approach, for example Gordon (1981, 1995), Gordon et al. (1983, 1987), Kotz (2013) and McDonough et al. (2010).
8. The organic composition of capital is the ratio of capitalists' advances on constant capital, that is, means of production and intermediate products, to advances on labour, that is, wages. According to Marx, this ratio has a tendency to rise because of the mechanisation of production associated with technical change. For the 'falling rate of profit due to a rising organic composition of capital' theories see Catephores (1989, pp. 166–87), Foley (1986, Chapters 8–9) and Shaikh (1978a, 1978b, 1987, 2011, 2016, Chapter 16).
9. This section draws on Hein (2014a, Chapter 5).
10. See Sylos-Labini (1979) for an excellent elaboration on these conditions.
11. In Kalecki (1954, Chapters 1–2, 1971, Chapters 5–6) the ratio of raw material costs to wage costs also affects functional income distribution. However, raw material costs have been ignored here, because we have assumed vertically integrated sectors.
12. On Kalecki's approach to money and finance and its compatibility with post-Keynesian monetary theory, see in particular Arestis (1996b), Dymski (1996), Lopez (2002), and Sawyer (1985, Chapter 5, 2001a, 2001b).
13. Kalecki's approach was inspired by his reading of Marx's (1885) schemes of reproduction in *Capital, Vol. 2*, which we have presented in Section 3.2 above. See Kalecki (1968a).
14. In the foreword to the English translation of his early works published in Poland in the 1930s, *Studies in the Theory of Business Cycles, 1933–1939*, there is a similar view: 'The studies also reflect the most essential features of my theory of the business cycle. I modified in my later work only the factors determining investment decisions' (Kalecki 1969a, p. 1).
15. For a survey of Kalecki's models of the business cycle and the respective investment functions in these models, see in particular Lopez G. and Assous (2010, Chapter 5), Sawyer (1985, Chapter 3) and Steindl (1981).
16. A growth trend can then only be generated by exogenous factors. As Steindl (1981, p. 132, emphasis in the original) points out, Kalecki's model 'can *alternatively* either produce a cycle or a trend'. Kalecki focussed on the cycle and therefore had to rely on external stimulus in order to generate a positive trend.
17. In a neoclassical model, this endogenous mechanism is the real rate of interest in the capital market, which is supposed to equilibrate real saving and real investment at full employment.
18. For different views and debates on Keynes's 'principle of effective demand', see Allain (2009, 2013), Chick (1983, Part II), Davidson (1972, Chapter 3, 1994/2011, Chapters 2–5), Hartwig (2007, 2011, 2013a, 2017) and Hayes (2007a, 2007b, 2013).
19. Neoclassical roots are also present in other parts of Keynes's *General Theory*. For example, Keynes (1936, pp. 16–17) accepts the 'first classical postulate' with respect to the labour market, that is a falling marginal productivity curve of labour, which implies an inverse relationship between the real wage rate and employment. Of course, in his approach the neoclassical causality between the real wage rate and employment is reversed. It is effective demand which determines employment, and through this channel the real wage rate is affected. Furthermore, he accepts the neoclassical marginal productivity theory of income distribution, as soon as full

employment is achieved: 'If we suppose the volume of output to be given, *i.e.* to be determined by forces outside the classical scheme of thought, then there is no objection to be raised against the classical analysis of the manner in which private self-interest will determine what in particular is produced, in what proportions the factors of production will be combined to produce it, and how the value of the final product will be distributed between them' (Keynes 1936, pp. 378–9).

20.   Keynes (1936, p. 138) also points out that there is an aggregation problem in the neoclassical approach, since it is not clear what physical productivity of a stock of capital with heterogeneous capital goods can mean and how it could be measured without using values/prices in order to aggregate the capital goods to a capital stock. As has become obvious in the Cambridge capital controversies of the 1950s and 1960s, in the case of a more-than-one-good economy, the aggregate neoclassical production function and the results derived from it are untenable (Harcourt 1969, 1972, Hein 2014a, Chapter 3). Relative prices need to be known in order to aggregate heterogeneous capital goods to the value of a capital stock and heterogeneous output goods to the value of final output, and thus to set up an aggregate neoclassical production function. Therefore, the marginal products of capital and labour in this production function cannot determine the real rate of interest and the real wage rate, because one of these distribution parameters has to be known in order to determine relative prices, as has been rigorously shown by Sraffa (1960). Therefore, the values of the capital stock and of output cannot be determined without having a distribution parameter, and thus functional income distribution, determined in the first place.

21.   See Keynes (1973, pp. 201–23, pp. 229–33), Hawtrey (1937), Ohlin (1937a, 1937b) and Robertson (1937, 1938a, 1938b, 1940).

22.   See in particular the work by Minsky (1975, 1977), as well as the surveys by Crotty (1992) and Fazzari and Mott (1986/87).

23.   On the monetary circuit school see Bossone (2001, 2003), Graziani (1989, 1994, 1996, 2003), Hein (2008, Chapter 10.2), Lavoie (1992, pp. 149–69, 2014, Chapter 4.3), Lavoie and Seccareccia (2016), Parguez (1996), Parguez and Seccareccia (2000), and Seccareccia (1996, 2003). On the relationship between the monetary circuit school and post-Keynesianism see Deleplace and Nell (1996), Fontana (2000) and Rochon (1999, 2003). On the relationship of the monetary circuit school with Marxian economics, see Graziani (1997). For a recent Sraffian perspective on the monetary circuit theory, see Cesaratto (2017), Cesaratto and Di Bucchianico (2020) and Cesaratto and Pariboni (2021). For a partly confusing debate in the 1980s in post-Keynesian economics on credit, finance, saving and investment, which has stimulated my interest in monetary circuit research, see Asimakopulos (1983, 1985, 1986a, 1986b, 1986/87), Davidson (1986/87), Graziani (1984, 1988), Kregel (1986/87), Richardson (1986), Snippe (1985), Terzi (1986, 1986/87), and Wray (1988).

24.   On the role of commercial banks in the monetary circuit school see, in particular, Bossone (2001, 2003).

25.   See Graziani (1989), Hein (2008, Chapter 10.2), Lavoie (1992, pp. 151–7), and Seccareccia (1996, 2003) for similar analyses.

26.   Rochon (2005) assumes that interest payments on short-term initial credit of the present circuit will take place at the start of the next circuit – or during future circuits. But it remains true that the means for the debtors to pay interest have to be injected into the circuit by the creditors, the commercial banks themselves.

27.   Here and in Figure 3.5, we assume that the government runs a deficit, that is, tax revenues fall short of the sum of government demand for goods and services plus government interest payments. If tax revenues exceed total government expenditures, and the government hence saves, it will have to buy bonds issued by the firm sector to allow the monetary circuit to be closed. Alternatively, in a model with deposits, it may increase its deposits, and long-term bank lending to firms will have to increase to close the circuit.

28.   For attempts at extending the monetary circuit theory to include issues of financialisation, see, for example, Sawyer (2016) and Sawyer and Passarella Veronese (2017).

4. Post-Keynesian constant price macroeconomic models

4.1 INTRODUCTION

Having presented the foundations of the principle of effective demand, and the roles of money, finance, investment and saving in the previous chapter, we will now develop some basic constant price post-Keynesian short-run macroeconomic models. Of course, these models are based on the principle of effective demand, and they consider the distribution of income between different social groups or classes. They also take into account the financing side of effective demand, that is, credit and interest on credit. The models are short-run models in the sense that all the stocks (capital, financial assets and liabilities) are taken as given and exogenous, as results of past developments. Also the labour force and labour supply are taken to be given and exogenous. Usually, neither the capital stock nor the labour force is fully utilised, which means that our model economies are characterised by the underutilisation of the capital stock and by unemployment, as normal states of affairs indicated already by Keynes (1936) and Kalecki (1935). We will analyse the short-run determination of aggregate demand, output and income and thus, with given labour productivity, also of employment, each within the period. Feedback effects on the next period's stocks of capital and financial assets and liabilities will not be the focus of this analysis.

In Section 4.2, we will outline the foundations of a closed economy model regarding production, finance, income and expenditures, on the one hand, and regarding interest, money and credit, and the role of the central bank, on the other hand. In Section 4.3, we will then present the basic model for this closed private economy without taxes and government expenditures and analyse the effects of changes in model parameters, like firms' animal spirits, rentiers' propensity to save, the profit share and the rate of interest. Section 4.4 will then explicitly introduce the government into the model and discuss the roles of taxes, government expenditures and government budget deficits. In Section 4.5, some open economy features will be included, introducing exports and imports of goods and services with the rest of the world and analysing the effects of exogenous changes in interest rates, income distribution and also the nominal exchange rate. In Section 4.6, we will then touch upon the role of wage inequality and examine the effects of relative income concerns in the consumption function of a basic model. Finally, in Section 4.7, the focus will be on the short-run macroeconomics of gender pay gaps.

4.2 THE MODEL ECONOMY

4.2.1 Production, Finance, Income and Expenditures

In our closed economy model with no government sector a homogeneous output (Y) is produced with a fixed coefficient production technology, using labour (N) and a non-depreciating capital stock (K) as inputs.[1] There is no overhead labour, and labour productivity ($y = Y/N$) is hence constant up to full capacity output given by the capital stock. This supply constraint is only reached by accident, and the economy usually operates below full capacity and potential output (Y^p) given by the capital stock, with a constant capital-potential output ratio ($v = K/Y^p$). Labour supply is not a constraint. There is always a reserve army of labour through several channels, like the variation of labour force participation rates of domestic labour, that is, female participation or life working time, and through migration.

We assume that long-term finance of the nominal capital stock (pK) consists of firms' accumulated retained earnings (E_F), on the one hand, and long-term credit ($B_F = B_{FR} + B_{FB}$), on the other hand, either granted by rentiers (B_{FR}) in terms of holding corporate bonds issued by the firms or in terms of loans granted by the banking sector (B_{FB}):

$$pK = E_F + B_{FR} + B_{FB}. \tag{4.1}$$

For the sake of simplicity, we thus ignore the emission of equity by firms and hence a market for shares, as well as a dividend rate on shares.[2]

The banking sector is a very rudimentary one, because we want to keep the initial model as simple as possible. Therefore, we abstract from a central bank and from central bank money for the most basic version and first only consider a 'pure credit economy', in which transactions are being paid for by transfers between accounts held with commercial banks. As explained in Chapter 3, from a monetary circuit perspective, banks provide short-term credit to firms in order to get the process of production started. At the end of each circuit they grant long-term credit to firms, and they provide deposits for the private sector. In order to simplify the exposition, we will not look at short-term credit, but only at the end of circuit position, that is, at the change in long-term loans granted by banks to firms and at the change in deposits held by rentiers. We assume that banks charge interest on loans but do not pay interest on deposits, so that we have interest-bearing financial assets (corporate bonds and long-term bank loans) and a non-interest bearing one (deposits) which is held for liquidity reasons. The rate of interest on loans is determined by the risk and liquidity concerns of credit-granting commercial banks and rentiers that hold corporate bonds, and the volumes of credit and deposits are endogenously determined in the system, as we will explain in more detail in the next section. We assume that the rate of interest on long-term loans charged by banks is the same as the rate of interest on corporate bonds issued by firms and held by rentiers. Finally, we assume that banks are owned by rentiers, that they operate without costs and that the interest on loans received is paid out as income to their owners immediately and completely.

The balance sheet matrix of our 'pure credit' model economy can be found in Table 4.1, which presents the stocks of assets (+) and liabilities (−) and the net worth of each sector and the economy as a whole at the beginning of a period. The added sums of each of the columns have to be equal to the added sums of each of the rows:

$$pK = E_F + B_{FR} + D_R. \tag{4.2}$$

This tells us that long-term finance of the capital stock (pK) consists of accumulated retained earnings (E_F), that is, firms' equity under the control of the owners or the managers of the firms, and the stocks of credit being granted by rentiers (B_{FR}) and by banks (B_{FB}). It becomes also clear that, to the degree that rentiers prefer to hold their financial assets in the most liquid

Table 4.1 Balance sheet matrix for a closed economy with neither a government nor a central bank

	Workers' households	Rentiers' households	Firms	Banks	Σ
Deposits		$+D_R$		$-D_R$	0
Loans		$+B_{FR}$	$-(B_{FR}+B_{FB})$	$+B_{FB}$	0
Capital			pK		pK
Σ	0	$+B_{FR}+D_R$	$+E_F$	0	$pK = B_{FR} + D_R + E_F$ $= B_{FR} + B_{FB} + E_F$

Table 4.2 Transaction flow matrix for a closed economy with neither a government nor a central bank

	Workers' households	Rentiers' households	Firms' current	Firms' capital	Banks	Σ
Consumption	$-pC_W$	$-pC_R$	$+pC_W + pC_R$			0
Investment			$+pI$	$-pI$		0
Wages	$+W$		$-W$			0
Retained profits			$-\Pi_F$	$+dE_F$		0
Distributed profits: Interest		$+R_F$	$-R_F$			0
Change in deposits		$-dD_R$			$+dD_R$	0
Change in loans		$-dB_{FR}$		$+dB_{FR} + dB_{FB}$	$-dB_{FB}$	0
Σ	0	0	0	0	0	0

form, that is, deposits (D_R) in this case, and thus refrain from directly crediting the firm sector, the banks have to step in and have to provide long-term credit to the firms of the same amount ($B_{FB}=D_R$). This is the same result as we have derived from the monetary circuit approach in Chapter 3.

Economic transactions over a period are summarised in the transaction flow matrix in Table 4.2. In this matrix, inflows to the sectors' accounts have a plus and outflows have a minus. In order to prevent black holes and to get the accounting right, the sum in each row as well as in each column has to be equal to zero. The level of production in our model economy in each period is determined by the principle of effective demand, that is, mainly by the firms' decisions to invest (pI), independently of prior saving (S), because, in principle, firms have access to additional credit (dB_{FB}) being generated 'out of nothing' by a developed banking sector. Workers hired for production purposes receive wages (W) which we assume to be consumed entirely (pC_W). By means of selling their output partly as consumption goods to workers (pC_W) and rentiers (pC_R), and partly as investment goods to other firms (pI), firms receive total revenues:

$$pY = pC_W + pC_R + pI. \tag{4.3}$$

For the sake of simplicity, we abstract from profits paid out to the owners/managers of the firms and from consumption out of these profits. Profits are thus partly retained in the firm sector (Π_F) and hence saved in order to partially finance the addition to the capital stock ($\Pi_F = dE_F$). The other part of gross profits is distributed to rentiers in terms of interest payments on the stock of debt issued by the firms and held by the rentiers or the banks at the beginning of each period [$R = iB = i(B_{FR} + B_{FB}) = R_{FR} + R_{FB}$]. Since the rentiers own the banks, the interest payments on bank loans are also received by rentiers' households and are therefore directly accounted in the rentiers' revenues – without tracing this flow through the banks in Table 4.2. The rate of interest (i) on loans is determined by the risk and liquidity concerns of the banks and the rentiers, as we will explain below. Total revenues are thus distributed between the three types of income, wages, retained profits and distributed profits to rentiers:

$$pY = W + \Pi = W + \Pi_F + R = W + \Pi_F + i\left(B_{FR} + B_{FB}\right). \tag{4.4}$$

Whereas workers spend what they get:

$$W = pC_W, \tag{4.5}$$

rentiers consume part of their income (pC_R) and save the rest (S_R), either by means of buying further corporate bonds issued by firms (dB_R) or by holding more non-interest bearing deposits (dD_R):

$$R = pC_R + S_R = pC_R + dB_{FR} + dD_R. \tag{4.6}$$

For firms to be able to obtain the required long-term finance for their investment:

$$pI = dE_F + dB_{FR} + dB_{FB}, \tag{4.7}$$

the unwillingness of the rentiers to provide this long-term finance through buying bonds, holding liquidity instead, has to be compensated by additional credit being granted by the banking sector ($dD_R = dB_{FB}$).

Since gross profits (Π), including retained profits and interest payments, are determined by the difference between revenues and wage payments, with workers not saving, from equations (4.3)–(4.5) we obtain that profits thus depend on investment expenditures of firms and consumption expenditures of rentiers, as we have already explained in Chapter 3 following Kalecki (1954, Chapter 3, 1971, Chapter 7):

$$\Pi = pC_R + pI. \tag{4.8}$$

Again, as in Chapter 3, it becomes clear that, with a given level of firms' investment, a reduction in the rentiers' propensity to consume, and thus an increase in their propensity to save, reduces firms' sales, revenues and profits. An increase in rentiers' liquidity preference, however, changes the firms' liability structure; it will lead to a decrease in corporate bonds held by rentiers and to an increase in long-term loans granted by commercial banks.

As Tables 4.1 and 4.2 show, the balance sheet matrix and transaction flow matrix are linked with each other. The stocks of debt inherited from the past, together with the rates of return on these stocks, determine some of the flows, that is, the interest payments of firms to rentiers and banks. And the flows in the current period will feedback on the stocks at the beginning of the next period, because investment adds to the capital stock and additional credit and deposit creation add to the respective stocks as well. However, since in this chapter we are interested in the short-run determination of the levels of output, income and employment, we will not treat these feedback effects here. In what follows, the capital stock, as well as the stock of debt, the stock of accumulated retained earnings and the stock of deposits, are each considered to be constant for the period under consideration, each inherited from the past. Some long-run dynamics will then be touched upon in Chapters 7–9.[3]

4.2.2 Endogenous Money and Exogenous Interest Rates with a Central Bank

In the next step, we will now introduce a central bank that supplies central bank money in the money market and sets the rate of interest in that market. The respective balance sheet matrix is shown in Table 4.3. In the money market – or, synonymously, the interbank market – the central bank supplies central bank money or reserves (M) to the commercial banks in exchange for good collateral, which is a certain fraction of the assets held by commercial banks $[(1 - b)B_{FB}]$, that is, bank credit granted to firms in our model. Commercial banks grant long-term credit (B_{FB}) to creditworthy firms, keep a fraction (bB_{FB}) as assets on their balance sheet and offer deposits to the non-financial sector of the economy, in our case only held by the rentiers' households (D_R). For the sake of simplicity, we still assume that commercial banks do not pay any interest on deposits. Furthermore, rentiers may also hold reserves (M_R) instead of deposits for liquidity purposes. Workers and firms will only transitorily make use of reserves and deposits for their transactions but will not hold these two non-interest bearing but most liquid financial assets. Since workers spend all their income on consumption, there are no financial assets to be held at the end of each period. Firms are the deficit sector in our model economy, and they will thus hold no non-interest bearing financial assets either at the end of each period, when all the sales and purchases have been done, but rather use any money and deposits to service and reduce their stock of debt. Therefore, in our

Table 4.3   Balance sheet matrix for a closed economy without a government but with a central bank

	Workers' households	Rentiers' households	Firms	Commercial banks	Central bank	Σ
Money/ reserves		$+M_R$		$+M_B$	$-M$	0
Deposits		$+D_R$		$-D_R$		0
Loans		$+B_{FR}$	$-(B_{FR} + B_{FB})$	$+bB_{FB}$	$+(1 - b)B_{FB}$	0
Capital			pK			pK
Σ	0	$+B_{FR} + D_R + M_R$	$+E_F$	0	0	$pK = E_F + B_{FR} + D_R + M_R = E_F + B_{FR} + B_{FB}$

model economy, only rentiers will hold stocks of deposits and reserves. Commercial banks may also hold reserves (M_B), either because of minimum reserve requirements and/or because of liquidity considerations.

The consistency of the balance sheet matrix for our model with a central bank and with central bank money requires the following equation to hold:

$$pK = E_F + B_{FR} + B_{FB} = E_F + B_{FR} + D_R + M_R. \tag{4.9}$$

Again, it becomes clear, as already derived from our monetary circuit analysis in Chapter 3, that commercial banks' long-term credit to firms has to be equal to deposits and reserves held by rentiers' households.

The transaction flow matrix for the model economy with a central bank in Table 4.4 is based on the one in Table 4.2 and includes the central bank, as well as the change in reserves issued by the central bank and held by rentiers' households and commercial banks. Rentiers can now use their saving per period either by means of buying additional corporate bonds issued by firms, holding more deposits with commercial banks or holding more reserves issued by the central bank. Commercial banks obtain more reserves from the central bank in exchange for additional collateral, which is a fraction of additional long-term loans commercial banks have granted to firms. These reserves are either demanded by, and thus forwarded to, rentiers' households instead of deposits, or they are held by the commercial banks themselves for liquidity purposes. Since the central bank is now holding a fraction of interest-bearing loans granted to firms, it also receives interest payments from the firm sector, and we assume that these payments are forwarded to the rentiers' households as owners of the commercial banks, and also of the central bank – since there is no government yet in our model economy.

With respect to the determination of interest rates, credit and money stocks, we follow the post-Keynesian 'horizontalist' monetary view pioneered by Kaldor (1970b, 1982, 1985), Lavoie (1984, 1996a, 2011b, 2014, Chapter 4) and Moore (1988a, 1988b, 1989a).[4] This view can be summarised as follows:

> Money is credit-driven; loans make deposits; deposits make reserves. The supply of and the demand for credit money are interdependent. The control instrument of the central bank is not a quantity but a price, the rate of interest.
>
> (Lavoie, 1992, p. 170)

This post-Keynesian theory of money and credit endogeneity has recently been confirmed by several central banks in their explanations of the operation of the monetary system and of money and credit creation, like the Bank of England (Jakab and Kumhof 2015, McLeay et al. 2014a, 2014b), the US Federal Reserve (Ihrig et al. 2021) or even the Deutsche Bundesbank (2017). In fact, the Bank of England authors positively refer to post-Keynesian and monetary circuit economists, like Graziani (1989), Howells (1995a), Kaldor and Trevithick (1981), Minsky (1986b, 1991), Moore (1979, 1983, 1988a) and Palley (1996a).[5]

According to the post-Keynesian approach, the central bank's monetary policy determines the base rate of interest in the money market, that is, the interbank market where the central banks and commercial banks interact. The central bank, as 'lender of last resort', is responsible for the liquidity and stability of the money market and the whole monetary system. Therefore, the central bank accommodates the generation of credit and hence deposits by

Table 4.4 Transaction flow matrix for a closed economy without a government but with a central bank

	Workers' households	Rentiers' households	Firms' current	Firms' capital	Commercial banks	Central bank	Σ
Consumption	$-pC_W$	$-pC_R$	$+pC_W + pC_R$				0
Investment			$+pI$	$-pI$			0
Wages	$+W$		$-W$				0
Retained profits			$-\Pi_F$	$+dE_F$			0
Distributed profits: Interest		$+R_F$	$-R_F$				0
Change in money/reserves		$-dM_R$			$-dM_B$	$+dM$	0
Change in deposits		$-dD_R$			$+dD_R$		0
Change in loans		$-dB_{FR}$		$+dB_{FR} + dB_{FB}$	$-bdB_{FB}$	$-(1-b)dB_{FB}$	0
Σ	0	0	0	0	0	0	0

commercial banks with the required amount of central bank money, under the condition that commercial banks can provide 'good collateral', that is, securities which meet the criteria set by the central bank. The amount of central bank money is thus determined by economic activity, payment conventions and liquidity preference, provided that commercial banks only grant credit to creditworthy borrowers in the credit market and thus have the securities, which are demanded by the central bank in exchange for central bank money. This implies that there is always some sort of 'rationing', in the sense that the willingness to pay the rate of interest demanded by the central bank is a necessary but not a sufficient condition for commercial banks to obtain reserves in the money market. To the extent that commercial banks can supply the required collateral, the central bank's money supply curve in the interbank market becomes horizontal.

Modern central banks supply central bank money and manage the short-term interest rates by applying a corridor system, as explained by Lavoie (2014, Chapter 4.4). The ceiling of this corridor is given by the lending facility rate at which commercial banks can obtain central bank money overnight, provided that they can offer good collateral. The floor is given by the deposit facility rate, which commercial banks receive holding reserves in their deposits with the central bank. Of course, as we have learnt in course of and after the Global Financial Crisis and the Great Recession 2007–09, central banks may decide to turn the deposit facility rate negative, and commercial banks may have to pay for holding liquidity on their accounts with the central bank. Usually, the money market rate should remain within the corridor given by the lending facility rate and the deposit facility rate. Whenever there is a lack of supply of reserves, which drives money market rates up, commercial banks can always obtain reserves overnight, provided they have good collateral, from the central bank at the lending facility rate (the old discount rate). Whenever there is excess supply of reserves in the money market, which drives money market rates down, commercial banks can deposit excess reserves at the deposit rate with the central bank. The central bank's target rate is within the corridor and the central bank tries to reach this target rate by managing and fine-tuning the supply of reserves to commercial banks.[6] Of course, central banks' targets do not have to be in the middle of the corridor (symmetric corridor system) but can also be (close to) the floor or the ceiling, as explained by Lavoie (2014, pp. 219–25).

Commercial banks determine the interest rate in the credit or financial market, where they interact with the non-financial sectors of the economy. Commercial banks set their lending interest rates by marking up the central bank's base rate, which they have to pay in the market for reserves, and then supply credit at this interest rate to those borrowers in the credit market, only firms in our simple model, whom they consider creditworthy. Again, the willingness of firms to pay the rate of interest set by commercial banks in the credit market is a necessary, but not a sufficient condition to obtain credit. There will always be some sort of 'credit rationing' for those firms who are unable to provide required collateral or own means of finance, or to meet other screening requirements applied by commercial banks. According to Wolfson (1996), in a post-Keynesian theory of credit rationing based on asymmetric expectations of borrowers and lenders in a world with fundamental uncertainty, credit rationing may occur due to differences in expectations between borrowers and lenders. Wolfson (1996) shows that credit standards and interest rates are both increased if commercial banks' state of confidence decreases, in particular during a financial crisis. Credit rationing and increasing spreads between credit and money market interest rates, because of rising risk and liquidity premia, as well as expectations of rising short-term interest rates in the future, then move together.

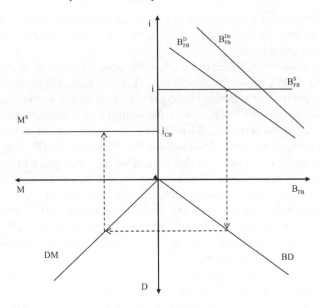

Figure 4.1   The horizontalist approach to endogenous money and credit

The horizontalist view on interest rates, money and credit is presented in Figure 4.1. The upper left quadrant shows the central bank's horizontal money supply curve (M^S) in the money market at a given base rate of interest (i_{CB}) set by the central bank, the central bank's target rate in the money market. In the upper right quadrant we find an interest rate inverse loan demand curve for bank credit (B^D_{FB}), which is the creditworthy loan demand from the perspective of the commercial banks. In contrast, we have the notional loan demand curve (B^{Dn}_{FB}), which also includes the part of loan demand that does not meet the creditworthiness standards of commercial banks. The loan supply curve (B^S_{FB}) of commercial banks is horizontal at a given rate of interest (i) calculated by marking up the central bank's base rate:

$$i = (1 + m_B) i_{CB}. \tag{4.10}$$

The mark-up (m_B) is determined by commercial banks' risk and liquidity premia, by other costs than refinancing costs, target profits in banking and by the degree of competition in the banking sector that affects target profits. The mark-up is also affected by commercial banks' expectations about future short-term interest rates in the money market, because banks are transforming maturities: They lend long-term in the credit market but they borrow short-term in the money market. Risk and liquidity premia, and hence mark-ups, will be stable during tranquil times, but may shift violently during times of heightened uncertainty and financial crisis.

The lower right quadrant with the loan-deposit curve (BD) shows that loans (B) make deposits (D). While granting credit to creditworthy firms, commercial banks simultaneously generate deposits, which firms will use for their expenditures, that is, for payments of wages, interest payments and purchases of investment goods from other firms. Households will partly spend these deposits when buying consumption goods from firms; firms will spend the deposits buying investment goods from other firms. In our model, workers' households will spend all their income, whereas rentiers' households save, and part of the saving is held as deposits with commercial banks.

However, in an economy with central bank money, not all the purchases will be paid for by shifting deposits held with commercial banks. There are also cash payments which constitute a demand for central bank money by the non-financial sector. Furthermore, commercial banks have to hold mandatory reserves with the central bank, and also excess reserves are held on the accounts of the commercial banks with the central bank. The lower left quadrant shows the deposit-reserves curve (DM) and displays that deposits (D) make reserves (M). For the sake of simplicity it is assumed that each 'making' takes place in fixed proportions. Whereas the loan-deposit curve is a 45° line for our model, the deposit-reserves curve will be affected by payment conventions, required reserve ratios and liquidity preference.

An increase in creditworthy loan demand, hence an outward shift in the B_{FB}^D-curve, will increase loan and money supply at given interest rates. Higher standards for creditworthiness associated with a more cautious credit supply will be associated with a downward shift in the creditworthy loan demand curve in Figure 4.1.

If liquidity preference and risk considerations of commercial banks and, hence, their mark-ups remain constant, the central bank's interest rate setting in the money market also determines the rate of interest in the credit market. Under these conditions, changes in the money market rate and in the credit market rate of interest are due to changes in the monetary policy stance. Changes in the central bank's base rate will therefore also shift the credit supply curve and affect credit demand and hence real economic activity financed by credit. However, in a deep financial and economic crisis, as for example 2007–09, we should observe:

- A rising spread between the credit market interest rate and the money market rate because of higher uncertainty, higher risks of default of borrowers and higher risk and liquidity premia.
- In particular, a rising gap between notional and creditworthy loan demand, and hence rising credit rationing, because of the application of tighter creditworthiness standards in the face of higher uncertainty and higher risks of default.
- And a clockwise rotation in the DM curve indicating rising liquidity preference of the non-financial sectors but also of commercial banks and hence a rise in the money-deposit and the money-loan ratio.

All this is shown in Figure 4.2.

Therefore, if commercial banks' liquidity and risk considerations, their expectations regarding the future short-term rate of interest, or the degree of competition in the banking sector, and hence their mark-ups change, monetary policy may not be able to determine the credit market rate of interest directly. Hence, a first asymmetry regarding the effectiveness of central banks' interest rate policies may arise: An increasing money market rate of interest will, at some point, always trigger an increasing credit market rate, because commercial banks have to recover costs of refinancing and have to gain minimum profits. But a decreasing money market rate may not be followed by a falling credit market rate if commercial banks' liquidity and risk premia increase due to rising uncertainty and rising default risks in an economic and financial crisis, if commercial banks expect a higher short-term rate in the future or if commercial banks' profit aspirations increase due to lower competition.

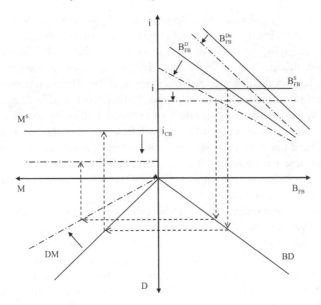

Figure 4.2   Interest rates, credit and money during the financial and economic crises 2007–09

A second asymmetry arises when we look at the effect of changing credit market interest rates on credit-financed expenditures and the volume of credit. A rising money market rate through the upward pressure on the credit market rate of interest is, in principle, always able to reduce the volume of credit-financed expenditures in an economic boom by means of forcing the credit supply curve upward – and thus terminating the economic boom. In times of recession, however, central banks may not be able to stimulate credit-financed demand and expand the volume of credit, even when they are successful in lowering the credit market rate through a lower policy rate in the money market. Depressed expectations of the private sector and/or rising cautiousness of commercial banks may shift the creditworthy demand curve inwards and/or make it vertical – and the famous 'investment trap' emerges, in which lower interest rates do not stimulate investment expenditures. We will have to come back to this asymmetry in the effectiveness of central banks' interest rates policies later on when discussing monetary policies in Chapters 5 and 6 of this book.

In particular the second asymmetry explains why unconventional measures and quantitative easing applied by many central banks during the Global Financial Crisis and the Great Recession 2007–09 and after have been of little effect in terms of stimulating aggregate demand, output and employment.[7] Of course, central banks that lower the standards of collateral and offer long-term reserves to commercial banks improve the balance sheets of the latter and secure their survival. Direct interventions of central banks into financial markets, increasing the demand for government and corporate bonds, lower long-term interest rates and in a sense circumvent risk-averse commercial banks with high liquidity preference. However, in a deep recession with depressed demand expectations of firms, and thus an inward shift of the credit demand curves (Figure 4.2), this is insufficient to stimulate deficit-financed investment expenditures and hence aggregate demand. Falling domestic interest rates triggered by unconventional monetary policies and a depreciation of the domestic currency, and thus an improvement of international price competitiveness of domestic producers, may stimulate exports, if these are highly price-elastic, and if the rest of the world is not applying similar policies. We know this has not been the case. Furthermore, expansionary macroeconomic effects of a currency devaluation are far from certain, if the effects on domestic income distribution are taken into account, as we will show further below and in Chapter 5. Therefore, quantitative easing policies have been effective in terms stabilising the financial sector and reducing interest rates and the debt burden of the deficit sectors of the economy, including the government, but have not been sufficient to stabilise aggregate demand, output and employment. For this purpose expansionary fiscal policies have been required, as has been extensively analysed by post-Keynesian authors.[8] We will return to these economic policy issues and implications in Chapters 5 and 6.

Before we move on to building a simple short-run macroeconomic model on the balance sheet and transaction flow matrices in Tables 4.3 and 4.4 by introducing some behavioural equations, a few comments on the post-Keynesian theory of exogenous interest rates and endogenous credit and money shown in Figures 4.1 and 4.2 are at place. Such type of presentations of the post-Keynesian monetary approaches have been used by several authors, like Fontana (2003, 2004a, 2004b, 2009a, Chapter 8), Fontana and Setterfield (2009b), Hein (2008, Chapter 6), Howells (2009) and Palley (1994a, 1996a, Chapter 7). But it has not been always clear what exactly is presented in these diagrams. This has then led to unresolved controversies, in particular about the slope of the money and the credit supply curves in the controversies between 'horizontalists' and 'structuralists'.[9]

In the horizontalist approach followed in this book, money and credit are stocks at the end (or the beginning) of a period, and Figures 4.1 and 4.2 thus present snapshots with given expectations regarding profitability, creditworthiness, risks of default and so on, and given liquidity preference of economic actors. The downward sloping credit demand curve can be explained using Kalecki's (1937) 'principle of increasing risk' and Keynes's (1936, Chapter 11) considerations of rising borrowers' risk with the increase of the firm's stock of debt at a point in time – without considering macroeconomic feedbacks, as explained in Chapter 3. Therefore, at a point in time, a higher rate of interest means a lower desire to debt-finance the capital stock, mainly because of rising borrowers' risk. Under the conditions of given parameters, as mentioned above, money supply and credit supply curves are both horizontal. In the course of a period these parameters will change endogenously through macroeconomic feedbacks, that is, credit-financed expenditures generate income, and also through exogenous shocks, and then lead to a new snapshot at the end of the period or the beginning of the next period. We have seen this for the results of the financial and economic crisis presented in Figure 4.2: A lower willingness to obtain credit for long-term finance of the capital stock shifts the demand for credit curve, tighter creditworthiness standards affect the gap between notional and creditworthy credit demand, higher risk and liquidity premia affect the mark-up and thus shift the credit supply curve, higher liquidity preferences of firms and banks affect the DM curve and a change in interest rate policies of the central bank shifts the money supply curve.

In the structuralist view, however, this clear distinction between different points in time has been blurred, and it has been argued that money supply and credit supply curves should be viewed to be necessarily upward sloping while credit and money demand increase, with a focus on an upward sloping credit supply curve (Dow 2006, Herr 1988a, 1988b, 1993, Howells 1995a, 1995b, 2006, Palley 1994a, 1996a, Chapter 7, 1996b, 2013c, Pollin 1991, Wray 1990,

1992a, 1992b, 1995).[10] As the main reason for an upward sloping money supply curve it has been argued that central banks might not always accommodate a higher demand for reserves, usually associated with an increase in credit. Horizontalists would argue that this is a change in the policy stance of central banks targeting a higher rate of interest in the money market, which shifts the horizontal money supply curve upward.

As main causes for an upward sloping credit supply curve it has been argued by structuralists that, with a higher volume of credit, commercial banks will charge a higher interest rate because of lower liquidity and higher risk, and hence an increase in the respective premia. Fontana (2003, 2004a, 2004b, 2009a, Chapter 8) and Fontana and Setterfield (2009b) have made the same argument for a stepwise increase of the credit supply curve from period to period. However, from a horizontalist perspective, it is not clear at all why a higher volume of credit and credit-financed expenditures should necessarily be associated with a loss of liquidity in the commercial banks' balance sheets and with higher risk to be taken by banks at the beginning of the next period, if the macroeconomic feedbacks within the period are taken into account. Of course, it is conceded that the commercial banks' long-term interest rate may rise with an increasing amount of credit granted, even when the central bank maintains the base rate in the money market at a constant level. Changes in the degree of competition in the banking sector and shifts in expectations and hence in liquidity preference or risk assessments of commercial banks may be a cause for this. What is disputed from a macroeconomic perspective, however, is the necessity of an increase of the loan rate in the face of rising demand for credit, due to necessarily decreasing liquidity of commercial banks and increasing indebtedness of credit-seeking firms and thus higher risk (Lavoie 1996a).

First, an increase in long-term credit does not necessarily mean decreasing liquidity of commercial banks. Rising loans mean rising deposits, the spending of which will remain within the banking sector. Individual banks may face liquidity constraints, but the banking sector as whole will not, as long as the demand for central bank money remains constant. If increasing credit is associated with increasing demand for central bank money, too, commercial banks might face liquidity problems if the central bank is not willing to accommodate increasing demand for reserves at a given rate of interest, and the loan rate of interest might rise because of a higher money market rate. However, this increase in interest rates is then caused by non-accommodation of the central bank. It is thus tantamount to an increase in the central bank's target base rate, that is, an upward shift in the central bank's horizontal supply curve of reserves. Similarly, increasing spending of firms financed by means of credit generates increasing realised profits. Therefore, an increasing degree of indebtedness of firms or a rising share of interest payments in total profits is by no means necessary. On the contrary, we might even observe a 'paradox of debt' (Steindl 1952), that is, increasing loan-financed investment, but falling debt-capital ratios of firms, and hence a fall in borrowers' and lenders' risk, when the macroeconomic effects of rising investment is taken into account. This has been shown, for example, by Hein (2012b) in an analytical growth model and by Godley (1999), Lavoie and Godley (2001/2) and Lavoie (2017b) in stock-flow consistent (SFC) numerical simulation models. Therefore, if we view the situations presented in Figures 4.1 and 4.2 as end (or beginning) of period stocks, then there is no reason to follow the structuralist or Fontana's approach and to assume that an increase in money or credit demand is necessarily related with higher interest rates. The horizontalist approach thus seems to be vindicated, and we will take the rate of interest in the financial market as an exogenous variable in what follows.

4.3   A CONSTANT PRICE CLOSED ECONOMY MODEL WITHOUT A GOVERNMENT

4.3.1   The Basic Model

Let us now start with the first model of pricing, distribution and aggregate demand for a closed economy without a government, based on the framework explained in the previous section. In oligopolistic or monopolistically competitive markets, firms have some price setting power. They determine the price (p) of the homogenous good in the goods market by applying a mark-up (m) to unit direct labour costs, the ratio of the nominal wage rate (w) and labour productivity (y), which is itself the ratio of real output per worker ($y = Y/N$). The mark-up and unit direct labour costs are both assumed to be constant up to full capacity output:

$$p = \left[1 + m(i)\right]\frac{W}{y}, \quad m > 0, \frac{\partial m}{\partial i} \geq 0. \tag{4.11}$$

The mark-up is affected by the degree of competition in the goods market and workers' bargaining power in the labour market, which each constrain the price setting power of the individual firm, as explained by Kalecki (1954, Chapter 1, 1971, Chapter 6) and outlined in Chapter 3 of this book (see also Hein 2014, Chapter 5.2). Furthermore, apart from profits, the mark-up has to cover overhead costs and is thus potentially affected by changes in interest costs of firms.[11] With the stock of debt of the firms given in the short run, a change in the rate of interest will induce an upward pressure on the mark-up, in particular if associated with weakened bargaining power of workers and/or a lower degree of competition in the goods market. Since in this chapter we abstract from inflation and assume the price level in the goods market to be constant, any change in the mark-up – with constant prices – means that nominal and real unit labour costs are immediately adversely affected.

As explained above in this chapter, the rate of interest in our model is a monetary category, with the short-term rate determined by central bank policies and the long-term rate also affected by liquidity and risk assessments of commercial banks and financial wealth holders, as well as their expectations regarding future short-term rates. The relevant rate of interest in our model is the long-term rate of interest corrected for inflation (expectations), which we will call the real rate of interest ($i_r = i - \hat{p}^e$). Since inflation is assumed away in this basic model, the real rate of interest is thus equal to the nominal rate of interest.

Following Kalecki, the mark-up determines the share of gross profits (Π) in national income (h) and thus also the share of wages (W) in national income ($\Omega = 1 - h$):

$$h = \frac{\Pi}{pY} = \frac{\Pi}{W + \Pi} = \frac{mW}{W + mW} = \frac{m}{1 + m}, \tag{4.12}$$

$$\Omega = 1 - h = \frac{W}{pY} = \frac{W}{W + \Pi} = \frac{W}{W + mW} = \frac{1}{1 + m}. \tag{4.13}$$

Functional income distribution is therefore affected by any change in the determinants of the mark-up, including potentially a change in the real rate of interest. Graphically, this determination of profit and wage shares by firms' pricing can be seen in Figure 4.3, which is based on the pricing equation (4.11) and shows the sums of wages and profits for an output level Y_1

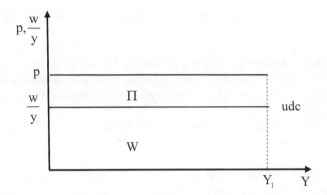

Figure 4.3   Mark-up pricing and income distribution without overhead labour costs

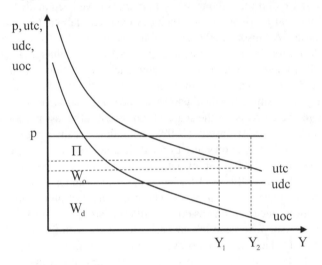

Figure 4.4   Mark-up pricing and income distribution with overhead labour costs

with constant unit direct labour costs (udc=w/y), mark-ups and prices. Whenever the level of output changes, with constant unit direct labour costs and prices, the sums of wages and profits will change, too, but their proportion and thus the functional distribution of income will remain unchanged.

Such a constancy of wage and profit shares with changes in aggregate demand and output is not in line with empirical observations: In the short-run course of the trade cycle, we rather observe falling wage shares in the upswing and the boom, but rising wage shares in the downswing and the recession (Hein 2014a, Chapter 1, Stockhammer 2017b).[12] This is due, in particular, to overhead labour costs and pro-cyclical total labour productivity (Kalecki 1971, Chapter 6, Rowthorn 1981, Lavoie 2009b, 2014, Chapters 4–5). In the upswing with rising economic activity, unit overhead labour costs (uoc) and unit total labour costs (utc) are falling, thus raising the profit share and lowering the wage share in national income accounting, whereas in the downswing we see the reverse. Including overhead labour costs, which are proportional to productive capacity and the capital stock, in the basic pricing and distribution model shown in Figure 4.3 gives Figure 4.4. Moving from output level Y_1 to the higher level Y_2, again with constant unit direct labour costs, mark-ups and prices, will yield the following:

- first, as before, a constant share of wages of direct labour in national income (W_d/pY),
- second, a falling share of overhead labour/managerial salaries in national income (W_o/pY),
- third, a falling share of overhead labour/managerial income in total labour income $[W_o/(W_d + W_o)]$,
- fourth, a fall in the total labour income share $[(W_d+W_o)/pY]$,
- fifth, a rise in the profit share in national income (Π/pY).

Of course, if demand and output fall, we will see the opposite movements of these income shares. Including overhead labour makes functional income distribution thus endogenous to aggregate demand and output in the short run.[13]

Regarding the share of direct labour, several attempts have been made to correct the wage share from the national accounts, which includes overhead labour remuneration, for (top-) management salaries. Atkinson (2009) correcting for the top 10 and the top 50 per cent in the UK, Glyn (2009) for the top 1 per cent in the USA and Dünhaupt (2011) for the top 0.1 per cent in the USA and Germany have presented such calculations. Apart from showing a more pronounced falling recent trend since the mid-1970s/early 1980s, such corrected wage shares still display some similar cyclical pattern as the wage share from the national accounts. However, the more one corrects for the share of top salaries, the less pronounced is the cyclical pattern, as can be seen in Atkinson's (2009) calculations for the share of the bottom 50 per cent in the UK, which hardly shows any cyclical fluctuations any more, but only a slightly downward sloping trend. Making use of data on supervisory and production labour for the USA provided by Mohun (2014), and taking supervisory labour as representing overhead labour, Rolim (2019) shows a similar result: The wage share of production workers displays no cyclical fluctuations but a continuous downward trend since the mid-1970/early 1980s. The wage share of supervisory/overhead labour varies inversely with the rate of capacity utilisation, whereas the profit share shows a pro-cyclical behaviour. Both display a rising trend since the mid-1970s/early 1980s. Rolim's (2019) VAR estimations, focussing on the interaction of the three income shares with capacity utilisation and hence economic activity, suggest that higher activity has no strong effect on the production workers' share of income, supporting again that this seems to be rather constant over the trade cycle, as assumed by Kalecki (1971, Chapter 6) – and in our simple model without overhead labour.

Saving in our model consists of retained earnings of firms (Π_F), the difference between total profits and rentiers' income (R), plus saving out of rentiers' income (S_R):

$$S = \Pi_F + S_R = \Pi - R + S_R = hpY - iB_F + s_R iB_F$$

$$= hpY - (1 - s_R)iB_F, \quad 1 \geq s_R > 0.$$

(4.14)

Rentiers' income ($R = iB_F$) is determined by the rate of interest and the stock of debt (B_F) at issuing price at the beginning of the period. Rentiers consume a fraction from their current income determined by their propensity to consume (c_R). Therefore, rentiers' saving is affected by their propensity to save out of their income ($s_R = 1 - c_R$), which is assumed to be positive and constant.[14]

In a monetary production economy, investment of firms (pI) is independent of any prior saving in the economy, because firms have access to finance generated endogenously by the banking sector, as explained above. The investment function proposed here contains Keynesian and Kaleckian features, which we have outlined in Chapter 3:

$$pI = pI_a + \beta pY - \theta iB_F, \quad I_a, \beta, \theta \geq 0. \tag{4.15}$$

First, following Keynes (1936), we assume that investment decisions of firms are determined by long-term expectations and by 'animal spirits', the 'spontaneous urge to action rather than inaction' (Keynes 1936, p. 161), which are represented by a shift parameter I_a in equation (4.15), representing autonomous investment. Second, investment is affected by (expected) sales and hence by income, represented by the accelerator term βpY. And third, we have included a negative effect of the interest payments on debt, represented by $-\theta iB_F$. Although a negative effect of the rate of interest on investment decisions is in line with Keynes's (1936) theory of investment based on the marginal efficiency of capital and the rate of interest, we rely more on Kalecki's (1937) concept of the 'principle of increasing risk', which is also addressed in Keynes's (1936) remarks on borrowers' and lenders' risk, as we have argued in Chapter 3. Higher interest payments have a negative effect on investment, because they reduce retained earnings and thus firms' own means of finance, which are important for their access to external means in incompletely competitive credit or financial markets. The amount of own means of finance of the firm is usually a criterion for creditworthiness and thus impacts the amount of external finance a firm can raise from rentiers by issuing corporate bonds and from commercial banks by obtaining loans. Furthermore, a drain of internal means of finance increases the risk of illiquidity of the firm relying on external finance and thus dampens the willingness to invest in the capital stock.

Equation (4.16) presents the goods market equilibrium condition, the equality of investment and saving decisions. In equation (4.17) we have the Keynesian/Kaleckian stability condition, a higher marginal response of saving with respect to income than investment:

$$pI = S, \tag{4.16}$$

$$\frac{\partial S}{\partial (pY)} > \frac{\partial (pI)}{\partial (pY)} \quad \Rightarrow \quad h > \beta \quad \Rightarrow \quad h - \beta > 0. \tag{4.17}$$

4.3.2 The Goods Market Equilibrium and the Effects of Changes in Model Parameters

Plugging equations (4.14) and (4.15) into equation (4.16), the goods market equilibrium value for income can be derived as in equation (4.18). Using the equilibrium value for income from equation (4.18) in equation (4.14) or (4.15), we can then calculate the respective equilibrium values for investment and saving, as provided in equation (4.19). Finally by using the definition of the profit share ($h = \Pi/pY$), we can derive from equation (4.18) also the equilibrium value of profits in equation (4.20). Graphically, equilibrium income and investment/saving are shown in Figure 4.5.

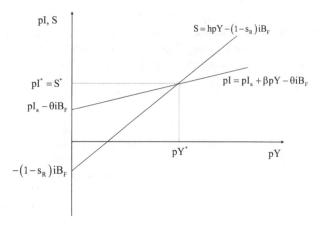

Figure 4.5   Short-run equilibrium income in a private closed economy

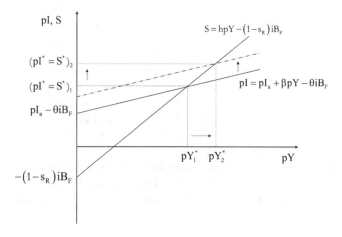

Figure 4.6   An increase in animal spirits/autonomous investment

$$pY^* = \frac{pI_a + (1 - s_R - \theta)iB_F}{h - \beta}, \tag{4.18}$$

$$pI^* = S^* = \frac{hpI_a + [\beta(1 - s_R) - \theta h]iB_F}{h - \beta}, \tag{4.19}$$

$$\Pi^* = \frac{h[pI_a + (1 - s_R - \theta)iB_F]}{h - \beta}, \tag{4.20}$$

As can easily be seen from equations (4.18), (4.19) and (4.20), an increase in long-term expectations and animal spirits, and thus in autonomous investment, will have expansionary effects

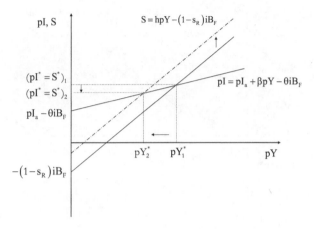

Figure 4.7   An increase in the rentiers' propensity to save

on all endogenous variables. This is shown in Figure 4.6. From equations (4.18), (4.19) and (4.19) we can also immediately see that an increase in the propensity to save out of rentiers' income reduces equilibrium income, investment and profits. The paradox of saving is thus valid with respect to all three endogenous variables. This is also shown in Figure 4.7 for equilibrium income and investment/saving. A rise in the profit share will have negative effects on equilibrium income, investment and profits, as is obvious from equations (4.18a), (4.19a) and (4.20a). Our economy is thus wage-led: A higher wage share in national income has an expansionary effect. We also have a 'paradox of costs' (Rowthorn 1981): Lowering the real wage rate and the wage share, and thus increasing the profit share, is detrimental to aggregate profits and hence the profit rate, that is, profits over the given nominal capital stock: $r = \Pi/pK$.

$$\frac{\partial(pY^*)}{\partial h} = \frac{-\left[pI_a + (1-s_R-\theta)iB_F\right]}{(h-\beta)^2} = \frac{-pY^*}{h-\beta} < 0, \tag{4.18a}$$

$$\frac{\partial(pI^*)}{\partial h} = \frac{-\beta\left[pI_a + (1-s_R-\theta)iB_F\right]}{(h-\beta)^2} = \frac{-\beta pY^*}{h-\beta} < 0, \tag{4.19a}$$

$$\frac{\partial\Pi^*}{\partial h} = \frac{-\beta\left[pI_a + (1-s_R-\theta)iB_F\right]}{(h-\beta)^2} = \frac{-\beta pY^*}{h-\beta} < 0. \tag{4.20a}$$

Figure 4.8 shows the contractionary effects of a higher profit share on equilibrium national income and investment/saving. Finally, a change in the interest rate has ambiguous effects on the equilibrium values of the model, as can be seen in equations (4.18b), (4.19b) and (4.20b):

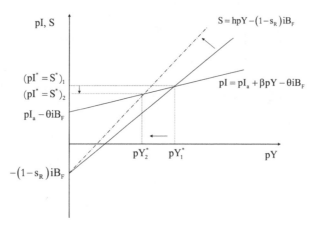

Figure 4.8   An increase in the profit share

$$\frac{\partial\left(pY^{*}\right)}{\partial i}=\frac{\left(1-s_{R}-\theta\right)B_{F}-pY^{*}\dfrac{\partial h}{\partial i}}{h-\beta},$$

(4.18b)

$$\frac{\partial\left(pI^{*}\right)}{\partial i}=\frac{\left[\beta\left(1-s_{R}\right)-\theta h\right]B_{F}-\beta pY^{*}\dfrac{\partial h}{\partial i}}{h-\beta},$$

(4.19b)

$$\frac{\partial\Pi^{*}}{\partial i}=\frac{h\left(1-s_{R}-\theta\right)B_{F}-\beta pY^{*}\dfrac{\partial h}{\partial i}}{h-\beta}.$$

(4.20b)

If the mark-up is interest-inelastic ($\partial h/\partial i = 0$) and the propensity to consume out of rentiers' income exceeds the marginal effect of internal funds on investment ($1-s_{R}-\theta>0$), a higher interest rate will trigger higher equilibrium values for income and profits, as can be seen in equations (4.18b) and (4.20b). A positive effect on equilibrium investment would also require a strong accelerator effect of income on investment decisions, as is obvious from equation (4.19b). This constellation is known as the 'puzzling case' (Lavoie 1995b). In the case of an interest-elastic mark-up ($\partial h/\partial i > 0$), the puzzling case effects may persist, in particular for equilibrium income and profits, if a higher interest rate has only a mild impact on the mark-up and the profit share, with dampening effects on equilibrium income, investment and profits. With strong effects of a change in the interest rate on the profit share, the impact of a higher rate of interest on equilibrium income, investment and profits may turn negative. And if the 'normal case' (Lavoie 1995b) conditions prevail, which means that the propensity to consume out of rentiers' income falls short of the marginal effect of internal funds on investment ($1-s_{R}-\theta<0$), a higher interest rate will trigger lower equilibrium values for income, profits and investment at any rate, irrespective of an interest-elastic or -inelastic profit share.

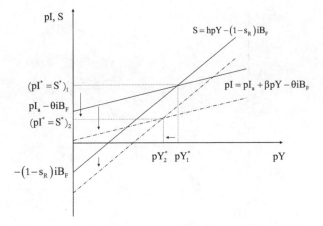

Figure 4.9   A rise in the interest rate with an interest-inelastic profit share I: The normal case – a fall in equilibrium income and investment/saving

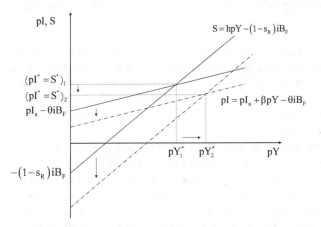

Figure 4.10   A rise in the interest rate with an interest-inelastic profit share II: The intermediate case – a rise in equilibrium income but a fall in investment/saving

Figures 4.9, 4.10 and 4.11 show the potential effects of a rise in the interest rate on equilibrium income and investment/saving for interest-inelastic mark-ups and profit shares. We start with the normal case in Figure 4.9, in which a higher interest rate has depressing effects on equilibrium income and investment/saving. As can be seen, the rise in the interest rate causes a strong downward shift of the investment function due to the high importance of internal means of finance for investment, that is, a high value of θ in the investment function in equation (4.15), but only a weak downward shift of the saving function because of a relatively high propensity to save out of rentiers' income.

If the importance of internal means of finance for investment, and thus the value of θ is somewhat lower, and the propensity to consume out of rentiers' income is somewhat higher, and thus the propensity to save lower, we may get an intermediate case as in Figure 4.10. The respective shifts of investment and saving functions triggered by a rise in the interest rate

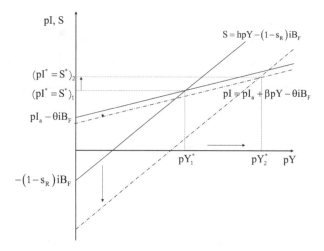

Figure 4.11   A rise in the interest rate with an interest-inelastic profit share III: The puzzling case – a rise in equilibrium income and investment/saving

cause an increase in equilibrium income but a fall in equilibrium investment/saving. A higher interest rate redistributes income from firms to rentiers' households which stimulates consumption more than it partially depresses investment. But the increase in aggregate demand is insufficient to cause an overall rise in investment because the accelerator effect is too weak relative to the internal means of finance effect, that is, the value of β is too low relative to θ in the investment function.

Finally, we may obtain the puzzling case of a rise in equilibrium income and investment/saving triggered by a rise in the interest rate, as shown in Figure 4.11. Here, a low effect of internal means of finance on investment and thus a low θ only mean a minor downward shift of the investment function, whereas a high rentiers' propensity to consume, and thus a low propensity to save, mean a strong downward shift in the saving function. A higher interest rate re-distributing income from firms to rentiers has a strong effect on consumption but only a weak partial effect on investment, and the rise in consumption demand then also increases equilibrium investment through the accelerator in the investment function.

Allowing for an interest-elastic mark-up and profit share in Figures 4.9–4.11 would mean a counter-clockwise rotation of the saving function. Therefore, the puzzling and intermediate cases become less likely, albeit not impossible.

Parametric changes in the stock of corporate debt inherited from the past have the same effects as changes in the interest rate, as should be obvious. A higher (lower) stock of debt means higher (lower) interest payments of the firm and higher (lower) interest incomes for the rentiers' households. In the puzzling case, a higher stock of debt has expansionary effects – the demand regime is 'debt-led'. In the normal case the effects will be contractionary, and the demand regime is 'debt-burdened':

$$\frac{\partial(pY^*)}{\partial B_F} = \frac{(1-s_R-\theta)i}{h-\beta},$$ (4.18c)

Table 4.5   Responses of equilibrium output/income, investment/saving and profits to changes in exogenous variables and parameters

	pY^*	$pI^* = S^*$	Π^*
pI_a	+	+	+
s_R	−	−	−
h	−	−	−
i	+/−	+/−	+/−
B_F	+/−	+/−	+/−

$$\frac{\partial(pI^*)}{\partial B_F} = \frac{\left[\beta(1-s_R)-\theta h\right]i}{h-\beta}, \tag{4.19c}$$

$$\frac{\partial\Pi^*}{\partial B_F} = \frac{h(1-s_R-\theta)i}{h-\beta}. \tag{4.20c}$$

If the mark-up and the profit share were considered to be affected not by the interest rate (i) but by interest payments (iB_F), we would have to add the same modifying effects via the profit share to equations (4.18c)–(4.20c) as explained for the effects of changes in the interest rate in equations (4.18b)–(4.20b) above.

Table 4.5 summarises the main features of the constant price, closed private economy short-run macroeconomic model based on the principle of effective demand. The economic policy implications of this simple model are quite straightforward. Any policies which increase autonomous investment expenditures have expansionary effects. The same is true for policies that manage to reduce the propensity to save out of household income, that is, rentiers' income in our model, or those that re-distribute incomes from profits to wages. The macroeconomic effects of interest rate policies of monetary authorities, however, will depend on the propensity to consume out of rentiers' income, the effect of internal means of finance on investment and also on the interest elasticity of the mark-up and hence the profit share. Depending on these model parameters different effects are possible. An increase in the rate of interest will thus, in theory, not necessarily have contractionary effects on the economy. We will come back to this question in Chapters 5 and 6, when it comes to discussing inflation-targeting interest rate policies.

4.4   THE GOVERNMENT IN THE CONSTANT PRICE CLOSED ECONOMY MODEL: TAXES AND GOVERNMENT EXPENDITURES

4.4.1   The Basic Model

In this section, we will now include the government in our basic constant price closed economy model. We keep all the assumptions regarding the private sector from the previous section. However, regarding the ownership of the central bank, we now assume that it is owned

Table 4.6 Balance sheet matrix for a closed economy with a government and a central bank

	Workers' households	Rentiers' households	Firms	Government	Commercial banks	Central bank	Σ
Money/reserves		$+M_R$			$+M_B$	$-M$	0
Deposits		$+D_R$			$-D_R$		0
Loans		$+B_{FR} + B_{GR}$	$-(B_{FR} + B_{FB})$	$-(B_{GR} + B_{GB})$	$+b(B_{FB} + B_{GB})$	$+(1-b)$ $(B_{FB} + B_{GB})$	0
Capital			pK				pK
Σ	0	$+B_{FR} + B_{GR} + D_R + M_R$	$+E_F$	$-(B_{GR} + B_{GB})$	0	0	$pK=$ $E_F + B_{FR} + D_R + M_R - B_{GB}$ $=E_F + B_{FR} + B_{FB}$

by the government and not by the rentiers. As can be seen in the balance sheet matrix in Table 4.6, which is an extension of the balance sheet matrix in Table 4.3, we treat the government as a debtor sector, issuing long-term government debt (B_G) to be held by rentiers (B_{GR}) or by banks (B_{GB}). A fraction $(1 - b)$ of government debt will be held by the central bank, together with a fraction of corporate debt, equivalent to reserves supplied to the economy, via commercial banks, and held by rentiers' households and commercial banks at the end of the period. Of course, governments have access to short-term finance in order to finance government expenditures, as explained in Chapter 3 on the monetary circuit. But as in the previous section of the current chapter, we assume the monetary circuit to be closed in each period, such that short-term finance is destroyed at the end of the period. The consistency of the balance sheet matrix requires the following equation to hold:

$$pK = E_F + B_{FR} + D_R + M_R - B_{GB} = E_F + B_{FR} + B_{FB}. \qquad (4.21)$$

Including the government in the transaction flow matrix in Table 4.7 means that, on the one hand, governments receive taxes on wages (T_W) from workers' households, on rentiers' income (T_R) from rentiers' households and on retained profits (T_F) from the firm sector. Governments' expenditures on consumption goods (G) go to the firm sector, and government interest payments (R_G) on the stock of government debt held by rentiers' households (iB_{GR}) and by commercial banks (ibB_{GB}), which are owned by rentiers' households, go to the rentiers' households. We assume again that banks do not pay interest on deposits and do not retain interest income from loans granted to firms and governments. Therefore we include interest revenues to banks, both from governments and firms, as direct payments to rentiers' households. The government's interest payments on the fraction of government debt held by the central bank [$i(1 - b)B_{GB}$] go to the central bank, and, similar to the commercial banks, the central bank distributes these interest revenues to its owner, the government. Therefore, also these payments are not included in the transaction flow matrix. Since the central bank may also hold corporate bonds, the interest revenues on these are also distributed to the government. Therefore, we consider the government interest payments to the rentiers' households to be net of those interest revenues received.

With a positive tax rate on wages, workers would pay taxes to the government, and we assume again that they do not save and spend their net income after taxes completely on consumption goods. Rentiers pay taxes to the government, consume part of their net income and save the other part by increasing their stock of reserve holdings, deposits and/or additional loans to the firm sector and/or the government. Firms' revenues derive from selling consumption goods and services to workers, rentiers and the government, and from selling investment goods to other firms. Firms pay taxes to the government, wages to workers and interest income to rentiers, and they keep the residual as retained earnings, which add to the equity owned by the firm. Together with further debt issued by the firm and held by rentiers and/or banks this contributes to long-term financing of investment. For commercial banks, the change in deposits held by rentiers has to be equal to the change in reserves held by commercial banks plus the change in the additional corporate and government bonds held by the commercial banks. For the central bank, the change in issued reserves held by rentiers and by banks has to be equal to the change in additional corporate and government bonds held by the commercial banks. Looking at the accounting identity of incomes and expenditures, we have:

Table 4.7 Transaction flow matrix for a closed economy with a government and a central bank

	Workers' households	Rentiers' households	Firms' current	Firms' capital	Government	Commercial banks	Central bank	Σ
Taxes	$-T_W$	$-T_R$	$-T_F$		$+T$			0
Government consumption			$+G$		$-G$			0
Consumption	$-pC_W$	$-pC_R$	$+pC_W + pC_R$					0
Investment			$+pI$	$-pI$				0
Wages	$+W$		$-W$					0
Retained profits			$-\Pi_F$	$+dE_F$				0
Interest payments		$+R_F + R_G$	$-R_F$		$-R_G$			0
Change in money/reserves		$-dM_R$				$-dM_B$	$+dM$	0
Change in deposits		$-dD_R$				$+dD_R$		0
Change in loans		$-dB_{FR} - dB_{GR}$		$+dB_{FR} + dB_{FB}$	$+dB_{GR} + dB_{GB}$	$-bd(B_{FB} + B_{GB})$	$-(1-b)d(B_{FB} + B_{GB})$	0
Σ	0	0	0	0	0	0	0	0

$$pY = pY_P + iB_G = pI + pC_R + pC_W + G + iB_G$$

$$= \Pi_F^{net} + T_F + R^{net} + T_R + W^{net} + T_W \qquad (4.22)$$

$$= \Pi_F^{net} + R^{net} + W^{net} + T,$$

with pY as total income, composed of income from production (pY_P) plus government interest payments (iB_G).

In order to simplify the further analysis, we will assume that the rates of interest on corporate and on government bonds are the same. Furthermore, we assume that the tax rate on wages is zero ($t_w = 0$) and that the tax rates on interest income and on retained profits are the same, such that we have a single tax rate on profits ($t_\Pi = t_F = t_R \geq 0$). Finally, to reduce the complexity of our modelling, we will also assume in what follows that the central bank will not hold corporate and government bonds (b = 1) and thus that there are no reserves in the system (M = 0). Governments will thus only pay interest on their stock of debt to rentiers and not receive any interest income via the central bank.

Income distribution in production is determined by mark-up pricing of firms, in the way explained and applied in the previous section. The mark-up may be interest-elastic. Furthermore, similar to long-term changes in the interest rate, also persistent changes in the tax rate on profits might trigger a change in the mark-up and hence in the profit share before taxation, because, from the perspective of the firm, this is equivalent to a change in overhead costs. In the case of a tax-elastic mark-up, an increase in the tax rate on profits will thus partly be at the expense of the wage share. Since we are assuming constant prices in this chapter, an interest or tax driven increase in the mark-up would mean a fall in nominal and real unit labour costs. Profit and wage shares in production are given as:

$$h = \frac{\Pi}{pY_P} = \frac{\Pi}{W + \Pi} = \frac{m}{1+m}, \quad m > 0, \frac{\partial m}{\partial i} \geq 0, \frac{\partial m}{\partial t_\Pi} \geq 0, \qquad (4.23)$$

$$\Omega = 1 - h = \frac{W}{pY_P} = \frac{1}{1+m}. \qquad (4.24)$$

Government expenditures on goods and services (G) are treated as autonomous and a policy variable. Government interest payments to rentiers, directly or via banks, (iB_G) are given by the exogenous interest rate, determined by interest rate policies of the central bank and by liquidity and risk assessment of commercial banks and rentiers, as explained above, and by the stock of government debt accumulated in the past. Government tax revenues are composed of taxes paid by firms and rentiers on their respective incomes and are thus endogenous with respect to economic activity, income distribution between labour and capital, the stock of government debt and the interest rate:

$$T = T_F + T_R = t_\Pi \Pi_F + t_\Pi R = t_\Pi \left(hpY_P - iB_F\right) + t_\Pi \left(iB_F + iB_G\right) = t_\Pi \left(hpY_P + iB_G\right). \qquad (4.25)$$

Since workers spend their net income after taxes and do not save, we have:

$$pC_W = W = (1 - h)pY_P. \qquad (4.26)$$

Retained profits after taxes are saved by definition:

$$\Pi_F^{net} = \left(1 - t_\Pi\right)\Pi_F = \left(1 - t_\Pi\right)\left(hpY_P - iB_F\right). \tag{4.27}$$

Rentiers save a certain fraction of their net income after taxes, which is composed of interest payments of firms and of governments:

$$S_R = \left(1 - t_\Pi\right)s_R i\left(B_F + B_G\right), \quad 1 \geq s_R > 0. \tag{4.28}$$

Summing up equations (4.27) and (4.28), we obtain for the private saving function in our model economy:

$$S = \Pi_F^{net} + S_R = \left(1 - t_\Pi\right)\left[hpY_P - iB_F + s_R i\left(B_F + B_G\right)\right]$$

$$= \left(1 - t_\Pi\right)\left\{hpY_P - i\left[\left(1 - s_R\right)B_F - s_R B_G\right]\right\}, \tag{4.29}$$

$$1 \geq s_R > 0, \quad 1 > t_\Pi \geq 0.$$

The investment function builds on the one introduced in the previous section. Firms' investment decisions are thus determined by autonomous investment, affected by Keynes's (1936) 'animal spirits', by the accelerator effect of output on investment and by internal means of finance, referring to Kalecki's (1937) 'principle of increasing risk'. On the latter, not only interest payments, as in the previous model, but also tax payments on retained earnings have a negative impact:

$$pI = pI_a + \beta pY_P - \theta\left[iB_F + t_\Pi\left(hpY_P - iB_F\right)\right]$$

$$= pI_a + \left(\beta - \theta t_\Pi h\right)pY_P - \theta\left(1 - t_\Pi\right)iB_F, \tag{4.30}$$

$$pI_a, \beta, \theta \geq 0, \quad \beta - \theta t_\Pi h > 0$$

In the investment function we assume that an increase of output and income in production has a positive effect on investment although it also raises tax payments on retained profits. We thus assume that $\beta - \theta t_\Pi h > 0$. The equilibrium condition is:

$$pI + G + iB_G = S + T, \tag{4.31}$$

and the stability condition with autonomous G and exogenous iB_G is given as:

$$\frac{\partial S}{\partial\left(pY_P\right)} + \frac{\partial T}{\partial\left(pY_P\right)} > \frac{\partial\left(pI\right)}{\partial\left(pY_P\right)}$$

$$\Rightarrow \left(1 - t_\Pi\right)h + t_\Pi h > \beta - \theta t_\Pi h \tag{4.32}$$

$$\Rightarrow \left(1 + \theta t_\Pi\right)h - \beta > 0.$$

4.4.2 The Goods Market Equilibrium and the Effects of Changes in Model Parameters

Plugging equations (4.25), (4.29) and (4.30) into equation (4.31), and assuming government expenditures on goods and services to be exogenous, yields equilibrium output and income from production:

$$pY_P^* = \frac{pI_a + G + (1-t_\Pi)i\left[(1-s_R-\theta)B_F + (1-s_R)B_G\right]}{(1+\theta t_\Pi)h - \beta}. \tag{4.33}$$

For total equilibrium income we have to add government interest payments:

$$pY^* = pY_P^* + iB_G$$

$$= \frac{pI_a + G + (1-t_\Pi)i\left[(1-s_R-\theta)B_F + (1-s_R)B_G\right] + \left[(1+\theta t_\Pi)h - \beta\right]iB_G}{(1+\theta t_\Pi)h - \beta} \tag{4.34}$$

$$= \frac{pI_a + G + i\left\{(1-t_\Pi)(1-s_R-\theta)B_F + \left[(1-t_\Pi)(1-s_R) + (1+\theta t_\Pi)h - \beta\right]B_G\right\}}{(1+\theta t_\Pi)h - \beta}.$$

Equilibrium gross profits from production are given by the profit share in equation (4.23) and equilibrium income from production in equation (4.33):

$$\Pi^* = hpY_P^* = \frac{h\left\{pI_a + G + (1-t_\Pi)i\left[(1-s_R-\theta)B_F + (1-s_R)B_G\right]\right\}}{(1+\theta t_\Pi)h - \beta}. \tag{4.35}$$

Finally, equilibrium tax revenues can also be determined making use of equilibrium profits or equilibrium income in production:

$$T^* = T_F + T_R = t_\Pi\left(\Pi^* + iB_G\right) = t_\Pi\left(hpY_P^* + iB_G\right)$$

$$= \frac{t_\Pi\left\langle h\left\{pI_a + G + i(1-t_\Pi)\left[(1-s_R-\theta)B_F + (1-s_R)\right]B_G\right\} + \left[(1+\theta t_\Pi)h - \beta\right]iB_G\right\rangle}{(1+\theta t_\Pi)h - \beta} \tag{4.36}$$

$$= \frac{t_\Pi\left\langle h\left[pI_a + G + (1-t_\Pi)(1-s_R-\theta)iB_F\right] + \left\{h\left[(1-t_\Pi)(1-s_R) + 1 + \theta t_\Pi\right] - \beta\right\}iB_G\right\rangle}{(1+\theta t_\Pi)h - \beta}$$

As can easily be seen in equations (4.34)–(4.36), an improvement of animal spirits has again expansionary effects on all endogenous variables, also in our model with a government. The paradox of saving remains valid, too. An increase in the propensity to save out of rentiers' income will reduce equilibrium income, profits and government tax revenues. It will also not come as a surprise that the introduction of the government does not change the wage-led nature of aggregate demand, which we have found for the model without a government in the previous section. A higher profit share will thus lower equilibrium output and income in production and, of course, also reduce equilibrium total income:

$$\frac{\partial\left(pY_P^*\right)}{\partial h} = \frac{-\left\{pI_a + G + i\left(1-t_\Pi\right)\left[\left(1-s_R-\theta\right)B_F + \left(1-s_R\right)B_G\right]\right\}\left(1+\theta t_\Pi\right)}{\left[\left(1+\theta t_\Pi\right)h - \beta\right]^2}$$

$$= \frac{-\left(1+\theta t_\Pi\right)pY_P^*}{\left(1+\theta t_\Pi\right)h - \beta} < 0$$

(4.33a)

Also the paradox of costs remains valid. A higher profit share, and thus a lower wage share and lower unit labour costs, will reduce aggregate equilibrium profits:

$$\frac{\partial\Pi^*}{\partial h} = \frac{-\beta\left\{pI_a + G + i\left(1-t_\Pi\right)\left[\left(1-s_R-\theta\right)B_F + \left(1-s_R\right)\right]B_G\right\}}{\left[\left(1+\theta t_\Pi\right)h - \beta\right]^2}$$

$$= \frac{-\beta pY_P^*}{\left(1+\theta t_\Pi\right)h - \beta} < 0.$$

(4.35a)

And since aggregate profits are reduced by an increase in the profit share, also equilibrium tax revenues of the government will be lower:

$$\frac{\partial T^*}{\partial h} = t_\Pi\frac{\partial\Pi^*}{\partial h} = \frac{-t_\Pi\beta pY_P^*}{\left(1+\theta t_\Pi\right)h - \beta} < 0.$$

(4.36a)

Looking at the effect of a change in the interest rate on equilibrium output and income in production, assuming an interest-inelastic mark-up, we obtain:

$$\frac{\partial\left(pY_P^*\right)}{\partial i} = \frac{\left(1-t_\Pi\right)\left[\left(1-s_R-\theta\right)B_F + \left(1-s_R\right)B_G\right]}{\left(1+\theta t_\Pi\right)h - \beta}.$$

(4.33b)

The impact of a higher interest rate will be positive in the puzzling case regarding the effect of redistribution between firms and rentiers $(1-s_R-\theta>0)$. But even in the normal case $(1-s_R-\theta<0)$, the effect of a rise in the interest rate on equilibrium output and income may be positive, because it increases the interest payments of the government to rentiers, which raises aggregate demand and output and may thus overcompensate for the depressing effect of the interest payments on corporate debt.

Similarly, a higher stock of government debt will raise equilibrium income, profits and tax revenues, whereas a higher stock of corporate debt will have expansionary effects in the puzzling case, or the debt-led regime, but contractionary impacts in the normal case, or the debt-burdened regime, derived in the previous section:

$$\frac{\partial\left(pY_P^*\right)}{\partial B_G} = \frac{\left(1-t_\Pi\right)\left(1-s_R\right)i}{\left(1+\theta t_\Pi\right)h - \beta} > 0,$$

(4.33c)

$$\frac{\partial\left(pY_P^*\right)}{\partial B_F} = \frac{\left(1-t_\Pi\right)\left(1-s_R-\theta\right)i}{\left(1+\theta t_\Pi\right)h-\beta}. \tag{4.33d}$$

Government expenditures on goods and services, which do not require any tax revenues or saving by the private sector in order to be executed, as we have shown in the monetary circuit analysis in Chapter 3, have expansionary effects on equilibrium income, profits and tax revenues:

$$\frac{\partial\left(pY_P^*\right)}{\partial G} = \frac{1}{\left(1+\theta t_\Pi\right)h-\beta} > 0, \tag{4.33e}$$

$$\frac{\partial\Pi^*}{\partial G} = \frac{h}{h\left(1+\theta t_\Pi\right)-\beta} > 0, \tag{4.35b}$$

$$\frac{\partial T^*}{\partial G} = \frac{t_\Pi h}{\left(1+\theta t_\Pi\right)h-\beta} > 0. \tag{4.36b}$$

The values of the income multiplier of government expenditures in equation (4.33e) of our model are negatively affected by the profit share, the tax rate on profits and by the responsiveness of firms' investment towards internal funds, and positively by the accelerator effect in the investment function.[15] Since the effect of government expenditures on tax revenues in equation (4.36) is positive, with equation (4.36b) showing the tax revenue multiplier, deficit-financed government expenditures are partly self-financing. A long-term financing gap would have to be covered by increasing government debt to be held by rentiers out of their higher income and saving. This means for the society as a whole, deficit-financed government expenditures always finance themselves through higher incomes, as the basis for higher tax revenues and higher demand for government bonds, as already Kalecki (1944) had clearly pointed out.

With given government expenditures for goods and services and interest payments to rentiers, an increase in the tax rate on profits has the following effect on equilibrium income:

$$\frac{\partial\left(pY_P^*\right)}{\partial t_\Pi} = \frac{-\theta h\left(pI_a +G\right)-i\left[\left(1-s_R-\theta\right)B_F +\left(1-s_R\right)B_G\right]\left[\left(1+\theta\right)h-\beta\right]}{\left[\left(1+\theta t_\Pi\right)h-\beta\right]^2}$$

$$= \frac{-\theta h p Y_P^* -i\left[\left(1-s_R-\theta\right)B_F +\left(1-s_R\right)B_G\right]}{\left(1+\theta t_\Pi\right)h-\beta} < 0 \tag{4.33f}$$

If the puzzling case conditions prevail $(1-s_R-\theta>0)$, an increase in the tax rate has a uniquely negative effect on equilibrium income generated in production, and with a given profit share also on equilibrium profits. The same is true for the normal case $(1-s_R-\theta<0)$, because we have $-\theta h p Y_P^* + \theta i B_F \leq 0$ in our model. In equilibrium, firms cannot pay out more interest income to the rentiers than their whole profits. The contractive effects of an increase in the tax rate will even be stronger if we allow for a tax-elastic mark-up and thus an increase in the profit share accompanying a rise in the tax rate on profits:

$$\frac{\partial\left(pY_P^*\right)}{\partial t_\Pi} = \frac{-\left[\theta h + \left(1 + \theta t_\Pi\right)\frac{\partial h}{\partial t_\Pi}\right]pY_P^* - i\left[\left(1 - s_R - \theta\right)B_F + \left(1 - s_R\right)B_G\right]}{\left(1 + \theta t_\Pi\right)h - \beta} < 0. \tag{4.33g}$$

The effect of a higher tax rate on tax revenues is undetermined. On the one hand, a higher tax rate raises tax revenues for a given level of income, but, on the other hand, a higher tax rate lowers equilibrium income, without or with a tax-elastic mark-up, as we have just seen:

$$\frac{\partial T^*}{\partial t_\Pi} = h p Y_P^* + i G_B + t_\Pi h \frac{\partial\left(pY_P^*\right)}{\partial t_\Pi}. \tag{4.36c}$$

Table 4.8 summarises the main properties of our constant price model with a government.

4.4.3 Equilibrium with a Balanced Government Budget

If the government decides to run a balanced budget, government expenditures on goods and services will be determined by tax revenues minus the interest payments on the government debt and will thus become endogenous. Alternatively, of course, but less realistically, we could also assume that government expenditures remain autonomous and the tax rate is endogenously adjusted in order to generate a balanced budget. We could also assume that tax payments are independent of income and are imposed on the private sector such that they match government expenditures on goods and services plus government interest payments. Here, we will only consider the first option. A balanced budget means:

Table 4.8 Responses of equilibrium income/output, profits and tax revenues to changes in exogenous variables and parameters

	pY^*	pY_P^*	Π^*	T^*
pI_a	+	+	+	+
s_R	−	−	−	−
h	−	−	−	−
i	+/−	+/−	+/−	+/−
B_F	+/−	+/−	+/−	+/−
B_G	+	+	+	+
G	+	+	+	+
t_Π	−	−	−	+/−

$$G + iB_G = T. \tag{4.37}$$

With this, the goods market equilibrium condition from equation (4.30) becomes:

$$pI = S. \tag{4.38}$$

The stability of the goods market equilibrium now requires:

$$\frac{\partial S}{\partial(pY_P)} > \frac{\partial(pI)}{\partial(pY_P)}$$

$$\Rightarrow (1 - t_\Pi)h > \beta - \theta t_\Pi h \tag{4.39}$$

$$\Rightarrow h\left[1 - t_\Pi(1 - \theta)\right] - \beta > 0.$$

Plugging the saving function (4.29) and the investment function (4.30) into equation (4.38) yields:

$$pY_P^* = \frac{pI_a + (1 - t_\Pi)i\left[(1 - s_R - \theta)B_F - s_R B_G\right]}{\left[1 - t_\Pi(1 - \theta)\right]h - \beta}. \tag{4.40}$$

As can easily be seen, equilibrium output and income from production are positively affected by animal spirits and negatively by the propensity to save out of rentiers' income and by the profit share, as in the previous model. The effects on overall income and on profits before taxation are in the same direction. The paradoxes of thrift and costs remain valid, and aggregate demand remains wage-led. Because of the balanced budget requirement, the effect of a change in the tax rate is now the opposite of what has been found in the previous model version:

$$\frac{\partial(pY_P^*)}{\partial t_\Pi} = \frac{i\left[s_R B_G - (1 - s_R - \theta)B_F\right] + (1 - \theta)hpY_P^*}{\left[1 - t_\Pi(1 - \theta)\right]h - \beta} > 0. \tag{4.40a}$$

The effect of an increase in the tax rate on equilibrium income generated in production is always positive, irrespective of puzzling or normal cases, because we have $(1 - \theta)hpY_P^* - (1 - \theta)iB_F > 0$ in our model. With a balanced budget, a higher tax rate allows for higher government demand for goods and services and thus generates a higher equilibrium level of production and therefore also higher equilibrium levels of overall income $(Y^* = Y_P^* + iB_G)$, profits before taxation $(\Pi^* = hY_P^*)$ and tax revenues $[T^* = t_\Pi(hY_P^* + iB_G)]$. The more progressive the tax system, that is, the higher the tax rate on profits with a zero tax rate on wages in our model, the higher will be equilibrium output and income. From these results it also follows that cutting the tax rate will have contractionary effects on equilibrium income, if governments follow a balanced budget approach and compensate the loss in tax revenues by a cut in government expenditures.

These expansionary effects of an increase in tax-financed government expenditures emerge because the depressing effects of higher taxes on private expenditures are lower than the increase in government expenditures, because a part of private income taxed and shifted to the government would have been saved. Furthermore, we have constrained the effects of the tax rate such that a higher tax rate does not undermine a positive effect of rising output on the incentive to invest in equation (4.30). The proof of an expansionary effect of tax-financed government expenditures is usually associated with the work of Haavelmo (1945), who derived a positive balanced budget multiplier built on the same idea – but assuming income independent tax revenues matching government expenditures.

These expansionary effects of a higher tax rate on equilibrium income in a balanced budget model will, however, be reduced, or may even turn contractionary, if the mark-up and the profit share become tax-elastic:

$$\frac{\partial \left(pY_P^* \right)}{\partial t_\Pi} = \frac{i\left[s_R B_G - \left(1 - s_R - \theta \right) B_F \right] + \left\{ \left(1 - \theta \right) h - \left[1 - t_\Pi \left(1 - \theta \right) \right] \frac{\partial h}{\partial t_\Pi} \right\} pY_P^*}{\left[1 - t_\Pi \left(1 - \theta \right) \right] h - \beta}. \tag{4.40b}$$

Such distributional effects of a higher tax rate on profits in favour of the profit share may thus undermine the positive results associated with the Haavelmo theorem.

4.4.4 Going beyond the Short Run: Government Debt Dynamics

Going beyond the short-run orientation in this chapter, we can finally take a look at government debt dynamics and the sustainability of government debt in the long run, if the government is running fiscal deficits, like in the model in Section 4.4.2. In the first step, sustainability can be defined as a constant government debt-nominal GDP ratio in the long run. A constant government debt-nominal GDP ratio ($B_G/pY = B_G/Y^n$) requires that government debt (B_G) and nominal GDP ($pY = Y^n$) grow at the same rate, which means that government debt will have to grow at the same rate as real GDP plus the price index grow:

$$\hat{B}_G = \frac{dB_G}{B_G} = \frac{d\left(pY \right)}{pY} = \left(\hat{pY} \right) = \hat{p} + \hat{Y}. \tag{4.41}$$

Since the nominal government deficit (D) is given by:

$$D = G + iB_G - T = dB_G, \tag{4.42}$$

equation (4.41) becomes:

$$\hat{B}_G = \frac{dB_G}{B_G} = \frac{D}{B_G} = \frac{\dfrac{D}{pY}}{\dfrac{B_G}{pY}} = \left(\hat{pY} \right) = \hat{p} + \hat{Y} \tag{4.43}$$

$$\Rightarrow \frac{B_G}{pY} = \frac{\dfrac{D}{pY}}{\hat{p} + \hat{Y}}.$$

With a constant government deficit-nominal GDP ratio and a constant nominal rate of growth of the economy, the government debt-GDP ratio will thus converge towards a definite value given by the ratio of the government deficit-nominal GDP ratio and the growth rate of nominal GDP. The latter is composed of the growth rate of real GDP and the growth rate of the price index, hence the rate of inflation.

The government deficit can be decomposed into a primary deficit ($D' = G - T$) and the interest payments on the stock of government debt (iB_G):

$$D = D' + iB_G.\tag{4.44}$$

Inserting this into equation (4.43) yields:

$$\frac{B_G}{pY} = \frac{\dfrac{D' + iB_G}{pY}}{\hat{p} + \hat{Y}}.\tag{4.45}$$

With a balanced primary budget ($D' = 0$), and hence a government deficit equal to government interest payments ($D = iB$), governments can thus service their debt with their current deficits and stabilise the government debt-GDP ratio – provided that nominal GDP growth is positive. Even a positive rate of inflation with zero real growth would satisfy this requirement. Therefore, no tax revenues have to be expended in order to pay interest to the holders of government bonds. Potentially restrictive distribution effects, that is, taxing the workers and the poor households in order to pay interest to the rich rentiers' households who can afford to save and to hold government bonds, can thus be avoided. Finally, rearranging equation (4.45) gives:

$$\frac{B_G}{pY} = \frac{\dfrac{D'}{pY}}{\hat{Y} + \hat{p} - i} = \frac{\dfrac{D'}{pY}}{\hat{Y} + \hat{p} - \left(i_r + \hat{p}\right)} = \frac{\dfrac{D'}{pY}}{\hat{Y} - i_r}.\tag{4.46}$$

If the growth rate of nominal GDP, that is, the sum of real GDP growth plus the inflation rate, exceeds the nominal interest rate on government debt, governments can also run a primary deficit-GDP ratio without compromising a long-run stable government debt-GDP ratio. If we consider that the nominal interest rate can be decomposed into the real interest and the rate of inflation ($i = i_r + \hat{p}$), the condition for stable government debt-GDP ratios is either that nominal GDP growth has to exceed the long-term nominal interest rate on government debt ($\hat{Y}^n = \hat{Y} + \hat{p} > i = i_r + \hat{p}$) or that the real GDP growth has to exceed the real rate of interest ($\hat{Y} > i_r$). These conditions for government debt sustainability have already been pointed out by Domar (1944), and they have been reiterated by Arestis and Sawyer (2004b, 2010a, 2010b), Hein and Martschin (2020, 2021), Sawyer (2020) and several others.[16] As shown recently by Blanchard (2019), in historical perspective (since the 1950s) in the USA, a rate of interest below GDP growth has rather been the norm than the exception, which has somewhat calmed the orthodox objections to government deficit spending and government debt.

However, if nominal GDP growth falls short of the nominal rate of interest, or real GDP growth is below the real rate of interest, stabilising the government debt-GDP ratio will require a primary surplus in the government budget – and thus implies the use of tax revenues in order to satisfy the income demands of the rentiers holding government debt. That is the reason why post-Keynesians, who heavily rely on fiscal policies in order to achieve non-inflationary full employment in the short and in the long run, insist that these policies have to be co-ordinated with central bank policies targeting long-term interest rates below GDP growth. We will explain this in more detail in Chapter 6 on post-Keynesian macroeconomic policies.

4.5   AN OPEN ECONOMY MODEL WITH CONSTANT PRICES

4.5.1   The Basic Model

In order to discuss some open economy issues, we can extend our model economy to include the foreign sector, the rest of the world (RoW), with which the domestic economy trades goods and services. Since this trade is not necessarily balanced, we also have to include the associated creditor-debtor relationships, which may have built up between the domestic economy and the RoW over time, that is, domestic debt held by the RoW, as well as foreign debt held by domestic economic actors. This generates the balance sheet matrix presented in Table 4.9, which is an extension of the balance sheet matrix in Table 4.6. We assume that only the private domestic sector has financial relationships with the RoW; debt issued by the domestic firm sector may be partially held by foreign actors (B_{FRoW}), and domestic rentiers may hold debt issued in the RoW (B_{RoWR}).

The consistency of the balance sheet matrix requires the following equation to hold:

$$pK = E_F + B_{FR} + B_{FRoW} + D_R + M_R - B_{GB}$$
$$= E_F + B_{FR} + B_{FB} + B_{FRoW}.$$

(4.47)

The transaction flow matrix for the open economy is presented in Table 4.10, as an extension of the matrix for the closed economy in Table 4.7. Of course, only the firm sector may sell export goods and services to the RoW (pEx), and we assume that only the firm sector is importing from the RoW (p_faIm); in the model further below it will only import raw materials and intermediate products. Since imports are denominated in foreign prices (p_f), in order to express imports in domestic currency, we also need the nominal exchange rate (a), expressing the price of a unit of foreign currency in domestic currency. Furthermore, the domestic firm sector pays interest income to the RoW (R_{FRoW}) and the domestic rentiers' households receive interest income from the RoW (R_{RoWR}). Finally, the RoW may change its holdings of domestic firms' debt (dB_{FRoW}), and domestic rentiers may increase their holding of debt issued in the RoW (dB_{RoWR}).

For consistency, we need for the relationship between the domestic economy and the RoW:

$$pEx - p_f a Im + R_{RoWR} - R_{FRoW} = dB_{RoWR} - dB_{FRoW}.$$

(4.48)

If the left-hand side of equation (4.48) is positive, that is, the sum of domestic export revenues plus capital income from the RoW exceeds the sum of domestic expenditures for imports plus capital income payments to the RoW ($pEx + R_{RoWR} > p_f aIm + R_{FRoW}$), the domestic economy is running a current account surplus, which implies that its net international investment position ($B_{RoWR} - B_{FRoW}$) improves to the same extent ($dB_{FRoW} < dB_{RoWR}$). If the left-hand side of

Table 4.9 *Balance sheet matrix for an open economy with a government and a central bank*

	Workers' households	Rentiers' households	Firms	Government	Commercial banks	Central bank	Rest of the world (RoW)	Σ
Money/ reserves		$+M_R$			$+M_B$	$-M$		0
Deposits		$+D_R$			$-D_R$			0
Loans		$+B_{FR} + B_{GR} + B_{RoWR}$	$-(B_{FR} + B_{FB} + B_{FRoW})$	$-(B_{GR} + B_{GB})$	$+b(B_{FB} + B_{GB})$	$+(1-b)(B_{FB} + B_{GB})$	$B_{FRoW} - B_{RoWR}$	0
Capital			pK					pK
Σ	0	$+B_{FR} + B_{GR} + B_{RoWR} + D_R + M_R$	$+E_F$	$-(B_{GR} + B_{GB})$	0	0	$B_{FRoW} - B_{RoWR}$	$pK = E_F + B_{FR} + B_{FRoW} + D_R + M_R - B_{GB} = E_F + B_{FR} + B_{FB} + B_{FRoW}$

99

Table 4.10   Transaction flow matrix for an open economy with a government and a central bank

	Workers' households	Rentiers' households	Firms' current	Firms' capital	Government	Commercial banks	Central bank	Rest of the world (RoW)	Σ
Taxes	$-T_W$	$-T_R$	$-T_F$		$+T$				0
Government consumption			$+G$		$-G$				0
Consumption	$-pC_W$	$-pC_R$	$+pC_W + pC_R$						0
Investment			$+pI$	$-pI$					0
Exports			$+pEx$					$-pEx$	0
Imports			$-p_aIm$					$+p_aIm$	0
Wages	$+W$		$-W$						0
Retained profits			$-\Pi_F$	$+dE_F$					0
Interest payments		$+R_{FR} + R_{GR} + R_{RoWR}$	$-(R_{FR} + R_{FRoW})$		$-R_{GR}$			$+R_{FRoW} - R_{RoWR}$	0
Change in money/reserves		$-dM_R$				$-dM_B$	$+dM$		0
Change in deposits		$-dD_R$				$+dD_R$			0
Change in loans		$-dB_{FR} - dB_{GR} - dB_{RoWR}$		$+dB_{FR} + dB_{FB} + dB_{FRoW}$	$+dB_{GR} + dB_{GB}$	$-bd(B_{FB} + B_{GB})$	$-(1-b)d(B_{FB} + B_{GB})$	$-dB_{FRoW} + dB_{RoWR}$	0
Σ	0	0	0	0	0	0	0	0	0

equation (4.48) is negative, that is, the sum of domestic export revenues plus capital income from the RoW falls short of the sum of domestic expenditures for imports plus capital income payments to the RoW ($pEx + R_{RoWR} < p_f aIm + R_{FRoW}$), the domestic economy is running a current account deficit. This implies that the net international investment position of the domestic economy declines to the same extent ($dB_{FRoW} > dB_{RoWR}$).

In the following model, which is a short-run version of the model by Hein and Vogel (2008, 2009),[17] we will make some further simplifying assumptions for the sake of clarity regarding the main arguments. We assume an open economy, which depends on imported inputs for production purposes and the output of which competes in international markets. Labour mobility between the domestic economy and the RoW is excluded. We take the prices of imported inputs and of the competing foreign final output to be exogenously given and to be moving in step. The nominal exchange rate is determined by monetary policies and international financial markets, and it is also considered to be exogenous for our purposes.[18] Foreign economic activity is taken to be exogenously given, too. Furthermore, we assume that the net international investment position of the domestic economy, which has been built up in the past, is zero, and hence the net international investment position of the RoW is zero as well, of course. This assumption allows us to ignore the cross-border capital income payments and to focus on exports and imports of goods and services. We also simplify the public sector and assume that the stock of government debt inherited from the past is zero, too; therefore we can abstract from government interest payments in the short-period model. Tax rates are also assumed to be zero, and we thus only include government demand for goods and services funded by government deficits – which of course, in a long-run analysis, would imply interest payments in future periods.

With these simplifications, we can start by modifying our pricing equation (4.11) from the closed economy model and discussing the effects on distribution and international price competitiveness. Then we will add a net-export equation to the macroeconomic model of the closed economy and examine the effects of changes in model parameters, that is, in saving propensities, income distribution, interest rates and nominal exchange rates.

4.5.2 Prices, Distribution and International Competitiveness

We assume again the technical conditions of production and hence labour productivity to be constant. Domestic prices are set by firms that mark-up constant unit variable costs, which now consist of labour costs and imported raw material and semi-finished product costs. The mark-up is again mainly determined by the degree of price competition in the goods market and by relative powers of firms and workers in the labour market, and it might be affected by changes in the exogenously given interest rate, as explained above. Of course, in an open economy foreign competition limits the price setting power of domestic firms. But also the wage setting power of workers and trade unions may be constrained, because firms may use the threat of relocation of production sites – which we do not consider in our model. Using the symbols introduced above, and denoting unit raw material and semi-finished product inputs per unit of output with μ we get the following price equation for the domestically produced good:

$$p = \left[1 + m(i)\right]\left(\frac{w}{y} + p_f\, a\mu\right), \quad m > 0, \frac{\partial m}{\partial i} \geq 0. \tag{4.49}$$

Following Kalecki (1954, Chapter 2, 1971, Chapter 6), the relationship between unit material costs and unit labour costs (z) is defined as:

$$z = \frac{p_f a\mu}{\dfrac{w}{y}}.$$

(4.50)

Therefore, the price equation can also be written as:

$$p = (1+m)\frac{w}{y}\left(1 + \frac{p_f a\mu}{\dfrac{w}{y}}\right) = (1+m)\frac{w}{y}(1+z).$$

(4.51)

The profit share (h) in domestic value added, consisting of domestic profits (Π) and wages (W), is given by:

$$h = \frac{\Pi}{pY} = \frac{\Pi}{\Pi+W} = \frac{m\dfrac{w}{y}(1+z)}{m\dfrac{w}{y}(1+z)+\dfrac{w}{y}} = \frac{m(1+z)}{m(1+z)+1} = \frac{1}{\dfrac{1}{m(1+z)}+1}.$$

(4.52)

The profit share in the open economy is hence determined by the mark-up and by the ratio of unit material costs to unit labour costs. The profit share will rise whenever the mark-up or the ratio of unit material costs to unit labour costs increases. An increase in the latter may be caused by a fall in the domestic wage rate, a rise in foreign prices or an increase in the nominal exchange rate, that is, a devaluation of the domestic currency. For the wage share in domestic income we obtain the reverse effects:

$$\Omega = 1-h = \frac{W}{pY} = \frac{W}{\Pi+W} = \frac{\dfrac{w}{y}}{m\dfrac{w}{y}(1+z)+\dfrac{w}{y}} = \frac{1}{m(1+z)+1}.$$

(4.53)

Before we can analyse the effects of changes in domestic distribution on aggregate demand, profits and investment in an open economy, we have to clarify the relationship between distribution and international competitiveness because the latter will affect net exports. We choose the real exchange rate (a_r) as an indicator for international price competitiveness:

$$a_r = \frac{ap_f}{p}.$$

(4.54)

An increase in the real exchange rate implies increasing international price competitiveness of domestic producers. From equation (4.54), it follows for the respective growth rates:

$$\hat{a}_r = \hat{a} + \hat{p}_f - \hat{p}. \tag{4.55}$$

Therefore, increasing price competitiveness can be caused by an increasing nominal exchange rate, hence a nominal depreciation of the domestic currency, higher foreign inflation or lower domestic inflation. The effect of changes in distribution on international price competitiveness depends on the cause of distributional change. Applying equations (4.49) and (4.54) we can consider three main cases.

First, if the change in distribution is caused by a change in the mark-up, ceteris paribus, we get an inverse relationship between the profit share and international competitiveness. A higher (lower) mark-up causes a higher (lower) profit share and falling (rising) international price competitiveness of domestic producers:

$$\frac{\partial a_r}{\partial m} = \frac{-ap_f\left(\dfrac{w}{y} + p_f a\mu\right)}{p^2} < 0. \tag{4.54a}$$

Second, if a change in the nominal wage rate changes distribution via the effect on the ratio of unit material costs to unit labour costs, we obtain a positive relationship between the profit share and international competitiveness: Falling (rising) nominal wages cause a rising (falling) profit share and increasing (decreasing) international price competitiveness:

$$\frac{\partial a_r}{\partial w} = \frac{-ap_f\left(1+m\right)\dfrac{1}{y}}{p^2} < 0. \tag{4.54b}$$

Third, if a change in the nominal exchange rate is the cause for redistribution, we also get a positive relationship between the profit share and international price competitiveness: An increasing (decreasing) nominal exchange rate – that is, a nominal depreciation (appreciation) – causes increasing (decreasing) international price competitiveness and the related increase (fall) in prices for imported raw materials in domestic currency raises (reduces) the profit share:

$$\frac{\partial a_r}{\partial a} = \frac{p_f p - ap_f\left(1+m\right)p_f\mu}{p^2} = \frac{p-\left(1+m\right)\mu ap_f}{\dfrac{p^2}{p_f}} > 0. \tag{4.54c}$$

Summing up, changes in the domestic profit share may be associated with either declining or improving international competitiveness, depending on the source of the distributional change:

$$a_r = a_r(h), \qquad \frac{\partial a_r}{\partial h} > 0, \text{ if } dz > 0 \text{ and } dm = 0,$$

$$\frac{\partial a_r}{\partial h} < 0, \text{ if } dz = 0 \text{ and } dm > 0. \tag{4.56}$$

4.5.3   The Goods Market Equilibrium and the Effects of Changes in Model Parameters

The saving and the investment functions remain the same as for the closed economy model in Section 4.3. We assume that workers do not save. Saving is thus composed of retained earnings of firms, the difference between total profits and rentiers' income (R) and saving out of rentiers' income (S_R). Therefore, saving depends on the profit share in domestic income, on the propensity to save out of rentiers' income and on rentiers' income, which is determined by the rate of interest (i) and the stock of corporate debt (B_F):

$$S = \Pi - R + S_R = hpY - \left(1 - s_R\right)iB_F, 1 \geq s_R > 0. \tag{4.57}$$

Investment decisions of firms are determined by long-term expectations and by 'animal spirits', represented by autonomous investment (pI_a), by (expected) sales and hence by income (βpY), and by interest payments on corporate debt ($-\theta iB_F$):

$$pI = pI_a + \beta pY - \theta iB_F, \ pI_a, \beta, \theta \geq 0. \tag{4.58}$$

Net exports, that is, the difference between the values of exports (pEx) and imports ($p_f aIm$), is positively affected by international price competitiveness of domestic firms, provided the Marshall-Lerner condition can be assumed to hold. This means that the sum of the absolute values of the price elasticities of exports and imports have to exceed unity. Under this condition, the real exchange rate will have a positive effect on net exports. But net exports also depend on the relative developments of foreign and domestic demand and thus on foreign and domestic income. If domestic income increases (decreases), ceteris paribus, net exports will decline (increase), with imports rising (falling). If foreign income in domestic currency ($p_f aY_f$) and thus foreign demand rises (falls), ceteris paribus, net exports will rise (fall), with exports rising (falling). Net exports thus depend on the real exchange rate and on domestic demand determined by domestic income, as well as foreign demand determined by foreign income. The coefficients on domestic and foreign incomes are affected by the income elasticities of the demand for imports and exports and hence by non-price competitiveness:[19]

$$NX = pEx - ap_f \ Im = \psi a_r\left(h\right) + \chi p_f aY_f - \phi pY, \quad \psi, \phi, \chi \geq 0. \tag{4.59}$$

Equation (4.60) presents the goods market equilibrium condition, the equality of planned leakages (saving) and planned injections (investment and net exports), including exogenous government demand for goods and services (G), and in (4.61) we have the Keynesian/Kaleckian stability condition, a higher marginal response of saving with respect to income than the one of investment plus net exports:

$$pI + G + NX = S, \tag{4.60}$$

$$\frac{\partial S}{\partial\left(pY\right)} > \frac{\partial\left(pI\right)}{\partial\left(pY\right)} + \frac{\partial NX}{\partial\left(pY\right)} \Rightarrow h - \beta + \phi > 0. \tag{4.61}$$

By plugging equations (4.57), (4.58) and (4.59) into equation (4.60), the goods market equilibrium value for income can be derived as in equation (4.62). Using the equilibrium value for income from equation (4.62) in equation (4.58), we can then calculate the respective equilibrium value for investment, as provided in equation (4.63). By using the definition of the profit share ($h = \Pi/pY$) we can also derive the equilibrium value of profits from equation (4.62), as is displayed in equation (4.64). Finally, we can insert the equilibrium value for income from equation (4.62) into equation (4.60) in order to find, as we do in equation (4.65), the equilibrium level of net exports. Graphically, equilibrium income, investment, net exports and saving are derived in Figure 4.12.

$$pY^* = \frac{G + pI_a + (1 - s_R - \theta)iB_F + \psi a_r + \chi p_f aY_f}{h - \beta + \phi}, \tag{4.62}$$

$$pI^* = \frac{pI_a(h + \phi) + \beta(G + \psi a_r + \chi p_f aY_f) + [\beta(1 - s_R) - \theta(h + \phi)]iB_F}{h - \beta + \phi}, \tag{4.63}$$

$$\Pi^* = \frac{h[G + pI_a + (1 - s_R - \theta)iB_F + \psi a_r + \chi p_f aY_f]}{h - \beta + \phi}, \tag{4.64}$$

$$NX^* = \frac{(h - \beta)(\psi a_r + \chi p_f aY_f) - \phi[G + pI_a + (1 - s_R - \theta)iB_F]}{h - \beta + \phi}. \tag{4.65}$$

As can easily be seen from equations (4.62)–(4.64), an increase in long-term expectations and animal spirits, and thus in autonomous investment, will have expansionary effects on equilibrium income, investment and profits. The same is true for an increase in government expenditures. The effect on equilibrium net exports in equation (4.65), however, will be negative, because the expansionary effect on income will raise imports without affecting exports. Graphically, an improvement in autonomous investment means an upward shift of the investment function, and thus the investment plus government expenditures plus net exports

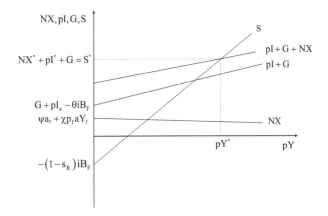

Figure 4.12   Short-run equilibrium income in an open economy with a government

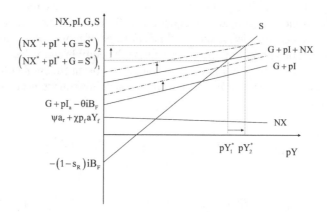

Figure 4.13   An increase in animal spirits/autonomous investment

function, in Figure 4.13, which will then lead to higher equilibrium income and investment but also to lower equilibrium net exports.

From equations (4.62)–(4.64), we can also see that an increase in the propensity to save out of rentiers' income has a negative effect on equilibrium income, investment and profits, whereas the effect on net exports is positive due to the reduction in domestic demand and imports. This means that the paradox of saving also holds in the open economy model. Graphically, an increase in the propensity to save out of rentiers' income means an upward shift of the saving function in Figure 4.14, which will then lead to lower equilibrium income and higher equilibrium net exports.

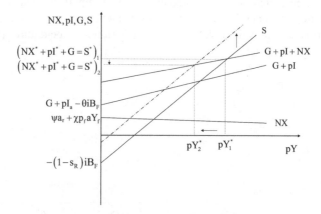

Figure 4.14   An increase in the propensity to save out of profits

For the effects of redistribution of income, that is, a change in the profit share, the open economy model does not generate unique results any more:

$$\frac{\partial(pY^*)}{\partial h} = \frac{\psi\dfrac{\partial a^r}{\partial h}(h-\beta+\phi)-\left[G+pI_a+(1-s_R-\theta)iB_F+\psi a_r+\chi p_f aY_f\right]}{(h-\beta+\phi)^2}$$

$$= \frac{\psi\dfrac{\partial a_r}{\partial h}-pY^*}{h-\beta+\phi}$$

(4.62a)

$$\frac{\partial(pI^*)}{\partial h} = \frac{\beta\left\{\psi\dfrac{\partial a_r}{\partial h}(h-\beta+\phi)-\left[G+pI_a+(1-s_R-\theta)iB_F+\psi a_r+\chi p_f aY_f\right]\right\}}{(h-\beta+\phi)^2}$$

$$= \frac{\beta\left(\psi\dfrac{\partial a_r}{\partial h}-pY^*\right)}{h-\beta+\phi}$$

(4.63a)

$$\frac{\partial\Pi^*}{\partial h} = \frac{h\psi\dfrac{\partial a_r}{\partial h}(h-\beta+\phi)+(\phi-\beta)\left[G+pI_a+(1-s_R-\theta)iB_F+\psi a_r+\chi p_f aY_f\right]}{(h-\beta+\phi)^2}$$

$$= \frac{h\psi\dfrac{\partial a_r}{\partial h}+(\phi-\beta)pY^*}{h-\beta+\phi},$$

(4.64a)

$$\frac{\partial NX^*}{\partial h} = \frac{(h-\beta)\psi\dfrac{\partial a_r}{\partial h}(h-\beta+\phi)+\phi\left[G+pI_a+(1-s_R-\theta)iB_F+\psi a_r+\chi p_f aY_f\right]}{(h-\beta+\phi)^2}$$

$$= \frac{(h-\beta)\psi\dfrac{\partial a_r}{\partial h}+\phi pY^*}{h-\beta+\phi}.$$

(4.65a)

As can be seen in equations (4.62a)–(4.65a), the effects of a change in the profit share on equilibrium income, investment, profits and net exports can be decomposed into the effects of redistribution on demand, holding the real exchange rate constant, and the effect through the change in the real exchange rate on net exports. The redistribution towards profits has a contractive effect on equilibrium income, and hence on investment and profits, and a positive effect on net exports (through the decline in income-determined imports), if we hold the real exchange rate constant, that is, if we assume $\partial a_r/\partial h = 0$. Graphically, this effect is shown by a counter-clockwise rotation of the saving function in Figure 4.15. However, if the increase in the profit share is associated with a rise in the real exchange rate, that is, $\partial a_r/\partial h > 0$, and

Macroeconomics after Kalecki and Keynes

thus with an improvement of the international price competitiveness of domestic producers (through a nominal devaluation of the currency or through a nominal wage cut), we have to include the stimulating effects on (net) exports. This is shown by upward shifts of the net export function, and thus in the investment plus government expenditures plus net exports function, in Figure 4.15. This stimulating effect will then counteract the contractive effect of redistribution on consumption and investment. If the net export effect via devaluation is weaker than the redistributive effect on domestic demand, equilibrium demand, production and income, as well as investment and profits, will still fall, and the economy will remain wage-led. This case is shown in Figure 4.15.

However, if the redistribution towards profit is weak, leading to a weak reduction in domestic demand, and the stimulating effect of the real devaluation on net exports is very strong, equilibrium demand, investment and profits may rise – and the economy will turn profit-led. This case is shown in Figure 4.16, which contains a less pronounced counter-clockwise rotation of the saving function and a more pronounced shift of the net export function, and then the sum of net export, investment and government expenditure functions. Adding the effect on net exports, a domestically wage-led economy may thus turn profit-led in total. In the empirical literature on estimating demand regimes, this is a result that has been found for some small open economies – and also for some commodity exporting and emerging market economies.[20] Mature, less open capitalist economies, however, seem to remain wage-led, even if a positive correlation of the profit share with net exports is found.

If the rise in the profit share is associated with a fall in the real exchange rate and hence in international price competitiveness (because of a rise in the mark-up), the overall effect will always be contractionary with respect to equilibrium income, profits and investment, as is shown in Figure 4.17.

These results imply that some caution is required when it comes to assessing the macroeconomic effects of a real devaluation of the domestic currency: Policies of real devaluation, which improve the international price competitiveness of domestic firms, either by means of nominal devaluation of the domestic currency or by wage cuts, will only stimulate aggregate demand, output and employment if the economy is in a profit-led demand regime. However, if the economy is in a wage-led regime, policies of real devaluation might stimulate net exports but the associated redistribution of income will have overall depressive effects on aggregate demand, output and employment – and also on investment in the capital stock. This also

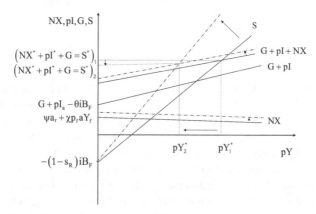

Figure 4.15 *An increase in the profit share associated with improved international price competitiveness – wage-led total demand*

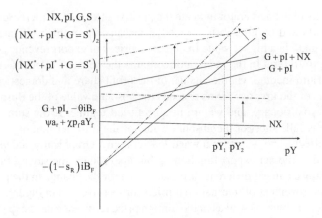

Figure 4.16   An increase in the profit share associated with improved international price competitiveness – profit-led total demand

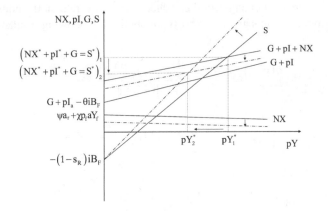

Figure 4.17   An increase in the profit share associated with a fall in international price competitiveness

becomes obvious if we look at the response of equilibrium income towards a rise in the nominal exchange rate, that is, a devaluation of the domestic currency:

$$
\frac{\partial\left(pY^{*}\right)}{\partial a}
$$

$$
= \frac{\left(\psi\dfrac{\partial a_{r}}{\partial a}+\chi p_{f}Y_{f}\right)\left(h-\beta+\phi\right)-\left[G+pI_{a}+\left(1-s_{R}-\theta\right)iB_{F}+\psi a_{r}+\chi p_{f}aY_{f}\right]\dfrac{\partial h}{\partial a}}{\left(h-\beta+\phi\right)^{2}} \tag{4.62b}
$$

$$
= \frac{\psi\dfrac{\partial a_{r}}{\partial a}+\chi p_{f}Y_{f}-pY^{*}\dfrac{\partial h}{\partial a}}{h-\beta+\phi}
$$

The first two terms in the numerator indicate the positive effects of an increase of the exchange rate on net exports and on equilibrium income, via an improvement of international price competitiveness and via a higher value in domestic prices of export revenues obtained in foreign prices. The third term in the numerator contains the negative effect of currency devaluation on equilibrium income, via the change in the profit share and domestic demand. If the sum of the values of the first two terms exceeds the absolute value of the third term, currency depreciation is expansionary, and we are in a profit-led regime. If the sum of the values of the first two terms falls short of the absolute value of the third term, a higher exchange rate has depressing effects, and we are in a wage-led economy. Graphically, a depreciation of the exchange rate shifts the net export function up but also rotates the saving function counterclockwise, so that we can get different cases, as shown for the change in the profit share associated with an improvement of international price competitiveness in Figures 4.15 and 4.16.

A rise in foreign income, as well as in the foreign price level, each have expansionary effects on equilibrium income, investment and profits, as can be seen in equations (4.62)–(4.64). The effect on net exports will also be positive if the level of income generated by domestic demand is stable, that is, if $h - \beta > 0$, which we assume to hold.

Finally, for the effects of changes in the exogenous interest rate on the equilibrium values of income, investment, profits and net exports we obtain the following results:

$$\frac{\partial(pY^*)}{\partial i} = \frac{(1-s_R-\theta)B_F - \frac{\partial h}{\partial i}pY^* + \frac{\partial a_r}{\partial h}\frac{\partial h}{\partial i}\psi}{h-\beta+\phi}, \tag{4.62c}$$

$$\frac{\partial(pI^*)}{\partial i} = \frac{[\beta(1-s_R-\theta)-\theta(h+\phi)]B_F - \frac{\partial h}{\partial i}\beta pY^* + \frac{\partial a_r}{\partial h}\frac{\partial h}{\partial i}\beta\psi}{h-\beta+\phi}, \tag{4.63b}$$

$$\frac{\partial\Pi^*}{\partial i} = \frac{(1-s_R-\theta)B_F - \frac{\partial h}{\partial i}(\beta-\phi)pY^* + \frac{\partial a_r}{\partial h}\frac{\partial h}{\partial i}h\psi}{h-\beta+\phi}, \tag{4.64b}$$

$$\frac{\partial NX^*}{\partial i} = \frac{-(1-s_R-\theta)\phi B_F + \frac{\partial h}{\partial i}\phi pY^* + \frac{\partial a_r}{\partial h}\frac{\partial h}{\partial i}(h-\beta)\psi}{h-\beta+\phi}. \tag{4.65b}$$

In our open economy model we have three channels for the effects of changes in the interest rate on the goods market equilibrium. First, there is the effect via the redistribution of income between rentiers (creditors) and firms (debtors), which is represented by the first term in the numerators of equations (4.62c)–(4.65b). As in the closed economy version of our model, an increase in interest rates will have expansionary effects on income, investment and profits, and negative effects on net exports through this channel, if the puzzling case conditions prevail. The latter requires a very high propensity to consume and thus a low propensity to save out of rentiers' income, a very low effect of interest payments on investment and a strong accelerator effect of income on investment. With a low propensity to consume and a high propensity to save out of rentiers' income and a strong effect of interest payments on investment, the normal case conditions will dominate and the effects of a rising rate of interest on income, investment and profits will be negative through this channel, and the effect on net exports will be positive.

Second, we may have a positive effect of a rising interest rate on the profit share, that is, an interest-elastic mark-up, because of increasing overhead costs. Through this channel, we have a negative effect on equilibrium income, investment and profits and a positive effect on net exports, because domestic demand in our economy is wage-led. This effect can be seen in the second term in the numerators of equations (4.62c)–(4.65b).

Third, as shown in the third terms of the numerators of equations (4.62c)–(4.65b), a change in the profit share triggered by a change in the interest rate will also be associated with a change in the real exchange rate and hence in the international price competitiveness of domestic producers. This will then also affect the equilibrium values of income, investment, profits and net exports. Since the change in the profit share in this case is triggered by a change in overhead costs, which will then affect the mark-up, we have good reason to assume that the higher profit share will be associated with a fall in the real exchange rate and hence with a real appreciation of the domestic currency and a reduction of the international price competitiveness of domestic producers. We will thus have a negative effect on equilibrium income, investment, profits and net exports through this channel. In an open economy model with capital mobility having an impact on the nominal and on the real exchange rate, we would also expect that a rise in domestic interest rates, ceteris paribus, would contribute to an appreciation of the domestic currency and thus to a loss of price competitiveness in international markets, further weakening aggregate demand. But this is not included in our simple model.

Summing up the three channels, we have that higher (lower) interest rates will have expansionary (contractionary) effects on equilibrium income, investment and profits – and cause lower (higher) net exports:

- if the puzzling case conditions for the effect of changes of interest rates on domestic demand with constant profit shares prevail,
- and if the distributional effects of changes in interest rates on wage and profit shares are small,
- and if the effect of the associated real appreciation of the domestic currency on net exports is small, too.

We are more likely to see contractionary (expansionary) effects of higher (lower) interest rates on equilibrium income, investment and profits – and higher (lower) net exports:

- if the normal case conditions for the effect of changes of interest rates on domestic demand with constant profit shares prevail,
- and/or if the distributional effects of changes in interest rates on wage and profit shares are high,
- and/or if the effect of the associated real appreciation of the domestic currency on net exports is strong.

For the effect of parametric changes in the stock of corporate debt, we obtain the same results, in particular if we make the mark-up depend on interest payments, which would then imply

Table 4.11   *Responses of equilibrium output/income, investment, profits and net exports to changes in exogenous variables and parameters*

	pY^*	pI^*	Π^*	NX^*
G	+	+	+	−
pI_a	+	+	+	−
s_R	−	−	−	+
h	+/−	+/−	+/−	−/+
a	+/−	+/−	+/−	+
p_f	+	+	+	+
Y_f	+	+	+	+
i	+/−	+/−	+/−	−/+
B_F	+/−	+/−	+/−	−/+

that a higher stock of corporate debt would be associated with a higher mark-up, too. Debt-led or debt-burdened regimes may arise, as already explained for the closed economy model.

Table 4.11 summarises the effects of changes in exogenous variables on equilibrium endogenous variables for the open economy model with constant prices. While the effects of changes in animal spirits/autonomous investment, government expenditures, the propensity to save, foreign prices and foreign income are unique, the effects of changes in the profit share, the nominal exchange rate, the interest rates and the stock of corporate debt are dependent on the demand regime.

4.6   MACROECONOMIC EFFECTS OF WAGE INEQUALITY[21]

Post-Keynesian macroeconomic models, and Kaleckian models in particular, have histori-cally focussed on the class division of society. The analysis has been concerned with the distribution of income (and partly wealth) between capital and labour and on the relationship of wage and profit shares with aggregate demand, like in the models we have presented in the previous sections, as well as with capital accumulation, when it comes to distribution and growth models.[22] However, we have ignored wage inequality. In the post-Keynesian litera-ture, in some contributions, a distinction has been made between direct labour and overhead labour, thus allowing for the differentiation of the working class into managers and workers (Lavoie 1995a, 1996c, 2009b, Rowthorn 1981). Other models, like ours in the previous sec-tions, which explicitly introduce finance, interest and credit have led to the distinction of the capitalist class into creditors and debtors (Hein 2008, 2014a, Chapter 9, Lavoie 1995b). When the focus turned towards the macroeconomics of finance-dominated capitalism, the distinc-tion between rentiers/shareholders, on the one hand, and corporations run by managers, on the other hand, has become important (Dutt 2016, Hein 2009, 2010, 2012a, 2014a, Chapter 10). In the current section we will now focus on models allowing for a division of the working class into high and low wage earners, the latter potentially emulating the consumption behaviour of the former financed by increasing indebtedness under certain conditions – also a feature of finance-dominated capitalism.

4.6.1 Kaleckian/post-Keynesian Macroeconomic Models with Different Types of Workers

Models with workers and managers, in which the latter are treated as overhead labour, make wage and profit shares endogenous to short-run changes in aggregate demand, as we have shown above in Section 4.3.1. Moving beyond this very short run and ignoring the features of endogenous unit managerial overhead costs, Palley (2005, 2015c, 2015d, 2017) has shown in a series of models that the introduction of a wage bill division between workers and managers can render an economy profit-led with respect to the profit share, but wage-led with respect to the workers' share of the wage bill – as compared to the manager's share. He also shows that a change in the wage-bill division, which affects wage dispersion and personal income inequality, can also change the character of the regime (Palley 2017). Increasing the workers' share of the wage bill at the expense of the managers' share makes the economy more likely to be wage-led for a given functional distribution of income between wages and profits. Similarly, if workers save and own part of the capital stock and thus receive parts of the profits, the ownership shares of the capital stock may affect the regime: A higher ownership share of the workers, which grants them a higher share of the profits, has expansionary effects on aggregate demand, capital accumulation and growth, because they have a higher propensity to consume out of their profit incomes than the capitalists. This feature thus makes the model economy more likely to be profit-led.

Another fashionable type of recent models has amended the traditional Kaleckian focus on functional income shares in the wage-led vs. profit-led debate by including wage dispersion together with interdependent consumption and financing norms of households. In these models, consumption decisions are no longer determined by the respective households' income, but may be affected by the consumption of some reference group and thus other households' income ('keeping up with the Joneses'). Furthermore, the ability to finance consumption exceeding the household's income by going into debt is required. In these models, wage inequality is often included by splitting the working class into low-wage and high-wage workers, where the former earn a fraction of the real wage rate of the latter (Detzer 2018, Kapeller and Schütz 2014, 2015, Kapeller et al. 2018). Other studies, however, have maintained the traditional two-class divide and assume that capitalists/rentiers also earn additional wage income, that is, high management salaries, which is a multiple of workers' wage income (Kim et al. 2014, Setterfield and Kim 2016, Setterfield et al. 2016, Zezza 2008). Consequently, in the models by Dutt (2016) and by Prante et al. (2022a), for example, the household sector is divided between top 10 per cent income households, representing the fraction of households which earn manager salaries and distributed profits, and the bottom 90 per cent of the income distribution, which earn wages and have only marginal or no profit incomes.

In order to combine personal or wage inequality with interdependent consumption norms, these models expand the traditional Kaleckian consumption function: Poor households may now emulate the consumption of richer households. In this way, these models are related to Veblen's (1899) 'conspicuous consumption', Duesenberry's (1949) 'relative income hypothesis' and the 'expenditure cascades' proposed by Frank et al. (2014). Since consumption exceeding income has to be financed by credit, financial norms of households and the banking system also play a major role. In this context, consumption emulation is a complex phenomenon affected by socio-cultural preferences, institutions, the (non-)provision of public goods (especially housing, education and healthcare) and the access to credit. It may thus be viewed as an indicator for the necessity to keep up consumption in an increasingly unequal and competitive society, in which access to credit is easily provided. In this way, with a focus on the USA, changing financial norms and consumption emulation behaviour, including housing, have often been linked to rising inequality and the rise in US household debt observed before the financial and economic crises 2007–09 (Barba and Pivetti 2009, Cynamon and Fazzari 2008, 2013, van Treeck 2014, 2015).

Whereas in the traditional Keynesian/Kaleckian models a distributional shift favouring high-income households (i.e. an increase of the profit share and/or of wage dispersion towards manager salaries) would cause a contraction of aggregate consumption, in the models mentioned here, the inclusion of consumption emulation allows for different outcomes. If the emulation effects are strong enough, they will lead to an increase in aggregate consumption, despite a falling wage share and rising inequality, and will thus modify the resulting demand regimes. Kapeller and Schütz (2015) develop a simple neo-Kaleckian model including unconstrained consumer debt and rising wage inequality. In their model, a *consumption-driven profit-led regime* may arise if emulation effects are relatively strong and negative demand effects, stemming from workers' debt burden, are relatively small. Kapeller and Schütz (2014) and Kapeller et al. (2018) present stock-flow-consistent models in which rising wage inequality in the traditional Keynesian/Kaleckian case leads to a contraction of aggregate demand, while, when coupled with Veblenian debt-financed consumption emulation, and with a Minsky banking system with endogenously changing risk perceptions of banks, the rise in wage inequality can trigger a 'Minsky-Veblen cycle'. While rising wage inequality initially leads to an expansion of aggregate demand driven by increasing credit to workers' households, banks' changing risk perceptions, due to increasing household indebtedness, eventually trigger a strong compression period that culminates in financial panic and finally leads to a sustained consolidation period. After this relatively stable period, it is assumed that risk perceptions behave in a 'Minskyian way', and thus the cycle repeats itself.

In Setterfield and Kim (2016, 2017), based on Kim et al. (2014), workers emulate very affluent households' consumption by taking up debt. In their model, the extent to which indebted working households are managing their repayment obligations is important. If households treat saving as a residual, determined only after consumption and debt servicing ('pecking order'), the likelihood of an emerging consumption-driven profit-led regime increases. The authors show how the inclusion of emulation and debt-financed consumption, coupled with redistribution away from workers, can turn otherwise wage-led results of the neo-Kaleckian model into profit-led ones.

Carvalho and Rezai (2016) implement effects of wage inequality in a neo-Kaleckian model by making the propensity to save from wages directly dependent on a measure of wage inequality. However, they assume that rising wage inequality always leads to a rising propensity to save out of wage income. Prante (2018) criticises this argument and shows in a simple post-Kaleckian model that the macroeconomic effects of personal and functional income distribution can either dampen or reinforce each other, depending on the specific consumption and financing norms of an economy. In the model of the following section we present a variation of the latter idea.

Macroeconometric estimations on the relative importance of real and financial wealth, credit supply, basic needs or relative income effects on consumption are still inconclusive, as reviewed by Prante (2018). For example, Behringer and van Treeck (2018), for a panel of

20 countries (1972–2007), find that, ceteris paribus, rising personal income inequality leads to a deterioration of the financial balances of the private household sector, which is interpreted as supporting the relative income hypothesis. Stockhammer and Wildauer (2016), however, in panel estimations for OECD countries (1980–2013) fail to find an effect of personal income inequality on consumption, which is interpreted as contradicting the relative income hypothesis. The authors find positive effects of the wage share, household debt and property and stock prices on consumption in their estimations. Moore and Stockhammer (2018) and Stockhammer and Wildauer (2018) support these findings regarding the irrelevance of the relative income hypothesis: Real estate prices were the most important drivers of household debt, whereas they do not find a significant impact of shifts in the income distribution on household sector indebtedness. Furthermore, Kim (2013, 2016) and Kim et al. (2015) in studies on the USA have found that although new credit to households will boost aggregate demand and output in the short run, the effects of household debt variables on output and growth are negative in the long run. These potentially contradictory short- and long-run effects of credit and debt on consumption, aggregate demand and growth have been included in a range of several further post-Keynesian/Kaleckian models (Dutt 2005, 2006, Hein 2012a, Chapter 5, 2012c, Nishi 2012a, Palley 1994b, Vasudevan 2017).

4.6.2 A Simple Macroeconomic Model with Wage Inequality and Potential Relative Income Effect on Consumption

In this section, we will provide the introduction of wage inequality into the closed economy model from Section 4.3. The model is a short-run level version, which draws on the distribution and growth model in Hein and Prante (2020). We assume again a closed private economy in which one good, which can be used for consumption and investment purposes, is produced with a constant coefficients production technology, that is, with a constant capital-potential output ratio and constant labour productivity and hence a constant labour-output ratio. We abstract again from overhead costs and overhead labour, as well as from the depreciation of the capital stock. Capitalists own the means of production and earn profits, which are partly consumed and partly saved. For the sake of simplicity, unlike the previous models, we do not explicitly consider the creditor-debtor relationships within the capitalist class, and we thus do not distinguish retained profits and distributed profits in terms of interest payments. Therefore, we have a single propensity to save out of profits, which is higher than the propensity to save out of wages, in particular because saving out of profits includes retained earnings of corporations.

Workers earn wages and, unlike the model in Section 4.3, the propensity to save out of wages is assumed to be positive, so that workers' households also own part of the stock of wealth, earn capital income from this wealth and benefit/suffer from positive/negative valuation effects related to this stock of wealth. Wealth dynamics and valuation effects are not explicitly modelled but are taken to be exogenous in our model, with potential effects on workers' propensity to consume out of wage income.[23] We assume that wages are unequally distributed across the model economy, mainly because of differentials in bargaining power of different types of workers, due to different degrees of unionisation, for example. Furthermore, we also assume that wage dispersion is positively associated with the profit share and negatively with the wage share in national income. In other words, if there is a fall (rise) in the overall wage share due to a fall (rise) in workers' and trade unions' bargaining power, we will assume that low-paid workers are affected more than proportionally. This seems to be a reasonable assumption, given the medium- to long-run developments in several developed capitalist economies from the early 1980s until the 2007–09 crises, in the era of neo-liberalism and finance-dominated capitalism, when a tendency of the labour income share to fall was associated with a rise in wage inequality and in wage dispersion, of course to different degrees in different countries (Glyn 2006, Tridico 2017).

As in the previous closed economy models in this chapter, the profit share (h) is determined by mark-up (m) pricing on unit variable costs consisting only of unit direct labour costs, which are assumed to be constant up to full capacity output:

$$h = h(m), \quad \frac{\partial h}{\partial m} > 0. \tag{4.66}$$

The mark-up is treated to be exogenous and determined by the degree of price competition in the goods market and by relative powers of capital and labour in the labour market, in the same way as explained above. Wage inequality (Γ) is affected by the profit share in the way just described:[24]

$$\Gamma = \Gamma(h), \quad \frac{\partial \Gamma}{\partial h} \geq 0. \tag{4.67}$$

The propensity to save out of wages (s_w) is co-determined by wage inequality.

$$s_w = s_{w0} - \eta \Gamma, \quad 0 \leq s_{w0} < 1. \tag{4.68}$$

If $\eta = 0$, wage inequality has no effect on the average propensity to save out of wages; high and low wage earners have the same propensity to save. If $\eta < 0$, we have a 'normal' or usually expected effect of inequality on consumption/saving out of wages due to absolute income effects. A rise in wage inequality will raise the average propensity to save out of wage income, because high wage earners have a higher propensity to save than low wage earners. However, if $\eta > 0$, we have 'puzzling' or unexpected effects of inequality on consumption/saving out of wages. Therefore, in this case, a rise in wage inequality will lower the average propensity to save out of wages and consumption out of wages will increase. This may be due to the persistence of basic needs of low-income workers, relative income considerations, improved access to credit and/or wealth effects on consumption.

Saving (S) is composed of saving out of profits and saving out of wages and hence determined by the propensity to save out of profits (s_Π) and the sum of profits (Π) and the propensity to save out of wages and the sum of wages (W). Saving is hence affected by the level of nominal income (pY), the functional propensities to save out of different income types and functional income distribution, as well as wage dispersion which itself is a function of the profit share:

$$S = s_\Pi \Pi + s_w W = \left[s_\Pi h + \left(s_{w0} - \eta \Gamma \right) \left(1 - h \right) \right] pY,$$

$$s_\Pi > s_{w0} - \eta \Gamma. \tag{4.69}$$

Compared to the previous sections, we assume a simplified neo-Kaleckian investment function, in which investment finance and a negative effect of the interest rate and of debt services are ignored. Investment (pI) is only determined by animal spirits or autonomous investment (pI_a) and by (expected) aggregate demand and hence by income via the accelerator mechanism:

$$pI = pI_a + \beta pY, \quad pI_a, \beta > 0. \tag{4.70}$$

From our closed private economy model in Section 4.3, we know that, without considering the effects of wage dispersion in the saving/consumption functions, with this investment function our model would only generate wage-led demand results. The goods market equilibrium is given by the equality of investment and saving decisions:

$$pI = S. \tag{4.71}$$

The goods market equilibrium stability condition, which for our comparative exercises below we assume to be met, is:

$$\frac{\partial S}{\partial(pY)} - \frac{\partial(pI)}{\partial(pY)} > 0 \quad \Rightarrow \quad s_\Pi h + \left(s_{w0} - \eta\Gamma\right)\left(1-h\right) - \beta > 0. \tag{4.72}$$

We thus obtain the following goods market equilibrium values for output/income and investment/saving:

$$pY^* = \frac{pI_a}{s_\Pi h + \left(s_{w0} - \eta\Gamma\right)\left(1-h\right) - \beta}, \tag{4.73}$$

$$pI^* = S^* = \frac{pI_a\left[s_\Pi h + \left(s_{w0} - \eta\Gamma\right)\left(1-h\right)\right]}{s_\Pi h + \left(s_{w0} - \eta\Gamma\right)\left(1-h\right) - \beta}. \tag{4.74}$$

The effects of a change in the profit share on the equilibrium values are as follows:

$$\frac{\partial(pY)^*}{\partial h} = \frac{-pI_a\left[s_\Pi - \left(s_{w0} - \eta\Gamma\right) - \left(1-h\right)\eta\dfrac{\partial\Gamma}{\partial h}\right]}{\left[s_\Pi h + \left(s_{w0} - \eta\Gamma\right)\left(1-h\right) - \beta\right]^2}$$

$$= \frac{-pY^*\left[s_\Pi - \left(s_{w0} - \eta\Gamma\right) - \left(1-h\right)\eta\dfrac{\partial\Gamma}{\partial h}\right]}{s_\Pi h + \left(s_{w0} - \eta\Gamma\right)\left(1-h\right) - \beta} \tag{4.73a}$$

$$\frac{\partial(pY)^*}{\partial h} > 0, \quad if : s_\Pi - \left(s_{w0} - \eta\Gamma\right) - \left(1-h\right)\eta\frac{\partial\Gamma}{\partial h} < 0, \tag{4.73a'}$$

$$\frac{\partial(pI)^*}{\partial h} = \frac{-\beta pI_a\left[s_\Pi - (s_{w0} - \eta\Gamma) - (1-h)\eta\frac{\partial\Gamma}{\partial h}\right]}{\left[s_\Pi h + (s_{w0} - \eta\Gamma)(1-h) - \beta\right]^2}$$

(4.74a)

$$= \frac{-\beta pY^*\left[s_\Pi - (s_{w0} - \eta\Gamma) - (1-h)\eta\frac{\partial\Gamma}{\partial h}\right]}{s_\Pi h + (s_{w0} - \eta\Gamma)(1-h) - \beta}$$

$$\frac{\partial(pI)^*}{\partial h} > 0, \quad \text{if}: s_\Pi - (s_{w0} - \eta\Gamma) - (1-h)\eta\frac{\partial\Gamma}{\partial h} < 0. \tag{4.74a'}$$

As can be seen in equations (4.73a) and (4.74a) and also in Figure 4.18, the effect of a rise in the profit share on the goods market equilibrium can be decomposed into the primary effect via a change in functional income shares and a secondary effect via induced changes in wage inequality. The effects through changes in functional income distribution can be seen in the first terms in brackets in the numerators of equations (4.73a) and (4.74a). They show uniquely falling equilibrium incomes and investment/saving in the face of a rising profit share, because we have assumed $s_\Pi - (s_{w0} - \eta\Gamma) > 0$ to hold. In Figure 4.18 this primary effect is indicated by a counter-clockwise rotation of the saving function from S_1 to S_{2A}, which means a downward shift of equilibrium income from pY_1^* to pY_{2A}^* and a respective reduction in equilibrium investment/saving. Without any further effects our model economy would thus be clearly wage led.

If there are further or secondary effects of changes in functional distribution on wage inequality, we may obtain different outcomes. If the rise in wage inequality, due to absolute income effects on consumption, causes a rise in the average propensity to save out of wage income ($\eta < 0$), the depressing effect of a rising profit share on equilibrium income and investment/saving will be reinforced, as can be seen in equations (4.73a) and (4.74a). In Figure 4.18, this effect means a further counter-clockwise rotation of the saving function towards S_{2B}, which causes a fall in equilibrium income to pY_{2B}^* and a respective reduction in equilibrium investment/saving. Hence, demand becomes even more wage-led.

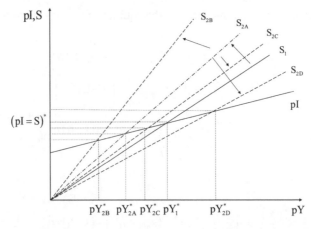

Figure 4.18   Potential effects of a rise in the profit share with relative income effects on consumption

However, if compensatory mechanisms with respect to workers' consumption are at work (basic needs, relative income concerns, credit availability, positive wealth effects), the average propensity to save out of wages may fall ($\eta > 0$), and this may then dampen the decrease in equilibrium income and investment/saving or even reverse it, as is evident in equations (4.73a) and (4.74a). Looking at Figure 4.18, in the first case, this secondary effect rotates the saving function slightly clockwise towards S_{2C}, so that the overall effect of a rise in the profit share and of redistribution on equilibrium income and investment/saving is still negative, but less so than without these effects. Equilibrium income will only fall to pY_{2C}^* and to the associated level of investment/saving, so that the economy is still wage-led, but less so than without these effects. Moreover, with strong compensatory effects, as shown by the rotation of the saving function towards S_{2D} and the higher equilibrium values at pY_{2D}^*, a rise in the profit share and the associated increase in wage inequality will now show expansionary effects on aggregate demand, income and investment/saving. Our economy becomes 'seemingly profit-led'. The results so far are still generating stable equilibria, that is, the stability condition $s_\Pi h + (s_{wo} - \eta\Gamma)(1 - h) - \beta > 0$ is still met. However, if inequality rises by too much and/or the responsiveness of saving/consumption with respect to inequality is too strong, such that the slope of the saving function in Figure 4.18 becomes smaller than the slope of the investment function, we will observe cumulatively unstable processes.

Summing up, what this simple model shows is that taking into account personal income or wage distribution together with basic needs, relative income concerns, credit availability or wealth effects, a basically wage-led demand economy may turn seemingly profit-led. But do these modifications mean that the focus on functional income shares and the wage-led vs. profit-led demand distinction in the basic post-Keynesian/Kaleckian models is useless? We do not believe so. Rising consumption in the face of falling wage shares and rising income/wage inequality is difficult to sustain due to the associated indebtedness problems, as found in several of the models, which we have referred to above. Therefore, at the end of the day, sustainable development has to rely on income-financed consumption demand, and here functional income shares matter again. In fact, the concern with functional income distribution mirrors a basic contradiction with respect to the role of wages in a capitalist economy: Wages are costs for the individual firm, but also a main source of demand for the firm sector as a whole! But if absolute income effects dominate at the end of the day, this means that if the average propensity to save is to rise with wage inequality (which can be assumed in the long run), then it is not only income shares, but also wage dispersion which matter here. This consequence has an interesting policy implication, as Palley (2017) has pointed out: Even if an economy were profit-led via an investment channel, as in Bhaduri and Marglin (1990) and Kurz (1990), or via a net export channel, as in Blecker (1989) and in our open economy model presented in Section 4.5, reducing wage dispersion would still be a reliable and sustainable way of boosting aggregate demand, output, income and employment.

4.7   MACROECONOMIC EFFECTS OF GENDER WAGE GAPS[25]

4.7.1   Gender and Macroeconomics

Recently, a rising number of authors have been concerned with integrating gender issues into post-Keynesian/Kaleckian macroeconomic models, thus linking two heterodox schools of thought, post-Keynesian economics and feminist economics.[26] These approaches have included the reproduction of labour in macroeconomic models, focussing on the disproportional share of women as compared to men in unpaid reproductive and care work (Braunstein et al. 2011, 2020). Most feminist post-Keynesian macroeconomic models have examined the effects of gender inequality on growth for developing countries, further taking into account the specific structural features of these economies, like a dual production structure, segregated labour markets, the balance-of-payments constraint and partly also the role of economic policies (Blecker and Seguino 2002, Seguino 2010, 2012, 2020, Seguino and Braunstein 2019).[27] Onaran (2015) and Onaran et al. (2019) have integrated several of these features into a more general gendered macroeconomic model on Kaleckian grounds, which has then also been estimated for the UK. This model integrates three dimensions of inequalities – functional income distribution between wages and profits, gender inequality, and wealth concentration, and their interactions. It includes the impact of fiscal policies, in particular the effects of government spending on social and physical infrastructure, as well as different types of taxation; and it analyses both the demand- and supply-side effects on output and employment.

Our ambition in this section is more modest, basic and mainly didactic and pedagogical. We will focus on the integration of a gender wage gap into our basic closed and open economy models presented above in this chapter. Since our simple model will be for a one-good economy, several features of emerging capitalist economies which figure prominently in parts of the literature referred to above cannot directly be included. Thus, the model can be viewed to refer more to developed capitalist economies. However, the main purpose is analytical, and it is meant to understand some channels of influence of changes in gender wage gaps on distribution and aggregate demand. We will start to examine the impact of closing the gender wage gap for a closed economy model and then look at a model for an economy which is open for foreign trade (but not for international capital or labour movements). This section presents short-run level versions of the Kaleckian distribution and growth models in Hein (2020). Long-run effects of reducing gender wage gaps on capital accumulation and productivity growth can be found in that paper.

4.7.2   The Closed Economy Model

4.7.2.1 Basic structure

In the basic version, we assume a closed economy without a government sector, as in Section 4.3 above. The economy is composed of two classes, capitalists and workers. We now assume that workers are split into male workers (N_M) and female workers (N_F), whereas no gender division is assumed for the capitalist class. Employment (N) thus consists of a male ($\rho = N_M/N$) and a female share ($1 - \rho = N_F/N$):

$$N = \rho N + (1-\rho) N. \tag{4.75}$$

We assume that male and female labour are generally in excess supply and pose no constraint to output. Capitalists own the means of production, hire male and female workers, organise the production process and decide about investment in the capital stock. Capitalists receive profits, which they partly consume and partly save – buying assets issued by the corporate sector and thus the capitalists themselves or depositing parts of the profits with a banking sector, which is also owned by the capitalists. We do not model the financial sector here, but only assume, as shown in detail in the previous sections, that capitalists have access to finance, that is, credit, generated by the financial sector 'out of nothing', for investment purposes. As in the previous section, we abstract from the creditor-debtor relationships within the capitalist class, and we thus do not distinguish retained profits and distributed profits in terms of interest payments.

We assume that a homogenous output (Y) for consumption and investment purposes is produced combining direct male or female labour and a given and non-depreciating capital stock (K). We thus ignore overhead labour costs, raw material and intermediate product cost, as well as capital stock depreciations. We assume a fixed coefficient production technology without technical progress, as before. Male and female workers operate the same technology and thus have the same labour productivity ($y = Y/N$):

$$\frac{Y}{N} = \frac{Y_M}{N_M} = \frac{Y_F}{N_F} = y = y_M = y_F, \tag{4.76}$$

with Y_M and Y_F denoting male and female output, respectively, each produced in combination with the respective (fraction of the homogenous) capital stock. The assumption of equality of male and female labour productivity (y_M, y_F) allows us to focus on true gender wage gaps. Because of historically, socially and institutionally given discrimination against women, nominal wages for female work (w_F) will only be a fraction of nominal wages for male work (w_M):

$$w_F = \varepsilon w_M, \quad 1 \geq \varepsilon > 0. \tag{4.77}$$

Therefore, we have ε as a gender wage equality parameter and $(1 - \varepsilon)$ for the gender wage gap. We assume that this parameter is determined by gender conflict, history, institutions and so on. We will treat this parameter as an exogenous variable, which can be affected by policies, and examine the macroeconomic effects of changes in this parameter. The assumption of equal male and female labour productivity but lower female wages indicates that our model refers to the gender wage gap adjusted for structural discrimination against women with respect to education, access to high skilled jobs, labour market segregation and so on, which are the focus of most of the literature referred to above.[28]

Nominal income (pY), that is, real income/output multiplied by the price level, in our model economy is distributed between male wages (W_M), female wages (W_F) and profits (Π):

$$pY = W_M + W_F + \Pi = w_M N_M + w_F N_F + rpK$$
$$= w_M \left[\rho + \varepsilon(1 - \rho) \right] N + rpK. \tag{4.78}$$

4.7.2.2 Pricing and distribution

Income distribution, both between capital and labour and between male and female workers, can again be derived starting from firms' mark-up pricing in an incompletely competitive goods market. We assume that firms mark-up unit labour costs, consisting of male and female wage costs per unit of output, and the mark-up (m) is determined by the degree of price competition in the goods market and the relative strength of capital and labour in the labour market:

$$p = (1+m)\frac{W_M + W_F}{Y} = (1+m)\frac{w_M N_M + w_F N_F}{Y}$$

$$= (1+m)\frac{w_M\left[\rho + \varepsilon(1-\rho)\right]}{y}, \quad m > 0. \tag{4.79}$$

For the further analysis we assume the determinants of the mark-up to be constant for the sake of simplicity, in order to analyse the 'pure' effects of a change in the gender wage gap. From equation (4.79) we get that profits are given by:

$$\Pi = m\left(w_M N_M + w_F N_F\right) = m w_M\left[\rho + \varepsilon(1-\rho)\right]N. \tag{4.80}$$

For the profit share in nominal income we thus obtain:

$$h = \frac{\Pi}{pY} = \frac{\Pi}{W_M + W_F + \Pi}$$

$$= \frac{m w_M\left[\rho + \varepsilon(1-\rho)\right]N}{(1+m)w_M\left[\rho + \varepsilon(1-\rho)\right]N} = \frac{m}{1+m}. \tag{4.81}$$

For the aggregate wage share (Ω) this means:

$$\Omega = 1 - h = \frac{W_M + W_F}{pY} = \frac{W_M + W_F}{W_M + W_F + \Pi}$$

$$= \frac{w_M\left[\rho + \varepsilon(1-\rho)\right]}{(1+m)w_M\left[\rho + \varepsilon(1-\rho)\right]} = \frac{1}{1+m}. \tag{4.82}$$

These are the well-known results from the very basic Kaleckian model without intermediate products, overhead labour and so on: Functional income distribution is only determined by the mark-up in firms' pricing, as has been shown in Section 4.3. But now we also have to determine the male (Ω_M) and the female (Ω_F) share of wages in national income:

$$\Omega_M = \frac{W_M}{pY} = \frac{W_M}{W_M + W_F + \Pi}$$

$$= \frac{w_M \rho}{(1+m)w_M\left[\rho + \varepsilon(1-\rho)\right]} = \Omega\frac{\rho}{\rho + \varepsilon(1-\rho)}, \tag{4.83}$$

$$\Omega_F = \frac{W_F}{pY} = \frac{W_F}{W_M + W_F + \Pi}$$

$$= \frac{w_M \varepsilon(1-\rho)}{(1+m)w_M\left[\rho + \varepsilon(1-\rho)\right]} = \Omega\frac{\varepsilon(1-\rho)}{\rho + \varepsilon(1-\rho)}. \tag{4.84}$$

The wage shares of male and female workers therefore depend on the overall wage share and the respective gender shares in this overall wage share. These shares are affected by the share of male and female workers in total employment and by the gender wage equality parameter and hence by the gender wage gap. An improvement towards gender wage equality and a reduction in the gender wage gap will have the following effects on income distribution:

$$\frac{\partial h}{\partial \varepsilon} = 0, \tag{4.81a}$$

$$\frac{\partial \Omega}{\partial \varepsilon} = 0, \tag{4.82a}$$

$$\frac{\partial \Omega_M}{\partial \varepsilon} = \frac{-\Omega \rho (1-\rho)}{\left[\rho + \varepsilon (1-\rho)\right]^2} = \frac{-\rho (1-\rho)}{(1+m)\left[\rho + \varepsilon (1-\rho)\right]^2} < 0, \tag{4.83a}$$

$$\frac{\partial \Omega_F}{\partial \varepsilon} = \frac{\Omega \rho (1-\rho)}{\left[\rho + \varepsilon (1-\rho)\right]^2} = \frac{\rho (1-\rho)}{(1+m)\left[\rho + \varepsilon (1-\rho)\right]^2} > 0. \tag{4.84a}$$

In this simple model, an improvement towards gender wage equality and a reduction of the gender wage gap will thus have no effect on the profit share and on the aggregate wage share, but it will improve the female wage share at the expense of the male wage share. An increase in the female nominal wage rate, keeping the male nominal wage rate constant and treating it as an anchor, thus reducing the gap between them, will increase the price level, because we assume a constant mark-up and constant labour productivity. This increase in the price level, however, will be less than proportional since male nominal costs remain constant, such that the female real the male wage rate and the female wage share will rise, and it will make the male real wage rate and the male wage share fall accordingly. This basic model is open to assuming that lowering the gender wage gap is associated with an improvement of workers' bargaining power in the labour market and thus with a lower mark-up and a lower profit share, as Onaran et al. (2019) have found for the UK. This would also be in line with the positive relationship between the profit share and wage inequality, addressed in the previous section. However, for analytical purposes we prefer to keep these two types of redistribution distinct in the current section. Their interaction, however, could easily be added to the following analysis.

4.7.2.3 Distribution, aggregate demand and output

For the goods market equilibrium we thus have to look at investment and saving, that is, income not consumed. As in the previous section, we assume again a simplified neo-Kaleckian investment function, in which investment finance and a negative effect of the interest rate and of debt services are ignored. Investment (pI) is thus only determined by animal spirits or autonomous investment (pI$_a$) and by (expected) aggregate demand and hence by income via the accelerator mechanism:

$$pI = pI_a + \beta pY, \quad pI_a, \beta > 0. \tag{4.85}$$

Aggregate saving (S) consists of saving out of profit (S_Π), saving out of male workers' wages (S_{WM}) and saving out of female workers' wages (S_{WF}). Each saving aggregate is determined by the respective propensity to save and the respective income, with s_Π denoting the propensity to save out of profits, s_{WM} the propensity to save out of male wages and s_{WF} the propensity to save out of female wages. We therefore obtain for the saving function:

$$S = S_\Pi + S_{WM} + S_{WF} = \left(s_\Pi h + s_{WM}\Omega_M + s_{WF}\Omega_F\right)pY, \quad 0 \le s_{WM}, s_{WF} < s_\Pi \le 1. \quad (4.86)$$

Since saving out of profits contains retained earnings of corporations, which cannot be consumed and are thus saved by definition, and since profits usually go to the high-income households, we assume the propensity to save out of profits to exceed each of the two propensities to save out of wages.[29] Whether the propensity to save out of female wages is higher or lower than the propensity to save out of male wages is an open question. On the one hand, female wages are lower than male wages and, according to Keynes's (1936, Chapter 8) absolute income hypothesis, we would expect a higher propensity to consume and thus a lower propensity to save out of female wages than out of male wages, as also expected by Onaran (2015). On the other hand, it has been found by Seguino and Sagrario Floro (2003) for semi-industrialised countries that rising relative income and more bargaining power of women increase aggregate saving rates. Potential causes are that women's income is more unstable and women's expenditures are dominated more by pre-cautionary motives. Interestingly, the estimations by Onaran et al. (2019) for the UK support the notion that the propensity to save out of female wages is higher than out of male wages.[30] In our following analysis, we will therefore consider both cases, $s_{WM} > s_{WF}$ and $s_{WM} < s_{WF}$.

Plugging in the determination of the male and female wage shares from equations (4.83) and (4.84) into equation (4.86) we obtain:

$$S = \left\{h\left[s_\Pi - \frac{s_{WM}\rho + s_{WF}\varepsilon(1-\rho)}{\rho + \varepsilon(1-\rho)}\right] + \left[\frac{s_{WM}\rho + s_{WF}\varepsilon(1-\rho)}{\rho + \varepsilon(1-\rho)}\right]\right\}pY. \quad (4.87)$$

The average propensity to save out of wages (s_w) is the weighted average of the propensity to save out of male and female wages, with weights given by the male and female share in wages:

$$s_W = \frac{S_W}{W} = \frac{S_{WM} + S_{WF}}{W_M + W_F}$$

$$= \frac{s_{WM}\Omega_M pY + s_{WF}\Omega_F pY}{\Omega pY} = \frac{s_{WM}\rho + s_{WF}\varepsilon(1-\rho)}{\rho + \varepsilon(1-\rho)}. \quad (4.88)$$

Using equation (4.88), the saving equation thus becomes:

$$S = \left\{h\left[s_\Pi - s_W(\varepsilon)\right] + s_W(\varepsilon)\right\}pY. \quad (4.89)$$

The propensity to save out of wages is here endogenous with respect to the degree of gender wage equality and thus the gender wage gap:

$$\frac{\partial s_W}{\partial \varepsilon} = \frac{-(1-\rho)\rho(s_{WM} - s_{WF})}{[\rho + \varepsilon(1-\rho)]^2}. \tag{4.88a}$$

An improvement towards gender wage equality and a decline in the gender wage gap will thus reduce the average propensity to save out of wages, if the propensity to save out of female wages falls short of the propensity to save out of male wages. It will raise the average propensity to save out of wages if the propensity to save out of female wages is higher than out of male wages.

For the goods market equilibrium we need the equality of planned saving and investment:

$$pI = S. \tag{4.90}$$

For the stability of the goods market equilibrium, it is required that saving responds more than investment to a change in income as the endogenous variable:

$$\frac{\partial S}{\partial(pY)} - \frac{\partial(pI)}{\partial(pY)} > 0 \;\Rightarrow\; h(s_\Pi - s_W) + s_W - \beta > 0. \tag{4.91}$$

Aggregate supply adjusts to demand, and saving adjusts to investment, by means of changes in income/output. We receive the equilibrium level of income (pY^*) by plugging equations (4.85) and (4.89) into equation (4.90):

$$pY^* = \frac{pI_a}{h(s_\Pi - s_W) + s_W - \beta}. \tag{4.92}$$

Inserting this value into equations (4.85) or (4.89) we also obtain equilibrium investment/saving:

$$pI^* = S^* = \frac{pI_a\left[h(s_\Pi - s_W) + s_W\right]}{h(s_\Pi - s_W) + s_W - \beta}. \tag{4.93}$$

Multiplying equilibrium income by the profit share determined in equation (4.81) yields equilibrium profits:

$$\Pi^* = \frac{hpI_a}{h(s_\Pi - s_W) + s_W - \beta}. \tag{4.94}$$

For this closed economy model with positive saving out of wages, it is well known that the paradox of saving applies, that is, a higher propensity to save out of any type of income will lower all the endogenous variables, the levels of income, investment/saving and profits.

Furthermore, as shown in Section 4.3, demand in such an economy is wage-led. A rise in the aggregate wage share, and thus a fall in the profit share, will lead to higher equilibrium levels of income and investment/saving:

$$\frac{\partial(pY)^*}{\partial h} = \frac{-pI_a(s_\Pi - s_W)}{\left[h(s_\Pi - s_W) + s_W - \beta\right]^2} < 0. \tag{4.92a}$$

$$\frac{\partial(pI)^*}{\partial h} = \frac{-\beta pI_a(s_\Pi - s_W)}{\left[h(s_\Pi - s_W) + s_W - \beta\right]^2} < 0. \tag{4.93a}$$

The paradox of costs, that is, a higher profit share that generates lower equilibrium profits, which will emerge if there is no saving out of wages, may but will not necessarily arise in the model with positive saving out of wages:

$$\frac{\partial \Pi^*}{\partial h} = \frac{s_W - \beta}{\left[h(s_\Pi - s_W) + s_W - \beta\right]^2}. \tag{4.94a}$$

A high propensity to save out of wages and a low accelerator effect of income on investment may undermine the paradox of costs.

For the improvement towards gender wage equality and a reduction in the gender wage gap, we obtain:

$$\frac{\partial(pY)^*}{\partial \varepsilon} = \frac{pI_a(1-h)(1-\rho)\rho(s_{WM} - s_{WF})}{\left\{\left[h(s_\Pi - s_W) + s_W - \beta\right]\left[\rho + \varepsilon(1-\rho)\right]\right\}^2} \tag{4.92b}$$

$$\frac{\partial(pI)^*}{\partial \varepsilon} = \frac{\beta pI_a(1-h)(1-\rho)\rho(s_{WM} - s_{WF})}{\left\{\left[h(s_\Pi - s_W) + s_W - \beta\right]\left[\rho + \varepsilon(1-\rho)\right]\right\}^2} \tag{4.93b}$$

$$\frac{\partial \Pi^*}{\partial \varepsilon} = \frac{hpI_a(1-h)(1-\rho)\rho(s_{WM} - s_{WF})}{\left\{\left[h(s_\Pi - s_W) + s_W - \beta\right]\left[\rho + \varepsilon(1-\rho)\right]\right\}^2} \tag{4.94b}$$

If the propensity to save out of female wages is lower than out of male wages, a reduction in the gender wage gap, and thus an increase in the female wage share at the expense of the male wage share, will be expansionary and lift the equilibrium levels of income, investment/saving and profits. The economy will thus be 'gender equality-led'. In the opposite case, however, if the propensity to save out of female wages exceeds that out of male wages, a reduction in the gender wage gap will reduce the equilibrium levels of income, investment/saving and profits. The economy will thus be 'gender equality-burdened'. In the next section we will examine if and how these results change in an economy which is open to foreign trade.

4.7.3 The Open Economy Model

4.7.3.1 Basic structure

To consider the macroeconomic effects of closing the gender wage gap in an open economy, we make use of the model introduced in Section 4.5, without considering exogenous government demand here. We thus assume an economy without economic activity of the state, which is open to foreign trade, but not to international movements of capital and labour. The economy depends on imported inputs for production purposes, and its output competes in international markets. We take the prices of imported inputs and of the competing foreign final output to be exogenously given. If they are changing, they are moving in step. The nominal exchange rate is determined by monetary policies and international financial markets and is also considered to be exogenous for our purposes. Foreign economic activity is also taken to be exogenously given.

4.7.3.2 Pricing, distribution and international competitiveness

We keep the assumptions regarding capital and labour inputs, the capital-potential output ratio and the labour productivity of male and female labour from the previous section. But, as in Section 4.5, we also consider imported raw material and semi-finished product inputs and assume that firms mark-up unit variable costs, consisting of unit labour costs and unit semi-finished product and material costs, which, by assumption, are completely imported. We denote unit raw material and semi-finished product inputs per unit of output again by μ, the nominal exchange rate by a and the price of a unit of imported foreign goods in foreign currency by p_f. The pricing equation for domestically produced goods thus becomes:

$$p = (1+m)\left\{\frac{w_M[\rho+\varepsilon(1-\rho)]}{y}+p_f a\mu\right\}, \quad m > 0. \tag{4.95}$$

The ratio z between unit material and semi-finished product costs and unit labour costs is given as:

$$z = \frac{p_f a\mu y}{w_M[\rho+\varepsilon(1-\rho)]}. \tag{4.96}$$

The price equation thus becomes:

$$p = (1+m)\frac{w_M[\rho+\varepsilon(1-\rho)]}{y}(1+z). \tag{4.97}$$

The profit share in domestic value added, consisting of domestic profits, male and female wages, is given by:

$$h = \frac{\Pi}{W_M + W_F + \Pi} = \frac{(1+z)m}{1+(1+z)m}. \tag{4.98}$$

As is well known from Section 4.5, the profit share in the open economy is hence determined by the mark-up and by the ratio of unit costs for imported material and semi-finished products to unit labour costs, now consisting of male and female labour costs. The aggregate wage share is given by:

$$\Omega = 1 - h = \frac{W_M + W_F}{W_M + W_F + \Pi} = \frac{1}{1 + (1+z)m}, \tag{4.99}$$

and the male and female wage shares are determined by:

$$\Omega_M = \frac{W_M}{W_M + W_F + \Pi} = \Omega \frac{\rho}{\rho + \varepsilon(1-\rho)} = \frac{\rho}{\left[1 + (1+z)m\right]\left[\rho + \varepsilon(1-\rho)\right]}, \tag{4.100}$$

$$\Omega_F = \frac{W_F}{W_M + W_F + \Pi} = \Omega \frac{\varepsilon(1-\rho)}{\rho + \varepsilon(1-\rho)} = \frac{\varepsilon(1-\rho)}{\left[1 + (1+z)m\right]\left[\rho + \varepsilon(1-\rho)\right]}. \tag{4.101}$$

The ratio of unit material and semi-finished product costs to unit wage costs in equation (4.96) is now affected by the gender wage equality parameter:

$$\frac{\partial z}{\partial \varepsilon} = \frac{-p_f e \mu y (1-\rho)}{w_M \left[\rho + \varepsilon(1-\rho)\right]^2} = \frac{-(1-\rho)z}{\left[\rho + \varepsilon(1-\rho)\right]} < 0. \tag{4.96a}$$

Therefore, any change in the gender wage gap will not only affect the distribution of wages between males and females, as in the closed economy case, it will also have an impact on the overall wage share and the profit share in the open economy case:

$$\frac{\partial h}{\partial \varepsilon} = \frac{-m(1-\rho)z}{\left[1 + (1+z)m\right]^2 \left[\rho + \varepsilon(1-\rho)\right]} < 0, \tag{4.98a}$$

$$\frac{\partial \Omega}{\partial \varepsilon} = \frac{(1-\rho)mz}{\left[1 + (1+z)m\right]^2 \left[\rho + \varepsilon(1-\rho)\right]} > 0, \tag{4.99a}$$

$$\frac{\partial \Omega_M}{\partial \varepsilon} = \frac{-(1-\rho)\rho(1+m)}{\left\{\left[1 + (1+z)m\right]\left[\rho + \varepsilon(1-\rho)\right]\right\}^2} < 0, \tag{4.100a}$$

$$\frac{\partial \Omega_F}{\partial \varepsilon} = \frac{(1-\rho)\left\{\rho(1+m) + mz\left[\rho + \varepsilon(1-\rho)\right]\right\}}{\left\{\left[1 + (1+z)m\right]\left[\rho + \varepsilon(1-\rho)\right]\right\}^2} > 0. \tag{4.101a}$$

An improvement of gender wage equality by narrowing the gender wage gap will raise the female wage share and reduce the male wage share for the same reasons as mentioned above for the closed economy. Furthermore, however, it will also increase the aggregate wage share and reduce the profit share in national income, because a rise in female wages, everything else constant, will lower the ratio of unit material and semi-finished product costs to unit labour costs.

International price competitiveness of domestic firms will again be indicated the real exchange rate, as in Section 4.5:

$$a_r = \frac{ap_f}{p}. \tag{4.102}$$

An increase in the real exchange rate implies increasing international price competitiveness of domestic producers. From equation (4.102), it follows for the respective growth rates:

$$\hat{a}_r = \hat{a} + \hat{p}_f - \hat{p}. \tag{4.103}$$

Therefore, higher price competitiveness can be caused by an increasing nominal exchange rate, hence a nominal depreciation of the domestic currency, increasing foreign prices or declining domestic prices. The effect of changes in profit and wage shares on international competitiveness will depend on the cause of distributional change, as we have explained in Section 4.5. If, everything else constant, the profit share rises because of an increase in the mark-up, domestic prices will rise and the real exchange rate and international price competitiveness of domestic producers will fall. If, however, the profit share rises because of an increase in the ratio of unit material and intermediate product costs to unit labour costs, which may be driven by a fall in nominal wages, a rise in foreign prices or a rise in the nominal exchange rate, hence a depreciation of the domestic currency, the international price competitiveness of domestic producers will rise.

The reduction of the gender wage gap and a rise of the gender wage equality parameter have a uniquely negative effect on the real exchange rate and thus on international price competitiveness:

$$\frac{\partial a_r}{\partial \varepsilon} = \frac{-(1-\rho)p_f a\mu y}{(1+m)w_M\{(1+z)[\rho+\varepsilon(1-\rho)]\}^2} = \frac{-(1-\rho)a_r}{(1+z)[\rho+\varepsilon(1-\rho)]} < 0. \tag{4.102a}$$

The explanation is straightforward: With constant male nominal wages, constant labour productivity and constant mark-ups, a reduction in the gender wage gap means an increase in the female nominal wage rate. This will raise average unit wage costs and domestic prices, although less than proportional, such that female real wages and wage shares rise by more than male real wages and wage shares fall. Therefore, the profit share falls simultaneously with the international price competitiveness of domestic producers. Again, we could assume here that a reduction in the gender wage gap by means of raising female wages is associated with a squeeze of the mark-up, either because it goes along with an improvement of workers' general bargaining power and/or because firms attempt to maintain international price competitiveness, as Blecker (1989) and Blecker and Seguino (2002) have argued. This would then reinforce the reduction in the profit share, on the one hand, but dampen or even prevent the fall in international price competitiveness, on the other hand. However, in what follows we will not explicitly consider this when we examine the effects on aggregate demand and income/output, in order to keep the analysis simple and tractable.

4.7.3.3 Distribution, aggregate demand and income/output

For the analysis of the effects of changes in the gender wage gap on aggregate demand, investment, profits and net exports, we start again with the goods market equilibrium condition for an open economy without economic activity of the state: Planned saving has to be equal to planned nominal investment and nominal net exports (NX), the difference between nominal exports (pEx) and nominal imports ($ap_f Im$) of goods and services:

$$S = pI + pEx - ap_f \, Im = pI + NX. \tag{4.104}$$

We can use the saving function (4.89) and the investment function (4.85) from the closed economy model, and specify the net export function as in Section 4.5 as follows:

$$NX = pEx - ap_f \, Im = \psi a_r(\varepsilon) + \chi ap_f Y_f - \phi pY, \quad \psi, \phi, \chi \geq 0. \tag{4.105}$$

Net exports are positively affected by the international price competitiveness of domestic producers, provided the Marshall-Lerner condition can be assumed to hold and the sum of the absolute values of the price elasticities of exports and imports exceeds unity. Under this condition, the real exchange rate will have a positive effect on net exports. However, net exports also depend on the relative developments of foreign and domestic demand. If domestic demand increases (decreases), ceteris paribus, net exports will decline (increase), because imports will rise (fall). Moreover, if foreign demand rises (falls), ceteris paribus, net exports will rise (fall). Net exports will thus depend on the real exchange rate, foreign income ($ap_f Y_f$) determining foreign demand (in domestic prices) and domestic income determining domestic demand. The coefficients on domestic and foreign incomes are affected by the income elasticities of the demand for exports and imports.

Stability of the goods market equilibrium in equation (4.104) requires that saving responds more to a change in the endogenous variable, the domestic level of income, than investment and net exports do together:

$$\frac{\partial S}{\partial(pY)} - \frac{\partial(pI)}{\partial(pY)} - \frac{\partial NX}{\partial(pY)} > 0 \Rightarrow h(s_\Pi - s_w) + s_w - \beta + \phi > 0. \tag{4.106}$$

Plugging equations (4.85), (4.89) and (4.105) into equation (4.104) and solving for domestic income and then using equilibrium domestic income to determine the equilibrium levels of investment, profits and net exports yields the following results:

$$pY^* = \frac{pI_a + \psi a_r + \chi ap_f Y_f}{h(s_\Pi - s_w) + s_w - \beta + \phi}, \tag{4.107}$$

$$pI^* = \frac{pI_a \left[h(s_\Pi - s_w) + s_w + \phi\right] + \beta\left[\psi a_r + \chi ap_f Y_f\right]}{h(s_\Pi - s_w) + s_w - \beta + \phi}, \tag{4.108}$$

$$\Pi^* = \frac{h\left(pI_a + \psi a_r + \chi ap_f Y_f\right)}{h\left(s_\Pi - s_W\right) + s_W - \beta + \phi},$$

(4.109)

$$NX^* = \frac{\left(\psi a_r + \chi ap_f Y_f\right)\left[h\left(s_\Pi - s_W\right) + s_W - \beta\right] - pI_a \phi}{h\left(s_\Pi - s_W\right) + s_W - \beta + \phi}.$$

(4.110)

For the effects of an improvement towards gender wage equality and a reduction in the gender wage gap, we obtain:

$$\frac{\partial(pY)^*}{\partial\varepsilon} = \frac{\dfrac{\partial a_r}{\partial\varepsilon}\psi - pY^*\left[\dfrac{\partial h}{\partial\varepsilon}\left(s_\Pi - s_W\right) + \dfrac{\partial s_W}{\partial\varepsilon}\left(1-h\right)\right]}{h\left(s_\Pi - s_W\right) + s_W - \beta + \phi},$$

(4.107a)

$$\frac{\partial(pI)^*}{\partial\varepsilon} = \frac{\beta\left\{\dfrac{\partial a_r}{\partial\varepsilon}\psi - pY^*\left[\dfrac{\partial h}{\partial\varepsilon}\left(s_\Pi - s_W\right) + \dfrac{\partial s_W}{\partial\varepsilon}\left(1-h\right)\right]\right\}}{h\left(s_\Pi - s_W\right) + s_W - \beta + \phi},$$

(4.108a)

$$\frac{\partial\Pi^*}{\partial\varepsilon} = \frac{h\left\langle\dfrac{\partial a_r}{\partial\varepsilon}\psi - pY^*\left\{\dfrac{\partial h}{\partial\varepsilon}\left[s_\Pi - s_W - \dfrac{1}{h}\left(h\left(s_\Pi - s_W\right) + s_W - \beta + \phi\right)\right] + \dfrac{\partial s_W}{\partial\varepsilon}\left(1-h\right)\right\}\right\rangle}{h\left(s_\Pi - s_W\right) + s_W - \beta + \phi},$$

(4.109a)

$$\frac{\partial NX^*}{\partial\varepsilon} = \frac{\dfrac{\partial a_r}{\partial\varepsilon}\psi\left[h\left(s_\Pi - s_W\right) + s_W - \beta\right] + \phi pY^*\left[\dfrac{\partial h}{\partial\varepsilon}\left(s_\Pi - s_W\right) + \dfrac{\partial s_W}{\partial\varepsilon}\left(1-h\right)\right]}{h\left(s_\Pi - s_W\right) + s_W - \beta + \phi}.$$

(4.110a)

Each of the equations (4.107a)–(4.110a) is written in such a way that the different channels through which an improvement in gender wage equality affects the endogenous variables of the model are clearly visible. First, we have the channel via the international price competitiveness of domestic producers $(\partial a_r/\partial\varepsilon)$ which affects foreign demand for domestically produced goods and hence exports. Second, we have the channel via the profit share $(\partial h/\partial\varepsilon)$ and third via gender wage distribution and the average propensity to consume out of wages $(\partial s_W/\partial\varepsilon)$, which will each affect domestic demand. For the interpretation of our results, we have to remember that we assume the stability condition for the goods market equilibrium in (4.105) to hold, which means that the denominators in equations (4.107a)–(4.110a) are all positive. From equation (4.98a) we have $\partial h/\partial\varepsilon < 0$, and from equation (4.102a) we know that $\partial e^r/\partial\varepsilon < 0$. Furthermore, from equation (4.88a) we know that $\partial s_W/\partial\varepsilon < 0$, if $s_{WM} > s_{WF}$, and $\partial s_W/\partial\varepsilon > 0$, if $s_{WM} < s_{WF}$.

Let us start with the first case, in which the propensity to save out of female wages is lower than out of male wages, hence that $s_{WM} > s_{WF}$ and $\partial s_W/\partial\varepsilon < 0$. In this case, domestic demand will clearly rise whenever the gender wage gap is reduced, because the profit share falls and also the average propensity to save out of wages declines. However, the effect on foreign demand and exports will be negative, because of a declining real exchange rate. The effect on total demand, domestic income/output and investment will depend on the relative strengths of these effects. If the expansionary effect on domestic demand dominates the contractionary effect on foreign demand, the numerators in equations (4.107a) and (4.107a) will be positive; equilibrium income and investment will rise and will hence be gender equality-led. As can clearly be seen in equations (4.107a) and (4.108a), this is the more (less) likely:

- the lower (higher) the price elasticity of exports indicated by ψ,
- the lower (higher) the effect of reducing the gender wage gap on the real exchange rate, $\partial a_r/\partial \varepsilon$,
- the higher (lower) the differential in the propensities to save out profits and out of aggregate wages, $(s_\Pi - s_w)$,
- the lower (higher) the profit share, h,
- and the stronger (weaker) the negative effects of an improvement of the gender wage equality are on the profit share, $\partial h/\partial \varepsilon$, and on the average propensity to save out of wages, $\partial s_w/\partial \varepsilon$.

If the contractionary effect of an improvement of gender wage equality on foreign demand dominates the expansionary effect on domestic demand, the numerator in equations (4.106a) and (4.107a) may turn negative, and the equilibrium levels of income and investment will decline. The economy will then be gender equality-burdened.

If the economy is gender equality-led, and the equilibrium levels of income and investment hence rise in the face of a reduction in the gender wage gap, the level of profits is likely to improve, too, but not necessarily so, as can be seen in equation (4.109a). Furthermore, net exports will certainly fall, as can be seen in equation (4.110a). In the gender equality-burdened case, in which the equilibrium levels of income and investment hence fall in the face of a reduction in the gender wage gap, profits will also fall, as will net exports, of course.

Turning to the second case, in which the propensity to save out of female wages is higher than out of male wages, hence $s_{WM} < s_{WF}$ and $\partial s_w/\partial \varepsilon > 0$, it is obvious that a gender equality-led demand and growth regime becomes less likely, although not impossible. The effect of lowering the gender wage gap on domestic demand may now already be negative if the dampening effect via the increase in the average propensity to save out of wages exceeds the expansionary effect via the reduction in the profit share. In this case, the term $(\partial h/\partial \varepsilon)(s_\Pi - s_w) + (\partial s_w/\partial \varepsilon)(1 - h)$ in the numerators of equations (4.107a) and (4.108a) will turn positive, which will make the numerators negative and we will see lower equilibrium levels of income/output and investment. Demand will be gender equality-burdened, and we will also see depressive effects on the equilibrium level of profits. The effect on equilibrium net exports will be positive, as already mentioned above. However, if the dampening effect via the increase in the average propensity to save out of wages falls short of the expansionary effect via the reduction in the profit share, the term $(\partial h/\partial \varepsilon)(s_\Pi - s_w)+(\partial s_w/\partial \varepsilon)(1 - h)$ in the numerators of equations (4.107a) and (4.108a) will turn negative, and domestic demand will increase. But still we have the negative effect via the fall in the real exchange rate on exports and net exports, which may make the economy gender equality-burdened, as in the first case.

Summing up, although a gender equality-led regime is logically not impossible, if the propensity to save out of female wages is higher than out of male wages, it is less likely in this case. If the propensity to save out of female wages is lower than out of male wages, a gender equality-led regime is a very likely outcome, in particular if the depressive real appreciation-export effect is not too strong relative to the expansionary domestic demand effect. Of course, these are only the short-run distribution and aggregate demand effects of improving gender wage equality. Further effects on productivity growth, in particular, should occur, as pointed out in a distribution and growth model context by Hein (2020) and in the gendered macroeconomics literature referred to above in this section.

NOTES

1. For a short overview of different production technologies being applied in macroeconomic models, see Blecker and Setterfield (2019, pp. 10–15).
2. Alternatively, the reader may assume that issuing corporate bonds in our model also includes issuing shares, such that both can be summarised as long-term outside finance, and that the interest rate in our model can then be viewed as a composite rate of return on outside finance, hence as a weighted average of the interest rate on corporate bonds and the dividend rate on equity. See Hein (2014a, Chapter 10) for such a procedure in a distribution and growth model context.
3. For more detailed analysis of the long-run dynamics of these variables in distribution and growth models based on similar foundations, see for example Hein (2008, Chapter 13, 2014a, Chapters 9–10).
4. See Hein (2008, Chapter 6.5) for an overview of the post-Keynesian views on interest, credit and money, and Lavoie (2014, Chapter 4, 2020a) for an extensive treatment. For introductions to and overviews of the post-Keynesian monetary theory, see also in particular Lavoie (2003a, 2006c, 2011b) and Lavoie and Seccareccia (2016).
5. Bindseil and König (2013), the first author from the European Central Bank and the second from the German Institute for Economic Research (DIW), also praised Basil Moore's (1988a) *Horizontalists and Verticalists* in a special issue of the *Review of Keynesian Economics*.
6. For example, in the Eurozone since 18 September 2019, the deposit facility rate has been at −0.5 per cent, the marginal lending facility rate at 0.25 per cent, and the main refinancing operations rate, the target rate, at 0 per cent (ECB 2021).
7. For assessments of central bank responses to the Great Financial Crisis and the Great Recession 2007–09, see Bibow (2015), D'Arista (2013), Fullwiler (2013), Herr (2014a), Lavoie (2010a, 2014 Chapter 4, 2016c), Lavoie and Fiebiger (2018) and Palley (2011, 2016, 2018).
8. For post-Keynesian assessments of macroeconomic policy responses to the 2007–09 Global Financial Crisis and the Great Recession, as well as the following Eurozone crisis, and the implications for macroeconomic theory and policy, see for example Arestis and Sawyer (2011), Bibow (2013a, 2013b, 2016), Blecker (2016c), Davidson (2009), Hein (2011b, 2013, 2013/14, 2018a), Hein and Detzer (2015b, 2015c), Hein and Martschin (2020, 2021), Hein and Truger (2011, 2012/13), Lavoie (2016b, 2016c, 2018), Palley (2012, 2013b), Skidelsky (2009) and the contributions to the books by Arestis and Sawyer (2012, 2014, 2017), Bitzenis et al. (2015), Dejuan et al. (2013), Hein et al. (2016) and Herr et al. (2017, 2019), for example.
9. For a review of the arguments in the horizontalists vs. structuralists debate, see Hein (2008, Chapter 6). For more recent contributions to the debate see Deleidi (2018, 2019, 2020) and the chapters in Rochon and Rossi (2017a).
10. Wray (2006), however, does not consider himself a structuralist any more.
11. The idea that lasting variations in interest rates may affect functional income distribution and hence the share of wages and gross profits in total income goes back to Sraffa (1960, p. 33). For modern versions, see also Panico (1985), Panico and Pinto (2017), Panico et al. (2012) and Pivetti (1991). In the post-Keynesian literature, we find it also in the work of Kaldor (1982, p. 63), Pasinetti (1974, pp. 139–41) and Hein (2006d, 2007, 2008, Part II). This idea is also compatible with Kalecki's (1954, p. 18) notion that the degree of monopoly and hence the mark-up 'may, but need not necessarily, increase' when overheads and hence interest costs increase. Empirical evidence supporting the distribution effect of changes in the monetary interest rate is also reviewed in Hein (2012a, Chapter 2, 2014a, Chapter 9, 2015), Hein and Schoder (2011), Lima and Setterfield (2010) and Rochon and Rossi (2006a, 2006b). Hein and Schoder (2011) have provided econometric support for such an effect for Germany and the USA in the period 1960–2007.
12. However, some studies argue that the wage share is finally rising in a boom, causing a profit squeeze crisis. See for example Kiefer and Rada (2015) and other studies referred to in the next footnote.

13.   This endogeneity has important implications for assessing the empirical estimation results regarding the demand and growth effects of changes in the wage share or the profit share, as Lavoie (1995a, 2009b, 2014, Chapters 4–5, 2017) has tirelessly pointed out (see also Blecker and Setterfield 2019, pp. 205–7, Rolim 2019). It raises severe doubts regarding those studies, like Barbosa-Filho and Taylor (2006), Carvalho and Rezai (2016), Diallo et al. (2011), Flaschel and Proaño (2007), Kiefer and Rada (2015), Nikiforos and Foley (2012) and Rezai (2015), which claim that there is a short-run positive causal effect of the profit share on aggregate demand and growth, that is, that demand and growth are profit-led.

14.   For the sake of simplicity we ignore an autonomous part in rentiers' consumption, unlike what we have assumed for Kalecki's consumption function out of profits in Chapter 3.

15.   The effectiveness of fiscal policies with regard to stabilising aggregate demand and economic activity, in particular in economic downswings when interest rate policies of central banks face severe limitations (zero lower bound, investment trap), has been shown recently by orthodox and heterodox authors alike, using different types of empirical methods. Multipliers have been shown to be time varying, with higher values in a recession. Particularly government investment has been estimated to have the highest multiplier effects. See, for example, Blanchard and Leigh (2013, 2014), Bouthevillain et al. (2009), Brancaccio and De Cristofaro (2020), Charles (2016b), Charles et al. (2015), Coenen et al. (2012, 2013), Gechert (2015), Gechert and Rannenberg (2018), Gechert et al. (2019), Hemming et al. (2002), Qazizada and Stockhammer (2015), Setterfield (2019) and Stockhammer et al. (2019).

16.   These results have recently also been confirmed in post-Keynesian/Kaleckian autonomous demand-driven growth models, in which government consumption expenditures are the non-capacity creating autonomous growth driver (Dutt 2020, Hein 2018c, Hein and Woodgate 2021).

17.   For similar open economy versions of the Kaleckian distribution and growth model, see Bhaduri and Marglin (1990) and Blecker (1989). More elaborated models have been presented by Blecker (1999, 2002, 2011) and Cassetti (2012), for example.

18.   For post-Keynesian exchange rate theories, see De Paula et al. (2017), Fritz et al. (2018), Harvey (2007/08, 2009, 2019), Herr (1992), Herr and Priewe (2006), Lavoie (2014, Chapter 7), Priewe (2008) and Priewe and Herr (2005). We will come back to exchange rate issues in Chapter 6.

19.   The coefficients indicate marginal effects of changes in the levels of domestic and foreign income on imports and exports, respectively, whereas the elasticities describe the effects of the growth rates of domestic and foreign income on the growth rates of imports and exports, respectively.

20.   See Hein (2014a, Chapter 7) for an overview of empirical studies and Hartwig (2014), Onaran and Galanis (2014) and Onaran and Obst (2016) for recent results on a broad set of countries. A recent overview of studies on emerging economies can be found in Jimenez (2020). For a discussion of different empirical results for wage- vs. profit-led demand and growth in different studies on the same countries and periods, see Blecker (2016a) and Stockhammer (2017a) and the remarks in Chapter 2.

21.   This section draws on Hein and Prante (2020) and presents a short-run level version of the growth model included in that contribution.

22.   For post-Keynesian distribution and growth models, see, for example, Blecker and Setterfield (2019, Chapters 3–4), Hein (2014a, Chapters 4–8) and Lavoie (2014, Chapter 6).

23.   We have to be careful not to confuse the propensity to save of workers' households with the propensity to save out of wages. What we assume here is that workers have two different propensities to save: A higher one out of their profits and a lower one out of the wages they receive. This may be justified by the fact that profits in large part are not paid out to households but are rather retained, increasing the value of the firms and thus also the wealth of the owners of the firms. This wealth effect might then feedback on consumption and saving out of wages for those workers who have accumulated financial assets.

24.   Wage inequality could be measured by the Gini coefficient of wage distribution amongst working households, or by the share of high wage households (top 0.1, 1 or 10 per cent) in the total wage bill.

25.   This section draws on Hein (2020) and presents short-run level versions of the growth models included in that contribution.

26.   See Seguino (2019) for several arguments, why post-Keynesians should be concerned with more general stratification issues in macroeconomics, with gender being an important one amongst them. On the relevance and the contribution of stratification for the explanation of economic development and financial and economic crises, see, for example, Berik et al. (2009) and Fukuda-Parr et al. (2013).

27.   See Onaran (2015) and Onaran et al. (2019), and in particular Seguino (2020) for a more comprehensive review of the feminist macroeconomics literature.

28.   These assumptions may raise the question, why, in our one-good economy, firms should hire male labour at all. However, it should be clear that this model is an extreme simplification of a more complex world determined by historical, social and institutional features. One of these features is a male dominated labour force.

29.   Since we assume the propensity to save out of male and female wages to be positive, it means that both types of workers accumulate financial assets and become co-owners of or creditors to the firms, and thus will also receive part of the profits generated in the firm sector. We will not follow this up, and therefore we have to be

careful not to confuse the propensity to save of female and male workers with the propensity to save out of female and male wages. In essence, what we assume here is that male and female workers have two different propensities to save each: A higher one out of their profits and a lower one out of the wages they receive. This may be justified by the fact that profits in large part are not paid out to households but are rather retained, increasing the value of the firms and thus also the wealth of the owners of the firms, who will be capitalists and also those workers who save. In a more elaborated model we should therefore also include consumption out of accumulated wealth.

30. See also Seguino (2020) on the unclear results regarding different saving propensities of men and women.

5. Post-Keynesian macroeconomic models with conflict inflation

5.1   INTRODUCTION

In this chapter we will now include inflation in our models from Chapter 4. In post-Keynesian macroeconomics inflation as a persistent process is of the conflicting claims type (Blecker and Setterfield 2019, Chapter 5, Hein 2006a, 2008, Chapter 16, Lavoie 2014, Chapter 8, Stockhammer 2008). Of course, a positive demand shock may generate a rise in prices if firms face short-run supply constraints. But this will only lead to inflation as a positive growth rate of the price index, which persists and may even accelerate, if, for example, workers resist a reduction of the real wage rate and a re-distribution of income at their expense, and a price-wage-price spiral emerges. Similar for a supply shock, which indicates an increasing claim of some actors in the economy, and which will generate inflation, if the claims of other actors do not give way. Wage-price-wage or price-wage-price spirals will emerge. Therefore, the distinction between demand-pull and cost-push inflation to be found in many textbooks is somewhat misleading and only refers to the trigger of an inflation process. Persistent inflation is always based on distribution conflict between different groups or sectors in the economy, workers, firms, rentiers, government or the foreign sector, either triggered by a demand shock or a supply shock.

The roots of the post-Keynesian conflicting claims theory of inflation go back at least to Joan Robinson's (1956, pp. 48–50, 1962, pp. 58–9) 'inflation barrier' for the rate of growth. This barrier is given by workers' resistance to accept lower real wages in an economy with a fully utilised capital stock, in which higher capital stock and GDP growth require lower consumption.[1] Interestingly, the notion of conflict inflation has also partially made it into the three equations model by Carlin and Soskice (2009, 2015, Chapter 3), as one variant of the 'new consensus macroeconomics' (NCM). However, although inflation in their model is generated by inconsistent distribution claims of workers and firms, there are neither any effects on income distribution nor any further effects on demand, output, employment or unemployment. In the post-Keynesian tradition, however, inconsistent income claims do not only generate inflation but also cause changes in income distribution. These changes may then feedback on aggregate demand, employment and thus inflation itself, as we will show in this chapter.

Kalecki (1971, Chapter 14) in his 'Class struggle and the distribution of income' had already pointed out that higher workers' bargaining power, which leads to accelerating nominal wage growth, may be able to squeeze firms' mark-ups and thus raise the wage share. Later, Rowthorn (1977, p. 177) argued:

> The working class can shift distribution in its favour by fighting more vigorously for higher wages, although the cost of such militancy is a faster rate of inflation, as capitalists try, with only partial success to protect themselves by raising prices.

Sylos-Labini (1979) has provided some support for Kalecki's and Rowthorn's views that trade union bargaining power may have an impact on the mark-up and hence on income distribution. Empirically, he has found an only partial pass through of changes in unit costs, in particular unit labour costs, to prices for manufacturing industries in several countries. Sylos-Labini (1979) provides the following explanation: It can be assumed that output prices and nominal wage rates and their respective growth rates within a sector or industry are uniform, but labour productivity and labour productivity growth amongst firms differ, as do therefore their mark-ups in pricing. The dominant and price determining firm is assumed to have the highest or at least an above average growth rate of labour productivity. An increase in the uniform nominal wage rate may therefore be shifted to prices completely by this price leading firm. However, other firms with lower productivity growth and higher unit labour cost growth than the price leader cannot completely shift their higher unit labour cost growth to prices, in order to remain competitive with the new ruling price being set by the price leader. The followers' mark-ups and hence the average mark-up of the industry will therefore be squeezed. For the industry as a whole on average, nominal unit labour cost growth will exceed output price inflation, and functional income distribution will shift in favour of wages. In the reverse case, when workers' and trade unions' bargaining power is weak and uniform nominal wages or nominal wage growth decline, the price setting firm will only have to adjust prices according to the lower productivity growth of its competitors and will hence be able to raise its mark-up.[2] Average nominal unit labour cost growth will fall short of average output price inflation in this case. The average mark-up of the industry will rise, and income will be re-distributed from wages to profits. Stockhammer et al. (2009, 2011) have reported empirical evidence for the partial adjustment of output price inflation to changes in nominal unit labour cost growth for the Eurozone and Germany. Onaran et al. (2011) find similar results for the USA, as do Onaran and Galanis (2014) for several G20 countries and Onaran and Obst (2016) for 15 EU countries.

In post-Keynesian macroeconomics, we find, basically, two ways of modelling the relationship between distributional conflict and inflation. A tradition going back to Marglin (1984a) and Dutt (1987) has presented models in which inconsistent distributional claims of firms and workers, which sum up to more than output/income, generate stable inflation at any level of employment. If workers' distributional claims are positively affected by the employment level, and hence negatively by the unemployment rate, this gives rise to a stable Phillips curve,[3] in which higher employment and lower unemployment are related to a higher rate of inflation and a higher wage share, as we will show below. However, the Robinsonian inflation barrier, in the sense of a level of employment at which inflation rates start rising, even without a further increase in employment, or a decrease in unemployment, disappears in this approach. Modern versions of such models can be found, for example, in Blecker and Setterfield (2019, Chapter 5), Lavoie (2014, Chapter 8) and Setterfield (2009a).

An alternative approach, deriving a short-run inflation barrier in the Robinsonian sense, with rising rates of inflation at a certain level of employment or unemployment, has been put forward by myself (Hein 2006a, 2008, Chapter 16) and by Stockhammer (2008), and then jointly in Hein and Stockhammer (2009a, 2010), as well as in Hein and Stockhammer (2009b, 2011b) for didactic purposes. Again assuming that the workers' distributional claims are positively related to employment, for given institutional environments regarding the goods market, the labour market and the social benefit system, which co-determine the distributional claims of firms and workers, these models generate only one level of employment at which inflation remains constant, which is called the 'stable inflation rate of employment' (SIRE). This is the level at which distributional claims of workers and firms are consistent with each other and thus sum up to total output/income. The SIRE is thus viewed as an inflation barrier for employment: Whenever employment rises above, inflation rates will rise together with the wage share; whenever it falls below, inflation rates will fall, as will the wage share.[4] This short-run behaviour of inflation has some similarities with the NAIRU theory as a core of the NCM, as put forward in the three equations model by Carlin Soskice (2009, 2015, Chapters 1–3).[5] However, as will be seen below, there are major differences between the post-Keynesian view of the inflation barrier and the NAIRU in the NCM. First, any deviations from the inflation barrier (SIRE, NAIRU) in the post-Keynesian model have distributional effects, between capital and labour and also between creditors and debtors, with further effects on aggregate demand and employment, which are absent in the NCM. Second, unlike the NCM, the inflation barrier (SIRE, NAIRU) is not viewed as a strong attractor (Sawyer 2002), neither by real balance effects nor by central bank interest rate policies. Third, the inflation barrier (SIRE, NAIRU) itself is affected by aggregate demand, output and employment through various channels and thus becomes endogenous with respect to the latter, and hence also to macroeconomic policies, at least in the medium or long run. Therefore, according to this approach, in empirical and econometric work there will be severe difficulties in finding a definite inflation barrier, SIRE or NAIRU, which is independent of aggregate demand and actual employment.[6]

In terms of the empirical predictions, the two post-Keynesian ways of modelling the relationship between distributional conflict and inflation might hence come to similar conclusions. The institutional environment together with the level of employment will affect distributional claims and thus inflation. With a given institutional environment, we should therefore expect that higher (lower) employment rates should be associated with higher (lower) inflation rates. Tendencies towards acceleration/deceleration of inflation at certain levels of employment/unemployment in the Hein and Stockhammer view may then be softened or even cancelled out by endogeneity processes, as we will show below.

The following models will present these post-Keynesian views on distribution conflict, inflation and employment. We will again start with a closed economy without government economic activity, that is, without government expenditures and taxation. First, we will examine the relationship between conflicting claims, employment, inflation and distribution between labour and capital. Here, we will outline the two post-Keynesian views on the matter. Then we will move on with the one based on Hein and Stockhammer (2009b, 2010, 2011b) for reasons to be specified in that section. We will take a look at the effects of changing inflation rates on distribution between rentiers as the creditors and firms as the debtors in our model. The next step will then integrate variations in inflation and the associated re-distribution of income into the closed economy macroeconomic model without a government, as intro-duced in Chapter 4. In this context, we will also examine the potentials and the limits of an inflation-targeting central bank, as proposed by the NCM, both in the short run with respect to stabilising the economy around the inflation barrier (SIRE, NAIRU) and beyond the short run with respect to the endogeneity of the inflation barrier (SIRE, NAIRU). In the next steps, we will then, following the procedure in Chapter 4, first introduce government expenditures and taxation and examine fiscal policies as a potential stabiliser of the system around the SIRE. In the next step, we will turn towards an open economy version of the model, including exports and imports and their determinants. Again, the inflation generation process that gives rise to a SIRE will be examined and then linked with the income generating process in the open economy. Finally, in this chapter, we will review some further channels of endogeneity of the distribution claims equilibrium, generating a SIRE, with respect to the goods market equilibrium determined by aggregate demand, apart from the endogeneity with respect to some macroeconomic policy tools and the real exchange rate discussed before.

While in Chapter 4, we focussed on a goods market equilibrium determined by short-run quantity adjustments, where we kept prices and thus also inflation expectations constant; in the current chapter we will now make use of different runs or periods, as already indicated above. Again, we will assume a short run, containing within-period quantity adjustments in the goods market with output and supply adjusting to demand, generating a temporary goods market equilibrium. This supposes that there is always some spare capacity, which can be mobilised in order to satisfy demand, both with respect to the labour force and to the capital stock inherited from the past. Of course, for this short run, we assume, as in Chapter 4, that the stocks of capital, as well as financial assets and liabilities are each given from past development. Furthermore, in this chapter, we will now assume that inflation expectations are given for this short period from workers' and capitalists' experience of the previous period, too. However, actual inflation generated within the short period may not coincide with inflation expectations. In this case, at least in the models proposed by Hein (2006a), Stockhammer (2008) and Hein and Stockhammer (2009a, 2009b, 2010, 2011b), inflation expectations will adapt from one short period to another – but, somewhat unrealistically, we still assume that capital and financial stocks do not change, in order to focus on the dynamics generated by adaptive inflation expectations only. Since inflation in these models is driven by distribution conflict, constant inflation will only emerge when we have reached a distribution equilibrium, in which the distributional claims of capital and labour are consistent with each other, taking into account the claims of other actors, the rentiers, governments and the foreign sector where appropriate. Furthermore, we will touch upon some persistence mechanisms, which may arise after several periods, that is, in the medium or long run, without systematically discussing capital and financial stock dynamics. In this sense, also this chapter stays in the realm of short-run macroeconomics – that is, assuming given capital and financial stocks.

5.2 MODELLING CONFLICT INFLATION AND INCOME DISTRIBUTION BETWEEN CAPITAL AND LABOUR IN A CLOSED ECONOMY WITHOUT A GOVERNMENT

We will start by modelling inflation for a closed private economy, as introduced in Sections 4.2–4.3. A single homogenous good is produced with homogenous direct labour and a fixed coefficients technology using a non-depreciating capital stock, which is financed in the long term by credit and accumulated retained earnings. Depreciations of the capital stock and overhead labour costs can thus be ignored again, and firms set prices (p) in oligopolistic markets by marking up (m) unit direct labour costs, the ratio of the nominal wage rate (w) and labour productivity (y). As explained in Chapter 4, the mark-up may be affected by overhead costs, in our model in particular by interest costs and hence the interest rate (i):

$$p = \left[1 + m(i)\right]\frac{w}{y}, \quad m > 0, \frac{\partial m}{\partial i} \geq 0. \tag{5.1}$$

By definition, the rate of price inflation is thus composed of the rate of growth of the mark-up, the rate of growth of unit direct labour costs, which itself is given as the growth rate of the nominal wage rate minus the growth rate of labour productivity:

$$\hat{p} = \left(\widehat{1+m}\right) + \hat{w} - \hat{y}. \tag{5.2}$$

Since our model is a short-run model, in what follows we assume labour productivity to be constant and hence $\hat{y} = 0$. However, the following arguments and results can easily be extended to include productivity growth, too. Functional income distribution in our model economy can be derived from the pricing equation (5.1). The wage share (Ω) is given as the share of wages (W) in national income (pY), which is equal to the ratio of the real wage rate ($w_r = w/p$) to labour productivity. The profit share is the share of gross profits (Π), including retained earnings, dividends, interest and rent, in national income ($h = 1 - \Omega$). Each share is uniquely determined by the mark-up:

$$\Omega = \frac{W}{pY} = \frac{w}{py} = \frac{w_r}{y} = \frac{1}{1+m}, \tag{5.3}$$

$$h = \frac{\Pi}{pY} = 1 - \Omega = 1 - \frac{w}{py} = 1 - \frac{w_r}{y} = \frac{m}{1+m}. \tag{5.4}$$

For the growth rate of the wage share we obtain from equation (5.3):

$$\hat{\Omega} = \hat{w} - \hat{p} - \hat{y}. \tag{5.5}$$

With a constant technology in the short run and hence zero productivity growth, the wage share rises (falls) whenever wage inflation exceeds (falls short of) price inflation, which means that also the real wage rate will rise (fall). As can be seen in equation (5.2) this is only possible if the mark-up falls (rises). Therefore, in order to deal with wage inflation, price inflation and income distribution, we have to treat the mark-up as a variable, too. One way will be to view the mark-up in equation (5.1) and the related wage and profit shares in equations (5.3) and (5.4) as firms' targets, which may not necessarily be realised at the end of the short period.

As indicated in the introduction, in post-Keynesian macroeconomics we find, basically, two principal ways of dealing with distribution conflict and inflation, and we will now outline and assess them in turn. We will assume that workers and firms have target income shares, expressed as target wage shares each. Workers have control over nominal wage growth in the labour market in order to reach their target wage share, and firms use active price setting – and hence price inflation – in the goods markets in order to reach their target. Workers' wage setting power in the labour market is constrained by the competition amongst workers for the existing jobs. On the one hand, this is affected by the structure and the institutions of the labour market allowing workers to organise and limit competition amongst themselves (union density, wage bargaining coverage, wage bargaining co-ordination, employment protection legislation) and by government interventions and the social benefit system setting a minimum floor to market wages (minimum wage legislation, unemployment benefits). On the other hand, the wage setting power of workers is related to the level of employment and unemployment, or to their rates of change, assuming that low (or falling) unemployment rates limit the competition amongst workers and put them in a better bargaining position vis-à-vis firms. Unemployment thus has the function of restricting workers' distribution claims through containing their bargaining power (Kalecki 1971, pp. 156–64). Firms' price setting power is affected by the well-known factors determining the mark-up in their pricing, in particular the degree of price competition amongst firms in the goods market (degree of market concentration, relevance of price competition, successful product differentiation, marketing), but potentially also by overhead costs, particularly by interest costs and hence the interest rate in our model.

5.2.1   The Blecker, Setterfield and Lavoie Approach

The first post-Keynesian approach towards distribution conflict and inflation can be presented following the elaborations in the textbooks by Blecker and Setterfield (2019, Chapter 5) and Lavoie (2014, Chapter 8). Similar presentations can also be found in Dutt (1987) and Cassetti (2003), based on Kaleckian distribution and growth models, and in the macroeconomic models by Setterfield (2006, 2009a), amongst others. According to this approach, nominal wage growth in the labour market can be determined as follows:[7]

$$\hat{w}_t = \varphi_1\left(\Omega_W^T - \Omega_{t-1}\right) + \varphi_2\hat{p}_{t-1}, \quad \varphi_1 > 0, 1 \geq \varphi_2 \geq 0. \tag{5.6}$$

Nominal wage growth will thus be positive (negative), whenever workers' target wage share (Ω_W^T) exceeds (undercuts) the realised wage share in the previous period, taking into account the past period's rate of price inflation.[8] The coefficient φ_1 indicates workers' and trade unions' responses to deviations from their distribution targets, and it is affected by their bargaining power and their conflict orientation. The coefficient φ_2 indicates the response of nominal wage growth to past and currently expected price inflation. As will be seen below, what is important for the result of the basic model is the assumption that this coefficient, which Lavoie (2014, p. 550) calls 'the rate of price "indexation"', is $\varphi_2 < 1$.

In my view, the assumption $\varphi_2 < 1$ lacks some plausibility, and it also contradicts my experience from the early 2000s in advising German trade unions in the metal sector prior to the wage bargaining rounds. If the trade unions feel that the past period wage share falls short of their target wage share, and they hence would like to raise the wage share in the current period, they know from equation (5.5) that nominal wage growth has to exceed expected inflation (as well as expected productivity growth if this were positive). If we assume adaptive expectations for the sake of simplicity in a Keynesian world dominated by fundamental uncertainty, as also Blecker and Setterfield (2019, Chapter 5) and Lavoie (2014, Chapter 8) do, inflation expectations for the current period should be equal to the past period's inflation $(p_t^e = p_{t-1})$. Therefore, the past period's inflation should thus be fully taken into account when pushing for nominal wage increases in the current period in order to raise the wage share. In other words, what trade unions usually try to do, at least, is to protect the purchasing power of nominal wages by demanding compensation for (expected) inflation. Furthermore, they usually ask for their share in productivity growth (which is zero in our model), in order to protect the wage share. Finally, particularly if they are in a strong bargaining position, they demand re-distribution and hence an increase in the wage share, represented by the term $\varphi_1\left(\Omega_W^T - \Omega_{t-1}\right)$ in equation (5.6). Assuming $\varphi_2 < 1$ is thus tantamount to believing that workers and trade unions systematically, period by period, underestimate price inflation, which is not very convincing. Of course, trade unions could be too weak to obtain nominal wage increases in line with or exceeding expected inflation. But this should then be integrated into the model by making the target wage share dependent on workers' and trade unions' bargaining power and not by implying some systematic inflation illusion.

But let us return to Blecker and Setterfield (2019, Chapter 5) and Lavoie (2014, Chapter 8). The growth rate of prices set by firms and hence the rate of price inflation is conceived as:

$$\hat{p}_t = \pi_1\left(\Omega_{t-1} - \Omega_F^T\right) + \pi_2\hat{w}_t, \quad \pi_1 > 0, 1 \geq \pi_2 \geq 0. \tag{5.7}$$

Price inflation will thus be positive (negative) if the firms' target wage share (Ω_F^T) falls short of (exceeds) the previous period's wage share, taking into account current period's wage inflation, which Lavoie (2014, p. 550) calls 'wage indexation'. The first term indicates firms' response to deviations from their distribution targets, and it is affected by firms' price setting power in the goods market. Similar to 'price indexation' in equation (5.6), it is assumed that usually wage indexation is incomplete, hence $\pi_2 < 1$. Again the assumption $\pi_2 < 1$ is difficult to accept, because if firms feel that they have to lower the current wage share and raise their profit share, because the past period's wage share has exceeded their target and the profit share has fallen short of target, they know from equation (5.5) that price inflation has to exceed wage inflation (assuming away productivity growth). Therefore, why should wage inflation only partially enter price inflation? Assuming $\pi_2 < 1$ would thus need some further explanation or justification as well.

However, let us now follow Blecker and Setterfield (2019, Chapter 5) and Lavoie (2014, Chapter 8) and assume that $\varphi_2 < 1$ and $\pi_2 < 1$. In equilibrium, the wage share should be constant over time ($\Omega_t = \Omega_{t-1}$), and hence we need $\hat{\Omega} = 0$. From equation (5.5), assuming $\hat{y} = 0$, equilibrium thus requires:

$$\hat{p}_t = \hat{w}_t = \hat{p}_{t-1} = \hat{w}_{t-1}. \tag{5.8}$$

Applying this condition to equations (5.6) and (5.7) yields equilibrium price and wage inflation, as well as the equilibrium wage share:

$$\hat{p}^* = \hat{w}^* = \frac{\varphi_1\pi_1\left(\Omega_W^T - \Omega_F^T\right)}{\varphi_1\left(1 - \pi_2\right) + \pi_1\left(1 - \varphi_2\right)}, \tag{5.9}$$

$$\Omega^* = \frac{\dfrac{\varphi_1\Omega_W^T}{1 - \varphi_2} + \dfrac{\pi_1\Omega_F^T}{1 - \pi_2}}{\dfrac{\varphi_1}{1 - \varphi_2} + \dfrac{\pi_1}{1 - \pi_2}}. \tag{5.10}$$

In a simplified case with $\varphi_2 = 0$ and $\pi_2 = 0$ this equilibrium would boil down to:

$$\hat{p}^* = \hat{w}^* = \frac{\varphi_1\pi_1\left(\Omega_W^T - \Omega_F^T\right)}{\varphi_1 + \pi_1}, \tag{5.11}$$

$$\Omega^* = \frac{\varphi_1 \Omega_W^T + \pi_1 \Omega_F^T}{\varphi_1 + \pi_1}. \tag{5.12}$$

If workers' target wage share exceeds the firms' target, positive equilibrium inflation will emerge, and neither group will reach its distribution target. The equilibrium wage share will be in between the two targets. Inflation thus permanently reconciles the diverging distribution targets. This is shown in Figure 5.1. In the opposite case, if the workers' target falls short of the firms' target, we should see a negative equilibrium inflation rate and hence continuously falling prices.

But let us further discuss the case in which $\Omega_W^T - \Omega_F^T > 0$. A larger gap between the targets will generate a higher equilibrium inflation rate, as can easily be seen in equations (5.9) or (5.11). The same is true for stronger responses to the deviations from targets, that is, higher values for φ_1, π_1:

$$\frac{\partial \hat{p}^*}{\partial \varphi_1} = \frac{\pi_1^2 \left(\Omega_W^T - \Omega_F^T \right)}{\left(\varphi_1 + \pi_1 \right)^2} > 0, \tag{5.11a}$$

$$\frac{\partial \hat{p}^*}{\partial \pi_1} = \frac{\varphi_1^2 \left(\Omega_W^T - \Omega_F^T \right)}{\left(\varphi_1 + \pi_1 \right)^2} > 0. \tag{5.11b}$$

A stronger response of workers and trade unions to deviations from their wage share targets will raise the equilibrium wage share, whereas as a stronger response of firms to deviations from their target will lower the equilibrium wage share:

$$\frac{\partial \Omega^*}{\partial \varphi_1} = \frac{\pi_1 \left(\Omega_W^T - \Omega_F^T \right)}{\left(\varphi_1 + \pi_1 \right)^2} > 0, \tag{5.12a}$$

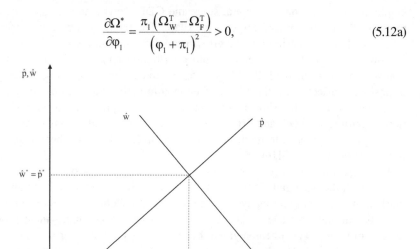

Figure 5.1   Conflicting claims equilibrium inflation in the Blecker, Setterfield and Lavoie approach

$$\frac{\partial \Omega^*}{\partial \pi_1} = \frac{-\varphi_1 \left(\Omega_W^T - \Omega_F^T \right)}{\left(\varphi_1 + \pi_1 \right)^2} < 0. \tag{5.12b}$$

As can be seen in equation (5.9), higher values of the 'indexation' indicators (φ_2, π_2) raise equilibrium inflation. And from equation (5.10), taking into account equations (5.12a) and (5.12b) it becomes clear that an increase in φ_2 raises the equilibrium wage share, whereas a higher π_2 lowers it.

Equations (5.9) and (5.10) also make clear that as soon as workers and firms fully take into account past price inflation when setting nominal wages and current wage inflation when setting prices, no equilibrium inflation and no equilibrium wage share can be derived any more. If $\varphi_2 = 1$ and (or) $\pi_2 = 1$, equations (5.9) and (5.10) have no solutions anymore. From equations (5.6) and (5.7) we can see that in this case the equilibrium condition in (5.8) can only be fulfilled if the distribution targets of workers and firms match, that is, only if $\Omega_{t-1} = \Omega_W^T = \Omega_F^T$. If this holds, wage and price inflation will remain constant at the past period's rate. We will see in the next section that this will be the main message of the Hein and Stockhammer approach.

But let us link distribution conflict and inflation to employment/unemployment in the Blecker, Setterfield and Lavoie approach before. Lavoie (2014, Chapter 8) is reluctant to directly base inflation on employment or unemployment levels, via workers' and/or firms' target wage shares, and rather prefers to make the workers' real wage or wage share target a positive function of the growth rate of the employment rate e = N/L, with N representing employment and L the labour force, composed of employed and unemployed labour L = N + U. The growth rate of the employment rate is hence given as $\hat{e} = \hat{N} - \hat{L} = g - g_n$, with employment growth, in the absence of productivity growth, given by the growth rate of the capital stock and of GDP (g), and labour force growth as the long-run maximum or the 'natural rate of growth' (g_n). With a constant labour force and hence $\hat{L} = g_n = 0$, the growth rate of the employment rate is equal to capital stock and GDP growth, and the latter can then be taken to positively affect workers' target wage share. The interaction between distribution targets, inflation, effective distribution and growth can then be examined (see also Cassetti 2003).

However, since this will lead us into distribution and growth theory, we rather follow Blecker and Setterfield (2019, Chapter 5.2.3) and assume that workers' target wage share is positively affected by the levels of economic activity and employment. We will adapt their model here for the short-run framework we have presented so far.[9] The basic assumptions regarding workers' and firms' wage share targets are also consistent with the Hein and Stockhammer approach to be discussed below; in fact they have been taken from Hein and Stockhammer (2010, 2011b).

The target wage share of workers ($\Omega_W^T = 1 - h_W^T$), implying also a target profit share of workers (h_W^T), on the one hand, depends on medium-run institutional circumstances of the labour market, the wage bargaining system and the social benefit system in general (union density, wage bargaining coverage, wage bargaining co-ordination, employment protection legislation, minimum wages, unemployment benefits, etc.). On the other hand, the workers' target wage share is affected by the rate of employment (e = N/L), and hence by the rate of unemployment (ue = U/L):

$$\Omega_W^T = 1 - h_W^T = \Omega_0 + \Omega_1 e, \quad 1 > \Omega_0 > 0, \Omega_1 \geq 0. \tag{5.13}$$

We can take the institutional environment to be constant in the short run. It is represented by both the constant Ω_0, as well as the coefficient Ω_1 indicating the response of the workers' and the trade unions' wage share target to the employment rate. Employment and unemployment will vary in the short run, depending on effective demand in the goods market, as we will discuss further below. With a given institutional environment, lower unemployment improves workers' or trade unions' bargaining power and thus their target wage share. Here we assume that workers and labour unions do not consider inflationary macroeconomic effects of their nominal wage demands and potentially restrictive monetary policy reactions, or negative effects on exports in an open economy. Therefore, neither coordination between trade unions in different firms or industries with an eye to avoiding macroeconomic externalities of wage bargaining is supposed, nor between wage bargaining parties and monetary policy.

The target wage share of firms ($\Omega_F^T = 1 - h_F^T$), or their target gross profit share (h_F^T), which covers retained earnings and interest payments to rentiers, is given by mark-up pricing on unit labour costs in incompletely competitive goods markets. For the short run, we can assume the firms' target profit and wage shares to be constant up to full capacity output.

$$h_F^T = 1 - \Omega_F^T = h_0, \quad 1 > h_0 > 0. \tag{5.14}$$

Plugging the respective target wage share functions (5.13) and (5.14) into equations (5.6) and (5.7) yields:

$$\hat{w}_t = \varphi_1\left(\Omega_0 + \Omega_1 e - \Omega_{t-1}\right) + \varphi_2 \hat{p}_{t-1}, \quad \varphi_1 > 0, 1 \geq \varphi_2 \geq 0, \tag{5.15}$$

$$\hat{p}_t = \pi_1\left(\Omega_{t-1} - 1 + h_0\right) + \pi_2 \hat{w}_t, \quad \pi_1 > 0, 1 \geq \pi_2 \geq 0. \tag{5.16}$$

Applying the equilibrium condition in equation (5.8) to equations (5.15) and (5.16) provides equilibrium wage and price inflation, as well as the equilibrium wage share:

$$\hat{p}^* = \hat{w}^* = \frac{\varphi_1 \pi_1 \left(\Omega_0 + \Omega_1 e + h_0 - 1\right)}{\varphi_1\left(1 - \pi_2\right) + \pi_1\left(1 - \varphi_2\right)}, \tag{5.17}$$

$$\Omega^* = \frac{\dfrac{\varphi_1}{1-\varphi_2}\left(\Omega_0 + \Omega_1 e\right) + \dfrac{\pi_1}{1-\pi_2}\left(1 - h_0\right)}{\dfrac{\varphi_1}{1-\varphi_2} + \dfrac{\pi_1}{1-\pi_2}}. \tag{5.18}$$

Figure 5.2 presents the workers' and the firms' target wage shares, as well as the equilibrium wage share in the upper panel and equilibrium wage and price inflation in the lower panel, each as a function of the employment rate. At the employment rate e_0, the distribution targets of workers and firms are consistent and equilibrium wage and price inflation are zero. Hence, we have constant nominal wage rates and constant prices, as can also be seen in equation (5.17). At employment rates above e_0, when workers' target wage shares exceed firms' target wage shares, a higher employment rate, and thus higher bargaining power of workers and trade unions, leads to higher equilibrium price and wage inflation, as well as to a higher wage share. This is also obvious from equations (5.17) and (5.18). We thus obtain the well-known Phillips curve. In this post-Keynesian framework, however, the increase in equilibrium inflation associated with a lower unemployment rate is also accompanied by an increase in the equilibrium wage share. At employment rates below e_0 workers' target wage shares fall short of the firms' target, equilibrium inflation rates will be negative and we will see falling prices, as can also be derived from equation (5.17).

An improved institutional environment in favour of workers and trade unions (higher union density, higher wage bargaining coverage, better wage bargaining co-ordination, more employment protection legislation, higher minimum wages, higher unemployment benefits, etc.) will raise the coefficients Ω_0 and Ω_1 in the workers' target wage share function and thus also equilibrium inflation and the equilibrium wage share for a given level of employment, as can be seen in equations (5.17) and (5.18). In Figure 5.2, this would mean an upward shift and a counter-clockwise rotation of the workers' target wage share curve, the equilibrium wage share curve and the equilibrium wage and price inflation curve, that is, the Phillips curve. A higher target mark-up of firms will mean an increase in the constant h_0 in the firms' target wage share function; it will also raise equilibrium inflation but lower the equilibrium wage share, as can be seen in equations (5.17) and (5.18). In Figure 5.2, this would mean a

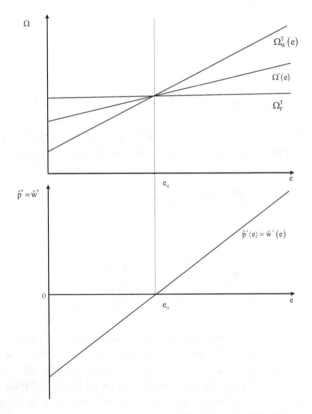

Figure 5.2   Conflicting claims, distribution and inflation in the Blecker and Setterfield approach

downward shift of the firms' target wage share curve and the equilibrium wage share curve, and an upward shift of the Phillips curve.

As already pointed out above, the smooth increase in equilibrium inflation with the employment rate depends on the incomplete 'indexation' of nominal wage growth and inflation, that is, on $\varphi_2 < 1$ and $\pi_2 < 1$. If we had $\varphi_2 = 1$ and $\pi_2 = 1$, equations (5.17) and (5.18) would have no solutions anymore. Inflation and the wage share would only be constant if the income claims of workers and firms were consistent, which means that $\Omega_0 + \Omega_1 e = 1 - h_0$ has to hold. The assumptions $\varphi_2 < 1$ and $\pi_2 < 1$ thus rule out an inflation barrier for the increase in employment beyond the level given by consistent income share claims. This will be the focus of the Hein and Stockhammer approach, which we will discuss next.

5.2.2   The Hein and Stockhammer Approach[10]

The alternative post-Keynesian approach to distribution conflict and inflation, based on the works by Hein (2006a, 2008, Chapter 16), Stockhammer (2008) and then Hein and Stockhammer (2009b, 2010, 2011b), rather derives an inflation barrier to the employment rate by focussing on the inclusion of plausible inflation expectations.[11] The basic model set up regarding target wages shares of workers and firms is the same as in the previous approach.

Workers' target wage is determined as in equation (5.13) by socio-institutional factors of the labour market, the wage bargaining system and the social benefit system, on the one hand, and by the employment rate, on the other hand, as explained above. The firms' target wage share is given as in equation (5.14) by their target profit share, with the latter being determined by the degree of price competition in the goods market and potentially by overhead costs, as also explained above. These income claims will be consistent if the two targets are consistent and the target wage shares of workers and firms are the same, or, which is equivalent, if the target wage share of workers and the target profit share of firms sum up to unity:

$$\Omega_W^T = \Omega_F^T \Rightarrow \Omega_W^T = 1 - h_F^T \Rightarrow \Omega_W^T + h_F^T = 1. \tag{5.19}$$

Using equations (5.13) and (5.14), equation (5.19) implies:

$$h_0 + \Omega_0 + \Omega_1 e^N = 1. \tag{5.20}$$

We thus obtain a 'consistent claims rate of employment', which, as we will explain below, can be viewed as a SIRE (e^N):

$$e^N = \frac{1 - h_0 - \Omega_0}{\Omega_1}. \tag{5.21}$$

This SIRE in our model can be viewed as the counterpart to a 'non-accelerating inflation rate of unemployment' (the NAIRU), which is given as $u^N = 1 - e^N$. Of course, the wage share at the SIRE will be equal to the target wage shares of workers, as well as to the target wage share of firms:

$$\Omega^N = \Omega_W^T = \Omega_F^T = \Omega_0 + \Omega_1 e^N = 1 - h_0. \tag{5.22}$$

Any deviation of the employment rate from the SIRE will mean inconsistent income claims. If $e > e^N$, the income claims will exceed the output to be distributed, that is, $\Omega_W^T + h_F^T > 1$. If $e < e^N$, income claims will fall short of the output to be distributed, that is, $\Omega_W^T + h_F^T < 1$. As Hein and Stockhammer (2009b, 2010, 2011b) point out, in the first case, an unexpected rise in inflation will make claims temporarily consistent with each other. In the second case, an unexpected fall in inflation will have the same effect. This can be shown as follows, starting with the following wage inflation equation – and still assuming productivity growth to be zero:

$$\hat{w}_t = \omega\left(e_t - e^N\right) + \hat{p}_{t-1}, \qquad \omega \ge 0. \tag{5.23}$$

In the case of $e > e^N$, workers and trade unions will raise nominal wage growth above expected inflation in order to obtain a target wage share which is higher than the wage share Ω^N at e^N. Assuming adaptive expectations, expected inflation in period t is given by inflation in period $t-1$, that is, $\hat{p}_t^e = \hat{p}_{t-1}$. The coefficient ω in equation (5.23) is positively related with the coefficient Ω_1 in the workers' target wage share equation (5.13) and indicates the required rise in wage inflation above expected price inflation, in order to reach the target wage share at the employment rate $e > e^N$. Since firms try to protect their constant target profit share from equation (5.14), higher wage inflation will also trigger higher price inflation in the goods market:

$$\hat{p}_t = \vartheta\omega\left(e_t - e^N\right) + \hat{p}_{t-1}, \qquad 1 \ge \vartheta \ge 0. \tag{5.24}$$

Inflation will hence rise compared to inflation expectations given by the previous period's inflation. The result is thus unexpected inflation ($\hat{p}^u$), which is the difference between inflation in the current period and the previous one:

$$\hat{p}_t^u = \hat{p}_t - \hat{p}_{t-1} = \vartheta\omega\left(e_t - e^N\right). \tag{5.25}$$

The coefficient ϑ in equations (5.24) and (5.25) can be seen as a pass-through factor for the increase in nominal unit labour cost growth to inflation. In the simplest case, in which all firms producing the single good in our model economy are operating with the same technology and thus have the same labour productivity and are exposed to the same increase in nominal wage growth, we can expect that the increase in nominal wage growth will be completely passed through to inflation; we will hence have $\vartheta = 1$. In this case, which was assumed in Hein (2006a, 2008, Chapter 16), wage and price inflation will be the same, firms will always be able to achieve their target profit share and workers' re-distribution attempts will be completely frustrated. This is also the case in the NCM model by Carlin and Soskice (2009, 2015).

However, as soon as we have some heterogeneity within the firm sector, firms will be faced with different growth rates of nominal unit labour costs. They may be operating with different technologies and/or different efficiencies of management. Alternatively, they may face firm or region specific increases in nominal wage growth, because there is no co-ordination of wage bargaining amongst workers and trade unions. In this case, only the firm with the lowest unit labour cost growth will be able to completely pass-through the increase in its unit labour costs to prices. The firms with higher nominal unit labour cost growth will have to follow the price-leading firm in order to protect market shares and will thus not be able to completely pass-through their higher nominal unit labour cost growth to price inflation. Therefore, for the firm sector as a whole we will have $\vartheta < 1$. This is the case assumed in Hein and Stockhammer (2009b, 2010, 2011b).

If $e > e^N$, although inflation is rising compared to previous periods' inflation and we will thus have unexpected inflation, price inflation will be lower than wage inflation, and the firm sector as a whole will not be able to protect its target profit share. We will thus see a falling profit share associated with unexpected inflation. The wage share will be rising but will not reach the workers' target.

If $e < e^N$, workers' bargaining power will be too weak to achieve nominal wage growth in line with expected inflation. This implies that due to low bargaining power, workers' target wage share is lower than the firms' target and, of course, also lower than Ω^N at e^N. Firms will thus be faced with nominal wage growth lower than expected inflation, which will then be partially passed through to actual inflation. We will thus see unexpected disinflation associated with rising profit shares and falling wage shares.

From equations (5.24) and (5.25) it is also clear that inflation will be constant and unexpected inflation will be zero, if the employment rate is equal to the SIRE, hence $e = e^N$. However, in the case $e \neq e^N$, we may also have constant inflation and zero unexpected inflation, if either workers' target wage share does not respond to a deviation of the employment rate from the SIRE, and hence $\omega = 0$, or if firms are unable to pass-through an increase in wage inflation to price inflation at all, and thus $\vartheta = 0$. In the first case, workers' target wage share is adjusted to the firms' target wage share, which would then be realised, of course. In the second case, the wage share would rise up to the workers' target and firms would be frustrated.

But let us come back to the cases in which ω and ϑ are both positive. With employment rates above e^N, we will thus see rising inflation, that is, positive unexpected inflation, a rising wage share and a falling profit share. With employment rates below e^N, we will observe falling inflation, that is, unexpected disinflation, a falling wage share and a rising profit share. With any deviation of the employment rate from e^N and thus mutually inconsistent wage share targets of workers and profit share targets of firms, unexpected inflation thus makes realised wage and profit shares temporarily consistent. Equation (5.20) becomes:

$$h_0 - h_2 \hat{p}^u + \Omega_0 + \Omega_1 e - \Omega_2 \hat{p}^u = h_0 + \Omega_0 + \Omega_1 e - \left(h_2 + \Omega_2 \right) \hat{p}^u = 1,$$

$$0 < h_0, \Omega_0 < 1, 0 \leq h_2, \Omega_1, \Omega_2.$$

(5.26)

Unexpected inflation can thus also be written as:

$$\hat{p}^u = \frac{h_0 + \Omega_0 + \Omega_1 e - 1}{h_2 + \Omega_2}.$$

(5.27)

If employment exceeds the SIRE, positive unexpected inflation is required, and if employment falls short of the SIRE, negative unexpected inflation, that is, unexpected disinflation, is required. The temporarily realised wage and profit shares thus become:

$$\Omega = \Omega_W^T - \Omega_2 \hat{p}^u = \Omega_0 + \Omega_1 e - \Omega_2 \hat{p}^u, \quad 1 > \Omega_0 > 0, \Omega_1, \Omega_2 \geq 0,$$

(5.28)

$$h = h_F^T - h_2 \hat{p}^u = h_0 - h_2 \hat{p}^u, \quad 1 > h_0 > 0, \ h_2 \geq 0.$$

(5.29)

The coefficients h_2 and Ω_2 indicate the effectiveness of firms and workers, respectively, to achieve their targets, and they are determined by the pass-through coefficient ϑ in equation (5.24). The lower the value of h_2, the higher the pass-through of a change in wage inflation to price inflation and the closer is the actual profit share to the firms' target profit share. The lower the value of Ω_2, the lower the pass through of a change in wage inflation to price inflation and the closer the actual wage share to the workers' target wage share. In the case of complete pass through of any increase in wage inflation to price inflation, we have $\vartheta=1$, $h_2=0$ and $\Omega_2 > 0$. Firms would thus always reach their target, while workers would not and would have to accept the full adjustment to make income shares temporarily consistent. In the case of no pass-through of an increase in wage inflation to price inflation, we have $\vartheta=0$, $\Omega_2 = 0$ and $h_2>0$. Workers would thus always reach their target, while firms would not and would have to accept the full adjustment to make income shares temporarily consistent. This can also be seen by plugging the value for $\hat{p}_t^u$ from equation (5.27) into equations (5.28) and (5.29):

$$\Omega = \frac{\left(\Omega_0 + \Omega_1 e\right) h_2 + \Omega_2 \left(1 - h_0\right)}{h_2 + \Omega_2},$$ (5.30)

$$h = \frac{h_0 \Omega_2 + h_2 \left(1 - \Omega_0 - \Omega_1 e\right)}{h_2 + \Omega_2}.$$ (5.31)

In equations (5.26)–(5.31) we treat the coefficients h_2 and Ω_2 as constants. Strictly speaking, this is only true for the first period when the employment rate deviates from the SIRE. With a partial pass-through ($1>\vartheta>0$), wage (dis-)inflation will exceed price (dis-)inflation, the wage share will move closer to the workers' target without reaching it, and Ω_2 will fall whereas h_2 will rise. In what follows we will not explicitly address this effect, which will only occur over several periods.

Figure 5.3 shows the target wage shares of workers from equation (5.13) and firms from equation (5.14), as well as the realised wage share from equation (5.30) as functions of the employment rate in the upper part, and the related unexpected inflation rate from equation (5.27) in the lower part. We show here unexpected inflation as a function of the employment rate and not the inflation rate, as in the usual Phillips curve. With positive unexpected inflation, the Phillips curve would shift up from period to period in employment rate-inflation space, whereas with unexpected disinflation, that is, negative unexpected inflation, the Phillips curve would shift downward from period to period. Distribution of income between firms and wage earners varies with the employment rate and hence with the level of economic activity, as does unexpected inflation. At the point of intersection of the target wage share curves of workers and firms, we have the SIRE (e^N); workers' and firms' targets are equal to the realised wage share and unexpected inflation is zero, that is, inflation rates are constant over time. Whenever employment exceeds the SIRE, and unemployment falls short of the NAIRU, inflation will accelerate because the sum of the income claims exceeds output/income, and unexpected inflation will arise, fuelling future inflation expectations. Simultaneously, with only a partial pass-through of wage inflation to price inflation, the wage share will rise without workers achieving their higher distribution targets. Whenever employment falls short of the SIRE, and unemployment thus exceeds the NAIRU, inflation will decelerate and with a partial pass-through of wage disinflation to price disinflation, the wage share will fall without reaching the workers' lower target.

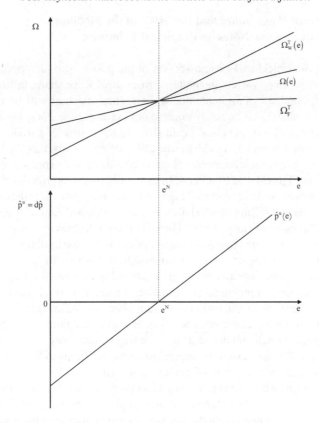

Figure 5.3 Conflicting claims, distribution and inflation in the Hein and Stockhammer approach

As already mentioned when discussing the Blecker and Setterfield approach, an improved institutional environment in favour of workers and trade unions (higher union density, higher wage bargaining coverage, better wage bargaining co-ordination, more employment protection legislation, higher minimum wages, higher unemployment benefits, etc.) will raise the coefficients Ω_0 and Ω_1 in the workers' target wage share function (5.13). This will lower the SIRE in equation (5.21), and for a given employment rate it will increase unexpected inflation in equation (5.27), as well as the realised wage share in equation (5.30), and, of course, it will simultaneously lower the realised profit share in equation (5.31). In Figure 5.3 this would mean an upward shift and a counter-clockwise rotation of the workers' target wage share curve, the realised wage share curve and the unexpected inflation curve. A higher target mark-up of firms will mean an increase in the constant h_0 in the firms' target wage share function (5.14). This will lower the SIRE in equation (5.21), for a given employment rate it will increase unexpected inflation in equation (5.27), it will lower the realised wage share in equation (5.30), and, of course, it will simultaneously increase the realised profit share in equation (5.31). In Figure 5.3 this would mean a downward shift of the firms' target wage share curve and in the realised wage share curve, as well as an upward shift of the unexpected inflation curve.

5.2.3   Pro-Cyclical Wage Share and the SIRE in the Medium to Long Run: Some Notes on Empirical Relevance

Both the Blecker, Setterfield and Lavoie version of the post-Keynesian approach, as well as the Hein and Stockhammer variant generate a pro-cyclical wage share; falling (rising) rates of unemployment, obtained in an economic upswing (downswing) will be associated with rising (falling) wage shares.[12] As already pointed out in Chapter 4, this is not in line with the empirical observations of a pro-cyclical profit share in the course of a trade cycle in several countries (Hein 2014a, Chapter 1, Stockhammer 2017b). Empirically, this can be explained by counter-cyclical unit overhead labour costs (Lavoie 2009b, 2014, Chapters 5–6), in particular, as we have shown in Figure 4.4 in Chapter 4. In the medium- to long-run development beyond the trade cycle, however, we have observed high and even rising rates of inflation accompanied by rising wage shares and falling profit shares in main developed capitalist economies in the course of the 1970s until the early 1980s. Then the reverse followed, that is, falling rates of inflation and falling wage shares in the course of the 1980s, at least until the crises of 2007–09 (Glyn 2006, Hein 2014a, Chapter 1, Stockhammer 2017b, Tridico 2017).

Our models thus display a positive short-run relationship between the wage share of direct labour, economic activity, employment and inflation, which, however, is not observable in the conventional wage share data of the national accounts, because the latter includes management salaries and hence overhead labour remuneration. However, medium- to long-run real world situations represented by national accounts data on wage shares may be consistent with what our model generates. But we have to be aware that these medium- to long-run developments are not only generated by variations of employment and unemployment rates, but also by those structural features which determine wage and profit share targets of firms and workers, as well as the means to reach these targets. With regard to firms' target income shares, these include those factors which determine the mark-up in firms' pricing in the goods market, like the degree of price competition, the firms' perception of workers' bargaining power, as well as persistent changes in overhead costs. With regard to workers' target income shares, those structural features of the labour market, the wage bargaining institutions and the social benefit system, which have an impact on workers' bargaining power, have to be considered. These include the employment protection legislation, union density, wage bargaining coverage, the degree of wage bargaining co-ordination, unemployment benefits replacement rate and duration, legal minimum wages, but also in an international framework the degree of openness of the economy with respect to trade and financial flows. Several studies have shown that the long-run falling trend in the wage share since the mid-1970s/early 1980s in mature capitalist economies has been caused by these, or a selection of these factors, amongst other causes.[13]

According to the Hein and Stockhammer (2010, 2011b) model, changes in these structural features will have an impact on the SIRE determined in equation (5.21) and in Figure 5.3, as explained in the previous section. It thus seems that this model generates similar results and implications as the mainstream NAIRU theory (Carlin and Soskice 2009, 2015, Chapter 2). Lowering workers' and trade unions' bargaining power through 'structural reforms' in the labour market and the social benefit system should thus increase the SIRE and reduce inflationary pressure, but also reduce the wage share. Of course, similar results with regard to the SIRE and inflationary pressure could be obtained by increasing price competition in the goods market or lowering overhead costs of firms – with dampening effects on the profit share. Whereas the distributive effects of structural reforms of the labour market and the social benefit system aimed at reducing workers' and trade unions' bargaining power seem to be well supported by the empirical literature, positive effects on long-run trends of employment rates or unemployment rates are not as clear.

First, as already mentioned above, econometric studies have had severe difficulties in finding a definite NAIRU (or SIRE), which is independent of aggregate demand and actual employment, as has been reviewed and pointed out by Cross (2014), Heimberger et al. (2017), Lang et al. (2020) and Stanley (2004), for example. Second, several empirical and econometric studies aiming at explaining international and/or intertemporal differences in long-run unemployment trends have had similar difficulties in uniquely relating these differences to structural features of the labour market and the social benefit system.[14] Usually, aggregate demand dynamics and macroeconomic policies have an important role to play when it comes to explaining long-run unemployment trends.[15]

As will be seen, these empirical findings are no surprise considering the post-Keynesian theory of the inflation barrier and the SIRE. Although structural features of the labour market, the social benefit system and the goods market have an impact on the SIRE, inflationary pressure and income distribution in the post-Keynesian approach, to be further developed in the next sections, there is no reason to believe that actual employment rates will automatically adjust towards the SIRE, or actual unemployment rates to the NAIRU. The latter can therefore not be seen as a strong attractor for medium-run unemployment rates, as Sawyer (2002) had already pointed out. Even the applications of macroeconomic policies, in particular inflation-targeting interest rate policies of the central bank, as recommended by the NCM, will not be able to adjust actual employment rates to the SIRE or actual unemployment rates to the NAIRU at any rate. Finally, demand determined employment rates, as well as macroeconomic policy interventions that are conducted in order to adjust employment towards the SIRE, will have an impact on the SIRE or the NAIRU. Hence, the SIRE or NAIRU is endogenous to aggregate demand and macroeconomic policies.

Therefore, in order to examine the relationship between distribution conflict, inflation, income distribution, aggregate demand and employment, we will continue in the next section by touching upon another distributional issue related to unexpected inflation, the distribution of income between creditors and debtors, or between rentiers and firms, before we then integrate the re-distributional processes accompanying unexpected inflation into the post-Keynesian macroeconomic models from Chapter 4.

5.3 UNEXPECTED INFLATION AND DISTRIBUTION BETWEEN RENTIERS AND FIRMS[16]

We are using the same basic private closed economy model as in Section 4.3 and assume that the capital stock of the firm sector is partly financed by accumulated retained earnings and partly by credit granted by rentiers, either directly or indirectly through the banking sector. Therefore, capital income or gross profits (Π) is split into retained profits of enterprise (Π_F) and rentiers' income (R), the firms' interest payments to rentiers' households:

$$\Pi = \Pi_F + R. \tag{5.32}$$

Using again i for the long-term nominal rate of interest paid on the stock of debt, we can define the long-term real interest rate for given inflation expectations ($\hat{p}^e$), the expected or the 'ex ante' real interest rate (i_r^e), as:

$$i_r^e = i - \hat{p}^e. \tag{5.33}$$

The actual or 'ex post' real interest rate (i_r) is furthermore affected by unexpected inflation ($\hat{p}^u$) and therefore becomes:

$$i_r = i - \hat{p} = i - (\hat{p}^e + \hat{p}^u) = i_r^e - \hat{p}^u. \tag{5.34}$$

Firms' payments to rentiers are given by the stock of corporate debt (B_F) at issue prices, or at face value, and the nominal rate of interest. Rentiers' nominal interest income (R) can be decomposed into a part compensating for the expected inflationary devaluation of the stock of nominal assets held by rentiers ($\hat{p}^e B_F$), and into expected real income determined by the 'ex ante' real rate of interest ($R_r^e = i_r^e B_F$):[17]

$$R = iB_F = (i_r^e + \hat{p}^e)B_F = i_r^e B_F + \hat{p}^e B_F = R_r^e + \hat{p}^e B_F. \tag{5.35}$$

Rentiers' 'real' ex post income (R_r) and firms' 'real' ex post interest payments are affected by unexpected inflation in the following way:

$$R_r = (i - \hat{p}^e - \hat{p}^u)B_F = (i_r^e - \hat{p}^u)B_F = i_r B_F = R_r^e - \hat{p}^u B_F. \tag{5.36}$$

Unexpected inflation therefore re-distributes real income between creditors and debtors and hence between rentiers and firms: Whenever there is positive unexpected inflation, real income payments of firms and hence real income received by rentiers is reduced, that is, the debtors gain and the creditors lose. With negative unexpected inflation, that is, unexpected disinflation, the reverse holds true. That is how real debt effects play out in our model.[18]

Summing up the post-Keynesian approach by Hein and Stockhammer (2010, 2011b) to the interaction of employment, inflation and distribution, we have the following results: Whenever employment deviates from the SIRE, and hence unemployment deviates from the NAIRU, positive or negative unexpected inflation and hence rising or falling rates of inflation will emerge together with re-distribution between capital and labour, on the one hand, and between firms and rentiers, on the other hand, as summarised in Table 5.1. The macroeconomic consequences of the distributional changes associated with unexpected inflation and

Table 5.1   *Inflation and distribution effects of deviations of the employment rate from the SIRE or of deviations of the unemployment rate from the NAIRU*

	$\hat{p}^u(e)$	$\Omega(e)$	$h(e)$	$\frac{\Pi_F}{\Pi}(e)$	$\frac{R}{\Pi}(e)$
$e > e^N$(SIRE) ue < NAIRU	+	+	−	+	−
$e = e^N$(SIRE) ue = NAIRU	0	0	0	0	0
$e < e^N$(SIRE) ue > NAIRU	−	−	+	−	+

the feedback effects on aggregate demand, output and employment/unemployment will be examined in the next section.

5.4 THE GOODS MARKET EQUILIBRIUM WITH DISTRIBUTION CONFLICT AND UNEXPECTED INFLATION IN A CLOSED ECONOMY WITHOUT A GOVERNMENT[19]

Integrating the distributional effects of conflict inflation into our model of Section 4.3, we can start with the saving and investment equations (4.14) and (4.15), as well as the goods market equilibrium (4.16), and rephrase them in real terms.[20] Saving, investment and income in real terms are the nominal values from Section 4.3 corrected for expected changes in the price level and hence for expected inflation. From the saving and investment functions in these real terms we can then derive a goods market equilibrium which would be realised if inflation expectation came true. Then we can examine the effects of unexpected inflation on saving, investment and the goods market equilibrium. The channels for these effects will be those developed above, that is, changes in wage and profit shares, on the one hand, and in the distribution of total profits between firms and rentiers via changes in the real interest rate, on the other hand.

Following our saving function from Section 4.3, saving in real terms (S_r) consists of retained earnings and saving out of rentiers' income. Workers are assumed not to save. Saving is thus determined by total profits, and hence the profit share (h) and real income (Y), the propensity to save out of rentiers' income (s_R), and rentiers' real income as a product of the real rate of interest (i_r) and the stock of corporate debt (B_F) granted by rentiers, either directly or via banks:

$$S_r = hY - (1 - s_R)i_r B_F, \quad 1 \geq s_R > 0. \tag{5.37}$$

Unexpected inflation will affect real saving thus via changes in the profit share and via changes in the real interest rate. As in Section 4.3, investment (I), now in real terms, is affected positively by autonomous investment (I_a), or 'animal spirits', and by an accelerator effect of real income, as well as negatively by real interest payments to rentiers, again as a product of the real interest rate and the stock of corporate debt:

$$I = I_a + \beta Y - \theta i_r B_F, \quad I_a, \beta, \theta \geq 0. \tag{5.38}$$

We assume that unexpected inflation per se will not affect autonomous investment or animal spirits, but it will have an impact on real investment through changes in the real interest rate. The goods market equilibrium in our model and the stability conditions are given as:

$$I = S_r, \tag{5.39}$$

$$\frac{\partial S_r}{\partial Y} > \frac{\partial I}{\partial Y} \Rightarrow h - \beta > 0. \tag{5.40}$$

From equations (5.37)–(5.39) we can now derive an 'ex ante' goods market equilibrium including the target or expected values for the profit share (h_0) and for the real interest rate (i_r^e)

in the saving and investment functions and solving for ex ante equilibrium income (Y^e), the equilibrium which would emerge if inflation expectations came true and unexpected inflation were zero:

$$Y^e = \frac{I_a + (1 - s_R - \theta) i_r^e B_F}{h_0 - \beta}.$$

(5.41)

The effect of changes in parameters, like animal spirits and autonomous investment, the propensity to save, the interest rate and the profit share, on this equilibrium have been analysed extensively in Section 4.3 and will not be repeated here. We will make use of some of these effects, regarding changes in the real interest rate and the profit share associated with unexpected inflation, as well as regarding changes in the interest rate triggered by monetary policy intervention, in the following analysis. But first, we have to relate the ex ante goods market equilibrium level of income to the corresponding employment rate.

With given labour productivity ($y = Y/N$) and a given labour force (L), the employment rate ($e = N/L$) is positively related to output and income in the following way:

$$e = \frac{N}{L} = \frac{N}{Y} \frac{Y}{L} = \frac{Y}{yL} = qY,$$

(5.42)

with $q = 1/(yL)$ as a constant, since y and L are assumed to be constant in the short run. Equations (5.41) and (5.42) thus imply the following ex ante goods market equilibrium rate of employment (e^e):

$$e^e = \frac{q\left[I_a + (1 - s_R - \theta) i_r^e B_F\right]}{h_0 - \beta}.$$

(5.43)

Since the equilibria in equations (5.41) and (5.43) are based on behavioural equations which include target profit shares and expected inflation, these equilibria are planned or 'ex ante' equilibria. They will only come true and persist if targets and expectations are met. But since the 'ex ante' goods market equilibrium employment rate in equation (5.43) may deviate from the SIRE determined in equation (5.21), such a deviation will then trigger unexpected inflation and the related processes of income re-distribution, both between capital and labour and between firms and rentiers, which we have summarised in Table 5.1. These effects have to be examined next in order to arrive at the 'ex post' or end of period equilibrium income and output, which includes the effects of unexpected inflation.

In order to be able to calculate the effects of changes in the inflation rate on the ex post goods market equilibrium employment rate, the distribution effects of unexpected inflation on the profit share from equation (5.29) and on rentiers' ex post real income from equation (5.36) have to be included in the goods market equilibrium employment rate from equation (5.43) which then turns into:

$$e^* = \frac{q\left[I_a + (1 - s_R - \theta)(i - p^e - p^u) B_F\right]}{h_0 - h_2 p^u - \beta} = \frac{q\left[I_a + (1 - s_R - \theta) i_r B_F\right]}{h - \beta}.$$

(5.44)

Since unexpected inflation causes a deviation from the 'ex ante' goods market equilibrium employment rate in equation (5.43), equation (5.44) does not define an equilibrium in the behavioural sense, with all targets and expectations being met. It is rather a temporary 'ex post' goods market equilibrium taking into account the distributional and thus demand effects of unexpected inflation. Since there is no positive or negative excess demand in the goods market, economic agents will not change the activity level defined in equation (5.44), but adjust inflation expectations in the next period according to unexpected inflation in the current period. However, unless the employment rate determined by the 'ex post' goods market equilibrium (e^*) matches the SIRE (e^N), unexpected inflation will occur again, causing again a deviation of the end of period 'ex post' from the 'ex ante' goods market equilibrium, triggering further adjustments, and so on.

From equation (5.44), the effect of unexpected inflation on the 'ex post' goods market equilibrium rate of employment can be derived as follows:

$$\frac{\partial e^*}{\partial p^u} = \frac{h_2 e^* - q\left(1 - s_R - \theta\right)B_F}{h_0 - h_2 p^u - \beta} = \frac{q\left[h_2 Y^* - \left(1 - s_R - \theta\right)B_F\right]}{h - \beta}. \tag{5.44a}$$

Since we assume that the denominator in equation (5.44a) remains positive in order to maintain the goods market equilibrium stability condition from (5.40),[21] the direction of the effects of unexpected inflation on the end of period employment rate depends on the sign of the numerator. Here we see the two effects of unexpected inflation. First, there is re-distribution between gross profits and wages, with unexpected inflation (disinflation) associated with a falling (rising) profit share and a rising (falling) wage share. Through this channel, unexpected inflation (disinflation) has a positive (negative) effect on economic activity and employment, as can be seen in the first term in the numerator ($h_2 e^*$). As already noticed in Section 4.3 for the constant price version, our closed economy model is unambiguously wage-led, as far as the effects of re-distribution between capital and labour on output and employment are concerned. Taken alone, this means that unexpected inflation would cause a further deviation of e^* from e^N.

Second, we have the re-distribution amongst the different types of total profits, with unexpected inflation (disinflation) reducing (raising) the share of rentiers' income in total profits (R/Π). The effect of re-distribution between firms and rentiers on economic activity through this channel, shown in the second term of the numerator $[-q(1 - s_R - \theta)B_F]$, is not clear in advance. It depends on the values of the rentiers' propensity to consume $(1 - s_R)$ and the sensitivity of firms' investment with respect to internal funds (θ). If the former exceeds the latter $(1 - s_R - \theta > 0)$, unexpected inflation and re-distribution at the expense of rentiers have a dampening effect on economic activity and employment. This is the 'puzzling case' already explained in Section 4.3. However, if the effect on firms' investment is stronger than that on rentiers' consumption $(1 - s_R - \theta < 0)$, unexpected inflation will have a stimulating effect on economic activity and employment, and the 'normal case' explained in Section 4.3 is obtained. For the sake of simplifying further exposition, we will assume that the 'normal case' prevails, that is, unexpected inflation will have an accelerating effect on aggregate demand and employment via re-distribution between firms and rentiers, too.[22] Therefore, taking our two channels together, we get an overall expansionary feedback effect of unexpected inflation on aggregate demand, output and the employment rate. Unexpected inflation will hence move the 'ex post' goods market equilibrium rate of employment farther away from the SIRE.[23]

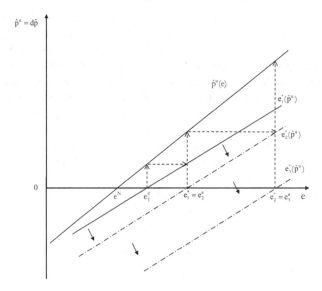

Figure 5.4   Stable inflation rate of employment (e^N), ex ante (e^e) and ex post (e^*) goods mar-
ket equilibrium rate of employment with a strong effect of unexpected inflation
on employment: Upward instability

Such a cumulative process is shown in Figure 5.4 for a strong effect of unexpected inflation on
the ex post goods market equilibrium rate of employment and in Figure 5.5 for a weak effect:
The initial 'ex ante' goods market equilibrium rate of employment e_1^e exceeds the short-run
SIRE (e^N) which triggers unexpected inflation, according to our unexpected inflation curve
$\hat{p}^u(e)$. Since unexpected inflation has a positive effect on the 'ex post' goods market equilibrium rate of employment, according to the $e_1^*(\hat{p}^u)$-curve, this will move the goods market
equilibrium to e_1^*, which is even farther away from the SIRE at e^N. With adaptive expectations, in the next period economic agents will make the inflation rate of the previous period
the expected rate; the previous period's ex post period equilibrium will become the current
period's 'ex ante' goods market equilibrium $e_1^* = e_2^e$. The 'ex post' goods market equilibrium
function in employment-unexpected inflation space will shift according to the $e_2^*(\hat{p}^u)$-curve.
Unexpected inflation will be triggered again and, as a result, the goods market equilibrium
rate of employment will diverge further from the SIRE to e_2^*, and so on. We will thus observe
a process of monotonous divergence of the goods market equilibrium rate of employment
from the SIRE. The same will be true if the ex ante goods market equilibrium rate of employment falls short of the SIRE initially, as can be seen in Figure 5.6. The distribution claims
equilibrium at the SIRE is thus highly unstable. Whenever the employment rate given by
the goods market deviates from the SIRE, and the rate of unemployment deviates from the
NAIRU, we will observe cumulative processes, that is, ever rising (falling) rates of employment and inflation, rising (falling) wage shares, falling (rising) profit shares and falling (rising) rentiers' shares in total profits – which, of course, require stabilisation.
An alternative way of looking at the dynamics included in our approach is focussing on
the interaction of the wage share with the employment rate, as for example in Blecker

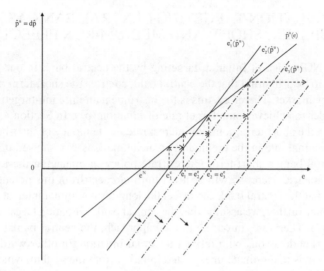

Figure 5.5   Stable inflation rate of employment (e^N), ex ante (e^e) and ex post (e^*) goods market equilibrium rate of employment with a weak effect of unexpected inflation on employment: Upward instability

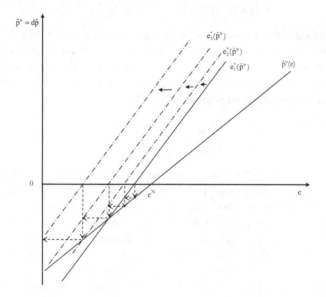

Figure 5.6   Stable inflation rate of employment (e^N), ex ante (e^e) and ex post (e^*) goods market equilibrium rate of employment: Downward instability

and Setterfield (2019, Chapter 5).[24] An analysis of our model within this framework can be found in Appendix II to this chapter. In the next steps we will now have to discuss if and how to stabilise the system by means of macroeconomic policies. First, we will turn to monetary policies, as suggested by the NCM, for example; then we will look at fiscal policies.

5.5   AN INFLATION-TARGETING CENTRAL BANK AS A STABILISER? SHORT- AND MEDIUM-RUN EFFECTS[25]

Examining the NCM idea of inflation targeting by the central bank in our post-Keynesian model, we have to bear in mind that the central bank controls the short-term nominal interest rate in the money market. Therefore, this is the instrument an inflation-targeting central bank can apply in order to achieve some target rate of inflation ($\hat{p}^T$). In Section 4.2 we explained the link between the short-term nominal interest rate in the money or inter-bank market and the long-term nominal rate in the credit and financial markets. We showed that the effectiveness of the central bank's short-term interest rate policy in managing the long-term rate is potentially asymmetric. Here we will abstract for a moment from this potential asymmetry, and we assume that the central bank can affect the long-term nominal interest rate. In order to simplify the matter further, we assume that the central bank's inflation target equals expected inflation ($\hat{p}^T = \hat{p}^e$). Therefore, in our simplified approach, the central bank's inflation target is not fixed but is endogenous with respect to actual inflation. In other words, the only aim of our central bank is to eliminate unexpected inflation from the system, which generates the following central bank reaction function:

$$i = i_{r0}^e + \hat{p} + \iota\left(\hat{p} - \hat{p}^T\right) = i_{r0}^e + \hat{p}^e + \hat{p}^u + \iota\left(\hat{p} - \hat{p}^e\right)$$

$$= i_{r0}^e + \hat{p}^e + \left(1 + \iota\right)\hat{p}^u, \quad i_{r0}^e \geq 0, \iota > 0,$$

(5.45)

with i_{r0}^e being the central bank's estimation of the real interest rate which generates a SIRE, and ι the reaction parameter with respect to unexpected inflation. From equation (5.44) we obtain the following effect of a change in the nominal interest rate being set by the central bank on the ex post goods market equilibrium employment rate (e^{CB}), assuming an interest-inelastic mark-up and target profit share in the short run:

$$\frac{\partial e^{CB}}{\partial i} = \frac{q\left(1 - s_R - \theta\right)B_F}{h - \beta}.$$

(5.44b)

For the 'normal case' ($1 - s_R - \theta < 0$) regarding the effects of re-distribution between firms and rentiers on capacity utilisation, and abstracting from the possibility of the 'puzzling case' ($1 - s_R - \theta > 0$), inflation-targeting monetary policies will have the required inverse effects on economic activity and employment. The SIRE may therefore be turned into an attractor by inflation-targeting monetary policies following the monetary policy rule in equation (5.45). The effects of changes in the nominal interest rate have to over-compensate for the effects of unexpected inflation on output and employment. This is no problem with employment exceeding the SIRE and unemployment falling short of the NAIRU and thus positive unexpected inflation. The central bank can always increase its instrument variable such that the nominal interest rate rises according to equation (5.45) and wipe out unexpected inflation by means of eliminating 'excess employment' from the system. This is shown in Figure 5.7.

For a stable monotonic adjustment, as in Figure 5.7, we need a steep ('ex post') goods market equilibrium employment curve incorporating monetary policy responses (e^{cb}), which indicates only weakly contractive effects of the interest rate policy of the central bank. Otherwise, we may obtain oscillating convergence, as shown in Figure 5.8, or even oscillating divergence of the employment rate determined by monetary policies away from the SIRE, as shown in

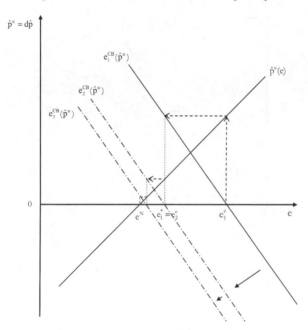

Figure 5.7 An inflation-targeting central bank monotonically stabilising the ex post goods market equilibrium rate of employment towards the SIRE

Figure 5.9. Therefore, central banks have to be careful in their responses in order to avoid excessive over- and undershooting which could destabilise the system. This is also the message of those post-Keynesian approaches advocating inflation-targeting monetary policies, like Fontana and Palacio-Vera (2007), Palley (2006, 2007a) and Setterfield (2006).

However, there are further limitations for monetary policies adjusting the goods market equilibrium rate of employment to the SIRE, which we have to consider – and which have led several post-Keynesian authors, like Arestis (1996a, 2011a, 2013), Arestis and Sawyer (2003, 2004a), Davidson (2006), Gnos and Rochon (2007), Hein (2002, 2006a, 2008, Chapter 16), Hein and Stockhammer (2009b, 2010, 2011b), Kriesler and Lavoie (2007), Lavoie (1996b), Rochon and Setterfield (2007), Setterfield (2009a), Smithin (2007) and Wray (2007) to abandon inflation targeting. Instead, as we will see in Chapter 6, those authors have proposed an alternative post-Keynesian macroeconomic policy mix to the NCM, in which wage/incomes policies and fiscal policies play major roles when it comes to stabilising output, employment and inflation. However, to be fair, those post-Keynesians who are not fundamentally critical of inflation-targeting interest rate policies of the central bank would also see major roles for wages/incomes and fiscal policies.

Addressing the problems of inflation-targeting interest rate policies, we can distinguish between short-run problems and medium-run problems, that is, problems which will only show up in the course of several periods. Let us tackle the short-run problems first. Here, the limits of inflation targeting arise when employment falls short of the SIRE and unemployment exceeds the NAIRU, and unexpected inflation is hence negative. This will be particularly problematic in a climate of low inflation and hence low nominal interest rates.

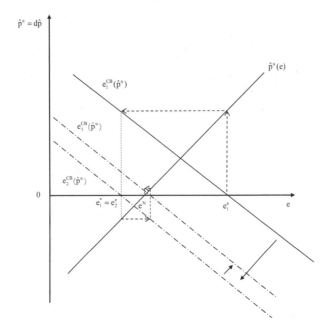

*Figure 5.8   An inflation-targeting central bank cyclically stabilising the ex post goods mar-
ket equilibrium rate of employment towards the SIRE*

First, with unexpected disinflation or even deflation, a negative nominal interest rate according to equation (5.45) might be required in order to stabilise the system. This is what central
banks cannot achieve due to the zero lower bound of their instrument variable, the short-term
nominal lending rate in the money market. Of course, as we explained in Section 4.2, the
deposit facility rate, which central banks pay to commercial banks that hold reserves with the
central bank, can become negative. But it is difficult to conceive that the main lending rate or
even the overnight lending facility rate turns negative. Furthermore, even if the main lending
rate were temporarily negative, what is at stake for inflation-targeting policies is the long-term
interest rate in the credit market, charged by profit-making commercial banks. It seems to be
unlikely that this could turn negative.

Second, another constraint for central bank policies to stimulate the economy when
employment falls short of the SIRE arises from the interaction of the central bank with the
commercial banking sector, as we explained in Section 4.2. Whereas the central bank can
always force commercial banks to increase long-term nominal interest rates in the credit market by means of increasing the base rate in the money market, commercial banks might not
follow the central bank in decreasing interest rates, in particular in a recession with increasing
uncertainty, defaults and risk assessments. Falling money market interest rates may therefore
be accompanied by constant or even rising credit market rates if commercial banks increase
their mark-ups during a recession.

Third, even if there is room for manoeuvre for the central bank to lower the short-term
interest rate and even if commercial banks keep mark-ups constant and lower credit market
rates, this may fail to have stimulating effects on private investment, if firms' 'animal spirits'

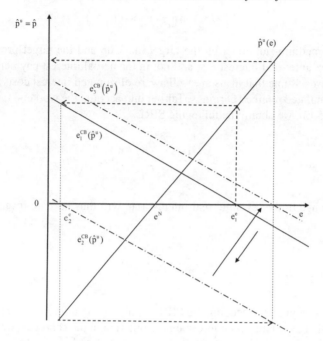

Figure 5.9 An inflation-targeting central bank de-stabilising the ex post goods market equilibrium rate of employment

(I_a) in the investment function are collapsing, and this collapse over-compensates the stimulating effects via re-distribution in favour of firms. This is the famous 'investment trap' situation, in which private investment does not respond positively to falling interest rates. Firms may then dispose of increasing means of internal finance but they will be reluctant to make use of them for real investment purposes.

Summing up the short-run limitations, central banks' inflation-targeting interest rate policies may be ineffective when expansionary intervention is needed most urgently, that is, in a deep recession or depression with deflationary pressure and a collapse of firms' 'animal spirits', as could be observed in the recent Great Recession 2008–09 and the COVID-19 crisis 2020. Therefore, central banks' capacities to adjust actual unemployment towards the NAIRU, and employment towards the SIRE, are asymmetric, and an inflation-targeting monetary policy strategy will be ineffective in periods of rising unemployment and persistent disinflation and finally deflation.

Taking a medium-run perspective, another problem of inflation-targeting interest rate policies arises. In Hein (2006a, 2008, Chapter 15) and Hein and Stockhammer (2010, 2011b), it has been argued that persistent changes in the 'ex ante' real interest rate affect firms' target profit share in the medium run and hence the SIRE.[26] Since, from the perspective of the firm, interest payments are costs which have to be covered by the mark-up on unit labour costs, persistent changes in the 'ex ante' real interest rate will cause medium-run changes in the firms' target mark-up, which will hence become interest-elastic (see also Section 4.3). Therefore, the firms' target profit share from equation (5.14) has to be expanded:

$$h_F^T = h_0 + h_3 i_r^e, \quad h_0 > 0, h_3 \geq 0. \tag{5.46}$$

Note that for a medium-run effect on the target mark-up and the target profit share, it is a change in the 'ex ante' real interest rate and not in the actual interest payments which is relevant, because we assume that firms are well aware of imputed interest costs on own capital, that is, on accumulated retained earnings. Taking into account the workers' target wage share from equation (5.13), we obtain the following SIRE:

$$e^N = \frac{1 - \Omega_0 - h_0 - h_3 i_r^e}{\Omega_1}. \tag{5.47}$$

A persistent change in the 'ex ante' real interest rate will thus have an inverse effect on the SIRE:

$$\frac{\partial e^N}{\partial i_r^e} = \frac{-h_3}{\Omega_1} < 0. \tag{5.47a}$$

In the case of employment exceeding the SIRE, applying the inflation-targeting interest rate rule from equation (5.45) may therefore stabilise inflation in the short run, but in the medium run the effects on the firms' target profit share may undermine the short-run stabilisation effects and may create unexpected inflation again, causing further central bank intervention, as is shown in Figure 5.10. With an employment rate e_1, unexpected inflation will be generated, triggering central banks to increase nominal and expected real interest rates, adjusting the employment rate towards the SIRE $e_2 = e_1^N$ in the short run. Higher interest rates, however, will force surviving firms to raise the target profit share and thus lower their target wage share curve towards Ω_{F2}^T, thus reducing the SIRE to e_2^N and triggering unexpected inflation at the employment rate e_2 again, as can be seen in Figure 5.10.

The increase in the ex ante real interest rate, however, will not only raise the target profit share of firms and reduce the SIRE, it will also raise the realised profit share. This can be shown as follows: With the target profit share from equation (5.46), unexpected inflation from equation (5.27) becomes:

$$\hat{p}^u = \frac{h_0 + h_3 i_r^e + \Omega_0 + \Omega_1 e - 1}{h_2 + \Omega_2}. \tag{5.48}$$

The realised profit share from equation (5.29) becomes:

$$h = h_F^T - h_2 \hat{p}^u = h_0 + h_3 i_r^e - h_2 \hat{p}^u,$$

$$1 > h_0 > 0, \quad h_2, h_3 \geq 0. \tag{5.49}$$

Substituting unexpected inflation using equation (5.48), this becomes:

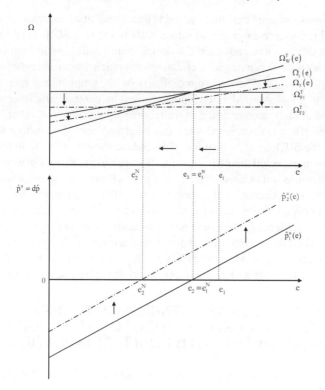

Figure 5.10   Persistent increase in the 'ex ante' real rate of interest and the SIRE

$$h = \frac{\Omega_2\left(h_0 + h_3 i_r^e\right) + h_2\left(1 - \Omega_0 - \Omega_1 e\right)}{h_2 + \Omega_2},$$ (5.50)

with

$$\frac{\partial h}{\partial i_r^e} = \frac{\Omega_2 h_3}{h_2 + \Omega_2} > 0.$$ (5.50a)

The increases in the ex ante real interest rate will thus raise the realised profit share, and this will then have depressing effects on aggregate demand in our wage-led economy.[27] On top of the short-run direct effects of the increase in the interest rate in equation (5.44b), we will thus have in the medium run:

$$\frac{\partial e^{CB}}{\partial i_r^e} = \frac{\partial e^{CB}}{\partial h} \frac{\partial h}{\partial i_r^e} = \frac{-e^{CB}}{h - \beta} \frac{\Omega_2 h_3}{h_2 + \Omega_2} = \frac{-\Omega_2 h_3 e^{CB}}{\left(h - \beta\right)\left(h_2 + \Omega_2\right)} < 0.$$ (5.44c)

There is no reason to assume that this second round effect of an increase in the ex ante real interest rate will reduce the employment rate exactly to the new SIRE at e_2^N in Figure 5.10. If the employment rate remains above e_2^N, the central banks will have to intervene anew, raise the interest rate with short-run negative effects on the employment rate, medium-run depressive effects on the SIRE and second round effects on the employment rate, and so on. The economy will thus show stagflation tendencies caused by central bank interventions, that is, falling employment rates accompanied by inflationary pressures. But other interactions are possible, too. The effect in equation (5.44c) may be strong enough to reduce the employment rate even below the SIRE at e_2^N, which will then induce the central bank to lower the interest rate in the face of unexpected disinflation, with short-run expansionary effects on the employment rate and medium-run positive effects on the SIRE and on the employment rate, too.[28] Whatever type of interaction of employment rate and SIRE will emerge, the SIRE, as well as the NAIRU, will become endogenous to inflation-targeting interest rate policies via the interest cost channel, with higher (lower) interest rates causing a lower (higher) SIRE and a higher (lower) NAIRU. Therefore, taking this channel into account, inflation-targeting interest rate policies do not seem to be an adequate policy strategy in order to stabilise the economy at a high SIRE. We will therefore look at the stabilising potential of fiscal policies in the next step.

5.6   FISCAL POLICIES AS A STABILISER: TAXES AND GOVERNMENT EXPENDITURES IN THE CLOSED ECONOMY MODEL WITH CONFLICT INFLATION

We will now introduce taxes and government expenditures into our closed economy model with conflict inflation, building on the constant price model variant from Section 4.4. We treat government's real expenditures on goods and services (G_r) again as an exogenous policy variable. For the sake of simplicity, we assume that with unexpected inflation, governments immediately adjust nominal spending within the period such that real expenditures remain at the planned level. Government's ex post real interest payments to rentiers, directly or via banks, are given by the real interest rate and the stock of government debt at issue prices ($i_r B_G$). As in the previous section, the ex ante real interest rate is determined by the interest rate policies of the central bank, by the liquidity preference of financial wealth holders and banks and by inflation expectations. Unexpected inflation may thus affect the real values of these payments, similarly as with real corporate debt services discussed above. In case of positive unexpected inflation, governments as the debtor gain in real terms and rentiers as the creditors lose, whereas with unexpected disinflation, we have re-distribution from the government to the rentiers.

The government's ex post real tax revenues are composed of taxes paid by firms and rentiers on their respective real incomes and are thus endogenous with respect to the level of economic activity in production (Y_p). They will also be affected by income distribution, both between capital and labour, indicated by the profit share in production, and between the state and the rentiers, which is affected by the real interest rate on the stock of government debt:

$$T_r = t_\Pi \left(hY_P - i_r B_F \right) + t_\Pi \left(i_r B_F + i_r B_G \right) = t_\Pi \left(hY_P + i_r B_G \right). \tag{5.51}$$

Re-distribution between firms and rentiers has no effect on the government's tax revenues, because we assume a uniform tax rate on all types of profits (t_Π), that is, retained earnings and rentiers' interest income. Again, we assume for the sake of simplicity that the tax rate on wages is zero. Unexpected inflation affects government's tax revenues in real terms via the associated income re-distribution. Positive (negative) unexpected inflation will be associated with a lower (higher) profit share, and it will lower (raise) the real rate of interest on government debt. The latter implies that the government as a debtor will benefit (suffer) from positive (negative) unexpected inflation by lower (higher) real values of its interest payments, but it will also suffer (benefit), but less so, as a recipient of taxes on rentiers' interest revenues.

Retained profits after taxes in real terms (Π_{Fr}^{net}) are saved by definition, and with a constant propensity to save (s_R) out of rentiers' income, saving in real terms is given by:

$$S_r = \Pi_{Fr}^{net} + S_{Rr} = \left(1 - t_\Pi\right)\left[hY_P - i_r B_F + s_R i_r\left(B_F + B_G\right)\right]$$

$$= \left(1 - t_\Pi\right)\left\{hY_P - i_r\left[\left(1 - s_R\right)B_F - s_R B_G\right]\right\}, \tag{5.52}$$

$$1 \geq s_R > 0,\ 1 > t_\Pi \geq 0.$$

Our investment function in real terms builds on the one applied in the previous section. Firms' investment decisions are thus determined by autonomous investment, affected by Keynes's (1936) 'animal spirits', by the accelerator effect of output on investment and by internal means of finance, referring to Kalecki's (1937) 'principle of increasing risk'. On the latter, not only real interest payments, as in the previous model, but also tax payments on retained earnings have a negative impact, as explained in Section 4.4:

$$I = I_a + \beta Y_P - \theta\left[i_r B_F + t_\Pi\left(hY_P - i_r B_F\right)\right]$$

$$= I_a + \left(\beta - \theta t_\Pi h\right)Y_P - \theta\left(1 - t_\Pi\right)i_r B_F, \tag{5.53}$$

$$I_a, \beta, \theta \geq 0,\ \beta - \theta t_\Pi h > 0$$

In the investment function we assume that an increase in output and income from production has a positive effect on investment although it also raises tax payments on retained profits; hence we require again that $\beta - \theta t_\Pi h > 0$. The equilibrium condition is:

$$I + G_r + i_r B_G = S_r + T_r, \tag{5.54}$$

and the stability condition is given as:

$$\frac{\partial S_r}{\partial Y_P} + \frac{\partial T_r}{\partial Y_P} > \frac{\partial I}{\partial Y_P} \Rightarrow \left(1 - t_\Pi\right)h + t_\Pi h > \beta - \theta t_\Pi h$$

$$\Rightarrow \left(1 + \theta t_\Pi\right)h - \beta > 0. \tag{5.55}$$

From these equations we can now derive the ex ante goods market equilibrium, again including distribution targets and inflation expectations into the behavioural functions above, that is, replacing the profit share by the firms' target share (h_0) and the real interest rate by the ex ante real rate (i_r^e). Plugging the so-modified equations (5.51)–(5.53) into equation (5.54), and assuming government expenditures on goods and services to be exogenous, yields ex ante equilibrium output and income from production:

$$Y_P^e = \frac{I_a + G_r + (1-t_\Pi)i_r^e\left[(1-s_R-\theta)B_F + (1-s_R)B_G\right]}{(1+\theta t_\Pi)h_0 - \beta}.$$

(5.56)

For total ex ante equilibrium income, we have to add ex ante real government interest payments:

$$Y^e = Y_P^e + i_r^e B_G$$

$$= \frac{I_a + G_r + i_r^e\left\{(1-t_\Pi)(1-s_R-\theta)B_F + \left[(1-t_\Pi)(1-s_R) + (1+\theta t_\Pi)h_0 - \beta\right]B_G\right\}}{(1+\theta t_\Pi)h_0 - \beta}.$$

(5.57)

The effect of changes in parameters (such as animal spirits and autonomous investment, the propensity to save, the interest rate, the profit share, government expenditures and the tax rate on profits) on this equilibrium were analysed extensively in Section 4.4 and will not be repeated here. We will make use of some of these effects, regarding changes in the real interest rate and the profit share associated with unexpected inflation and related to government expenditures and taxation, in the following analysis.

Making use of equation (5.42) again and assuming $q = 1/(yL)$ to be constant, we obtain the ex ante goods market equilibrium rate of employment (e^e) implied by equation (5.56):

$$e^e = \frac{q\left\{I_a + G_r + (1-t_\Pi)i_r^e\left[(1-s_R-\theta)B_F + (1-s_R)B_G\right]\right\}}{(1+\theta t_\Pi)h_0 - \beta}.$$

(5.58)

The ex ante goods market equilibrium employment rate in equation (5.58) may deviate from the SIRE determined in equation (5.21). Such a deviation will then trigger unexpected (dis-) inflation and the related processes of income re-distribution, both between capital and labour and between firms and rentiers, which we have summarised in Table 5.1. To arrive at the ex post goods market equilibrium employment rate, the distribution effects of unexpected inflation on the profit share from equation (5.29) and on rentiers' ex post real income from equation (5.36) have to be included in the goods market equilibrium employment rate from equation (5.58), which then turns into:

$$e^* = \frac{q\left\{I_a + G_r + (1-t_\Pi)(i_r^e - p^u)\left[(1-s_R-\theta)B_F + (1-s_R)B_G\right]\right\}}{(1+\theta t_\Pi)(h_0 - h_2\hat{p}^u) - \beta}$$

$$= \frac{q\left\{I_a + G_r + (1-t_\Pi)i_r\left[(1-s_R-\theta)B_F + (1-s_R)B_G\right]\right\}}{(1+\theta t_\Pi)h - \beta}.$$

(5.59)

Unexpected (dis-)inflation will have the following effect on the ex post goods market equilibrium employment rate:

$$\frac{\partial e^*}{\partial p^u} = \frac{\left(1+\theta t_\Pi\right)h_2 e^* - q\left(1-t_\Pi\right)\left[\left(1-s_R-\theta\right)B_F + \left(1-s_R\right)B_G\right]}{\left(1+\theta t_\Pi\right)\left(h_0 - h_2\hat{p}^u\right)-\beta}$$

$$= \frac{q\left\{\left(1+\theta t_\Pi\right)h_2 Y^* - \left(1-t_\Pi\right)\left[\left(1-s_R-\theta\right)B_F + \left(1-s_R\right)B_G\right]\right\}}{\left(1+\theta t_\Pi\right)h-\beta}$$

(5.59a)

Again, assuming the denominator to remain positive so as to satisfy the goods market equilibrium stability condition (5.55), the effect of unexpected inflation on the employment rate via re-distribution between capital and labour $[(1+\theta t_\Pi)h_2 e^*]$ will be positive. The effects via re-distribution between creditors and debtors $\{-q(1-t_\Pi)[(1-s_R-\theta]B_F + (1-s_R)B_G\}$, however, is not clear in advance, even if we assume again the normal case conditions with respect to corporate debt to hold $(1-s_R-\theta<0)$, because we also have to consider that unexpected inflation will reduce rentiers' real income from holding government bonds and thus consumption demand from that income. In what follows, we will assume that this effect will be small enough to keep the numerator in equation (5.59a) positive. If this is the case, unexpected inflation (disinflation) will raise (lower) ex post aggregate demand and employment and will thus move the latter farther away from the SIRE, as in the model above without a government. Incompatible distribution claims and unexpected (dis-)inflation will thus have the cumulative diverging effects of the employment rate from the SIRE shown in Figures 5.4–5.6 and make the equilibrium at the SIRE thus highly unstable.

Let us now look at the stabilising potentials of fiscal policies, either using government expenditures or the tax rate on profits as policy instruments. Government expenditures have a uniquely positive effect on the ex post equilibrium levels of output and thus also on the related employment rate taking into account fiscal policy effects (e^{FP}):

$$\frac{\partial e^{FP}}{\partial G_r} = \frac{q}{\left(1+\theta t_\Pi\right)h-\beta} > 0.$$

(5.59b)

Therefore, lowering government expenditures when the employment rate exceeds the SIRE and increasing it when the employment rate falls short of the SIRE will always be able to stabilise the economy around the SIRE. Fontana (2009b), Setterfield (2007b) and Sawyer (2009b) have therefore suggested replacing the central bank's inflation-targeting interest rate policies, as proposed by the NCM, by government's fiscal policies in order to stabilise the SIRE or the NAIRU. According to Settersfield (2007b, p. 417, emphasis in the original), there is good reason – even within the NCM framework – to conclude that 'fiscal policy is at least as, if not, *more* potent as an instrument of stabilization policy than is monetary policy'. The interest rate rule in equation (5.45) could thus be replaced by a government expenditure rule of the following type:

$$G_r = G_{r0} + G_{r1}\left(e^N - e\right), \quad G_{r0} \geq 0, G_{r1} > 0,$$

(5.60)

with G_{r0} as the expenditure level to reach the SIRE and G_{r1} as the reaction coefficient towards deviation of the employment rate from the SIRE. The adjustment processes will be similar to those shown in Figures 5.7 or 5.8 for contractive monetary policies. Of course, government expenditure policies also have to make sure not to over- or undershoot the SIRE target or to run into a destabilising process, as in Figure 5.9, by choosing too high a reaction coefficient. Compared to central bank interest policies, however, government expenditures as an adjustment policy tool have the advantage of being effective also in deep recessions with deflationary tendencies and poor entrepreneurial animal spirits, when monetary policies are facing the zero lower bound and investment trap problems. This is shown in Figure 5.11.

Furthermore, government expenditure policies have no medium-run detrimental effects on the SIRE, unlike central bank interest rate policies. Of course, in order to be effective, both in the short and the medium run, aggregate demand-managing fiscal policies need the cooperation of the central bank's interest rate policy in order to avoid rising interest rates when government deficits and debt, associated with expansionary policies, start to rise. We have shown in Section 4.4 that long-run stable government debt-GDP ratios require a real (nominal) interest rate on government bonds below long-run real (nominal) GDP growth.

The alternative government fiscal policy tool to manage aggregate demand, employment and inflation is the tax rate, in our model the tax rate on total profits, both on retained earnings and interest incomes of the rentiers. Raising the tax rate with constant government expenditures has the following effect on the ex post goods market equilibrium rate of employment including the fiscal policy intervention:

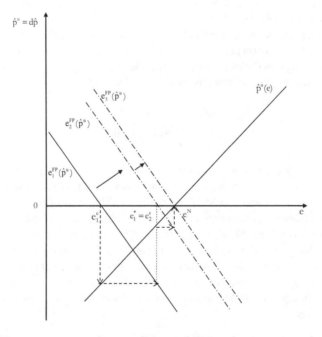

Figure 5.11   *Government expenditure policies stabilising the ex post goods market equilibrium rate of employment towards the SIRE*

$$\frac{\partial e^{FP}}{\partial t_\Pi} = \frac{-\theta h e^* - q i_r \left[\left(1 - s_R - \theta\right) B_F + \left(1 - s_R\right) B_G \right]}{\left(1 + \theta t_\Pi\right) h - \beta}$$

$$= \frac{-q \left\{ \theta h Y_p^* + i_r \left[\left(1 - s_R - \theta\right) B_F + \left(1 - s_R\right) B_G \right] \right\}}{\left(1 + \theta t_\Pi\right) h - \beta} < 0$$

(5.59c)

An increase in the tax rate has a uniquely negative effect on equilibrium income generated in production and thus on the related employment rate. This is true, both for the puzzling case conditions $(1 - s_R - \theta > 0)$ and for the normal case conditions $(1 - s_R - \theta < 0)$, because we have $\theta h Y_p^* - \theta i_r B_F \geq 0$ in our model, that is, firms cannot pay out more interest income to the rentiers than their whole profits. With these results, we could also replace the central bank interest rate rule from equation (5.45) in order to stabilise inflation by a fiscal policy tax rule:

$$t_\Pi = t_{\Pi 0} + t_{\Pi 1} \left(e - e^N \right), \quad t_{\Pi 0} \geq 0, \, t_{\Pi 1} > 0,$$

(5.61)

with $t_{\Pi 0}$ as the tax rate to reach the SIRE and $t_{\Pi 1}$ as the reaction coefficient towards deviation of the employment rate from the SIRE. Whenever the employment rate exceeds the SIRE and unexpected inflation arises, government would have to raise the tax rate on profits. When the employment rate falls short of the SIRE and unexpected disinflation is observed, the tax rate would have to be lowered. The adjustment processes would thus again be similar to those shown in Figures 5.7 or 5.8 for contractive monetary policies. Government tax policies also have to avoid over- or undershooting the SIRE target, or to run into a destabilising process as in Figure 5.9. But similar to central bank interest rate policies, and unlike government expenditure policies, choosing the tax rate as an adjustment policy tool runs the risk of being ineffective in deep recessions with deflationary tendencies and poor corporative or entrepreneurial animal spirits. Low and falling animal spirits might then induce firms not to invest (or to increase their investment) despite lower tax rates and higher net retained earnings. Of course, we also have to consider the effects of profit tax cuts on rentiers' income and their consumption expenditures. A very high rentiers' propensity to consume could thus generate positive effects on aggregate demand and employment. But if these effects are small, then the effectiveness of the tax policy instrument may be asymmetric in the short run, similar to central bank's interest rate policies. Whereas raising tax rates does not face a constraint bringing the economy down to the SIRE level, lowering tax rates in order to lift the economy up to the SIRE level might not work, because it is an indirect stimulus which has to rely on the responses by the firm sector, in particular.

Furthermore, the changing tax rate has detrimental medium-run effects on the SIRE – again, similar to central bank interest rate policies – if we assume the mark-up in the firm's pricing equation to be tax-elastic in the medium run. We had introduced and examined the effects of a tax-elastic mark-up in Section 4.4 for the constant price version of the model. In our conflicting claims inflation model of the current chapter a tax-elastic mark-up means that the firms' target profit share from equation (5.46) is affected by the tax rate on profits and has to be expanded as follows:

$$h_F^T = h_0 + h_3 i_r^e + h_4 t_\Pi, \quad 1 > h_0 > 0, \, h_3, h_4 \geq 0.$$

(5.62)

Taking into account the workers' target wage share from equation (5.13), we obtain the following SIRE:

$$e^N = \frac{1 - \Omega_0 - h_0 - h_3 i_r^e - h_4 t_\Pi}{\Omega_1}. \tag{5.63}$$

A change in the tax rate on profits will thus have a medium-run inverse effect on the SIRE:

$$\frac{\partial e^N}{\partial t_\Pi} = \frac{-h_4}{\Omega_1} < 0. \tag{5.63a}$$

In the case of employment exceeding the SIRE and the government raising the tax rate on profits according to equation (5.61), this will stabilise inflation in the short run by reducing aggregate demand, output and employment. But, similar to the effect of inflation-targeting interest rate policies of the central bank, in the medium run the effects on the firms' target profit share may undermine the short-run stabilisation effects and may create unexpected inflation again, that is, 'tax-push inflation' requiring further tax hikes. We will thus see again the effects, as shown in Figure 5.10.

In Section 5.5, we have also analysed the second round effect of an increase in the interest rate via a higher target profit share on the goods market equilibrium employment rate. A similar effect will arise here. The increase in the tax rate on profits will not only raise the target profit share of firms and reduce the SIRE, it will also raise the realised profit share in the medium run. With the target profit share from equation (5.62), unexpected inflation from equation (5.27) becomes:

$$\hat{p}^u = \frac{h_0 + h_3 i_r^e + h_4 t_\Pi + \Omega_0 + \Omega_1 e - 1}{h_2 + \Omega_2}. \tag{5.64}$$

The realised profit share from equation (5.29) turns into:

$$h = h_F^T - h_2 \hat{p}^u = h_0 + h_3 i_r^e + h_4 t_\Pi - h_2 \hat{p}^u,$$
$$1 > h_0 > 0, h_2, h_3, h_4 \geq 0. \tag{5.65}$$

Substituting unexpected inflation using equation (5.64), this becomes:

$$h = \frac{\Omega_2 \left(h_0 + h_3 i_r^e + h_4 t_\Pi \right) + h_2 \left(1 - \Omega_0 - \Omega_1 e \right)}{h_2 + \Omega_2}, \tag{5.66}$$

with

$$\frac{\partial h}{\partial t_\Pi} = \frac{\Omega_2 h_4}{h_2 + \Omega_2} > 0. \tag{5.66a}$$

The increase in the tax rate on profits will thus raise the realised profit share via the target profit share, and this will then have depressive effects on aggregate demand in our wage-led economy. On top of the short-run direct effects of the increase in the tax rate on profits in equation (5.59c), we will thus have in the medium run:

$$\frac{\partial e^{FP}}{\partial t_{\Pi}} = \frac{\partial e^{FP}}{\partial h}\frac{\partial h}{\partial t_{\Pi}} = \frac{-\left(1+\theta t_{\Pi}\right)e^{FP}}{\left(1+\theta t_{\Pi}\right)h-\beta}\frac{\Omega_2 h_4}{h_2+\Omega_2}$$

$$= \frac{-\Omega_2 h_4\left(1+\theta t_{\Pi}\right)e^{FP}}{\left[\left(1+\theta t_{\Pi}\right)h-\beta\right]\left(h_2+\Omega_2\right)} < 0.$$

(5.59d)

This second-round effect will move the employment rate towards the lower SIRE. It will depend on the parameter values, whether, by a fluke, it will then exactly meet the new SIRE, or whether it will over- or undershoot, triggering further changes in the tax rate on profits. Again, whatever type of interaction of the employment rate and SIRE will emerge, the SIRE, as well as the NAIRU, will become endogenous to the tax policies of the government via the effects of the tax rate on target profit shares. A higher (lower) tax rate on profits will cause a lower (higher) SIRE and a higher (lower) NAIRU. Therefore, taking this channel into account, too, the tax rate on profits does not seem to be an adequate policy tool in order to stabilise the economy at a high SIRE.

In our formal model in this section, we have assumed the tax rate on wages to be zero. However, in case taxes on wages are positive, the effects of choosing the tax rate on wages as a fiscal policy tool can also be briefly reviewed without going into the analytical details. A higher (lower) tax rate on wages will reduce (increase) workers' net income, therefore consumption out of wages for a given propensity to consume, thus it will lower (raise) aggregate demand and hence the goods market equilibrium employment rate. Therefore, governments could also make use of the tax rate on wages in a similar way as discussed for the tax rate on profits, shown in equation (5.61), in order to adjust economic activity and employment to the SIRE level. Reducing the tax rate on wages will even be more effective than lowering taxes on profits when the economy is below the SIRE level, because workers have a higher propensity to consume. However, the tax rate on wages will also have detrimental medium-run effects if it is used as a policy tool in order to bring the economy down to the SIRE level, and if the workers' real wage rate and wage share target is related to net income or their share in net income after taxes, as is supposed in Figure 5.11. In this case, a higher tax rate on wages will reduce the goods market equilibrium rate of employment from e_1 towards e_2, which equals the SIRE e_1^N. However, a higher tax rate will induce workers to raise their target wage share and the target wage share curve will shift up from Ω_{W1}^T to Ω_{W2}^T, such that the SIRE will fall to e_2^N, and at e_2 we will thus have unexpected inflation again.

The second-round effect of a rising tax rate on wages, through a medium-run change in functional income distribution, on the goods market equilibrium employment rate will be definitely positive. Since a higher tax rate causes a higher target wage share of workers, this will then lead to a higher realised wage share, and thus to a lower profit share, as we have shown above in Section 5.2. In a wage-led economy, this will then trigger an increase in aggregate demand, output and employment:

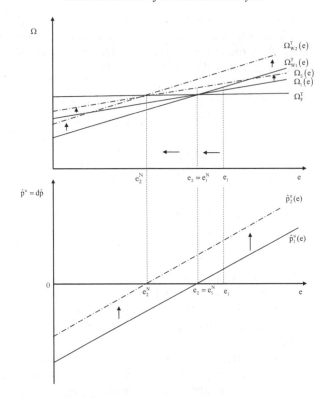

Figure 5.12   An increase in the tax rate on wages and the SIRE

$$\frac{\partial e^{FP}}{\partial t_w} = \frac{\partial e^{FP}}{\partial h} \frac{\partial h}{\partial \Omega_w^T} \frac{\partial \Omega_w^T}{\partial t_w} > 0, \quad \frac{\partial e^{FP}}{\partial h} < 0, \quad \frac{\partial h}{\partial \Omega_w^T} < 0, \quad \frac{\partial \Omega_w^T}{\partial t_w} > 0. \qquad (5.59e)$$

Whereas the short-run effect of an increase in the tax rate on wages will lower the employment rate towards the SIRE, the medium-run effects will decrease the SIRE, on the one hand, but raise the employment rate, on the other hand, triggering unexpected inflation again. If policymakers then raise the tax rate again, short-run effects will reduce inflationary pressure, but in the medium run, the SIRE will fall, employment will rise and unexpected inflation will emerge again – the economy will be moved into stagflation, that is, lower employment rates and tax-push inflation.[29]

Summing up our discussion, it has turned out that government expenditure policies are an efficient tool to stabilise the economy around some SIRE. Rising government deficits and debts associated with expansionary policies might need the support of and co-ordination with the interest rate policies of the central bank in order to avoid unsustainable government debt dynamics. Active tax policies that are pursued in order to manage the macro-economy are inferior to government expenditure policies. In the short run, the effectiveness may be asymmetric, because the demand and employment effects have to rely on adequate responses of the households and firms, which may not come forth, in particular in deep recessions.

Furthermore, raising tax rates to dampen inflationary levels of economic activity may not be effective in the medium run if distribution targets of firms and workers are geared towards after tax income shares. Whereas discretionary tax policies have some severe downsides as short-run macroeconomic stabilisation policies, the tax and social benefit system will have to play a role when it comes to medium-run stabilisation via the distribution of disposable income. We will touch upon these issues in Chapter 6.

5.7 CONFLICT INFLATION IN THE OPEN ECONOMY MACROECONOMIC MODEL

Let us now introduce conflict inflation into the open economy model presented in Section 4.5. We keep the basic assumption regarding production and finance from that model, which is a short-run version of the model by Hein and Vogel (2008, 2009).[30] This means that we assume an open economy, which depends on imported inputs for production purposes and the output of which competes in international markets. Labour mobility between the domestic economy and the rest of the world (RoW) is excluded. We take foreign price inflation with regard to imported inputs and the competing foreign final output as exogenously given. The nominal exchange rate will be treated as an exogenous parameter, which might be affected by monetary policies, liquidity preference and expectations of financial wealth holders.[31] Foreign economic activity is taken to be exogenously given, too. Furthermore, as in Section 4.5, we assume that the net international investment position of the domestic economy, which has been built up in the past, is zero, and hence the net international investment position of the RoW is zero, too, so that we can ignore the cross-border interest payments and, in the short run, focus on exports and imports of goods and services. To keep the model as simple as possible, we assume that the stock of government debt inherited from the past is zero, too. Therefore, we can abstract from government interest payments in the short-run model. Tax rates are also assumed to be zero, and we thus only include government real demand for goods and services funded by government deficits – which of course, in a medium-run analysis, would imply interest payments in future periods. We start by analysing the inflation generation process and then we move to linking it with the income generation process. For the inflation generation process we again follow the Hein and Stockhammer (2010, 2011b) approach. An open economy extension of the Blecker, Setterfield and Lavoie approach can be found in Blecker (2011) and Lavoie (2014, Chapter 8.9).

5.7.1 Inflation and Distribution

In Section 4.5, we started with the pricing equation of domestic producers of the single good in our model economy, which we reproduce here:

$$p = \left[1 + m(i)\right]\left(\frac{w}{y} + p_f a\mu\right), \quad m > 0, \frac{\partial m}{\partial i} \geq 0, \tag{5.67}$$

with μ denoting unit raw material and semi-finished product inputs per unit of output imported from abroad, p_f for foreign prices in foreign currency and a for the nominal exchange rate, indicating the price of a unit of foreign currency in domestic currency. An increase in the nominal exchange thus means a devaluation of the domestic currency, whereas a decrease implies an appreciation. From equation (5.67) we can derive the potential sources of inflation in our open economy:

$$\hat{p} = \xi_1\left(\hat{w}-\hat{y}\right)+\xi_2\left(\hat{p}_f+\hat{a}+\hat{\mu}\right)+\left(\widehat{1+m}\right), \tag{5.68}$$

with $\xi_1 = \dfrac{\left(1+m\right)w/y}{p}$, $\xi_2 = \dfrac{\left(1+m\right)p_f a\mu}{p}$, and hence $\xi_1+\xi_2 = 1$. With a constant technology in the short run, and hence $\hat{y}=0$ and $\hat{\mu}=0$, and a constant mark-up in firms' pricing, given by the structural features of the goods market, and hence $\left(\widehat{1+m}\right)=0$, domestic price inflation may thus be driven by domestic wage inflation, foreign price inflation and/or a continuous devaluation of the domestic currency:

$$\hat{p} = \xi_1\hat{w}+\xi_2\left(\hat{p}_f+\hat{a}\right). \tag{5.69}$$

Defining the ratio of unit material costs to unit labour costs:

$$z = \frac{p_f a\mu}{\dfrac{w}{y}}, \tag{5.70}$$

we can derive the profit and wage shares determined by firms' pricing:

$$h = \frac{\Pi}{pY} = \frac{\Pi}{\Pi+W} = \frac{m\left(1+z\right)}{m\left(1+z\right)+1} = \frac{1}{\dfrac{1}{m\left(1+z\right)}+1}. \tag{5.71}$$

$$\Omega = 1-h = \frac{W}{pY} = \frac{W}{\Pi+W} = \frac{1}{m\left(1+z\right)+1}. \tag{5.72}$$

The profit share is thus positively related to the mark-up and the ratio of unit material to unit labour costs. A higher ratio z means that unit imported material costs in the pricing equation (5.67) rise relative to unit domestic labour costs. With given unit labour costs, total unit variable costs and a given mark-up, prices and unit profits will rise. This then implies a higher profit share and a lower wage share in domestic income. Therefore, even with a constant mark-up, a fall in the ratio z will mean a lower profit share and a rise in this ratio implies a higher profit share. The growth rate of z is given as:

$$\hat{z} = \hat{p}_f+\hat{a}+\hat{\mu}-\left(\hat{w}-\hat{y}\right), \tag{5.73}$$

and with given technological coefficients in the short run, that is, $\hat{y}=0$ and $\hat{\mu}=0$, this boils down to:

$$\hat{z} = \hat{p}_f+\hat{a}-\hat{w}. \tag{5.74}$$

If nominal wage rate growth is equal to foreign inflation plus the growth rate of the nominal exchange rate, that is, the rate of depreciation of the domestic currency, the z-ratio will be constant, and with a given mark-up, also the profit share in equation (5.71) and the wage share in equation (5.72) will be constant. A constant z also implies from equation (5.69) that the rate of domestic wage inflation, equal to foreign inflation plus the rate of depreciation, is equal to domestic price inflation:

$$\hat{z} = 0 \implies \hat{p}_f + \hat{a} = \hat{w} = \hat{p}. \tag{5.74a}$$

If foreign inflation plus the rate of depreciation of the domestic currency exceeds domestic wage inflation, the z-ratio will rise, the profit share will rise and the wage share will fall, and domestic price inflation will also exceed domestic wage inflation:

$$\hat{z} > 0 \implies \hat{p}_f + \hat{a} > \hat{p} > \hat{w}. \tag{5.74b}$$

If foreign inflation plus the rate of depreciation of the domestic currency falls short of domestic wage inflation, the z-ratio will fall, the profit share will fall and the wage share will rise, and domestic price inflation will also fall short of domestic wage inflation:

$$\hat{z} < 0 \implies \hat{w} > \hat{p} > \hat{p}_f + \hat{a}. \tag{5.74c}$$

Different from the closed economy model, domestic wage inflation that exceeds given foreign inflation plus a given rate of depreciation of the domestic currency will raise the wage share even though wage inflation may be fully passed through to price inflation, which we now assume for the sake of simplicity.

We will now suppose that the target profit share is given by the constant mark-up in firms' price setting and the expectation of a constant medium-run z-ratio, that is, the condition in (5.74a). Foreign inflation is perceived to be exogenously given, as is the rate of depreciation of the domestic currency, which for simplicity we can set equal to zero ($\hat{a} = 0$) and thus assume a constant nominal exchange rate in the short run. A medium-run increase in the foreign inflation trend (relative to trend domestic wage and price inflation) or a depreciation of the domestic currency will raise the firms' target profit share, which thus becomes dependent on the expected real exchange rate (a_r^e) in the medium run. The expected real exchange rate is given as:

$$a_r^e = \frac{a^e p_f^e}{p^e}, \tag{5.75}$$

and

$$\hat{a}_r^e = \hat{a}^e + \hat{p}_f^e - \hat{p}^e. \tag{5.76}$$

A higher nominal exchange rate or higher foreign trend inflation relative to domestic trend inflation will thus raise the medium-run target profit share – via the increase in the z-ratio. Note that we conceive this as a slow process over a few periods, similar to the effect of the ex ante real interest rate on the target profit share, discussed above for the closed economy model. Our medium-run target profit share for the open economy is thus given by:

$$h_F^T = h_0 + h_3 i_r^e + h_5 a_r^e, \quad 1 > h_0 > 0, h_3, h_5 \geq 0. \tag{5.77}$$

The introduction of the real exchange into the firms' target profit share can also be found in Blecker (2011) and Lavoie (2014, Chapter 8). Unlike these authors, we assume that the real exchange rate has no direct effect on the workers' and trade unions' target wage share, because, in our model economy, workers only demand domestically produced consumption goods, which are not directly affected by the real exchange rate. We thus keep the workers' target wage share function from the closed economy without a government also for the open economy model:

$$\Omega_W^T = 1 - h_W^T = \Omega_0 + \Omega_1 e, \quad 1 > \Omega_0 > 0, \Omega_1 \geq 0. \tag{5.78}$$

From equations (5.81) and (5.82) we can again derive our SIRE:

$$e^N = \frac{1 - \Omega_0 - h_0 - h_3 i_r^e - h_5 a_r^e}{\Omega_1}. \tag{5.79}$$

A short-run increase in wage inflation, and also in price inflation according to equation (5.69), will mean unexpected wage and price inflation, if we again assume adaptive expectations. This will lower the actual profit share below the firms' target share, even if all firms fully pass-through the increase in wage inflation to price inflation, because the actual z-ratio will fall. It will also keep the actual wage share below the workers' target wage share, because higher wage inflation will induce higher price inflation, albeit at a lower rate. This will make ex post income shares temporarily consistent with each other:

$$\Omega = \Omega_W^T - \Omega_2 \hat{p}^u = \Omega_0 + \Omega_1 e - \Omega_2 \hat{p}^u,$$
$$1 > \Omega_0 > 0, \Omega_1, \Omega_2 \geq 0, \tag{5.80}$$

$$h = h_F^T - h_2 \hat{p}^u = h_0 + h_3 i_r^e + h_5 a_r^e - h_2 \hat{p}^u,$$
$$1 > h_0 > 0, h_2, h_3, h_5 \geq 0. \tag{5.81}$$

Unexpected inflation can thus be written as:

$$\hat{p}^u = \frac{h_0 + h_3 i_r^e + h_5 a_r^e + \Omega_0 + \Omega_1 e - 1}{h_2 + \Omega_2}. \tag{5.82}$$

Substituting unexpected inflation into equation (5.81) yields the realised profit share:

$$h = \frac{\left(h_0 + h_3 i_r^e + h_5 a_r^e\right)\Omega_2 + h_2\left(1 - \Omega_0 - \Omega_1 e\right)}{h_2 + \Omega_2}, \tag{5.83}$$

and for the realised wage share, we obtain:

$$\Omega = \frac{\left(\Omega_0 + \Omega_1 e\right)h_2 + \Omega_2\left(1 - h_0 - h_3 i_r^e - h_5 a_r^e\right)}{h_2 + \Omega_2}. \tag{5.84}$$

In the short run, a higher (lower) employment rate will raise (lower) the workers' target wage share according to equation (5.78), raise (lower) unexpected inflation in equation (5.82), raise (lower) the realised wage share according to equation (5.84) and lower (raise) the realised profit share in equation (5.83). We will thus get the effects shown in Figure 5.3 again. Furthermore, a higher (lower) employment rate will also lower (raise) the real exchange rate, through the effects on domestic inflation, as can be seen in equation (5.76).

In the medium run, an increase (decline) in the (expected) real exchange rate will raise (lower) the target profit share in equation (5.77), lower (raise) the SIRE in equation (5.79), raise (lower) unexpected inflation in equation (5.82), raise (lower) the realised profit share in equation (5.83) and lower (raise) the realised wage share in equation (5.84). A medium-run change in the expected real exchange rate will thus have similar effects as a change in the expected real interest rate, discussed above for the closed economy model and shown in Figure 5.10. We will discuss the demand effects of these medium-run changes further below in the context of the open economy aggregate demand and employment model, after the discussion of the short-run properties of the model.

5.7.2 The Goods Market Equilibrium with Distribution Conflict and the Effects of Unexpected Inflation in an Open Economy

For the analysis of distribution conflict, unexpected inflation and aggregate demand, we keep the saving and investment equation from Section 5.4. Saving in real terms (S_r) consists of retained earnings and saving out of rentiers' income. Workers are assumed not to save. Saving is thus determined by total profits and hence the profit share (h) and real income (Y), the propensity to save out of rentiers' income (s_R), and rentiers' real income as a product of the real rate of interest (i_r) and the stock of corporate debt (B_F) granted either directly or via banks:

$$S_r = hY - \left(1 - s_R\right)i_r B_F, \quad 1 \geq s_R > 0. \tag{5.85}$$

Investment (I) in real terms is affected positively by autonomous investment (I_a) or 'animal spirits' and by an accelerator effect of real income, as well as negatively by real interest payments to rentiers, again as a product of the real interest rate and the stock of corporate debt:

$$I = I_a + \beta Y - \theta i_r B_F, \quad I_a, \beta, \theta \geq 0. \tag{5.86}$$

As in Section 5.6, we assume government expenditures in real terms (G_r) to be exogenous policy instruments, and we disregard government indebtedness and interest payments, as mentioned above.

As in the fixed price model in Section 4.5, net exports in real terms are positively affected by international price competitiveness of domestic firms, provided the Marshall-Lerner condition can be assumed to hold. The real exchange rate will thus have a positive effect on net exports. But net exports also depend on the relative developments of foreign and domestic demand

and thus on foreign and domestic real income. The coefficients on domestic and foreign real incomes are affected by the income elasticities of the demand for imports and exports:[32]

$$NX_r = Ex - a_r Im = \psi a_r + \chi a_r Y_f - \phi Y, \quad \psi, \chi, \phi \geq 0 \tag{5.87}$$

Equation (5.88) presents the goods market equilibrium condition, the equality of planned leakages (saving) and planned injections (investment, net exports, government expenditures), and in (5.89) we have the Keynesian/Kaleckian stability condition, a higher marginal response of saving with respect to domestic income than the one of investment plus net exports:

$$I + G_r + NX_r = S_r, \tag{5.88}$$

$$\frac{\partial S_r}{\partial Y} > \frac{\partial I}{\partial Y} + \frac{\partial NX_r}{\partial Y} \Rightarrow h - \beta + \phi > 0. \tag{5.89}$$

Including inflation expectations and the target profit share in the behavioural functions (5.85)–(5.87), we can derive the ex ante equilibrium output:

$$Y^e = \frac{G_r + I_a + \left(1 - s_R - \theta\right)i_r^e B_F + a_r^e\left(\psi + \chi Y_f\right)}{h_0 + h_3 i_r^e + h_5 a_r^e - \beta + \phi}. \tag{5.90}$$

The effects of changes in parameters, like animal spirits and autonomous investment, the propensity to save out of rentiers' income, the interest rate and the profit share, government expenditures and the real exchange rate or foreign income, on this equilibrium have been analysed extensively in Section 4.5 and will not be repeated here. We will make use of some of these effects, regarding changes in the real interest rate, the profit share and the real exchange rate associated with unexpected inflation in the short run, and regarding medium-run changes in the expected real exchange rate and its determinants in what follows. With the assumption of a constant $q = 1/(yL)$, we obtain the ex ante equilibrium employment rate:

$$e^e = \frac{q\left[G_r + I_a + \left(1 - s_R - \theta\right)i_r^e B_F + a_r^e\left(\psi + \chi Y_f\right)\right]}{h_0 + h_3 i_r^e + h_5 a_r^e - \beta + \phi}. \tag{5.91}$$

If this employment rate deviates from the SIRE in equation (5.79), unexpected inflation will be generated, which will then affect the ex post real interest rate ($i_r^e - \hat{p}^u = i_r$), real exchange rate ($a_r^e - a_2 \hat{p}^u = a_r$) and profit share ($h_F^T - h_2 \hat{p}^u = h_0 + h_3 i_r^e + h_5 a_r^e - h_2 \hat{p}^u = h$) in the course of the short period. We thus get the following ex post employment rate at the end of the short period:

$$e^* = \frac{q\left[G_r + I_a + \left(1 - s_R - \theta\right)\left(i_r^e - p^u\right)B_F + \left(a_r^e - a_2 p^u\right)\left(\psi + \chi Y_f\right)\right]}{h_0 + h_3 i_r^e + h_5 a_r^e - h_2 \hat{p}^u - \beta + \phi}$$

$$= \frac{q\left[G_r + I_a + \left(1 - s_R - \theta\right)i_r B_F + a_r\left(\psi + \chi Y_f\right)\right]}{h - \beta + \phi} \tag{5.92}$$

with the following effect of unexpected inflation:

$$
\frac{\partial e^*}{\partial p^u} = \frac{h_2 e^* - q\left[\left(1-s_R-\theta\right)B_F + a_2\left(\psi + \chi Y_f\right)\right]}{h_0 + h_3 i_r^e + h_5 a_r^e - h_2 p^u - \beta + \phi}
$$

$$
= \frac{q\left[h_2 Y^* - \left(1-s_R-\theta\right)B_F - a_2\left(\psi + \chi Y_f\right)\right]}{h - \beta + \phi}
$$

(5.92a)

Again assuming the goods market stability condition (5.89) to be fulfilled, the direction of the effect of unexpected inflation on the employment rate is composed of the three terms in the numerator, which indicate the three channels of influence. According to the first term, a rising wage share and a falling profit share associated with unexpected inflation will raise domestic demand, which is wage-led. Following the second term, lower real interest payments of the firms to the rentiers caused by unexpected inflation will increase effective demand and employment, if we assume the normal case to prevail $(1-s_R-\theta<0)$ and hence the real interest effect on investment to be stronger than on rentiers' consumption. So far, unexpected inflation would thus mean a further increase in the employment rate, rising further above the SIRE, as in the closed economy model in Section 5.4. Of course, for unexpected disinflation we will have the reverse effects, that is, a further fall below the SIRE. However, in an open economy we also have to consider the effects of unexpected inflation on the real exchange rate in the third term of the numerator. In case of unexpected inflation, the real exchange rate will fall and the domestic currency will appreciate in real terms. On the one hand, this lowers the international price competitiveness of domestic producers. On the other hand, with given foreign income and a given foreign propensity to spend on domestic exports, this will lower foreign demand for domestic goods through this real income channel. With unexpected disinflation, we would see the reverse effects. Therefore, this third channel will have a partially stabilising effect moving the employment rate back towards the SIRE. Whether this effect is stronger than the destabilising effects via re-distribution between capital and labour and between firms and rentiers is an empirical question.

In what follows, we will thus have to distinguish between two cases. In the first case of a short-run unstable SIRE, the demand and employment effects of unexpected inflation via re-distribution between capital and labour and between firms and rentiers dominate over the net export effects: $h_2 Y^* - \left(1-s_R-\theta\right)B_F - a_2\left(\psi + \chi Y_f\right) > 0$. In the second case of a short-run stable SIRE, the net export effects of unexpected inflation dominate over the re-distribution effects on domestic demand: $h_2 Y^* - \left(1-s_R-\theta\right)B_F - a_2\left(\psi + \chi Y_f\right) < 0$. These two cases have close similarities with our distinction between wage- and profit-led demand in Section 4.5. However, the wage- vs. profit-led distinction assumes functional income distribution to be exogenous and examines the effects of changes in wage and profit shares on aggregate demand, as well as growth and employment (Hein 2014a, Chapter 7, Lavoie and Stockhammer 2013b). In the current chapter, wage and profit shares are endogenous and interact with output and the employment rate. But it is clear that the unstable case means that unexpected inflation and a rising wage share are associated with rising aggregate demand, output and employment rates; it is thus associated with an overall wage-led demand regime. The stable case in our model means that unexpected inflation and a rising wage share are associated with falling aggregate demand, output and employment rates, as in a profit-led demand regime. We will now discuss these two regimes in turn and also integrate medium-run effects of changes in the expected real exchange rate.

5.7.3   The Case of the Short-Run Unstable SIRE

The short-run unstable case for the open economy shares the characteristics of the interaction of unexpected (dis-)inflation and the employment rate of the closed economy model discussed in Section 5.4 and can graphically be described by Figures 5.4–5.6. The negative (positive) effect of positive (negative) unexpected inflation on net exports will dampen but not prevent the instability. In the medium run, over several periods, continuous positive (negative) unexpected inflation implies that the domestic wage and price inflation trend will exceed (fall short of) foreign inflation, which will lead to a fall (rise) in the expected real exchange rate, as well as to a fall (rise) in the ratio z of unit material to unit wage costs. According to equation (5.77), firms' target profit share will thus decrease (increase) and, according to equation (5.79), the SIRE will rise (fall) and follow the actual employment rate:

$$\frac{\partial e^N}{\partial a_r^e} = \frac{-h_5}{\Omega_1} < 0. \tag{5.79a}$$

Since a falling (rising) target profit share of firms also means a falling (rising) realised profit share, according to equation (5.83), the latter will further stimulate (dampen) aggregate demand, output and employment in equation (5.92). The medium-run effect of a change in the expected real exchange rate on the goods market equilibrium employment rate via the change in the target and the actual profit share, taking into account equation (5.83), are given as:

$$\frac{\partial e^*}{\partial a_r^e} = \frac{\partial e^*}{\partial h}\frac{\partial h}{\partial a_r^e} = \frac{-e^*}{h-\beta+\phi}\frac{h_5}{h_2+\Omega_2}$$

$$= \frac{-h_5 e^*}{(h-\beta+\phi)(h_2+\Omega)} < 0. \tag{5.92b}$$

Due to the endogeneity of the SIRE and further demand effects of medium-run changes in the target profit share, we may thus have self-reinforcing downward (upward) processes of both the ex post goods market equilibrium rate of employment and the SIRE. Figure 5.13 shows such a scenario for a downward process. Initially, the employment rate e_1 falls short of the SIRE at e_1^N, which causes unexpected disinflation, a fall in the wage share and a rise in the real exchange rate. The latter, however, is insufficient to raise net exports more than domestic demand falls. Therefore the employment rate falls further to e_2. The increase in the real exchange rate raises the target profit share and lowers the target wage share of firms in the medium run from Ω_{F1}^T to Ω_{F2}^T and therefore reduces the SIRE to e_2^N. By a fluke, we may arrive at $e_2^N = e_2$, and the economy will rest there. However, a slight deviation of employment from this new SIRE will further lower domestic demand, output and the employment rate towards e_3, and so on. Of course, other – maybe cyclical – downward processes are possible, but they will not be discussed here. What is important for our purposes is to have shown that the SIRE in the open economy becomes endogenous to the real exchange rate, which itself is affected by the goods market equilibrium employment rate.

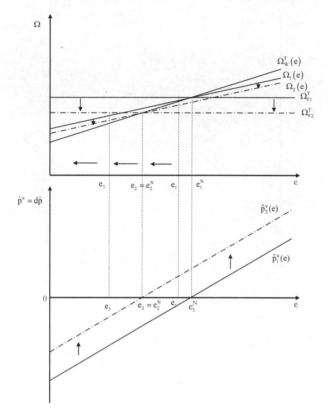

Figure 5.13 Short-run unstable and medium-run endogenous SIRE in an open economy

5.7.4 The Case of the Short-Run Stable SIRE

In the short-run stable case, the negative (positive) effect of positive (negative) unexpected inflation on net exports will dominate over the re-distributive effects on domestic demand, prevent cumulative instability and move the employment rate back towards the SIRE. However, unless this effect leads to an immediate return of the employment rate towards the SIRE, medium-run positive (negative) unexpected inflation effects on the expected real exchange rate also have to be considered in this case. As explained above, these cause a change in the target profit share in equation (5.77), the SIRE in equation (5.79), the realised profit share in equation (5.83), with a second-round effect on the employment rate in equation (5.92). A potential scenario is shown in Figure 5.14. Initially, the employment rate e_1 falls short of the SIRE at e_1^N, which causes unexpected disinflation, a fall in the wage share and a rise in the real exchange rate. The latter is now sufficient to raise net exports more than domestic demand falls. Therefore the employment rate rises to e_2. The increase in the real exchange rate raises the target profit share and lowers the target wage share of firms in the medium run from Ω_{F1}^T to Ω_{F2}^T and therefore reduces the SIRE to e_2^N. This also implies that the actual profit share rises and the wage share falls. Furthermore, since $e_2 < e_2^N$ in our example, domestic inflation will fall further, improving the real exchange rate, which will then move the employment rate

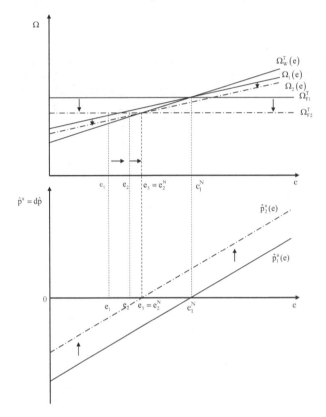

Figure 5.14   Short-run stable and medium-run endogenous SIRE in an open economy

towards $e_3 = e_2^N$. The SIRE will thus stabilise, but at a lower level due to the disequilibrium effects of unexpected disinflation on the expected real exchange rate and thus on the firms' target profit share. Of course, as in the unstable case, other disequilibrium paths are possible, which we do not want to explore here any further. Again, what is important, also for the stable case, is that the SIRE in the open economy becomes endogenous to the real exchange rate, which itself is affected by the goods market equilibrium employment rate.

Our results, both for the unstable and the stable case, thus undermine the optimistic view regarding the stabilising potential of real exchange rate movements in the open economy NCM model proposed by Carlin and Soskice (2015, Chapter 9). In their model, net exports are a positive function of the real exchange rate, and the nominal exchange rate is a negative function of the domestic interest rate, following an uncovered interest rate parity theory of the exchange rate.[33] With accelerating (decelerating) inflation, the real exchange rate falls (rises) with dampening effects on the employment rate and thus on the inflation rate leading the economy back to the SIRE or the NAIRU. Therefore, in their NCM approach, the central bank will have to raise (lower) the interest rate by less than in the closed economy case, because of the effects of accelerating (decelerating) inflation on the real exchange rate, on the one hand, and because of the effects of higher (lower) interest rates on the nominal exchange rate, on the other hand. However, this NCM approach ignores the distribution and demand effects of accelerating (decelerating) inflation in the short-run, as well as the endogeneity of the SIRE (and the NAIRU) with respect to the real exchange in the medium run (and with respect to the real interest rate), which are each prominent in our post-Keynesian approach.

From these results it follows that also in the open economy framework the SIRE is far from being a strong attractor in the short run, in particular if aggregate demand remains wage-led. Furthermore, even without adjustments of the nominal exchange rate, real exchange rate dynamics associated with unexpected (dis-)inflation feeds back on the SIRE in the medium run. Therefore, one cannot expect to reach a high SIRE (or a low NAIRU) without macroeconomic economic policy interventions and aggregate demand management. For these, government expenditure policies seem to be the appropriate tool, also in the open economy, because government tax policies and central bank interest rate policies face similar constraints in the open economy as those pointed out for the closed economy. We will derive the overall macroeconomic policy implications from our post-Keynesian model in more detail in Chapter 6. Before doing so, however, let us point out a few further endogeneity channels of the SIRE, which have been discussed in the literature.

5.8 FURTHER MEDIUM- TO LONG-RUN ENDOGENEITY CHANNELS FOR THE SIRE AND THE NAIRU[34]

While discussing the post-Keynesian closed and open economy macroeconomics models with conflict inflation, we have already pointed out several endogeneity channels of the SIRE (or the NAIRU) with respect to the expected real interest rate and the tax rate on profits or on wages, as well as to the expected real exchange rate. While the interest and tax rate channels are related to economic policy interventions that attempt to stabilise the SIRE, the real exchange rate channel may already arise from the disequilibrium process in which the employment rate deviates from the SIRE, without any policy intervention. This channel may then be reinforced by nominal exchange rate policies. In this section we will now integrate three further endogeneity channels of the SIRE (or the NAIRU) with respect to the actual employment or unemployment rate determined in the goods market. We only indicate the effects on the SIRE and the NAIRU for a closed economy model but ignore the associated feedback effects on the goods market equilibrium rate of employment, which may then give rise to complex interacting dynamics in the medium run, as indicated in the previous sections.

5.8.1 Persistence Mechanisms in the Labour Market

Labour market-related mechanisms for unemployment persistence have already been suggested by Blanchard and Summers (1987, 1988) and Ball (1999) and have recently been further explored by Ball (2014), Stockhammer and Sturn (2012) and Stockhammer et al. (2014), for example. Applying union wage bargaining or insider-outsider models, persistent unemployment and an increasing share of long-term unemployment in total unemployment, with the associated loss of skills and access to firms by the long-term unemployed, will decrease the pressure of a given rate of unemployment on labour unions' or insiders' target wage shares and hence on nominal wage demands. This will then require an increasing rate of unemployment in order to stabilise inflation.

This can be integrated into our model as follows. Assume that the share of the long-term unemployed in total unemployment increases when the unemployment rate exceeds some threshold, which is given by frictional unemployment caused by the 'normal' working of the labour market in the face of changing demand patterns and structural as well as regional change. The employment rate hence falls short of a 'full employment' rate (e^f) associated with this rate of unemployment. Since the share of long-term unemployment in total unemployment will now increase, we obtain the following effect of actual employment on the workers' target wage from equation (5.13):

$$\Omega_W^T = \Omega_0 + \Omega_1 \left[e + \Omega_3 \left(e^f - e \right) \right], \ 1 > \Omega_0 > 0, \Omega_1, \Omega_3 \geq 0. \tag{5.93}$$

When the goods market equilibrium rate of employment persistently falls short of full employment ($e^f - e > 0$), long-term unemployment will arise and the workers' target wage share for a given total rate of employment will increase. Combining equation (5.93) with the firms' target profit share from equation (5.14) we get for the SIRE:

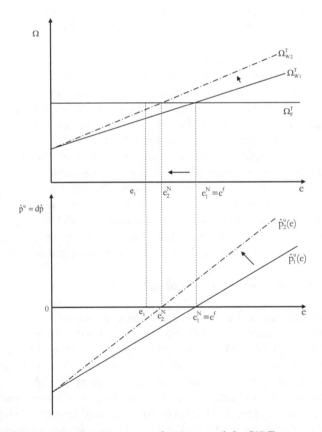

Figure 5.15   Labour market persistence mechanisms and the SIRE

$$e^N = \frac{1 - \Omega_0 - \Omega_1\Omega_3\left(e^f - e\right) - h_0}{\Omega_1}.$$
(5.94)

Whenever the employment rate determined by the goods market falls short of the 'full employment' rate, it will decrease the SIRE and hence increase the NAIRU.

$$\frac{\partial e^N}{\partial\left(e^f - e\right)} = -\Omega_3 < 0.$$
(5.94a)

Figure 5.15 shows the negative effect of labour market persistence mechanisms on the SIRE, assuming that the initial SIRE is associated with full employment in the above sense. If the goods market equilibrium rate of employment e_1 persistently falls short of this, the stable inflation rate of employment will thus decrease below the full employment rate, from e_1^N to e_2^N.[35]

Note that a readjustment of the SIRE to the full employment rate requires that the goods market equilibrium rate of employment will have to exceed the SIRE for a considerable period of time, facilitating the reintegration of the long-term unemployed.

5.8.2 Wage Aspirations Based on Conventional Behaviour

Following an argument suggested by Setterfield and Lovejoy (2006), Skott (2005) and Stockhammer (2008), we can assume that workers' distribution targets are affected by actual distribution. If there is persistent deviation of the actual wage share from the target wage share, caused by a deviation of the goods market equilibrium rate of employment from the SIRE, wage earners adjust their targets accordingly. Simply put, workers will get used to the actual distribution of income and incorporate it into their distribution target. Therefore, in the medium run, the target wage share of workers from equation (5.13) becomes:

$$\Omega_W^T = \Omega_0 + \Omega_1 e + \Omega_4\left(\Omega - \Omega_W^T\right) = \frac{\Omega_0 + \Omega_1 e + \Omega_4\Omega}{1 + \Omega_4},$$
(5.95)

$$1 > \Omega_4 > 0, \Omega_1, \Omega_4 \geq 0.$$

Combining equation (5.95) with the firms' target profit share from equation (5.14), the SIRE becomes:

$$e^N = \frac{\left(1 - h_0\right)\left(1 + \Omega_4\right) - \Omega_0 - \Omega_4\Omega}{\Omega_1}.$$
(5.96)

A deviation of the actual wage share from the workers' target share has the following effect on the stable inflation rate of employment:

$$\frac{\partial e^N}{\partial\Omega} = -\frac{\Omega_4}{\Omega_1} < 0.$$
(5.96a)

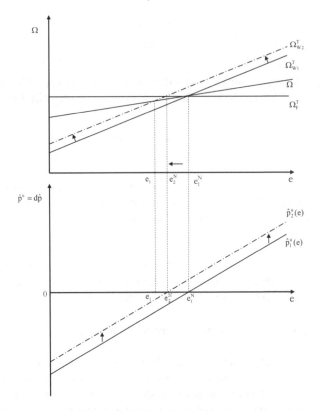

Figure 5.16   Endogenous wage aspirations and the SIRE

A positive deviation of the actual wage share from the workers' target, caused by employment falling short of the SIRE, finally reduces the SIRE and raises the NAIRU, because workers adjust their target wage share towards the actual wage share. This is shown in Figure 5.16, in which the SIRE decreases from e_1^N to e_2^N. Of course, the process also works in the other direction. Employment exceeding the SIRE, and unemployment falling short of the NAIRU, will be associated with a wage share below the workers' target, and the workers will finally adjust their targets and hence increase the SIRE towards the employment rate determined by the goods market and reduce the NAIRU towards actual unemployment.

5.8.3   The Effect of Investment in the Capital Stock

The effects of investment in the capital stock on employment and the NAIRU have been explored by Arestis and Sawyer (2004a, 2005), Rowthorn (1995, 1999) and Sawyer (2002).[36] The capital stock in relation to output may directly affect the stable inflation rate of employment and hence the NAIRU if firms' target mark-up and profit share are positively related to capacity utilisation ($u = Y/K$) in the medium to long run. Lower current investment will lead to a lower future capital stock and to higher medium- to long-run capacity utilisation, if there is a constant growth rate in the non-capacity creating autonomous components of demand, for example government expenditures in the closed economy or exports driven by the growth of foreign income in the open economy. Higher capacity utilisation will then lead to higher target mark-ups and profit shares of firms:

$$h_F^T = h_0 + h_1 u, \ h_0 > 0, h_1 \geq 0. \tag{5.97}$$

Taking into account workers' target wage share from equation (5.13), we get for the SIRE:

$$e^N = \frac{1 - \Omega_0 - h_0 - h_1 u}{\Omega_1}. \tag{5.98}$$

From this, we obtain for the effect of capacity utilisation, which, under the conditions mentioned above, is negatively affected by the capacity effects of investment in the medium to long run:

$$\frac{\partial e^N}{\partial u} = -\frac{h_1}{\Omega_1} < 0. \tag{5.98a}$$

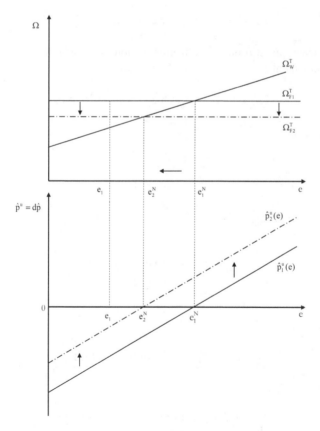

Figure 5.17 Low investment in the short run, higher capacity utilisation in the long run and the SIRE

Again, the process should also operate in reverse. Any rise in investment will have short-run positive effects on aggregate demand and employment, and in the medium to long run we will see the positive effects on productive capacity, which should lower capacity utilisation and hence firms' target mark-ups and profit shares, and therefore raise the SIRE.

Figure 5.17 shows the negative effects associated with weak investment, aggregate demand and employment in the short run, which will raise capacity in the medium to long run, triggering higher target mark-ups and profit shares. Therefore, the SIRE will decrease from e_1^N to e_2^N.

APPENDIX 5.I: A PRO-CYCLICAL PROFIT SHARE IN THE HEIN AND STOCKHAMMER MODEL

The Hein and Stockhammer (2009b, 2010, 2011b) model of the inflation barrier from Section 5.2.2 is able to generate a pro-cyclical profit share, instead of a pro-cyclical wage share, if the firms' target profit share includes a strong effect of the employment rate and workers' nominal wage demands show only weak responses towards unexpected inflation. This can be shown as follows. We take workers' target wage share from equation (5.13):

$$\Omega_W^T = 1 - h_W^T = \Omega_0 + \Omega_1 e, \quad 1 > \Omega_0 > 0, \Omega_1 \geq 0, \tag{5.13}$$

and we modify firms' target profit share from equation (5.14) such that it also depends positively on the employment rate:

$$h_F^T = 1 - \Omega_F^T = h_0 + h_1 e, \quad 1 > h_0 > 0, h_1 \geq 0. \tag{5.14A}$$

The SIRE then becomes:

$$e^N = \frac{1 - h_0 - \Omega_0}{h_1 + \Omega_1}, \tag{5.21A}$$

and unexpected inflation becomes:

$$\hat{p}^u = \frac{h_0 + \Omega_0 + \left(h_1 + \Omega_1\right)e - 1}{h_2 + \Omega_2}. \tag{5.27A}$$

The realised wage and profit shares are then:

$$\Omega = \frac{\Omega_0 h_2 + \Omega_2\left(1 - h_0\right) + \left(\Omega_1 h_2 - \Omega_2 h_1\right)e}{h_2 + \Omega_2}, \tag{5.30A}$$

$$h = \frac{h_0 \Omega_2 + h_2\left(1 - \Omega_0\right) + \left(h_1 \Omega_2 - h_2 \Omega_1\right)e}{h_2 + \Omega_2}. \tag{5.31A}$$

With

$$\frac{\partial \Omega}{\partial e} = \frac{\Omega_1 h_2 - \Omega_2 h_1}{h_2 + \Omega_2}, \tag{5.30Aa}$$

and

$$\frac{\partial h}{\partial e} = \frac{h_1 \Omega_2 - h_2 \Omega_1}{h_2 + \Omega_2}, \tag{5.31Aa}$$

it is clear that if $h_1 \Omega_2 - h_2 \Omega_1 > 0$, we will have $\dfrac{\partial h}{\partial e} > 0$ and $\dfrac{\partial \Omega}{\partial e} < 0$. A strong response of firms' target profit share with respect to employment and a low response of the workers' target wage share, that is, a high value of h_1 and a low value of Ω_1, and a weak response of workers' nominal wage setting towards unexpected inflation and a high response of firms' price setting, that is, a high value of Ω_2 and a low value h_2, may thus generate a pro-cyclical profit share, even if we disregard overhead labour. The result is shown in Figure 5.A.I.

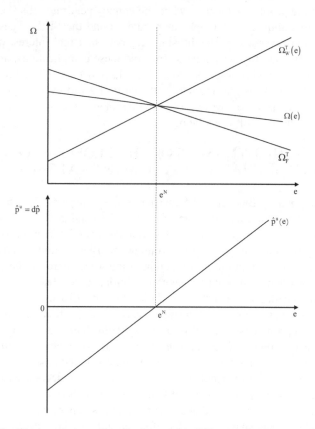

Figure 5.A.I   Conflicting claims, distribution and inflation in the Hein and Stockhammer approach with a pro-cyclical profit share

Table 5.A.I   Inflation and distribution effects of deviations of the employment rate from the SIRE or of deviations of the unemployment rate from the NAIRU: The case of a pro-cyclical profit share

	$\hat{p}^u(e)$	$\Omega(e)$	$h(e)$	$\dfrac{\Pi_F}{\Pi}(e)$	$\dfrac{R}{\Pi}(e)$
$e > e^N(\text{SIRE})$ $ue < \text{NAIRU}$	+	−	+	+	−
$e = e^N(\text{SIRE})$ $ue = \text{NAIRU}$	0	0	0	0	0
$e < e^N(\text{SIRE})$ $ue > \text{NAIRU}$	−	+	−	−	+

For this case, the distributional results of deviations of the employment rate from the SIRE from Table 5.1 have to be modified, so that we get Table 5.A.I. Such distributional effects, of course, would also modify the demand generation processes for the closed and the open economy models in Sections 5.4 and 5.7. Since domestic demand in our model is wage-led, an increase (fall) in the profit (wage) share when the employment rate exceeds the SIRE, and a fall (rise) in the profit (wage) share when the employment rate falls short of the SIRE, would contribute to stabilising the employment rate around the SIRE. These effects could thus dampen or even reverse the destabilising real debt and real interest payment effects and would thus complicate further analysis. To avoid these complications, and also because the demand effects of changing wage or profit shares have been estimated to be rather weak (Onaran and Galanis 2014), we abstract from the case of a pro-cyclical profit share in our model versions in this chapter. However, it has to be remembered that the wage share in our model is only the wage share of direct labour.

APPENDIX 5.II: THE DYNAMICS OF THE CLOSED ECONOMY MODEL IN A WAGE SHARE–EMPLOYMENT RATE SPACE

Following the approach by Blecker and Setterfield (2019, Chapter 5.3), where the dynamic interaction of the wage share and the rate of capacity utilisation is analysed in a distribution and growth framework, we can also analyse our short-run interaction between the wage share and the employment rate in a similar framework. Blecker and Setterfield, first, look at an aggregate demand (AD) curve as a function of the wage share (or the profit share) and distinguish between wage- and profit-led demand, similar to our distinction in Chapter 4 of this book. Second, they define a distributive relationship, or a distributive curve (DC), which presents the wage share as a function of the rate of capacity utilisation. This distributive curve may then represent a profit squeeze, that is, a falling profit share with rising capacity utilisation, or a wage squeeze, that is, a falling wage share with rising capacity utilisation. Blecker and Setterfield (2019, p. 227) then distinguish three cases: The first case of a wage-led demand regime with a wage squeeze distributive regime is stable. The second case of a wage-led demand regime with a weak profit squeeze distributive regime is stable, too. Graphically, this second case is given by an aggregate demand curve that is steeper than the distributive curve in capacity utilisation-wage share space. The third case, however, with a wage-led demand regime and a strong profit-squeeze distributive regime is unstable. Here, the distributive curve is steeper than the aggregate demand curve. In our model, the positive effect of the employment rate on the wage share is akin to the Blecker and Setterfield (2019) profit-squeeze distributive regime. However, in our model, we also have the effects on unexpected inflation and the effects on distribution between creditors (rentiers) and debtors (firms), which are all absent in the Blecker and Setterfield (2019, Chapter 5.3) model.

In our model, we can look at the end of period, 'ex post' employment rate as a function of the profit share, and thus the wage share, in equation (5.44), which we reproduce here, as representing the demand or employment regime:

$$e^* = \frac{q\left[I_a + \left(1 - s_R - \theta\right)i_r B_F\right]}{h - \beta} = \frac{q\left[I_a + \left(1 - s_R - \theta\right)i_r B_F\right]}{1 - \Omega - \beta}.$$

(5.44)

The counterpart is equation (5.30) of the realised wage share as a function of the employment rate, also repeated here, representing the distributive regime:

$$\Omega = \frac{\left(\Omega_0 + \Omega_1 e\right)h_2 + \Omega_2\left(1 - h_0\right)}{h_2 + \Omega_2}.$$

(5.30)

The respective slopes are given by:

$$\frac{\partial e^*}{\partial \Omega} = \frac{q\left[I_a + \left(1 - s_R - \theta\right)i_r B_F\right]}{\left(1 - \Omega - \beta\right)^2} > 0,$$

(5.44A)

$$\frac{\partial \Omega}{\partial e} = \frac{\Omega_1 h_2}{h_2 + \Omega_2} > 0.$$

(5.30A)

Our model thus generates a wage-led demand and employment regime associated with a profit squeeze distributive regime. Furthermore, whereas the distributive curve in equation (5.30) has a constant slope given in equation (5.30A), the slope of the employment curve from equation (5.44) is increasing with the wage share, as can be seen in equation (5.44A).[37] The higher the wage share, the stronger the effects of a marginal increase in the wage share on the employment rate. Graphically, our model thus generates a linear distributive curve [$\Omega(e)$] and a non-linear progressively rising employment curve [$e^*(\Omega)$], as shown in Figure 5.A.II, with an unstable equilibrium at e^N and Ω^N.

Any deviation from the distribution claims equilibrium at e^N and Ω^N leads to cumulative deviations. However, due to the non-linear employment function, we arrive at a stable low activity equilibrium at e_1 and Ω_1, well below the SIRE. We know that in our model framework, this is associated with falling inflation rates, associated with re-distribution between profits and wages and, in particular, with re-distribution between rentiers (creditors) and firms (debtors). These destabilising effects are ignored when looking at the interaction between employment rate and wage share only. That is one of the reasons why we prefer to continue with our modelling framework instead of the more elegant and more compact one proposed by Blecker and Setterfield (2019, Chapter 5.3) and other authors.

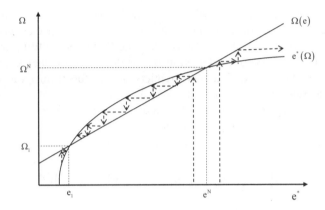

Figure 5.A.II   Interaction of wage share and employment rate in the closed economy model – ignoring real interest rate effects

NOTES

1. See Hein (2014a, Chapter 4.4) for a full model.
2. The price adjustment of the price leader will therefore be asymmetric.
3. The Phillips curve goes back to the statistical work of Phillips (1958) on the negative relationship between nominal wage growth and the rate of unemployment in the UK, 1861–1957. It was then re-interpreted as a negative relationship between the unemployment rate and price inflation by Samuelson and Solow (1960), which became a core element of the neoclassical synthesis, dominating macroeconomics in the 1950s and 1960s. For further details, see Snowdon and Vane (2005, Chapter 3).
4. In a Kaleckian distribution and growth model context, I had called this distributional claims equilibrium a 'stable inflation rate of capacity utilisation' (SIRCU) (Hein 2006c, 2008, Chapter 16).
5. Stockhammer (2008) clearly distinguishes between a 'NAIRU theory', versions of which can be found in monetarist, new Keynesian, post-Keynesian and Marxian approaches, and a 'NAIRU story', which relates unemployment to regulated labour markets, too high workers' bargaining power and income claims, and which is not shared by post-Keynesians and several Marxian authors.
6. Empirical concerns and critique of estimations of the NAIRU, as included in Lang et al. (2020) and Stanley (2004), therefore, do not apply to the post-Keynesian view of the inflation barrier (SIRE, NAIRU) as an endogenous phenomenon with respect to effective demand and actual employment.
7. In what follows, time indices will only be used if equations contain a time lag.
8. The modelling follows Blecker and Setterfield (2019, Chapter 5.2.1) and Lavoie (2014, Chapters 8.3–8.4) with the exception that both have formulated the model in terms of target and actual real wages, whereas we have chosen target and actual wage shares. However, with zero labour productivity growth these formulations are equivalent.
9. Blecker and Setterfield (2019, Chapter 5.2.3) use the rate of capacity utilisation as an indicator for economic activity, have it affect both target wage shares of workers and firms, also include endogenous productivity growth, but omit a wage indexation term in their price Phillips curve.
10. This section draws on and further elaborates on Hein and Stockhammer (2010, 2011b).
11. Interestingly, also Lavoie (2006b) in a post-Keynesian amendment of the NCM accepts a short-run inflation barrier, which is then endogenised in the medium to long run, similar to the procedure in Hein and Stockhammer (2010, 2011b).
12. In Appendix I, we show that a modification of the firms' target profit share may allow for a pro-cyclical profit share in the Hein and Stockhammer (2009b, 2010, 2011b) model under certain conditions, and we explain why we abstract from this case in the following model analyses.
13. For studies on the determinants of long-run trends of wage and profit shares, and on the causes of re-distribution from labour to capital, in particular in the recent era of finance-dominated capitalism since the late 1970s/early 1980s, see for example Dünhaupt (2017), Guschanski and Onaran (2018), Hein (2015), Hein and Detzer (2015a), Hein et al. (2017a, 2017b, 2018), Jayadev (2007), Kohler et al. (2019), Kristal (2010), Setterfield (2007a, 2021) and Stockhammer (2017b).

14. See, for example, Baccaro and Rei (2007), Baker et al. (2004), Ball (1999, 2014), Bassanini and Duval (2006), Blanchard and Wolfers (2000), Girardi et al. (2020), Howell (2011), Logeay and Tober (2006), Stockhammer (2011), Stockhammer and Sturn (2012), Stockhammer and Klär (2010), Stockhammer et al. (2014), Storm and Naastepad (2012, Chapter 2), Vergeer and Kleinknecht (2012) and the recent meta analysis by Brancaccio et al. (2020).

15. Hein and Truger (2005a, 2005b) have shown that relatively high unemployment rates in Germany in international comparison from the early 1990s until the early 2000s cannot be explained by those structural features which are said to determine the NAIRU but rather by a restrictive macroeconomic policy mix – or a restrictive macroeconomic policy regime. We will return to the role of macroeconomic policy regimes for aggregate demand and growth in Chapter 8 of this book.

16. This section is based on and elaborates on Hein and Stockhammer (2010, 2011b).

17. Repayment of debt is not considered explicitly. It can be assumed that debt is rolled over when we move from period to period.

18. On the relevance of real debt effects for economic downturns and recessions, see already Fisher (1933) and Keynes (1936, p. 264), as well as our remarks in Chapter 3.

19. This section draws on Hein and Stockhammer (2010, 2011b) and presents a short-run level version of the distribution and growth model presented in that paper.

20. Our way of modelling the income generating process, in line with our model in Section 4.3, is different from other post-Keynesian alternative models to the NCM, which have accepted a simple interest rate inverse IS curve, like Atesoglu and Smithin (2006), Lavoie (2006b), Rochon and Setterfield (2007) and Setterfield (2006). For post-Keynesian approaches to effective demand and income generation allowing for real debt and different distribution effects, as in the model presented here, see also Hein (2006a, 2008, Chapter 16), Hein and Stockhammer (2010, 2011b), Setterfield (2009a) and Stockhammer (2008).

21. Of course if unexpected inflation is very high and the pass-through of wage inflation to price inflation is very low, implying a strong re-distribution in favour of labour and a high value of h_2, the goods market may turn unstable. However, we will not discuss this case here.

22. See Hein and Stockhammer (2010) for the inclusion of the 'puzzling case' in the present model. Empirically, Hein and Schoder (2011) have found the 'normal case' for the USA and Germany in the period from 1960 to 2007.

23. Interestingly, similar considerations can be found in Keynes (1936, p. 262), when he discusses the effects of money wage cuts and related disinflation or deflation: 'A reduction of money-wages will somewhat reduce prices. It will, therefore, involve some re-distribution of real income (a) from wage earners to other factors entering into marginal prime cost whose remuneration has not been reduced, and (b) from entrepreneurs to rentiers to whom a certain income fixed in terms has been guaranteed . . . The transfers from wage earners to other factors of production is likely to diminish the propensity to consume. The effect of the transfer from entrepreneurs to rentiers is more open to doubt. But if rentiers represent on the whole the richer section of the community and those whose standard of life is least flexible, then the effect of this will be unfavourable'.

24. See also Stockhammer (2004b) who analyses the dynamic stability of the SIRE/NAIRU in a post-Kaleckian distribution and growth model. He finds that with wage-led demand and growth, as in our short-run model, the NAIRU may be unstable, whereas with profit-led demand and growth it may turn stable. However, he does not consider the impact of changes in inflation on distribution between creditors and debtors and the related demand and growth effects.

25. This section draws on and further elaborates on Hein and Stockhammer (2010, 2011b).

26. Lima and Setterfield (2010) provide an overview of empirical studies on the interest cost channel, according to which changes in the interest rate affect firms' costs of production and hence their pricing decisions. They report ample evidence for the existence of such an effect in developed capitalist economies. Lima and Setterfield (2014) present explicit attempts at modelling the interest-cost effects in a more complex dynamic post-Keynesian macroeconomic model.

27. Such distributional effects of monetary policies and the interest rate have been analysed and confirmed by Argitis and Michopolou (2010), Argitis and Pitelis (2001, 2006), Duménil and Lévy (2005), Dünhaupt (2012), Epstein and Jayadev (2005), Epstein and Power (2003), Hein and Schoder (2011), Moore (1989b), Niggle (1989) and Rochon and Rossi (2006a, 2006b), for the USA and several other countries. Kappes (2021) has presented a recent review of the empirical literature on monetary policy and personal income distribution. Of course, following the Kaleckian approach explained in Chapter 3, functional distribution is affected by several other factors, like the bargaining power of workers, the degree of price competition amongst firms, the sectoral composition of the economy and, in an international context, by the imported material costs relative to domestic wage costs (Hein 2015). Therefore, we should not expect that periods of low interest rates, like since the 1990s, should be associated automatically with high or rising wage shares and falling inequality in the personal distribution of income. See also the references for empirical studies on the determinants of long-run trends of wage and profit shares in footnote 13.

28. See Prante et al. (2020, 2022b) for interactive simulations of the effects of an interest-elastic mark-up in a similar modelling framework.
29. Bibow (2006) has analysed tax push inflation for the cases of Germany and the Eurozone from 1999 until 2005, focussing on a series of hikes of indirect taxes and administered prices in the context of fiscal restrictions raising measured inflation. He does not include these in a conflicting claims inflation model like ours. However, if introduced in our model, increases in indirect taxes and administered prices for public goods and services, for example, will have the same effects as increases in tax rates on wages, in particular, if we assume that workers' and trade unions' real wage and distribution targets are geared towards real purchasing power of wages in terms of consumption goods.
30. For further open economy models with conflict inflation, see Bastian and Setterfield (2020), Blecker (1999, 2011), Cassetti (2012), Lavoie (2014, Chapter 8.9) and Vera (2014), for example.
31. For post-Keynesian exchange rate theories, see De Paula et al. (2017), Fritz et al. (2018), Harvey (2007/08, 2009, 2019), Herr (1992), Herr and Priewe (2006), Lavoie (2014, Chapter 7), Priewe (2008) and Priewe and Herr (2005). We will elaborate more on exchange rate determination in Chapter 6.
32. The coefficients indicate marginal effects of changes in the levels of domestic and foreign income on imports and exports, respectively, whereas the elasticities describe the effects of the growth rates of domestic and foreign income on the growth rates of imports and exports, respectively.
33. Uncovered interest rate parity theory means that we have $i - i_f = \left(a^e - a\right)/a$ (Carlin and Soskice 2015, p. 316).

    The difference between the domestic interest rate and the foreign interest rate (i_f) thus compensates for an expected depreciation of the domestic currency vis-à-vis the foreign currency, that is, an expected increase in the nominal exchange rate. This approach implies that in foreign exchange equilibrium with a constant nominal exchange rate, domestic and foreign interest rates should be equal – both in nominal terms and in real terms. For post-Keynesian alternative exchange rate theories, in which a constant exchange rate is consistent with a hierarchy of interest rates due to different liquidity premia of different currencies, or different currency premia, see De Paula et al. (2017), Fritz et al. (2018), Herr and Priewe (2006), Priewe (2008) and Priewe and Herr (2005).
34. This section is based on and elaborates on Hein and Stockhammer (2010).
35. See Prante et al. (2020, 2022b) for interactive simulations of what they call labour market hysteresis.
36. For empirical work on the effects of the capital stock on long-run unemployment see Alexiou and Pitelis (2003), Arestis and Biefang-Frisancho Mariscal (2000), Arestis et al. (2006, 2007), Girardi et al. (2020), Stockhammer (2004a) and Stockhammer and Klär (2010).
37. This nonlinearity of aggregate demand, the rate of capacity utilisation and the employment rate in our case, with respect to the wage share (or the profit share), has been pointed out and explored more extensively by Köhler (2018) and Prante (2019).

6. A post-Keynesian co-ordinated macroeconomic policy mix*

6.1 INTRODUCTION

From our post-Keynesian models presented in Chapter 5, it follows that the new consensus macroeconomics (NCM) policy framework has to be completely revised in order to achieve a high and stable medium- to long-run employment rate with stable inflation rates and inflation expectations. In Chapter 2, we have already outlined the main differences between a post-Keynesian macroeconomic policy mix and the NCM policy mix. For convenience, we repeat this overview here again in Table 6.1. In the orthodox NCM approach, put forward by, for example, Carlin and Soskice (2009, 2015), inflation-targeting monetary policies are the main stabilising economic policy tool. Central bank policies applying the interest rate tool have short-run real effects on unemployment, but in the long run only the inflation rate is affected. Fiscal policies are to support inflation-targeting monetary policies by balancing the public budget over the cycle. Only for deep recessions, in which monetary policy becomes ineffective, are active fiscal policies recommended for short-run stabilisation. The labour market, together with the social security system, determines equilibrium unemployment, the non-accelerating inflation rate of unemployment (NAIRU), in the long run, and the speed of adjustment towards this rate in the short run. Regarding international economic policies, mainstream economics would be rather in favour of free trade, free capital flows and flexible exchange rates, reaping the presumed benefits from comparative advantages and the related international division of labour. In the Carlin and Soskice (2009, 2015) NCM approach, exchange rate adjustments take over part of the stabilisation, such that less active interest rate policies by the central bank are required. Since, at least in the long run, there is a clear division of labour between the different areas of economic policymaking, ex ante co-ordination is not required – each area of policymaking would have to follow its tasks as outlined.

From our post-Keynesian models a completely different policy mix has to be derived, as summarised in Table 6.1, too. In this chapter, we will develop this post-Keynesian approach for monetary, wage and fiscal policies and will then consider some open economy issues. The macroeconomic policy mix based on post-Keynesian models advocates the co-ordination of economic policies between the different areas, both in the short and the medium to long run, because there is no clear-cut assignment of policymakers and their instruments to just one specific economic policy target, that is, full employment, stable inflation, equitable distribution of income and wealth, international balance and financial stability. The following elaborations are based on Hein and Stockhammer (2009b, 2010, 2011b). A similar post-Keynesian economic policy mix has been advocated by Arestis (2010, 2013) and Arestis and Sawyer (2010a) based on slightly different models. Historically, such a post-Keynesian macroeconomic policy mix can already be found in Kalecki's contributions in the mid-1940s towards the end of World War II, as has recently been pointed out by Hein and Martschin (2020).[1] European Economic

Table 6.1   Macroeconomic policy recommendations: New consensus models (NCM) and post-Keynesian models (PKM) compared

	NCM	PKM
Monetary policy	Inflation targeting by means of interest rate policies, which affects unemployment in the short run, but only inflation in the long run	Target low interest rates which mainly affect distribution, and stabilise monetary, financial and real sectors by applying other instruments (lender of last resort, credit controls, etc.)
Fiscal policy	Supports monetary policy in achieving price stability by balancing the budget over the cycle	Real stabilisation in the short and in the long run with no autonomous deficit targets; reduction of inequality
Labour market and wage/incomes policy	Determines the NAIRU in the long run and the speed of adjustment in the short run; focus should be on flexible nominal and real wages	Affects price level/inflation and distribution; focus on stable nominal wage and nominal unit labour cost growth, as well as compressed wage structure
International economic policies	Free trade, free capital flows and flexible exchange rates	Regulated capital flows, managed exchange rates, infant industry protection, regional and industrial policies
Economic policy co-ordination	Clear assignment in the long run; co-ordination at best only in the short run	No clear assignment; economic policy co-ordination required in the short and the long run, both nationally and internationally

Source: Based on Hein (2017a, p. 154).

and Monetary Union (EMU) applications of the post-Keynesian/Kaleckian macroeconomic policy approach have been proposed by Arestis (2011b), Arestis and Sawyer (2011, 2013), Hein (2017c, 2018a, 2019d), Hein and Detzer (2015b, 2015c), Hein and Martschin (2020), Hein and Truger (2005c, 2011), Hein et al. (2012b) and Sawyer (2013), for example.

6.2   MONETARY POLICY

From the criticism of inflation-targeting monetary policies developed in Chapter 5, that is, its short-run asymmetric effects on long-term market interest rates and effective demand and its long-run adverse cost and inflation pressure effects, different implications for more adequate monetary policies can be drawn. Applying the distinction made by Rochon and Setterfield (2007), either an 'activist' position or a 'parking-it' approach for central bank interest rate policies has been proposed in post-Keynesian monetary macroeconomics.

The proponents of the 'activist' approach confirm the central bank's responsibility for stable inflation and regard the interest rate as an appropriate tool to achieve this goal. Post-Keynesian monetary economics is held to be generally consistent with inflation targeting by central banks and with the application of an interest rate operation procedure (Fontana and Palacio-Vera 2007, Palley 2007a, Setterfield 2006). Contrary to the NCM, however, the post-Keynesian authors are aware of long-run real effects of inflation-targeting monetary policies. Furthermore, they demand more careful counter-cyclical stabilisation by means of interest rate policies, as well as more reasonable, that is higher, inflation targets. Of course, post-Keynesian proponents of activist interest rate policies see the limits of these policies in stabilising the economy in a deep recession and advocate activist fiscal policies for this purpose, too.

The 'parking-it' approach, however, refrains from recommending fine-tuning the economy by means of interest rate policies but focusses on the long-run distribution effects of the central bank interest rate policy and therefore recommends stabilising the long-term rate of interest at a certain level (Arestis and Sawyer 2010b, Gnos and Rochon 2007, Hein and Stockhammer 2010, 2011b, Lavoie 1996b, Rochon and Setterfield 2007, Setterfield 2009a, Smithin 2007, Wray 2007). This is very much in line with our arguments presented in Chapter 5 and follows from the models we have presented there. Different interest rate targets have been suggested. Wray (2007) proposes targeting a zero nominal short-term interest rate in the money market.[2] This would then, of course, generate positive nominal interest rates in the credit market which reflect risk assessments and liquidity preference, in particular. Smithin (2004, 2007) suggests that central banks should target a long-term real interest rate equal to zero, or as close to zero as possible, allowing rentiers to maintain their stock of real wealth but not to obtain a real income from financial wealth, at least not allow them to participate in real income growth. Lavoie (1996b) and Setterfield (2009a) favour targeting a long-term real rate of interest equal to productivity growth, which allows rentiers to participate in real growth and keeps distribution between rentiers, on the one hand, and firms and labourers, on the other hand, constant.[3]

Since we have abstracted from productivity growth in our models in Chapter 5, the rules proposed by Smithin (2004, 2007) and by Lavoie (1996b) and Setterfield (2009a) boil down essentially to the same, and we arrive at the following target long-term nominal rate of interest (i^T):

$$i^T = i_r^T + \hat{p} = i_r^T + \hat{p}^e + \hat{p}^u, \tag{6.1}$$

with i_r^T as the target real rate of interest being given by long-run productivity growth ($i_r^T = \hat{y}$), which is zero in our short-run models.

With a constant labour force, labour productivity growth is equal to real GDP growth. In line with Arestis and Sawyer (2010a, 2010b), Hein and Detzer (2015a, 2015b) and Hein and Martschin (2020, 2021), we can thus specify a pragmatic interest rate rule for developed capitalist economies, with little long-run change in trend employment. The target long-term nominal interest rate (i^T) for central banks should be slightly above the rate of inflation ($\hat{p}$) but below nominal GDP growth ($\hat{Y}^n = \hat{Y} + \hat{p}$), or a slightly positive long-term real rate of interest ($i_r^T = i^T - \hat{p}$) below real GDP growth ($\hat{Y}$) should be targeted:

$$\hat{p} \leq i^T \leq \hat{Y} + \hat{p} = \hat{Y}^n \quad \Leftrightarrow \quad 0 \leq i_r^T \leq \hat{Y}. \tag{6.2}$$

These real or nominal long-term interest rates will also be used as benchmarks for the macroeconomic policy regime analysis included in Chapter 8. Achieving such a long-term interest rate ensures that financial wealth in real terms is protected against inflation, on the one hand, which seems to be a condition for a monetary production economy based on creditor-debtor relationships to function. On the other hand, however, reaching the so-defined target rate

Macroeconomics after Kalecki and Keynes

makes sure that re-distribution in favour of income derived from the production of goods and services (retained profits of firms and wages of workers) will foster investment in the capital stock, aggregate demand and employment. As we have shown in Section 4.4, keeping the interest rate below GDP growth (either in nominal or real terms) makes sure that the government does not have to run primary surpluses in order to service its debt and keep its debt-GDP ratio constant. Regressive distribution effects of servicing government debt will thus be avoided, because the government does not have to raise taxes (from the working and the middle class) in order to pay interest (to the rich rentiers holding government debt). Interest payments can be made out of additional credit granted by rentiers while keeping the debt-GDP ratio constant. A similar argument is also true for other deficit sectors, like the corporate sector: Servicing the debt and keeping debt-income or debt-capital ratios constant does not require squeezing wages or retained earnings.

In order to reach the target rate of interest, central banks will have to adjust their policy instrument, the nominal interest rate, so that a constant target real rate of interest emerges. This implies adjusting the nominal interest rate to unexpected inflation at the end of each period. As we have explained in Section 4.2, the long-term nominal rate of interest in the credit and financial market (i) is determined by the base rate of interest in the money market under direct control of the central bank (i_{CB}) and by the mark-up applied by commercial banks and other financial intermediaries (m_B):

$$i = \left(1 + m_B\right)i_{CB}. \tag{6.3}$$

The mark-up is affected by liquidity and risk assessments, as well as by the degree of competition in the credit and financial markets. Therefore, in order to achieve their long-term interest rate target, central banks also need to assess the mark-up applied by commercial banks and set the short-term rate of interest accordingly:

$$i_{CB} = \frac{i^T}{\left(1 + m_B\right)} = \frac{i_r^T + \hat{p}}{\left(1 + m_B\right)} = \frac{i_r^T + \hat{p}^e + \hat{p}^u}{\left(1 + m_B\right)}. \tag{6.4}$$

As is obvious from equation (6.4), the mark-up applied by commercial banks in setting the long-term interest rate may constrain the central bank in achieving its long-term nominal interest rate target. This is true, in particular, in times of crisis and rising uncertainty when this mark-up may become volatile and may increase in an unpredictable way. Central banks may then have to directly intervene in financial markets, purchasing government and corporate bonds, thus raising bond prices and bringing long-term interest rates on bonds down to their target rates.

There is broad agreement amongst post-Keynesians that such 'quantitative easing policies' (QE), as the response to the 2007–09 financial and economic crises and the 2020 COVID-19 crisis, in the face of the failure of inflation-targeting policies by means of short-term interest rate setting, will primarily affect long-term interest rates, capital gains of asset holders and balance sheets of commercial banks, as well as the exchange rate in an open economy (Lavoie 2016b, Lavoie and Fiebiger 2018). The expansionary effects on aggregate demand and credit, however, are rather limited unless they are supported by active and expansionary fiscal policies. Furthermore, in the medium run, as we have shown in Section 5.7, a real depreciation, as one of the main channels of QE, may fuel conflict inflation, lower the stable inflation rate or employment (SIRE) and raise the profit share. This will then have depressive effects on domestic demand, and on overall demand and employment, if aggregate demand is wage-led. At the international level QE may trigger a depreciation spiral, as Palley (2011) has pointed out. Furthermore, quantitative easing coupled with negative interest rates in the money market might increase financial fragility since it fuels indebtedness and risk taking (Palley 2016a, 2018). This will be the case both for negative central bank lending rates to subsidise commercial banks and for negative central bank deposit rates to promote portfolio changes towards longer-term interest bearing assets.

Although monetary policy of the central bank in our approach should thus neither pursue an inflation target nor make any attempt at adjusting the employment rate to some target rate, central banks remain responsible for the orderly working of the monetary and financial system and hence for financial stability (Arestis and Sawyer 2010a, 2010b). This includes the definition of credit standards for refinance operations with commercial banks, the implementation of reserve requirements and even credit controls, in order to channel credit into desirable areas and to avoid credit-financed bubbles in certain markets.[4] Above all, central banks have to act as lender of last resort for the banking sector in order to prevent systemic liquidity crises[5] and as the guarantor of government debt in order to prevent sovereign debt crises and relieve governments from financial market pressure. The latter has been and is still an important lesson to learn in order to fully overcome the Eurozone crisis and the underlying design failure of the Eurozone, that is, the lack of a convincing lender of last resort for the member countries' governments and of a guarantee of public debt, as Arestis and Sawyer (2011), Goodhart (1998), Hein (2013/14, 2018a), Hein and Detzer (2015a, 2015b), Wray (2012, Chapter 5.7) and others have pointed out.

6.3   INCOMES AND WAGE POLICY

The NCM view on the role of wage formation and wage bargaining calls for nominal and real wage flexibility by means of structural reforms in the labour market, and decentralisation of wage bargaining in order to accelerate the adjustment towards the NAIRU in the short run and in order to reduce the NAIRU itself in the medium to long run. This view cannot be sustained on the basis of our model. Nominal wage flexibility generates unexpected inflation whenever employment rates deviate from the SIRE and unemployment rates deviate from the NAIRU. This is associated with re-distribution between capital and labour, on the one hand, and it affects distribution between rentiers and firms, on the other. In a wage-led closed economy, nominal and real wage flexibility makes actual employment (unemployment) diverge further from the SIRE (NAIRU) in our model, as we have shown in Section 5.4. In an open economy, only a strong real exchange rate effect on net exports may temporarily contain or reverse this instability, as we have discussed in Section 5.7. Furthermore, short-run deviations of employment (unemployment) rates from the SIRE (NAIRU) affect the SIRE (NAIRU) in the medium to long run and turn the latter endogenous with respect to effective demand, employment and macroeconomic policies through various channels. This is true both in the closed and in the open economy, as we have also shown in Chapter 5. Finally, going beyond the short and medium run with given technical conditions of production, wage moderation and re-distribution at the expense of labour will also be associated with weak real wage-induced productivity growth and innovations, which will further add to the weakening of long-run growth prospects.[6]

In order to avoid the destabilising effects of nominal and real wage flexibility, post-Keynesians advocate stable nominal wage growth (or stable nominal unit labour cost growth if productivity growth is positive) in line with stable inflation and hence allocating the role of nominal stabilisation to incomes or wage policies (see, for example, Arestis 1996a, 2013, Arestis and Sawyer 2010a, Davidson 2006, Hein and Stockhammer 2010, 2011b, and Setterfield 2006).[7] Therefore, nominal unit labour costs should grow at a rate similar to the country's inflation target, set by the central bank, the parliament or the government. This means that nominal wage growth $\hat{w}$ should equal the sum of long-run growth of labour productivity ($\hat{y}$) and the target inflation rate $\hat{p}^T$:

$$\hat{w} = \hat{y} + \hat{p}^T. \tag{6.5}$$

Following this wage rule will contribute to stable inflation at the target rate and also keep income shares constant, provided that the mark-up in firms' pricing remains constant and that imported material costs in an open economy grow in line with domestic unit labour costs, as we have pointed out in Chapter 5. Under these conditions, the destabilising distribution effects of nominal and real wage flexibility in wage-led economies will be avoided, too.

The following questions arise regarding the kind of productivity growth that should be included in the wage norm in equation (6.5). Should we include short-run or trend productivity growth? Furthermore, should we include firm-specific, industry or economy-wide productivity growth? Since labour productivity moves pro-cyclically, rising in an upswing and falling in a downswing, in particular because of overhead labour (see Chapter 4.3), focussing on trend productivity growth instead of actual productivity growth will have a stabilising effect on aggregate demand and employment. In a boom, it will contribute to a falling overall wage share, with dampening effects on aggregate demand in a wage-led economy, and in a recession it will contribute to a rising overall wage share with stabilising effects on aggregate demand in a wage-led economy.

Including economy-wide trend productivity growth in the nominal wage growth equation will also favour structural change, both within industries and in the economy as a whole. Such an orientation will favour high productivity growth firms and industries at the expense of low productivity growth firms and industries. Firms and industries will have to improve labour productivity by increasing efficiency and the speed of introduction of labour-saving technological change in order to survive; undercutting each other by lower wage growth will not be an option any more. Focussing on economy-wide trend productivity growth while setting wages will also restrict wage dispersion and is thus a core element of a 'solidaristic wage policy' (Schulten 2002). To the extent that wage and income policies manage to reduce wage dispersion and wage inequality, the demand effects seem to be favourable, too, irrespective of whether a change in functional income distribution has wage- or profit-led effects on aggregate demand, as has been shown and argued by Palley (2017).

Implementing the wage norm in equation (6.5) is tantamount to flattening our unexpected inflation Phillips curve (5.27) from Chapter 5 and making it horizontal in the optimal case. For convenience, we reproduce the Phillips curve from Chapter 5 here:

$$\hat{p}^u = \frac{h_0 + \Omega_0 + \Omega_1 e - 1}{h_2 + \Omega_2}. \tag{6.6}$$

In the context of our model we have two ways of integrating nominal stabilisation by means of wage or incomes policies. The first way is to increase the values of h_2 and Ω_2 in equation (6.6). This implies making the unexpected inflation curve flatter by means of reducing workers' and firms' inflation push in the face of unexpected inflation, which means increasing firms' and workers' willingness to accept deviations of actual distribution from their respective targets.

The second way is to make the target wage shares of workers and firms compatible for a relevant range of employment rates, as has been argued by Hein (2004, 2006a, 2008, Chapter 16), Hein and Stockhammer (2010, 2011b) and Kriesler and Lavoie (2007). In the context of our model this requires reformulating the workers' target wage share from equation (5.13) in Chapter 5 to:

$$\Omega_W^T = 1 - h_W^T = 1 - h_F^T = h_0, \text{ if} : e_1^N < e < e_2^N$$

and   (6.7)

$$\Omega_W^T = 1 - h_W^T = \Omega_0 + \Omega_1 e, \text{ if} : e < e_1^N \text{ or } e_2^N < e.$$

The SIRE, and hence also the NAIRU, become a range, and the unexpected inflation curve from equation (6.8) becomes a zero horizontal line between e_1^N and e_2^N, as shown in Figure 6.1:

$$\hat{p}_t^u = \frac{h_0 + \Omega_0 + \Omega_1 e - 1}{h_2 + \Omega_2}, \text{ if} : e < e_1^N \text{ or } e_2^N < e$$

and   (6.8)

$$\hat{p}_t^u = 0, \text{ if} : e_1^N < e < e_2^N.$$

In the first way, that is, raising the values of h_2 and Ω_2, variations in the employment rate will still have weak effects on unexpected inflation and income distribution. Any deviation from the SIRE will thus trigger further deviation tendencies and real stabilisation will be required by economic policies. In the second way, the optimal way, variations in the employment rate between e_1^N and e_2^N do not trigger any unexpected inflation and re-distribution of income, and hence no deviation processes will set in. In this case, demand management is free to choose a high level of employment close to e_2^N without violating stable inflation rates and stable income distribution.

Drawing on industrial relations literature,[8] it seems that a high degree of wage bargaining co-ordination at the national level, strong labour unions and employer organisations and hence organised labour markets should be particularly suitable for pursuing this nominal and real stabilisation role of wage bargaining. Co-ordination may take place against different institutional backgrounds, that is, bargaining at the national level, pattern bargaining at the sectoral level, involvement of the government in the bargaining process itself, but also by setting statutory minimum wages or by the declaration of general applicability of bargaining results.

The stabilising effects of the implementation of the wage norm in equation (6.5), guided by economy-wide trend productivity growth and the target rate of inflation, are obvious, as is shown in Figure 6.1. In the range of employment rates between e_1^N and e_2^N, positive or negative

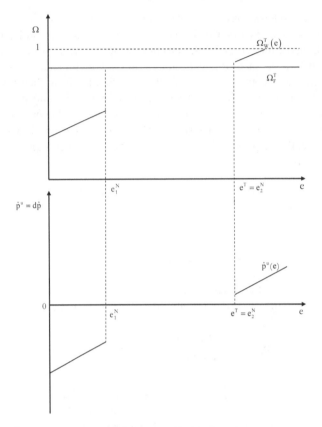

Figure 6.1   Results of a post-Keynesian macroeconomic policy mix

demand shocks with related effects on the employment rate will not generate any effects on wage and price inflation as well as income distribution. These shocks will thus not create further instability tendencies, such as those which we have shown in Chapter 5.

But even if, unlike our models in Chapter 5, firms change their target mark-ups and their target wage shares in response to changes in aggregate demand, output and employment, for example in long-lasting booms or in severe recessions, following the wage norm in equation (6.5) will contribute to stability in a wage-led economy. This is shown in Figure 6.2, where we assume that workers and trade unions, within the range of the employment rates e_1 and e_2, which are now no longer stable inflation rates of employment, follow the wage norm from equation (6.5), whereas firms apply a pro-cyclical target mark-up. The workers' target wage share curve is thus horizontal, whereas the firms' target wage share curve is downward sloping, and we only have a single SIRE again at e^N, at which we assume that inflation is not only constant but also at the target rate.

In a boom, employment exceeds e^N in Figure 6.2, price inflation rises above the target rate and exceeds constant wage inflation given by equation (6.5), wage shares fall and profit shares rise. In a wage-led demand regime, this will dampen aggregate demand and employment and contribute to bringing the economy back to stable inflation at e^N. The reverse will happen in

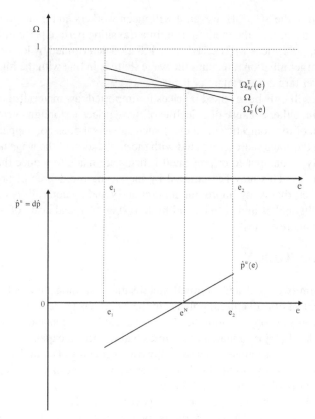

Figure 6.2   Constant target wage share of workers and pro-cyclical target profit share of firms

a recession, in which employment falls below e^N. Price inflation falls below constant wage inflation given by equation (6.5), wage shares rise and profit shares fall. This will stimulate aggregate demand and contribute to bringing the employment rate back to the stable inflation rate at e^N. In a wage-led demand regime, following the wage norm in equation (6.5) will thus dampen cyclical fluctuations. It implies that workers will have to accept falling wage shares in a boom and will see rising wage shares in a recession. On average over some cycles, this would contribute to stabilising functional income distribution together with inflation.

So far we have discussed the advantages of co-ordinated wage policies following the wage norm in equation (6.5) in the case of positive and negative demand shocks, and for constant and pro-cyclical target profit shares of firms. Let us finally take a look at a supply shock in an open economy framework, as presented in Section 5.7. There we have seen that an increase in import prices for raw materials and intermediate products leads to higher domestic prices and a lower wage share with contractive effects on aggregate demand in the short run. In the medium run, firms' target profit share will rise and their target wage share will fall, even with constant mark-ups, because of an increase in the ratio z of unit material costs to unit wage costs. Without wage bargaining co-ordination, this will then mean a lower SIRE in the medium run. Wage bargaining co-ordination applying the wage norm in equation (6.5) will prevent such a fall in the SIRE. However, it will mean workers and trade unions will have to accept a lower wage share in the medium run. In a transition period, price inflation driven by the increases in import prices will exceed wage inflation determined by long-run productivity growth plus the target inflation rate, until the wage share is in line with the higher target profit share and the lower target wage share of firms.

Such a process will only be reversed if prices for imported raw materials and semi-finished products fall again, either because of a decline of these prices in foreign currency or because of an appreciation of the domestic currency. If such a reversal does not happen, the decline in real wages and in the wage share associated with the application of the wage norm form equation (6.5) can only be dampened or prevented if firms are made to reduce their target mark-ups and profit shares. This may be achieved by increasing the degree of price competition in the goods market, that is, by improving market entry and by controlling or even breaking up monopolies, oligopolies and cartels, and by lowering overhead costs of firms, that is, by lowering taxes or interest rates.

6.4   FISCAL POLICY

Because of the limits of real and nominal stabilisation via monetary policy, as shown in Chapter 5, the neglect of active fiscal policies in the NCM has turned out to be a major problem. This has not only become clear in the 2007–09 Great Recession and in the 2020 COVID-19 crisis, in which all major capitalist economies had to turn to expansionary fiscal policies in order to stabilise and stimulate a depressed private economy. The deficiency of the NCM in this respect was already highlighted by several post-Keynesian critics well before the recent crises. In particular, Arestis and Sawyer (2003, 2004a, 2004b) have shown that the arguments against activist fiscal policies and government deficit spending, like crowding out and the Ricardian equivalence hypothesis, presuppose the stability of full employment equilibrium and the dominance of rational model-consistent expectations of economic actors and thus ignore fundamental uncertainty, aggregate demand failures and Keynesian unemployment. They also pointed out some empirical evidence on fiscal multipliers which lent no support for the neglect of active fiscal policies in the NCM.

This effectiveness of fiscal policies with regard to stabilising aggregate demand and economic activity, in particular in economic downswings when interest rate policies of central banks face severe limitations (zero lower bound, weak animal spirits of firms), has been supported recently again by orthodox and heterodox authors, using different types of empirical methods.[9] Fiscal multipliers have been shown to be time varying, with higher values in a downswing and recession than in an economic upswing. Government expenditures have higher multiplier effects than variations in taxation, with the highest multiplier values for government investment. In effect, in the course of the recent crises, there has been a broad agreement amongst economists and policymakers that fiscal stimulus in a deep recession should be applied, if the stimulus is 'timely, targeted and temporary', as Elmendorf and Furman (2008, p. 5) have famously put it. Such a view of fiscal policies as a short-run stabiliser has also found its place in recent versions of the NCM, as in Carlin and Soskice (2015, Chapter 14). They argue that fiscal policy is important in deep recessions, when monetary policy is constrained by the zero lower bound for the interest rate or by fixed exchange rate regimes. Also the relevance of short-run automatic stabilisers is acknowledged. However, in the long run, government deficits have to be constrained or reversed, assuming that long-run full employment equilibrium and the full employment growth path are independent of aggregate demand and demand management fiscal policies. Lavoie and Seccareccia (2017) have termed this approach 'new fiscalism'.[10] However, in a sense, this approach is not so new, because new Keynesian mainstream macroeconomists have returned to the view of fiscal policy as a short-run emergency policy tool, that allows for demand stabilising fiscal deficits, which should then be repaid in good times, which already prevailed in the neoclassical synthesis of the 1950s/60s (Snowdon and Vane 2005, Chapter 3).

The post-Keynesian view on fiscal policy, as can be derived from our models in Chapters 4 and 5, is different from 'new fiscalism', as has recently been summarised again by Arestis (2012, 2015).[11] In the post-Keynesian view, fiscal policy has a permanent role to play. First, lack of aggregate demand for reaching non-inflationary full employment output levels may not only be a short-run deep recession phenomenon, but may be a medium- to long-run problem, in particular in mature monetary production economies. Second, fiscal policy does not only affect aggregate demand in the short and the long run, but it also has an impact on the supply conditions and thus on potential output and potential growth in the long run. In other words, aggregate demand management by fiscal policies is not only required to reach the SIRE in the short and the long run, but also affects the SIRE itself in the long run through various channels, as we have pointed out in Chapter 5. Therefore, in a post-Keynesian model real stabilisation is the task of fiscal policies, both in the short run and in the long. Furthermore, since fiscal policies are responsible for short- and long-run demand management, it goes without saying that fiscal policies can also contribute to preventing accelerating inflation, which means employment rates determined in the goods market exceeding the SIRE. Based on these considerations a government expenditure rule of the following type can be suggested:

$$G_r = G_{r0} + G_{r1}\left(e^T - e\right), \quad G_{r0} \geq 0, G_{r1} > 0, \tag{6.9}$$

with G_{r0} as the expenditure level to reach the target employment rate (e^T) and G_{r1} as the reaction coefficient towards deviation of the employment rate from the target rate. The employment target should, of course, be the maximum employment rate achievable without triggering unexpected inflation, that is, $e^T = e_{N2}$ in Figure 6.1.

Making use of government expenditures in order to stabilise aggregate demand in the short and in the long run means accepting the emanating government deficits (with given tax rates) in the short run and the related government debts in the long run. This is equivalent to a 'functional finance' approach proposed by Lerner (1943). The functional finance view implies that government deficits should mop up the excess of private sector planned saving over planned investment at the SIRE level of economic activity. In a closed economy, government deficit spending (D), that is, the difference between government expenditures for goods and services (G) plus government interest payments on the stock of government debt (iB_G) and government revenues (T), has thus to compensate for the difference between private sector saving (S) and investment (pI) at the SIRE activity level of the economy:

$$D = G + iB_G - T = S - pI. \tag{6.10}$$

Applying government deficit spending in this way assures that there is always enough saving in the economy as a whole to fund government deficits, as, for example, already Kalecki (1944) and Lerner (1943) have argued, and as we have shown in the monetary circuit model in Section 3.5. Crowding out will not occur, provided that the central bank does not raise the interest rate when governments expand their fiscal deficits. Furthermore, as we have shown in Section 4.4, if central banks keep the nominal interest rate below nominal GDP growth in the long run, government debt-GDP ratios will stabilise even with primary deficits and hence without regressive distribution effects of government tax policies.[12]

In order to stabilise the economy at the SIRE level of economic activity, governments should vary expenditures and not the tax rate, to avoid those short-run asymmetric and long-run detrimental effects, which we have highlighted in Section 5.6. There, we have shown that lowering the tax rate in a deep recession with the employment rate below the SIRE might not be sufficient to stimulate aggregate demand and investment, if firms' sales expectations are depressed. Raising the tax rate in a boom with the employment rate above the SIRE might have long-run detrimental effects on the SIRE, because a higher tax rate will lower (raise) the firms' (workers') target wage share.

Whereas changing tax rates to stabilise aggregate demand and employment faces some severe limitations, and therefore the variation of government expenditures with given tax rates should be preferred, the structure of tax rates, together with government social transfers, will affect the distribution of disposable income and thus aggregate demand and employment in the short and in the long run. The structure of tax rates and social transfers will thus also have an impact on the required government fiscal deficits (or surpluses) for aggregate demand management, both in the short and in the long run. Generally, the more progressive the tax system, that is, the higher the tax rate on profits (or on high incomes) relative to the tax rate on wages (or on low incomes), and the more generous social transfers are, the more effective automatic stabilisers will be in the short run. In a boom, a progressive tax system and falling government deficits (or rising government surpluses) will dampen the growth of disposable income and aggregate demand, whereas in a recession social transfers and rising government deficits (or falling government surpluses) will contribute to stabilising disposable income, consumption and aggregate demand. Furthermore, the more re-distributive the tax and transfer system is, the lower will be the gap between private saving and private investment in the long run – assuming this gap to be positive in most of the cases. Therefore, re-distributive government tax and social policies will not only reduce the inequality in disposable incomes and thus contribute to social cohesion, it will also contribute to stabilising aggregate demand and employment in the short and in the long run.

The functional finance approach to fiscal policy has recently gained prominence again in the context of 'modern money theory' (MMT), in particular in the USA (Kelton 2020, Mosler 1997/98, Mitchell et al. 2019, Tcherneva 2006, Wray 1998, 2002, 2012). Starting from the chartalist view, according to which money is a creature of the state (Lerner 1947),[13] it has been argued that there are no limits to government deficit expenditures (and hence also to government debt) other than potential output at which inflationary pressure will arise. Several MMT proponents argue that the governments' power to spend should be used for an 'employer of last resort' policy (ELR). Governments should offer employment to everybody for a basic wage and thus create a buffer stock employment, which will rise in an economic downswing and on which the private sector can draw in the economic upswing.[14]

In the debates on MMT it has been clarified that such a view on fiscal policy can only hold for a sovereign money system, in which domestic currency is the unit of account, taxes and government expenditures are paid in that currency, the central bank can issue the currency without constraints, public debt is issued in the domestic currency and no exchange rate target exists, that is, in a system of floating exchange rates, which is supposed to assure that persistent current account deficits and indebtedness in foreign currency are prevented.[15] Only under these conditions can it be argued that there are no financial constraints on government deficits and debt, that there is no crowding out and that government deficits rather reduce overnight interest rates in the money market, instead of raising these rates and the long-term interest rate in the financial markets (Lavoie 2013). As pointed out by Epstein (2019a, 2019b), it is difficult for other countries than the USA to meet all these criteria. Furthermore, whereas the confusing consolidation of the government and the central bank in most of the contributions of the MMT proponents can be remedied without undermining the main conclusions, as Lavoie (2013) has shown, the open economy issues around functional finance require more careful consideration. Relying on floating exchange rates seems to ignore important detrimental feedback effects of exchange rate variations on aggregate demand and inflation, which we pointed out in Chapters 4 and 5.

6.5   THE INTERNATIONAL DIMENSION

Our open economy models in Chapters 4 and 5 have shown that variations in the nominal and the real exchange rate do not have unique effects on domestic output and employment, if distributional effects are taken into account. A nominal and real depreciation of the domestic currency thus does not necessarily have expansionary effects, and it may also lead to the acceleration of conflict inflation in the domestic economy. Furthermore, from Thirlwall's (1979) law and empirical studies on that law, we know that non-price competitiveness may be more relevant than price competitiveness for exports and imports in the long run.[16] Therefore, income elasticities of exports and imports and growth differentials between the domestic and the foreign economies may be far more important than price elasticities, when it comes to explaining current account imbalances.[17]

From these considerations it follows that, similar to central bank policies with respect to the rate of interest, post-Keynesian macroeconomic policies should aim at stabilising or 'parking' the exchange rate at a level which is consistent with a balanced current account and not treat it as a short-run adjustment tool for external rebalancing. However, whereas central bank interest rate policies will have a direct, albeit asymmetric, effect on long-term interest rates in credit and financial markets, according to our post-Keynesian approach, 'parking' the exchange rate is not an easy task, since there is no unified post-Keynesian view on the determinants of the exchange rate, as also becomes clear in the review of Lavoie (2014, Chapter 7), for example. Therefore, in the open economy models of Chapters 4 and 5 we have treated the real exchange as exogenous and not directly and uniquely related to domestic economic activity.

When it comes to explaining exchange rates, post-Keynesians seem to agree on a rejection of orthodox theories of purchasing power parity and uncovered interest rate parity (Lavoie 2014, Chapter 7). According to purchasing power theory, the nominal exchange rate is determined by domestic and foreign price levels, which themselves depend on money supply. Changes in the nominal exchange rate should thus compensate for inflation differentials between the domestic and the foreign economies and lead to balanced current accounts. According to uncovered interest rate parity theory, the difference between the domestic interest rate (i) in financial markets and the foreign interest rate (i_f) compensates for an expected appreciation (depreciation) of the domestic currency vis-à-vis the foreign currency, that is, an expected increase (fall) in the nominal exchange rate (Carlin and Soskice 2015, p. 316):

$$i - i_f = \frac{a^e - a}{a}. \tag{6.11}$$

In this approach, the causality runs from the differential of the expected and the current exchange rate to the required interest rate differential to keep the foreign exchange market in equilibrium. This approach implies that for a constant (expected) nominal exchange rate ($a^e - a = 0$) in long-run equilibrium, domestic and foreign interest rates should be equal – both in nominal terms and in real terms. Stabilising the exchange rate would thus mean domestic central banks targeting the world long-term interest rate, and there would be no leeway for gearing interest rate policies towards domestic requirements, that is, targeting a long-term interest rate below the domestic trend rate of growth, as proposed in Section 6.2 above.

Several monetary Keynesians have presented a variant of this theory, including currency risk and a relative currency premium (o) in the explanation of the long-term equilibrium interest rates consistent with constant exchange rates (De Paula et al. 2017, Fritz et al. 2018, Herr 1992, Herr and Priewe 2006, Priewe 2008, Priewe and Herr 2005):

$$i - i_f = \frac{a^e - a}{a} - o. \tag{6.12}$$

The currency premium, indicating the asset-protecting property of a currency, determines the position of the respective currency in the international currency hierarchy. This is then associated with a reversed hierarchy of interest rates, that is, countries with low (high) currency risk and a high (low) currency premium will have low (high) long-term equilibrium interest rates.[18] Currency risk and the currency premium may negatively depend on the accumulated net foreign debt (Smithin 2002/03) and positively on low domestic inflation rates, stable exchange rates, as well as the liquidity and the openness of the financial market (Harvey 2019, Herr 1992). Also in this approach, the control of the central bank over the domestic interest rate in countries with high currency risk and a low currency premium is severely constrained. Only in the long run can control be regained by a policy of stabilising domestic inflation and the exchange rate, as well as a policy orientation towards avoiding or reducing debt in foreign currency, which should each improve the currency premium and allow for lower interest rates and stable exchange rates (Harvey 2019).

Lavoie (2000, 2003b, 2014, Chapter 7) acknowledges that the (expected) exchange rate may be related to international interest rate differentials. However, he argues that the causality is from interest rate differentials towards the differential between the future (expected) and the spot exchange rate. National central banks thus keep control over the domestic interest rate. However, lowering the domestic interest rate may trigger capital outflows to countries with higher interest rates, which will then impose a depreciation pressure on the national currency. A lower domestic interest rate will hence not be associated with an expected appreciation of the domestic currency in a flexible exchange rate system, but with a depreciation. However, if low domestic interest rates contribute to stimulating domestic growth, capital flows may then be reversed; inflows to the domestic economy may rise again and lead to an appreciation of the domestic currency (Lavoie 2000). All of this will depend on which kind of motivation governs international capital flows – long-run growth perspectives or short-run profitability based on interest rate arbitrage.

Arestis (2013) makes a similar argument, also based on the causality from interest rates to exchange rates. If equity flows dominate in the long run over other financial asset flows, a rise in the domestic interest rate might even lead to a depreciation of the domestic currency, via the growth prospect effects on the portfolio of international financial investors, rather than to an appreciation, via interest rate effects on their portfolio composition.

Of course, both Lavoie (2000, 2003b, 2014, Chapter 7) and Arestis (2013) also take into account the potentially disturbing effects of uncertainty, volatile expectations and short-run speculative financial flows on exchange rate fluctuations, as in particular pointed out by Harvey (2007/08, 2009, 2019), but also by Herr (2011) and the monetary Keynesians mentioned above. They conclude that the stabilisation of exchange rates thus requires regulating international capital flows.

These considerations might thus constrain the ability of central banks to set domestic interest rates below domestic nominal GDP growth, as proposed above. But from this brief discussion, we can also conclude that domestic macroeconomic policies aiming at domestic demand generation at SIRE levels should be conducive to stable exchange rates, hence avoiding the potentially destabilising effects of exchange rate variations in the short and in the medium run pointed out in Chapter 5. This implies that central banks should target domestic long-term interest rates slightly below trend GDP growth and should thus not aim at directly manipulating the exchange rate by interest rate policy. Wage policies should contribute to achieving a stable target inflation rate, having nominal wages grow at trend domestic productivity growth plus the domestic target rate of inflation. The latter should be in line with the target inflation rates of the main trading partners. Also in the open economy, fiscal policy is then free to manage domestic demand such that the SIRE is reached – without constraints given by deficit or debt targets or ceilings. Such a policy mix should be conducive to avoiding 'beggar-thy-neighbour policies', that is, persistent trade and current account surpluses, on the one hand, as well as persistent current account deficits and rising indebtedness in foreign currency, on the other hand.

To the extent that full employment at the SIRE level is associated with a current account deficit and the accumulation of debt in foreign currency, the required improvement of the current account should be gained by raising non-price competitiveness (Arestis 2010, 2013, Arestis and Sawyer 2010a, Hein and Detzer 2015b, 2015c). Following Thirlwall's (1979) law, increasing the balance of payments constrained growth rate, or reducing current account deficits at a given growth rate, requires improving the income elasticity of exports and decreasing the income elasticity of imports. Not only for this purpose are active industrial and regional policies, linked with public investment in infrastructure, education and R&D, essential, but also for overcoming regional and sectoral supply-side bottlenecks, as Arestis (2010, 2013) and Arestis and Sawyer (2010a) have pointed out. Apart from several practical problems pointed out in the debate on the ELR programme (see footnote 14), the exclusive focus of demand managing fiscal policies on ELR programmes, as proposed by several MMT proponents (see footnote 15), seems to be severely limited against the background of required industrial and regional policies.

To provide a stable international framework for such a macroeconomic policy mix, international cooperation would be favourable. This should include a system of managed exchange rates with symmetrical adjustment obligations in case of current account imbalances, in line with Keynes's (1942) proposal of an International Clearing Union (Davidson 1982, 2009, 2011, Chapter 17). Current account deficit countries would have to dampen domestic demand in the short run to reduce their imports and improve non-price competitiveness in the long run to increase their exports. Current account surplus countries would have to stimulate domestic demand in order to raise imports. Furthermore, capital controls would be needed in order to reduce speculation, uncertainty and volatility. Of course, such an approach could be further developed and amended towards providing stable finance of medium-run current account deficits for investment purposes in catching-up emerging capitalist economies, as suggested by Kalecki and Schumacher (1943) for the post-World War II world economy,[19] and also proposed by Hein and Detzer (2015b, 2015c) recently for overcoming the imbalances in the Eurozone.

6.6　SUMMING UP: A POST-KEYNESIAN CO-ORDINATED MACROECONOMIC POLICY MIX

The post-Keynesian macroeconomic policy mix requires ex ante co-ordination of macroeconomic policies at the national and the international level, because potentially each of the economic policy actors and their instruments affect most of the targets of macroeconomic policies (Table 6.1). In this framework or policy mix, wage policies, and hence wage

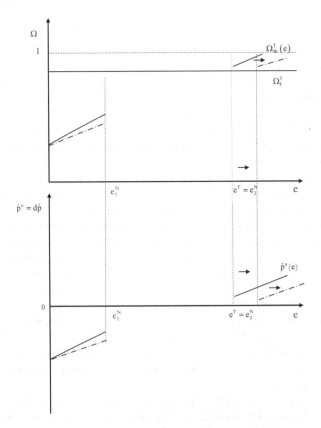

Figure 6.3　Expansionary macroeconomic policies raising the SIRE through the labour market persistence mechanisms and a lower target wage share of workers

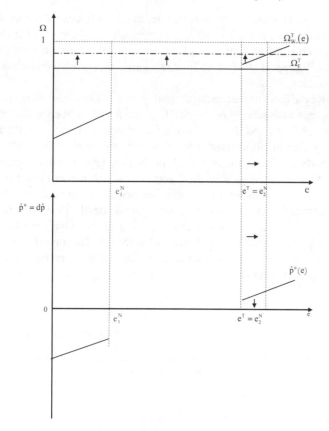

Figure 6.4   Lower interest rate and/or expansionary fiscal policies raising the SIRE through a lower mark-up and a higher target wage share of firms

bargaining parties, are mainly responsible for stable inflation rates and hence for nominal stabilisation. Such wage policies also contribute to stabilising the distribution of income. Fiscal policies are responsible for demand management, keeping effective demand at a level sufficient to maintain high non-inflationary employment, and hence for real stabilisation in the short and in the long run. Focussing (part of) government expenditures on public investment, R&D and education will help to overcome supply-side bottlenecks and to tackle regional and sectoral imbalances. In Chapter 9 we will argue that this type of fiscal policies will have to be geared towards the required socio-ecological transformation in the face of climate change and other ecological constraints and that it can contribute to long-run sustainable development. Progressive income and wealth taxes together with social transfers aiming at a more equal distribution of disposable income will contribute to stabilising the macroeconomy via automatic stabilisers. Interest rate policies by the central bank should not aim at fine-tuning the economy in either real or in nominal terms – that is, should not interfere with the tasks of wage and fiscal policies – but should instead focus on stable distribution between rentiers, on the one hand, and firms and labourers, on the other hand, in order to avoid destabilising distribution effects of changes in the interest rate. In addition, central banks should focus on providing and maintaining financial stability, in particular on their role of lender of last resort for the banking sector and as guarantor of government debt. Furthermore, the international environment should support stable exchange rates and current account balances, as outlined in the previous section.

Such a post-Keynesian macroeconomic policy mix should also take into account the medium- to long-run endogeneity of the SIRE, as reviewed in Section 5.8, and should thus try to 'test the waters' now and then. Allowing for employment rates slightly above the SIRE level will trigger rising inflation rates in the short run, but increase the SIRE and reduce the NAIRU in the medium run, on the one hand through the labour market persistence channel, which will affect the target wage shares of workers, as is shown in Figure 6.3. On the other hand, government policies that stimulate public and private investment, as well as low interest rate policies of central banks, will increase aggregate demand in the short run and will also lower the target profit shares of firms in the long run and thus also contribute to raising the SIRE and reducing the NAIRU, as is shown in Figure 6.4. Through this endogeneity channel, the functional distribution of market incomes may also be changed in favour of the wage share, without triggering ever-rising rates of inflation.

NOTES

*   This chapter partly draws on Hein and Stockhammer (2010, 2011b) and further develops the arguments provided there.

1.   See Kalecki (1943b, 1943c, 1944, 1945) and Kalecki and Schumacher (1943). See also Łaski (2019, Chapter 5) and Sawyer (2020), both with a focus on Kaleckian fiscal policies.

2.   Forstater and Mosler (2005, p. 535) even argued that the 'natural, nominal, risk free rate of interest is zero under relevant contemporary institutional arrangements'.

3.   This approach is based on Pasinetti's (1980–81, 1981) 'natural rate of interest', which is then called the 'fair rate of interest'. See Lavoie (1997) and Seccareccia and Lavoie (2016).

4.   On capital requirements and reserve requirements, and asset-based reserve requirements in particular, see Goodhart (2009), Detzer (2012) and Palley (2004, 2007b, 2010), for example.

5.   On the lender of last resort role of central banks and the fulfilment of this role in the cases of the Federal Reserve in the USA and the ECB in the Eurozone in and after the 2007–09 Global Financial Crisis and the Great Recession, see for example Herr (2014a).

6.   See Bhaduri (2006) and Hein (2014a, Chapter 8) on theoretical models, and Hartwig (2013b, 2014), Hein and Tarassow (2010), Naastepad (2006), Storm and Naastepad (2011) and Vergeer and Kleinknecht (2010/11, 2012, 2014) for empirical results.

7.   Keynes explicitly recommended the introduction of incomes policy, in order to prevent the deterioration of international price competitiveness in a period of appreciation of the British currency in 1925 and then to avoid cost-push inflation in a war economy in 1939/40, as Brown (1990) explains. Furthermore, in Keynes's theoretical work he provided several arguments in favour of rigid nominal wages in order to stabilise a monetary production economy, as we have outlined in Section 3.4.

8.   See Hall and Franzese (1998), Kittel and Traxler (2001), Soskice (1990), Traxler (1999) and Traxler and Kittel (2000), for example. For a recent review of minimum wages, collective bargaining system and economic development in Asia and Europe, see, for example, the contributions in van Klaveren et al. (2015).

9.   See, for example, Blanchard and Leigh (2013, 2014), Bouthevillain et al. (2009), Brancaccio and De Cristofaro (2020), Charles (2016b), Charles et al. (2015), Coenen et al. (2012, 2013), Gechert (2015), Gechert and Rannenberg (2018), Gechert et al. (2019), Hemming et al. (2002), Qazizada and Stockhammer (2015), Setterfield (2019) and Stockhammer et al. (2019).

10.   See also the other contribution to the special issue 'The political economy of the New Fiscalism' in the *European Journal of Economics and Economic Policies: Intervention*, 2017, 14 (3).

11.   See also the other contributions to the inaugural issue of the *Review of Keynesian Economics* in 2012 on fiscal policies.

12. See also the recent autonomous demand-led growth models driven by government expenditures, which derive similar long-run equilibrium and stability conditions for the related government debt dynamics, by Dutt (2020), Hein (2018c) and Hein and Woodgate (2021).

13. For a critical discussion of this broad claim, see Febrero (2009) and Rochon and Vernengo (2003), for example.

14. For proposals and controversial debates of ELR programmes, see Epstein (2019a, 2019b), Landwehr (2020), Levrero (2019), Mitchell and Wray (2005), Mitchell et al. (2019, Chapter 19), Mosler (1997/98), Sawyer (2003, 2004), Theurl and Tamesberger (2021) and Wray (1998, 2012), for example.

15. For the recent post-Keynesian debate assessing the consistency and the relevance of MMT, see for example Epstein (2019a, 2019b), Fiebiger (2016a), Fiebiger et al. (2012), Lavoie (2013), Palley (2015a, 2015b, 2020), Prates (2020), Tymoigne and Wray (2015) and Vernengo and Pérez Caldentey (2020). See also the contributions to the special issue of the *Real World Economics Review*, Issue 89, 2019, on 'modern monetary theory and its critics'.

16. For Thirlwall's law and empirical studies on that law, see, for example, Blecker (2016b, 2021), Blecker and Setterfield (2019, Chapter 9), Hein (2014a, Chapter 4), Lavoie (2014, Chapter 7.6.5), McCombie (2011, 2019), McCombie and Thirlwall (2004), Setterfield (2011), Thirlwall (2002, Chapters 4–5, 2011, 2013, Chapter 5, 2019) and the contributions to the special issue of the *Review of Keynesian Economics*, 2019, 7 (4) on 'Thirlwall's Law at 40'.

17. This view has recently been applied in the debate on current account imbalances in the Eurozone and on ways to reduce the huge German current account surplus by Hein and Truger (2014, 2017) and by Storm and Naastepad (2015).

18. Of course, this approach is inspired by Chapter 17 of Keynes (1936), in which the interest rate on other assets than money is explained by the liquidity premium on money, as we have explained in Chapter 3 of this book. A lower liquidity premium has to be compensated by a higher interest rate.

19. For a review of the discussion of Keynes's plan of an International Clearing Union by Balogh, Schumacher and Kalecki, see recently Faudot (2021).

7. From short-run macroeconomics to long-run distribution and growth: a systematic comparison of different paradigms and approaches*

7.1 INTRODUCTION

So far in this book the focus has been on short-run macroeconomics, assuming constant conditions of production, a constant capital stock and thus constant potential output, a constant labour force, as well as constant stocks of financial assets and liabilities. This was meant to explain the determinants of distribution, output, employment and inflation in a monetary production economy from a post-Keynesian perspective and to derive the main macroeconomic policy implications. Since in the chapters that follow we would like to touch upon some recent issues in modern capitalism, namely those that are associated with financialisation and led to the Global Financial Crisis and the Great Recession 2007–09 or the current challenges of the ecological crisis, some basic knowledge about different theories of distribution and growth is required. This means moving beyond the short run as defined above. This will then allow us to discuss the role of macroeconomic policies in a growth context. Recent books by Blecker and Setterfield (2019), Foley et al. (2019), Hein (2014a) and Lavoie (2014, Chapter 6) contain detailed and extensive presentations of orthodox and heterodox distribution and growth theories, and post-Keynesian approaches in particular. Therefore, in the current chapter, we will only present the basic versions in a unified modelling framework making use of the method of model closures in order to distinguish between different approaches. Although the focus will be on different versions of post-Keynesian distribution and growth theories, we will also include classical and orthodox Marxian, as well as old and new neoclassical theories, for the sake of comparison.

Using model closures in order to compare different approaches in the area of distribution and growth has been around for a while. As acknowledged by Marglin (1984b, p. 530), Sen (1963) introduced this concept, comparing neoclassical and neo-Keynesian approaches – the latter are today rather termed post-Keynesian models in the tradition of Kaldor and Robinson (Hein 2014a, Chapter 4). Marglin (1984a, 1984b) has used this method in order to compare neoclassical, neo-Marxian and neo-Keynesian, that is, post-Keynesian, models. Amadeo (1986) has compared a Marxian, a post-Keynesian Kaldor-Robinson and a Kaleckian case in a unified framework. Similarly and much more elaborately and extensively, Dutt (1990) has provided a comparison of neoclassical, neo-Marxian, post-Keynesian Kaldor-Robinson (what he calls neo-Keynesian) and Kalecki-Steindl approaches. The latter is in essence what we have termed the neo-Kaleckian model (Hein 2014, Chapter 6). The post-Kaleckian approach based on Bhaduri and Marglin (1990) and Kurz (1990) has then been included by Hein (2017b) in such an exercise. In Section 7.2, we will briefly review the major distinguishing features of the main approaches towards (functional) income distribution and growth. Section 7.3 will contain the basic model for the comparison of different approaches by means of model closure. In Sections 7.4 and 7.5, old and new neoclassical growth theory will be presented within this framework, while Section 7.6 will contain the classical and orthodox Marxian approaches. In Section 7.7, the post-Keynesian Kaldor-Robinson distribution and growth model will be presented, and in Section 7.8 the different versions of the Kalecki-Steindl theory, the neo-Kaleckian and the post-Kaleckian variants will be shown. In Section 7.9, we will discuss the Sraffian supermultiplier growth model in our unified framework. The final Section 7.10 will integrate endogenous productivity growth into a basic Kaleckian model and make use of Kaldorian and Marxian ideas for this purpose.

7.2 THE DISTINGUISHING FEATURES OF ORTHODOX AND HETERODOX THEORIES OF DISTRIBUTION AND GROWTH

The theories of distribution and growth can be broadly separated into orthodox approaches and heterodox approaches, as in Table 7.1. As already mentioned, in this chapter we are only interested in the basic structures of the models, the main chains of causalities and interdependencies, as well as in the determinations of long-run growth equilibria or trends.

The orthodox approaches contain the neoclassical microeconomic theory of distribution, as included in the general equilibrium theory going back to Walras (1874/1954), the neoclassical macroeconomic theory of distribution, based on Wicksell (1893) and Clark (1899), and then in particular the old neoclassical growth models proposed by Solow (1956) and Swan (1956) and finally the new neoclassical growth theories starting with the works of Romer (1986) and Lucas (1988). The latter are nowadays mainly included in mainstream textbooks and taught in mainstream academic programmes.[1] In principle, the neoclassical approach explains both income distribution and growth in a unified and integrated framework taken from its foundations in allocation theory based on 'first principles'. These are given production technologies (i.e. production functions), given preferences (i.e. utility functions), given initial endowments of economic agents and the assumption of strictly utility and profit maximising behaviour of economic agents in perfectly competitive markets. Assuming marginal productivity remuneration of the factors of production, the technology of production thus determines the income shares of the factors of production.

When it comes to growth, in the *old neoclassical growth models* à la Solow (1956), flexible factor prices and smooth substitution between capital and labour guarantee the adjustment

Table 7.1   Distribution and growth theories

Orthodox		Heterodox				
			Post-Keynesian			
				Kalecki-Steindl		
Old neoclassical (Solow, Swan)	New neoclassical (Romer, Lucas)	Classical/ Marxian	Kaldor-Robinson	Neo-Kaleckian (Dutt, Rowthorn)	Post-Kaleckian (Bhaduri/ Marglin, Kurz)	Sraffian supermultiplier (Serrano)

towards an exogenously given full employment equilibrium growth rate, the 'natural rate of growth', determined by non-explained rates of labour force growth and technical progress. In the modern version of neoclassical growth theory, that is, in the *new neoclassical or endogenous growth theory*, productivity growth and hence the natural rate of growth are determined endogenously in a way which is consistent with neoclassical first principles. In this approach it is technology, either externalities of the production process, or the technologies applied in the purposeful generation of growth-enhancing human capital or research and development (R&D), as well as preferences, in particular the time preference of households regarding present and future consumption, which determine productivity growth and, with a given rate of labour force growth, thus the natural rate of growth.

Either assuming Say's law to hold in the long run, or making it hold via a flexible real interest rate in the market for loanable funds, old and new neoclassical distribution and growth models ignore the Keynesian problem of the non-neutrality of money and the importance of effective demand for long-run growth. Furthermore, they have to face the critique of the 'Cambridge controversies in the theory of capital', questioning the very existence of uniquely downward sloping factor demand curves in price-quantity space. This then questions the smooth substitution of factors of production guided by relative factor prices in a more-than-one-good economy, which are important for the adjustment towards the natural rate of growth and thus the full employment growth path (Harcourt 1969, 1972, Lazzarini 2011, Hein 2014a, Chapter 3.6).

Based on this critique, heterodox approaches, like classical and Marxian theories, as well as different post-Keynesian approaches, include a degree of freedom in the determination of relative prices and thus in functional income distribution. Some information about distribution is required, in order to calculate long-run equilibrium prices. This can then be derived from different socio-economic distribution theories. Furthermore, in heterodox theories, income distribution, capital accumulation and growth are interrelated, albeit in different ways, as we will see below.

The *classical authors*, such as Adam Smith (1776) and David Ricardo (1817), as well as Karl Marx (1867, 1885, 1894) assume that functional income distribution is determined by socio-institutional factors and power relationships between capital and labour determining a conventional real wage rate. For a given production technology, the rate of profit then becomes a residual variable. As an alternative based on Sraffa's (1960, p. 33) ideas, some neo-Ricardian authors, like Panico (1985) and Pivetti (1991), have proposed taking the rate of profit as being determined by the monetary interest rates, making the real wage rate the residual variable. With functional income distribution given in either way, the rate of profit, together with capitalists' propensity to save and to accumulate, determines the long-run equilibrium rates of capital accumulation and growth.[2] In this approach the validity of Say's law in Ricardo's version is assumed: Profits saved are completely used for investment and accumulation, so that no problems of effective demand for the economy as a whole arise in long-run growth. However, the validity of Say's law is not accepted by all classical economists, as Sowell (1972) has pointed out. As we have shown in Chapter 3, also Marx's theory allows for an interpretation in which aggregate demand, finance, credit and interest rates matter for the determination of long-run accumulation and growth, as for example also Argitis (2001) and Hein (2006b, 2019b) have made clear.

For those classical authors accepting Say's law, this does not mean that the growth path is characterised by full employment (Garegnani 1978, 1979). On the contrary, unemployment is considered to be a persistent feature of capitalism constraining distribution claims of workers and thus providing the conditions for positive profits, capital accumulation and growth. Furthermore in this perspective, capital accumulation feeds back on the rate of profit in the long run and causes a tendency of the rate of profit to fall. This is either due to the specific nature of technical progress causing a falling productivity of capital, as in Marx's (1867, 1894) notion of a rising 'organic composition of capital', or it is caused by the falling marginal productivity of land which may not be compensated for by productivity enhancing technical progress, as in Ricardo's (1817) theory of differential rent.

From a (post-)Keynesian perspective, this classical and orthodox Marxian approach, of course, suffers from the assumption of the long-run neutrality of money and from the lack of any role for effective demand in long-run growth theory. Therefore, the *first generation of post-Keynesian distribution and growth theories* put forward by Nicholas Kaldor (1955/56, 1957, 1961) and Joan Robinson (1956, 1962) have relied on John Maynard Keynes's (1936) and Michal Kalecki's (1935, 1939) 'principle of effective demand' and have attempted to extend it to the long period and hence to growth and distribution issues (Blecker and Setterfield 2019, Chapter 3, Hein 2014a, Chapter 4, Lavoie 2014, Chapter 6). From this perspective, in a monetary production economy, investment by firms is independent of prior saving and is the driving force of the growth process, because firms have access to finance independently of any prior saving in the economy. For the macro-economy, saving will have to adjust to investment. Since the post-Keynesian approach by Kaldor and Robinson assumes the long-run full or normal utilisation of productive capacities given by the capital stock,[3] this adjustment has to take place through changes in income distribution, assuming a higher propensity to save out of profits than out of wages. And this will only happen if prices in the goods markets are more flexible than nominal wages in the labour market, such that a change in investment and aggregate demand can trigger a change in functional income distribution via the change in prices relative to more rigid nominal wages. The causality known from the classicals and the orthodox Marxian interpretation is thus reversed: The rate of profit is determined by the rate of accumulation and growth, as well as by the propensities to save out of profits and out of wages.

Obviously, the assumption of long-run growth with a normal or full rate of capacity utilisation and the related requirements of goods market prices being more flexible than nominal wages in the long run, in order to generate the required re-distribution and adjustment of saving to investment, poses some problems. First, it is not clear why in organised oligopolistic goods markets price reactions should be speedier than quantity responses, in particular in periods of shrinking demand. Second, even if prices were highly flexible, it is not clear why nominal wages should be more rigid in the long run and, in particular, why workers should accept a lower real wage rate or wage share whenever capital accumulation accelerates. Of course, Robinson (1962, pp. 58–9) discussed the exceptional case of the 'inflation barrier', when there is a tendency of the real wage rate to be forced below some conventional or target level, and workers start to resist, generating a price-wage-price spiral. However, it remains unclear why workers should accept a lower real wage rate at any level of the wage rate when unemployment is low and growth is high.

Alternatively, in the *second generation of post-Keynesian models* based on Michal Kalecki's (1954, 1971) and Josef Steindl's (1952) works, the independence of capital accumulation of firms from saving at the macroeconomic level is connected with a determination of income distribution by relative economic powers of capital and labour, mainly through firms' mark-up pricing on constant unit labour costs up to full capacity output in imperfectly competitive goods markets, as we have explained in detail in Chapter 3. Functional income distribution and hence the profit share are thus explained by the relative economic powers of capital and labour affecting the mark-up in firms' pricing, and the rate of capacity utilisation, as an accommodating variable in the long run, is determined by aggregate demand growth and hence by capital accumulation and consumption (Blecker and Setterfield 2019, Chapter 4, Hein 2014a, Chapters 5–11, Lavoie 2014, Chapter 6).

For the closed economy, the effects of distributional changes on equilibrium capacity utilisation and growth then mainly depend on the relative weights of demand/utilisation and profitability determinants in the investment function. The neo-Kaleckian model based on the works of Rowthorn (1981) and Dutt (1984, 1987) contains a strong accelerator effect of demand and no direct effect of profitability in the investment function. In its closed economy version without saving out of wages, it generates uniquely depressing effects of re-distribution at the expense of the wage share on the rates of capacity utilisation, capital accumulation, growth and profit. The post-Kaleckian model, based on the works of Bhaduri and Marglin (1990) and Kurz (1990), however, also contains a direct profitability effect in the investment function. Therefore, its closed economy version without saving out of wages is able to generate different regimes of demand and growth, hence positive or negative effects of a lower wage share on capacity utilisation, capital accumulation, growth and the rate of profit, depending on the relative weights of accelerator and profitability terms in the investment function and on the differential in the propensities to save from profits and from wages. Including international trade also allows for profit-led demand and growth in an otherwise neo-Kaleckian model, as Blecker (1989) has shown even before Bhaduri and Marglin (1990) and Kurz (1990).[4]

The treatment of the rate of capacity utilisation as a long-run endogenous variable in Kaleckian models has been criticised by Marxian and Harrodian authors and has been debated for a while. The critics, like Duménil and Lévy (1999), Shaikh (2009) and Skott (2010, 2012), have argued that the Kaleckian notion of an endogenous rate of capacity utilisation beyond the short run is not sustainable, that Kaleckian models thus face the problem of Harrodian instability, that is, cumulative divergence of actual capacity utilisation from the normal or the target rate of utilisation of firms, and that the Kaleckian results of the paradox of saving and a potential paradox of costs, and hence wage-led demand and growth, cannot be validated beyond the short run. As has been reviewed by Hein et al. (2011, 2012a), Hein (2014a, Chapter 11) and Lavoie (2014, Chapter 6.5), Kaleckian authors have defended their model by downgrading the relevance of a long-run equilibrium in which the goods market equilibrium rate of utilisation equals the firms' target rate, or by arguing that the target rate of utilisation turns endogenous with respect to the goods market equilibrium rate in the long run.

Alternatively, starting with Allain (2015) and Lavoie (2016a), several Kaleckian authors have accepted an exogenous normal or target rate of capacity utilisation for the long-run growth equilibrium and have turned towards introducing a *Sraffian supermultiplier* process into their models of distribution and growth in order to defend this approach against the Harrodian and Marxian critique.[5] Initially a Sraffian supermultiplier model driven by autonomous demand was proposed by Serrano (1995a, 1995b).[6] In these models, the autonomous growth rate of a non-capacity creating component of aggregate demand, that is, autonomous consumption, residential investment, exports or government expenditures, determines long-run growth. Under the conditions that Harrodian instability in the investment function is not too strong, the models generate a stable adjustment towards the normal rate of capacity utilisation in the long run. A change in the propensity to save or in the profit share will have no effect on the long-run growth rate but will affect the traverse and thus the long-run growth path. The paradox of saving and the possibility of a paradox of costs from the short run thus disappear with respect to the long-run growth rate, but they remain valid with respect to the long-run growth path.[7]

7.3 THE BASIC MODEL FOR A SYSTEMATIC COMPARISON OF DISTRIBUTION AND GROWTH THEORIES BY MEANS OF MODEL CLOSURES

We will now compare the basic features of each of the approaches outlined above making use of a very simple model and then apply different closures, according to the different theories. In essence we will start with two equations for the basic model and will then add four equations for each approach, in order to close the model. Each approach can then be described graphically in a two quadrant system by the relationship between the rate of growth and the rate of profit, on the one hand, and by an endogenous variable adjusting the rate of profit to its long-run equilibrium value, on the other hand.

We assume a closed economy without a government sector, which is composed of two classes, workers and capitalists. Workers offer labour power to capitalists and receive wages, which they use in order to purchase consumption goods. We assume that the classical saving hypothesis holds, such that there is no saving from wages. Capitalists own the means of production and receive profits, which are partly consumed and partly saved – buying assets issued by the corporate sector and thus the capitalists themselves, or depositing parts of the profits with the financial sector, which is also owned by the capitalists and not explicitly modelled here. Capitalists control the capital stock, hire labour, organise the production process and decide about investment and thus the expansion of the capital stock. For the latter they draw on their own means of finance, issue stocks or corporate bonds or draw on credit endogenously generated and granted by the financial sector. By assumption all these transactions take place within the capitalist class, and they are not modelled here.

In our model economy, a homogenous output (Y) is produced combining direct labour and a non-depreciating capital stock in the production process. The homogeneous output can be used for consumption and investment purposes. For the sake of simplicity we refrain from the consideration of overhead labour and depreciation of the capital stock, as well as raw materials and intermediate products. The rate of profit (r) relating the flow of profits (Π) to the nominal capital stock (pK) can be decomposed into the profit share (h), relating profits to nominal income (pY), the rate of capacity utilisation (u), relating actual output to potential output given by the capital stock (Y^p), and the inverse of the capital-potential output ratio (v), relating the capital stock to potential output:

$$r = \frac{\Pi}{pK} = \frac{\Pi}{pY} \frac{Y}{Y^p} \frac{Y^p}{K} = hu\frac{1}{v}. \tag{7.1}$$

Our assumption regarding saving translates into the following saving rate (σ), which relates the flow of total saving (S) to the value of the capital stock:

$$\sigma = \frac{S}{pK} = \frac{s_\Pi \Pi}{pK} = s_\Pi r = s_\Pi hu\frac{1}{v}, \quad 0 < s_\Pi \leq 1. \tag{7.2}$$

With zero saving out of wages, the saving rate is determined by the propensity to save out of profits (s_Π) and by the profit rate, where the components of the latter are given from equation (7.1). It should be noted that in the neoclassical growth theory there is no distinction between saving out of profits and saving out of wages, but just an average propensity to save out of income. With our classical saving hypothesis, the average propensity to save out of income (s) is given by $s = s_\Pi h$, and it will hence rise with an increase in the propensity to save out profits and with the profit share.

7.4   THE OLD NEOCLASSICAL GROWTH MODEL

Starting with the old neoclassical growth model in the tradition of Solow (1956) and Swan (1956), we obtain the following closure. In long-run equilibrium, capacity utilisation is at its normal or target rate (u_n). Profit maximising firms use the capital stock at the optimal rate – and labour is fully employed through a flexible real wage rate in the labour market:

$$u = u_n. \tag{7.3n}$$

Functional income distribution and thus the profit share in the neoclassical model are determined by the production technology, assuming marginal productivity remuneration. With a Cobb/Douglas production function, the profit share is given by the output elasticity of capital and is hence exogenous for the growth process with a given production function:

$$h = \bar{h}. \tag{7.4n}$$

From equations (7.1), (7.3n) and (7.4n), the capital-potential output ratio remains as a variable which may adjust the profit rate to its value required by the growth equilibrium. The latter is given by the natural rate of growth (g_n), composed of the sum of labour force growth and the rate of technical progress, each of which is assumed to be exogenous.

$$g = g_n. \tag{7.5n}$$

Finally, in the neoclassical model, investment is identically equal to saving. It is thus the saving decisions of the households which determine investment of the firms, and the saving rate thus determines the rate of capital accumulation (g):

$$\sigma = \frac{S}{pK} \equiv g = \frac{pI}{pK}. \tag{7.6n}$$

Equation (7.6n) is what Harrod (1939) used to call the 'warranted rate of growth'. In the neoclassical model, the warranted rate of growth will now adjust towards the natural rate of growth through a variation in the capital-potential output ratio.

Graphically, the old neoclassical growth model is presented in Figure 7.1. On the right-hand side, we have the relationship between the rate of profit and the saving rate (equation 7.2), the latter being identical with the rate of capital accumulation (equation 7.6n). On the left-hand side, we have the relationship between the rate of profit and the capital-potential output ratio (equation 7.1), assuming the profit share to be given technologically and capacity utilisation

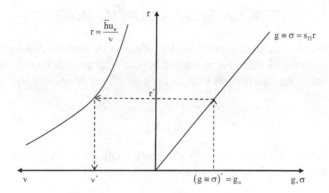

Figure 7.1   The old neoclassical growth theory

Table 7.2   Effects of changes in exogenous variables on endogenous variables in the old neoclassical growth model

Exogenous variables	Endogenous variables		
	$(\sigma \equiv g)^*$	r^*	v^*
g_n	+	+	−
h	0	0	+
u_n	0	0	+
s_Π	0	−	+

at its normal rate. In long-run growth equilibrium, the natural rate of growth determines the equilibrium growth rate of capital accumulation (the warranted rate), and with a given propensity to save thus the equilibrium rate of profit. The latter will adjust to its equilibrium value through changes in the capital-potential output ratio, that is, through substitution between capital and labour guided by flexible real wages and real interest rates in the labour and capital markets, responding to changes in factor supply and demand.

With the natural rate of growth as an exogenous variable, together with the propensity to save out of profits (determined by time preference in more elaborated models), the profit share (given by production technology) and the normal rate of utilisation (determined by profit maximisation) as exogenous variables, too, the warranted rate of growth, the rate of profit and the capital-potential output ratio become the endogenous variables in the old neoclassical growth model (Table 7.2). A higher (lower) natural rate of growth will cause a higher (lower) warranted rate of growth, a higher (lower) rate of profit and a lower (higher) capital-potential output ratio. A higher (lower) propensity to save out of profits, and thus a clockwise (counterclockwise) rotation of the g–σ-curve, will have no effect on the equilibrium rates of growth and capital accumulation but will cause a lower (higher) rate of profit and a higher (lower) capital-potential output ratio. Finally, a higher (lower) profit share or a higher (lower) normal rate of utilisation will lead to an upward (downward) shift of the r-curve in Figure 7.1 and will thus have no effect on the equilibrium rates of growth and capital accumulation but will cause a higher (lower) capital-potential output ratio.

7.5   THE NEW NEOCLASSICAL GROWTH MODELS

Turning to the new neoclassical growth models inspired by Romer (1986) and Lucas (1988) we obtain the following closure. As in the old neoclassical growth model, utilisation of the capital stock in long-run equilibrium is at its optimal, target or normal level – and labour is fully employed, too:

$$u = u_n. \tag{7.3ng}$$

Factor income shares and thus the profit share are again given by production technology, assuming marginal productivity remuneration:

$$h = \bar{h}. \tag{7.4ng}$$

But unlike the old neoclassical growth model, the capital-potential output ratio is no longer a passively adjusting variable. It is now a constant, either determined by macroeconomic externalities, like knowledge spill-overs, exactly compensating for falling marginal productivities of the capital stock at the microeconomic levels, as in the AK model. Alternatively, productivity growth generated by human capital or R&D expenditures in the respective models exactly compensates for falling marginal productivity of capital. Taking the AK model as the most simple and workhorse model of new neoclassical growth theory, with a production function $Y = AK_B$, and A as constant productivity of the broad capital stock, including physical and human capital (K_B) (Hein 2014a, Chapter 3.5), we obtain:

$$v = \frac{1}{A}. \tag{7.5ng}$$

Finally, as in the old neoclassical growth model, investment is identically equal to saving:

$$\sigma = \frac{S}{pK} \equiv g = \frac{pI}{pK} \tag{7.6ng}$$

Figure 7.2 presents the new neoclassical growth theory, using the same functions as for the old neoclassical model, but now the causality is reversed. The capital-potential output ratio turns out to be the exogenous variable in our model setup, itself determined by externalities or by technology and preferences with respect to the generation of technological progress through human capital accumulation or R&D expenditures. The other exogenous variables are again the propensity to save out of profits (determined by time preference), the profit share and the normal rate of utilisation (determined by technology and profit maximisation). The endogenous variables are now the rate of profit and the rates of accumulation and growth (Table 7.3).

A higher (lower) broad capital productivity and thus a lower (higher) capital-potential output ratio cause a higher (lower) rate of profit and higher (lower) equilibrium rates of accumulation and growth. A higher (lower) profit share or a higher (lower) normal rate of utilisation, and thus an upward (downward) shift of the r-curve, has the same effects. A higher (lower) propensity to save, hence a clockwise (counter-clockwise) rotation of the g–σ-curve, causes a higher (lower) equilibrium rate of capital accumulation and growth but has no effect on the equilibrium profit rate.

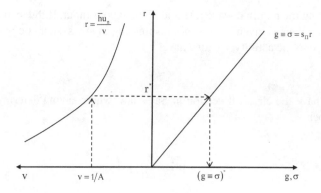

Figure 7.2 The new neoclassical growth theory

Table 7.3 Effects of changes in exogenous variables on endogenous variables in the new neoclassical growth theory

Exogenous variables	Endogenous variables	
	$(\sigma \equiv g)^*$	r^*
v	–	–
h	+	+
u_n	+	+
s_Π	+	0

7.6 THE CLASSICAL AND ORTHODOX MARXIAN DISTRIBUTION AND GROWTH MODELS

Discussing the classical and orthodox Marxian closure in our model, we have again that productive capacities given by the capital stock are used at their normal or target rate in the long-run growth equilibrium:

$$u = u_n. \tag{7.3cm}$$

Usually, in the classical and orthodox Marxian approach we have unemployment in the long-run growth equilibrium. Functional income distribution is determined by socio-institutional factors and distribution conflict – either over the real wage rate or over the rate of interest, as explained above. Let us here focus on the subsistence or conventional real wage rate (w_r^s), which for a given production technology and thus a given labour-output ratio ($l_0 = N/Y$) determines the profit share:

$$h = \frac{pY - wN}{pY} = 1 - w_r^s l_0, \tag{7.4cm}$$

with w representing the nominal wage rate and N the labour input. If the technical conditions of production are taken as given, that is, not responding in any systematic way to changes in distribution or economic activity, we also have:

$$v = \bar{v}. \tag{7.5cm}$$

And finally, we have the classical version of Say's law, where saving determines investment in the capital stock:

$$\sigma = \frac{S}{pK} \equiv g = \frac{pI}{pK}. \tag{7.6cm}$$

Figure 7.3 presents the classical/orthodox Marxian distribution and growth model. On the right-hand side, we have the relationship between the rate of profit and the saving and accumulation rate from equations (7.2) and (7.6cm). And on the left-hand side, we have the rate of profit from equation (7.1), for a given capital-potential output ratio and a normal rate of capacity utilisation only depending on the profit share. Distribution conflict determines the profit share, thus the profit rate, and the latter, together with the propensity to save out of profits, determines equilibrium capital accumulation and growth.

The exogenous variables in the classical/orthodox Marxian model are thus the profit share, the capital-potential output ratio, the normal rate of capacity utilisation and the propensity to save out of profits (Table 7.4). A higher (lower) profit share, as well as a higher (lower) normal rate of utilisation, the latter through a clockwise (counter-clockwise) rotation of the r-curve, will cause a higher (lower) profit rate and a higher (lower) equilibrium rate of capital accumulation and growth. Should technical change trigger a higher capital-potential output ratio, hence a counter-clockwise rotation of the r-curve, a lower rate of profit and thus also lower equilibrium capital accumulation and growth will result, as in Marx's (1894) falling rate of profit and over-accumulation crisis theory. Finally, a higher (lower) propensity to save, hence a clockwise (counter-clockwise) rotation of the g–σ-curve, will cause a higher (lower) equilibrium rate of accumulation and growth but will have no effect on the equilibrium profit rate. These results are structurally similar to the ones in the new neoclassical growth theory – although based on a very different type of model – as already pointed out by Kurz and Salvadori (2003).

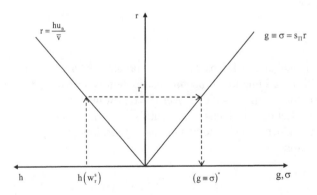

Figure 7.3   The classical/orthodox Marxian distribution and growth theory

Table 7.4   Effects of changes in exogenous variables on endogenous variables in the classical/orthodox Marxian distribution and growth theory

Exogenous variables	Endogenous variables	
	$(\sigma \equiv g)^*$	r^*
v	−	−
h	+	+
u_n	+	+
s_Π	+	0

7.7   THE POST-KEYNESIAN KALDOR-ROBINSON MODEL

The textbook version of the first generation post-Keynesian distribution and growth model in the tradition of Kaldor and Robinson (Blecker and Setterfield 2019, Chapter 3.4, Hein 2014a, Chapter 4.4, Lavoie 2014, Chapter 6.1) provides the following closure. In the long-run growth equilibrium, the utilisation rate of productive capacities given by the capital stock is at its normal or target rate:

$$u = u_n. \tag{7.3kr}$$

Labour, however, is usually not fully employed. The capital-potential output ratio is an exogenous variable, which is itself affected by the nature of technical progress. However, it is not systematically related to the rate of profit or economic activity:

$$v = \bar{v}. \tag{7.4kr}$$

With a constant and given normal rate of utilisation and a given capital-potential output ratio, the profit share becomes the variable adjusting the profit rate (equation 7.1) to its equilibrium value. The distinguishing feature of the post-Keynesian approach, as mentioned above, is the independence of firms' investment decisions from households' saving decisions. This means that we now have an investment function separately from the saving function in equation (7.2):

$$g = g(\alpha, r), \quad \frac{\partial g}{\partial \alpha} > 0, \frac{\partial g}{\partial r} > 0. \tag{7.5kr}$$

Following Kaldor (1957, 1961) and Robinson (1956, 1962), investment decisions are determined by firms' 'animal spirits' (α), describing the 'spontaneous urge to action rather than inaction' (Keynes 1936, p. 161), and by the (expected) rate of profit. Profits and thus the profit rate are considered to have a positive influence on investment decisions, as retained profits provide internal funds for investment, and furthermore they alleviate the access of firms to external funds in incompletely competitive financial markets. Equation (7.6kr) is the goods market equilibrium, in which the accumulation rate and the saving rate have to be equal:

$$g^* = \frac{pI}{pK} = \sigma^* = \frac{S}{pK}. \tag{7.6kr}$$

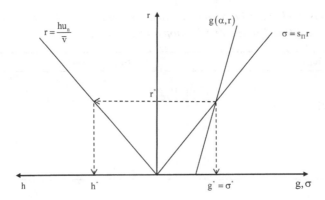

Figure 7.4   The post-Keynesian Kaldor-Robinson distribution and growth theory

The Kaldor-Robinson distribution and growth model is presented in Figure 7.4. On the right-hand side, we have the accumulation rate and the saving rate, each as a function of the rate of profit. And on the left-hand side, we have the relationship of the profit rate and the profit share for a given normal rate of capacity utilisation and a given capital-potential output ratio. The point of intersection of investment and saving functions determines the long-run equilibrium accumulation and growth rate, as well as the associated equilibrium profit rate, with the profit share as the adjusting variable. Higher equilibrium growth will trigger a higher profit rate, a higher profit share and thus a lower wage share.

In the post-Keynesian Kaldor-Robinson model, we have as exogenous variables and parameters those determining the investment and saving function, which are animal spirits, the responsiveness of investment with respect to the profit rate ($\partial g/\partial r$) and the propensity to save out of profits, as well as the exogenously given normal rate of utilisation and capital-potential output ratio (Table 7.5). Any rise (fall) in animal spirits, hence a rightwards (leftwards) shift in the g-curve, or in the responsiveness of investment to the profit rate, hence a clockwise (counter-clockwise) rotation in the g-curve, will cause higher (lower) equilibrium rates of accumulation, growth and profit, and a higher (lower) profit share. A higher (lower) propensity to save, thus a clockwise (counter-clockwise) rotation in the σ-curve, has a negative (positive) effect on the equilibrium values of accumulation, growth, the profit rate and the profit share. The paradox of thrift is thus valid for long-run growth, too. Finally, any change in the

Table 7.5   Effects of changes in exogenous variables on endogenous variables in the post-Keynesian Kaldor-Robinson distribution and growth model

Exogenous variables	Endogenous variables		
	$\sigma^* = g^*$	r^*	h^*
v	0	0	+
u_n	0	0	−
α	+	+	+
$\partial g/\partial r$	+	+	+
s_{Π}	−	−	−

capital-potential output ratio or in the normal rate of utilisation will have no effects on the equilibrium accumulation, growth and profit rates but will only affect the equilibrium profit share. A change in the capital-potential output ratio (rotation in the r-curve) will be positively related with the profit share, whereas a change in the normal rate of utilisation (rotation in the r-curve, too) will have an inverse effect on the profit share.

7.8 THE POST-KEYNESIAN KALECKI-STEINDL DISTRIBUTION AND GROWTH MODELS

The second generation post-Keynesian distribution and growth theory is the one based on the contributions by Kalecki (1954, 1971) and Steindl (1952). We present here the textbook version of the neo-Kaleckian and post-Kaleckian models (Blecker 2002, Blecker and Setterfield 2019, Chapter 4, Hein 2014a, Chapter 6, Lavoie 2014, Chapter 6.2). As explained above, the rate of capacity utilisation becomes an endogenous variable in the Kalecki-Steindl approach. The profit share, and thus functional income distribution, is mainly determined by the mark-up in firms' pricing in imperfectly competitive markets. In our simple closed private one-good economy model, it is thus only the mark-up (m) on constant unit labour costs which determines the profit share:

$$h = h(\bar{m}), \quad \frac{\partial h}{\partial m} > 0. \tag{7.3ks}$$

The mark-up itself is affected by several factors, as we have explained in Chapter 3, such as the degree of competition in the goods market, the bargaining power of workers and unit overhead costs, which we all treat as constant and given. The capital-potential output ratio is also considered as an exogenous variable determined by technology, which does not systematically respond to distribution and activity variables in the model:

$$v = \bar{v}. \tag{7.4ks}$$

With the profit share and the capital-potential output ratio as exogenously given, the rate of capacity utilisation becomes the variable adjusting the profit rate (equation 7.1) to its equilibrium value. The determinants in the Kalecki-Steindl investment function are basically similar to the ones in the Kaldor-Robinson model. We have again firms' or managements' animal spirits (α), sometimes taken to represent the firms' assessment of the long-run growth trend of the economy. Furthermore, the (expected) rate of profit is of relevance, because it indicates internal means of finance required for attracting external investment finance, according to Kalecki's (1937) 'principle of increasing risk'. Also, the dynamics of demand are reflected in the rate of profit through changes in capacity utilisation (equation 7.1). Unlike the Kaldor-Robinson model, however, Kaleckians and Steindlians prefer to include the constituting elements of the profit rate in the investment function, because, as in particular Bhaduri and Marglin (1990) have argued, the source of a change in the profit rate may be important when it comes to the discussion of the effects on firms' investment decisions. Therefore, on top of animal spirits, the three principal determinants of the profit rate from equation (7.1) can be included in the Kalecki-Steindl accumulation function:

$$g = g(\alpha, h, u, v), \quad \frac{\partial g}{\partial \alpha} > 0, \frac{\partial g}{\partial h} \geq 0, \frac{\partial g}{\partial u} > 0, \frac{\partial g}{\partial v} = 0. \tag{7.5ks}$$

Investment decisions will thus positively depend on the profit share and the rate of capacity utilisation, because each will increase the (expected) rate of profit, ceteris paribus. Here, it is important to understand that we are talking about partial effects on investment decisions, applying the ceteris paribus clause, and are not yet considering the further feedback effects through the model. However, neo-Kaleckians would insist that even the partial effect of a change in the profit share is irrelevant for firms' decisions to invest (and hence that $\partial g/\partial h = 0$). Regarding changes in the capital-potential output ratio through technical change, the partial effects on investment decisions are not clear. On the one hand, a higher capital-potential output ratio means a lower rate of profit which should dampen investment. On the other hand, however, a higher capital-potential output ratio means that a certain increase in demand requires a higher increase in the capital stock than before, which should boost investment. The sign of the sum of these two opposing effects is not clear ex ante, so that any direct effect of changes in the capital-potential output ratio on investment is disregarded in what follows. Finally, equation (7.6ks) is again the familiar goods market equilibrium condition:

$$g^* = \frac{pI}{pK} = \sigma^* = \frac{S}{pK}. \tag{7.6ks}$$

Figure 7.5 presents the general post-Keynesian Kalecki-Steindl distribution and growth model. On the right-hand side, we have the accumulation rate and the saving rate, each as a function of the rate of profit – bearing in mind that we have to take into account potentially different effects of the components of the profit rate on investment. And on the left-hand side we have the relationship of the profit rate with the rate of capacity utilisation, for a given profit share and a given capital-potential output ratio. The point of intersection of the investment and saving functions determines the long-run equilibrium accumulation and growth rate, as well as the associated equilibrium profit rate, with capacity utilisation as the adjusting variable. Higher equilibrium growth will trigger a higher equilibrium rate of utilisation and a higher profit rate. Higher growth will thus not come at the expense of the workers' share in

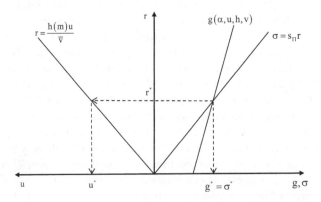

Figure 7.5   The post-Keynesian Kalecki-Steindl distribution and growth theory

national income, which will remain constant, as long as the determinants of the mark-up do not change.[8]

In the Kalecki-Steindl approach, we have again the parameters and coefficients of the saving and investment functions as exogenous variables: Animal spirits, the responsiveness of investment with respect to capacity utilisation ($\partial g/\partial u$) and with respect to the profit share ($\partial g/\partial h$), which is zero in the neo-Kaleckian model) and the propensity to save out of profits (Table 7.6). Furthermore, we have the capital-potential output ratio, a change of which will only affect the relationship between the equilibrium profit rate and the utilisation rate, because we have disregarded any unique direct effect on investment. And finally, we have the profit share, which will affect the left-hand side of Figure 7.5 but potentially also the right-hand side through the effects on capital accumulation. Any rise (fall) in animal spirits, hence a rightwards (leftwards) shift in the g-curve, or in the responsiveness of investment with respect to capacity utilisation or the profit share, thus a clockwise (counter-clockwise) rotation in the g-curve, will cause higher (lower) equilibrium rates of accumulation, growth, profit and capacity utilisation. A higher (lower) propensity to save out of profits, thus a clockwise (counter-clockwise) rotation in the σ-curve, will cause lower (higher) equilibrium rates of accumulation, growth, profit and capacity utilisation – the paradox of thrift again. An increase in the capital-potential output ratio will only have positive effects on equilibrium capacity utilisation, through a counter-clockwise rotation in the r-curve, but will have no effects on the equilibrium rates of accumulation and profit. Finally, changes in the profit share will either have positive or negative effects on the equilibrium rates of capital accumulation, growth and profit, depending on whether we apply the neo- or the post-Kaleckian approach towards the determinants of investment, as we will analyse graphically in more detail below.

In the graphical presentation of the model, any change in the profit share will affect both the r-curve and potentially the g-curve in the Kalecki-Steindl model. On the one hand, a higher (lower) profit share will cause a clockwise (counter-clockwise) rotation of the r-curve in Figure 7.5. On the other hand, a higher (lower) profit share will cause a rotation of the g-curve. Here the direction will depend on the relative importance of the profit share and the rate of utilisation in the investment function. Let us focus on a reduction of the profit share in what follows – caused by a reduction in the mark-up; for an increase in the mark-up and the profit share, the arguments below apply in reverse.

Table 7.6   Effects of changes in exogenous variables on endogenous variables in the Kalecki-Steindl growth theory

Exogenous variables	Endogenous variables		
	$\sigma^* = g^*$	r^*	u^*
v	0	0	+
h	–/+	–/+	–/+
α	+	+	+
$\partial g/\partial u$	+	+	+
$\partial g/\partial h$	+	+	+
s_Π	–	–	–

With a strong responsiveness of investment towards utilisation ($\partial g/\partial u$) and a very weak or even zero reaction towards the profit share ($\partial g/\partial h$), as assumed in the neo-Kaleckian model, a fall in the profit share and thus a lower profit share and a higher rate of utilisation for every rate of profit, hence a counter-clockwise rotation of the r-curve, will also trigger a clockwise rotation of the g-curve in the g–r-space, as shown in Figure 7.6. Every rate of profit will be associated with a higher rate of utilisation, and firms' investment will respond positively; the g-curve will rotate clockwise. This will then cause higher equilibrium rates of accumulation, growth, profit and capacity utilisation. The economy will be in a wage-led demand and a wage-led growth regime or, as Bhaduri and Marglin (1990) have termed it, in a stagnationist demand and wage-led growth regime. Furthermore, the paradox of costs (Rowthorn 1981) applies: A higher wage share triggers a higher profit rate.

However, the wage-led demand/wage-led growth regime is only one possible regime, if we consider a positive and somewhat stronger direct effect of the profit share on capital accumulation, as has been argued by Bhaduri and Marglin (1990) and Kurz (1990). In this case, a lower profit share, triggering a higher rate of utilisation for every profit rate, hence the counter-clockwise rotation of the r-curve, will be associated with a counter-clockwise rotation of the g-curve, too. Each rate of profit is associated with a lower profit share, and firms will accumulate at a lower rate. If this rotation of the g-curve is not too pronounced, we may still get wage-led demand, hence higher equilibrium utilisation, but profit-led growth, thus lower equilibrium capital accumulation and growth. Furthermore, the equilibrium profit rate comes down, too, and the paradox of costs disappears. Bhaduri and Marglin (1990) call this a 'stagnationist conflict' or a 'profit squeeze' constellation: Although re-distribution in favour of wages is expansionary with respect to aggregate demand and capacity utilisation, it will not be supported by capitalists, because it will mean a lower rate of profit to them and also a lower rate of accumulation and growth. Figure 7.7 shows this intermediate case.

Finally, if the effect of the profit share on investment is very pronounced, a lower profit share will cause a more considerable counter-clockwise rotation of the g-curve, as in Figure 7.8, and we will see profit-led demand and profit-led growth. A lower profit share will thus cause lower equilibrium rates of capacity utilisation, capital accumulation, growth and profit. Bhaduri and Marglin (1990) call this an exhilarationist demand and a profit-led growth regime. The model

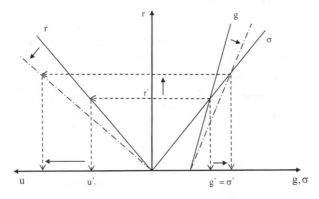

Figure 7.6   A reduction in the profit share in the Kalecki-Steindl growth theory: The neo-Kaleckian model and the wage-led demand/wage-led growth regime of the post-Kaleckian model

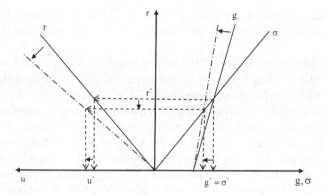

Figure 7.7   A reduction in the profit share in the Kalecki-Steindl growth theory: The intermediate case with wage-led demand and profit-led growth in the post-Kaleckian model

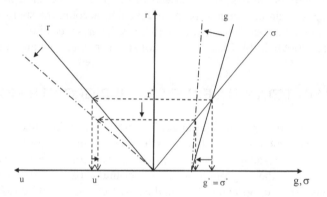

Figure 7.8   A reduction in the profit share in the Kalecki-Steindl growth theory: The profit-led demand and profit-led growth regime in the post-Kaleckian model

generates basically the same results as the classical/orthodox Marxian and the new neoclassical growth theories, but here in a demand-led growth framework without having to assume Say's law to hold.

In the graphical derivation of the potential regimes in the post-Kaleckian framework, we have focussed on the relative responsiveness of capital accumulation towards the rate of capacity utilisation and the profit share. It should be added that the regimes will also depend on the propensity to save out of profits, which determines the slope of the σ-curve. It is easy to see graphically that the higher (lower) the propensity to save out of profits, the more likely wage-led (profit-led) regimes are in the face of re-distribution of income.

The post-Kaleckian model closure thus provides a very flexible instrument. It allows for the derivation of different demand and growth regimes depending on model parameter values and thus encompasses several of the other approaches discussed in this chapter – from the new growth theory and the classical/orthodox Marxian approach generating profit-led growth to the neo-Kaleckian wage-led demand and growth models, with an intermediate regime of wage-led demand and profit-led growth in between. The determination of the dominating demand and growth regime in a specific country during a specific period then becomes an empirical issue.

Starting with Bowles and Boyer (1995), several empirical studies, using different estimation techniques and yielding partly contradictive results, have been presented, as has been reviewed by Blecker (2016a), Stockhammer (2017a) and Stockhammer and Onaran (2013), for example. The literature applying the single equations estimation approach tends to find wage-led demand regimes also for open economies, with some exceptions for small very open economies and for emerging and commodity exporting countries.[9] Studies using an aggregative or systems approach, however, tend to find profit-led results.[10] The major reason for these difference seems to be that the Kaleckian authors applying the single equations or structural approach are looking for medium- to long-run effects of changes in functional income distribution on aggregate demand, capital accumulation and growth, whereas the Goodwinian proponents of the aggregative or systems approach are focussing on short-run interdependencies between distribution and economic activity, as Blecker (2016a) has pointed out. Furthermore, the Goodwinian authors finding positive effects of the profit share on capital accumulation and economic activity do not seem to properly take into account the short-run endogeneity of the profit share with respect to economic activity in the presence of overhead labour costs, as Lavoie (1995a, 2009b, 2014, Chapters 4–5, 2017a) has pointed out and we have shown in Chapter 4.[11]

7.9   THE SRAFFIAN SUPERMULTIPLIER GROWTH MODEL

For the presentation of the Sraffian supermultiplier growth model invented by Serrano (1995a, 1995b), we take autonomous consumption growth as determining long-run growth of the system, as in Lavoie's (2016a) adaption of this approach into an otherwise Kaleckian distribution and growth model.[12] In the long-run growth equilibrium, capacity utilisation will converge towards the firms' target or normal rate, as in the post-Keynesian Kaldor-Robinson model or in the neoclassical and classical/orthodox Marxian models:

$$u = u_n. \qquad\qquad (7.3\text{sm})$$

Income distribution is exogenous for growth:

$$h = \bar{h}. \qquad\qquad (7.4\text{sm})$$

Sraffian Supermultiplier authors seem to rely on a classical/Marxian determination of the real wage rate, which then determines the profit share, as we have used above for the classical/orthodox Marxian model $[h = h(w_r^s)]$. Kaleckian authors adopting autonomous growth as a driver of their models have the profit share determined by firms' mark-up pricing in an oligopolistic or monopolistic goods market, as in our Kaleckian models outlined above $[h = h(m)]$.

The capital-potential output ratio can again be considered as an exogenous variable determined by the state of technology, which does not systematically respond to distribution and activity variables in the model:[13]

$$v = \bar{v}. \qquad\qquad (7.5\text{sm})$$

With these three variables given, the rate of profit in equation (7.1) is already determined before we consider saving and investment, as in the new neoclassical growth theory and the classical/orthodox Marxian model. Therefore, the profit rate cannot be treated as the adjusting variable anymore, unlike the old neoclassical, the post-Keynesian Kaldor-Robinson and the Kalecki-Steindl approaches. However, the supermultiplier growth model shares a feature with those other post-Keynesian models, namely that investment is independent of saving also in the long run. Firms' net investment follows the expected trend rate of growth of output and sales, such that potential output given by the capital stock grows in line with expected demand. Following Dutt's (2019, 2020) proposal of 'reasonable' expectations, we assume that firms' expectations about the trend rate of growth of the economy adjust to the autonomous growth rate, which is the growth rate of autonomous consumption (γ) in the current model. Furthermore, we assume that firms will slow down (accelerate) the rate of capital accumulation whenever the actual rate of capacity utilisation falls short of (exceeds) the normal or the target rate of utilisation. We thus obtain the following investment function:

$$g = g\left[\gamma, \left(u - u_n\right)\right], \quad \frac{\partial g}{\partial \gamma} = 1, \frac{\partial g}{\partial \left(u - u_n\right)} > 0. \tag{7.5sm}$$

The goods market equilibrium is again given by the equality of the decisions to save and to invest:

$$g^* = \frac{pI}{pK} = \sigma^* = \frac{S}{pK}. \tag{7.6sm}$$

In order to allow for a long-run adjustment of saving and investment with a given normal rate of profit ($r_n = \overline{h}u_n / \overline{v}$) and thus a normal rate of capacity utilisation (since the capital-potential output ratio is exogenous as are the factors that determine the profit share), we include autonomous consumption growth in the saving function. We thus modify the saving equation (7.2) by including an autonomous consumption-capital rate (c_a):

$$\sigma = s_\Pi r - c_a, \quad 0 < s_\Pi \leq 1. \tag{7.2sm}$$

The autonomous consumption-capital rate is given as:

$$c_a = \frac{pC_{a0}e^{\gamma t}}{pK}, \tag{7.7sm}$$

with C_{a0} as autonomous consumption in period t=0 and γ as the constant growth rate of autonomous consumption. The autonomous consumption-capital rate will rise (fall) whenever the growth rate of autonomous consumption exceeds (falls short of) the rate of capital accumulation in the disequilibrium process:

$$\hat{c}_a > 0, \quad \text{if} : \gamma > g. \tag{7.7sma}$$

The supermultiplier distribution and growth model is presented in Figure 7.9. On the left-hand side we have the rate of profit as a function of capacity utilisation with the profit share and the

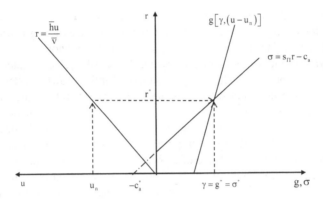

Figure 7.9   A Sraffian supermultiplier growth model

capital-potential output ratio given by mark-up pricing and technology. In the long-run growth equilibrium, however, the rate of capacity utilisation adjusts towards the normal or target rate of the firms. Only in the short run may capacity utilisation deviate from the normal rate and thus the profit rate from the normal profit rate. In the long run, however, the adjustment towards the normal rate of capacity utilisation also fully determines the rate of profit in long-run equilibrium, which then will be at the normal rate of profit ($r^* = r_n = hu_n/v$). On the right-hand side, we have the accumulation and the saving rates determined by the rate of profit. As explained, capital accumulation in the long-run is determined by the autonomous growth rate of the system, autonomous consumption in our case. In the short run, accumulation may deviate from the autonomous growth rate, if capacity utilisation deviates from the normal rate of utilisation, which also means that the rate of profit deviates from the normal rate of profit, as mentioned above. The saving rate includes the autonomous consumption-capital rate. With a constant growth rate of autonomous consumption, the autonomous consumption-capital rate becomes an endogenous variable, which adjusts the saving rate towards the accumulation rate and turns both equal to the autonomous growth rate in long-run equilibrium.

For clarification, we can graphically examine the adjustment towards long-run equilibrium growth for three cases. An increase in the growth rate of autonomous consumption, as shown in Figure 7.10, will shift the accumulation function to the right. This will temporarily lead to a goods market equilibrium rate of accumulation exceeding the new autonomous growth rate, associated with the rates of profit and utilisation exceeding the respective normal rates. Since the rate of capital accumulation is higher than the autonomous growth rate, the autonomous consumption-capital rate will fall and thus shift the saving function to the right as well, until we have a goods market equilibrium, in which the accumulation rate and the autonomous growth rate will be equal and the autonomous consumption-capital rate will be constant. Comparing the old and new equilibrium, an increase in the autonomous growth rate leads to higher equilibrium accumulation and saving rates and to a lower equilibrium autonomous consumption-capital rate.

An increase in the propensity to save out of profits, as shown in Figure 7.11, means a clockwise rotation of the saving rate function. The rates of capacity utilisation and profits fall below their respective normal rates, and the goods market equilibrium rate of capital accumulation falls below the autonomous growth rate. The latter implies that the autonomous

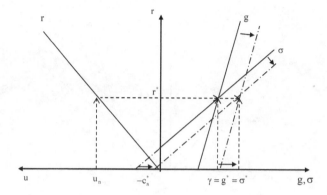

Figure 7.10   An increase in the autonomous growth rate in a Sraffian supermultiplier growth model

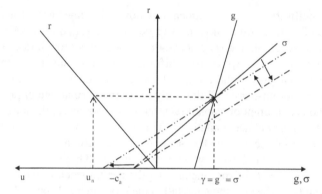

Figure 7.11   An increase in the propensity to save out of profits in a Sraffian supermultiplier growth model

consumption-capital rate rises, shifting the saving rate function to the left, which increases the goods market equilibrium rate of capital accumulation until it is equal to the autonomous growth rate, and the autonomous consumption-capital is thus constant. An increase in the propensity to save from profits has therefore no effect on the long-run equilibrium rates of capital accumulation, profit and capacity utilisation but only raises the equilibrium autonomous consumption-capital rate. The paradox of saving thus disappears regarding the long-run equilibrium rates of capacity utilisation, profit and accumulation. However, during the adjustment process, a higher propensity to save causes lower rates of capacity utilisation, profit and accumulation. A lower rate of accumulation means that in the new growth equilibrium the capital stock will be lower than it would have been without the increase in the propensity to save. A higher (lower) propensity to save thus leads to a lower (higher) growth path but not a lower (higher) growth rate, as in the other post-Keynesian distribution models.

Finally, we can look at the effects of a lower profit share, as shown in Figure 7.12. A lower profit share will rotate the profit rate function in the left quadrant. Since every profit rate on the vertical axis will now be associated with higher rate of capacity utilisation, this will stimulate investment and the accumulation function will rotate clockwise, if we have a dominant

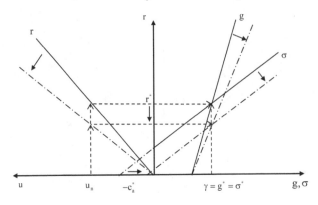

Figure 7.12　A fall in the profit share in a Sraffian supermultiplier growth model

effect of capacity utilisation in the investment function, as assumed here. The rates of capacity utilisation and profit rise above their respective normal rates, and the goods market equilibrium rate of capital accumulation rises above the autonomous growth rate. The autonomous consumption-capital rate falls, which will shift the saving rate function to the right, thereby reducing the goods market equilibrium rate of capital accumulation towards the autonomous growth rate. A lower profit share will thus only lower the normal rate of profit and the equilibrium autonomous consumption-capital rate, but it will not affect the long-run equilibrium rates of capacity and capital accumulation. The paradox of costs and wage-led demand and growth disappear with respect to the long-run growth rate. But also in this case, the traverse towards the new long-run equilibrium will be associated with higher rates of utilisation, profit and capital accumulation. The latter means that the capital stock in the new equilibrium is higher than it would have been without the fall in the profit share. A lower (higher) profit share thus leads to a higher (lower) growth path, but not to a higher (lower) growth rate, as in the wage-led growth variant of the Kaleckian distribution and growth model.

In the supermultiplier growth model, we thus have the rate of capital accumulation, and thus the rate of growth, the profit rate and the autonomous consumption-capital rate as endogenous variables. The capital-potential output ratio, the profit share and the normal rate of capacity

Table 7.7　Effects of changes in exogenous variables on endogenous variables in the Sraffian supermultiplier growth theory

Exogenous variables	Endogenous variables		
	$\sigma^* = g^*$	r^*	c_a^*
v	0	−	−
h	0	+	+
u_n	0	+	+
γ	+	0	−
$\partial g / \partial (u - u_n)$	0	0	0
s_Π	0	0	+

utilisation are exogenous variables which together determine the normal and long-run equilibrium rate of profit, and also affect the long-run equilibrium autonomous consumption-capital rate, but have no effect on long-run equilibrium capital accumulation and growth (Table 7.7). The long-run accumulation and growth rate is exclusively determined by the exogenous growth rate of autonomous demand, which also has an impact on the equilibrium autonomous consumption-capital rate. The responsiveness of investment to the deviation of capacity utilisation from the normal or target rate has no effect on any long-run endogenous equilibrium variable, whereas the propensity to save only affects the autonomous consumption-capital rate.

7.10 ENDOGENISING PRODUCTIVITY GROWTH: A KALECKI-STEINDL-KALDOR-MARX MODEL

In this chapter, we do not attempt to discuss the role of technological progress in all the different paradigms and models.[14] We will only present a simple and stylised extension of the Kaleckian distribution and growth model from Section 7.8, making use of some arguments on the determinants of technological progress by Kaldor and Marx. We will then use this approach in Chapter 8 to assess the contribution of macroeconomic policies to current stagnation tendencies.

Starting with Rowthorn (1981), Dutt (1990, Chapter 5), Taylor (1991, Chapter 10) and Lavoie (1992, Chapter 6), several authors have introduced endogenous technological change and labour productivity growth into Kaleckian distribution and growth models, as reviewed and elaborated in Hein (2014a, Chapter 8). Relying on Kaldor's (1957) technical progress function, labour productivity growth can be assumed to be positively affected by capital stock growth due to capital-embodied technological change. Alternatively, Kaldor's (1966) 'Verdoorn's Law' argued that labour productivity growth is positively affected by demand and output growth, in particular in manufacturing, due to dynamic returns to scale. Of course, both versions are related, since capital stock growth and output growth move in step, if Harrod-neutral technical progress is assumed and we have a constant equilibrium rate of capacity utilisation in the long run. Harrod-neutral technical progress means that labour productivity increases, but the capital-potential output ratio remains constant. Adding a Marxian component to the story, following Marx (1867, Chapter 25) and integrating a wage-push variable into the productivity growth function of the model, it can be argued that a higher real wage rate or a higher wage share induces capitalists to speed up the implementation of labour-augmenting technological progress in order to protect the profit share. Therefore, equation (7.8) is obtained for long-run productivity growth ($\hat{y}$), with k_i representing a set of further institutional factors that determine productivity growth, like government technology policies and R&D expenditures, the education system, learning by doing and so on:[15]

$$\hat{y} = \hat{y}\left(g^*, h, k_i\right), \quad \frac{\partial \hat{y}}{\partial g^*} > 0, \frac{\partial \hat{y}}{\partial h} < 0, \frac{\partial \hat{y}}{\partial k_i} > 0. \tag{7.8}$$

Furthermore, we can assume that the goods market equilibrium rate of capital accumulation is positively affected by productivity growth, because of capital-embodied technological change, in particular. Firms have to invest in new capital stock in order to benefit from technological inventions generated in R&D. Taking into account the exogenous parameters determining the goods market equilibrium rate of accumulation in the Kaleckian distribution and growth model outlined in Section 7.8, we arrive at the following equation for equilibrium capital accumulation, taking productivity growth to be exogenous:

$$g^* = g^*\left(\alpha, h, s_\Pi, \hat{y}\right), \quad \frac{\partial g^*}{\partial \alpha} > 0, \frac{\partial g^*}{\partial h} < 0, \frac{\partial g^*}{\partial s_\Pi} < 0, \frac{\partial g^*}{\partial \hat{y}} > 0. \tag{7.9}$$

Here we assume a neo-Kaleckian model or the wage-led growth case of the post-Kaleckian model, that is, $\partial g^*/\partial h < 0$.[16] Equations (7.8) and (7.9) describe a demand-determined endogenous growth model, and Figure 7.13 presents the long-run equilibrium values for capital accumulation (g^{**}) and productivity growth ($\hat{y}^{**}$) and thus the endogenous potential or 'natural' growth rate.[17] Any fall in the goods market equilibrium rate of capital accumulation (g^*), triggered by a fall in animal spirits or a rise in the profit share or in the propensity to save out of profits, thus causes a leftward shift in the g^*-curve. Thus lower long-run equilibrium rates of capital accumulation and productivity growth, and hence potential growth, emerge.

Furthermore, a rise in the profit share will not only affect the g^*-curve but also the productivity function, as is shown in Figure 7.14. In this case, both curves get shifted and the long-run growth equilibrium falls from g_1^{**}, y_1^{**} to g_2^{**}, y_2^{**}. Re-distribution at the expense (in favour)

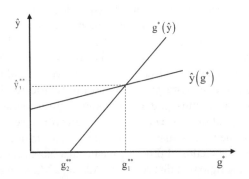

Figure 7.13   A Kalecki-Steindl-Kaldor-Marx endogenous growth model

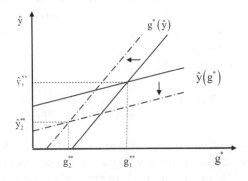

Figure 7.14   A rise in the profit share in the Kalecki-Steindl-Kaldor-Marx endogenous growth model

of wages is thus detrimental to (benefits) long-run capital accumulation, productivity growth and thus potential growth – in our closed economy model.

NOTES

*   This chapter is based on and further elaborates on Hein (2017b).
1. See, for example, for the new neoclassical growth models, Aghion and Howitt (2009) and Barro and Sala-i-Martin (2004), and for a simplified overview Hein (2014a, Chapter 3).
2. For an introduction to the classical approach to distribution and growth, see Blecker and Setterfield (2019, Chapter 2), Harris (1987), Hein (2018d, Chapter 2), Kurz and Salvadori (2003) and Pasinetti (1974, Chapter 1), and for an overview of Marxian theories see Hein (2018d, Chapter 3) and Shaikh (1978a).
3. Kaldor even assumed full employment in his early essentially one-sector equilibrium growth models, which he abandoned in his later work, that is, in Kaldor (1966).
4. See also our elaboration on wage- and profit-led demand regimes in an open economy in Chapter 4.
5. See Allain (2019, 2021), Dutt (2019, 2020), Hein and Woodgate (2021), Lavoie and Nah (2020), Nah and Lavoie (2017, 2019a, 2019b) and Palley (2019) for the introduction of autonomous demand growth into Kaleckian distribution and growth models.
6. The supermultiplier model has been developed and applied by several authors, such as Cesaratto (2015), Cesaratto and Di Bucchianico (2020), Cesaratto et al. (2003), Dejuan (2005), Deleidi and Mazzucato (2019), Di Bucchianico (2021), Fazzari et al. (2013, 2020), Freitas and Christianes (2020), Freitas and Serrano (2015, 2017), Pariboni (2016) and Vieira Mandarino et al. (2020), amongst others. For empirical applications, see Fiebiger (2018), Fiebiger and Lavoie (2019), Girardi and Pariboni (2016), Girardi et al. (2020), Perez-Montiel and Manera (2020) and Perez-Montiel and Pariboni (2022).
7. For a critical assessment of these models, see, for example, Nikiforos (2018) and Skott (2017, 2019).
8. Obviously, here we could now discuss feedback effects of economic activity on income distribution through changes in the degree of competition, workers' bargaining power or unit overhead costs. However, this would go beyond our simple overview. See Dutt (2012) for a detailed review and discussion, as well as Assous and Dutt (2013), Hein and Stockhammer (2010, 2011b), Lavoie (2010c) and Stockhammer (2004b), amongst several others, for modelling attempts. See also Chapter 5 of this book.
9. In the single equations or structural approach, functional income distribution is considered to be exogenous and the effects of changes of the profit share (or the wage share) on the components of aggregate demand, consumption, investment, exports and imports, are estimated separately, controlling for other influences, and then summed up. See for recent multi-country studies applying this approach, Hartwig (2014), Jimenez (2020), Onaran and Galanis (2014) and Onaran and Obst (2016). For reviews of the results of single equations estimations studies, see Hein (2014a, Chapter 7) and Stockhammer and Onaran (2013), and for more recent reviews focussing on emerging capitalist economies, see Akcay et al. (2022) and Jimenez (2020).
10. The aggregative or systems approach directly estimates the effect of changes in the profit share (or wage share) on economic activity and takes into account the feedback effect of GDP growth on distribution. For studies applying this approach, mainly to the US economy, see Barbosa-Filho and Taylor (2006), Carvalho and Rezai (2016), Diallo et al. (2011), Flaschel and Proaño (2007), Kiefer and Rada (2015), Nikiforos and Foley (2012) and Rezai (2015).
11. See also Blecker and Setterfield (2019, pp. 205–7) and Rolim (2019).
12. Alternatively, we could also treat government expenditure growth as autonomous growth rate, like in Allain (2015) or in Hein and Woodgate (2021), or export growth, like in Nah and Lavoie (2017). For textbook presentations of supermultiplier growth models, see Blecker and Setterfield (2019, Chapter 7) and Lavoie (2014, Chapter 6).
13. Kaleckian-type supermultiplier models with technical progress, like Allain (2021) and Nah and Lavoie (2019a), usually assume Harrod neutrality, which means that the capital-potential output ratio remains constant, while labour productivity grows.
14. For a discussion of technical progress in classical and Marxian theories, see, for example, Blecker and Setterfield (2019, Chapter 2), Foley et al. (2019, Chapters 7–9) and Hein (2018d, Chapters 2–3), for old and new neoclassical growth theory, see Foley et al. (2019, Chapter 11) and Hein (2014a, Chapter 3), and for the different versions of post-Keynesian distribution and growth theory, see Blecker and Setterfield (2019, Chapter 5), Hein (2014a, Chapters 4 and 8) and Lavoie (2014, Chapter 6.9).
15. For empirical estimations of this productivity growth function, as well as an overview of other results of productivity growth functions estimations, see Hein and Tarassow (2010) and the overview in Hein (2014a, Chapter 8).
16. For an inclusion of intermediate and profit-led demand and growth regimes, see Hein (2014a, Chapter 8) and Hein and Tarassow (2010).
17. For analytical treatments see Hein (2014a, Chapter 8, 2016, 2018a).

8. Macroeconomic demand and growth regimes in finance-dominated capitalism, stagnation tendencies and the macroeconomic policy regimes

8.1 INTRODUCTION

In Chapters 4 and 5 we distinguished between wage- and profit-led effects of changes in functional income distribution on aggregate demand, between the normal and the puzzling case when discussing the effects of changes in the interest rate on aggregate demand and between debt-led and debt-burdened effects of changes in the stock of corporate debt on aggregate demand. In Chapter 7, we then extended the distinction between wage- and profit-led regimes to long-run growth in the context of the post-Kaleckian distribution and growth model. All these distinctions between different regimes or cases have referred to the effects of the change of a single exogenous variable or parameter of the model, that is, the wage or profit share, the rate of interest or the stock of debt in the short run, on the equilibrium values of the model, that is, equilibrium income and capacity utilisation or equilibrium accumulation and growth. In this chapter we will now change the perspective and rather examine the sources, the financing and the drivers of demand and growth. We will start in Section 8.2 with the concept of macroeconomic demand and growth regimes in finance-dominated capitalism, which focusses on examining the sources of demand and the way the demand components are financed. Then, in Section 8.3, we will present some results on demand and growth regimes before the 2007–09 Global Financial Crisis and Great Recession, the changes in regimes in the course of and after these crises and the emanating tendency towards stagnation. In Section 8.4 we will explain these regimes, the regime changes and the related tendencies towards stagnation in a stylised Kaleckian distribution and growth model, relying on the framework we introduced in Chapter 7. In Section 8.4 we will address the recent debate on growth drivers in post-Keynesian economics and comparative political economy. The concept of a macroeconomic policy regime, integrating the post-Keynesian notion of a desirable or functional macroeconomic policy mix developed in Chapter 6, is introduced and applied. From this, we will conclude that current stagnation tendencies can be viewed to a large extent as the result of 'stagnation policy' (Steindl 1976, 1979).

8.2 THE MAIN MACROECONOMIC FEATURES OF FINANCE-DOMINATED CAPITALISM AND THE CONCEPT OF DEMAND AND GROWTH REGIMES

The Kaleckian/post-Keynesian concept of macroeconomic demand and growth regimes has been applied to the period of financialisation of modern capitalism or of finance-dominated capitalism. In this period, since the late 1970s/early 1980s starting in the USA and the UK, the capitalist economies have been exposed to the liberalisation of financial markets, the development of new financial instruments and an overall increasing role of finance in the operation of the economies, to different degrees in different countries (Epstein 2005).[1] The changes in the structure, institutions and power relationships in modern finance-dominated capitalism have been reviewed and summarised in Detzer et al. (2017), Guttmann (2016), Palley (2009a, 2012, 2013b, 2021a, 2021b), Sawyer (2013/14) and van der Zwan (2014), for example. From a macroeconomic perspective, these changes have had important implications for (1) income distribution, (2) investment in the capital stock, (3) consumption and (4) the build-up of global and regional (e.g. European) current account imbalances, as explained in Hein (2012a, 2014a, Chapter 10) and Hein and van Treeck (2010a), for example.[2]

1. With regard to distribution, financialisation has been conducive to a rising gross profit share, including retained profits, dividends and interest payments, and thus a falling labour income share, on the one hand, and to increasing inequality of wages and top management salaries and thus of wage dispersion and of personal or household incomes, on the other hand. Hein (2012a, Chapter 2, 2015) has reviewed the evidence for a set of developed capitalist economies since the early 1980s and finds ample empirical support for falling labour income shares and increasing inequality in the personal/household distribution of market incomes with only a few exceptions, increasing inequality in the personal/household distribution of disposable income in most of the countries and an increase in the income share of the very top income earners particularly in the USA and the UK, but also in several other countries for which data is available, with rising top management salaries as one of the major driving forces.

   Reviewing the empirical literature on the determinants of functional income distribution against the background of the Kaleckian theory of income distribution, it is argued in Hein (2015) that features of finance-dominated capitalism have contributed to the falling labour income share since the early 1980s through three main channels: The falling bargaining power of trade unions, rising profit claims imposed in particular by increasingly powerful rentiers and a change in the sectoral composition of the economy in favour of the financial corporate sector at the expense of the non-financial corporate sector or the public sector with higher labour income shares.[3] Dünhaupt (2017), Dünhaupt and Hein (2019), Hein et al. (2017a, 2017b, 2018) and Kohler et al. (2019) have supported these channels in recent studies making use of variations and extensions of the Kaleckian framework.

2. Regarding investment in the capital stock, financialisation has meant increasing shareholder power vis-à-vis firms and workers, the demand for an increasing rate of return on equity held by rentiers and an alignment of management with shareholder interests through short-run performance-related pay schemes, such as bonuses, stock option programmes and so on. On the one hand, this has imposed short-termism on management and has caused a decrease in management's animal spirits with respect to real investment in the capital stock and long-run growth of the firm and an increasing preference for financial investment, generating high profits in the short run. On the other hand, it has drained internal means of finance available for real investment purposes from non-financial corporations, through increasing dividend payments and share buybacks in order to boost stock prices and thus shareholder value. These 'preference' and 'internal means of finance' channels each have partially negative effects on firms' real investment in capital

stock, as has been modelled by Dallery (2009) and Stockhammer (2005/06) based on the post-Keynesian theory of the firm, for example. At the macroeconomic level, this may then lead to contractionary effects on income, growth and profits. However, it may also lead to higher income and profits, so-called 'profits without investment regimes', if consumption out of profits, rentiers' income or wages, government expenditures or net exports rise sufficiently, as has been shown by Hein (2009, 2010, 2012a, Chapter 3), Hein and van Treeck (2010b) and van Treeck (2009a, 2009b).[4]

Empirical and econometric evidence for the 'preference' and 'internal means of finance' channels of financialisation in business investment has been supplied by Barradas (2017), Davis (2016, 2017, 2018a, 2018b), Feiner Solis (2021), Orhangazi (2008), Onaran et al. (2011), Stockhammer (2004c), Tori and Onaran (2017, 2018) and van Treeck (2008). These studies confirm a depressing effect of increasing shareholder value orientation on investment in the capital stock, in particular for the USA but also for other economies, like the France, Germany, the UK and other Western European countries.[5]

3. Regarding consumption, financialisation has generated an increasing potential for wealth-based and debt-financed consumption in some countries. This created the potential to compensate for the depressing demand effects of financialisation, which have been imposed on the economy via re-distribution and income-financed consumption and via the depressing impact of shareholder value orientation on real investment. Stock market and housing price booms have each increased notional wealth against which households were willing to borrow. Changing financial norms, new financial instruments (credit card debt, home equity lending) and the deterioration of creditworthiness standards, triggered by the securitisation of mortgage debt and 'originate and distribute' strategies of commercial banks, made credit increasingly available to low-income, low-wealth households, in particular. This potentially allowed for consumption to rise faster than median income and thus to stabilise aggregate demand. But it also generated increasing debt-income ratios of private households.

Several authors, like Barba and Pivetti (2009), Cynamon and Fazzari (2008, 2013), Guttmann and Plihon (2010), van Treeck and Sturn (2012, 2013) and van Treeck (2014) have presented extensive case studies on wealth-based and debt-financed consumption, with a focus on the USA. In these studies, Veblen's (1899) 'conspicuous consumption', Duesenberry's (1949) 'relative income hypothesis' and the 'expenditure cascades' proposed by Frank et al. (2014) figure prominently and provide arguments for why poor and middle-income households may emulate the consumption of richer households ('keeping up with the Joneses') by means of debt-financed consumption expenditures. Some studies have also highlighted the relevance of debt-financed expenditures on basic needs in the face of stagnating or even falling real wages and rising inequalities. Consumption emulation can thus be seen as a complex response towards rising inequalities, which is affected by socio-cultural preferences, institutions, the (non-)provision of public goods (especially housing, education and healthcare) and the access to credit.

Macroeconometric estimations on the relative importance of real and financial wealth, credit supply, basic needs or relative income effects on consumption are still inconclusive, as reviewed by Prante (2018). Some studies, like Carvalho and Rezai (2016) and Brown (2004) for the USA, find negative effects of rising inequality of personal/household incomes on consumption and thus no indication for the relative income hypothesis. Darku (2014) for Canada, however, obtains negative effects of rising inequality on saving rates of private households, in line with the relative income hypothesis. Behringer and van Treeck (2018) for a panel of 20 countries (1972–2007) find that, ceteris paribus, rising personal income inequality leads to a deterioration of the financial balances of the private household sector, which is interpreted as supporting the relative income hypothesis. Stockhammer and Wildauer (2016), however, in panel estimations for OECD countries (1980–2013) fail to confirm an effect of personal income inequality on consumption, which is interpreted as contradicting the relative income hypothesis. The authors find positive effects of the wage share, household debt and property and stock prices on consumption in their estimations. Moore and Stockhammer (2018) and Stockhammer and Wildauer (2018) support these findings regarding the irrelevance of the relative income hypothesis: Real estate prices were the most important drivers of household debt, whereas they do not find a significant impact of shifts in the income distribution on household sector indebtedness. Several other studies have also shown that financial and housing wealth was a significant determinant of consumption, particularly in the USA, but also in countries like the UK, France, Italy, Japan and Canada (Boone and Girouard 2002, Ludvigson and Steindel 1999, Onaran et al. 2011). Finally, Kim (2013, 2016, 2020) and Kim et al. (2015) have found in studies on the USA that although new credit to households will boost aggregate demand and output in the short run, the effects of household debt variables on output and growth are negative in the long run. This indicates the contradictory effects of the flow of new credit and the stock of debt on consumption. These potentially contradictory short- and long-run effects of credit and debt on consumption, aggregate demand and growth have been included in a range of Kaleckian distribution and growth models (Dutt 2005, 2006, Hein 2012a, Chapter 5, 2012c, Nishi 2012b, Setterfield and Kim 2016, 2017, Setterfield et al. 2016).

4. The liberalisation of international capital markets and capital accounts in the period of finance-dominated capitalism has allowed for rising and persistent current account imbalances at the global, but also at the regional levels, in particular within the Eurozone. This has been analysed by several authors, including Akcay et al. (2022), Hein (2012a, Chapter 6, 2014a, Chapter 10), Hein and Martschin (2020), Hein and Mundt (2012, 2013), Horn et al. (2009), Stockhammer (2010, 2012, 2015), UNCTAD (2009) and van Treeck and Sturn (2012, 2013). Several countries have thus compensated the lack of domestic demand, caused by rising inequality and weak investment in the capital stock, by rising net exports and current account surpluses. Simultaneously, other countries, in particular those with dynamic credit-financed consumption demand, built up rising import surpluses and current account deficits. The current account deficits of the debt-financed model have been matched by the current account surpluses of the export-led model. Financialisation contributed to these developments to the extent that the deregulation and liberalisation of international capital markets and capital accounts allowed current account imbalances to persist and deficits to be financed over longer periods. However, these rising current account imbalances were accompanied by rising foreign indebtedness of the current account deficit countries, speculative capital movements, exchange rate volatilities and potential (and actual) currency crises (Herr 2011).

Under the conditions of the dominance of finance, income re-distribution at the expense of labour and low-income households, and weak investment in the capital stock, different demand and growth regimes have thus emerged. These can be analysed by looking at the sources of demand and at the way demand is financed. The empirical examination and clustering of macroeconomic demand and growth regimes under financialisation has been introduced by Hein (2011b, 2011c) and then used in several studies with slightly differing labelling of regimes for the period before the Global Financial Crisis and the Great Recession (2007–09).[6] In these studies, the following regimes have been distinguished: (1) an export-led mercantilist (ELM) regime, (2) a weakly export-led (WEL) regime, (3) a domestic demand-led (DDL) regime and (4) a debt-led private demand (boom) (DLPD) regime.

Empirically, these demand and growth regimes have been assessed by considering, first, the financial balances of the main macroeconomic sectors. These are:

- The private sector financial balance ($FB_P = S - pI$), as the difference between private saving (S) and private investment (pI), and with the private household sector, the financial and non-financial corporate sectors as sub-sectors.
- The government sector financial balance ($FB_G = T - G$), as the difference between tax revenues and social security contributions (T) and government expenditures (G).
- The external sector financial balance ($FB_E = pIm - pEx + FI^{net}$), as the difference between domestic imports (pIm) generating foreign sector revenues and domestic exports (pEx) which are equivalent to foreign sector expenditures. The external sector balance also includes the net revenues from the cross-border payments for factors of production, that is, wages and capital incomes, as well as cross-border transfers (FI^{net}), which may be positive or negative for the external sector, of course.

The sectoral financial balances of a country should sum up to zero, apart from statistical discrepancies, because a positive financial balance of one sector needs a respective negative financial balance of another sector – a creditor needs a debtor and vice versa:

$$FB_P + FB_G + FB_E = 0. \tag{8.1}$$

The second step in the determination of demand and growth regimes involves examining the growth contributions of the main demand aggregates. These are the growth contributions of private consumption (C_{HH}) and public consumption (C_G), as well as private and public investment (I), which sum up to the growth contribution of domestic demand, and finally the growth contribution of the balance of goods and services, that is, of net exports (NX). The growth contributions of the demand aggregates should sum up to real GDP growth of the respective country:

$$\hat{Y}_t = \frac{dY_t}{Y_{t-1}} = \frac{dC_{HHt}}{Y_{t-1}} + \frac{dC_{Gt}}{Y_{t-1}} + \frac{dI_t}{Y_{t-1}} + \frac{dNX_t}{Y_{t-1}}. \tag{8.2}$$

Therefore, looking at these two sets of indicators provides some information on the main sources of demand and growth, on how demand is financed and on the related deficit dynamics (Table 8.1).

The ELM regime shows positive financial balances of the private domestic sectors as a whole, which are mainly matched by negative financial balances of the external sector, indicating current account surpluses. There are high growth contributions of the positive balance

Table 8.1   Classification of demand-led growth regimes under financialisation

Export-led mercantilist (ELM)	• Positive financial balances of the private sector and the private household sector, • Negative financial balances of the external sector, • Positive balance of goods and services, • Positive growth contributions of net exports.
Weakly export-led (WEL)	Either • Positive financial balances of the private sector, • Negative financial balances of the external sector, • Positive balance of goods and services, • Negative growth contributions of net exports. Or • Negative but improving financial balances of domestic sectors, • Positive but declining financial balances of external sector, • Negative but improving net exports, • Positive growth contributions of net exports.
Domestic demand-led (DDL)	• Positive financial balances of the private household sector and positive or balanced financial balances of the private sector as a whole, • Balanced or positive financial balances of the external sector, • Growth is almost exclusively driven by domestic demand, • Around zero growth contribution of net exports.
Debt-led private demand boom (DLPD)	• Negative or close to balance financial balances of the private sector, • Positive financial balances of the external sector, • Significant growth contributions of domestic demand and private consumption demand in particular, • Negative growth contributions of net exports.

Source: Based on Dünhaupt and Hein (2019, p. 458).

of goods and services, and thus, rising net exports and current account surpluses, and small or even negative growth contributions of domestic demand.

The WEL regime either shows positive financial balances of the domestic sectors, negative financial balances of the external sector, and hence current account surpluses, but negative growth contributions of the balance of goods and services and thus falling net exports and current account surpluses. Alternatively, we may have negative financial balances of the domestic sectors, positive financial balances of the external sector, and hence current account deficits, but positive growth contributions of the balance of goods and services and thus improving net exports and hence falling current account deficits.

The DDL regime is characterised by positive financial balances of the private household sector, while the government and, to some extent, the corporate sector are running deficits. The external sector is usually roughly balanced, seeing only small deficits or surpluses. Domestic demand contributes positively to growth (without being driven by credit-financed private consumption), and there are only slightly negative or positive growth contributions of the balance of goods and services.

The DLPD regime is characterised by deficits of the private domestic sectors as a whole, which are, on the one hand, driven by corporate deficits and, on the other hand, by negative or close to zero financial balances of the private household sector. The latter implies that major parts of the private household sector have negative saving rates out of current income and finance these deficits by increasing their stock of debt or by decreasing their stock of assets. The deficits of the private domestic sectors are usually mirrored by positive financial balances of the external sector, that is, by current account deficits. Growth is mainly driven by private domestic demand, and private consumption demand in particular, to a large degree financed by credit, while the balance of goods and services negatively contributes to growth.

8.3   DEMAND AND GROWTH REGIMES BEFORE THE 2007–09 CRISES, THE CHANGE IN REGIMES IN THE COURSE OF AND AFTER THESE CRISES AND THE TENDENCY TOWARDS STAGNATION

Against the background of falling wage shares and rising income inequality, as shown in Table 8.2 for major developed capitalist economies, in the pre-2007–09 crises period, debt-financed private consumption and partially debt-financed real estate investment have been the main drivers of growth in the DLPD regime countries. This led to rising, and then unsustainable, household debt dynamics, as well as to rising current account deficits and thus unsustainable foreign debt dynamics in some countries. In the counterpart ELM countries, rising net exports and current account surpluses have partly compensated for weak domestic demand caused by the features of finance-dominated capitalism and have become the main drivers of

Table 8.2 Distribution trends for selected OECD countries before and after the Global Financial Crisis and the Great Recession 2007–09

		Adjusted wage share	Top income share	Gini coefficients
USA	Before	−	+	+
	After	−	+	+
UK	Before	0	+	+
	After	−	−	0
Spain	Before	−	+	0
	After	−	−	+
Germany	Before	−	+	+
	After	0	NA	+
Sweden	Before	−	+	+
	After	0	0	0
France	Before	−	+	0
	After	+	0	−

Notes: + tendency to increase, − tendency to decrease, 0 no tendency, NA no data.
Before: Early 1990s until the crisis 2007–09; after: After the crisis 2007–09.
Source: Based on Hein et al. (2017a, p. 164).

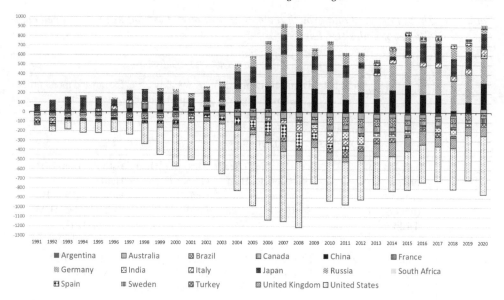

Data source: IMF (2021), author's presentation.

Figure 8.1   Current account balance, major countries, 1991–2020, in billions of US dollars

demand and growth. These developments have been associated with rising current account imbalances at the global scale (Figure 8.1) and unsustainable foreign debt dynamics in some counterpart current account deficit countries, which have followed the DLPD regime.

As is well known, these unsustainable debt dynamics then led to the Global Financial Crisis and the Great Recession (2007–09), as well as to the Eurozone crisis starting in 2010.[7] The financial crisis was triggered by the subprime mortgage crisis in the USA and spread over the globe via the financial contagion channel in globally integrated financial markets and via the international trade channel in globally integrated goods markets.

Some recent studies have examined the shift of regimes from the period before the Global Financial Crisis and the Great Recession to the period after these crises for developed capitalist economies:[8] Dodig et al. (2016) for 15 OECD countries, Dünhaupt and Hein (2019) for 3 Baltic Sea countries, Hein (2019a) for 6 OECD countries and the initial Eurozone (EA-12), Hein and Martschin (2020) for 11 initial Eurozone countries and the EA-12 as a whole and Hein et al. (2021) for 30 OECD countries. The following pattern has been found, as shown in Table 8.3: ELM countries before the 2007–09 crises have mainly maintained this regime or have become WEL in the course of and after the crises. The only exception is Finland, which turned DDL. WEL regimes before the crises kept this regime or even became ELM, Canada being the exception, which moved towards DDL, stabilised by government deficits. DDL regimes before the crises moved towards WEL or even ELM regimes after the crises. The only exceptions are France, which remained DDL, and Turkey, which has shown some indication of a DLPD regime after the crises. Finally, DLPD countries before the crisis either shifted to WEL or even ELM regimes after the crisis, or they turned towards DDL regimes stabilised by high government deficits.

Table 8.3 *Shift of demand and growth regimes according to five studies on developed capitalist economies (DCEs)*

		Post 2007–09 crisis			
		Debt-led private demand (boom) (DLPD)	Domestic demand-led with high public sector deficits (DDL)	Weakly export-led (WEL)	Export-led mercantilist (ELM)
	Debt-led private demand (boom) (DLPD)		New Zealand (Hea) UK (Dea, H, Hea) USA (Dea, H, Hea) South Africa (Dea)	Australia (Hea) Greece (Dea, Hea, H/M) Portugal (Hea) Slovakia (Hea) Spain (Hea)	Estonia (Dea, D/H, Hea) Hungary (Dea, Hea) Ireland (Hea, H/M) Latvia (D/H) Spain (H, H/M)
	Domestic demand led (DDL)	Turkey (Dea)	France (Dea, H, Hea, H/M)	Italy (Dea, Hea) Poland (Dea, Hea) Portugal (Dea, H/M)	EA-12 (H, H/M) Italy (H/M)
Pre-2007–09 crisis	Weakly export-led (WEL)		Canada (Hea)	Czech Rep. (Hea) Iceland (Hea) Norway (Hea)	Denmark (D/H, Hea) Slovenia (Hea)
	Export-led mercantilist (ELM)		Finland (Hea, H/M)	Austria (Hea) Belgium (H/M) Japan (Dea, Hea) Sweden (Dea, H, Hea)	Austria (H/M) Belgium (Hea) Germany (Dea, H, Hea, H/M) Korea (Hea) Luxembourg (Hea) Netherlands (Hea, H/M) Switzerland (Hea)

Notes: Dea: Dodig et al. (2016), 2001–08, 2008–14; D/H: Dünhaupt and Hein (2019), 1995–2008, 2009–16; H: Hein (2019a), 1999–2007, 2008–16; Hea: Hein et al. (2021), 2000–08, 2009–16; H/M: Hein and Martschin (2020), 2001–09, 2010–19.

Source: Based on Akcay et al. (2022, p. 83).

This polarisation of post-crisis regimes in the developed OECD countries, with ELM or WEL regimes, on the one hand, and DDL regimes stabilised by government deficits, on the other hand, has been accompanied by a tendency of major emerging capitalist economies to remain DDL or even move towards DLPD regimes, as has recently been analysed by Akcay et al. (2022). Even before the 2007–09 crises, the distribution trends in the emerging capitalist economies were more diverse and did not show the unique trend towards falling wage shares and rising income inequality, as in the developed capitalist economies, as can be seen

Table 8.4   Distribution trends for selected emerging capitalist economies before and after the Global Financial Crisis and the Great Recession 2007–09

		Wage share	Top income share (Top 1 per cent and top 10 per cent)	Gini coefficient for disposable income
Argentina	2004–08	+	+	–
	2009–17	+	NA	–
Brazil	2004–08	+	+	–
	2009–17	+	0	0
China	2004–08	–	+	+
	2009–17	+	–	–
India	2004–08	–	+	+
	2009–17	–	+	+
Mexico	2000–08	–	NA	–
	2009–18	–	NA	–
Russia	2004–08	+	+	0
	2009–17	0	–	–
South Africa	2004–08	–	+	0
	2009–17	+	+	0
Turkey	2000–08	–	–	–
	2009–19	+	+	0

Notes: + tendency to increase, – tendency to decrease, 0 no tendency, NA no data..
Source: Based on Akcay et al. (2022, p. 91).

in Table 8.4. Also after these crises there is no obvious and unique pattern, as analysed by Akcay et al. (2022). Looking at the shift of regimes in the emerging capitalist economies from the pre-crises period (2000–08) to the crises and post-crises period (2009–19), only Russia and Mexico have become more export-oriented, Russia moving from WEL in the first period towards ELM in the second, and Mexico moving from DDL towards WEL (Table 8.5). For the other six countries, the regimes became less export oriented. South Africa has remained DLPD, and Turkey has turned towards this regime from a DDL type. India remained DDL stabilised by government deficits, and Brazil and Argentina shifted towards this regime, too, from WEL in the case of Brazil and from ELM in the case of Argentina. China moved from ELM to WEL. Some of the emerging capitalist economies have thus provided the global counterpart for the tendency towards WEL and ELM regimes in the developed capitalist economies.

From a global perspective, current account imbalances have been slightly reduced in and after the crises when compared to the years before. However, they are still much more pronounced than in the 1990s and the early 2000s (Figure 8.1). The high current account surpluses of the ELM countries (Germany, Italy, Spain, the Eurozone as a whole, Sweden,

Table 8.5 *Shift of demand and growth regimes in emerging capitalist economies from 2000–08 to 2009–19*

		Second period (2009–19)			
		Debt-led private demand (DLPD)	Domestic demand-led with high public sector deficits (DDL)	Weakly export-led (WEL)	Export-led mercantilist (ELM)
First period (2000–08)	Debt-led private demand (DLPD)	South Africa			
	Domestic demand led with high public sector deficits (DDL)	Turkey	India	Mexico	
	Weakly export-led (WEL)		Brazil		Russia
	Export-led mercantilist (ELM)		Argentina	China	

Source: Based on Akcay et al. (2022, p. 87).

Japan, China and Russia) are matched by the current account deficits of domestic demand-led economies with high public sector deficits (in particular the USA, the UK and France) and of emerging market and/or commodity exporting countries (Argentina, Australia, Brazil, Canada, India, South Africa and Turkey). The risks of such a global situation are obvious. If ever more economies, like currently the whole Eurozone, move towards an ELM regime, the world economy will face an aggregation problem. It will become increasingly difficult to generate the related current account deficits in other regions of the world. Stagnation tendencies are then the inescapable consequences of this failure of demand generation and demand management at the global level.

Since global demand stabilisation has relied on public sector financial deficits in the mature DDL economies, as well as on public and private sector deficits in emerging market economies, further risks and dangers have built up. First, high government deficits and debt in mature DDL economies as stabilisers of national and global demand may be reversed for political reasons (debt ceilings, debt brakes), although there may be no risks of over-indebtedness of governments, if debt can be issued in the country's own currency and is backed by the respective central bank, as in the case of the USA and the UK, for example. Second, capital inflows into emerging market economies may be unstable and face 'sudden stops' because of changes in expectations and/or over-indebtedness in foreign currency of these countries. And third, there are the risks of politically induced protection measures in order to reduce current account deficits, which are considered to be too high.

Apart from these short- to medium-run problems, there has arisen a long-run stagnation problem associated with weak investment and capital stock growth, which has led to the re-emergence of the debate about secular stagnation and stagnation policy, both in mainstream economics (Gordon 2015, Summers 2014, 2015, Teulings and Baldwin 2014a, 2014b, von Weizsäcker and Krämer 2021a, 2021b) and in post-Keynesian economics (Blecker 2016d,

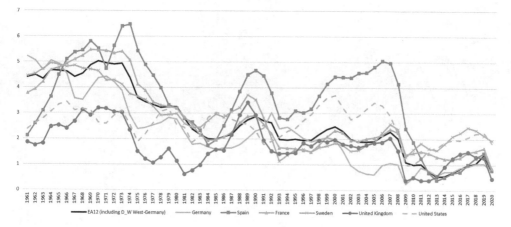

Data source: European Commission (2021), author's calculations.

Figure 8.2   *Growth rate of the real net capital stock (at 2015 prices), selected countries, 1961–2020, in per cent*

Cynamon and Fazzari 2015, 2016, Hein 2016, 2018a, 2019a, 2021, 2022a, 2022b, Onaran 2016a, Palley 2012, 2016b, van Treeck 2015). Due to the effects of financialisation on investment, as outlined above, growth contributions of investment were already weak before the 2007–09 crises and have become even weaker in the crises and post-crises period (Hein 2019a, Hein et al. 2021). In a long-run perspective, capital stock growth in major developed capitalist economies has seen a downward trend, only interrupted by the new economy boom in the second half of the 1990s, with particularly low growth rates in the period after the Great

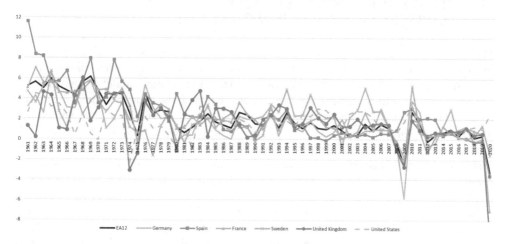

Data source: European Commission (2021), author's calculations.

Figure 8.3   *Growth rate of real GDP (at 2015 prices) per person employed, selected countries, 1961–2020, in per cent*

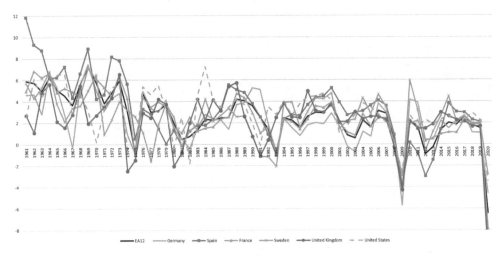

Data source: European Commission (2021), author's calculations.

Figure 8.4   Growth rate of real GDP (at 2015 prices), selected countries, 1961–2020, in per cent

Recession (Figure 8.2). This has led or at least contributed to falling growth rates of labour productivity, which also became particularly low after the Great Recession (Figure 8.3), as well as to the falling trend of real GDP growth rates (Figure 8.4).

8.4   REGIMES, REGIME CHANGES AND STAGNATION TENDENCIES IN A STYLISED KALECKIAN DISTRIBUTION AND GROWTH MODEL[9]

The macroeconomic features of finance-dominated capitalism and the emerging regimes outlined in Section 8.2 have been modelled by applying stock-flow consistent models, either small scale analytical models or large scale numerical simulation models.[10] Here we will constrain ourselves to presenting the two extreme demand and growth regimes before the crisis, the DLPD and ELM regimes, in a stylised Kaleckian model of distribution and growth, which is based on the model structure introduced in Chapter 7. We will study two countries in that framework, an import surplus and current account deficit country and an export surplus and current account surplus country. Then we will discuss the effects of rising inequality and behavioural changes in the period leading to the Global Financial Crisis and the Great Recession, generating the DLPD and the ELM regimes. Next we will briefly look at the changes in the course of and after the crises, leading to the replacement of the DLPD regime by a DDL regime stabilised by government deficits as (another) global counterpart to the ELM regime. Finally, we will assess the observed tendency towards stagnation accompanying these regimes and regime changes with the help of a slight extension of the model by endogenous productivity growth, as already indicated in Chapter 7.

We assume an open economy with a primitive government sector, which only appears as a deficit-spending sector drawing on money and credit generated in the financial sector, so that taxation issues can be ignored. The private sector is composed of two classes, workers and capitalists, the latter including the financial capitalists or the rentiers. Capitalists own the means of production and receive profits, which are partly consumed and partly saved, buying assets issued by the corporate sector, and thus the capitalists themselves, or by the government. Alternatively, parts of the saved profits may also become deposits with the banking sector, which is also owned by the capitalists and not explicitly modelled here. Capitalists control the capital stock, hire labour, organise the production process and decide about investment and thus the expansion of the capital stock. For the latter, they draw on their own means of finance, issue stocks or corporate bonds or draw on credit endogenously generated and granted by the financial sector. By assumption, these transactions take place within the capitalist class, and they are not modelled here. Workers offer labour power to capitalists and receive wages, which they partly use in order to purchase consumption goods and partly save. However, the propensity to save out of wages is much lower than the propensity to save out of profits, because the workers' households are the low-income households with a higher propensity to consume out of income than the high-income capitalists' or rentiers' households. Furthermore, a part of the profits is retained within the corporate sector and is thus saved by definition.

In the model economy, again a homogenous output (Y) is produced combining direct labour (N) and a non-depreciating capital stock (K) in the production process. We assume again a fixed coefficients production technology with a constant labour-output ratio ($l_0 = N/Y$) and a constant capital-potential output ratio ($v = K/Y^p$). The homogeneous output can be used for consumption and investment purposes. For the sake of simplicity, overhead labour and depreciation of the capital stock, as well as (imported) raw materials and intermediate products are not considered, unlike the open economy models in Chapters 4 and 5, but in line with the basic distribution and growth models in Chapter 7. The rate of profit (r), relating the flow of profits (Π) to the nominal capital stock (pK), can again be decomposed into the profit share (h), relating profits to nominal income (pY), the rate of capacity utilisation (u), relating actual output to potential output given by the capital stock (Y^p), and the inverse of the capital-potential output ratio (v), relating the capital stock to potential output:

$$r = \frac{\Pi}{pK} = \frac{\Pi}{pY}\frac{Y}{Y^p}\frac{Y^p}{K} = hu\frac{1}{v}. \tag{8.3}$$

Our assumption regarding saving translates into the following domestic saving rate (σ), which relates the flow of total domestic saving (S) to the value of the capital stock:

$$\sigma = \frac{S_\Pi + S_W + S_G}{pK} = \frac{s_\Pi\Pi + s_W W - D}{pK} = s_\Pi h\frac{u}{v} + s_W(1-h)\frac{u}{v} - \delta$$

$$= \left[(s_\Pi - s_W)h + s_W\right]\frac{u}{v} - \delta, \quad 0 \le s_W < s_\Pi \le 1, \ \delta \ge 0. \tag{8.4}$$

Total saving is composed of saving out of profits (S_Π), saving out of wages (S_W) and government saving (S_G), which is zero or negative in our model, because we ignore taxation and only allow for government deficits ($D = -S_G \geq 0$). A government deficit is thus equivalent to government expenditures. The saving rate is determined by the propensities to save out of profits (s_Π) and out of wages (s_W), by the components of the profit rate from equation (8.3), as well as by the government deficit or expenditure rate (δ), which relates government deficits and expenditures to the capital stock and which is treated as a long-run exogenous policy parameter. A rise in the profit share raises the saving rate, as does an increase in capacity utilisation, the functional propensities to save and a reduction in the government deficit rate.

As explained in Chapter 7, in the Kaleckian distribution and growth models the rate of capacity utilisation is treated as a medium- to long-run endogenous variable. The profit share, and thus functional income distribution, is mainly determined by the mark-up (m) in firms' pricing in imperfectly competitive markets, as explained in Chapters 3 and 4:[11]

$$h = h(m), \quad \frac{\partial h}{\partial m} > 0. \tag{8.5}$$

The mark-up itself is affected by several factors, such as the degree of price competition in the goods market, the bargaining power of workers and also by unit overhead costs, which are all treated as exogenously given here. The capital-potential output ratio is also considered as an exogenous variable determined by technology, which does not systematically respond to distribution and activity variables in the model:

$$v = \bar{v}. \tag{8.6}$$

With the profit share and the capital-potential output ratio as exogenously given variables, the rate of capacity utilisation becomes the variable adjusting the profit rate (equation 8.3) to its equilibrium value required by the goods market equilibrium. As first determinant in the investment function in Kaleckian models, we have firms' or managements' animal spirits (α), sometimes taken to represent the firms' assessment of the long-run growth trend of the economy. Furthermore, the (expected) rate of profit is of relevance, because it indicates the internal means of finance required for attracting external investment finance, according to Kalecki's (1937) 'principle of increasing risk'. Also the dynamics of demand as a determinant of investment are reflected in the rate of profit through changes in capacity utilisation. Apart from animal spirits, we can thus include the three determinants of the profit rate from equation (8.3) into the Kaleckian accumulation function, in line with the procedure regarding the Kaleckian model in Chapter 7:

$$g = g(\alpha, h, u, v), \quad \frac{\partial g}{\partial \alpha} > 0, \quad \frac{\partial g}{\partial h} \geq 0, \quad \frac{\partial g}{\partial u} > 0, \quad \frac{\partial g}{\partial v} = 0. \tag{8.7}$$

Investment decisions will thus positively depend on the profit share and the rate of capacity utilisation, because each increase the (expected) rate of profit, ceteris paribus. Neo-Kaleckians, however, would insist that the partial effect of a change in the profit share is irrelevant for firms' decisions to invest and hence that $\partial g / \partial h = 0$. In order to simplify the further exposition, but also for empirical reasons, this view is followed here.[12] Regarding exogenous changes in the capital-potential output ratio through technical change, the partial effects on investment decisions are not clear in general, as explained in Chapter 7. On the one hand, a higher capital-potential output ratio means a lower rate of profit, which should dampen investment. On the other hand, however, a higher capital-potential output ratio means that a certain increase in demand determined output requires a higher increase in the capital stock, which should boost investment. The sign of the sum of these two opposing effects is not clear ex ante, so that any direct effect of changes in the capital-potential output ratio on investment is disregarded in what follows. We treat the capital potential-output ratio as a constant, even in the face of technical change.[13]

The net export rate (b) is given by the relationship between net exports (NX), as the difference between exports (pEx) and imports ($p_f a$Im) in domestic currency, and the capital stock. It is negatively affected by domestic demand and capacity utilisation triggering rising imports and positively affected by foreign income and capacity utilisation (u_f) generating rising exports. Also the real exchange rate ($a_r = ap_f/p$), given by the nominal exchange rate (a), the foreign price level (p_f) and the domestic price level (p), may have a positive effect on net exports, if exports and imports are price sensitive and the Marshall-Lerner condition holds. For simplicity we assume here that the real exchange rate is positively related to the profit share:[14]

$$b = \frac{pEx - p_f a\,Im}{pK} = \frac{NX}{pK} = b\left[u, u_f, a_r(h)\right],$$

$$\frac{\partial b}{\partial u} < 0, \frac{\partial b}{\partial u_f} > 0, \frac{\partial b}{\partial a_r} \geq 0, \frac{\partial a_r}{\partial h} > 0. \tag{8.8}$$

Finally, equation (8.9) provides the goods market equilibrium condition for the open economy:

$$g^* + b^* = \sigma^*. \tag{8.9}$$

Next, an export and current account deficit economy, as well as an export and current account surplus economy are presented with the help of this stylised neo-Kaleckian distribution and growth model, as shown in Figures 8.5a and 8.5b. In the right-hand quadrants we have the determination of the long-run goods market equilibrium from equation (8.9), with the domestic saving rate from equation (8.4) and the accumulation rate from equation (8.7) as positive functions of the rate of profit (or its components), and the net export rate from equation (8.8) as a negative function of the domestic demand and capacity utilisation, for given profit share, real exchange rate and foreign growth rate. Note that the net export rate is negative for the export deficit country in Figure 8.5a and positive for the export surplus country in Figure 8.5b. The goods market equilibrium then determines the equilibrium rates of capital accumulation, domestic saving (with the government deficit rate as an exogenous component) and net export, as well as the equilibrium rate of capacity utilisation and, for a given profit share and capital-potential output ratio, also the equilibrium rate of profit in the left-hand quadrants.

In the model, an improvement of animal spirits, that is, a rightwards shift of the g- and the g + b-functions in Figures 8.5a and 8.5b, leads to higher equilibrium rates of accumulation, profit and utilisation in both economies. Lower propensities to save out of wages or out of profits, that is, a counter-clockwise rotation of the σ-function, or a higher government deficit rate, that is, an upward shift of the σ-function, will also cause higher equilibrium rates of accumulation, profit and utilisation in both regimes. The paradox of saving is thus valid again. Since the net export-capital rate is negatively affected by domestic demand, higher animal

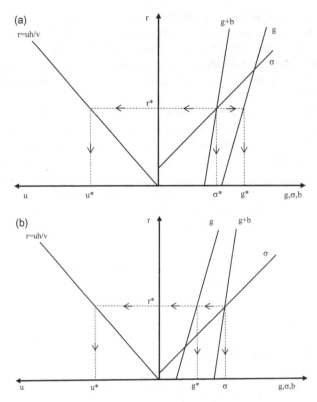

Figure 8.5   A basic Kaleckian distribution and growth approach. (a) An export and current account deficit economy. (b) An export and current account surplus economy

spirits, lower propensities to save and higher government deficit rates will each lead to lower equilibrium net export-capital rates. If foreign demand and capacity utilisation are higher or the real exchange rate rises and the domestic currency thus depreciates, the $g + b$-function will shift to the right and we will see higher equilibrium rates of accumulation, profit, utilisation and net exports.

Any rise in the profit share will affect both the r-function in the left quadrant and also the g-function in the right quadrant, as we have outlined in Chapter 7 and as can be seen in Figures 8.6a and 8.6b. On the one hand, a higher profit share causes a clockwise rotation of the r-function, because any rate of capacity utilisation is now related with a higher rate of profit and any rate of profit with a lower rate of capacity utilisation. On the other hand, the change in the profit share will also affect the g- and the g + b-functions. With a strong responsiveness of investment to utilisation ($\partial g / \partial u$) and a very weak or zero direct reaction to the profit share ($\partial g / \partial h$), as assumed in the neo-Kaleckian model, a higher profit share and thus a lower rate of utilisation for every rate of profit trigger a counter-clockwise rotation of the g- and thus also the g + b-functions in the right quadrant of Figures 8.6a and 8.6b. Every rate of profit is now associated with a lower rate of utilisation, and firms' investment responds accordingly.

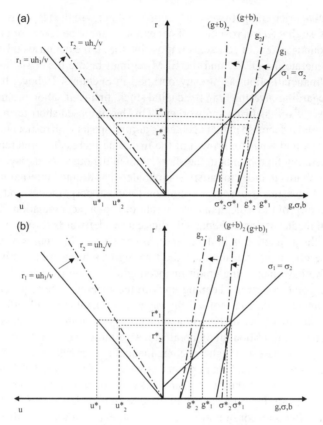

Figure 8.6   *A rising profit share in isolation in a basic neo-Kaleckian approach. (a) An*
export and current account deficit economy. (b) An export and current account
surplus economy

Finally, if the rise in the profit share takes place in a single country in isolation, net exports
will slightly improve, because we have assumed that the increase in the profit share is associated with an improvement of international price competitiveness, so that the change of the
g + b-curve slightly deviates from the change of the g-curve. We assume here that the net
export effect of re-distribution is weak, and, therefore, taking the effects together, we can see
that both countries in Figures 8.6a and 8.6b are wage led: A rise in the profit share, ceteris
paribus, will lead to a fall in the equilibrium rates of capacity utilisation, profit and capital
accumulation. This is in line with much of the empirical literature on estimating the wage-
or profit-led regimes applying the single equations or structural estimation approach. These
studies find wage-led demand regimes for open economies, with some exceptions for small
very open economies and for emerging and commodity exporting countries.[15] The equilibrium net export rates ($b^* = \sigma^* - g^*$) in our model will rise in both regimes, assuming that
the increase in the profit share and the concomitant improvement of price competitiveness
raising exports and the fall in domestic capacity utilisation dampening imports take place in
isolation. Obviously, if the rise in the profit share takes place globally, thus in both regimes,

neither will relative price competitiveness be improved nor will the respective export markets remain constant, so that an improvement of net exports cannot be taken for granted any more for individual countries and, of course, is impossible for all the countries taken together.[16]

In order to generate the DLPD and the ELM regimes before the crisis in Figure 8.7, further effects of financialisation, as already outlined in Section 8.2 above, have to be taken into account. Regarding investment in the capital stock, financialisation has meant increasing shareholder power vis-à-vis firms and workers. This has imposed short-termism on management and has caused a decrease in management's animal spirits with respect to real investment in the capital stock and long-run growth of the firm, and increasing preference for financial investment, generating high profits in the short run. On the other hand, paying out dividends and buying back shares in order to satisfy shareholders has drained internal means of finance available for real investment purposes from non-financial corporations and thus required a higher total rate of profit to execute a certain rate of capital accumulation. The 'preference' and the 'internal means of finance' channels thus cause a leftwards shift and a counter-clockwise rotation of the g-function in both regimes, as can be seen in Figures 8.7a and 8.7b.

Regarding the effects on consumption the two regimes have to be distinguished. In the DLPD regime we have increasing credit-financed consumption in particular. This has been due to relative income concerns ('keeping up with the Joneses'), the requirements to sustain necessary consumption in the face of falling wages, considerable wealth effects on consumption associated with stock price and housing price booms and improved access to consumption credit due to financial innovations and liberalisation, reinforced by the stock price and housing booms. A rising profit share and higher income inequality are thus associated with lower propensities to save out of wages and out of profits, as well as with a lower differential between the two propensities. We observe thus a counter-clockwise rotation in the domestic saving function of Figure 8.7a, assuming little change in the government deficit rate. In the ELM regime, any expansionary effects on consumption have been absent for several, partly different reasons in different countries: A more developed welfare state providing basic consumption and public goods, absence of house price booms, a less deregulated credit market and so on. For the sake of simplicity, the σ-function in Figure 8.7b has not been changed, ignoring potentially contractionary effects of rising inequality in personal and household incomes. These would lead to higher average propensities to save out of wages and out of profits and to a higher differential between these two rates, which would rotate the σ-function clockwise. But we ignore this here.

Regarding net exports and the current account balance, we can ignore the effects of redistribution on relative price competitiveness, because profit shares and rates have improved globally in both types of regimes. Therefore, the b-function is mainly affected by relative demand dynamics and non-price competitiveness. In the DLPD economy, low foreign demand from ELM countries and high domestic demand dynamics decrease net exports and increase current account deficits; the g + b-function in Figure 8.7a therefore shows a more pronounced leftward shift than the g-function. In the ELM economy, low domestic demand dynamics due to regressive re-distribution dampens imports, and high foreign demand dynamics, particularly from the DLPD economies, raises exports, so that we have rising net exports and current account surpluses. In Figure 8.7b, therefore, although the accumulation function is shifted leftwards, the g + b-function gets slightly shifted to the right.

As can be seen in Figures 8.7a and 8.7b, re-distribution and changes in economic behaviour under the conditions of financialisation lead to the following changes in medium- to long-run equilibrium positions in the two regimes. We obtain that a higher profit share raises the

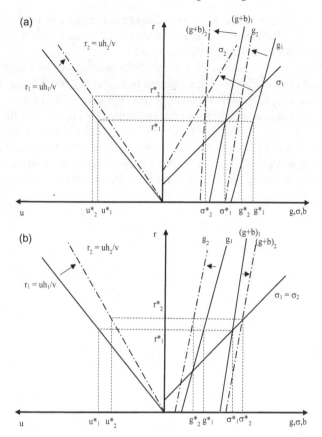

Figure 8.7 *Distributional and behavioural changes before the crisis generating the DLPD and the ELM regimes. (a) The DLPD regime: Rising profit share, falling average propensity to save due to relative income effects and credit-financed consumption, and rising current account deficits. (b) The ELM regime: Rising profit share, rising average propensity to save due to higher profit share, and rising current account surpluses*

equilibrium profit rates in both regimes. This is accompanied by a fall in equilibrium capital stock growth, which means that we have 'profits without investment' regimes in both cases (Hein 2014a, Chapter 10). However, in the DLPD case in Figure 8.7a this is accompanied by a rise in the equilibrium rate of capacity utilisation. Demand thus turns 'seemingly profit-led' here, a regime which we have already explained in Chapter 4 while dealing with wage inequality. High domestic demand dynamics in this regime also cause lower net exports and thus rising current account deficits. The ELM regime in Figure 8.7b displays a fall in equilibrium capacity utilisation and thus remains wage-led but shows higher net exports and current account surpluses. This overall constellation has then given rise to unsustainable private debt dynamics in the DLPD economies, which in countries not able to issue debt in their own currencies was coupled with unsustainable foreign debt dynamics. These unsustainable debt dynamics then triggered the financial crisis and led to the collapse of both pre-crisis regimes in the course of the Global Financial Crisis and the Great Recession, as has been analysed in more detail in Hein (2012b, Chapter 6), for example.[17]

The core macroeconomics behind the regime shifts in the developed capitalist economies in the course of and after the 2007–09 crises, as indicated in Section 8.3, can also be analysed with the help of our simple model. Whereas several pre-crises ELM countries stayed ELM also after the crises, and hence continue to be represented by Figure 8.7b, the DLPD regimes turned towards DDL regimes stabilised by government deficits or towards ELM regimes. These shifts are shown in Figures 8.8a and 8.8b. We focus here on the most important changes that trigger the shift in regimes in order to keep the figures clearly arranged and ignore minor and country specific changes. For example, for both regime shifts in the course of and after

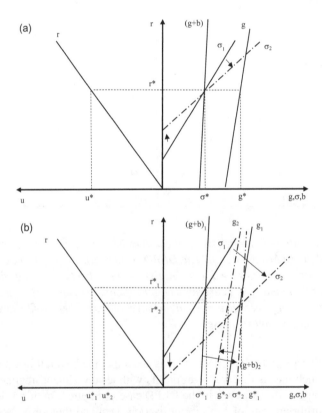

Figure 8.8   *Regime shifts in the course and after the 2007–09 crises. (a) From the DLPD regime to the DDL regime stabilised by government deficits: Constant profit share and inequality, higher propensity to save out of wage and profit income, higher government deficits, constant current account deficits. (b) From the DLPD to the ELM regime: Constant profit share and inequality, higher propensity to save out of income, lower government deficits, reduced animal spirits, improved international price competitiveness and positive net exports and current account*

the crises we keep functional and personal income distribution constant, although empirical analysis tells us that some indicators of income inequality have worsened also after the crises in several pre-crises DLPD countries, as shown in Tables 8.2 and 8.4.[18]

Furthermore, for the shift from the DLPD to the DDL regime stabilised by government deficits shown in Figure 8.8a, we ignore further changes in the parameters of the accumulation and net export functions. The change in regime is thus only triggered by the change in the saving function. The requirement for deleveraging of private households in the course of and after the crisis, rising uncertainty and precautionary saving, together with tightened credit standards have increased the propensity to save out of profits and out of wages and thus rotated the σ-function counter-clockwise in Figure 8.8a. Furthermore, higher government deficits in order to stabilise the economy during and after the crises have shifted this function upward – in Figure 8.8a to such an extent that the original pre-crisis equilibrium is maintained, but this is just for simplification and should not be taken for granted. As a result we get that the private household deficit is substituted by a higher government sector deficit without changing any other features of the regime: Considerable net export or current account deficits, weak capital accumulation, but rates of capacity utilisation and profit maintained.

For the shift from the DLPD to the ELM regime shown in Figure 8.8b, we take into account shifts in the accumulation and the net export functions, too. For the saving function we have again an increase in the propensities to save out wages and out of profits, for the same reasons as mentioned above, which lead to a clockwise rotation of the σ-curve. Furthermore, government austerity policies reducing the government deficit-capital ratio also shift the σ-curve down. Austerity policies and depressed overall demand also reduce firms' animal spirits and shift the g-function to the left. The depressive effects of lower private and public consumption and lower investment are partly compensated for by improved net exports. These are generated by depressed domestic demand relative to higher foreign demand (from DDL economies stabilised by government deficits and from some previous ELM countries which have become less export oriented after the crises) and by improved international price competitiveness. The latter has been associated with further re-distribution at the expense of labour and low-income households, which we ignore here in the graphical presentation for the sake of simplicity. Together, these changes cause a rightward shift of the g + b-function with b now being positive. These changes lead to a fall in the equilibrium rates of capital accumulation, profit and capacity utilisation and a rise of the equilibrium net export-capital rate – which is now positive, as can be seen in Figure 8.8b.

As we have pointed out above in Section 8.3, these shifts in regimes in the developed capitalist economies, together with DLPD and DDL regimes in emerging economies in the post-crises period, have been associated with persistent current account imbalances at the global level – with the related instability potentials. Apart from these short- to medium-run problems of stability of such a global constellation associated with the polarisation of the demand and growth regimes, we can also address the long-run stagnation problem associated with the still persisting 'profits without investment' patterns in the post-crises regimes in our model. For this purpose, we can follow the introduction of endogenous productivity growth into the simple Kaleckian distribution and growth model from Section 7.10.

In the first step, we introduce exogenous productivity growth into the determination of the equilibrium rate of capital accumulation and growth determined in the model above. We assume that capital accumulation is positively affected by productivity growth, because of capital embodied technological change, in particular. Firms have to invest in new capital stock in order to benefit from technological inventions. Taking into account the exogenous parameters determining the goods market equilibrium rate of accumulation derived above, we arrive at the following equation for equilibrium capital accumulation:

$$g^* = g^*\left(y, \alpha, h, s_w, s_\Pi, \delta, u_f, a_r\right),$$

$$\frac{\partial g^*}{\partial y} > 0, \frac{\partial g^*}{\partial \alpha} > 0, \frac{\partial g^*}{\partial h} < 0, \frac{\partial g^*}{\partial s_w} < 0, \frac{\partial g^*}{\partial s_\Pi} < 0, \frac{\partial g^*}{\partial \delta} > 0, \frac{\partial g^*}{\partial u_f} > 0, \frac{\partial g^*}{\partial a_r} > 0.$$

(8.10)

Productivity growth, animal spirits, the government deficit-capital rate, foreign capacity utilisation and the real exchange rate have positive effects on the goods market equilibrium rate of capital accumulation, whereas the profit share, as well as the propensities to save out of wages and out of profits have negative effects each.

Relying on Kaldor's (1957) technical progress function, labour productivity growth is assumed to be positively affected by capital stock growth due to capital-embodied technological change. Following Marx (1867), a higher real wage rate or a higher wage share induces capitalists to speed up the implementation of labour augmenting technological progress in order to protect the profit share. We thus obtain for long-run productivity growth:

$$\hat{y} = \hat{y}\left(g^*, h, k_i\right), \quad \frac{\partial \hat{y}}{\partial g^*} > 0, \frac{\partial \hat{y}}{\partial h} < 0, \frac{\partial \hat{y}}{\partial k_i} > 0,$$

(8.11)

with k_i representing a set of further institutional factors determining productivity growth, like government technology policies and R&D expenditures, the education system and so on.

Equations (8.10) and (8.11) describe the demand-determined endogenous growth model, a basic version of which we have already introduced in Chapter 7. Figure 8.9 presents the long-run equilibrium values for capital accumulation (g_1^{**}) and productivity growth ($\hat{y}_1^{**}$) and thus the endogenous potential or 'natural' growth rate. The fall in the goods market equilibrium rate of capital accumulation which we have seen for the DLPD and the ELM regimes before the crises, which then has persisted in the post-crises DDL and ELM regimes, causes a leftward shift in the g^*-curve and thus lower long-run equilibrium rates of capital accumulation and productivity growth. Furthermore, since the demand and growth regimes in finance-dominated capitalism have also seen a fall in the wage and a rise in the profit share, this has had an independent negative effect on long-run productivity growth, shifting the $\hat{y}$-curve down. The latter may also be affected by a fall in government expenditures on R&D and education associated with post-crises austerity policies. With these shifts, the long-run growth equilibrium falls from g_1^{**}, y_1^{**} to g_2^{**}, y_2^{**}.

Summing up the results of our Kalecki-Steindl-Kaldor-Marx endogenous growth model, post-crises stagnation tendencies – and falling potential growth – can be explained by those financialisation features that generate low capital stock growth (i.e. depressed animal spirits of the management of non-financial corporations), high propensities to save out of the different types of income after the crises, low government expenditure and deficit rates (in particular in the ELM countries) and high profit shares. Moreover, rising profit shares have an independent depressing effect on the innovation

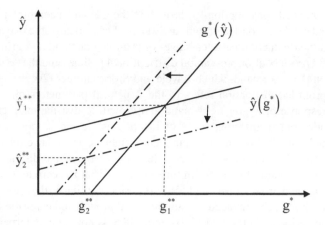

Figure 8.9   Stagnation in a Kalecki-Steindl-Kaldor-Marx endogenous growth model

activities of firms and on productivity growth, too, which is also negatively affected by falling government expenditures on R&D and education. Several of these determinants of stagnation are thus affected by economic policies, which induced Steindl (1976, 1979) to focus on 'stagnation policy' in order to explain long-run stagnation trends in modern capitalism (Hein 2016, 2018a). In the following section, we will therefore turn to a more explicit discussion of the role of institutions, power relationships and economic policies for the demand and growth regimes in finance-dominated capitalism, for the shift of regimes in the course of and after the 2007–09 crises and for the prevailing stagnation tendencies.

8.5   GROWTH DRIVERS, REGIME SHIFTS, MACROECONOMIC POLICY REGIMES AND STAGNATION POLICY

8.5.1   Comparative and International Political Economy, Post-Keynesian Macroeconomics and Demand and Growth Regimes

Recently, the post-Keynesian/Kaleckian demand-led growth regime approaches have reso-nated in the comparative political economy (CPE) and in the international political economy (IPE) literature. In an attempt at overcoming the implications of the NCM as the supply side-dominated macroeconomic backbone of much of the CPE research, in particular of the 'varieties of capitalism' (VoC) approach (i.e. Carlin and Soskice 2009, 2015, Hall and Soskice 2001, Hope and Soskice 2016), Baccaro and Pontusson (2016, 2018) have made use of the post-Keynesian categories of demand-led macroeconomic growth regimes, which we have explained in the previous and the current chapter of this book.[19] However, they do not pay sufficient attention to the different analytical levels of the distinction between wage-led/profit-led regimes, on the one hand, and DLPD/ELM regimes, on the other, in post-Keynesian research (Hein et al. 2021). Baccaro and Pontusson (2016, 2018) argue wage-led growth dur-ing the 'golden age' period (1950s–70s) of modern capitalism has been succeeded by differ-ent regimes, in particular in the period from the mid-1990s until 2008: Export-led growth in

Germany, debt-financed consumption-led growth in the UK and a combination of export-led and debt-financed consumption-led growth in Sweden. Theoretically, the two authors have not clearly followed the distinction between wage- or profit-led demand and growth regimes, on the one hand, and pro-labour or pro-capital distributional policies and the resulting economic developments, on the other hand, which Lavoie and Stockhammer (2013b) have pointed out. The wage- or profit-led distinction refers to the structural parameters of an economy that determine the response of aggregate demand and growth to distributional changes (mainly saving propensities out of different types of income, as well as responsiveness of invest-ment, exports and imports towards distributional variables), as we have referred to in detail in Chapters 4, 5 and 7 of this book. This is different from the actual distributional and eco-nomic policies being followed in a certain time period – what Baccaro and Pontusson (2016) refer to as the wage-led growth post-World War II period. Similarly, they do not consider that the distinction between debt-financed consumption-led growth and export-led growth, which they apply to the period from the mid-1990s until 2008, is not the counterpart of a wage-led growth regime, as discussed in the Kaleckian distribution and growth literature. Therefore, these regimes cannot be seen as successors or a replacement of wage-led demand and growth. The distinction between debt-financed consumption-led demand and growth and export-led demand and growth refers to the sources of demand and growth. In other words, a country can be structurally wage-led, follow a pro-capital distributional policy strategy, as the ones dominating since late 1970s/early 1980s period of finance-dominated capitalism, and then generate either a DLPD regime or an ELM regime, as should be clear from the analysis pro-vided in this book.

Also post-Keynesians have provided attempts at linking their macroeconomic demand and growth regime approaches to the CPE and IPE literature on institutional varieties of capital-ism or on welfare state models in modern capitalism. Stockhammer (2022) has recently sum-marised some potential post-Keynesian macroeconomic foundations for CPE, which should broaden the approach suggested by Baccaro and Pontusson (2016) and would help to over-come the dominance of NCM macroeconomics in CPE with its supply-side focus, the long-run neutrality of money, the lack of aggregate demand and macroeconomic policy effects for long-run economic performance. Stockhammer (2022) points out three core macroeco-nomic foundations that post-Keynesians can provide for CPE: First, the Kaleckian distinction of wage-led and profit-led demand regimes; second, the post-Keynesian theory of money, finance, financialisation and Minskyan financial instability; and, third, the focus on path-dependent growth and demand-led technological progress. This is very much in line with what we have presented so far.

Behringer and van Treeck (2018, 2019) have made use of the traditional VoC approach in order to explain debt-led consumption-driven and export-driven regimes before the 2007–09 crises. In their view, it is the type of re-distribution, rooted in the institutional structure of an economy, which then determines the demand regime. Co-ordinated market economies (CME), typically Germany, have seen a fall in the wage share in the context of wage modera-tion in organised labour markets with relatively strong trade unions in international compari-son, but only small increases in household income inequality and only slight increases in top income shares, and have generated export-led regimes with current account surpluses. Liberal market economies (LME) with deregulated labour markets and weak trade unions, typically the USA, have seen considerable increases in top income shares, and a more stable functional income distribution, because high management salaries enter into the wage share. They have generated current account deficits and the dominance of a debt-financed consumption-led regime due to the dominance of relative rather than absolute income concerns for the determination of consumption expenditures, as we have explained above.

Although we see the merits in looking at the type of re-distribution in order to explain the different demand regimes and to link this with the social and institutional structures of the economy, we feel that Behringer and van Treeck's (2018, 2019) line of reasoning is somewhat incomplete. For the relative income hypothesis and debt-financed consumption to take effect, we do not only need an increase in income inequality but also the desire or the need of households to go into debt for consumption purposes and thus the related demand for credit, as well as the willingness of the financial sector to supply this hardly creditworthy demand for credit. This means we need a broader institutional analysis in order to identify the conditions for the relative income hypothesis to take effect, both with respect to the development of the different types of re-distribution and with respect to the concomitant consumption behaviour. Furthermore, the inherent instabilities, both within debt-financed consumption and export-led regimes, and thus endogenous collapses of and changes in regimes have to be considered. For this purpose, the CME/LME distinction from the VoC approach seems to be too narrow, static and limited.

This is also the view taken by Stockhammer and Ali (2018) in their analysis of Eurozone regimes leading to the Eurozone crisis. They see the shortcomings in VoC analysis in the exclusive focus on labour market institutions and in a lack of an adequate treatment of finance and financial instability, as well as in a downplaying of the role of fiscal policies. Financial instability and economic policies, however, figure prominently in post-Keynesian analysis when it comes to explaining the demand and growth regimes in finance-dominated capitalism and the polarisation of these regimes within the Eurozone, too, as we have also argued. The features thus also provide a more complete explanation of the imbalances, with the current account deficit debt-led countries of the Eurozone periphery, on the one hand, and the current account surplus export-led countries in the Eurozone centre, on the other hand, leading then to the Eurozone crisis.

Stockhammer et al. (2016) have also been critical of traditional VoC analysis. Instead they have linked the European growth regimes before the 2007–09 crises with different types of working class restructuring in these regimes, looking at indicators for financialisation, industrial upgrading and working class coherence. Building on post-Keynesian macroeconomics, neo-Gramscian IPE and the French regulation theory, they distinguish three country groups or regimes: The 'North' (Germany, Austria, the Netherlands) with export orientation and heavy outsourcing to the countries of the 'East', retreat of the working regime and union decline, weak real wage growth and rising wage dispersion; the 'East' (Poland, Czech Republic, Slovakia, Hungary, Slovenia) with catching up and dependent integration into global value chains, a strong decline in union density, rapid real wage growth but rising wage dispersion; and the 'South' (Greece, Ireland, Italy, Portugal, Spain) with debt-driven growth based on a property and financial bubble, moderate decline in union density, moderate increase in real wages and stable wage dispersion.

These contributions show that the integration of CPE and IPE with post-Keynesian macroeconomics seems to be a promising route of research for a better understanding of the varieties and dynamics of modern capitalism. This is in line with the relevance of institutional and political factors for the emergence and the change in the demand and growth regimes discussed in the previous sections of this chapter. However, the contributions reviewed so far have not looked at the regime changes in the course of and after the 2007–09 crises and the respective drivers. Therefore, we turn to these issues in the next section.

8.5.2   Causes for for Regime Shifts and Growth Drivers

Hein (2019a), Hein and Martschin (2020) and Hein et al. (2021) have argued that the type of shift of the previously DLPD economies in the course of and after the 2007–09 crises has depended, on the one hand, on the requirements of private sector deleveraging after the financial crisis and, on the other hand, on the ability and willingness to run deficit-financed and stabilising fiscal policies. Hein et al. (2021) have also related these shifts of macroeconomic regimes to the welfare models approach based on Esping-Andersen (1990) and Hay and Wincott (2012), who distinguish between the Anglo-Saxon/liberal, the Continental European/ cooperative, the Scandinavian, the Central and Eastern European and the Mediterranean welfare models. According to these contributions, the institutional constraints imposed on national fiscal policies in the Eurozone, the absence of relevant fiscal policies at the Eurozone level and the turn towards austerity policies when the Eurozone crisis started in 2010, including substantial downsizing of welfare provision in some crisis countries, explain to a large extent why in particular European DLPD countries turned WEL or ELM after the Global Financial Crisis and the Great Recession. The collapse of domestic demand caused by the requirements for the private sectors to deleverage was reinforced by austerity policies of the public sector, which made imports collapse, net exports rise and the current account in these countries improve and in several cases even turn positive. Those DLPD countries before the crisis, which were able to make use of expansionary deficit-financed fiscal policies, in particular the UK and the USA, however, compensated private deleveraging by rising public deficits. This stabilised aggregate demand in their countries and through the import channel also in the global economy.

Kohler and Stockhammer (2021) have recently provided a more systematic cross-country analysis of the underlying growth drivers before and after the 2007–09 crises in 30 OECD countries. To explain the emergence of the different post-crises regimes, they consider the requirements of deleveraging in the context of a financial boom-bust cycle, the role of fiscal policies and the relevance of price and non-price competitiveness for exports. Generalising the claims being made in Hein (2019a), Hein and Martschin (2020) and Hein et al. (2021), they find that the former two drivers have had a major role to play, that is, the need for deleveraging generated by high private debt and the (lack of) expansionary deficit-financed fiscal policies. They also find that differences and changes in international price competitiveness are not systematically related to growth performance and thus have been overstated in some of the previous CPE literature on macroeconomic regimes. Furthermore, they abandon the regime distinction, which had been developed for the pre-crisis period, and rather focus on the distinction of the different growth drivers for the clustering of countries in the post-crises period. Jungmann (2021) has extended and applied the growth driver approach by Kohler and Stockhammer (2021) to a set of 19 emerging capitalist economies and has found mixed results. This seems to be in line with the findings of Akcay et al. (2022) regarding the different pattern of regime changes of emerging capitalist economies as compared to advanced capitalist economies referred to above.

8.5.3 Demand and Growth Regimes, Macroeconomic Policy Regimes and Stagnation Policy[20]

Hein and Martschin (2021) have kept the typology for macroeconomic regimes in finance-dominated capitalism, based on the examination of growth contributions of demand aggregates and of sectoral financial balances. In an attempt at understanding the role of macroeconomic policies for regime shifts and extending the research by Kohler and Stockhammer (2021), they have linked this approach with the post-Keynesian notion of macroeconomic policy regimes developed and applied in the early 2000s (Fritsche et al. 2005, Hein and Truger 2005a, 2005b, 2005c, 2009, Herr and Kazandziska 2011).[21] The concept of a 'macroeconomic policy regime' has been used to assess international and intertemporal comparative differences in macroeconomic performances of countries or regions. It describes the set of monetary, fiscal and wage or income policies, as well as their co-ordination and interaction, against the institutional background of a specific economy, including the degree of openness and the exchange rate regime. This concept supposes that macroeconomic policies have not only short-run effects on economic performance, as in the NCM, but also have a long-run impact on output, income, employment, inflation, distribution and growth, as in the post-Keynesian macroeconomic and distribution and growth models presented in this book. The post-Keynesian macroeconomic policy mix presented in Chapter 6 is used as a benchmark supporting a stable DDL regime. It is supposed that deviations from this benchmark should contribute to moving to the long-run unstable DLPD or WEL regimes and should thus have detrimental long-run effects on macroeconomic performance with regard to income, employment, inflation, distribution, financial stability and growth.

Applying indicators for the stances of monetary and fiscal policies, for wage policies and income distribution and for price and non-price competitiveness, Hein and Martschin (2021) have shown for the four largest Eurozone countries, France, Germany, Italy and Spain, how the country-specific macroeconomic policy regimes have supported the shift (or non-shift) of macroeconomic regimes from the pre- to the post-crises period. First, the macroeconomic regimes under finance-dominated capitalism outlined in Section 8.2 are analysed, as can be seen in Table 8.6. According to these results, Spain has moved from a DLPD regime before the crises towards an ELM regime in the course of the Global Financial Crisis and the Great Recession (2007–09), which was then succeeded by the Eurozone crisis starting in 2010. Germany kept the ELM regime, France kept the DDL regime, and Italy, as well as the core Eurozone as a whole, the EA-12, moved from a DDL to an ELM regime.

In the course of this process, the (core) Eurozone has externalised its pre-crises current internal account imbalances. Whereas its current account used to be roughly balanced with the rest of the word, while showing increasing internal imbalances between current account surplus and deficit countries, it has become a current account surplus region, free-riding on demand created in the rest of the world (Figure 8.10). This shift in the EA-12 regime has been associated with a particularly weak recovery of the Eurozone from the 2007–09 crises in international comparison, with the USA as a reference, as can be seen in Figure 8.11. As already pointed out above, this recovery of the developed capitalist world has been particularly weak in historical comparison and has triggered the renewed debate on secular stagnation in orthodox economics (Gordon 2015, Summers 2014, 2015). Furthermore, the recovery of the core Eurozone has not only been much weaker than that of the USA, it also has been

Table 8.6 Indicators for the demand and growth regimes in Spain, Germany, France and Italy, average annual values for the periods 2001–09 and 2010–19.

	Spain		Germany		France		Italy		EA-12	
	2001–09	2010–19	2001–09	2010–19	2001–09	2010–19	2001–09	2010–19	2001–09	2010–19
Financial balances of external sector as a share of nominal GDP, per cent	5.61	-1.41	-4.00	-7.24	-0.42	0.81	1.04	-0.94	-0.63	-2.75
Financial balances of public sector as a share of nominal GDP, per cent	-1.32	-6.03	-2.44	0.18	-3.45	-4.06	-3.28	-2.83	-2.63	-2.53
Financial balances of private sector as a share of nominal GDP, per cent	-4.29	7.44	6.43	7.05	3.87	3.25	2.24	3.77	3.22	5.31
– Financial balance of private household sector as a share of nominal GDP, per cent	-2.73	0.89	5.52	5.27	2.78	3.09	2.47	1.24	2.21	2.77
– Financial balance of the corporate sector as a share of nominal GDP, per cent	-1.56	6.55	0.91	1.78	1.08	0.16	-0.23	2.53	1.01	2.54
Real GDP growth, per cent	2.36	1.03	0.53	1.96	1.19	1.35	0.18	0.22	1.04	1.34
Growth contribution of domestic demand including stocks, percentage points	2.61	0.34	0.02	1.74	1.43	1.36	0.36	-0.16	0.96	1.01
– Growth contribution of private consumption, percentage points	1.34	0.27	0.19	0.73	0.97	0.55	0.23	0.05	0.62	0.43
– Growth contribution of public consumption, percentage points	0.87	0.04	0.25	0.38	0.38	0.29	0.22	-0.09	0.40	0.18
– Growth contribution of gross fixed capital formation, percentage points	0.47	-0.05	-0.18	0.56	0.24	0.39	0.00	-0.12	0.09	0.32
Growth contribution of the balance of goods and services, percentage points	-0.25	0.69	0.51	0.21	-0.25	-0.01	-0.18	0.39	0.09	0.34
– Growth contribution of exports, percentage points	0.46	1.41	1.42	2.04	0.34	1.15	-0.02	0.98	0.87	1.94
– Growth contribution of imports, percentage points	-0.71	-0.75	-0.92	-1.83	-0.59	-1.21	-0.16	-0.60	-0.79	-1.68
Net exports of goods and services as a share of nominal GDP, per cent	-3.56	2.48	4.81	6.25	0.35	-1.03	0.05	1.78	1.82	3.53
Regime	DLPD	ELM	ELM	ELM	DDL	DDL	DDL	ELM	DDL	ELM

Notes: DLPD: Debt-led private demand boom, DDL: Domestic demand-led, ELM: Export-led mercantilist, data source: European Commission (2019a), authors' calculations.

Source: Based on Hein and Martschin (2021, pp. 500–501).

270

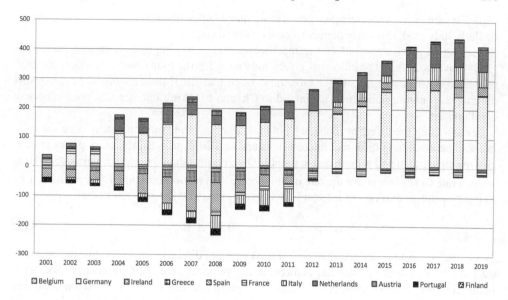

Data source: European Commission (2019a), authors' presentation.

Source: Based on Hein and Martschin (2021, p. 502).

Figure 8.10 Current account balance in core Eurozone countries, 2001–19 (in bn euros)

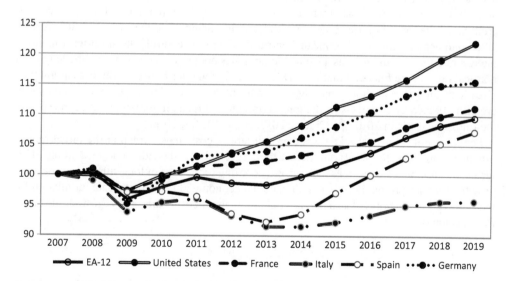

Data source: European Commission (2019a), authors' presentation.

Source: Based on Hein and Martschin (2021, p. 503).

Figure 8.11 Real GDP in Spain, Germany, France, Italy, the EA-12 and the USA, 2007–19, 2007 = 100

highly asymmetric, with Germany performing much better in comparison to Spain and particularly Italy (and also other periphery crisis countries).

Turning to the assessment of the macroeconomic policy regime, Hein and Martschin (2021) have examined the following policy indicators for the four countries, which are each related to the rules or targets for monetary, wage and fiscal policies in the post-Keynesian macroeconomic policy mix explained in Chapter 6, taking into account open economy conditions.

For assessing the effect of monetary policies of the central bank, the focus is on the relationship between long-term real interest rates and real GDP growth. Monetary policy conducive to employment and growth and to a stable DDL regime should target a nominal long-term interest rate (i) slightly above the rate of inflation ($\hat{p}$) but below nominal GDP growth ($\hat{Y}^n$), or a slightly positive real rate of interest ($i_r = i - \hat{p}$) below real GDP growth ($\hat{Y} = \hat{Y}^n - \hat{p}$):

$$\hat{p} \le i \le \hat{Y}^n \quad \Leftrightarrow \quad 0 \le i_r \le \hat{Y}. \tag{8.12}$$

Of course, it is acknowledged that central banks cannot directly control long-term real interest rates in the credit or financial markets at any point in time but only control short-term nominal money market rates. Nevertheless, the use of this and other tools, like open market operations in financial markets in the context of quantitative easing, will have an impact on long-term nominal rates and, taking into account some persistence in inflation trends, also on long-term real rates beyond the short run. However, as pointed out in Chapters 4–6, this impact might be asymmetric, since raising short-term rates will always drive up long-term rates, whereas lowering short-term rates might not be able to bring long-term rates down in a deep and persistent recession with rising risk assessments and liquidity preference of financial and non-financial actors. That is why also short- and long-term real interest rates are considered. Since the four countries under examination are members of the Eurozone, it is further taken into account that the European Central Bank (ECB) controls the short-term nominal interest rate for the Eurozone as a whole. So far, it has not targeted country-specific long-term nominal rates in the financial market.[22] Different inflation rates between countries might then already mean different short- and long-term real interest rates. The differentials in the latter are also affected by country-specific long-term nominal rates, in particular since the start of the Eurozone crisis in 2010 (De Grauwe 2012, Hein 2013/14, 2018a).

For wage policy, it is checked whether unit labour costs have grown at the target rate of inflation, which for the four countries is the target rate for the Eurozone as a whole. This means that nominal wages (w) should grow according to the sum of long-run average or trend growth of labour productivity ($\hat{y}$) in the national economy plus the target rate of inflation for the Eurozone as a whole ($\hat{p}^T$), so that nominal unit labour costs (nulc = w/y) grow at the target rate of inflation:

$$\hat{w} = \hat{y} + \hat{p}^T \quad \Leftrightarrow \quad \hat{w} - \hat{y} = \hat{p}^T. \tag{8.13}$$

Furthermore, it is taken into account that rising or falling nominal unit labour cost growth will not proportionally affect the rate of inflation because of incomplete pass-through. Therefore, also changes in functional income distribution, that is, in the labour income share, are considered. For the assessment of the effects of wage policies via functional income distribution, it is taken into account that aggregate demand in all four countries examined has been estimated to be wage-led (Hein 2014a, Chapter 7, Onaran and Obst 2016).

For fiscal policy, government financial balances and the financial balances of the other sectors can be examined, as indicated by equation (8.1). However, since this equation is an accounting identity, it does not allow clear conclusions to be drawn regarding deliberate and discretionary fiscal policy interventions, as included in the post-Keynesian macroeconomic policy mix for real government expenditures (G_r):

$$G_r = G_{r0} + G_{r1}\left(e^T - e\right), \quad G_{r0} \geq 0, G_{r1} > 0, \tag{8.14}$$

with G_{r0} as the expenditure level to reach a target employment rate e^T associated with non-inflationary full employment, that is, the SIRE, and G_{r1} as the reaction coefficient towards deviations of the employment rate from the target rate. Hein and Martschin (2021) use the changes of the cyclically adjusted budget balance-potential GDP ratio (CBR) of the government and relate this to the change in the output gap to assess the short-run discretionary responsiveness of fiscal policies. They are not directly examining equation (8.14) and do not identify potential output with the target full employment level of output, because of the well-known empirical measurement problems and endogeneity features of potential output (Heimberger and Kapeller 2017). Therefore, they do not look at the levels of CBRs and output gaps but only at the annual changes. If output gaps and CBRs move in the same direction, fiscal policies are counter-cyclical, lowering (increasing) structural deficits or increasing (lowering) structural surpluses in an economic upswing (downswing). If output gaps and CBRs move in opposite directions, fiscal policies are pro-cyclical; governments are lowering (increasing) structural deficits or increasing (lowering) structural surpluses in an economic downswing (upswing).[23] Furthermore, the share of public investment in GDP as an indicator for the growth orientation of fiscal policies is considered, although this might be an incomplete indicator, because also government consumption expenditures in education, for example, may improve productivity growth.

Finally, Hein and Martschin (2021) also consider the open economy conditions, since they will have an impact on the effectiveness of domestic macroeconomic policies, on the one hand, and will also directly affect the demand and growth regime. They look at the degree of openness measured by export and import shares of GDP and the development of price competitiveness, measured by real effective exchange rates. Unlike our theoretical models, an increase of this rate indicates an appreciation and thus a loss of international price competitiveness. To take into account non-price competitiveness, the OEC economic complexity index (OEC 2020) is considered, following Kohler and Stockhammer (2021).

In Table 8.7 the empirical indicators for the pre-crises and the crises and post-crises periods for the four countries can be found, and Table 8.8 contains the assessment of the stances of monetary, fiscal and wage policies, as well as the development of the open economy conditions. We briefly summarise Hein and Martschin's (2021) main findings for each country, which are also based on country-specific studies on financialisation and the crisis by other authors.[24]

Spain's macroeconomic policy regime in the period 2001–09 contributed to the emergence of the DLPD regime in this period. The extremely low real interest rates and easy access to credit stimulated deficit-financed investment and private household consumption, the latter in the face of falling wage shares. Fiscal policy followed a more counter-cyclical stance on average, and high public investment-GDP ratios supported private investment through crowd-ing-in effects. As a result of these developments, large private sector deficits occurred, and private consumption and investment became the main drivers of growth, while housing and asset price bubbles were swelling. The downside of this trend was Spain's loss of international price competitiveness. Combined with low non-price competitiveness and the economy's comparatively high growth rates, this led to negative growth contributions of net exports and a worsening current account and thus, to large financial surpluses of the external sector.

The strong shift in Spain's macroeconomic policy regime over the second period has con-tributed to the shift of the demand and growth regime towards ELM. After the financial crisis, Spanish households and corporations had to reduce financial liabilities and deleveraged heav-ily. Tightening credit standards, rising real long-term interest rates and falling labour income shares dampened private domestic demand in the wage-led Spanish economy. Pro-cyclical fiscal austerity measures when the Eurozone crisis started squeezed domestic demand further. Net exports, and in particular exports, thus became the only growth driver, benefitting from the improved international price competitiveness caused by wage moderation and from higher growth in foreign economies, while non-price-competitiveness remained low.

The macroeconomic policy regime of Germany also contributed considerably to its ELM demand and growth regime in the period 2001–09: A restrictive monetary policy stance, pro-cyclically restrictive fiscal policies and weak public investment constrained domestic demand, which was further curbed by deflationary wage policies leading to decreasing labour income shares in a wage-led economy. Depressed domestic demand, together with improved interna-tional price competitiveness and, in particular, high non-price competitiveness, left growth to be exclusively driven by external demand. This resulted in current account surpluses and external sector deficits associated with this ELM regime, generating only mediocre growth in international comparison.

The gradual change in the German macroeconomic policy regime in the second period has had an impact on the demand and growth regime, without changing its ELM nature. However, the ELM regime became less extreme. The shift to expansionary monetary conditions as well as the rise in the labour income share fostered private investment and consumption demand, making them the main drivers of Germany's more favourable growth performance over the second period. Growth contributions of net exports declined but remained positive, so that export and current account surpluses continued to rise. Relatively dynamic private domestic and foreign demand allowed for fiscal consolidation as reflected by decreasing public sector deficits. This was reinforced by the introduction of the 'debt brake' that limited federal budget expenses (Detzer and Hein 2016). Therefore, although changes within the German macroeco-nomic policy regime towards the stimulation of domestic demand occurred, they were not strong enough to reverse the ELM demand and growth regime.

The macroeconomic policy regime in France provided the grounds for the French DDL regime in the first period. Growth was driven by domestic demand and mainly by private con-sumption, as enabled by a roughly stable labour income share in a wage-led economy. Wage policies also contributed to generating inflation at the target rate. Public expenditures contrib-uted positively to growth, too, by an on average rather counter-cyclical fiscal policy stance and, in particular, by high public investment. Consequently, the financial surpluses of the private sector were almost completely absorbed by corresponding public sector deficits, with only minor foreign sector deficits, and thus current account surpluses on a declining trend.

Table 8.7 Indicators for the macroeconomic policy regimes in Spain, Germany, France and Italy, average annual values for the periods 2001–09 and 2010–19

	Spain		Germany		France		Italy	
	2001–09	2010–19	2001–09	2010–19	2001–09	2010–19	2001–09	2010–19
Monetary policy								
Short-term real interest rate, per cent	−0.26	−0.31	1.87	−1.26	1.17	−0.69	0.50	−0.83
Long-term real interest rate, per cent	0.90	2.45	2.83	−0.39	2.27	0.69	1.84	2.15
Long-term real interest rate minus real GDP growth, percentage points	−1.46	1.41	2.31	−2.35	1.08	−0.66	1.66	1.93
Wage policy								
Nominal unit labour costs, annual growth, per cent	3.19	−0.26	0.93	1.73	2.15	0.85	3.32	0.78
Inflation rate (HCPI), per cent	2.92	1.26	1.67	1.41	1.87	1.28	2.30	1.26
Labour income share*, per cent	56.39	54.21	56.72	57.53	56.22	58.00	52.08	52.84
Change in labour income share from previous decade	−3.90	−2.18	−2.32	0.81	−0.87	1.78	−2.34	0.76
Fiscal policy								
Cyclically adjusted budget balance (CBR) (as percentage of potential GDP), annual change, percentage points	−0.87	0.33	0.41	0.47	−0.35	0.24	0.16	0.20
Output gap (as percentage of potential GDP), annual change, percentage points	−0.86	0.66	−0.83	0.25	−0.57	0.26	−0.75	0.17
Number of years with pro-cyclical fiscal policy (co: contractionary; ex: expansionary)	3 (3 co)	8 (4 co, 4 ex)	3 (3 co)	6 (3 co, 3 ex)	4 (2 co, 2 ex)	7 (4 co, 3 ex)	6 (3 co, 3 ex)	9 (3 co, 6 ex)
Public investment in per cent of GDP	4.35	2.63	2.11	2.26	3.95	3.70	3.13	2.48
Open economy								
Change in real effective exchange rate, vis-à-vis 37 industrial countries, per cent	2.22	−1.59	0.14	0.22	1.45	−0.58	2.71	−0.71
OEC economic complexity index	0.94	0.90	1.97	1.92	1.47	1.41	1.32	1.36
Real exports of goods and services, per cent of GDP	26.29	32.71	35.06	45.56	26.02	29.79	24.07	28.88
Real imports of goods and services, per cent of GDP	30.59	30.18	30.09	38.82	25.07	30.14	24.14	26.76

* Compensation per employee as percentage of GDP at market prices per person employed, data source: European Commission (2019a), OEC (2020), authors' calculations.

Source: Based on Hein and Martschin (2021, p. 512).

Table 8.8 *Macroeconomic policy regimes and demand and growth regimes in Spain, Germany, France and Italy for the periods 2001–09 and 2010–19*

	Spain		Germany		France		Italy	
	2001–09	2010–19	2001–09	2010–19	2001–09	2010–19	2001–09	2010–19
Monetary policy stance	+	–	–	+	–	+	–	–
Wage policy stance	–	–	–	+	+/–	–/+	–	–/+
Fiscal policy stance	+	–	+/–	–	+	–/+	–	–
Open economy conditions	–	+	0/+	0/+	–/0	0	–/0	0
Demand and growth regime	DLPD	ELM	ELM	ELM	DDL	DDL	DDL	ELM

Notes: DLPD: Debt-led private demand boom, DDL: Domestic demand-led, ELM: Export-led mercantilist.

+: Expansionary stance, –: Contractionary stance, 0: Neutral stance.

Monetary policy:

+: Negative real long-term interest rate–real GDP growth differential.

–: Positive real long-term interest rate–real GDP growth differential.

Wage policy:

+: Nominal unit labour cost growth close to ECB inflation target and rising labour income share.

–: Nominal unit labour cost growth far away from ECB inflation target and falling labour income share.

–/+: Nominal unit labour cost growth far away from ECB inflation target and rising labour income share.

+/–: Nominal unit labour cost close to ECB inflation target and falling labour income share.

Fiscal policy:

+: Counter-cyclical in many years, high public investment-GDP ratio.

–: Pro-cyclical in many years, low public investment-GDP ratio.

+/–: Counter-cyclical in many years, low public investment-GDP ratio.

–/+: Pro-cyclical in many years, high public investment-GDP ratio.

Open economy conditions:

+: Real depreciation.

–: Real appreciation, with low non-price competitiveness (complexity index).

–/0: Real appreciation, with intermediate non-price competitiveness (complexity index).

0/+: Small real appreciation, with high non-price competitiveness (complexity index).

0: Small real depreciation, with intermediate non-price competitiveness (complexity index).

Source: Based on Hein and Martschin (2021, p. 515).

276

The French demand and growth regime was not considerably altered from 2001–09 to 2010–19 and remained DDL. The macroeconomic policy regime contributed to this with an on average expansionary monetary policy stance and a slightly rising labour income share in a wage-led economy, both of which were favourable to private domestic demand. High public investments supported domestic demand whereas pro-cyclical fiscal policies were partly contractionary.

The Italian macroeconomic policy regime in the first period was very restrictive and contributed to a stagnating DDL regime. Demand was exclusively driven by private household consumption which, in the traditional bank-based Italian financial system, could not increase beyond current income levels (Gabbi et al. 2016), and by government consumption. Investment was constrained by low growth expectations and high real interest rates. Price-sensitive Italian exports, with only intermediate non-price competitiveness, suffered from real exchange rate appreciation, leading to falling net exports.

The Italian macroeconomic policy regime remained highly restrictive in the crises and post-crises period and enforced the shift in the demand and growth regime, from stagnant DDL to stagnant ELM. High real long-term interest rates and restrictive monetary conditions, pro-cyclical fiscal policies in two recessions and severe cuts of public investment constrained domestic demand in the face of stagnating household income over the whole period. Together with the improvement of international price competitiveness, this made net exports the only rising component of aggregate demand, leading to export and current account surpluses in this period and making Italy a stagnating ELM economy.

These comparative country case studies have shown that the macroeconomic policy regime has had an important impact on the emerging type of demand and growth regime and the changes in regimes after the 2007–09 crises. This impact has not only been exerted by fiscal policies, as pointed out by Hein (2019a), Hein and Martschin (2020), Hein et al. (2021) and Kohler and Stockhammer (2021), for example, but by the whole macroeconomic policy mix or regime. It is thus the combination of monetary, wage and fiscal policies, together with the open economy conditions, which has to be analysed in order to assess the role of economic policies for regime changes.

Methodologically, first, Hein and Martschin's (2021) approach supports the usefulness of the identification of demand and growth regimes according to growth contributions of the main demand components and financial balances of the macroeconomic sectors also for the post-2007–09 crises period. This allows for an understanding of the demand sources of growth (or stagnation, if there is a lack of demand), of how these sources are financed and of potential financial instabilities and fragilities which emerge as a result. Second, when it comes to the economic policy drivers of demand and growth regimes, as well as their respective changes, it has been shown that the exclusive focus on fiscal policies may be too limited and that it is the macroeconomic policy regime that matters; that is, the combination and interaction of monetary, fiscal and wage policies, as well as the open economy conditions.

These findings regarding the role of the macroeconomic policy regime for the demand and growth regimes are very much in line with Steindl's (1976, 1979) argument that economic stagnation is to a large degree the result of 'stagnation policy' (Hein 2016, 2018a, 2022b). Analysing the shift from the post-World War II 'golden age' period of modern capitalism with high growth and low unemployment towards the neo-liberal period with low growth and high unemployment since the mid-1970s, Joseph Steindl (1979) highlighted the switch towards 'stagnation policy'. He had already referred to this change in policy three years earlier: 'thus we witness stagnation not as an incomprehensible fate, as in the 1930s, but stagnation as policy' (Steindl 1976, p. xvii). In this context, Steindl (1979) refers to Kalecki's (1943b) 'Political aspects of full employment', in which Kalecki argued that, although governments might know how to maintain full employment in a capitalist economy, they will not do so, because of capitalists' opposition. Whereas in Kalecki (1943b), the opposition of the capitalist class towards full employment policies gave rise to a 'political business cycle', Steindl (1979, p. 9) argues that business opposition towards full employment policies generates a 'political trend' causing or contributing to stagnation. In his later work he related this political trend also to the increasing dominance of finance (Bhaduri and Steindl 1985, Steindl 1989).[25]

We can finally clarify the channels and the long-run effects of a restrictive macroeconomic policy regime, and thus of stagnation policy, with the help of our Kalecki-Steindl-Kaldor-Marx model shown in equations (8.10) and (8.11) and in Figure 8.9 in Section 8.4:

- Decreasing government (deficit) expenditures, that is, a fall in the government deficit and expenditure rate (δ), have a directly negative effect on long-run growth.
- Austerity policies and structural reforms weaken overall private expectations, animal spirits and firms' assessment of long-run growth (α).
- Lowering productivity enhancing public expenditures on R&D and education (k_i) weaken long-run productivity growth and private capital accumulation.
- Weakening workers' and trade unions' bargaining power through policies of labour and financial market deregulation, favouring the dominance of shareholders, abandoning aggregate demand management and accepting high rates of unemployment, each raise the total profit share (h) with a negative effect on aggregate demand, capital accumulation and growth in a wage-led economy. Only in small, very open economies or in emerging commodity exporting economies may the related real depreciation of the exchange rate (a_r) be strong enough to raise net exports sufficiently to increase total demand and growth and make the economy profit-led.
- Generating or accepting rising inequality and a higher profit share in the distribution of incomes through various channels, as well as generating higher uncertainty and thereby precautionary saving, leads to a rise in the average propensities to save out of profits and out of wages (s_Π, s_w) and thus to an increase in the aggregate propensity to save [$s = s_w + (s_\Pi - s_w)h$].
- Finally, not explicitly addressed in the model in Section 8.4 but in the post-Keynesian macroeconomic models in Chapters 4 and 5, raising real rates of interest through tight monetary policies has a negative effect on aggregate demand, if the normal case conditions prevail, and increasing the rate of interest above GDP growth will have contractionary effects in the long run.

If long-run stagnation were to be avoided, these stagnation policies would have to be reversed. The macroeconomic core of such an income-led recovery strategy would be the post-Keynesian macroeconomic policy mix outlined in Chapter 6, as can easily be compared. Several post-Keynesian authors have proposed such a macroeconomic recovery strategy after the 2007–09 crises, some of them linking it with financial market re-regulation, gender equality concerns and/or targeting government investment to the required socio-ecological transformation in the face of climate change and other ecological constraints.[26] The latter will be more closely examined in the next chapter.

NOTES

1. Epstein (2005, p. 3) famously argued in an often quoted passage that 'financialization means the increasing role of financial motives, financial markets, financial actors and financial institutions in the operation of the domestic and international economies'.
2. See also Hein (2019a, 2022a), Hein and Mundt (2012, 2013), Stockhammer (2010, 2012, 2015), van Treeck and Sturn (2012, 2013), the contributions in Hein et al. (2015, 2016) and several others
3. For detailed empirical studies supporting these different channels, see the references in Hein (2015).
4. The possibility of 'profits without investment regimes' should not come as a surprise, if Kalecki's (1954, 1972) theory of profits is applied, as we have outlined in Chapter 3.
5. For assessments, including the role of globalisation, offshoring and monopolisation for weak corporate investment, see Auvray and Rabinovich (2019), Auvray et al. (2021), Durand and Gueuder (2018), Fiebiger (2016b) and Kliman and Williams (2014).
6. See also Hein (2012a, Chapters 6 and 8, 2013, 2013/14) and Hein et al. (2012b).
7. For theoretical and empirical studies on the Global Financial Crisis, the Great Recession and also the following Eurozone crisis, see the contributions in Arestis and Sawyer (2012), Bitzenis et al. (2015), Dejuan et al. (2013), Hein et al. (2015, 2016) and Radosevic and Cvijanovic (2015), amongst several others.
8. Different allocations of countries to regimes across the studies are due to different time periods and slightly changing specifications of criteria.
9. This section draws on and further elaborates on the model structure used in Hein (2018d, Chapter 13).
10. See, for example, Belabed et al. (2018), Dallery and van Treeck (2011), Detzer (2018), Dutt (2005, 2006, 2016), Duwicquet (2020), Hein (2009, 2010, 2012a, 2012c, 2014a, Chapter 10), Kapeller and Schütz (2015), Isaac and Kim (2013), Lavoie (2008), Prante et al. (2022a), Setterfield and Kim (2016, 2017), Setterfield et al. (2016), Ryoo and Kim (2014), Ryoo and Skott (2008), Skott and Ryoo (2008), van Treeck (2009a) and Vieira Mandarino et al. (2020), amongst several others.
11. Since we ignore raw materials, there are no effects of raw material costs on domestic income distribution, other than in the open economy models in Chapters 4 and 5.
12. Most of the empirical estimations of the post-Kaleckian model find only little or no significant effects of profitability variables on investment. See Hartwig (2014) and Onaran and Galanis (2014) for recent multi-country studies and Hein (2014a, Chapter 7), Blecker (2016a) and Stockhammer (2017a) for reviews.
13. Technical change is thus assumed to be 'Harrod-neutral', as in many post-Keynesian/Kaleckian distribution and growth models (Hein 2014a, Chapter 8). While the labour-output ratio declines and labour productivity rises through technical change, the capital-potential output ratio remains constant.
14. See Hein (2014a, Chapter 7) and Hein and Vogel (2008, 2009) for a more detailed elaboration on the open economy Kaleckian distribution and growth model used here.
15. See for recent multi-country studies Hartwig (2014), Onaran and Galanis (2014) and Onaran and Obst (2016). For reviews of the results of single equations estimations studies, see Hein (2014a, Chapter 7) and Stockhammer and Onaran (2013), and for more recent reviews focussing on emerging capitalist economies, see Akcay et al. (2022) and Jimenez (2020). For comparative reviews of single equations estimation results and systems estimations with partly contradictive results, see Blecker (2016a) and Stockhammer (2017a).
16. See Onaran and Galanis (2014) for supportive estimation results showing that globally simultaneous hikes of the profit share drastically reduce potentially positive effects on net exports and thus make overall wage-led results even more likely.
17. See also the references in footnote 7.
18. See also the detailed analyses in Hein et al. (2017a, 2017b, 2018), for example.
19. See also the assessments by Piore (2016) and Streeck (2016).
20. This section draws on and further elaborates on Hein and Martschin (2021).
21. Herr and Priewe (2005, 2006), Kazandziska (2015, 2019) and Priewe and Herr (2005) have extended this approach to emerging capitalist economies, including further features, like the financial system or industrial policies.
22. See Bibow (2015), Herr (2014a) and Lavoie (2015b) on different aspects of ECB crises and post-crises policies.
23. See Hein and Truger (2009) for experiments with other indicators for the assessment of the stance of fiscal policies, using trend GDP growth as reference value for the growth of different fiscal expenditure categories.
24. See, for example, Ferreiro et al. (2016) on Spain, Detzer and Hein (2016) on Germany, Cornilleau and Creel (2016) on France and Gabbi et al. (2016) on Italy.
25. See Hein et al. (2015) for a review of the analysis of the transition towards finance-dominated capitalism in different Marxian and post-Keynesian approaches, amongst them the contributions by Josef Steindl.
26. See, for example, Arestis (2010), Cynamon and Fazzari (2010), Hein (2012a, Chapters 7–8, 2016, 2018a), Hein and Martschin (2020), Hein and Mundt (2012, 2013), Hein and Truger (2011, 2012/13), Obst et al. (2020), Onaran (2016a, 2016b), Onaran et al. (2017), Palley (2009b, 2012, Part II, 2013b, Chapters 11–12) and Pollin (2010), amongst several others.

9. Facing ecological constraints: implications and challenges for short- and long-run macroeconomic stability and macroeconomic policies

9.1 INTRODUCTION

The limits to economic growth imposed by nature have been pointed out by many authors over several decades. Already in the 1970s, the works by Daly (1973, 1974), Meadows et al. (1972) and Georgescu-Roegen (1971), for example, warned about the degradation of the earth's carrying capacity. According to these views, which became the foundations of ecological economics (Costanza 1989, Gowdy and Erickson 2005), economic activities are embedded in nature, or in the bio-physical system, and are constrained by the first and second laws of thermodynamics (the conservation of energy and the law of entropy), the complexity of intertwined natural processes and the exhaustibility of natural resources. Although some consistencies and complementarities of ecological economics with post-Keynesian economics have been pointed out by several authors some time ago, the integration of the implications of environmental constraints into post-Keynesian demand-driven macroeconomic models has only recently been attempted, as also pointed out by Rezai and Stagl (2016).

In this chapter, we will deal with some of the recent debates addressing the macroeconomic implications of ecological constraints. We will start with a review of the relationship between post-Keynesian and ecological economics. Then, we will touch on the immediately pressing problem of climate change and the required ecological transformation. In this context, concepts of de-growth and green growth will be discussed. Finally, we will touch upon the implications of low or even zero long-run growth imposed by ecological constraints for macroeconomic stability in a monetary production economy. Here the question of a growth imperative given by endogenous money and credit, positive interest rates and the requirement of positive profit rates will be examined, in particular. In this context, we will also briefly address the issue of stabilising employment in a zero-growth economy.

9.2 POST-KEYNESIAN ECONOMICS AND ECOLOGICAL ECONOMICS

Several authors have argued that post-Keynesian economics and ecological economics have some common features – both share the five pre-suppositions of heterodox economics, which we have discussed in Chapter 2 of this book. Already Bird (1982) pointed out from a post-Keynesian perspective that fundamental uncertainty undermines neoclassical environment and resource economics with its concept of inter-temporal optimisation in perfect future markets and efficient allocation of resources inter- and intra-generationally in the face of scarce and depleting resources. Berr (2009) argued that Keynes's work is consistent with sustainable development and a strong sustainability approach. Keynes's view on uncertainty is considered to be in line with a strong precautionary principle, because substitution of scarce resources and reversibility of damages cannot be generally expected due to hysteresis and path dependencies and so on. Berr (2015, p. 460) underlines this perspective and argues that 'post-Keynesian thinking, despite having rarely focussed on environmental (or more broadly, sustainable development) issues, possesses instruments that can turn it into a legitimate force in this domain'. Both, Bird (1982) and Berr (2009, 2015), also refer to the role of economic and political power, distributional issues and the role of policies when it comes to dealing with ecological constraints, with Berr (2009, 2015) pointing out the relevance of Kalecki's contributions in this respect. Gowdy (1991), from an ecological economics perspective, agrees that what he calls 'bioeconomics' and post-Keynesian economics have much in common in terms of the underlying methodological framework, the emphasis on the role of production rather than exchange and the indeterminacy of the social rate of discount, which plays a major role for inter-temporal equilibria in neoclassical environmental and resource economics. However, he points out that there are different and potentially conflicting attitudes towards growth in these two heterodox schools.

A comprehensive comparison of post-Keynesian and ecological economics has been put forward by Kronenberg (2010), concluding that there are some complementarities between these schools of thought. Whereas ecological economics has pointed out that growth of the global economy may be incompatible with improving welfare given the environmental constraints, the post-Keynesian approaches have analysed the determination and the dynamics of growth in a capitalist, monetary production economy. According to Kronenberg, both approaches can be synthesised, because they already show several similarities in basic concepts.[1] He focuses on four areas: Production and pricing theory, consumption theory, economic dynamics and economic policy.

Regarding production and pricing, Kronenberg (2010) argues that both heterodox schools reject the aggregate neoclassical production function and its properties (continuous substitution between capital, labour and land, relative marginal productivities determining relative factor prices, no relevance of intermediate products). Instead ecological and post-Keynesian economics rely on fixed coefficient/Leontief-type production functions with constant input-output ratios for a given technology in the short run. Post-Keynesian theory of production is thus considered to be consistent with the laws of nature – an increase in output requires an increase in intermediate inputs, given by the short-run constant input-output ratios. Of course, due to technical change, input-output ratios may change over time, but the laws of thermodynamics are always respected. Prices are assumed to be determined by costs of production – and hence include an impact of energy used in production – and show no direct responses to changes in demand.[2]

With regard to consumption theory, referring to Lavoie (2009c), Kronenberg (2010) points out that both post-Keynesian and ecological economics reject the hyper-rational utility maximising *homo economicus* from neoclassical economics and argue that, under the conditions of fundamental uncertainty, individuals apply procedural rationality and show satisficing behaviour. Consumer behaviour is thus driven by habits and conventions. Substitution guided by relative scarcities is downgraded, and fundamental uncertainty also requires the precautionary principle, which is highlighted in ecological economics, in particular.

Concerning economic dynamics, Kronenberg (2010) underlines that post-Keynesian theory is inherently dynamic, as has become clear in the distribution and growth theory after Keynes, built on the contributions by Harrod (1939), Kaldor (1957), Kalecki (1954) and Joan Robinson (1956). As we have also pointed out in Chapters 2 and 7 of this book, a major message of these approaches is that growth is demand determined and path dependent. According to Kronenberg (2010), this is consistent with the notion of irreversibility and the rise of entropy in ecological economics. Ecological economics could thus be linked with post-Keynesian macroeconomics, first, because of the elementary link between distribution and growth, and second, because of the importance of fundamental uncertainty, irreversibility and path dependence.

With regard to economic policies, this implies that government intervention is required to stabilise the long-run growth rate, according to Kronenberg (2010). In ecological economics growth has to be made consistent with ecological constraints, in post-Keynesian economics with full employment. For a synthesis, on the one hand, post-Keynesians have to become aware that there are ecological issues and constraints to take into account when designing full employment policies, as has already been pointed out by Robinson (1972), Eichner and Kregel (1975), and Schefold (1985). Full employment policies would have to be linked with policies tackling climate change and energy security, for example. Ecological economists, on the other hand, have to take into account the macroeconomic and employment implications of environmentally consistent GDP growth, which in their view may mean zero growth or even de-growth.

While some consistencies of post-Keynesian and ecological economics have been accepted for a while, the integration of ecological constraints into post-Keynesian demand-led macroeconomic models has only accelerated recently. Fontana and Sawyer (2013, 2014, 2016) provide important conceptual attempts in this respect, making use of monetary circuit and post-Keynesian growth theory. They present a simple post-Kaleckian demand-led growth model and distinguish the warranted growth rate, that is, the growth rate which keeps the goods market equilibrium output and capacity utilisation at the firms' targets, and the full employment growth rate from the growth rate allowed by a sustainable 'ecological footprint'.[3] They argue that these growth rates are independent of each other and that there are no automatic adjustments that align them. Since achieving an ecologically sustainable growth rate will require major adjustments of the growth in the capital stock and the effective labour force, economic policy interventions will be crucial for the transition towards ecological sustainability. Several ecological macroeconomic models with post-Keynesian features and post-Keynesian macroeconomic models with ecological considerations have been developed during the last decade, and we will touch upon some of them in the context of the following sections.

9.3   GREEN GROWTH, ZERO GROWTH OR DE-GROWTH TO FIGHT CLIMATE CHANGE?

The urgency of a socio-ecological transition in the face of climate change is broadly recognised in academic research, and it has become a top priority on the international political agenda, as has become clear with the Paris Agreement 2015, attempting to limit global warming to well below 2°C, preferably to 1.5°C compared to pre-industrial levels (UN 2015). According to the IPCC (2018), the global net carbon dioxide (CO_2) emissions will have to fall by about 45 per cent by 2030 and to zero by 2050 in order to reach a maximum global mean temperature increase of 1.5°C by 2100. However, the ideas and proposals concerning how to reach these goals vary a lot. Several approaches assume – or trust in – the possibility of decoupling economic growth from negative environmental impact by stimulating green investments and green growth, like the European Green Deal (European Commission 2019b) or the OECD Green Growth Strategy (OECD 2015). Others are sceptical and argue that a non-growing or even a de-growing economy is necessary if we are to achieve ecological sustainability (Jackson 2017, Victor 2008). Largely influenced by the work by Daly (1973, 1996), who presents the concept of a stationary state economy, zero-growth and de-growth proponents, like Hickel (2019), Hickel and Kallis (2020), Kallis (2011), Kallis et al. (2012) and Mastini et al. (2021), suggest that in order to meet ambitious ecological targets, we will need to go through a process of sustainable de-growth. This involves the downscaling of material throughput, that is, a decrease of material production and consumption that will most likely lead to stagnant or shrinking real GDP. However, the latter is considered to be not necessarily problematic, because it is claimed that real GDP is not a good indicator for social welfare, human development and well-being for many reasons. For example, real GDP excludes several welfare enhancing activities (i.e. private care work), on the one hand, and it includes repair costs of destruction as positive contributions (i.e. repair of environmental or war damages), on the other hand. Furthermore, fair or equal distribution seems to be more important for human well-being and happiness than the level of real GDP.

While all these are valid concerns, we hold that real GDP is nonetheless a good indicator for the level of economic activity and employment in a monetary production economy, as are wage and profit shares in GDP for income distribution. Therefore, it is important to analyse the relationship between greenhouse gas emissions and real GDP, on the one hand, and to study the macroeconomic effects of de-growth and examine its stability, on the other hand. However, such analyses are missing in some of the de-growth contributions mentioned above.

The relationship of CO_2 emissions and real GDP can be shown, making use of an extension of the Kaya identity (Kaya and Yokoburi 1997). We start with the relationship between real GDP (Y), the use of energy (J) and the related CO_2 and other greenhouse gas emissions (E):

$$E = \frac{E}{J}\frac{J}{Y}Y = qjY,$$

(9.1)

with q for the CO_2-energy ratio, the carbon footprint of the use of energy, and j for the energy-real GDP ratio, the energy intensity of real GDP. For the respective growth rates, we have:

$$\hat{E} = \hat{q} + \hat{j} + \hat{Y}.$$

(9.2)

The reduction in CO_2 emissions can thus be achieved by a reduction in the carbon footprint of energy and in the energy intensity of real GDP, that is, by green technological change and/or by a reduction in real GDP. Proponents of green growth assume that CO_2 emissions can be reduced to zero by significant reductions in the carbon footprint and in the energy intensity, such that real GDP does not have to shrink, but may even rise. We would thus see absolute decoupling of emissions and real GDP. De-growth proponents do not share this technology optimism and hold that real GDP will have to fall in order to reduce CO_2 emissions. Mastini et al. (2021), for example, suggest a 'Green New Deal without growth'. As with green growth proponents, de-growth proponents also support public investments and industrial policies for a green energy transition but argue that reaching the IPCC targets also requires lower real GDP and hence de-growth in terms of GDP.

The relationship between real GDP, population (P), labour force (L), employment (N) and hours worked (H) is given in the following way:

$$Y = \frac{Y}{H} \frac{H}{N} \frac{N}{L} \frac{L}{P} P = ynelP, \tag{9.3}$$

with y as labour productivity per hour worked, n as hours worked per person, e as the employment rate and l as the labour force participation rate. For the respective growth rates we have:

$$\hat{Y} = \hat{y} + \hat{n} + \hat{e} + \hat{l} + \hat{P}. \tag{9.4}$$

By definition, therefore, real GDP can thus fall

- through a decline in productivity, that is, through sectoral change towards more labour intensive sectors of production with lower labour productivity, usually towards green industries and service sectors,
- through a decline in hours worked per person, that is, through shortening daily, weekly, monthly or annual working time,
- through a decline in the employment rate, that is, an increase in the unemployment rate,
- through a decline in the labour force participation rate, that is, through longer periods of education and earlier retirements or through the exclusions of certain groups from the labour market, or
- through a fall in population.

Substituting equation (9.4) into equation (9.2) shows all the logical possibilities by means of which CO_2 emissions can be reduced:

$$\hat{E} = \hat{q} + \hat{j} + \hat{y} + \hat{n} + \hat{e} + \hat{l} + \hat{P}. \tag{9.5}$$

Macroeconomic de-growth or zero-growth scenarios have been modelled by Victor (2012) and Jackson and Victor (2020) for the Canadian economy, for example. Victor (2012) provides, amongst others, a stable de-growth scenario in a demand-driven model with a neoclassical aggregate production function and without fully modelling the financial sector. In this scenario, over a 30-years period from 2005 to 2035, greenhouse gas emissions fall by 80 per cent and GDP per capita falls by 40 per cent to the level of 1976. This is mainly achieved through a cut of working time by 70 per cent, which allows unemployment to stay roughly stable. The other exogenous drivers of such a de-growth scenario are population growth, which is assumed to be zero, government expenditures, which fall by 50 per cent, and a significant rise in carbon taxes, which lowers the emission intensity of real GDP through incentives for technical change towards green technologies.

Jackson and Victor (2020) present a stock-flow consistent (SFC) macroeconomic simulation model for Canada, based on the theoretical SFC approach by Godley and Lavoie (2007), which therefore also models stock-flow interactions in the monetary and financial sector. In the model, higher labour productivity increases real wages, which then increases consumption leading to a kind of growth imperative. Again, working time reduction per person is used to reduce GDP growth and to maintain employment. The authors present a carbon reduction scenario in which green investments (in renewable energies and the electrification of transport) are introduced to reduce Canada's carbon emissions. A sustainable prosperity scenario then assumes a constant population, a decline of working hours per person and significant transfer payments to mitigate inequality, on top of green investment. This sustainable stability scenario generates constant real GDP for a 50-years period, from 2017 to 2067, and achieves zero net carbon emission by 2040. Government debt-GDP ratios slightly rise but then stabilise.

Pollin (2018) remains rather critical of de-growth or even zero-growth strategies to bring CO_2 emissions down to zero fast enough at the global scale. Rather, he proposes green growth, at least during a long transition period. The overwhelming factor pushing emissions down should be massive growth in energy efficiency and clean renewable energy investments. This would raise GDP somewhat but bring down the emissions-GDP ratio ($E/Y = qj$). He claims that, between 2000 and 2014, 21 countries, including the USA, Germany, the UK, Spain and Sweden, managed to absolutely decouple GDP growth from CO_2 emissions. To generalise this for the world economy, Pollin (2018) proposes a Green New Deal, a worldwide programme to invest between 1.5 and 2 per cent of global GDP every year in energy efficiency (in the stock of buildings, automobiles and public transportation systems) and clean renewable energy supplies (solar, wind, biomass). According to his calculations, this would allow global CO_2 emissions to be reduced by 40 per cent within 20 years and also living standards and employment to be raised. Following this global strategy, within 40 to 50 years, CO_2 emissions could be eliminated altogether. Pollin (2021) links such a strategy with active industrial policies and argues that investment in energy efficiency and renewable energies of even 2.5 per cent of global GDP per year between 2024 and 2050 would bring down CO_2 emissions to zero at the end of this 25-years period. Pollin (2020) argues that the European Green Deal (European Commission 2019b) is basically in line with such a strategy but needs to be scaled up massively.

Priewe (2022) is also critical of zero-growth or de-growth strategies to achieve the Paris goals. His analysis shows that since 1990 emerging economies (including China and India, of course) have been the key contributors to greenhouse gas emissions. Similar to Pollin (2018), Priewe's different scenarios of a global transition towards zero CO_2 emissions show that the reduction of the emissions-GDP ratio is far more important than reducing real GDP growth. Zero growth per se is thus not considered to be effective in terms of reaching the Paris goals. Priewe rather advocates low green growth, and in the long run even zero growth, for the global North and moderate green growth for the global South as an economic policy orientation.

But what are the effective economic policy instruments for green growth? Dafermos et al. (2017) have developed a stock-flow-fund ecological macroeconomic model, which combines the SFC approach of Godley and Lavoie (2007) with the flow-fund model of Georgescu-Roegen (1971). The model was estimated and calibrated using global data. Based on this model, Dafermos and Nikolaidi (2019) have examined different green fiscal policy options for the ecological transition: Carbon taxes, green subsidies and green public investment. They show that carbon taxes reduce emissions and global warming, but they increase financial instability, because they have a negative effect on firms' profitability and hence also their access to credit. Green subsidies to the private sector and green public investment improve ecological efficiency. However, their positive environmental effects are partially offset by their macroeconomic rebound effects via the investment-GDP multiplier, which raises output and emissions, as also pointed out by Rezai et al. (2013). Therefore, Dafermos and Nikolaidi (2019) recommend a green fiscal policy mix of carbon taxes and green investments, which provide better overall outcomes.

Dafermos et al. (2018) have also made use of the Dafermos et al. (2017) stock-flow-fund ecological macroeconomic model and have analysed the effects of climate change on financial stability. Furthermore, they have evaluated the effects of green quantitative easing (QE) policies of central banks. They find that climate change affects financial asset prices and the financial position of firms and banks. By destroying firms' capital and reducing their profitability, climate change reduces the liquidity position of firms, increases the rates of default, lowers the prices of corporate bonds and thus raises interest rates. This increases financial instability in the economy, with negative effects on credit generation and overall economic activity. Green corporate QE policies of central banks can help to reduce climate change-induced financial instability, stimulate green investment and contribute to restricting CO_2 emissions and global warming. Its effectiveness, however, will depend on the interest rate elasticity of green investments.

Green fiscal policies as the core of any Green New Deal, accompanied by green QE policies of central banks, have obvious links with the post-Keynesian macroeconomic policy mix, which we have developed in Chapter 6, and with alternative macroeconomic policy regimes and recovery strategies after the recent crises, which we have pointed out in Chapter 8. However, distributional issues would have to be included in such a Green New Deal as well. Chancel and Piketty (2015) and Ivanova and Wood (2020), for example, have shown that the CO_2 and other greenhouse gas emissions are concentrated at the top end of personal or household income distribution. Chancel and Piketty (2015) in their global analysis find that the top 1 per cent richest Americans, Luxemburgers, Singaporeans and Saudi Arabians are the highest individual CO_2 emitters in the world. They conclude that the within-country inequality in CO_2 emissions matters more and more to explain the global dispersion of CO_2 emissions. Ivanova and Wood (2020) in their study on the EU show that the top 1 per cent of EU households have the highest per capita carbon footprint. The top 10 per cent of the population account for 27 per cent of the EU carbon footprint, which is much higher than that of the bottom 50 per cent of the population. This is, to a large degree, caused by the emissions related to individual mobility and transport, in particular flights. Income distribution and the related consumption patterns thus matter a lot when it comes to explaining CO_2 emissions, and they have to be taken into account in ecological transformation policies. Further research in this area seems to be required.

9.4   CAN ZERO GROWTH BE STABLE IN A MONETARY PRODUCTION ECONOMY?[4]

9.4.1   Some Views on the Feasibility of Zero Growth

Although there are different views on how to cope with the current and pressing problem of climate change, it is clear and broadly agreed that in the long run environmental constraints will require lower and maybe even zero growth of real GDP. This is true even if climate change can be stopped by a timely and successful reduction of CO_2 emissions to zero, because other ecological constraints, like the depletion of exhaustible resources, the limits of sinks and so on, may then become binding. The question thus arises whether stable zero growth in a monetary production economy with endogenous credit generation, positive interest and profit rates is possible at all. According to Fontana and Sawyer (2022), a zero-growth economy would have to resolve the following issues. The first is concerned with bringing net investment down to zero. The second relates to the issue of whether zero growth is compatible with positive profits and hence with capitalism. The third relates to the relationship between zero growth, endogenous credit and positive interest rates, and the stability of the financial system. Here the question of a growth imperative given by a positive rate of interest arises. Fourth, the question of full employment in a stationary economy with productivity growth arises. We will address all these questions in the current section.

Some de-growth proponents are rather sceptical whether de-growth or even a stationary economy are possible within a capitalist system (Berend Blauwhof 2012, Kallis 2011, Kallis et al. 2012). Specifically, it is argued that growth is a systemic requirement of capitalism, either because of an inherent pressure on capitalists to accumulate, as claimed in Marxian theory (Harvey 2007), or because of a growth imperative exerted by endogenous credit and a positive interest rate, as derived in some Keynesian-inspired theory (Binswanger 2009). Richters and Siemoneit (2019) provide a systematic and instructive discussion about growth imperatives and growth drivers, which goes beyond our macroeconomic discussion in this chapter.

From a macroeconomic perspective, several authors have tried to single out the conditions for a stationary economy in a systematic way. Lange (2018) analyses the conditions for sustainable economies without growth in different theories. He concludes that post-Keynesian theory can be compatible with zero growth. In a scenario with technological change, reductions in working hours and compensatory wage increases are found to be necessary to avoid rising unemployment. Furthermore, positive profits must be matched with a sufficiently high level of consumption out of profits. Consumption out of profits and out of wages must equal overall income, which in other words means that saving must be equal to zero. However, his study does not include any analysis of the conditions under which such a stationary economy is dynamically stable.

Rosenbaum (2015) tackles the issue of stable zero growth and technological progress using a Kaleckian model with fixed capital costs. Prices are set as a mark-up over unit total costs, which is problematic because unit fixed capital costs, and thus unit total costs, vary with the level of output. Target rate of return pricing would thus be an adequate approach. He introduces depreciation and discusses different cases for zero growth and its stability. However, as shown by Monserand (2020), there are several inconsistencies in the model, which mean that, overall, Rosenbaum (2015) is not proving what he claims, that is, the consistency of positive profits with stable zero growth under certain circumstances.

Monserand (2019) provides a more convincing approach of discussing zero or de-growth in a basic neo-Kaleckian distribution and growth model. He analyses the possibility of an equilibrium with a zero or negative rate of accumulation while keeping the Keynesian goods market equilibrium stability condition. He shows that the integration of autonomous consumption and/or government deficits allow for a stable goods market equilibrium with zero investment but positive profits. However he only focuses on the existence and stability of the goods market equilibrium without looking at the financial side and the related issue of financial stability in long-run dynamics.

Analysing the viability of positive interest rates in a stationary economy, Berg et al. (2015) combine an SFC model with an input-output approach. They show that an equilibrium, that is, constant stock-flow ratios, is possible, depending on the parameters regarding the propensity to consume out of wealth and the rate of interest on deposits, which is the only income from financial assets received by households, who also receive all the firms' profits. In their model, the government runs a balanced budget. This is also the case in Cahen-Fourot and Lavoie (2016), who consider an SFC model for a stationary economy and an endogenous determination of debt in the stationary state in order to show that models with credit-money and positive interest rates are compatible with a stationary economy. They show the latter is possible through the balancing of saving out of income with consumption out of wealth. Similarly, Jackson and Victor (2015) also find that a minimum consumption out of wealth is required for a stationary state in their SFC model with a more differentiated banking sector, including a central bank and commercial banks. However, in Cahen-Fourot and Lavoie (2016), the dynamic adjustment towards the stationary state is not considered, while Berg et al. (2015) and Jackson and Victor (2015) provide numerical robustness checks but no general stability analysis.

Richters and Siemoneit (2017) have clarified in their review of several models that a stationary state with positive profits and interest rates is only possible under the condition that each sector is running neither financial deficits nor surpluses.[5] The latter means that there are no retained profits in the corporate sector, that there are balanced government budgets and that saving out of household income is compensated for by consumption out of wealth or some other autonomous consumption – in an open economy we would also need a current account balance. Only under these conditions will the ratios of financial assets or liabilities to income (or the capital stock) remain constant and thus prevent systemic financial fragility and instability, that is, ever rising debt-income ratios of the deficit sectors. However, Richters and Siemoneit (2017) also do not examine the dynamic stability of a zero-growth equilibrium.

Building on the conditions pointed out by Richters and Siemoneit (2017), Hein and Jimenez (2022) have clarified in a stepwise process, starting with national income accounting and a monetary circuit approach for a closed economy without technical change, that a stationary state is compatible with positive profits, endogenous credit and a positive interest rate. In a Kaleckian distribution and growth model driven by autonomous government demand, they have then examined the conditions under which a stationary equilibrium is dynamically stable. We will follow their three-step approach and then add some considerations about the issue of technical change, productivity growth and full employment in a stationary economy at the end.

9.4.2   An Accounting Perspective on Zero Growth

For a stationary goods market equilibrium, effective demand must be sufficient to generate and reproduce stationary output over time. From national income accounting, output (Y_p), here net of depreciation, is given as the sum of private consumption out of rentiers' income (C_R) and out of wages (C_W), government consumption expenditures (G), net investment (I), revenues from exports of goods and services (Ex) minus expenditures on imports of goods and services (Im), all variables in real terms:

$$Y_p = C_R + C_W + G + I + Ex - Im. \tag{9.6}$$

It is assumed that depreciations are re-invested, so that the focus can be on output and income net of depreciations. For total income (Y), government interest payments to rentiers ($R_{GR} = iB_{GR}$) are included, with B_{GR} for the stock of government debt and i for the rate of interest on that debt. This income has to be added to the income generated in production, which is equal to the sum of total wages (W) and total profits ($\Pi = \Pi_F + R_{FR}$). Profits from production are the sum of retained profits (Π_F) and distributed profits (including interest and dividends) equal to rentiers' income from firms (R_{FR}). Assuming that both wages and profits are taxed, wages can be split into net wages and taxes on wages ($W = W^{net} + T_W$), retained profits into net retained profits and taxes on retained profits ($\Pi_F^T = \Pi_F^{net} + T_F$), rentiers' income from firms into their net income from firms and taxes on that income ($R_{FR} = R_{FR}^{net} + T_{FR}$) and rentiers' income from the government into net interest revenues from the government and taxes on these revenues ($R_{GR} = R_{GR}^{net} + T_{GR}$). Rentiers' total net income is $R^{net} = R_{FR}^{net} + R_{GR}^{net} = R_{FR} - T_{FR} + R_{GR} - T_{GR}$, and rentiers' total tax payments are $T_R = T_{FR} + T_{GR}$. For total income it thus obtained:

$$Y = Y_P + iB_{GR} = I + C_R + C_W + G + iB_{GR} + Ex - Im = \Pi_F + R_{FR} + R_{GR} + W$$

$$= \Pi_F^{net} + T_F + R_{FR}^{net} + T_{FR} + R_{GR}^{net} + T_{GR} + W^{net} + T_W = \Pi_F^{net} + R^{net} + W^{net} + T. \tag{9.7}$$

From this, it follows for the sectoral financial balances:

$$\Pi_F^{net} - I + R^{net} - C_R + W^{net} - C_W + T_W + T_F + T_R - G - iB_{GR} + Im - Ex$$

$$= FB_F + FB_R + FB_W + FB_G + FB_E = 0. \tag{9.8}$$

with $FB_F = \Pi_F^{net} - I$ as the corporate financial balance, $FB_R = S_R = R^{net} - C_R$ as the rentiers' households financial balance, equivalent to saving out of rentiers' income, $FB_W = S_W = W^{net} - C_W$ as the workers' households financial balance, equivalent to saving out of wages, $FB_G = T_W + T_F + T_R - G - iB_{GR} = T - G - iB_{GR}$ as the government financial balance, and $FB_E = Im - Ex$ as the foreign/external sector financial balance.

For a stationary economy at some target level of output ($Y_{P,I=0}^T$) zero net investment is required, that is, I = 0. For such an economy to be financially stable, the financial balances of the different macroeconomic sectors should each be balanced at the stationary target level of output to avoid ever-rising debt-income ratios of any sector. Otherwise, some sectors would continuously build up financial assets over time whereas others would accumulate the counterpart financial liabilities. Rising financial assets-income ratios, as well as increasing financial liabilities-income ratios, would be the consequence, violating the condition for financial stability of a stationary economy. For equation (9.8), this implies that saving out of net rentiers' income and out of net wages have each to be zero ($S_R = S_W = 0$), governments will have to run a balanced budget ($T - G - iB_{GR} = 0$)[6] and net exports and hence the current account have to be equal to zero, too (Ex − Im = 0). This implies that equation (9.7) becomes:

$$Y = Y_{P,I=0}^T + iB_{GR} = C_R + C_W + G + iB_{GR} = R_{FR} + R_{GR} + W$$

$$= R_{FR}^{net} + T_{FR} + R_{GR}^{net} + T_{GR} + W^{net} + T_W = R^{net} + W^{net} + T. \tag{9.9}$$

Since retained profits are zero, taxes are now given as the sum of taxes on rentiers' income and taxes on wages $(T = T_R + T_W)$. The condition of zero financial balances of each financial sector also implies:

$$C_R = R^{net} = R^{net}_{FR} + R^{net}_{GR} = \Pi^{net} + \left(iB_{GR}\right)^{net}. \tag{9.10}$$

It can therefore be concluded that a zero-growth economy is consistent with positive net profits and a positive rate of interest, if rentiers' consumption is positive. In other words, positive profits and a positive rate of interest do not require a growing economy from this accounting perspective.

9.4.3   Zero Growth in a Monetary Circuit Model

Fontana and Sawyer (2013, 2014, 2016) have already indicated the usefulness of the monetary circuit approach for the examination of the role of credit and interest in a stationary economy. Hein and Jimenez (2022) have then provided an explicit analysis. The literature on and the basic features of the monetary circuit approach have already been presented in Chapter 3 of this book. It should be remembered that this approach is firmly based on endogenous credit money. A key feature is the ability of the banking sector to create credit money. Expenditures can only take place if the economic agent is able to finance such expenditure, that is, if the agent has access to credit money, which can be generated by the banking sector 'out of nothing'.

Hein and Jimenez (2022) make use of a simple model of a pure credit economy for a closed economy without a central bank and hence without central bank money. The model economy is composed of five sectors, as shown in the balance sheet matrix in Table 9.1. The commercial banking sector is able to generate short-term credit (B^S), as well as to grant long-term credit (B). Other sectors may hold deposits with the banking sector. Such deposits are the most liquid financial asset in the model economy. It is assumed that the interest rate on short-term credit and deposits is zero and that any interest on long-term credit received by banks is immediately transferred to the rentiers as the owners of the banks. The second sector is a firm sector whose capital stock (K) is long-term financed by equity held by shareholders/rentiers (E_R) and by the firms themselves as accumulated retained earnings (E_F). The firm sector thus does not issue debt and is not financing its capital stock by long-term credit. The government sector is the indebted sector in the model and has issued long-term bonds in the past, which

Table 9.1   *Balance sheet matrix for a zero-growth closed economy without a central bank*

	Workers' households	Rentiers' households	Firms	Government	Banks	Σ
Deposits		$+D_R$			$-D_R$	0
Loans		$+B_{GR}$		$-(B_{GR} + B_{GB})$	$+B_{GB}$	0
Equity		$+E_R$	$-E_R$			
Capital			K			K
Σ	0	$+E_R + B_{GR} + D_R$	$+E_F$	$-(B_{GR} + B_{GB})$	0	$K = E_F + E_R$

are held by rentiers (B_{GR}) and by banks (B_{GB}). The rentiers' households hold equity issued by the firms and long-term bonds issued by the government and may also hold deposits with the banks (D_R). The workers' households do not hold any assets nor issue liabilities. The stock accounting consistency requires:

$$K = E_F + E_R. \tag{9.11}$$

For a zero-growth equilibrium economy, with zero net investment ($I=0$) and with initial government debt, inherited from past positive growth periods, and thus interest payments of the government to the rentiers ($iB_G = iB_{GR} + iB_{GB}$), the accounting equation (9.9) for income and expenditures holds again.

Furthermore, the prevention of systemic financial stability requires that the financial balances of each sector have to be equal to zero. This means that retained profits of the firm sector are zero and the rentiers receive all the profits as dividends. Saving out of workers' and out of rentiers' income needs to be zero, too. This means that workers and rentiers have to spend their net income after taxes for consumption goods. Furthermore, the government will have to run a balanced budget.

Figure 9.1 shows the four phases of the monetary circuit for a zero-growth economy with initial government debt, where F represents firms, Gov the government, HH_R rentiers' households and HH_W workers' households. In the first phase of the circuit, short-term initial finance (with no interest rate being charged on such finance) is provided by the banks to the firms (B_F^s) and to the government (B_G^s). The initial finance for firms consists of wages (W) and profits/dividends (Π) to be paid in advance to workers' and rentiers' households ($B_F^s = W + \Pi$). The initial finance for the governments consists of planned government consumption expenditures (G) plus government interest payments on the stock of debt to the rentiers ($B_G^s = G + iB_G$).

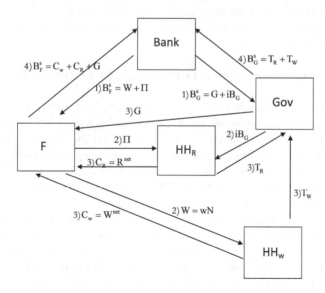

Figure 9.1   A monetary circuit for a zero-growth closed economy with a government, without a central bank and without interest on initial finance

The initial finance allows income payments to be made in advance to the rentiers' and workers' households in the second phase. These include the interest payments from the government to the rentiers (iB_G), the profits/dividends from the firms to the rentiers (Π) and wages paid by firms, which are equal to the nominal wage rate multiplied by the number of employees ($W = wN$).

Income received then allows for expenditures in the third phase (i.e. the reflux phase). Rentiers and workers pay taxes (T_R, T_w) to the government and spend their net incomes on consumption goods ($C_R = R^{net}, C_w = W^{net}$). The government now also spends its initial finance on government consumption (G).

The expenditures in the third phase make sure that the firms and the government receive the funds which enable them in the fourth phase to repay initial finance and hence short-term credit to the banks and thus to close the circuit. In the course of the monetary circuit, profits of firms are realised and a positive interest rate on government debt is also consistent with a stable stationary economy. Endogenous credit creation (and destruction) with positive interest rates and profits is thus possible in a stationary economy and, as such, does not impose a growth bias on the economy.

Table 9.2 presents the transaction flow matrix for our simple zero-growth economy. It displays the transactions between different sectors within a period and reflects the structure of the national accounting system. The top eight rows represent output and income from the spending and income approach and show for each sector zero net saving. The lower part represents the changes in financial assets and liabilities, the sum of which for each sector also has to be zero in a stable stationary economy, in which no sector should build up financial assets or liabilities. Of course, the portfolio structure of each sector may change, within the constraints given by consistent accounting. For example, if liquidity preference of the rentiers' household rises and they prefer to hold more deposits instead of government bonds, this implies (given a constant net asset position) that they have to reduce credit granted to the government while banks increase their long-term credit to the government. In other words, in a stable zero-growth economy, portfolio shifts are possible as long as net saving of each sector remains zero.

9.4.4   An Autonomous Demand-Led Growth Model with Zero Growth

In order to analyse the dynamic stability of a zero-growth equilibrium, Hein and Jimenez (2022) apply a Kaleckian distribution and growth model driven by autonomous government expenditure growth, as initially developed by Hein (2018c) and then modified by Hein and Woodgate (2021). We introduced the autonomous demand-led growth models, or the Sraffian supermultiplier models, and the integration of autonomous demand growth into Kaleckian distribution and growth models in Chapter 7 of this book. There, further references on this approach and also its discussion and critique can be found.

The dynamic model by Hein and Jimenez (2022) is a closed economy one-good model, as the ones we have used in previous chapters of this book. It is built on the closed economy model structure presented in the previous sections. To simplify the model, only taxes on capital income are considered. The model structure can thus also be presented by the balance sheet matrix in Table 9.1, ignoring deposits, and by the transaction flow matrix in Table 9.2, ignoring taxes on wages and potential changes in the portfolio composition in the lower part of that table.

Table 9.2 *Transaction flow matrix for a zero-growth closed economy without a central bank*

	Workers' households	Rentiers' households	Firms' current	Firms' capital	Government	Banks	Σ
Taxes	$-T_W$	$-T_R$			$+T_W + T_R$		0
Government consumption			$+G$		$-G$		0
Consumption	$-C_W$	$-C_R$	$+C_W + C_R$				0
Investment							0
Wages	$+W$		$-W$				0
Retained profits							0
Distributed profits/dividends		$+\Pi$	$-\Pi$				0
Interest payments		$+R_G$			$-R_G$		0
Σ	0	0	0	0	0	0	
Change in deposits		$-/+dD_R$				$+/-dD_R$	0
Change in loans		$-/+dB_{GR}$			$+/-B_{GR}$ $+/-B_{GB}$	$-/+dB_{GB}$	0
Change in equity		$-/+dE_R$		$+/-dE_F$			0
Σ	0	0	0	0	0	0	0

293

In the short run, defined by given government expenditures- and government debt-capital ratios, the model may generate a goods market equilibrium with positive capital accumulation and saving-capital ratios. In the long run, however, when government expenditures- and government debt-capital ratios become endogenous, the model converges towards the autonomous growth rate of government expenditures, which is set equal to zero. Hein and Jimenez (2022) examine the conditions under which this long-run convergence will lead to stable equilibria for government expenditures – and government debt-capital ratios – and thus to a stable stationary economy with positive profits and a positive rate of interest.

In the model, the pre-tax profit share in production ($h = \Pi/Y_p$) is determined by mark-up pricing of firms in an oligopolistic goods market. With given institutional conditions in the goods market, prices are constant, and the price level can be set at $p = 1$, such that nominal and real variables coincide. Since retained earnings in a stable stationary economy have to be zero, rentiers receive all the profits from production (hY_p) as dividends and the interest paid by the government on the stock of debt, either directly or indirectly via the banks they own ($iB_G = iB_{GR} + iB_{GB}$). It is assumed that workers do not save. Only rentiers save a fraction of their net income after taxes $[(1 - t_R)(hY_p + iB_G)]$, with a given tax rate (t_R), according to their propensity to save (s_R). Furthermore, they consume a fraction of their wealth ($B_G + K$) according to their propensity to consume out of wealth (c_{RW}), which in effect lowers their saving out of current income accordingly. Normalising all variables by the firms' capital stock, such that we have a rate of capacity utilisation ($u = Y_p/K$), a government debt-capital ratio ($\lambda = B_G/K$), a profit rate in production ($r = \Pi/K = hu$), the saving-capital ratio and hence the saving rate ($\sigma = S/K$) is given as:

$$\sigma = s_R\left(1 - t_R\right)\left(hu + i\lambda\right) - c_{RW}\left(1 + \lambda\right)$$

$$= s_R\left(1 - t_R\right)hu + \lambda\left[is_R\left(1 - t_R\right) - c_{RW}\right] - c_{RW}, \quad (9.12)$$

$$1 \geq s_R > 0, \ c_{RW} \geq 0.$$

Firms adjust the capital stock via net investment (I) according to the expected trend rate of growth of output and sales (α), which determines their animal spirits, such that potential output given by the capital stock grows in line with expected demand. They will slow down (accelerate) the rate of capital accumulation ($g = I/K$) whenever the actual rate of capacity utilisation falls short of (exceeds) the normal or the target rate of utilisation (u_n):

$$g = \alpha + \beta\left(u - u_n\right), \ \beta > 0. \quad (9.13)$$

Government expenditures (G) for goods and services, that is, government consumption, grow at a constant rate γ and drive the model. The government expenditures-capital ratio ($\delta = G/K$) is given as:

$$\delta = \frac{G_0 e^{\gamma t}}{K}. \quad (9.14)$$

Since it is assumed that only rentiers' income is taxed, the tax-capital ratio ($\tau = T/K$) is given by:

$$\tau = t_R \left(hu + i\lambda \right), \quad 1 > t_R \geq 0. \tag{9.15}$$

The balanced budget condition required for stable long-run zero growth, which is assumed to hold also for the short run, is given as:

$$\tau = t_R \left(hu + i\lambda \right) = \delta + i\lambda. \tag{9.16}$$

In a stationary economy with a stock of government debt inherited from the past and a positive rate of interest to be paid on that debt, governments thus need a primary surplus in order to run a balanced budget.

9.4.4.1 Short-run equilibrium

In the short run, firms will vary capacity utilisation to adjust output to demand, with given government expenditures- and debt-capital ratios. With a balanced government budget, the goods market equilibrium is given by:

$$\sigma + \tau = g + \delta + i\lambda \quad \Rightarrow \quad \sigma = g. \tag{9.17}$$

The Keynesian/Kaleckian stability condition for the short-run goods market equilibrium is:

$$\frac{\partial \sigma}{\partial u} - \frac{\partial g}{\partial u} > 0 \quad \Rightarrow \quad s_R \left(1 - t_R \right) h - \beta > 0. \tag{9.18}$$

From equations (9.12), (9.13), (9.14), (9.16) and (9.17), the short-run goods market equilibrium rate of capacity utilisation with a balanced government budget is obtained:

$$u^* = \frac{\alpha - \beta u_n + c_{RW} + \left[c_{RW} - s_R \left(1 - t_R \right) i \right] \lambda}{s_R \left(1 - t_R \right) h - \beta}. \tag{9.19}$$

The corresponding short-run equilibrium values for the rate of profit and the rate of accumulation are:

$$r^* = hu^* = \frac{h \left\{ \alpha - \beta u_n + c_{RW} + \left[c_{RW} - s_R \left(1 - t_R \right) i \right] \lambda \right\}}{s_R \left(1 - t_R \right) h - \beta}, \tag{9.20}$$

$$g^* = \frac{\left(\alpha - \beta u_n \right) s_R \left(1 - t_R \right) h + \beta \left\{ c_{RW} + \left[c_{RW} - s_R \left(1 - t_R \right) i \right] \lambda \right\}}{s_R \left(1 - t_R \right) h - \beta}, \tag{9.21}$$

Furthermore, from the balanced budget condition in equation (9.16), the rate of utilisation associated with this balanced budget can be derived:

$$u = \frac{\delta + \left(1 - t_R \right) i\lambda}{t_R h}. \tag{9.22}$$

From equations (9.19) and (9.22) the short-run equilibrium tax rate required for a balanced budget is obtained:

$$t_R^* = \frac{\left(s_R h - \beta\right)\left(\delta + i\lambda\right)}{h\left(\alpha - \beta u_n + c_{RW} + s_R \delta\right) + \left[c_{RW}h + \left(s_R h - \beta\right)i\right]\lambda}. \tag{9.23}$$

Using this equilibrium tax rate, the short-run equilibrium values for the rates of capacity utilisation, profit and capital accumulation can also be written as follows:

$$u^* = \frac{\alpha - \beta u_n + c_{RW}\left(1 + \lambda\right) + s_R \delta}{s_R h - \beta}, \tag{9.24}$$

$$r^* = \frac{h\left[\alpha - \beta u_n + c_{RW}\left(1 + \lambda\right) + s_R \delta\right]}{s_R h - \beta}, \tag{9.25}$$

$$g^* = \frac{\left(\alpha - \beta u_n\right)s_R h + \beta\left[c_{RW}\left(1 + \lambda\right) + s_R \delta\right]}{s_R h - \beta}. \tag{9.26}$$

Figure 9.2 illustrates a possible short-run equilibrium. As can be seen, in the short run, firms' assessment of the trend rate of growth may be different from the growth rate of autonomous demand, which is set to zero here. Therefore, even if with zero net financial balances of each sector at the normal rate of capacity utilisation (i.e., a balanced government budget and consumption out of wealth exactly compensating saving out of rentiers' income), capacity utilisation may deviate from that normal rate, and capital accumulation, saving and growth may hence be positive in the short run.

Table 9.3 contains the short-run comparative statics of the model, which are of the usual neo-Kaleckian type, which should be well known from Chapter 7 of this book and also from the short-run level versions of the model in Chapters 4 and 5. The paradox of thrift holds, and now there are also positive wealth effects on all endogenous variables. Aggregate demand is wage-led. Higher tax rates and higher government expenditures are expansionary because of the positive balanced budget multiplier. Higher interest rates are contractionary with an exogenous tax rate, as can be seen in equations (9.19)–(9.21), because of an inverse relationship with

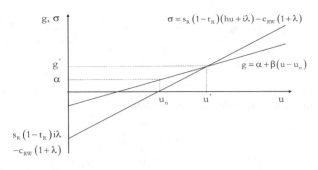

Figure 9.2   Short-run equilibrium

Table 9.3 *Response of stable zero-growth equilibrium to changes in exogenous variables in the short run and in the long run*

	Short run			Long run				
	u^*	r^*	g^*	u^{**}	r^{**}	g^{**}	$\delta^{**}>0$	$\lambda^{**}>0$
s_R	−	−	−	0	0	0	−	+
c_{RW}	+	+	+	0	0	0	+	−
$\hat{h}$	−	−	−	0	+	0	+/−	+
u_n	−	−	−	+	+	0	+/−	+
i	−/0	−/0	−/0	0	0	0	−	+
t_R	+	+	+	0	0	0	+	−
δ	+	+	+					
λ	+/−	+/−	+/−					

Note: In the short run, there are two possible cases regarding t_R and δ: In case 1, t_R is exogenous while δ is endogenous, while in case 2, δ is exogenous and t_R endogenous.

government expenditures. However, if government expenditures are exogenous, a higher interest rate has no effect, as is obvious from equations (9.24)–(9.26). A higher tax rate or higher government expenditures are expansionary; the same is true for a higher government-debt capital ratio if government expenditures are exogenous, but not necessarily if the tax rate is exogenous.

9.4.4.2 Long-run equilibrium

For the long run, Dutt's (2019, 2020) idea of reasonable expectations on behalf of the firms is applied. It is assumed that firms' expectations about the trend rate of growth of the economy adjust towards the autonomous growth rate of government expenditures, equal to zero in the model economy:

$$\alpha = \gamma = 0. \tag{9.27}$$

The goods market equilibrium will thus adjust towards the normal rate of capacity utilisation and the autonomous growth rate of government expenditures, as shown in Figure 9.3.

For the long-run equilibrium, however, it has to be considered that the government expenditures- and debt-capital ratios are endogenous in the long run, and it has to be examined whether these ratios will converge towards some stable long-run equilibrium. The time rates of change $\dot{x} = \partial x/\partial t$ of the two ratios are given as:

$$\dot{\delta} = \delta(\gamma - g) = \delta\left[\gamma - \alpha - \beta(u^* - u_n)\right], \tag{9.28}$$

$$\dot{\lambda} = \delta + i\lambda - \tau - \lambda g. \tag{9.29}$$

A balanced budget ($\delta + i\lambda - \tau = 0$) turns equation (9.29) into:

$$\dot{\lambda} = -\lambda g = -\lambda\left[\alpha + \beta(u^* - u_n)\right]. \tag{9.30}$$

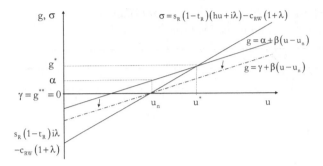

Figure 9.3   Long-run equilibrium

For the long-run equilibrium, the endogenous government expenditures- and debt-capital ratios have to be constant, and hence $\dot{\delta}=0$ and $\dot{\lambda}=0$ in equations (9.28) and (9.30) are needed. This generates the following trivial long-run equilibrium, with r_n as the normal rate of profit, that is, the rate of profit at normal capacity utilisation:

$$u^{**} = u_n,$$
(9.31)

$$r^{**} = hu_n = r_n,$$
(9.32)

$$g^{**} = \gamma = 0,$$
(9.33)

$$\delta^{**} = 0,$$
(9.34)

$$\lambda^{**} = 0.$$
(9.35)

However, also more meaningful long-run equilibria with positive government expenditures- and debt-capital ratios can be derived. Plugging the long-run equilibrium rate of capacity utilisation from equation (9.31) into the short-run goods market equilibrium rate of capacity utilisation from equation (9.19) gives:

$$u_n = \frac{\alpha + c_{RW} + \left[c_{RW} - s_R \left(1 - t_R \right) i \right] \lambda}{s_R \left(1 - t_R \right) h}.$$
(9.36)

Rearranging, and including the long-run requirement of a stationary economy ($\alpha = \gamma = 0$), provides the long-run equilibrium government debt-capital ratio:[7]

$$\lambda^{**} = \frac{s_R \left(1 - t_R \right) hu_n - c_{RW}}{c_{RW} - s_R \left(1 - t_R \right) i}.$$
(9.37)

Furthermore, from the balanced budget condition in equation (9.16), using equations (9.31) and (9.37), the related long-run equilibrium government expenditures-capital ratio is obtained:

$$\delta^{**} = t_R hu_n - \left(1 - t_R\right) i \lambda^{**}$$

$$= t_R hu_n - \frac{\left(1 - t_R\right) i \left[s_R \left(1 - t_R\right) hu_n - c_{RW}\right]}{c_{RW} - s_R \left(1 - t_R\right) i}. \tag{9.38}$$

The dynamic stability of the non-zero equilibria in equations (9.37) and (9.38) can be examined making use of the dynamic equations (9.28) and (9.30) together with the short-run goods market equilibrium in equation (9.24). The corresponding Jacobian matrix is given by:

$$J = \begin{pmatrix} \dfrac{\partial \dot{\delta}}{\partial \delta} & \dfrac{\partial \dot{\delta}}{\partial \lambda} \\[2ex] \dfrac{\partial \dot{\lambda}}{\partial \delta} & \dfrac{\partial \dot{\lambda}}{\partial \lambda} \end{pmatrix}. \tag{9.39}$$

Evaluated at the long-run equilibrium values δ^{**} and λ^{**}, the following elements of the Jacobian are obtained:

$$\frac{\partial \dot{\delta}}{\partial \delta} = \frac{-\beta s_R \delta^{**}}{s_R h - \beta}, \tag{9.28a}$$

$$\frac{\partial \dot{\delta}}{\partial \lambda} = \frac{-\beta c_{RW} \delta^{**}}{s_R h - \beta}, \tag{9.28b}$$

$$\frac{\partial \dot{\lambda}}{\partial \delta} = \frac{-\beta s_R \lambda^{**}}{s_R h - \beta}, \tag{9.30a}$$

$$\frac{\partial \dot{\lambda}}{\partial \lambda} = \frac{-\beta c_{RW} \lambda^{**}}{s_R h - \beta}. \tag{9.30b}$$

For the local stability in this 2×2 dynamic system, the trace of the Jacobian in (9.39) has to be negative and the determinant needs to be non-negative:

$$TrJ^{**} = \frac{\partial \dot{\delta}}{\partial \delta} + \frac{\partial \dot{\lambda}}{\partial \lambda} = \frac{-\beta s_R \delta^{**}}{s_R h - \beta} + \frac{-\beta c_{RW} \lambda^{**}}{s_R h - \beta} = \frac{-\beta \left(s_R \delta^{**} + c_{RW} \lambda^{**}\right)}{s_R h - \beta}, \tag{9.40}$$

$$DetJ^{**} = \frac{\partial \dot{\delta}}{\partial \delta} \frac{\partial \dot{\lambda}}{\partial \lambda} - \frac{\partial \dot{\delta}}{\partial \lambda} \frac{\partial \dot{\lambda}}{\partial \delta} = 0. \tag{9.41}$$

A determinant equal to zero implies a zero root model, with a continuum of locally stable equilibria, which means that the long-run equilibrium government expenditures- and debt-capital ratios are path-dependent. Since $s_R h - \beta > 0$ has to hold for short-run goods market equilibrium stability, positive long-run equilibrium values for the government expenditures- and debt-capital ratios δ^{**} and λ^{**} ensure that $\mathrm{TrJ}^{**} < 0$, such that a stable long-run equilibrium is obtained. Therefore, the conditions for positive equilibrium values for δ^{**} and λ^{**} in equations (9.37) and (9.38) are important. For $\lambda^{**} > 0$ in equation (9.37), it is required that

$$s_R \left(1 - t_R\right) hu_n > c_{RW} > s_R \left(1 - t_R\right) i \quad \Rightarrow \quad r_n > \frac{c_{RW}}{s_R \left(1 - t_R\right)} > i, \tag{9.37a}$$

or that

$$s_R \left(1 - t_R\right) hu_n < c_{RW} < s_R \left(1 - t_R\right) i \quad \Rightarrow \quad r_n < \frac{c_{RW}}{s_R \left(1 - t_R\right)} < i. \tag{9.37b}$$

Since condition (9.37b) implies that the rate of interest on safe government bonds exceeds the rate of profit in production, which will make production difficult to sustain, given the 'risks and troubles' involved here, the condition (9.37a) is economically more meaningful and is used in the further considerations.

If λ^{**} is positive, for δ^{**} in equation (9.38) to assume positive values, too, it is necessary that
$$\frac{t_R hu_n \left[c_{RW} - s_R \left(1 - t_R\right) i\right] - \left(1 - t_R\right) i \left[s_R \left(1 - t_R\right) hu_n - c_{RW}\right]}{c_{RW} - s_R \left(1 - t_R\right) i} > 0, \text{ which implies:}$$

$$\frac{c_{RW} t_R hu_n}{\left(1 - t_R\right) \left(s_R hu_n - c_{RW}\right)} > i$$

$$\Rightarrow \frac{c_{RW}}{s_R \left(1 - t_R\right)} > \frac{i r_n}{t_R r_n + \left(1 - t_R\right) i} = \frac{i}{t_R + \left(1 - t_R\right) i / r_n}. \tag{9.38a}$$

Since $r_n > i$ implies that $\dfrac{i}{t_R + \left(1 - t_R\right) i / r_n} > i$, for positive and stable long-run equilibria for both δ^{**} and λ^{**} in a stationary economy, it is required that:

$$s_R \left(1 - t_R\right) hu_n > c_{RW} > \frac{s_R \left(1 - t_R\right) ihu_n}{t_R r_n + \left(1 - t_R\right) i}, \tag{9.42}$$

which is equivalent to

$$hu_n > \frac{c_{RW}}{s_R \left(1 - t_R\right)} > \frac{ihu_n}{t_R hu_n + \left(1 - t_R\right) i}$$

$$\Rightarrow r_n > \frac{c_{RW}}{s_R \left(1 - t_R\right)} > \frac{i}{t_R + \left(1 - t_R\right) i / r_n}. \tag{9.43}$$

The normal rate of profit, that is, the rate of profit at normal capacity utilisation in long-run equilibrium, has to exceed the rate of interest scaled by the denominator in equation (9.43). This will allow the propensity to consume out of wealth relative to the rentiers' propensity to save out of their net income to assume a value consistent with a stable long-run equilibrium. If the conditions for the parameter values in equation (9.43) are not met, the long-run equilibrium values in equations (9.31), (9.32), (9.33), (9.37) and (9.38) will not be stable. Any deviation will not bring the system back to this stationary equilibrium.

The comparative dynamics for changes in the long-run equilibrium with respect to exogenous parameters are also summarised in Table 9.3. In the long run, utilisation is given by the normal rate and capital accumulation and growth by the zero-growth rate of autonomous government expenditures. Of course, a higher target rate of utilisation raises the long-run equilibrium rate of capacity utilisation, and a higher profit share raises the long-run equilibrium profit rate. The propensities to save out of rentiers' income and to consume out of wealth, as well as the interest rate and the tax rate, have no effects on the long-run equilibrium rates of utilisation and accumulation and only affect long-run equilibrium government expenditures- and debt-capital ratios, usually in opposite directions.

The results based on the Kaleckian distribution and growth model driven by autonomous government demand show that under some specific conditions regarding the values of the rate of profit, the rate of interest and the propensities to consume out of wealth and to save out of income, stable zero growth with endogenous credit, positive real interest rates and positive profit rates is possible. If these conditions are met, there is no growth imperative in a monetary production economy. However, one must recall that the model by Hein and Jimenez (2022) contains several restrictive assumptions:

- It has been assumed that, in the long run, firms' investment is only determined by the autonomous growth rate of the system, the zero-growth rate of government expenditures. This rules out long-run effects of animal spirits, competitive pressures, financial factors and so on, on investment in the aggregate.
- It has been assumed that the firm sector only re-invests depreciations and does not retain any profits net of depreciations, but pays out these profits to the rentiers' household sector (in the model in terms of dividends). Of course, this does not need to hold for each individual firm, but it has to hold in the aggregate.
- It has been assumed that the government balances its budget, at least in the long run (for the sake of simplicity, also a short-run balanced budget was assumed). This rules out any long-run requirements for government demand stabilisation in the functional finance sense, which we have elaborated on in Chapter 6 of this book. However, if there is no saving of the private sector at full employment, government deficits are not required from a functional finance perspective.
- Regarding distribution, the model only considers functional income distribution, but it does not address personal income inequality or wealth inequality in a zero-growth economy, as for example the SFC models by Jackson and Victor (2016) and Janischewski (2022).
- The model is only for a closed economy. However, the basic principles could also be applied to an open economy. In particular, this would then also require balanced current accounts, at least in the long run.

- The model has assumed constant technical conditions of production in a one-good economy and has only addressed goods market and systemic financial market stability; the latter in the sense of constant net assets- and net liabilities-income ratios of each macroeconomic sector. The model has not tackled the issue of stable employment and hence unemployment in a zero-growth economy under the conditions of technical progress, productivity growth and structural change. This is what we will briefly address in the next section.

9.4.5 Some Thoughts on Stable Employment and Zero Growth

In order to discuss the issue of stable employment and hence unemployment in a zero-growth economy with technical progress, productivity growth and structural change, we can start with rearranging equation (9.3), which then shows the principle statistical determinants of the employment rate – and thus the rate of unemployment:

$$\frac{N}{L} = \frac{Y}{\dfrac{Y}{H}\dfrac{H}{N}\dfrac{L}{P}p} \Rightarrow e = \frac{Y}{ynlP}. \tag{9.44}$$

From this it follows:

$$\hat{e} = \hat{Y} - \hat{P} - \hat{l} - \hat{n} - \hat{y}. \tag{9.45}$$

With zero growth – and thus constant real GDP – the employment rate will fall, according to population growth, growth in the labour force participation rate, growth of working time per person employed and productivity growth. In order to maintain a high rate of employment, and thus a low rate of unemployment, in a zero-growth economy with productivity growth, the following options or combinations of them are available:

- a slowdown in productivity growth through structural change towards green industries and services with higher labour intensity and lower labour productivity,
- a reduction of hours worked per person, that is, through shortening daily, weekly, monthly or annual working time,
- a decline in the labour force participation rate, that is, through longer periods of education and earlier retirements, or a politically and socially unacceptable exclusion of certain groups from the labour market, or
- through a fall in population via birth and immigration controls.

Since population growth and thus labour force growth in mature economies have come to a halt, and have sometimes already reversed, in these economies, the major role in preventing rising unemployment will have to be played by reducing productivity growth, by all types of cutting working time and by reducing the effective labour force participation rate through longer education periods and earlier retirements.

The increase in labour intensity and the slowdown in labour productivity growth can be expected to occur with structural change towards a green economy with more labour intensive and less capital and nature intensive methods of production. This has been pointed out both by de-growth proponents, like Jackson and Victor (2011, 2020) and Victor (2012), as well as in the green growth and Green New Deal concepts by Pollin (2018, 2020, 2021), amongst others.

Cutting weekly, annual (more holidays) and life-long (longer periods of education, sabbaticals, early retirements) working time in order to deal with the unemployment issue in a low or zero-growth economy is the focus of many contributions in the area of ecological macroeconomics, like Fontana and Sawyer (2022), Jackson and Victor (2011, 2020), Lange (2018), Rezai et al. (2013) and several others. It has also been part of Keynes's (1930b) long-run vision in his 'Economic possibilities of our grandchildren'. However, to make this affordable and socially acceptable for the majority of employees, it will have to be associated with income re-distribution, in particular towards low wage earners. This may take place through secondary re-distribution by the state, via progressive taxation and improved social transfers, different sorts of basic income schemes and so on, which each lead to a decoupling of work and income (Strunk et al. 2022). But it may also be achieved through improving primary distribution of market incomes via higher wage shares and a more compressed wage structure.

The required change in distribution to make shorter working time socially acceptable, however, will have several feedbacks on the macroeconomy, which have to be considered, as also pointed out by Rezai et al. (2013) and Taylor et al. (2016), for example. First, a higher wage share and a more egalitarian income distribution will have aggregate demand effects, which may be wage-led or profit-led, as we have discussed in Chapters 4 and 5 of this book. In the model by Hein and Jimenez (2022) presented in the previous section of this chapter, these effects will only be short-run and will not affect long-run growth, determined by the zero-growth rate of autonomous government expenditures. However, in other post-Keynesian models, like the Kaleckian models outlined in Chapter 7, also long-run growth effects are expected. In a wage-led regime, this will then stimulate demand and growth, potentially violating the environmental constraints. This problem might be reinforced by increasing propensities to consume, because of more leisure and a shift of consumption patterns towards higher emission (more travelling, more flights). In a profit-led regime, a higher wage share will reduce demand and growth, and shrinking real GDP will raise unemployment. In each case, further demand management interventions by the government will be required. Second, raising the wage share will stimulate the efforts of firms to introduce even more labour-saving technical progress, as we have outlined in Chapter 7 of this book. This will further raise labour productivity and potential output and thus require stabilising government intervention, too.

Summing up, a socio-economic and -ecological transformation in order to respect the environmental constraints is a huge challenge and requires a significant transformation of capitalism as we know it. Green New Deal concepts, as outlined above in this chapter, would have to be more closely linked with the post-Keynesian macroeconomic policy mix, as explained in Chapter 6.[8] In such a policy mix, fiscal policy has a major role to play, not only in terms of stabilising aggregate demand at non-inflationary full employment levels in the short and in the long run. Such fiscal policies, in particular, but not only, public investments, have to be targeted towards the required socio-ecological transformation, and they have to be linked with industrial and regional policies. Central banks can support such policies by targeting low long-term interest rates and by stabilising the financial system, making use of other instruments, like ecologically targeted quantitative easing and credit controls. Incomes policies will have a major role to play, in order to support stable inflation, on the one hand, but also to contribute to a more egalitarian distribution of income in a low or even zero-growth environment, on the other hand. Furthermore, consumption patterns would have to change and shift away from energy- and emission-intense individual consumption towards more labour-intense forms of collective consumption. Finally, international co-ordination of such a policy approach is most important, respecting the need of emerging economies to develop, on the one hand, and the planetary boundaries, on the other hand.

NOTES

1. For more detailed comparisons of ecological and post-Keynesian economics, see also the contributions in Holt et al. (2009).
2. For a recent attempt at tackling environmental sustainability from a Sraffian perspective making use of linear production theory, see Hahnel (2017). For some basics on renewable and exhaustible resources in the Sraffian model, see Kurz and Salvadori (1995, Chapter 12).
3. 'The Ecological Footprint adds up all the productive areas for which a population, a person or a product competes. It measures the ecological assets that a given population or product requires to produce the natural resources it consumes (including plant-based food and fiber products, livestock and fish products, timber and other forest products, space for urban infrastructure) and to absorb its waste, especially carbon emissions' (Global Footprint Network 2022).
4. This section draws on and further elaborates on Hein and Jimenez (2022).
5. Their review includes models from Berg et al. (2015), Binswanger (2009, 2015), Cahen-Fourot and Lavoie 2016), Douthwaite (2000), Farley et al. (2013), Godley and Lavoie (2007), Jackson and Victor (2015) and Lietaer et al. (2012).
6. Hein and Jimenez (2022) argue that even for a government which can issue debt in its own currency and which is supported by a national central bank, ever rising government debt-income ratios pose some financial instability risk, in particular in an open economy with capital mobility.
7. The same results can be derived by starting from the goods market equilibrium formulation in equation (9.24) together with equations (9.16) for the balanced government budget and (9.31) for the long-run equilibrium rate of capacity utilisation.
8. See Herr (2022) for an attempt at outlining some ideas of some institutional requirements based on the works of Keynes and Schumpeter.

10. Perspectives for post-Keynesian economics*

In this book, in Chapters 4–6, we presented some of the foundations of post-Keynesian macroeconomics, we developed a comprehensive post-Keynesian macroeconomic model, with variants both for the closed and the open economy, and we derived a full post-Keynesian macroeconomic policy mix. Furthermore, we embedded the post-Keynesian macroeconomic models and macroeconomic policy implications into the post-Keynesian research programme more generally in Chapter 2 and outlined the theoretical roots of post-Keynesian macroeconomics, in particular in the works of Kalecki and Keynes, in Chapter 3. Finally, we presented the application of post-Keynesian macroeconomics in some recent areas of research in Chapters 8 and 9. These include the work on macroeconomic regimes in finance-dominated capitalism, regime changes, growth drivers, stagnation tendencies and the role of macroeconomic policy regimes in all that, on the one hand, and the research on the macroeconomic implications of ecological constraints to growth and the urgent socio-ecological transformation, on the other hand. For this purpose, we had to move from short-run macroeconomics to long-run distribution and growth theories. Therefore, the different versions of the basic post-Keynesian distribution and growth models, in comparison to their neoclassical and classical/orthodox Marxian competitors, were presented in Chapter 7. Since the main content of each of the chapters of this book was already summarised in the introduction, we shall not repeat this here.

This final chapter will rather be linked to the overview on post-Keynesian economics provided in Chapter 2, and it will provide some thoughts on the perspectives for post-Keynesian economics. In Chapter 2, we argued that post-Keynesian economics has generated a considerable body of research in the areas of macroeconomics, employment and unemployment, distribution and growth, money, credit and finance, international money and finance, financialisation, financial instability and financial crises, the economics of European integration, as well as development and emerging-market economics. This research has provided solid foundations for alternative macroeconomic policies, which we have developed in the course of this book. In Chapter 2, we also pointed out that post-Keynesian economics since Kalecki and Keynes has only survived as a contested and embattled minority in economics, and we outlined the academic infrastructure which has supported this survival. Against this background, the question about the perspectives of post-Keynesian economics arises, given the experiences of the 2007–09 Global Financial Crisis and Global Recession, the 2020 COVID-19 crisis and the socio-ecological transformation needed in the face of the ecological crises.

The perspectives and future tasks for post-Keynesian economics have been discussed intensively after the 2007–09 crises, as for example reviewed by Dequech (2012), King (2012c), Lavoie (2012) and Lee (2012). Regarding the relationship with mainstream economics, some authors, like Colander (2009) and Fontana and Gerrard (2006), argued that post-Keynesians should observe the developments within orthodox/mainstream economics more closely, avoid attacking a textbook 'strawman', use modelling methods which are acceptable to mainstream economists, engage in dialogue and cooperate with mainstream economists. The goal in doing so should be to convince mainstream economists of the relevance of post-Keynesian economics. Others, like Davidson (2009), based on a narrow definition of 'Post Keynesian economics', only including the first strand outlined in Section 2.3, the fundamentalist Keynesians, argued that post-Keynesians should actively fight orthodox economics, with the aim of convincing mainstream economists that their approach is wrong.

Like Stockhammer and Ramskogler (2009), but for somewhat different reasons, I would consider both strategies to be misguided, because they over-estimate the potential for constructive dialogue or controversies, given the contradicting presuppositions of orthodox and heterodox economics, as presented in Section 2.2. In addition, these strategies seem to overrate the willingness of mainstream economists to enter into such dialogues or controversies, given their power and superior access to university positions, financing funds, political influence and so on. Furthermore, I would side with King (2008b, 2012c), who argues, contrary to the first strategy, that the developments and openness within mainstream macroeconomics should not be overrated and, contrary to the second, that it carries the severe risk of running into fundamental methodological debates and into 'sectarian intolerance'.

Dismissing any strategy targeting orthodox economics in the first place, however, does not imply that post-Keynesians should avoid dialogue or controversies with mainstream economists. On the contrary, to the extent that they are possible, these may be helpful to develop and sharpen the post-Keynesian research programme, which should focus on 'useful explanations of ongoing socio-economic transformations', as Stockhammer and Ramskogler (2009, p. 228) suggest. Such engagement is also required for post-Keynesians to have an impact on the economic policy stance, still to a large degree dominated by orthodox recommendations, and shift it towards policies that are more favourable to full employment, a more equal distribution of income and financially and environmentally sustainable development.[1] However, in my view, the primary target cannot be to convince and change orthodox/mainstream economists, but to contribute to a change in attitudes and power relations in the economy and the society as a whole. Only if this is successful, will the power relations in academia have the potential to change, as well. In such a perspective, a dialogue with 'orthodox dissenters' (Lavoie 2012) could play an important role, maybe with a strong focus on economic policies.[2] What are the implications of this perspective for post-Keynesian economics in the future?

First, post-Keynesians should improve their research programme in those areas which are underdeveloped, without giving up their strengths in macroeconomics and macroeconomic policies. This could include a closer examination of potential links with modern experimental and behavioural economics, in order to strengthen the behavioural functions in post-Keynesian macroeconomic models.[3] It would mean further integration of ecological constraints into post-Keynesian macroeconomic models, as pointed out in Chapter 9 of this book, and further interaction with ecological economics, in particular. It would mean continuing working on the macroeconomics of social segregation (gender, etc.), as we have pointed out in Section 4.7 on the macroeconomics of the gender wage gap, and continuing with the interaction with feminist economics, for example. It should also mean re-focussing on the political economy dimension and the social embeddedness of economic processes and economic policies, which is part of the tradition of Kalecki and Steindl, in particular, but has also been important in the other strands of post-Keynesian economics. The research on demand and growth regimes in finance-dominated capitalism, growth drivers and macroeconomic policy regimes is an example of this, which has already led to a more intense exchange between post-Keynesian economists and researchers in critical and comparative political economy and in international political economy, as we outlined in Chapter 8. These are just examples, which are not meant to be comprehensive or exclusive. Overall, post-Keynesianism can certainly benefit from closer cooperation with other heterodox schools, like ecological economics, institutional economics, different strands of Marxian economics (French regulation school, social structure of accumulation approach) and with critical and comparative political economy and international political economy. In this way, they can contribute to the development of a more comprehensive, but open and pluralistic alternative economics, or better political economy research programme.

Second, post-Keynesians would have to focus and concentrate on defending and improving the heterodox academic infrastructure, regarding university positions, research funding, graduate programmes, journals and appropriate journal rankings, associations and networks, conferences and summer schools, which was outlined in Section 2.5. As should be self-evident, cooperation in securing university positions, graduate programmes and research funding, at department, faculty, university levels and beyond, should not be restricted to other heterodox economists, but would have to include other progressive social scientists, business economists, engineers, scientists and so on. This means also further improving international networking, as has been shown, for example, by the establishment of a new research area on 'effective demand, income distribution and finance' in the European Association of Evolutionary Political Economy (EAEPE) a few years ago, in which post-Keynesians exchange research output with other heterodox schools of thought.[4] It also means establishing new national (and international) post-Keynesian networks and societies, as for example recently the Italian Post-Keynesian Network. Furthermore, post-Keynesian and heterodox economists should continue to make use of windows of opportunity that arise in the course of crises, in order to attract public funding. Recent examples for the period after the 2007–09 crises are, amongst several others, the successful applications for massive European Union funding for the international research project Financialisation, Economy, Society and Sustainable Development (FESSUD, 2011–16) with 15 international partners, and for the international Master programmes Economic Policies in the Age of Globalisation (EPOG, 2013–19) and Economic Policies for the Global Transition (EPOG+, 2020–25).[5] In particular, the ecological crisis and the need for a socio-ecological transformation should be another such window of opportunity.

Third, in order to have an impact on economic policies and to contribute to a more progressive social environment for academic research, post-Keynesians need to maintain and to improve their cooperation with trade unions, social movements and progressive political parties, as well as with research institutes and think tanks outside the university sector. For example, the Forum Macroeconomics and Macroeconomic Policies (FMM), founded as Research Network Macroeconomics and Macroeconomic Policies in 1996, which has been hosting one of the most important international post-Keynesian conferences during the last decades, has been organisationally based at and funded by the Macroeconomic Policy Institute (IMK) of the Hans Böckler Foundation, a foundation for research promotion and co-determination, affiliated with the German trade unions.[6] I would argue that both the worldwide post-Keynesian network and German and international trade unions have benefitted from this kind of cooperation. Last, but not least, post-Keynesians should, of course, actively participate and intervene in public economic and economic policy debates. If successful, this may even feedback positively on the academic debate. The resonance 'modern mone(tar)y theory' (MMT) has achieved in the US political arena is an example of how successful post-Keynesian interventions in the economic policy discourse can force mainstream economics to deal with post-Keynesian or other heterodox approaches in the academic arena – although they are, of course, not convinced (Mankiw 2020).

NOTES

*   This chapter partly draws on Hein (2014b) and further develops the considerations outlined there.
1. Such a strategy is also incompatible with Lee's (2012) suggestion to ignore mainstream economics when doing heterodox research. It might be compatible with what Earl and Peng (2012) call 'strategies of stealth'. See King (2012c) for a discussion.
2. The edited book by Fontana and Setterfield (2009a) on *Macroeconomics and Macroeconomic Pedagogy*, with chapters by open-minded orthodox authors and by post-Keynesians on the NCM and post-Keynesian amendments and alternatives, has been such an attempt. Also the annual conferences of the Forum for Macroeconomics and Macroeconomic Policies (FMM) in Berlin have tried to organise discussions of open-minded orthodox economists with post-Keynesians and other heterodox economists in their plenary sessions (www.fmm-macro.net). The success in terms of continuous debate and interaction, however, has been rather limited, in my view.
3. See, for example, King (2013) for a balanced assessment of the potentials.
4. For the EAEPE, see www.eaepe.org.
5. For the FESSUD research project see fessud.org, and for the EPOG Master programmes see www.epog.eu.
6. For the FMM, see www.fmm-macro.net, Gechert et al. (2017) and Hein and Priewe (2009).

Appendix

A.   RULES FOR CALCULATIONS WITH GROWTH RATES[1]

The growth rate of variable x is given by:

$$\hat{x} = \frac{dx}{x} = \frac{\partial x}{\partial t}\frac{1}{x} = \frac{\partial \log x}{\partial t}. \tag{A1}$$

Starting from:

$$y = \alpha x, \tag{A2a}$$

with α as a constant, differentiating with respect to time and dividing by y yields:

$$\frac{\partial y}{\partial t}\frac{1}{y} = \frac{\partial x}{\partial t}\frac{\alpha}{\alpha x}, \tag{A2b}$$

which gives:

$$\hat{y} = \hat{x}. \tag{A2c}$$

Starting from:

$$y = x + z, \tag{A3a}$$

differentiating with respect to time and dividing by y yields:

$$\frac{\partial y}{\partial t}\frac{1}{y} = \frac{\partial x}{\partial t}\frac{1}{x}\frac{x}{y} + \frac{\partial z}{\partial t}\frac{1}{z}\frac{z}{y}, \tag{A3b}$$

which gives:

$$\hat{y} = \hat{x}\frac{x}{y} + \hat{z}\frac{z}{y}. \tag{A3c}$$

Starting from:

$$y = xz, \tag{A4a}$$

differentiating with respect to time and dividing by y yields:

$$\frac{\partial y}{\partial t}\frac{1}{y} = \frac{\partial x}{\partial t}\frac{z}{xz} + \frac{\partial z}{\partial t}\frac{x}{xz}, \tag{A4b}$$

which gives:

$$\hat{y} = \hat{x} + \hat{z}. \tag{A4c}$$

Starting from:

$$y = \frac{x}{z}, \tag{A5a}$$

differentiating with respect to time and dividing by y yields:

$$\frac{\partial y}{\partial t}\frac{1}{y} = \frac{z}{x}\left(\frac{\partial x}{\partial t}\frac{z}{z^2} - \frac{\partial z}{\partial t}\frac{x}{z^2}\right), \tag{A5b}$$

which gives:

$$\hat{y} = \hat{x} - \hat{z}. \tag{A5c}$$

Starting from:

$$y = x^{\alpha}z^{\beta}, \tag{A6a}$$

with α and β as constants, taking logs:

$$\log y = \alpha \log x + \beta \log z, \tag{A6b}$$

differentiating with respect to time yields:

$$\frac{\partial \log y}{\partial t} = \alpha \frac{\partial \log x}{\partial t} + \beta \frac{\partial \log z}{\partial t}. \tag{A6c}$$

This is equal to:

$$\frac{\partial y}{\partial t}\frac{1}{y} = \alpha \frac{\partial x}{\partial t}\frac{1}{x} + \beta \frac{\partial z}{\partial t}\frac{1}{z}, \tag{A6d}$$

and therefore we obtain:

$$\hat{y} = \alpha\hat{x} + \beta\hat{z}. \tag{A6e}$$

B. RULES OF DIFFERENTIATION[2]

Constant function rule

$$y = f(x) = a, \text{ with a constant,} \tag{B1a}$$

$$\frac{\partial y}{\partial x} = f'(x) = 0 \tag{B1b}$$

Power function rule

$$y = f(x) = ax^n \tag{B2a}$$

$$\frac{\partial y}{\partial x} = f'(x) = nax^{n-1} \tag{B2b}$$

Sum-difference rule

$$y = f(x) = g(x) \pm h(x) \tag{B3a}$$

$$\frac{\partial y}{\partial x} = f'(x) = g'(x) \pm h'(x) \tag{B3b}$$

Product rule

$$y = f(x) = g(x)h(x) \tag{B4a}$$

$$\frac{\partial y}{\partial x} = f'(x) = g'(x)h(x) + g(x)h'(x) \tag{B4b}$$

Quotient rule

$$y = f(x) = \frac{g(x)}{h(x)} \tag{B5a}$$

$$\frac{\partial y}{\partial x} = f'(x) = \frac{g'(x)h(x) - g(x)h'(x)}{\left[h(x)\right]^2} \tag{B5b}$$

The total differential

$$y = f(x, z) \tag{B6a}$$

$$dy = \frac{\partial y}{\partial x} dx + \frac{\partial y}{\partial z} dz \qquad \text{(B6b)}$$

Chain rule

$$y = f(x,z) \text{ and } x = g(z) \qquad \text{(B7a)}$$

$$\frac{dy}{dz} = \frac{\partial y}{\partial x} \frac{dx}{dz} + \frac{\partial y}{\partial z} \qquad \text{(B7b)}$$

NOTES

1.   See, for example, Carlin and Soskice (2006, pp. 465–8) and Westphal (1994, pp. 551–2).
2.   See, for example, Chiang (1984, Chapter 7).

References

Aghion, P. and Howitt, P. (2009), *The Economics of Growth*, Cambridge, MA: MIT Press.

Akcay, Ü., Hein, E. and Jungmann, B. (2022), 'Financialisation and macroeconomic regimes in emerging capitalist countries before and after the Great Recession', *International Journal of Political Economy*, **51**(2), 77–100.

Alexiou, C. and Pitelis, C. (2003), 'On capital shortages and European unemployment: a panel data investigation', *Journal of Post Keynesian Economics*, **25**(4), 613–631.

Allain, O. (2009), 'Effective demand and short-term adjustment in the General Theory', *Review of Political Economy*, **21**(1), 1–22.

Allain, O. (2013), 'Effective demand: securing the foundations', *Review of Political Economy*, **25**(4), 653–660.

Allain, O. (2015), 'Tackling the instability of growth: a Kaleckian-Harrodian model with an autonomous expenditure component', *Cambridge Journal of Economics*, **39**(5), 1351–1371.

Allain, O. (2019), 'Demographic growth, Harrodian (in)stability and the supermultiplier', *Cambridge Journal of Economics*, **43**(1), 85–106.

Allain, O. (2021), 'A supermultiplier model of the natural rate of growth', *Metroeconomica*, **72**(3), 612–634.

Amadeo, E.J. (1986), 'Notes on capacity utilisation, distribution and accumulation', *Contributions to Political Economy*, **5**(1), 83–94.

Arestis, P. (1992), *The Post-Keynesian Approach to Economics: An Alternative Analysis of Economic Theory and Policy*, Aldershot, UK: Edward Elgar Publishing.

Arestis, P. (1996a), 'Post-Keynesian economics: towards coherence', *Cambridge Journal of Economics*, **20**(1), 111–135.

Arestis, P. (1996b), 'Kalecki's role in post Keynesian economics: an overview', in J.E. King (ed.), *An Alternative Macroeconomic Theory: The Kaleckian Model and Post-Keynesian Economics*, Boston: Kluwer Academic Publishers.

Arestis, P. (2006), 'New monetary policy and Keynes', *European Journal of Economics and Economic Policies: Intervention*, **3**(2), 245–262.

Arestis, P. (2009), 'New consensus macroeconomics and Keynesian critique', in E. Hein, T. Niechoj and E. Stockhammer (eds.), *Macroeconomic Policies on Shaky Foundations: Whither Mainstream Economics?*, Marburg: Metropolis.

Arestis, P. (2010), 'Economic policies after the new concensus macroeconomics', in S. Dullien, E. Hein, A. Truger and T. van Treeck (eds.), *The World Economy in Crisis – The Return of Keynesianism?*, Marburg: Metropolis.

Arestis, P. (2011a), 'Keynesian economics and the new consensus in macroeconomics', in E. Hein and E. Stockhammer (eds.), *A Modern Guide to Keynesian Macroeconomics and Economic Policies*, Cheltenham, UK: Edward Elgar Publishing.

Arestis, P. (2011b), 'European Economic and Monetary Union policies from a Keynesian perspective', in E. Hein and E. Stockhammer (eds.), *A Modern Guide to Keynesian Macroeconomics and Economic Policies*, Cheltenham, UK: Edward Elgar Publishing.

Arestis, P. (2012), 'Fiscal policy: a strong macroeconomic role', *Review of Keynesian Economics*, Inaugural Issue, 93–108.

Arestis, P. (2013), 'Economic theory and policy: a coherent post-Keynesian approach', *European Journal of Economics and Economic Policies: Intervention*, **10**(2), 243–255.

Arestis, P. (2015), 'Coordination of fiscal with monetary and financial stability policies can better cure unemployment', *Review of Keynesian Economics*, **3**(2), 233–247.

Arestis, P. (2017), 'Monetary policy since the Global Financial Crisis', in P. Arestis and M. Sawyer (eds.), *Economic Policies since the Global Financial Crisis. International Papers in Political Economy*, Basingstoke, UK: Palgrave Macmillan.

Arestis, P. and Biefang-Frisancho Mariscal, I. (2000), 'Capital stock, unemployment and wages in the UK and Germany', *Scottish Journal of Political Economy*, **47**(5), 487–503.

Arestis, P. and Sawyer, M. (2003), 'Reinventing fiscal policy', *Journal of Post Keynesian Economics*, **26**(1), 3–25.

Arestis, P. and Sawyer, M. (2004a), *Re-examining Monetary and Fiscal Policy for the 21st Century*, Cheltenham, UK: Edward Elgar Publishing.

Arestis, P. and Sawyer, M. (2004b), 'On fiscal policy and budget deficits', *European Journal of Economics and Economic Policies: Intervention*, **1**(2), 61–74.

Arestis, P. and Sawyer, M. (2005), 'Aggregate demand, conflict and capacity in the inflationary process', *Cambridge Journal of Economics*, **29**(6), 959–974.

Arestis, P. and Sawyer, M. (eds.) (2009), *Unemployment: Past and Present*, Basingstoke, UK: Palgrave Macmillan.

Arestis, P. and Sawyer, M. (2010a), '21st century Keynesian economic policy', in P. Arestis and M. Sawyer (eds.), *21st Century Keynesian Economics. International Papers in Political Economy*, Basingstoke, UK: Palgrave Macmillan.

Arestis, P. and Sawyer, M. (2010b), 'What monetary policy after the crisis?', *Review of Political Economy*, **22**(4), 499–515.

Arestis, P. and Sawyer, M. (2011), 'The design faults of the Economic and Monetary Union', *Journal of Contemporary European Studies*, **19**(1), 21–32.

Arestis, P. and Sawyer, M. (eds.) (2012), *The Euro Crisis. International Papers in Political Economy*, Basingstoke, UK: Palgrave Macmillan.

Arestis, P. and Sawyer, M. (2013), *Economic and Monetary Union Macroeconomic Policies: Current Practices and Alternatives*, Basingstoke, UK: Palgrave Macmillan.

Arestis, P. and Sawyer, M. (eds.) (2014), *Fiscal and Debt Policies for the Future. International Papers in Political Economy*, Basingstoke, UK: Palgrave Macmillan.

Arestis, P. and Sawyer, M. (eds.) (2017), *Economic Policies since the Global Financial Crisis. International Papers in Political Economy*, Basingstoke, UK: Palgrave Macmillan.

Arestis, P., Baddeley, M. and Sawyer, M. (2006), 'Is capital stock a determinant of unemployment?', in E. Hein, A. Heise and A. Truger (eds.), *Wages, Employment, Distribution and Growth. International Perspectives*, Basingstoke, UK: Palgrave Macmillan.

Arestis, P., Baddeley, M. and Sawyer, M. (2007), 'The relationship between capital stock, unemployment and wages in nine EMU countries', *Bulletin of Economic Research*, **59**(2), 125–139.

Argitis, G. (2001), 'Intra-capitalist conflicts, monetary policy and income distribution', *Review of Political Economy*, **13**(4), 453–470.

Argitis, G. and Michopoulou, S. (2010), 'Monetary policy, interest payments, income distribution and the macroeconomy', *Review of Applied Economics*, **6**(1–2), 29–39.

Argitis, G. and Pitelis, C. (2001), 'Monetary policy and the distribution of income: evidence for the United States and the United Kingdom', *Journal of Post Keynesian Economics*, **23**(4), 617–638.

Argitis, G. and Pitelis, C. (2006), 'Global finance, income distribution and capital accumulation', *Contributions to Political Economy*, **25**(1), 63–81.

Arnon, A. (1994), 'Marx, Minsky and monetary economics', in G. Dymski and R. Pollin (eds.), *New Perspectives in Monetary Economics. Explorations in the Tradition of Hyman P. Minsky*, Ann Arbor: University of Michigan Press.

Asimakopulos, A. (1983), 'Kalecki and Keynes on finance, investment, and savings', *Cambridge Journal of Economics*, **7**(3/4), 221–233.

Asimakopulos, A. (1985), 'Finance, savings and investment in Keynes's economics: a comment', *Cambridge Journal of Economics*, **9**(3), 405–407.

Asimakopulos, A. (1986/87), 'Finance, liquidity, saving and investment', *Journal of Post Keynesian Economics*, **9**(1), 79–90.

Asimakopulos, A. (1986a), 'Finance, investment, and saving: a reply to Terzi', *Cambridge Journal of Economics*, **10**(1), 81–82.

Asimakopulos, A. (1986b), 'Richardson on Asimakopulos on finance: a reply', *Cambridge Journal of Economics*, **10**(2), 199–201.

Assous, M. and Dutt, A.K. (2013), 'Growth and income distribution with the dynamics of power in labour and goods markets', *Cambridge Journal of Economics*, **37**(6), 1407–1430.

Atesoglu, H.S. and Smithin, J. (2006), 'Inflation targeting in a simple macroeconomic model', *Journal of Post Keynesian Economics*, **28**(4), 673–688.

Atkinson, A.B. (2009), 'Factor shares: the principal problem of political economy?', *Oxford Review of Economic Policy*, **25**(1), 3–16.

Auvray, T. and Rabinovich, J. (2019), 'The financialisation–offshoring nexus and the capital accumulation of US non-financial firms', *Cambridge Journal of Economics*, **43**(5), 1183–1218.

Auvray, T., Durand, C., Rabinovich, J. and Rikap, C. (2021), 'Corporate financialization's conservation and transformation: from Mark I to Mark II', *Review of Evolutionary Political Economy*, **2**(3), 431–457.

Baccaro, L. and Pontusson, J. (2016), 'Rethinking comparative political economy: the growth model perspective', *Politics & Society*, **44**(2), 175–207.

Baccaro, L. and Pontusson, J. (2018), 'Comparative political economy and varieties of macroeconomics', Max Planck Institute for the Study of Societies, Cologne, MPIfG Discussion Paper 18/10.

Baccaro, L. and Rei, D. (2007), 'Institutional determinants of unemployment in OECD countries: does the deregulatory view hold water?', *International Organization*, **61**(3), 527–569.

Baker, D., Glyn, A., Howell, D.R. and Schmitt, J. (2004), 'Labour market institutions and unemployment: a critical assessment of the cross-country evidence', in D.R. Howell (ed.), *Fighting Unemployment: The Limits of the Free Market Orthodoxy*, Oxford: Oxford University Press.

Ball, L. (1999), 'Aggregate demand and long-run unemployment', *Brooking Papers on Economic Activity*, **2**, 189–251.

Ball, L. (2014), 'Long-term damage from the Great Recession in OECD countries', *European Journal of Economics and Economic Policies: Intervention*, **11**(2), 149–160.

Barba, A. and Pivetti, M. (2009), 'Rising household debt: its causes and macroeconomic implications – a long-period analysis', *Cambridge Journal of Economics*, **33**(1), 113–137.

Barbosa-Filho, N. and Taylor, L. (2006), 'Distributive and demand cycles in the US economy – a structuralist Goodwin model', *Metroeconomica*, **57**(3), 389–411.

Barradas, R. (2017), 'Financialisation and real investment in the European Union: beneficial or prejudicial effects?', *Review of Political Economy*, **29**(3), 376–413.

Barro, R.J. and Sala-i-Martin, X. (2004), *Economic Growth*, 2nd edition, Cambridge, MA: MIT Press.

Bassanini, A. and Duval, R. (2006), 'The determinants of unemployment across OECD countries: reassessing the role of policies and institutions', *OECD Economic Studies*, **1**, 7–86.

Bastian, E.F. and Setterfield, M. (2020), 'Nominal exchange rate shocks and inflation in an open economy: towards a structuralist inflation targeting agenda', *Cambridge Journal of Economics*, **44**(6), 1271–1299.

Behringer, J. and van Treeck, T. (2018), 'Income distribution and the current account', *Journal of International Economics*, **114**(C), 238–254.

Behringer, J. and van Treeck, T. (2019), 'Income distribution and growth models: a sectoral balances approach', *Politics & Society*, **47**(3) 303–332.

Belabed, C., Theobald, T. and van Treeck, T. (2018), 'Income distribution and current account imbalances', *Cambridge Journal of Economics*, **42**(1), 47–94.

Berend Blauwhof, F. (2012), 'Overcoming accumulation: is a capitalist steady-state economy possible?', *Ecological Economics*, **84**, 252–261.

Berg, M., Hartley, B. and Richters, O. (2015), 'A stock-flow consistent input–output model with applications to energy price shocks, interest rates, and heat emissions', *New Journal of Physics*, **17**(1), 1–21.

Berik, G., van der Meulen Rodgers, Y. and Seguino, S. (2009), 'Feminist economics of inequality, development, and growth', *Feminist Economics*, **15**(3), 1–33.

Bernanke, B.S. and Gertler, M. (1995), 'Inside the black box: the credit channel of monetary policy transmission', *Journal of Economic Perspectives*, **9**(4), 27–48.

Bernanke, B.S., Gertler, M. and Gilchrist, S. (1996), 'The financial accelerator and the flight to quality', *The Review of Economics and Statistics*, **78**(1), 1–15.

Berr, E. (2009), 'Keynes and sustainable development', *International Journal of Political Economy*, **38**(3), 22–38.

Berr, E. (2015), 'Sustainable development in a post Keynesian perspective: why eco-development is relevant to post-Keynesian economics', *Journal of Post Keynesian Economics*, **37**(3), 459–480.

Bertocco, G. (2017), *Crisis and the Failure of Economic Theory. The Responsibility of Economists for the Great Recession*, Cheltenham, UK: Edward Elgar Publishing.

Bertocco, G. and Kalajzic, A. (2019), 'Great Recession and macroeconomic theory: a useless crisis?', *Review of Political Economy*, **31**(3), 382–406.

Bhaduri, A. (1986), *Macroeconomics: The Dynamics of Commodity Production*, Basingstoke, UK: Palgrave Macmillan.

Bhaduri, A. (2006), 'Endogenous economic growth: a new approach', *Cambridge Journal of Economics*, **30**(1), 69–83.

Bhaduri, A. and Marglin, S. (1990), 'Unemployment and the real wage: the economic basis for contesting political ideologies', *Cambridge Journal of Economics*, **14**(4), 375–393.

Bhaduri, A. and Steindl, J. (1985), 'Monetarism as a social doctrine', in P. Arestis and T. Skouras (eds.), *Post-Keynesian Economic Theory*, Sussex: Wheatsheaf.

Bibow, J. (2006), 'Inflation persistence and tax-push inflation in Germany and in the Euro Area: a symptom of macroeconomic mismanagement?', IMK Studies 01-2006, Duesseldorf: Macroeconomic Policy Institute (IMK) at the Hans Boeckler Foundation.

Bibow, J. (2013a), 'At the crossroads: the euro and its central bank guardian (and saviour?)', *Cambridge Journal of Economics*, **37**(3), 609–626.

Bibow, J. (2013b), 'On the Franco-German euro contradiction and ultimate euro battleground', *Contributions to Political Economy*, **32**(1), 127–149.

Bibow, J. (2015), 'The euro's savior? Assessing the ECB's crisis management performance and potential for crisis resolution', IMK Study 42, Duesseldorf: Macroeconomic Policy Institute (IMK) at Hans Boeckler Foundation.

Bibow, J. (2016), 'Making the euro viable: the Euro Treasury Plan', *European Journal of Economics and Economic Policies: Intervention*, **13**(1), 72–86.

Bindseil, U. and König, P.J. (2013), 'Basil Moore's *Horizontalists and Verticalists*: an appraisal 25 years later', *Review of Keynesian Economics*, **4**(1), 383–390.

Binswanger, M. (2009), 'Is there a growth imperative in capitalist economies? A circular flow perspective', *Journal of Post Keynesian Economics*, **31**(4), 707–727.

Binswanger, M. (2015), 'The growth imperative revisited: a rejoinder to Gilányi and Johnson', *Journal of Post Keynesian Economics*, **37**(4), 648–660.

Bird, P.J.W.N. (1982), 'Neoclassical and Post Keynesian environmental economics', *Journal of Post Keynesian Economics*, **4**(4), 586–593.

Bitzenis, A., Karagiannis, N. and Marangos, J. (eds.) (2015), *Europe in Crisis: Problems, Challenges and Alternative Perspectives*, New York: Palgrave Macmillan.

Blanchard, O. (2019), 'Public debt and low interest rates', *American Economic Review*, **109**(4), 1197–1229.

Blanchard, O. and Leigh, D. (2013), 'Growth forecast errors and fiscal multipliers', *American Economic Review: Papers and Proceedings*, **103**(3), 117–120.

Blanchard, O. and Leigh, D. (2014), 'Learning about fiscal multipliers from growth forecast errors', *IMF Economic Review*, **62**(2), 179–212.

Blanchard, O. and Summers, L.H. (1987), 'Hysteresis in unemployment', *European Economic Review*, **31**(1–2), 288–295.

Blanchard, O. and Summers, L.H. (1988), 'Beyond the natural rate hypothesis', *American Economic Review*, **78**(2), 182–187.

Blanchard, O. and Wolfers, J. (2000), 'The role of shocks and institutions in the rise of European unemployment: the aggregate evidence', *Economic Journal*, **110**(462), 1–33.

Blecker, R.A. (1989), 'International competition, income distribution and economic growth', *Cambridge Journal of Economics*, **13**(3), 395–412.

Blecker, R.A. (1999), 'Kaleckian macro models for open economies', in J. Deprez and J.T. Harvey (eds.), *Foundations of International Economics. Post-Keynesian Perspectives*, London, New York: Routledge.

Blecker, R.A. (2002), 'Distribution, demand and growth in neo-Kaleckian macro-models', in M. Setterfield (ed.), *The Economics of Demand-Led Growth*, Cheltenham, UK: Edward Elgar Publishing.

Blecker, R.A. (2011), 'Open economy models of distribution and growth', in E. Hein and E. Stockhammer (eds.), *A Modern Guide to Keynesian Macroeconomics and Economic Policies*, Cheltenham, UK: Edward Elgar Publishing.

Blecker, R.A. (2016a), 'Wage-led versus profit-led demand regimes: the long and the short of it', *Review of Keynesian Economics*, **4**(4), 373–390.

Blecker, R.A. (2016b), 'The debate over "Thirlwall's Law": balance-of-payments-constrained growth reconsidered', *European Journal of Economics and Economic Policies: Intervention*, **13**(3), 275–290.

Blecker, R.A. (2016c), 'Finance, distribution and the role of government: heterodox foundations for understanding the crisis', *Studies in Political Economy*, **97**(1), 75–85.

Blecker, R.A. (2016d), 'The US economy since the crisis: slow recovery and secular stagnation', *European Journal of Economics and Economic Policies: Intervention*, **13**(2), 203–214.

Blecker, R.A. (2021), 'Thirlwall's law is not a tautology, but some empirical tests of it nearly are', *Review of Keynesian Economics*, **9**(2), 175–203.

Blecker, R.A. and Seguino, S. (2002), 'Macroeconomic effects of reducing gender wage inequality in an export-oriented, semi-industrialized economy', *Review of Development Economics*, **6**(1), 103–119.

Blecker, R.A. and Setterfield, M. (2019), *Heterodox Macroeconomics: Models of Demand, Distribution and Growth*, Cheltenham, UK: Edward Elgar Publishing.

Boone, L. and Girouard, N. (2002), 'The stock market, the housing market and consumer behaviour', *OECD Economic Studies*, **2**, 175–200.

Bossone, B. (2001), 'Circuit theory of banking and finance', *Journal of Banking and Finance*, **25**(5), 857–890.

Bossone, B. (2003), 'Thinking of the economy as a circuit', in L.-P. Rochon and S. Rossi (eds.), *Modern Theories of Money*, Cheltenham, UK: Edward Elgar Publishing.

Bouthevillain, C., Caruana, J., Checherita, C., Cunha, J., Gordo, E., Haroutunian, S., Langenus, G., Hubic, A., Manzke, B., Pérez, J. and Tommasino, P. (2009), 'Pros and cons of various fiscal measures to stimulate the economy', *Banco de Espana Economic Bulletin*, July/August, 123–144.

Bowles, S. and Boyer, R. (1995), 'Wages, aggregate demand, and employment in an open economy: an empirical investigation', in G.A. Epstein and H.M. Gintis (eds.), *Macroeconomic Policy after the Conservative Era*, Cambridge, UK: Cambridge University Press.

Brancaccio, E. and De Cristofaro, F. (2020), 'Inside the IMF "mea culpa": a panel analysis on growth forecast errors and Keynesian multipliers in Europe', *PSL Quarterly Review*, **73**(294), 225–239.

Brancaccio, E., De Cristofaro, F. and Giammetti, R. (2020), 'A meta-analysis on labour market deregulation and employment performance: no consensus around the IMF-OECD consensus', *Review of Political Economy*, **32**(1), 1–21.

Braunstein, E., Bouhia, R. and Seguino, S. (2020), 'Social reproduction, gender equality and economic growth', *Cambridge Journal of Economics*, **44**(1), 126–156.

Braunstein, E., van Staveren, I. and Tavani, D. (2011), 'Embedding care and unpaid work in macroeconomic modeling: a structuralist approach', *Feminist Economics*, **17**(4), 5–31.

Brown, C. (2004), 'Does income distribution matter for effective demand? Evidence from the United States', *Review of Political Economy*, **16**(3), 291–307.

Brown, H.P. (1990), 'Would Keynes have endorsed incomes policies?', *Review of Political Economy*, **2**(2), 127–137.

Cahen-Fourot, L. and Lavoie, M. (2016), 'Ecological monetary economics: a post-Keynesian critique', *Ecological Economics*, **126**, 163–168.

Carlin, W. and Soskice, D. (2006), *Macroeconomics: Imperfections, Institutions & Policies*, Oxford: Oxford University Press.

Carlin, W. and Soskice, D. (2009), 'Teaching intermediate macroeconomics using the 3-equation model', in G. Fontana and M. Setterfield (eds.), *Macroeconomic Theory and Macroeconomic Pedagogy*, Basingstoke, UK: Palgrave Macmillan.

Carlin, W. and Soskice, D. (2015), *Macroeconomics: Institutions, Instability, and the Financial System*, Oxford: Oxford University Press.

Carvalho, F.C.d. (1992), *Mr Keynes and the Post Keynesians: Principles of Macroeconomics for a Monetary Production Economy*, Aldershot, UK: Edward Elgar Publishing.

Carvalho, L. and Rezai, A. (2016), 'Personal income inequality and aggregate demand', *Cambridge Journal of Economics*, **40**(2), 491–505.

Cassetti, M. (2003), 'Bargaining power, effective demand and technical progress: a Kaleckian model of growth', *Cambridge Journal of Economics*, **27**(3), 449–464.

Cassetti, M. (2012), 'Macroeconomic outcomes of changing social bargains: the feasibility of a wage-led open economy reconsidered', *Metroeconomica*, **63**(1), 64–91.

Catephores, G. (1989), *An Introduction to Marxist Economics*, Basingstoke, UK: Palgrave Macmillan.

Cesaratto, S. (2015), 'Neo-Kaleckian and Sraffian controversies on the theory of accumulation', *Review of Political Economy*, **27**(2), 154–182.

Cesaratto, S. (2017), 'Initial and final finance in the monetary circuit and the theory of effective demand', *Metroeconomica*, **68**(2), 228–258.

Cesaratto, S. and Di Bucchianico, S. (2020), 'Endogenous money and the theory of long period effective demand', *Bulletin of Political Economy*, **14**(1), 1–38.

Cesaratto, S. and Pariboni, R. (2021), 'Keynes's finance, the monetary and demand-led circuits: a Sraffian assessment', Working Paper No. 851, University of Siena.

Cesaratto, S., Serrano, F. and Stirati, A. (2003), 'Technical change, effective demand and employment', *Review of Political Economy*, **15**(1), 33–52.

Chancel, L. and Piketty, T. (2015), *Carbon and Inequality: From Kyoto to Paris*, Paris: Paris School of Economics.

Charles, S. (2008a), 'Corporate debt, variable retention rate and the appearance of financial fragility', *Cambridge Journal of Economics*, **32**(5), 781–795.

Charles, S. (2008b), 'A post-Keynesian model of accumulation with a Minskyan financial structure', *Review of Political Economy*, **20**(3), 319–331.

Charles, S. (2008c), 'Teaching Minsky's financial instability hypothesis: a manageable suggestion', *Journal of Post Keynesian Economics*, **31**(1), 125–138.

Charles, S. (2016a), 'Is Minsky's financial instability hypothesis valid?', *Cambridge Journal of Economics*, **40**(2), 427–436.

Charles, S. (2016b), 'An additional explanation for the variable Keynesian multiplier: the role of the propensity to import', *Journal of Post Keynesian Economics*, **39**(2), 187–205.

Charles, S., Dallery, T. and Marie, J. (2015), 'Why the Keynesian multiplier increases during hard times: a theoretical explanation based on rentier's saving behaviour', *Metroeconomica*, **66**(3), 451–473.

Chiang, A.C. (1984), *Fundamental Methods of Mathematical Economics*, 3rd edition, Auckland et al.: McGraw Hill.

Chick, V. (1983), *Macroeconomics after Keynes*, Oxford: Philip Allan.

Clarida, R., Gali, J. and Gertler, M. (1999), 'The science of monetary policy: a new Keynesian perspective', *Journal of Economic Literature*, **37**(4), 1661–1707.

Clark, J.B. (1899), *The Distribution of Wealth: A Theory of Wages, Interest and Profits*, New York: Macmillan, reprint: New York: Cosimo, 2005.

Coenen, C., Erceg, C.J., Freedman, C., Furceri, D., Kumhof, M., Lalonde, R., Laxton, D., Lindé, J., Mourougane, A., Muir, D., Mursula, S., de Resende, C., Roberts, J., Roeger, W., Snudden, S., Trabandt, M. and in't Veld, J. (2012), 'Effects of fiscal stimulus in structural models', *American Economic Journal: Macroeconomics*, **4**(1), 22–68.

Coenen, G., Straub, R. and Trabandt, M. (2013), 'Gauging the effects of fiscal stimulus packages in the Euro Area', *Journal of Economic Dynamics and Control*, **37**(2), 367–386.

Colander, D. (2009), 'How did macro theory get so far off track, and what can heterodox macroeconomists do to get it back on track?', in E. Hein, T. Niechoj and E. Stockhammer (eds.), *Macroeconomic Policies on Shaky Foundations: Whither Mainstream Economics?*, Marburg: Metropolis.

Colander, D., Föllmer, H., Haas, A., Goldberg, M., Juselius, K., Kirman, A., Lux, T. and Sloth, B. (2009), 'The financial crisis and the systemic failure of academic economics', Kiel Working Paper No. 1489, Kiel Institute for the World Economy.

Cornilleau, G. and Creel, J. (2016), 'Financialisation and the crises in the export-led mercantilist German economy', in E. Hein, D. Detzer and N. Dodig (eds.), *Financialisation and the Financial and Economic Crises: Country Studies*, Cheltenham, UK: Edward Elgar Publishing.

Costanza, R. (1989), 'What is ecological economics?', *Ecological Economics*, **1**(1), 1–7.

Cross, R. (2014), 'Unemployment: natural rate epicycles or hysteresis?', *European Journal of Economics and Economic Policies: Intervention*, **11**(2), 136–148.

Crotty, J. (1986), 'Marx, Keynes and Minsky on the instability of the capitalist growth process and the nature of government economic policy', in S.W. Helburn and D.F. Bramhall (eds.), *Marx, Keynes, Schumpeter: A Centennial Celebration of Dissent*, New York: M.E. Sharpe.

Crotty, J. (1992), 'Neoclassical and Keynesian approaches to the theory of investment', *Journal of Post Keynesian Economics*, **14**(4), 483–496.

Crotty, J. (1993), 'Rethinking Marxian investment theory: Keynes-Minsky instability, competitive regime shift and coerced investment', *Review of Radical Political Economics*, **25**(1), 1–26.

Cynamon, B.Z. and Fazzari, S.M. (2008), 'Household debt in the consumer age: source of growth – risk of collapse', *Capitalism and Society*, **3**(2), 1–30.

Cynamon, B.Z. and Fazzari, S.M. (2010), 'The Great Recession and perspectives on Keynesian policy', in S. Dullien, E. Hein, A. Truger and T. van Treeck (eds.), *The World Economy in Crisis – The Return of Keynesianism?*, Marburg: Metropolis.

Cynamon, B.Z. and Fazzari, S.M. (2013), 'Inequality and household finance during the consumer age', Working Paper No. 752, Annandale-on-Hudson, NY: Levy Economics Institute of Bard College.

Cynamon, B.Z. and Fazzari, S.M. (2015), 'Rising inequality and stagnation in the US economy', *European Journal of Economics and Economic Policies: Intervention*, **12**(2), 170–172.

Cynamon, B.Z. and Fazzari, S.M. (2016), 'Inequality, the Great Recession and slow recovery', *Cambridge Journal of Economics*, **40**(2), 373–399.

D'Arista, J. (2013), 'State of the art: the US central bank at 100', *International Journal of Political Economy*, **42**(3), 5–23.

Dafermos, Y. (2018), 'Debt cycles, instability and fiscal rules: a Godley-Minsky synthesis', *Cambridge Journal of Economics*, **42**(5), 1277–1313.

Dafermos, Y. and Nikolaidi, M. (2019), 'Fiscal policy and ecological sustainability: a post-Keynesian perspective', in P. Arestis and M. Sawyer (eds.), *Frontiers of Heterodox Macroeconomics. International Papers in Political Economy*, Basingstoke, UK: Palgrave Macmillan.

Dafermos, Y., Nikolaidi, M. and Galanis, G. (2017), 'A stock-flow-fund ecological macroeconomic model', *Ecological Economics*, **131**, 191–207.

Dafermos, Y., Nikolaidi, M. and Galanis, G. (2018), 'Climate change, financial stability and monetary policy', *Ecological Economics*, **152**, 219–234.

Dallery, T. (2009), 'Post-Keynesian theories of the firm under financialization', *Review of Radical Political Economics*, **41**(4), 492–515.

Dallery, T. and van Treeck, T. (2011), 'Conflicting claims and equilibrium adjustment processes in a stock-flow consistent macroeconomic model', *Review of Political Economy*, **23**(2), 189–211.

Daly, H.E. (1973), *Toward a Steady-State Economy,* San Francisco: W.H. Freeman.

Daly, H.E. (1974), 'Steady-state economics versus growthmania: a critique of the orthodox conceptions of growth, wants, scarcity, and efficiency', *Policy Sciences*, **5**(2), 149–167.

Daly, H.E. (1996), *Beyond Growth: The Economics of Sustainable Development*, Boston: Beacon Press.

Darku, A. (2014), 'Income inequality, status seeking, and savings rates in Canada', *Canadian Studies in Population,* **41**(3–4), 88–104.

Davidson, P. (1972), *Money and the Real World*, London: Macmillan.

Davidson, P. (1982), *International Money and the Real World*, Basingstoke, UK: Palgrave Macmillan.

Davidson, P. (1986/87), 'Finance, funding, saving, and investment', *Journal of Post Keynesian Economics*, **9**(1), 101–110.

Davidson, P. (1994/2011), *Post Keynesian Macroeconomic Theory*, 2nd edition in 2011, Aldershot, UK: Edward Elgar Publishing.

Davidson, P. (2002), *Financial Markets, Money and the Real World*, Cheltenham, UK: Edward Elgar Publishing.

Davidson, P. (2006), 'Can, or should, a central bank target inflation?', *Journal of Post Keynesian Economics*, **28**(4), 689–703.

Davidson, P. (2007), *John Maynard Keynes*, Basingstoke, UK: Palgrave Macmillan.

Davidson, P. (2009), *The Keynes Solution: The Path to Global Economic Prosperity*, Basingstoke, UK: Palgrave Macmillan.

Davidson, P. (2015), *Post-Keynesian Theory and Policy: A Realistic Analysis of the Market Oriented Capitalist Economy*, Cheltenham, UK: Edward Elgar Publishing.

Davis, L.E. (2016), 'Identifying the "financialization" of the non-financial corporation in the US economy: a decomposition of firm-level balance sheets', *Journal of Post Keynesian Economics*, **39**(1), 115–141.

Davis, L.E. (2017), 'Financialization and investment: a survey of the empirical literature', *Journal of Economic Surveys*, **31**(5), 1332–1358.

Davis, L.E. (2018a), 'Financialization and the nonfinancial corporation: an investigation of firm level investment behavior in the United States', *Metroeconomica*, **69**(1), 270–301.

Davis, L.E. (2018b), 'Financialization, shareholder orientation and the cash holdings of US corporations', *Review of Political Economy*, **30**(1), 1–27.

De Brunhoff, S. (1976), *Marx on Money,* New York: Urizen Books.

De Grauwe, P. (2012), 'The governance of a fragile Eurozone', *Australian Economic Review*, **45**(3), 255–268.

De Paula, L.F., Fritz, B. and Prates, D.M. (2017), 'Keynes at the periphery: currency hierarchy and challenges for economic policy in emerging economies', *Journal of Post Keynesian Economics*, **40**(2), 183–202.

Dejuan, O. (2005), 'Paths of accumulation and growth: towards a Keynesian long-period theory of output', *Review of Political Economy*, **17**(2), 231–252.

Dejuan, O., Febrero, E. and Uxo, J. (eds.) (2013), *Post-Keynesian Views of the Crisis and Its Remedies*, Abingdon: Routledge.

Deleidi, M. (2018), 'Post Keynesian endogenous money theory: a theoretical and empirical investigation of the credit demand schedule', *Journal of Post Keynesian Economics*, **41**(2), 185–209.

Deleidi, M. (2019), 'Endogenous money theory: horizontalists, structuralists and the credit market', *Bulletin of Political Economy*, **13**(1), 21–53.

Deleidi, M. (2020), 'Post-Keynesian endogenous money theory: horizontalists, structuralists and the paradox of illiquidity', *Metroeconomica,* **71**(1), 156–175.

Deleidi, M. and Mazzucato, M. (2019), 'Putting austerity to bed: technical progress, aggregate demand and the supermultiplier', *Review of Political Economy*, **31**(3), 315–335.

Deleplace, G. and Nell, E. (1996), 'Introduction: monetary circulation and effective demand', in G. Deleplace and E. Nell (eds.), *Money in Motion*, Basingstoke, UK: Palgrave Macmillan.

Dequech, D. (2012), 'Post Keynesianism, heterodoxy and mainstream economics', *Review of Political Economy*, **24**(2), 353–368.

Detzer, D. (2012), 'New instruments for banking regulation and monetary policy after the crisis', *European Journal of Economics and Economic Policies: Intervention*, **9**(2), 233–254.

Detzer, D. (2018), 'Inequality, emulation and debt: the occurrence of different growth regimes in the age of financialisation in a stock-flow consistent model', *Journal of Post Keynesian Economics*, **41**(2), 284–315.

Detzer, D. and Hein, E. (2016), 'Financialisation and the crises in the export-led mercantilist German economy', in E. Hein, D. Detzer and N. Dodig (eds.), *Financialisation and the Financial and Economic Crises: Country Studies*, Cheltenham, UK: Edward Elgar Publishing.

Detzer, D., Dodig, N., Evans, T., Hein, E., Herr, H. and Prante, F.J. (2017), *The German Financial System and the Financial and Economic Crisis*, Cham et al.: Springer International.

Deutsche Bundesbank (2017), 'The role of banks, non-banks and the central bank in the money creation process', *Monthly Report*, April, 13–33.

Di Bucchianico, S. (2021), 'Inequality, household debt, ageing and bubbles: a model of demand-side secular stagnation', Working Paper No. 160/2020, Institute for International Political Economy (IPE), Berlin School of Economics and Law.

Diallo, M., Flaschel, P., Krolzig, H. and Proaño, C. (2011), 'Reconsidering the dynamic interaction between real wages and macroeconomic activity', *Research in World Economy*, **2**(1), 77–93.

Dixon, R.J. and Thirlwall, A.P. (1975), 'A model of regional growth-differences on Kaldorian lines', *Oxford Economic Papers*, **27**(2), 201–214.

Dobusch, L. and Kapeller, J. (2012), 'A guide to paradigmatic self-marginalization: lessons for post-Keynesian economists', *Review of Political Economy*, **24**(3), 469–487.

Dodig, N., Hein, E. and Detzer, D. (2016), 'Financialisation and the financial and economic crises: theoretical framework and empirical analysis for 15 countries', in E. Hein, D. Detzer, and N. Dodig (eds.), *Financialisation and the Financial and Economic Crises: Country Studies*, Cheltenham, UK: Edward Elgar Publishing.

Domar, E.D. (1944), 'The "burden of the debt" and national income', *American Economic Review*, **34**(4), 794–828.

Domar, E.D. (1946), 'Capital expansion, rate of growth and employment', *Econometrica*, **14**(2), 137–147.

Dostaler, G. (2007), *Keynes and His Battles*, Cheltenham, UK: Edward Elgar Publishing.

Douthwaite, R. (2000), *The Ecology of Money*, Bristol: Green Books.

Dow, S. (2006), 'Endogenous money: structuralist', in P. Arestis and M. Sawyer (eds.), *A Handbook of Alternative Monetary Economics*, Cheltenham, UK: Edward Elgar Publishing.

Duesenberry, J.S. (1949), *Income, Saving and the Theory of Consumer Behavior*, Cambridge, MA: Harvard University Press.

Dullien, S. (2011), 'The new consensus from a traditional Keynesian and a post-Keynesian perspective: a worthwhile foundation for research or just a waste of time?', *Économie Appliquée*, **64**(1), 173–200.

Duménil, G. and Lévy, D. (1999), 'Being Keynesian in the short term and classical in the long term: the traverse to classical long-term equilibrium', *The Manchester School*, **67**(6), 684–716.

Duménil, G. and Lévy, D. (2005), 'Costs and benefits of neoliberalism: a class analysis', in G.A. Epstein (ed.), *Financialization and the World Economy*, Cheltenham, UK: Edward Elgar Publishing.

Dünhaupt, P. (2011), 'Financialization, corporate governance and income distribution in the USA and Germany: introducing an adjusted wage share indicator', in T. Niechoj, Ö. Onaran, E. Stockhammer, A. Truger and T. van Treeck (eds.), *Stabilising an Unequal Economy? Public Debt, Financial Regulation, and Income Distribution*, Marburg: Metropolis.

Dünhaupt, P. (2012), 'Financialization and the rentier income share – evidence from the USA and Germany', *International Review of Applied Economics*, **26**(4), 465–487.

Dünhaupt, P. (2017), 'Determinants of labour's income share in the era of financialisation', *Cambridge Journal of Economics*, **41**(1), 283–306.

Dünhaupt, P. and Hein, E. (2019), 'Financialisation, distribution, and macroeconomic regimes before and after the crisis: a post-Keynesian view on Denmark, Estonia, and Latvia', *Journal of Baltic Studies*, **50**(4), 435–465.

Durand, C. and Gueuder, M. (2018), 'The profit-investment nexus in an era of financialisation, globalisation and monopolisation: a profit-centred perspective', *Review of Political Economy*, **30**(2), 126–153.

Dutt, A.K. (1984), 'Stagnation, income distribution and monopoly power', *Cambridge Journal of Economics*, **8**(1), 25–40.

Dutt, A.K. (1987), 'Alternative closures again: a comment on "Growth, distribution and inflation"', *Cambridge Journal of Economics*, **11**(1), 75–82.

Dutt, A.K. (1990), *Growth, Distribution and Uneven Development*, Cambridge, UK: Cambridge University Press.

Dutt, A.K. (2005), 'Conspicuous consumption, consumer debt and economic growth', in M. Setterfield (ed.), *Interactions in Analytical Political Economy: Theory, Policy and Applications*, Armonk, NY: M.E. Sharpe.

Dutt, A.K. (2006), 'Maturity, stagnation and consumer debt: a Steindlian approach', *Metroeconomica*, **57**(3), 339–364.

Dutt, A.K. (2011), 'Economic growth and income distribution: Kalecki, the Kaleckians and their critics', in P. Arestis (ed.), *Microeconomics, Macroeconomics and Economic Policies*, Basingstoke, UK: Palgrave Macmillan.

Dutt, A.K. (2012), 'Distributional dynamics in Post Keynesian growth models', *Journal of Post Keynesian Economics*, **34**(3), 431–451.

Dutt, A.K. (2016), 'Growth and distribution in heterodox models with managers and financiers', *Metroeconomica*, **67**(2), 364–396.

Dutt, A.K. (2019), 'Some observations on models of growth and distribution with autonomous demand growth', *Metroeconomica*, **70**(2), 288–301.

Dutt, A.K. (2020), 'Autonomous demand growth, distribution, and fiscal and monetary policy in the short and long runs', in H. Bougrine and L.-P. Rochon (eds.), *Economic Growth and Macroeconomic Stabilization Policies in Post-Keynesian Economics: Essays in Honour of Marc Lavoie and Mario Seccareccia, Book Two*, Cheltenham, UK: Edward Elgar Publishing.

Dutt, A.K. and Amadeo, E.J. (1990), *Keynes's Third Alternative: The Neo-Ricardian Keynesians and the Post Keynesians*, Aldershot, UK: Edward Elgar Publishing.

Duwicquet, V. (2020), 'Financialization, dividends, and accumulation of capital', *Journal of Post Keynesian Economics*, **44**(2), 239–282.

Dymski, G.A. (1996), 'Kalecki's monetary economics', in J.E. King (ed.), *An Alternative Macroeconomic Theory: The Kaleckian Model and Post-Keynesian Economics*, Boston: Kluwer.

Earl, P.E. and Peng, T.C. (2012), 'Brands of economics and the Trojan horse of pluralism', *Review of Political Economy*, **24**(3), 451–467.

ECB (2021), European Central Bank, Key ECB interest rates, https://www.ecb.europa.eu/stats/policy _and_exchange_rates/key_ecb_interest_rates/html/index.en.html.

Ederer, S., Hein, E., Niechoj, T., Reiners, S., Truger, A. and van Treeck, T. (2012), *Interventions: 17 Interviews with Unconventional Economists (2004 – 2012)*, Marburg: Metropolis.

Ehnts, D. (2017), *Modern Monetary Theory and European Macroeconomics*, London: Routledge.

Eichner, A.S. (1976), *The Megacorp and Oligopoly*, Cambridge, UK: Cambridge University Press.

Eichner, A.S. (ed.) (1978), *A Guide to Post-Keynesian Economics*, White Plains, NY: M.E. Sharpe.

Eichner, A.S. and Kregel, J.A. (1975), 'An essay on post-Keynesian theory: a new paradigm in economics', *Journal of Economic Literature*, **13**(4), 1293–1311.

Elmendorf, D.W. and Furman, J. (2008), 'If, when, how: a primer on fiscal stimulus', Hamilton Project Strategy Paper, Washington, DC: Brookings Institution.

Epstein, G.A. (2005), 'Introduction: financialization and the world economy', in G.A. Epstein (ed.), *Financialization and the World Economy*, Cheltenham, UK: Edward Elgar Publishing.

Epstein, G.A. (2019a), 'The institutional, empirical and policy limits of "modern money theory"', Working Paper No. 481, Political Economy Research Institute (PERI), University of Massachusetts Amherst.

Epstein, G.A. (2019b), *What's Wrong with Modern Money Theory? A Policy Critique*, Cham, Switzerland: Palgrave.

Epstein, G.A. (2020), 'The MMT free lunch mirage can lead to a perverse outcome', *Challenge: The Magazine of Economic Affairs*, **63**(1), 2–13.

Epstein, G.A. and Jayadev, A. (2005), 'The rise of rentier incomes in OECD countries: financialization, central bank policy and labor solidarity', in G.A. Epstein (ed.), *Financialization and the World Economy*, Cheltenham, UK: Edward Elgar Publishing.

Epstein, G.A. and Power, D. (2003), 'Rentier incomes and financial crises: an empirical examination of trends and cycles in some OECD countries', *Canadian Journal of Development Studies*, **24**(2), 229–248.

Esping-Andersen, G. (1990), *The Three Worlds of Welfare Capitalism*, Cambridge, UK: Polity Press.

European Commission (2019a), Annual Macro-Economic Database (AMECO), November, https://ec .europa.eu/info/business-economy-euro/indicators-statistics/economic-databases/macroeconomic -database-ameco/ameco-database_en#database.

European Commission (2019b), The European Green Deal: Communication from the Commission to the European Parliament, the European Council, the Council, The European Economic and Social Committee and the Committee of The Regions, https://ec.europa.eu/info/sites/info/files/european -green-deal-communication_en.pdf.

European Commission (2021), Annual Macro-Economic Database (AMECO), November, https://ec .europa.eu/info/business-economy-euro/indicators-statistics/economic-databases/macro-economic -database-ameco_en.

Farley, J., Burke, M., Flomenhoft, G., Kelly, B., Murray, D., Posner, S., Putnam, M., Scanlan, A. and Witham, A. (2013), 'Monetary and fiscal policies for a finite planet', *Sustainability*, **5**(6), 2802–2826.

Faudot, A. (2021), 'The Keynes Plan and Bretton Woods debates: the early radical criticism by Balogh, Kalecki and Schumacher', *Cambridge Journal of Economics*, **45**(4), 751–769.

Fazzari, S.M. and Mott, T. (1986/87), 'The investment theories of Kalecki and Keynes: an empirical study of firm data, 1970–1982', *Journal of Post Keynesian Economics*, **9**(2), 171–187.

Fazzari, S.M., Ferri, P.E. and Variato, A.M. (2020), 'Demand-led growth and accommodating supply', *Cambridge Journal of Economics*, **44**(3), 583–605.

Fazzari, S.M., Ferri, P.E., Greenberg, E.G. and Variato, A.M. (2013), 'Aggregate demand, instability, and growth', *Review of Keynesian Economics*, **1**(1), 1–21.

Febrero, E. (2009), 'Three difficulties with neo-chartalism', *Journal of Post Keynesian Economics*, **31**(3), 523–541.

Feiner Solis, S. (2021), 'The effectiveness and risks of loose monetary policy under financialisation', Working Paper No. 159/2021, Institute for International Political Economy (IPE), Berlin School of Economics and Law.

Feiwel, G.R. (1975), *The Intellectual Capital of Michal Kalecki*, Knoxville: The University of Tennessee Press.

Felderer, B. and Homburg, S. (1992), *Macroeconomics and New Macroeconomics*, 2nd edition, Berlin: Springer.

Ferreiro, J., Gálvez, C. and González, A. (2016), 'Financialisation and the economic crisis in Spain', in E. Hein, D. Detzer and N. Dodig, N. (eds.), *Financialisation and the Financial and Economic Crises: Country Studies*, Cheltenham, UK: Edward Elgar Publishing.

Fiebiger, B. (2016a), 'Fiscal policy, monetary policy and the mechanics of modern clearing and settlement systems', *Review of Political Economy*, **28**(4), 590–608.

Fiebiger, B. (2016b), 'Rethinking the financialisation of non-financial corporations: a reappraisal of US empirical data', *Review of Political Economy*, **28**(3), 354–379.

Fiebiger, B. (2018), 'Semi-autonomous household expenditures as the *causa causans* of postwar US business cycles: the stability and instability of Luxemburg-type external markets', *Cambridge Journal of Economics*, **42**(1), 155–175.

Fiebiger, B. and Lavoie, M. (2019), 'Trend and business cycles with external markets: non-capacity generating semi-autonomous expenditures and effective demand', *Metroeconomica*, **70**(2), 247–262.

Fiebiger, B., Fullwiler, S., Kelton, S. and Wray, L.R. (2012), 'Modern monetary theory: a debate', PERI Working Papers No. 279, Universtity of Massachusetts, Amherst.

Fisher, I. (1933), 'The debt-deflation theory of great depressions', *Econometrica*, **1**(4), 337–357.

Flaschel, P. and Proaño, C. (2007), 'AS-AD disequilibrium dynamics and the Taylor interest rate policy rule: Euro-Area based estimation and simulation', in P. Arestis, E. Hein and E. Le Heron (eds.), *Aspects of Modern Monetary and Macroeconomic Policies*, Basingstoke, UK: Palgrave Macmillan.

Foley, D.K. (1986), *Understanding Capital: Marx's Economic Theory*, Cambridge, MA: Harvard University Press.

Foley, D.K., Michl, T.R. and Tavani, D. (2019), *Growth and Distribution*, 2nd edition, Cambridge, MA and London: Harvard University Press.

Fontana, G. (2000), 'Post Keynesians and circuitists on money and uncertainty: an attempt at generality', *Journal of Post Keynesian Economics*, **33**(1), 27–48.

Fontana, G. (2003), 'Post Keynesian approaches to endogenous money: a time framework explanation', *Review of Political Economy*, **15**(3), 291–314.

Fontana, G. (2004a), 'Rethinking endogenous money: a constructive interpretation of the debates between horizontalists and structuralists', *Metroeconomica*, **55**(4), 367–385.

Fontana, G. (2004b), 'Hicks on monetary theory and history: money as endogenous money', *Cambridge Journal of Economics*, **28**(1), 73–88.

Fontana, G. (2009a), 'Whither new consensus macroeconomics? The role of government and fiscal policy in modern macroeconomics', in E. Hein, T. Niechoj and E. Stockhammer (eds.), *Macroeconomic Policies on Shaky Foundations: Whither Mainstream Economics?*, Marburg: Metropolis.

Fontana, G. (2009b), *Money, Uncertainty and Time*, Abingdon: Routledge.

Fontana, G. and Gerrard, B. (2006), 'The future of Post Keynesian economics', *Banca Nazionale del Lavoro Quarterly Review*, **59**(236), 49–80.

Fontana, G. and Palacio-Vera, A. (2002), 'Monetary policy rules: what are we learning?', *Journal of Post Keynesian Economics*, **24**(4), 547–568.

Fontana, G. and Palacio-Vera, A. (2004), 'Monetary policy uncovered: theory and practice', *International Review of Applied Economics*, **18**(1), 25–41.

Fontana, G. and Palacio-Vera, A. (2007), 'Are long-run price stability and short-run output stabilization all that monetary policy can aim for?', *Metroeconomica*, **58**(2), 269–298.

Fontana, G. and Sawyer, M. (2013), 'Post-Keynesian and Kaleckian thoughts on ecological macroeconomics', *European Journal of Economics and Economic Policies: Intervention*, **10**(2), 256–267.

Fontana, G. and Sawyer, M. (2014), 'The macroeconomics and financial system requirements for a sustainable future', Financialisation, Economy, Society and Sustainable Development (FESSUD) Working Paper, No. 53, University of Leeds.

Fontana, G. and Sawyer, M. (2016), 'Towards post-Keynesian ecological macroeconomics', *Ecological Economics*, **121**, 186–195.

Fontana, G. and Sawyer, M. (2022), 'Would a zero growth economy be achievable and be sustainable?', *European Journal of Economics and Economic Policies: Intervention*, **19**(1), 89–102.

Fontana, G. and Setterfield, M. (eds.) (2009a), *Macroeconomics and Macroeconomic Pedagogy*, Basingstoke, UK: Palgrave Macmillan.

Fontana, G. and Setterfield, M. (2009b), 'A simple (and teachable) macroeconomic model with endogenous money', in G. Fontana and M. Setterfield (eds.), *Macroeconomics and Macroeconomic Pedagogy*, Basingstoke, UK: Palgrave Macmillan.

Forstater, M. and Mosler, W. (2005), 'The natural rate of interest is zero', *Journal of Economic Issues*, **39**(2), 535–542.

Foster, J.B. (2014), *The Theory of Monopoly Capitalism: An Elaboration of Marxian Political Economy*, New York: Monthly Review Press.

Frank, R.H., Levine, A.S. and Dijk, O. (2014), 'Expenditure cascades', *Review of Behavioral Economics*, **1**(1–2), 55–73.

Freitas, F. and Christianes, R. (2020), 'A baseline supermultiplier model for the analysis of fiscal policy and government debt', *Review of Keynesian Economics*, **8**(3), 313–338.

Freitas, F. and Serrano, F. (2015), 'Growth rate and level effects, the stability of the adjustment of capacity to demand and the Sraffian supermultiplier', *Review of Political Economy*, **27**(3), 258–281.

Freitas, F. and Serrano, F. (2017), 'The Sraffian supermultiplier as an alternative closure for heterodox growth theory', *European Journal of Economics and Economic Policies: Intervention*, **14**(1), 70–91.

Friedman, M. (1953), 'The methodology of positive economics', in M. Friedman, *Essays in Positive Economics*, Chicago: Chicago University Press.

Fritsche, U., Heine, M., Herr, H., Horn, G. and Kaiser, C. (2005), 'Macroeconomic regime and economic development: the case of the USA', in E. Hein, T. Niechoj, T. Schulten and A. Truger (eds.), *Macroeconomic Policy Coordination in Europe and the Role of the Trade Unions*, Brussels: ETUI.

Fritz, B., de Paula, L.F. and Prates, D.M. (2018), 'Global currency hierarchy and national policy space: a framework for peripheral economies', *European Journal of Economics and Economic Policies: Intervention*, **15**(2), 208–218.

Froyen, R.T. (2002), *Macroeconomics: Theories and Policies*, 7th edition, Upper Saddle River, NJ: Prentice Hall.

Fukuda-Parr, S., Heintz, J. and Seguino, S. (2013), 'Critical perspectives on financial and economic crises: heterodox macroeconomics meets feminist economics', *Feminist Economics*, **19**(3), 4–31.

Fullwiler, S.C. (2013), 'An endogenous money perspective on the post-crisis monetary policy debate', *Review of Keynesian Economics*, **1**(2), 171–194.

Gabbi, G., Ticci, E. and Vozzella, P. (2016), 'The transmission channels between the financial and the real sectors in Italy and the crisis', in E. Hein, D. Detzer and N. Dodig (eds.), *Financialisation and the Financial and Economic Crises: Country Studies*, Cheltenham, UK: Edward Elgar Publishing.

Garegnani, P. (1978), 'Notes on consumption, investment and effective demand, Part I', *Cambridge Journal of Economics*, **2**(4), 335–353.

Garegnani, P. (1979), 'Notes on consumption, investment and effective demand, Part II', *Cambridge Journal of Economics*, **3**(1), 63–82.

Gechert, S. (2015), 'What fiscal policy is most effective? A meta regression analysis', *Oxford Economic Papers*, **67**(3), 553–580.

Gechert, S. and Rannenberg, A. (2018), 'Which fiscal multipliers are regime-dependent? A meta-regression analysis', *Journal of Economic Surveys*, **32**(4), 1160–1182.

Gechert, S., Niechoj, T., Stockhammer, E., Truger, A. and Watt, A. (2017), 'Editorial: towards pluralism in macroeconomics? 20th anniversary conference of the FMM research network', *European Journal of Economics and Economic Policies: Intervention*, **14**(2), 125–130.

Gechert, S., Horn, G. and Paetz, C. (2019), 'Long-term effects of fiscal stimulus and austerity in Europe', *Oxford Bulletin of Economics and Statistics*, **81**(3), 647–666.

Georgescu-Roegen, N. (1971), *The Entropy Law and the Economic Process*, Cambridge, MA: Harvard University Press.

Girardi, D. and Pariboni, R. (2016), 'Long-run effective demand in the US economy: an empirical test of the Sraffian supermultiplier model', *Review of Political Economy*, **28**(4), 523–544.

Girardi, D., Paternesis Meloni, W. and Stirati, A. (2020), 'Reverse hysteresis? Persistence effects of autonomous demand expansion', *Cambridge Journal of Economics*, **44**(4), 835–869.

Global Footprint Network (2022), Ecological Footprint, https://www.footprintnetwork.org/our-work/ecological-footprint/.

Glyn, A. (2006), *Capitalism Unleashed: Finance, Globalization, and Welfare*, Oxford: Oxford University Press.

Glyn, A. (2009), 'Functional distribution and inequality', in W. Salverda, B. Nolan and T.M. Smeeding (eds.), *The Oxford Handbook of Economy Inequality*, Oxford: Oxford University Press.

Glyn, A. and Sutcliffe, B. (1972), *Capitalism in Crisis*, New York: Pantheon.

Gnos, C. and Rochon, L.-P. (2007), 'The new consensus and post-Keynesian interest rate policy', *Review of Political Economy*, **19**(3), 369–386.

Godley, W. (1999), 'Money and credit in a Keynesian model of income determination', *Cambridge Journal of Economics*, **23**(4), 393–411.

Godley, W. and Lavoie, M. (2007), *Monetary Economics: An Integrated Approach to Credit, Money, Income, Production and Wealth*, Basingstoke, UK: Palgrave Macmillan.

Goodfriend, M. and King, R.G. (1997), 'The new neoclassical synthesis and the role of monetary policy', in B.S. Bernanke and J.J. Rotemberg (eds.), *NBER Macroeconomics Annual: 1997*, Cambridge, MA: MIT Press.

Goodhart, C.A.E. (1998), 'The two concepts of money: implications for the analysis of optimal currency areas', *European Journal of Political Economy*, **14**(3), 407–432.

Goodhart, C.A.E. (2009), *The Regulatory Response to the Financial Crisis*, Cheltenham, UK: Edward Elgar Publishing.

Goodwin, R. (1967), 'A growth cycle', in C.H. Feinstein (ed.), *Capitalism and Economic Growth*, Cambridge, UK: Cambridge University Press.

Gordon, D.M. (1981), 'Capital-labor conflict and the productivity slowdown', *American Economic Review*, **71**(2), 30–35.

Gordon, D.M. (1995), 'Growth, distribution, and the rules of the game: social structuralist macro foundations for a democratic economic policy', in G.A. Epstein and H.M. Gintis (eds.), *Macroeconomic Policy after the Conservative Era*, Cambridge, UK: Cambridge University Press.

Gordon, D.M., Weisskopf, T.E. and Bowles, S. (1983), 'Long swings and the nonreproductive cycle', *American Economic Review*, **73**(2), 152–157.

Gordon, D.M., Weisskopf, T.E. and Bowles, S. (1987), 'Power, accumulation and crisis: the rise and the demise of the postwar social structure of accumulation', in Union for Radical Political Economics (ed.), *The Imperiled Economy, Book I: Macroeconomics from a Left Perspective*, New York: Union for Radical Political Economics.

Gordon, R.J. (2015), 'Secular stagnation: a supply side view', *American Economic Review: Papers and Proceedings*, **105**(5), 54–59.

Gowdy, J.M. (1991), 'Bioeconomics and post Keynesian economics: a search for common ground', *Ecological Economics*, **3**(1), 77–87.

Gowdy, J.M. and Erickson, J.D. (2005), 'The approach of ecological economics', *Cambridge Journal of Economics*, **29**(2), 207–222.

Graziani, A. (1984), 'The debate on Keynes' finance motive', *Economic Notes*, **1**(1), 15–34.

Graziani, A. (1988), 'The financement of economic activity in Keynes's thought', in H. Hagemann and O. Steiger (eds.), *Keynes' General Theory nach fünfzig Jahren*, Berlin: Duncker & Humblot.

Graziani, A. (1989), 'The theory of the monetary circuit', *Thames Paper in Political Economy*, Spring, 1–26.

Graziani, A. (1994), 'Monetary circuits', in P. Arestis and M. Sawyer (eds.), *The Elgar Companion to Radical Political Economy*, Aldershot, UK: Edward Elgar Publishing.

Graziani, A. (1996), 'Money as purchasing power and money as a stock of wealth in Keynesian economic thought', in G. Deleplace and E. Nell (eds.), *Money in Motion*, Basingstoke, UK: Palgrave Macmillan.

Graziani, A. (1997), 'The Marxist theory of money', *International Journal of Political Economy*, **27**(2), 26–50.

Graziani, A. (2003), *The Monetary Theory of Production*, New York: Cambridge University Press.

Guschanski, A. and Onaran, Ö. (2018), 'Determinants of the wage share: a cross-country comparison using sectoral data', *CESifo Forum*, **19**(2), 44–54.

Guttmann, R. (2016), *Finance-led Capitalism: Shadow Banking, Re-Regulation, and the Future of Global Markets*, Basingstoke, UK: Palgrave Macmillan.

Guttmann, R. and Plihon, D. (2010), 'Consumer debt and financial fragility', *International Review of Applied Economics*, **24**(3), 269–283.

Haavelmo, T. (1945), 'Multiplier effects of a balanced budget', *Econometrica*, **13**(4), 311–318.

Hahnel, R. (2017), *Income Distribution and Environmental Sustainability*, London, New York: Routledge.

Hall, P.A. and Franzese, R.J. (1998), 'Mixed signals: central bank independence, coordinated wage bargaining, and European Monetary Union', *International Organization*, **52**(3), 505–535.

Hall, P.A. and Soskice, D. (2001), *Varieties of Capitalism: The Institutional Foundations of Comparative Advantage*, Oxford: Oxford University Press.

Hamouda, O.F. and Harcourt, G.C. (1988), 'Post Keynesianism: from criticism to coherence?', *Bulletin of Economic Research*, **40**(1), 1–33.

Harcourt, G.C. (1969), 'Some Cambridge controversies in the theory of capital', *Journal of Economic Literature*, **7**(2), 369–405.

Harcourt, G.C. (1972), *Some Cambridge Controversies in the Theory of Capital*, Cambridge, UK: Cambridge University Press.

Harcourt, G.C. (2006), *The Structure of Post-Keynesian Economics: The Core Contributions of the Pioneers*, Cambridge, UK: Cambridge University Press.

Harcourt, G.C. and Kenyon, P. (1976), 'Pricing and the investment decision', *Kyklos*, **29**(3), 449–477.

Harcourt, G.C. and Kerr, P. (2009), *Joan Robinson*, Basingstoke, UK: Palgrave Macmillan.

Harcourt, G.C. and Kriesler, P. (eds.) (2013), *The Oxford Handbook of Post-Keynesian Economics*, 2 Volumes, Oxford: Oxford University Press.

Harris, D.J. (1987), 'Classical growth models', in J. Eatwell, M. Milgate and P. Newman (eds.), *The New Palgrave: A Dictionary of Economics,* Vol. 1, London, New York and Tokyo: Palgrave Macmillan.

Harrod, R.F. (1939), 'An essay in dynamic theory', *The Economic Journal*, **49**(193), 14–33.

Harrod, R.F. (1951), *The Life of John Maynard Keynes*, London: Macmillan.

Hartwig, J. (2007), 'Keynes vs. the Post Keynesians on the principle of effective demand', *European Journal of the History of Economic Thought*, **14**(4), 725–739.

Hartwig, J. (2011), 'Aggregate demand and aggregate supply: will the real Keynes please stand up?', *Review of Political Economy*, **23**(4), 613–618.

Hartwig, J. (2013a), 'Effective demand: securing the foundations', *Review of Political Economy*, **25**(4), 672–678.

Hartwig, J. (2013b), 'Distribution and growth in demand and productivity in Switzerland (1950–2010)', *Applied Economics Letters*, **20**(10), 938–944.

Hartwig, J. (2014), 'Testing the Bhaduri–Marglin model with OECD panel data', *International Review of Applied Economics*, **28**(4), 419–435.

Hartwig, J. (2017), 'The comparative statics of effective demand', *Review of Political Economy*, **29**(2), 360–375.

Harvey, D. (2007), *The Limits to Capital*, London: Verso.

Harvey, J.T. (2007/8), 'Teaching Post Keynesian exchange rate theory', *Journal of Post Keynesian Economics,* **30**(2), 147–168.

Harvey, J.T. (2009), *Currencies, Capital Flows and Crises: A Post Keynesian Analysis of Exchange Rate Determination*, London: Routledge.

Harvey, J.T. (2018), 'Intermediate macroeconomics: the importance of being Post Keynesian', *Journal of Post Keynesian Economics*, **41**(1), 83–98.

Harvey, J.T. (2019), 'Exchange rates and the balance of payments: reconciling an inconsistency in Post Keynesian theory', *Journal of Post Keynesian Economics*, **42**(3), 390–415.

Hawtrey, R.G. (1937), 'Alternative theories of the rate of interest: three rejoinders', *The Economic Journal*, **47**(187), 436–443.

Hay, C. and Wincott, D. (2012), *The Political Economy of European Welfare Capitalism*, Basingstoke, UK: Palgrave Macmillan.

Hayes, M.G. (2006), *The Economics of Keynes: A New Guide to the General Theory*, Cheltenham, UK: Edward Elgar Publishing.

Hayes, M.G. (2007a), 'The point of effective demand', *Review of Political Economy*, **19**(1), 55–80.

Hayes, M.G. (2007b), 'Keynes's Z function, heterogeneous output, and marginal productivity', *Cambridge Journal of Economics*, **31**(5), 741–753.

Hayes, M.G. (2013), 'Effective demand: securing the foundations', *Review of Political Economy*, **25**(4), 661–671.

Hayes, M.G. (2019), *John Maynard Keynes*, Cambridge, UK: Polity Press.

Heimberger, P. and Kapeller, J. (2017), 'The performativity of potential output: pro-cyclicality and path dependency in coordinating European fiscal policies', *Review of International Political Economy*, **24**(5), 904–928.

Heimberger, P., Kapeller, J. and Schuetz, B. (2017), 'The NAIRU determinants: what's "structural" about unemployment in Europe?', *Journal of Policy Modeling*, **39**(5), 883–908.

Hein, E. (2002), 'Monetary policy and wage bargaining in the EMU: restrictive ECB policies, high unemployment, nominal wage restraint and inflation above the target', *Banca Nazionale del Lavoro Quarterly Review*, **55**(222), 299–337.

Hein, E. (2004), 'Money, credit and the interest rate in Marx's economics: on the similarities of Marx's monetary analysis to post-Keynesian economics', *International Papers in Political Economy*, **11**(2), 1–43.

Hein, E. (2006a), 'Wage bargaining and monetary policy in a Kaleckian monetary distribution and growth model: trying to make sense of the NAIRU', *European Journal of Economics and Economic Policies: Intervention*, **3**(2), 305–329.

Hein, E. (2006b), 'Money, interest and capital accumulation in Karl Marx's economics: a monetary interpretation and some similarities to post-Keynesian approaches', *European Journal of the History of Economic Thought*, **13**(1), 113–140.

Hein, E. (2006c), 'On the (in-)stability and the endogeneity of the "normal" rate of capacity utilisation in a post-Keynesian/Kaleckian "monetary" distribution and growth model', *Indian Development Review*, **4**(1), 129–150.

Hein, E. (2006d), 'Interest, debt and capital accumulation – a Kaleckian approach', *International Review of Applied Economics*, **20**(3), 337–352.

Hein, E. (2007), 'Interest rate, debt, distribution and capital accumulation in a post-Kaleckian model', *Metroeconomica*, **58**(2), 310–339.

Hein, E. (2008), *Money, Distribution Conflict and Capital Accumulation: Contributions to 'Monetary Analysis'*, Basingstoke, UK: Palgrave Macmillan.

Hein, E. (2009), 'Financialisation in a comparative static, stock-flow consistent post-Kaleckian distribution and growth model', *Ekonomiaz: Basque Economic Review*, **72**(3), 120–139.

Hein, E. (2010), 'Shareholder value orientation, distribution and growth – short- and medium-run effects in a Kaleckian model', *Metroeconomica*, **61**(2), 302–332.

Hein, E. (2011a), 'Review of Lopez G., J., Assous, M., *Michal Kalecki* (Basingstoke, UK: Palgrave Macmillan, 2010)', *European Journal of Economics and Economic Policies: Intervention*, **8**(2), 405–406.

Hein, E. (2011b), 'Redistribution, global imbalances and the financial and economic crisis – the case for a Keynesian New Deal', *International Journal of Labour Research*, **3**(1), 51–73.

Hein, E. (2011c), 'Financialisation, re-distribution, and the financial and economic crisis – a Kaleckian perspective', in T. Niechoj, Ö. Onaran, E. Stockhammer, A. Truger and T. van Treeck, T. (eds.), *Stabilising an Unequal Economy? Public Debt, Financial Regulation, and Income Distribution*, Marburg: Metropolis.

Hein, E. (2012a), *The Maroeconomics of Finance-dominated Capitalism – and Its Crisis*, Cheltenham, UK: Edward Elgar Publishing.

Hein, E. (2012b), 'The rate of interest as a macroeconomic distribution parameter: horizontalism and post-Keynesian models of distribution and growth', *Bulletin of Political Economy*, **6**(2), 107–132, reprinted in L.-P. Rochon and S. Rossi (eds.) (2017), *Advances in Endogenous Money Analysis*, Cheltenham, UK: Edward Elgar Publishing.

Hein, E. (2012c), 'Finance-dominated capitalism, re-distribution, household debt and financial fragility in a Kaleckian distribution and growth model', *PSL Quarterly Review*, **65**(260), 11–51.

Hein, E. (2013), 'Finance-dominated capitalism, re-distribution and the financial and economic crises: a European perspective', in O. Dejuan, E. Febrero and J. Uxo (eds.), *Post-Keynesian Views of the Crisis and Its Remedies*, Abingdon: Routledge.

Hein, E. (2013/14), 'The crisis of finance-dominated capitalism in the Euro Area, deficiencies in the economic policy architecture and deflationary stagnation policies', *Journal of Post Keynesian Economics*, **36**(2), 325–354.

Hein, E. (2014a), *Distribution and Growth after Keynes: A Post-Keynesian Guide*, Cheltenham, UK: Edward Elgar Publishing.

Hein, E. (2014b), 'State and perspectives of post-Keynesian economics – views of a non-methodologist', in S. Dullien, E. Hein and A. Truger (eds.), *Makroökonomie, Entwicklung und Wirtschaftspolitik/ Macroeconomics, Development and Economic Policies: Festschrift für/for Jan Priewe*, Marburg: Metropolis.

Hein, E. (2015), 'Finance-dominated capitalism and re-distribution of income – a Kaleckian perspective', *Cambridge Journal of Economics*, **39**(3), 907–934.

Hein, E. (2016), 'Secular stagnation or stagnation policy? Steindl after Summers', *PSL Quarterly Review*, **69**(276), 3–47.

Hein, E. (2017a), 'Post-Keynesian macroeconomics since the mid-1990s – main developments', *European Journal of Economics and Economic Policies: Intervention*, **14**(2), 131–172.

Hein, E. (2017b), 'The Bhaduri/Marglin post-Kaleckian model in the history of distribution and growth theories – an assessment by means of model closures', *Review of Keynesian Economics*, **5**(2), 218–238.

Hein, E. (2017c), 'An alternative macroeconomic policy approach for the Eurozone', in H. Herr, J. Priewe and A. Watt (eds.), *Saving the Euro – Redesigning Euro Area Economic Governance*, London: Social Europe.

Hein, E. (2018a), 'Stagnation policy in the Eurozone and economic policy alternatives: a Steindlian/ neo-Kaleckian perspective', *Wirtschaft und Gesellschaft*, **44**(3), 315–348.

Hein, E. (2018b), 'The principle of effective demand – Marx, Kalecki, Keynes and beyond', in T.-H. Jo, L. Chester and C. D'Ippoliti (eds.), *Handbook of Heterodox Economics*, London: Routledge.

Hein, E. (2018c), 'Autonomous government expenditure growth, deficits, debt and distribution in a neo-Kaleckian growth model', *Journal of Post Keynesian Economics*, **41**(2), 216–238.

Hein, E. (2018d), *Verteilung und Wachstum: Eine paradigmenorientierte Einführung unter besonderer Berücksichtigung der post-keynesianischen Theorie*, 2. grundlegend überarbeitete und stark erweiterte Auflage, Marburg: Metropolis.

Hein, E. (2019a), 'Financialisation and tendencies towards stagnation: the role of macroeconomic regime changes in the course of and after the financial and economic crisis 2007–2009', *Cambridge Journal of Economics*, **43**(4), 975–999.

Hein, E. (2019b), 'Karl Marx – an early post-Keynesian? A comparison of Marx's economics with the contributions by Sraffa, Keynes, Kalecki and Minsky', *European Journal of Economics and Economic Policies: Intervention*, **16**(2), 238–259.

Hein, E. (2019c), 'Review of Toporowski, J., *Michal Kalecki: An Intellectual Biography, Volume 1: Rendezvouz in Cambridge, 1899–1939* (Basingstoke, UK: Palgrave Macmillan, 2013) and *Michal Kalecki: An Intellectual Biography, Volume II: By Intellect Alone 1939–1970* (Basingstoke, UK: Palgrave Macmillan, 2018)', *European Journal of Economics and Economic Policies: Intervention*, **16**(3), 420–426.

Hein, E. (2019d), 'Stagnation policy in the Eurozone and post-Keynesian economic policy alternatives', in J. Jespersen and F. Olesen (eds.), *Progressive Post-Keynesian Economics: Dealing with Reality*, Cheltenham, UK: Edward Elgar Publishing.

Hein, E. (2020), 'Gender issues in Kaleckian distribution and growth models: on the macroeconomics of the gender wage gap', *Review of Political Economy*, **32**(4), 640–664.

Hein, E. (2021), '*Saving and Investment in the Twenty-First Century: The Great Divergence* – some comments from a post-Keynesian perspective', *European Journal of Economics and Economic Policies: Intervention*, **18**(3), 293–302.

Hein, E. (2022a), 'Financialisation and stagnation – a macroeconomic regime perspective', in L.R. Wray and F. Dantas (eds.), *The Handbook of Economic Stagnation*, London et al.: Academic Press.

Hein, E. (2022b), 'Stagnation policy: a Steindlian perspective', in L.R. Wray and F. Dantas (eds.), *The Handbook of Economic Stagnation*, London et al.: Academic Press.

Hein, E. and Detzer, D. (2015a), 'Finance-dominated capitalism and income distribution: a Kaleckian perspective on the case of Germany', *Italian Economic Journal*, **1**(2), 171–191.

Hein, E. and Detzer, D. (2015b), 'Post-Keynesian alternative policies to curb macroeconomic imbalances in the Euro Area', *Panoeconomicus*, **62**(2), 217–236.

Hein, E. and Detzer, D. (2015c), 'Coping with imbalances in the Euro Area: policy alternatives addressing divergences and disparities between member countries', *Wirtschaft und Management: Schriftenreihe zur wirtschaftswissenschaftlichen Forschung und Praxis*, **22**, 13–50.

Hein, E. and Jimenez, V. (2022), 'Zero growth and macroeconomic stability: a post-Keynesian approach', *European Journal of Economics and Economic Policies: Intervention*, **19**(1), 41–60.

Hein, E. and Lavoie, M. (2019), 'Post-Keynesian economics', in R. Dimand and H. Hagemann (eds.), *The Elgar Companion to John Maynard Keynes*, Cheltenham, UK: Edward Elgar Publishing.

Hein, E. and Martschin, J. (2020), 'The Eurozone in crisis – a Kaleckian macroeconomic regime and policy perspective', *Review of Political Economy*, **32**(4), 563–588.

Hein, E. and Martschin, J. (2021), 'Demand and growth regimes in finance-dominated capitalism and the role of the macroeconomic policy regime: a post-Keynesian comparative study on France, Germany, Italy and Spain before and after the Great Financial Crisis and the Great Recession', *Review of Evolutionary Political Economy*, **2**(3), 493–527.

Hein, E. and Mundt, M. (2012), 'Financialisation and the requirements and potentials for wage-led recovery – a review focussing on the G20', Conditions of Work and Employment Series No. 37, Geneva: ILO.

Hein, E. and Mundt, M. (2013), 'Financialisation, the financial and economic crisis, and the requirements and potentials for wage-led recovery', in M. Lavoie and E. Stockhammer (eds.), *Wage-Led Growth: An Equitable Strategy for Economic Recovery*, Basingstoke, UK: Palgrave Machmillan.

Hein, E. and Prante, F.J. (2020), 'Functional distribution and wage inequality in recent Kaleckian growth models', in H. Bougrine and L.-P. Rochon (eds.), *Economic Growth and Macroeconomic Stabilization Policies in Post-Keynesian Economics: Essays in Honour of Marc Lavoie and Mario Seccareccia, Book Two*, Cheltenham, UK: Edward Elgar Publishing.

Hein, E. and Priewe, J. (2009), 'The Research Network Macroeconomics and Macroeconomic Policies (FMM) – past, present and future', *European Journal of Economics and Economic Policies: Intervention*, **6**(2), 166–173.

Hein, E. and Schoder, C. (2011), 'Interest rates, distribution and capital accumulation – a post-Kaleckian perspective on the US and Germany', *International Review of Applied Economics*, **25**(6), 693–723.

Hein, E. and Stockhammer, E. (2009a), 'A Post Keynesian macroeconomic policy mix as an alternative to the new consensus approach', in P. Arestis and M. Sawyer (eds.), *Unemployment: Past and Present*, Basingstoke, UK: Pagrave Macmillan.

Hein, E. and Stockhammer, E. (2009b), 'A post-Keynesian alternative to the new consensus model', in G. Fontana and M. Setterfield (eds.), *Macroeoconomic Theory and Macroeconomic Pedagogy*, Basingstoke, UK: Palgrave Macmillan.

Hein, E. and Stockhammer, E. (2010), 'Macroeconomic policy mix, employment and inflation in a post-Keynesian alternative to the new consensus model', *Review of Political Economy*, **22**(3), 317–354.

Hein, E. and Stockhammer, E. (eds.) (2011a), *A Modern Guide to Keynesian Macroeconomics and Economic Policies*, Cheltenham, UK: Edward Elgar Publishing.

Hein, E. and Stockhammer, E. (2011b), 'A post-Keynesian macroeconomic model of inflation, distribution and employment', in E. Hein and E. Stockhammer (eds.), *A Modern Guide to Keynesian Macroeconomics and Economic Policies*, Cheltenham, UK: Edward Elgar Publishing.

Hein, E. and Tarassow, A. (2010), 'Distribution, aggregate demand and productivity growth – theory and empirical results for six OECD countries based on a post-Kaleckian model', *Cambridge Journal of Economics*, **34**(4), 727–754.

Hein, E. and Truger, A. (2005a), 'What ever happened to Germany? Is the decline of the former European key currency country caused by structural sclerosis or by macroeconomic mismanagement?', *International Review of Applied Economics*, **19**(1), 3–28.

Hein, E. and Truger, A. (2005b), 'A different view of Germany's stagnation', *Challenge: The Magazine of Economic Affairs*, **48**(6), 64–94.

Hein, E. and Truger, A. (2005c), 'Macroeconomic coordination as an economic policy concept – opportunities and obstacles in the EMU', in E. Hein, T. Niechoj, T. Schulten and A. Truger (eds.), *Macroeconomic Policy Coordination in Europe and the Role of the Trade Unions*, Brussels: ETUI.

Hein, E. and Truger, A. (2009), 'How to fight (or not to fight) a slowdown', *Challenge: The Magazine of Economic Affairs*, **52**(2), 52–75.

Hein, E. and Truger, A. (2011), 'Finance-dominated capitalism in crisis – the case for a Keynesian New Deal at the European and the global level', in P. Arestis and M. Sawyer (eds.), *New Economics as Mainstream Economics*, Basingstoke, UK: Palgrave Macmillan.

Hein, E. and Truger, A. (2012/13), 'Finance-dominated capitalism in crisis – the case for a global Keynesian New Deal', *Journal of Post Keynesian Economics*, **35**(2), 183–210.

Hein, E. and Truger, A. (2014), 'Fiscal policy and rebalancing in the Euro Area: a critique of the German debt brake from a post-Keynesian perspective', *Panoeconomicus*, **61**(1), 21–38.

Hein, E. and Truger, A. (2017), 'Opportunities and limits of rebalancing the Eurozone via wage policies: theoretical considerations and empirical illustrations for the case of Germany', *PSL Quarterly Review*, **70**(283), 421–447.

Hein, E. and van Treeck, T. (2010a), 'Financialisation' in post-Keynesian models of distribution and growth – a systematic review', in M. Setterfield (ed.), *Handbook of Alternative Theories of Economic Growth*, Cheltenham, UK: Edward Elgar Publishing.

Hein, E. and van Treeck, T. (2010b), 'Financialisation and rising shareholder power in Kaleckian/post-Kaleckian models of distribution and growth', *Review of Political Economy*, **22**(2), 205–233.

Hein, E. and Vogel, L. (2008), 'Distribution and growth reconsidered – empirical results for six OECD countries', *Cambridge Journal of Economics*, **32**(3), 479–511.

Hein, E. and Vogel, L. (2009), 'Distribution and growth in France and Germany: single equation estimations and model simulations based on the Bhaduri/Marglin model', *Review of Political Economy*, **21**(2), 245–272.

Hein, E. and Woodgate, R. (2021), 'Stability issues in Kaleckian models driven by autonomous demand growth – Harrodian instability and debt dynamics', *Metroeconomica*, **72**(2), 388–404.

Hein, E., Lavoie, M. and van Treeck, T. (2011), 'Some instability puzzles in Kaleckian models of growth and distribution: a critical survey', *Cambridge Journal of Economics*, **35**(3), 587–612.

Hein, E., Lavoie, M. and van Treeck, T. (2012a), 'Harrodian instability and the "normal rate" of capacity utilisation in Kaleckian models of distribution and growth – a survey', *Metroeconomica*, **63**(1), 139–169.

Hein, E., Truger, A. and van Treeck, T. (2012b), 'The European financial and economic crisis: alternative solutions from a (post-)Keynesian perspective', in P. Arestis and M. Sawyer (eds.), *The Euro Crisis. International Papers in Political Economy*, Basingstoke, UK: Palgrave Macmillan.

Hein, E., Detzer, D. and Dodig, N. (eds.) (2015), *The Demise of Finance-Dominated Capitalism: Explaining the Financial and Economic Crises*, Cheltenham, UK: Edward Elgar Publishing.

Hein, E., Detzer, D. and Dodig, N. (eds.) (2016), *Financialisation and the Financial and Economic Crises: Country Studies*, Cheltenham, UK: Edward Elgar Publishing.

Hein, E., Dünhaupt, P., Alfageme, A. and Kulesza, M. (2017a), 'Financialisation and distribution before and after the crisis: patterns for six OECD countries', in P. Arestis and M. Sawyer (eds.), *Economic Policies since the Global Financial Crisis. International Papers in Political Economy*, Basingstoke, UK: Palgrave Macmillan.

Hein, E., Dünhaupt, P., Kulesza, M. and Alfageme, A. (2017b), 'Financialisation and distribution from a Kaleckian perspective: the US, the UK and Sweden compared – before and after the crisis', *International Journal of Political Economy*, **46**(4), 233–266.

Hein, E., Dünhaupt, P., Alfageme, A. and Kulesza, M. (2018), 'A Kaleckian perspective on financialisation and distribution in three main Eurozone countries before and after the crisis: France, Germany and Spain', *Review of Political Economy*, **30**(1), 41–71.

Hein, E., Paternesi Meloni, W. and Tridico, P. (2021), 'Welfare models and demand-led growth regimes before and after the financial and economic crisis', *Review of International Political Economy*, **28**(5), 1196–1223.

Heine, M and Herr, H. (2013), *Volkswirtschaftslehre: Paradigmenorientierte Einführung in die Mikro- und Makroökonomie*, 4th edition, München: Oldenbourg.

Heinrich, M. (1991), *Die Wissenschaft vom Wert*, Hamburg: VSA.

Hemming, R., Kell, M. and Mahfouz, S. (2002), 'The effectiveness of fiscal policy in stimulating economic activity: a review of the literature', International Monetary Fund Working Paper No. 02/208, Washington, DC: IMF.

Herr, H. (1988a), 'Theorie einer monetären Produktionswirtschaft', *Ökonomie und Gesellschaft*, **6**, 66–98.

Herr, H. (1988b), *Geld, Kredit und ökonomische Dynamik in marktvermittelten Ökonomien – die Vision einer Geldwirtschaft*, 2nd edition, München: Florentz.

Herr, H. (1992), *Geld, Währungswettbewerb und Währungssysteme: Theoretische und historische Analyse einer internationalen Geldwirtschaft*, Frankfurt a.M., New York: Campus.

Herr, H. (1993), 'Makroökonomische Budgetbeschränkung und Kreditmarkt', in H.J. Stadermann and O. Steiger (eds.), *Der Stand und die nächste Zukunft der Geldforschung: Festschrift für Hajo Riese zum 60. Geburtstag*, Berlin: Duncker & Humblot.

Herr, H. (2011), 'International monetary and financial architecture', in E. Hein and E. Stockhammer (eds.), *A Modern Guide to Keynesian Macroeconomics and Economic Policies*, Cheltenham, UK: Edward Elgar Publishing.

Herr, H. (2014a), 'The European Central Bank and the US Federal Reserve as lender of last resort', *Panoeconomicus*, **61**(1), 59–78.

Herr, H. (2014b), 'An analytical framework for the post-Keynesian macroeconomic paradigm', *Izmir Review of Social Sciences*, **1**(2), 73–105.

Herr, H. (2022), 'Transformation of capitalism to enforce ecologically sustainable GDP growth: lessons from Keynes and Schumpeter', *European Journal of Economics and Economic Policies: Intervention*, **19**(1), 159–173.

Herr, H. and Kazandziska, M. (2011), *Macroeconomic Policy Regimes in Western Industrial Countries*, London: Routledge.

Herr, H. and Priewe, J. (2005), 'Beyond the "Washington Consensus": macroeconomic policies for development', *Internationale Politik und Gesellschaft*, **2**(1), 72–97.

Herr, H. and Priewe, J. (2006), 'The Washington Consensus and (non-)development', in L.R. Wray and M. Forstater (eds.), *Money, Financial Instability and Stabilization Policy*, Cheltenham, UK: Edward Elgar Publishing.

Herr, H., Priewe, J. and Watt, A. (eds.) (2017), *Saving the Euro – Redesigning Euro Area Economic Governance*, London: Social Europe.

Herr, H., Priewe, J. and Watt, A. (eds.) (2019), *Still Time to Save the Euro*, Berlin: Social Europe.

Hickel, J. (2019), 'Degrowth: a theory of radical abundance', *Real World Economic Review*, **87**, 54–68.

Hickel, J. and Kallis, G. (2020), 'Is green growth possible?', *New Political Economy*, **25**(4), 469–486.

Hicks, J.R. (1937), 'Mr. Keynes and the "Classics": a suggested interpretation', *Econometrica*, **5**(2), 147–159.

Holt, R.P.F. and Pressman, S. (eds.) (2001), *A New Guide to Post-Keynesian Economics*, London: Routledge.

Holt, R.P.F., Pressman, S. and Spash, C.L. (eds.) (2009), *Post Keynesian and Ecological Economics: Confronting Environmental Issues*, Cheltenham, UK: Edward Elgar Publishing.

Hope, D. and Soskice, D. (2016), 'Growth models, varieties of capitalism and macroeconomics', *Politics & Society*, **44**(2), 209–226.

Horn, G., Joebges, H., Zwiener, R. (2009), 'From the financial crisis to the world economic crisis (II): global imbalances – causes of the crisis and solution strategies for Germany', IMK Policy Brief, December 2009, Duesseldorf: Macroeconomic Policy Institute (IMK) at Hans-Boeckler Foundation.

Howell, D. (2011), 'Institutions, aggregate demand and cross-country employment performance: alternative theoretical perspectives and the evidence', in E. Hein and E. Stockhammer (eds.), *A Modern Guide to Keynesian Macroeconomics and Economic Policies*, Cheltenham, UK: Edward Elgar Publishing.

Howells, P (1995a), 'The demand for endogenous money', *Journal of Post Keynesian Economics*, **18**(1), 89–106.

Howells, P. (1995b), 'Endogenous money', *International Papers in Political Economy*, **2**(2), 1–41.

Howells, P. (2006), 'The endogeneity of money: empirical evidence', in P. Arestis and M. Sawyer (eds.), *A Handbook of Alternative Monetary Economics*, Cheltenham, UK: Edward Elgar Publishing.

Howells, P. (2009), 'Money and banking in realistic macro model', in G. Fontana and M. Setterfield (eds.), *Macroeconomics and Macroeconomic Pedagogy*, Basingstoke, UK: Palgrave Macmillan.

Ihrig, J, Weinbach, G. and Wolla, C. (2021), 'Teaching the linkage between banks and the Fed: R.I.P. money multiplier', *Page One Economics: Econ Primer*, Federal Reserve Bank of St. Louis.

International Monetary Fund (IMF) (2021), World Economic Outlook Data Mapper, October 2021, https://www.imf.org/external/datamapper/datasets/WEO.

IPCC (2018), Intergovernmental Panel on Climate Change, Global Warming of 1.5°C, https://www.ipcc.ch/sr15/.

Isaac, A.G. and Kim, Y.K. (2013), 'Consumer and corporate debt: a neo-Kaleckian synthesis', *Metroeconomica*, **64**(2), 244–247.

Ivanova, D. and Wood, R. (2020), 'The unequal distribution of household carbon footprints in Europe and its link to sustainability', *Global Sustainability*, **3**(e18), 1–12.

Jackson, T. (2017), *Prosperity without Growth: Foundations of the Economy of Tomorrow*, 2nd edition, London: Routledge.

Jackson, T. and Victor, P.A. (2011), 'Productivity and work in the "green economy": some theoretical reflections and empirical tests', *Environmental Innovation and Societal Transformation*, **1**(1), 101–108.

Jackson, T. and Victor, P.A. (2015), 'Does credit create a "growth imperative"? A quasi-stationary economy with interest-bearing debt', *Ecological Economics*, **120**, 32–48.

Jackson, T. and Victor, P.A. (2016), 'Does slow growth lead to rising inequality? Some theoretical reflections and numerical simulations', *Ecological Economics*, **121**, 206–219.

Jackson, T. and Victor, P.A. (2020), 'The transition to a sustainable prosperity – a stock-flow-consistent ecological macroeconomic model for Canada', *Ecological Economics*, **177**, 1–14.

Jakab, Z. and Kumhof, M. (2015), 'Banks are not intermediaries of loanable funds – and why this matters', Bank of England Working Paper No. 529, London.

Janischewski, A. (2022), 'Inequality, non-linear consumption behaviour and monetary growth imperatives', *European Journal of Economics and Economic Policies: Intervention*, **19**(1), 61–88.

Jayadev, A. (2007), 'Capital account openness and the labour share of income', *Cambridge Journal of Economics*, **31**(4), 423–443.

Jespersen, J. (2009), *Macroeconomic Methodology: A Post-Keynesian Perspective*, Cheltenham, UK: Edward Elgar Publishing.

Jimenez, V. (2020), 'Wage shares and demand regimes in Central America: an empirical analysis 1970–2016', Working Paper No. 151/2020, Institute for International Political Economy (IPE), Berlin School of Economics and Law.

Jungmann, B. (2021), 'Growth drivers in emerging capitalist economies before and after the Global Financial Crisis', Working Paper No. 172/2021, Institute for International Political Economy (IPE), Berlin School of Economics and Law.

Kaldor, N. (1955/56), 'Alternative theories of distribution', *Review of Economic Studies*, **23**(2), 83–100, reprinted in N. Kaldor (1980), *Collected Economic Essays, Vol. 1: Essays on Value and Distribution*, 2nd edition, London: Duckworth.

Kaldor, N. (1957), 'A model of economic growth', *The Economic Journal*, **67**(268), 591–624, reprinted in N. Kaldor (1960), *Collected Economic Essays, Vol. 2: Essays on Economic Stability and Growth*, London: Duckworth.

Kaldor, N. (1961), 'Capital accumulation and economic growth', in F.A. Lutz and D.C. Hague (eds.), *The Theory of Capital*, London: Macmillan, reprinted in N. Kaldor (1978), *Collected Economic Essays, Vol. 5: Further Essays on Economic Theory*, London: Duckworth.

Kaldor, N. (1966), *Causes of the Slow Rate of Economic Growth in the United Kingdom*, Cambridge, UK: Cambridge University Press, reprinted in N. Kaldor (1978), *Collected Economic Essays, Vol. 5: Further Essays on Economic Theory*, London: Duckworth.

Kaldor, N. (1970a), 'The case for regional policies', *Scottish Journal of Political Economy*, **17**(3), 337–348, reprinted in N. Kaldor (1978), *Collected Economic Essays, Vol. 5: Further Essays on Economic Theory*, London: Duckworth.

Kaldor, N. (1970b), 'The new monetarism', *Lloyds Bank Review*, **97**, 1–17.

Kaldor, N. (1982), *The Scourge of Monetarism*, Oxford: Oxford University Press.

Kaldor, N. (1985), 'How monetarism failed', *Challenge: The Magazine of Economic Affairs*, **28**(2), 4–13.

Kaldor, N. and Trevithick, J. (1981), 'A Keynesian perspective on money', *Lloyds Bank Review*, **139**, 1–19.

Kalecki, M. (1932), 'Koniunktura a inflacja' (The business cycle and inflation), *Polska Gospodarcza*, **13**(48), 1411–1415, English translation in J. Osiatynski (ed.) (1990), *Collected Works of Michal Kalecki, Vol. I: Capitalism: Business Cycles and Full Employment*, Oxford: Clarendon Press.

Kalecki, M. (1933), *Proba teorii koniunktury (Essay on the Business Cycle Theory)*, Warszawa: Intstytut Badania Koniunktur Gospodarczych, English translation in J. Osiatynski (ed.) (1990), *Collected Works of Michal Kalecki, Vol. I: Capitalism: Business Cycles and Full Employment*, Oxford: Clarendon Press.

Kalecki, M. (1935), 'A macrodynamic theory of business cycles', *Econometrica*, **3**(3), 327–344, reprinted in J. Osiatynski (ed.) (1990), *Collected Works of Michal Kalecki, Vol. I: Capitalism: Business Cycles and Full Employment*, Oxford: Clarendon Press.

Kalecki, M. (1936), 'Some remarks on Keynes's theory', English translation of original Polish version, *Australian Economic Papers*, **21**, 1982, 245–253, reprinted in J. Osiatynski (ed.) (1990), *Collected Works of Michal Kalecki, Vol. I: Capitalism: Business Cycles and Full Employment*, Oxford: Clarendon Press.

Kalecki, M. (1937), 'The principle of increasing risk', *Economica*, **4**(16), 440–447.

Kalecki, M. (1939), *Essays in the Theory of Economic Fluctuations*, London: George Allen & Unwin, reprinted in J. Osiatynski (ed.) (1990), *Collected Works of Michal Kalecki, Vol. I: Capitalism: Business Cycles and Full Employment*, Oxford: Clarendon Press.

Kalecki, M. (1943a), *Studies in Economic Dynamics*, London: Allen and Unwin, reprinted in J. Osiatynski (ed.) (1991), *Collected Works of Michal Kalecki, Vol. II: Capitalism: Economic Dynamics*, Oxford: Clarendon Press.

Kalecki, M. (1943b), 'Political aspects of full employment', *Political Quarterly*, **14**(4), 322–331, reprinted in J. Osiatynski (ed.) (1990), *Collected Works of Michał Kalecki, Vol. I: Capitalism: Business Cycles and Full Employment,* Oxford: Clarendon Press.

Kalecki, M. (1943c), 'The burden of the national debt', *Bulletin of the Oxford University Institute of Statistics*, **5**(5), 76–80, reprinted in J. Osiatynski (ed.) (1997), *Collected Works of Michał Kalecki, Vol. VII: Studies in Applied Economics 1940–1967*, Oxford: Clarendon Press.

Kalecki, M. (1944), 'Three ways to full employment', in Oxford University Institute of Statistics (ed.), *The Economics of Full Employment*, Oxford: Basil Blackwell, reprinted in J. Osiatynski (ed.) (1990), *Collected Works of Michał Kalecki, Vol. I: Capitalism: Business Cycles and Full Employment*, Oxford: Clarendon Press.

Kalecki, M. (1945), 'Full employment by stimulating private investment?', *Oxford Economic Papers*, **7**(1), 83–92, reprinted in J. Osiatynski (ed.) (1990), *Collected Works of Michał Kalecki, Vol. I, Capitalism: Business Cycles and Full Employment*, Oxford: Clarendon Press.

Kalecki, M. (1954), *Theory of Economic Dynamics: An Essay on Cyclical and Long-Run Changes in Capitalist Economy*, London: Allen and Unwin, reprinted in J. Osiatynski (ed.) (1991), *Collected Works of Michal Kalecki, Vol. II: Capitalism: Economic Dynamics*, Oxford: Clarendon Press.

Kalecki, M. (1968a), 'The Marxian equations of reproduction and modern economics', *Social Science Information*, **7**(6), 73–79.

Kalecki, M. (1968b), 'Trends and business cycles reconsidered', *Economic Journal*, **78**(310), 263–276, reprinted in M. Kalecki, *Selected Essays on the Dynamics of the Capitalist Economy, 1933–1970*, Cambridge, UK: Cambridge University Press, 1971.

Kalecki, M. (1969a), *Studies in the Theory of Business Cycles, 1933–1939*, Oxford: Basil Blackwell.

Kalecki, M. (1969b), *Introduction to the Theory of Growth in a Socialist Economy*, Oxford: Basil Blackwell, reprinted in J. Osiatynski (ed.) (1991), *Collected Works of Michal Kalecki, Vol. IV: Socialism: Economic Growth and Efficiency of Investment*, Oxford: Clarendon Press.

Kalecki, M. (1971), *Selected Essays on the Dynamics of the Capitalist Economy, 1933 – 1970*, Cambridge, UK: Cambridge University Press.

Kalecki, M. (1972), *Selected Essays on the Economic Growth of the Socialist and the Mixed Economy*, Cambridge, UK: Cambridge University Press.

Kalecki, M. and Schumacher, E.F. (1943), 'International clearing and long-term lending', *Bulletin of the Institute of Statistics Oxford Supplement*, **5**(S5), 29–33, reprinted in J. Osiatynski (ed.) (1997), *Collected Works of Michal Kalecki, Vol. VII: Studies in Applied Economics, 1940–1967, Miscellenea*, Oxford: Clarendon Press.

Kallis, G. (2011), 'In defence of de-growth', *Ecological Economics*, **70**(5), 873–880.

Kallis, G., Kerschner, C. and Martinez-Alier, J. (2012), 'The economics of degrowth', *Ecological Economics*, **84**, 172–180.

Kapeller, J. and Schütz, B. (2014), 'Debt, boom, bust: a theory of Minsky–Veblen cycles', *Journal of Post Keynesian Economics*, **36**(4), 781–814.

Kapeller, J. and Schütz, B. (2015), 'Conspicuous consumption, inequality and debt: the nature of consumption driven profit-led regimes', *Metroeconomica,* **66**(1), 51–70.

Kapeller, J. and Springholz, F. (2021), *Heterodox Economics Directory*, 6th edition, http://heterodoxnews.com/hed/.

Kapeller, J., Landesmann, M., Mohr, F.X. and Schütz, B. (2018), 'Government policies and financial crises: mitigation, postponement or prevention?', *Cambridge Journal of Economics*, **42**(2), 309–330.

Kappes, S.A. (2021), 'Monetary policy and personal income distribution: a survey of the empirical literature', *Review of Political Economy*, advance access, doi:10.1080/09538259.2021.1943159.

Kaya, Y. and Yokoburi, K. (1997), *Environment, Energy, and Economy: Strategies for Sustainability*, Tokyo et al.: United Nations University Press.

Kazandziska, M. (2015), 'Macroeconomic policy regimes in emerging markets: the case of Latvia', *European Journal of Economics and Economic Policies: Intervention*, **12**(3), 318–352.

Kazandziska, M. (2019), *Macroeconomic Policy Regimes in Emerging Countries: The Case of Central Eastern Europe*, Marburg: Metropolis.

Kelton, S. (2020), *The Deficit Myth: Modern Monetary Theory and How to Build a Better Economy*, New York: Public Affairs.

Kenway, P. (1980), 'Marx, Keynes and the possibility theory of crisis', *Cambridge Journal of Economics*, **4**(1), 23–36.

Keynes, J.M. (1913), *Indian Currency and Finance*, reprinted in: *The Collected Writings of J.M. Keynes, Vol. I*, London: Macmillan, 1971.

Keynes, J.M. (1919), *The Economic Consequences of the Peace*, reprinted in: *The Collected Writings of J.M. Keynes, Vol. II*, London: Macmillan, 1971.

Keynes, J.M. (1920), *A Treatise on Probability*, reprinted in: *The Collected Writings of J.M. Keynes, Vol. VIII*, London: Macmillan, 1971.

Keynes, J.M. (1922), *A Revision of the Treaty*, reprinted in: *The Collected Writings of J.M. Keynes, Vol. III*, London: Macmillan, 1971.

Keynes, J.M. (1923), *A Tract on Monetary Reform*, reprinted in: *The Collected Writings of J.M. Keynes, Vol. IV*, London: Macmillan, 1971.

Keynes, J.M. (1930a), *A Treatise on Money*, 2 Volumes, reprinted in: *The Collected Writings of J.M. Keynes, Vol. V-VI*, London: Macmillan, 1973.

Keynes, J.M. (1930b), 'Economic possibilities of our grandchildren', reprinted in *The Collected Writings of J.M. Keynes, Vol. IX*, London: Macmillan, 1972.

Keynes, J.M. (1931), *Essays in Persuasion*, reprinted in: *The Collected Writings of J.M. Keynes, Vol. IX*, London: Macmillan, 1972.

Keynes, J.M. (1933a), 'A monetary theory of production', reprinted in *The Collected Writings of J.M. Keynes, Vol. XIII*, London: Macmillan, 1987.

Keynes, J.M. (1933b), *Essays in Biography*, reprinted in *The Collected Writings of J.M. Keynes, Vol. X*, London: Macmillan, 1972.

Keynes, J.M. (1936), *The General Theory of Employment, Interest, and Money*, reprinted in *The Collected Writings of J.M. Keynes, Vol. VII*, London: Macmillan, 1973.

Keynes, J.M. (1937), 'The General Theory of Employment', *Quarterly Journal of Economics*, **51**(2), 209–223, reprinted in *The Collected Writings of J.M. Keynes, Vol. VII*, London: Macmillan, 1973.

Keynes, J.M. (1942), 'Proposal for an International Clearing Union', reprinted in *The Collected Writings of J.M. Keynes*, Vol. XXV, London: Macmillan, 1980.

Keynes, J.M. (1943), 'The long-term problem of full employment', reprinted in *The Collected Writings of J.M. Keynes*, Vol. XXVII, London: Macmillan, 1980.

Keynes, J.M. (1973), *The General Theory and After, Part II: Defence and Development*, in *The Collected Writings of J.M. Keynes*, Vol. XIV, London: Macmillan.

Keynes, J.M. (1979), *The General Theory and After: A Supplement*, in *The Collected Writings of John Maynard Keynes*, Vol. XXIX, London: Macmillan.

Kiefer, D. and Rada, C. (2015), 'Profit maximizing goes global: the race to the bottom', *Cambridge Journal of Economics,* **39**(5), 1333–1350.

Kim, Y.K. (2013), 'Household debt, financialization, and macroeconomic performance in the United States, 1951–2009', *Journal of Post Keynesian Economics,* **35**(4), 675–694.

Kim, Y.K. (2016), 'Macroeconomic effects of household debt: an empirical analysis', *Review of Keynesian Economics,* **4**(2), 127–150.

Kim, Y.K. (2020), 'Household debt accumulation and the Great Recession of the United States: a comparative perspective', *Review of Radical Political Economics,* **52**(1), 26–49.

Kim, Y.K., Setterfield, M. and Mei, Y. (2014), 'A theory of aggregate consumption', *European Journal of Economics and Economic Policies: Intervention,* **11**(1), 31–49.

Kim, Y.K., Setterfield, M. and Mei, Y. (2015), 'Aggregate consumption and debt accumulation: an empirical examination of US household behaviour', *Cambridge Journal of Economics,* **39**(1), 93–112.

King, J.E. (2002), *A History of Post Keynesian Economics Since 1936,* Cheltenham, UK: Edward Elgar Publishing.

King, J.E. (2008a), *Nicholas Kaldor,* Basingstoke, UK: Palgrave Macmillan.

King, J.E. (2008b), 'Heterodox macroeconomics: what, exactly, are we against?', in L.R. Wray and M. Forstater (eds.), *Keynes and Macroeconomics after 70 Years: Critical Assessments of the General Theory,* Cheltenham, UK: Edward Elgar Publishing.

King, J.E. (2009), 'Microfoundations?', in E. Hein, T. Niechoj and E. Stockhammer (eds.), *Macroeconomic Policies on Shaky Foundations: Whither Mainstream Economics?,* Marburg: Metropolis.

King, J.E. (ed.) (2012a), *The Elgar Companion to Post Keynesian Economics,* 2nd edition, Cheltenham, UK: Edward Elgar Publishing.

King, J.E. (2012b), *The Microfoundations Delusion: Metaphor and Dogma in the History of Macroeconomics,* Cheltenham, UK: Edward Elgar Publishing.

King, J.E. (2012c), 'Post Keynesians and others', *Review of Political Economy,* **24**(2), 305–319.

King, J.E. (2013), 'Should post-Keynesians make a behavioural turn?', *European Journal of Economics and Economic Policies: Intervention,* **10**(2), 231–242.

King, J.E. (2015), *Advanced Introduction to Post Keynesian Economics,* Cheltenham, UK: Edward Elgar Publishing.

Kirman, A. (2010), 'The economic crisis is a crisis for economic theory', *CESifo Economic Studies,* **56**(4), 498–535.

Kittel, B. and Traxler, F. (2001), 'Lohnverhandlungssysteme und Geldpolitik', *Wirtschaft und Gesellschaft,* **27**(1), 11–40.

Kiyotaki, N. and Moore, J. (1997), 'Credit cycles', *Journal of Political Economy,* **105**(2), 211–248.

Kliman, A. and Williams, S.D. (2014), 'Why "financialisation" hasn't depressed US productive investment', *Cambridge Journal of Economics,* **39**(1), 67–92.

Knapp, G.F. (1905), *Staatliche Theorie des Geldes,* 3rd edition 1921, Munich, Leipzig: Duncker & Humblot.

Köhler, K. (2018), 'The limits to profit-wage redistribution: endogenous regime shifts in Kaleckian models of growth and distribution', Working Paper No. 112/2018, Institute for International Political Economy (IPE), Berlin School of Economics and Law.

Kohler, K. and Stockhammer, E. (2021), 'Growing differently? Financial cycles, austerity, and competitiveness in growth models since the Global Financial Crisis', *Review of International Political Economy,* advance access, doi:10.1080/09692290.2021.1899035.

Kohler, K., Guschanski, A. and Stockhammer, E. (2019), 'The impact of financialisation on the wage share: a theoretical clarification and empirical test', *Cambridge Journal of Economics,* **43**(4), 937–974.

Kotz, D.M. (2013), 'Social structures of accumulation, the rate of profit, and economic crises', in J. Wicks-Lim and R. Pollin (eds.), *Capitalism on Trial: Explorations in the Tradition of Thomas E. Weisskopf,* Cheltenham, UK: Edward Elgar Publishing.

Kregel, J. (1973), *The Reconstruction of Political Economy: An Introduction to Post-Keynesian Economics,* London: Macmillan.

Kregel, J. (1986/87), 'A note on finance, liquidity, saving, and investment', *Journal of Post Keynesian Economics,* **9**(1), 91–100.

Kriesler, P. and Lavoie, M. (2007), 'The new consensus on monetary policy and its post-Keynesian critique', *Review of Political Economy*, **19**(3), 387–404.

Kristal, T. (2010), 'Good times, bad times: postwar labor's share of national income in capitalist democracies', *American Sociological Review*, **75**(5), 729–763.

Kronenberg, T. (2010), 'Finding common ground between ecological economics and post-Keynesian economics', *Ecological Economics*, **69**(7), 1488–1494.

Kurz, H.D. (1990), 'Technical change, growth and distribution: a steady-state approach to "unsteady" growth', in H.D Kurz, *Capital, Distribution and Effective Demand*, Cambridge, UK: Polity Press.

Kurz, H.D. (2010), 'On the dismal state of a dismal science?', *Homo Oeconomicus*, **27**(3), 369–389.

Kurz, H.D. and Salvadori, N. (1995), *Theory of Production: A Long-Period Analysis*, Cambridge, UK: Cambridge University Press.

Kurz, H.D. and Salvadori, N. (2003), 'Theories of economic growth: old and new', in N. Salvadori (ed.), *The Theory of Economic Growth: A 'Classical' Perspective*, Cheltenham, UK: Edward Elgar Publishing.

Landwehr, J. (2020), 'The case for a job guarantee policy in Germany – a political-economic analysis of the potential benefits and obstacles', Working Paper No. 150/2020, Institute for International Political Economy (IPE), Berlin School of Economics and Law.

Lang, D., Setterfield, M. and Shikaki, I. (2020), 'Is there scientific progress in macroeconomics: the case of the NAIRU', *European Journal of Economics and Economic Policies: Intervention*, **17**(1), 19–38.

Lange, S. (2018), *Macroeconomics without Growth*, Marburg: Metropolis Verlag.

Łaski, K. (2019), *Lectures in Macroeconomics: A Capitalist Economy without Unemployment*, edited by J. Osiatynski and J. Toporowski, Oxford: Oxford University Press.

Lavoie, M. (1984), 'The endogenous flow of credit and the post-Keynesian theory of money', *Journal of Economic Issues*, **18**(3), 771–797.

Lavoie, M. (1992), *Foundations of Post-Keynesian Economic Analysis*, Aldershot, UK: Edward Elgar Publishing.

Lavoie, M. (1995a), 'The Kaleckian model of growth and distribution and its neo-Ricardian and neo-Marxian critiques', *Cambridge Journal of Economics*, **19**(6), 789–818.

Lavoie, M. (1995b), 'Interest rates in post-Keynesian models of growth and distribution', *Metroeconomica*, **46**(2), 146–177.

Lavoie, M. (1996a), 'Horizontalism, structuralism, liquidity preference and the principle of increasing risk', *Scottish Journal of Political Economy*, **43**(3), 275–300.

Lavoie, M. (1996b), 'Monetary policy in an economy with endogenous credit money', in G. Deleplace and E.J. Nell (eds.), *Money in Motion*, Basingstoke, UK: Palgrave Macmillan, reprinted in M. Lavoie (2020a), *Post-Keynesian Monetary Theory: Selected Essays*, Cheltenham, UK: Edward Elgar Publishing.

Lavoie, M. (1996c), 'Unproductive outlays and capital accumulation with target-return pricing', *Review of Social Economy*, **54**(3), 303–321.

Lavoie, M. (1997), 'Fair rates of interest in post-Keynesian political economy, in J. Texeira (ed.), *Issues in Modern Political Economy*, Brasilia: University of Brasilia Press, reprinted in M. Lavoie (2020a), *Post-Keynesian Monetary Theory: Selected Essays*, Cheltenham, UK: Edward Elgar Publishing.

Lavoie, M. (1999), 'The credit-led supply of deposits and the demand for money: Kaldor's reflux mechanism as previously endorsed by Joan Robinson', *Cambridge Journal of Economics*, **23**(1), 103–113.

Lavoie, M. (2000), 'A Post Keynesian view of interest parity theorems', *Journal of Post Keynesian Economics*, **23**(1), 163–179.

Lavoie, M. (2003a), 'A primer on endogenous credit-money', in L.-P. Rochon and S. Rossi (eds.), *Modern Theories of Money: The Nature and the Role of Money in Capitalist Economies*, Cheltenham, UK: Edward Elgar Publishing, reprinted in M. Lavoie (2020a), *Post-Keynesian Monetary Theory: Selected Essays*, Cheltenham, UK: Edward Elgar Publishing.

Lavoie, M. (2003b), 'Interest parity, risk premia, and Post Keynesian analysis', *Journal of Post Keynesian Economics*, **25**(2), 237–249.

Lavoie, M. (2006a), *Introduction to Post-Keynesian Economics*, Basingstoke, UK: Palgrave Macmillan.

Lavoie, M. (2006b), 'A post-Keynesian amendment to the new consensus on monetary policy', *Metroeconomica*, **57**(2), 165–192.

Lavoie, M. (2006c), 'Endogenous money: accommodationist', in P. Arestis and M. Sawyer (eds.), *Handbook on Alternative Monetary Economics*, Cheltenham, UK: Edward Elgar Publishing, 17–34, reprinted in M. Lavoie (2020a), *Post-Keynesian Monetary Theory: Selected Essays*, Cheltenham, UK: Edward Elgar Publishing.

Lavoie, M. (2006d), 'Do heterodox theories have anything in common? A post-Keynesian point of view', *European Journal of Economics and Economic Policies: Intervention*, **3**(1), 87–112.

Lavoie, M. (2008), 'Financialisation issues in a post-Keynesian stock-flow consistent model', *European Journal of Economics and Economic Policies: Intervention*, **5**(2), 331–356.

Lavoie, M. (2009a), 'Taming the new consensus: hysteresis and some other post-Keynesian amendments', in G. Fontana and M. Setterfield (eds.), *Macroeconomics and Macroeconomic Pedagogy*, Basingstoke, UK: Palgrave Macmillan.

Lavoie, M. (2009b), 'Cadrisme within a Kaleckian model of growth and distribution', *Review of Political Economy*, **21**(3), 371–393.

Lavoie, M. (2009c), 'Post Keynesian consumer choice theory and ecological economics', in R.P.F. Holt, S. Pressman and C.L. Spash (eds.), *Post Keynesian and Ecological Economics: Confronting Environmental Issues,* Cheltenham, UK: Edward Elgar Publishing.

Lavoie, M. (2010a), 'Changes in central bank procedures during the subprime crisis and their repercussions for monetary theory', *International Journal of Political Economy*, **39**(3), 3–23.

Lavoie, M. (2010b), 'The possible perverse effects of declining wages', *International Journal of Pluralism and Economic Education*, **1**(3), 260–275.

Lavoie, M. (2010c), 'Surveying long-run and short-run stability issues with the Kaleckian model of growth', in M. Setterfield (ed.), *Handbook of Alternative Theories of Economic Growth*, Cheltenham, UK: Edward Elgar Publishing.

Lavoie, M. (2011a), 'History and methods of post-Keynesian economics', in E. Hein and E. Stockhammer (eds.), *A Modern Guide to Keynesian Macroeconomics and Economic Policies*, Cheltenham, UK: Edward Elgar Publishing.

Lavoie, M. (2011b), 'Money, credit and central banks in post-Keynesian economics', in E. Hein and E. Stockhammer (eds.), *A Modern Guide to Keynesian Macroeconomics and Economic Policies*, Cheltenham, UK: Edward Elgar Publishing.

Lavoie, M. (2012), 'Perspectives for post-Keynesian economics', *Review of Political Economy*, **24**(2), 312–335.

Lavoie, M. (2013), 'The monetary and fiscal nexus of neo-chartalism: a friendly critique', *Journal of Economic Issues*, **48**(1), 1–31.

Lavoie, M. (2014), *Post-Keynesian Economics: New Foundations*, Cheltenham, UK: Edward Elgar Publishing.

Lavoie, M. (2015a), 'Review of Carlin, W. and Soskice, D., *Macroeconomics: Institutions, Instability, and the Financial System* (Oxford: Oxford University Press, 2015)', *European Journal of Economics and Economic Policies: Intervention*, **12**(1), 135–142.

Lavoie, M. (2015b), 'The Eurozone: similarities to and differences from Keynes's Plan', *International Journal of Political Economy*, **44**(1), 3–17.

Lavoie, M. (2016a), 'Convergence towards the normal rate of capacity utilization in neo-Kaleckian models: the role of non-capacity creating autonomous expenditures', *Metroeconomica*, **67**(1), 172–201.

Lavoie, M. (2016b), 'Understanding the global financial crisis: contributions of post-Keynesian economics', *Studies in Political Economy*, **97**(1), 58–75.

Lavoie, M. (2016c), 'Rethinking monetary theory in light of Keynes and the crisis', *Brazilian Keynesian Review*, **2**(2), 174–188.

Lavoie, M. (2017a), 'The origins and evolution of the debate on wage-led and profit-led regimes', *European Journal of Economics and Economic Polices: Intervention*, **14**(2), 200–221.

Lavoie, M. (2017b), 'Assessing some structuralist claims through a coherent stock-flow framework', in L.-P. Rochon and S. Rossi (eds.), *Advances in Endogenous Money Analysis*, Cheltenham, UK: Edward Elgar Publishing.

Lavoie, M. (2018), 'Rethinking macroeconomic theory before the next crisis', *Review of Keynesian Economics*, **6**(1), 1–21.

Lavoie, M. (2020a), *Post-Keynesian Monetary Theory: Selected Essays*, Cheltenham, UK: Edward Elgar Publishing.

Lavoie, M. (2020b), 'Was Hyman Minsky a post-Keynesian economist?', *Review of Evolutionary Political Economy*, **1**(1), 85–101.

Lavoie, M. and Fiebiger, B. (2018), 'Unconventional monetary policies, with a focus on quantitative easing', *European Journal of Economics and Economics Policies: Intervention*, **15**(2), 139–146.

Lavoie, M. and Godley, W. (2001/2), 'Kaleckian models of growth in a coherent stock-flow consistent framework: a Kaldorian view', *Journal of Post Keynesian Economics*, **24**(2), 277–312.

Lavoie, M. and Nah, W.J. (2020), 'Overhead labour costs in a neo-Kaleckian growth model with autonomous non-capacity creating expenditures', *Review of Political Economy*, **32**(4), 511–537.

Lavoie, M. and Seccareccia, M. (2016), 'Money and banking', in L.-P. Rochon and Rossi, S. (eds.), *An Introduction to Macroeconomics: A Heterodox Approach to Economic Analysis*, Cheltenham, UK: Edward Elgar Publishing.

Lavoie, M. and Seccareccia, M. (2017), 'Editorial to the special issue: the political economy of the New Fiscalism', *European Journal of Economics and Economic Policies: Intervention*, **14**(3), 291–295.

Lavoie, M. and Stockhammer, E. (eds.) (2013a), *Wage-Led Growth: An Equitable Strategy for Economic Recovery*, Basingstoke, UK: Palgrave Macmillan.

Lavoie, M. and Stockhammer, E. (2013b), 'Wage-led growth: concept, theories and policies', in M. Lavoie and E. Stockhammer (eds.), *Wage-Led Growth: An Equitable Strategy for Economic Recovery*, Basingstoke, UK: Palgrave Macmillan.

Lazonick, W. and O'Sullivan, M. (2000), 'Maximizing shareholder value: a new ideology for corporate governance', *Economy and Society*, **29**(1), 13–35.

Lazzarini, A. (2011), *Revisiting the Cambridge Capital Controversies: A Historical and Analytical Study*, Pavia: Pavia University Press.

Lee, F. (1998), *Post Keynesian Price Theory*, Cambridge, UK: Cambridge University Press.

Lee, F. (2012), 'Heterodox economics and its critics', *Review of Political Economy*, **24**(2), 337–351.

Lee, F. and Cronin, B.C., assisted by McConnel, S. and Dean, E. (2010), 'Research quality rankings of heterodox journals in a contested discipline', *American Journal of Economics and Sociology*, **69**(5), 1409–1452.

Lerner, A.P. (1943), 'Functional finance and the federal debt', *Social Research*, **10**(1), 38–51.

Lerner, A.P. (1947), 'Money as a creature of the state', *American Economic Review*, **37**(2), 312–317.

Levrero, E.S. (2019), 'On the criticisms of and obstacles to the Employer of Last Resort proposal', *International Journal of Political Economy*, **48**(1), 41–59.

Lietaer, B., Sally, G. and Arnsperger, C. (2012), *Money and Sustainability: The Missing Link*, Charmouth, Dorset/UK: Triarchy Press.

Lima, G.T. and Meirelles, A.J.A. (2007), 'Macrodynamics of debt regimes, financial instability and growth', *Cambridge Journal of Economics*, **31**(4), 563–580.

Lima, G.T. and Setterfield, M. (2010), 'Pricing behaviour and the cost push channel of monetary policy', *Review of Political Economy*, **22**(1), 19–40.

Lima, G.T. and Setterfield, M. (2014), 'The cost channel of monetary transmission and stabilization policy in a post-Keynesian macrodynamic model', *Review of Political Economy*, **26**(2), 258–281.

Logeay, C. and Tober, S. (2006), 'Hysteresis and the NAIRU in the Euro Area', *Scottish Journal of Political Economy*, **53**(4), 409–429.

Lopez, G., J. (2002), 'Two versions of the principle of effective demand: Kalecki and Keynes', *Journal of Post Keynesian Economics*, **24**(4), 609–622.

Lopez, G., J. and Assous, M. (2010), *Michal Kalecki*, Basingstoke, UK: Palgrave Macmillan.

Lucas, R.E. (1988), 'On the mechanics of economic development', *Journal of Monetary Economics*, **22**(1), 3–42.

Ludvigson, S. and Steindel, C. (1999), 'How important is the stock market effect on consumption?', *Federal Reserve Bank of New York Economic Policy Review*, July, 29–51.

Mankiw, N.G. (2020), 'A skeptic's guide to modern monetary theory', *American Economic Review: Papers and Proceedings*, **110**(May), 141–144.

Marglin, S.A. (1984a), 'Growth, distribution and inflation: a centennial synthesis', *Cambridge Journal of Economics*, **8**(2), 115–144.

Marglin, S.A. (1984b), *Growth, Distribution and Prices*, Cambridge, MA: Harvard University Press.

Marx, K. (1861–1863), *Theorien über den Mehrwert. Zweiter Teil, Marx-Engels-Werke,* Volume 26.2, Berlin: Dietz Verlag, 1967.

Marx, K. (1867), *Das Kapital. Kritik der politischen Ökonomie, Erster Band: Der Produktionsprozeß des Kapitals,* 4th edition, 1890, edited by F. Engels, reprinted as *Marx-Engels-Werke,* Volume 23, Berlin: Dietz Verlag 1962, Englisch translation: *Capital. A Critique of Political Economy, Volume 1: The Process of Capitalist Production,* New York: International Publisher, 1967.

Marx, K. (1885), *Das Kapital. Kritik der politischen Ökonomie, Zweiter Band: Der Zirkulationsprozeß des Kapitals,* 2nd edition, 1893, edited by F. Engels, reprinted as *Marx-Engels-Werke,* Volume 24, Berlin: Dietz Verlag 1963, Englisch translation: *Capital. A Critique of Political Economy, Volume 2: The Process of Circulation of Capital,* New York: International Publisher, 1967.

Marx, K. (1894), *Das Kapital. Kritik der politischen Ökonomie, Dritter Band: Der Gesamtprozeß der kapitalistischen Produktion,* edited by F. Engels, reprinted as *Marx-Engels-Werke,* Volume 25, Berlin: Dietz Verlag 1964, English translation: *Capital. A Critique of Political Economy, Volume 3: The Process of Capitalist Production as A Whole,* New York: International Publisher, 1967.

Mastini, R., Kallis, G. and Hickel, J. (2021), 'A green new deal without growth?', *Ecological Economics,* **179**, 1–9.

McCombie, J. (2011), 'Criticisms and defences of the balance-of-payments constrained growth model: some old, some new', *PSL Quarterly Review,* **64**(259), 353–392.

McCombie, J. (2019), 'Why Thirlwall's Law is not a tautology: more on the debate over the law', *Review of Keynesian Economics,* **7**(4), 429–443.

McCombie, J. and Thirlwall, A.P. (eds.) (2004), *Essays on Balance of Payments Constrained Growth: Theory and Evidence,* New York: Routledge.

McDonough, T., Reich, M. and Kotz, D.M. (eds.) (2010), *Contemporary Capitalism and Its Crises: Social Structure of Accumulation Theory for the 21st Century,* Cambridge, UK: Cambridge University Press.

McLeay, M., Radia, A. and Thomas, R. (2014a), 'Money in the modern economy: an introduction', *Bank of England Quarterly Bulletin,* **54**(1), 4–13.

McLeay, M., Radia, A. and Thomas, R. (2014b), 'Money creation in the modern economy', *Bank of England Quarterly Bulletin,* **54**(1), 14–27.

Meadows, D.H., Meadows, D.L., Randers, J. and Behrens, W.W. (1972), *The Limits to Growth,* New York: Universe Books.

Meirelles, A.J.A. and Lima, G.T. (2006), 'Debt, financial fragility, and economic growth: a post Keynesian macromodel', *Journal of Post Keynesian Economics,* **29**(1), 93–115.

Minsky, H.M. (1975), *John Maynard Keynes,* London and Basingstoke, UK: Palgrave Macmillan.

Minsky, H.M. (1977), 'The financial instability hypothesis', *Challenge: The Magazine of Economic Affairs,* **20**(1), 20–27.

Minsky, H.M. (1986a), *Stabilizing an Unstable Economy,* New Haven, CT: Yale University Press, 2nd edition, New York: McGraw-Hill, 2008.

Minsky, H.M. (1986b), 'Money and crisis in Schumpeter and Keynes', in H.-J. Wagener and J.W. Drukker (eds.), *The Economic Law of Motion of Modern Society: A Marx-Keynes-Schumpeter Centennial.* Cambridge, UK, New York and Sydney: Cambridge University Press.

Minsky, H.M. (1991), 'Endogeneity of money', in E.J. Nell and W. Semmler (eds.), *Nicholas Kaldor and Mainstream Economics: Confrontation or Convergence?,* New York: St. Martin's Press.

Mitchell, W. and Wray, L.R. (2005), 'In defense of Employer of Last Resort: a response to Malcolm Sawyer', *Journal of Economic Issues,* **39**(1), 235–244.

Mitchell, W., Wray, L.R. and Watts, M. (2019), *Macroeconomics,* London: Red Globe Press, Macmillan.

Modigliani, F. (1944), 'Liquidity preference and the theory of interest and money', *Econometrica,* **12**(1), 45–88.

Mohun, S. (2014), 'Unproductive labor in the U.S. economy 1964–2010', *Review of Radical Political Economics,* **46**(3), 355–379.

Monserand, A. (2019), 'De-growth in a neo-Kaleckian model of growth and distribution: a theoretical compatibility and stability analysis', Centre d'économie de l'Université Paris Nord (CEPN), Working Paper, No. 2019-01.

Monserand, A. (2020), 'A note on zero growth and structural change in a post Keynesian growth model', *Journal of Post Keynesian Economics,* **43**(1), 131–138.

Moore, B.J. (1979), 'The endogenous money stock', *Journal of Post Keynesian Economics*, **2**(1), 49–70.

Moore, B.J. (1983), 'Unpacking the Post Keynesian black box: bank lending and the money supply', *Journal of Post Keynesian Economics*, **5**(4), 537–556.

Moore, B.J. (1988a), *Horizontalists and Verticalists: The Macroeconomics of Credit Money*, Cambridge, UK: Cambridge University Press.

Moore, B.J. (1988b): 'The endogenous money supply', *Journal of Post Keynesian Economics*, **10**(3), 372–385.

Moore, B.J. (1989a), 'The endogeneity of credit money', *Review of Political Economy*, **1**(1), 65–93.

Moore, B.J. (1989b), 'The effects of monetary policy on income distribution', in P. Davidson and J. Kregel (eds.), *Macroeconomic Problems and Policies of Income Distribution*, Aldershot: Edward Elgar Publishing.

Moore, G.L. and Stockhammer, E. (2018), 'The drivers of household indebtedness reconsidered: an empirical evaluation of competing arguments on the macroeconomic determinants of household indebtedness in OECD countries', *Journal of Post Keynesian Economics*, **41**(4), 547–577.

Mosler, W. (1997/98), 'Full employment and price stability', *Journal of Post Keynesian Economics*, **20**(2), 167–182.

Naastepad, C.W.M. (2006), 'Technology, demand and distribution: a cumulative growth model with an application to the Dutch productivity growth slowdown', *Cambridge Journal of Economics*, **30**(3), 403–434.

Nah, W.J. and Lavoie, M. (2017), 'Long-run convergence in a neo-Kaleckian open-economy model with autonomous export growth', *Journal of Post Keynesian Economics*, **40**(2), 223–238.

Nah, W.J. and Lavoie, M. (2019a), 'Convergence in a neo-Kaleckian model with endogenous technical progress and autonomous demand growth', *Review of Keynesian Economics*, **7**(3), 275–291.

Nah, W.J. and Lavoie, M. (2019b), 'The role of autonomous demand growth in a neo-Kaleckian conflicting-claims framework', *Structural Change and Economic Dynamics*, **51**(C), 427–444.

Neilson, D.H. (2019), *Minsky*, Cambridge, UK and Medford, MA: Polity Press.

Nell, E. (2002), 'On realizing profits in money', *Review of Political Economy*, **14**(4), 519–530.

Niggle, C. (1989), 'Monetary policy and changes in income distribution', *Journal of Economic Issues*, **23**(3), 809–822.

Nikiforos, M. (2018), 'Some comments on the Sraffian supermultiplier approach to growth and distribution', *Journal of Post Keynesian Economics*, **41**(1), 659–674.

Nikiforos, M. and Foley, D.K. (2012), 'Distribution and capacity utilization: conceptual issues and empirical evidence', *Metroeconomica*, **63**(1), 200–229.

Nikiforos, M. and Zezza, G. (2017), 'Stock-flow consistent macroeconomic models: a survey', *Journal of Economic Surveys*, **31**(5), 1204–1239.

Nikolaidi, M. and Stockhammer (2017), 'Minsky models: a structured survey', *Journal of Economic Surveys*, **31**(5), 1304–1331.

Nishi, H. (2012a), 'A dynamic analysis of debt-led and debt-burdened growth regimes with Minskian financial structure', *Metroeconomica*, **63**(4), 634–660.

Nishi, H. (2012b), 'Household debt, dynamic stability, and change in demand creation patterns', *Review of Political Economy*, **24**(4), 607–622.

Obst, T., Onaran, Ö. and Nikolaidi, M. (2020), 'The effects of income distribution and fiscal policy on aggregate demand, investment and the budget balance: the case of Europe', *Cambridge Journal of Economics*, **44**(6), 1221–1243.

OEC (2020), Observatory of Economic Complexity, https://oec.world/en.

OECD (2015), *Towards Green Growth? Tracking Progress*, OECD Green Growth Studies, Paris: OECD Publishing.

Ohlin, B. (1937a), 'Alternative theories of the rate of interest: three rejoinders', *The Economic Journal*, **47**(187), 423–427.

Ohlin, B. (1937b), 'Some notes on the Stockholm theory of savings and investment', *The Economic Journal*, **47**(185), 53–69.

Onaran, Ö. (2015), 'The role of gender equality in an equality-led sustainable development strategy', Greenwich Papers in Political Economy, No. GPERC26, Greenwich Political Economy Research Centre.

Onaran, Ö. (2016a), 'Secular stagnation and progressive economic policy alternatives', *European Journal of Economics and Economic Policies: Intervention*, **13**(2), 229–240.

Onaran, Ö. (2016b), 'Wage- versus profit-led growth in the context of globalization and public spending: the political aspects of wage-led recovery', *Review of Keynesian Economics*, **4**(4), 458–474.

Onaran, Ö. and Galanis, G. (2014), 'Income distribution and growth: a global model', *Environment and Planning A: Economy and Space*, **46**(10), 2489–2513.

Onaran, Ö. and Obst, T. (2016), 'Wage-led growth in the EU15 member-states: the effects of income distribution on growth, investment, trade balance and inflation', *Cambridge Journal of Economics*, **40**(6), 1517–1551.

Onaran, Ö., Stockhammer, E. and Grafl, L. (2011), 'Financialisation, income distribution and aggregate demand in the USA', *Cambridge Journal of Economics*, **35**(4), 637–661.

Onaran, Ö., Andersen, L., Cozzi, C., Dahl, S., Nissen, T., Obst, T. and Tori, D. (2017), 'An investment and equality led sustainable development strategy for Europe', Greenwich Papers in Political Economy, GPERC 46, Greenwich Political Economy Research Centre.

Onaran, Ö., Oyvat, C. and Fotoupoulo, E. (2019), 'The effects of gender inequality, wages, wealth concentration and fiscal policy on macroeconomic performance', Greenwich Papers in Political Economy, No. GPERC71, University of Greenwich, Institute of Political Economy, Governance, Finance and Accountability.

Orhangazi, Ö. (2008), 'Financialisation and capital accumulation in the non-financial corporate sector: a theoretical and empirical investigation on the US economy, 1973–2003', *Cambridge Journal of Economics*, **32**(6), 863–886.

Palley, T.I. (1994a), 'Competing views on the money supply process', *Metroeconomica*, **45**(1), 67–88.

Palley, T.I. (1994b), 'Debt, aggregate demand, and the business cycle: an analysis in the spirit of Kaldor and Minsky', *Journal of Post Keynesian Economics*, **16**(3), 371–390.

Palley, T.I. (1996a), *Post Keynesian Economics: Debt, Distribution and the Macro Economy*, London: Macmillan.

Palley, T.I. (1996b), 'Accommodationism versus structuralism: time for an accommodation', *Journal of Post Keynesian Economics*, **18**(4), 585–594.

Palley, T.I. (2004), 'Asset-based reserve requirements: reasserting domestic monetary control in an era of financial innovation and instability', *Review of Political Economy*, **16**(1), 43–58.

Palley, T.I. (2005), 'Class conflict and the Cambridge theory of distribution', in B. Gibson (ed.), *Joan Robinson's Economics: A Centennial Celebration*, Cheltenham, UK: Edward Elgar Publishing.

Palley, T.I. (2006), 'A Post-Keynesian framework for monetary policy: why interest rate operating procedures are not enough', in C. Gnos and L.-P. Rochon (eds.), *Post-Keynesian Principles of Economic Policy*, Cheltenham, UK: Edward Elgar Publishing.

Palley, T.I. (2007a), 'Macroeconomics and monetary policy: competing theoretical frameworks', *Journal of Post Keynesian Economics*, **30**(1), 61–78.

Palley, T.I. (2007b), 'Asset-based reserve requirements: a response', *Review of Political Economy*, **19**(4), 575–578.

Palley, T.I. (2009a), 'The macroeconomics of financialization: a stages of development approach', *Ekonomiaz: Basque Economic Review*, **72**(3), 34–51.

Palley, T.I. (2009b), 'After the bust: the outlook for macroeconomics and macroeconomic policies', in E. Hein, T. Niechoj and E. Stockhammer (eds.), *Macroeconomic Policies on Shaky Foundations: Whither Mainstream Economics?*, Marburg: Metropolis.

Palley, T.I. (2010), 'Asset price bubbles and monetary policy: why central banks have been wrong and what should be done', *European Journal of Economics and Economic Policies: Intervention*, **7**(1), 91–107.

Palley, T.I. (2011), 'Quantitative easing: a Keynesian critique', *Investigacion Económica*, **70**(277), 69–86.

Palley, T.I. (2012), *From Crisis to Stagnation: The Destruction of Shared Prosperity and the Role of Economics*, Cambridge, UK: Cambridge University Press.

Palley, T.I. (2013a), 'Gattopardo economics: the crisis and the mainstream response of change that keeps things the same', *European Journal of Economics and Economic Policies: Intervention*, **10**(2), 193–206.

Palley, T.I. (2013b), *Financialization: The Economics of Finance Capital Domination*, Basingstoke, UK: Palgrave Macmillan.

Palley, T.I. (2013c), 'Horizontalists, verticalists and structuralists: the theory of endogenous money reassessed', *Review of Keynesian Economics*, **1**(4), 406–424.

Palley, T.I. (2015a), 'Money, fiscal policy, and interest rates: a critique of modern monetary theory', *Review of Political Economy*, **27**(1), 1–23.

Palley, T.I. (2015b), 'The critics of modern money theory (MMT) are right', *Review of Political Economy*, **27**(1), 45–61.

Palley, T.I. (2015c), 'A neo–Kaleckian–Goodwin model of capitalist economic growth: monopoly power, managerial pay and labour market conflict', *Cambridge Journal of Economics*, **38**(6), 1355–1372.

Palley, T.I. (2015d), 'The middle class in macroeconomics and growth theory: a three-class neo-Kaleckian-Goodwin model', *Cambridge Journal of Economics*, **39**(1), 221–243.

Palley, T.I. (2016a), 'Why negative interest rate policy (NIRP) is ineffective and dangerous', *Real-World Economics Review*, **76**, 5–15.

Palley, T.I. (2016b), 'Inequality, the financial crisis and stagnation: competing stories and why they matter', *Real World Economics Review*, **74**, 1–18.

Palley, T.I. (2017), 'Wage- vs. profit-led growth: the role of the distribution of wages in determining regime character', *Cambridge Journal of Economics*, **41**(1), 49–61.

Palley, T.I. (2018), 'The natural interest rate fallacy: why negative interest rate policy may worsen Keynesian unemployment', *Investigación Económica*, **77**(304), 7–39.

Palley, T.I. (2019), 'The economics of the super-multiplier: a comprehensive treatment with labor markets', *Metroeconomica*, **70**(2), 325–340.

Palley, T.I. (2020), 'What's wrong with modern money theory: macro and political economic restraints on deficit-financed fiscal policy', *Review of Keynesian Economics*, **8**(4), 472–493.

Palley, T.I. (2021a), *Neoliberalism and the Road to Inequality and Stagnation*, Cheltenham, UK: Edward Elgar Publishing.

Palley, T.I. (2021b), 'Financialization revisited: the economics and political economy of the vampire squid economy', *Review of Keynesian Economics*, **9**(4), 461–492.

Panico, C. (1980), 'Marx's analysis of the relationship between the rate of interest and the rate of profit', *Cambridge Journal of Economics*, **4**(4), 363–378.

Panico, C. (1985), 'Market forces and the relation between the rate of interest and profit', *Contributions to Political Economy*, **4**(1), 37–60.

Panico, C. (1988), 'Marx on the banking sector and the interest rate: some notes for a discussion', *Science and Society*, **52**(3), 310–325.

Panico, C. and Pinto, A. (2017), 'Income inequality and the financial industry', *Metroeconomica*, **69**(1), 39–59.

Panico, C., Pinto, A. and Puchet Anyul, M. (2012), 'Income distribution and the size of the financial sector: a Sraffian analysis', *Cambridge Journal of Economics*, **36**(6), 1455–1477.

Parguez, A. (1996), 'Beyond scarcity: a reappraisal of the theory of the monetary circuit', in G. Deleplace and E. Nell (eds.), *Money in Motion*, Basingstoke, UK: Palgrave Macmillan.

Parguez, A. and Seccareccia, M. (2000), 'The credit theory of money: the monetary circuit approach', in J. Smithin, J. (ed.), *What is Money?*, London, New York: Routledge.

Pariboni, R. (2016), 'Household consumer debt, endogenous money and growth: a supermultiplier-based analysis', *PSL Quarterly Review*, **69**(278), 211–233.

Pasinetti, L.L. (1962), 'Rate of profit and income distribution in relation to the rate of economic growth', *Review of Economic Studies*, **4**(29), 267–279, reprinted in L.L. Pasinetti (1974), *Growth and Income Distribution. Essays in Economic Theory*, Cambridge, UK: Cambridge University Press.

Pasinetti, L.L. (1974), *Growth and Income Distribution. Essays in Economic Theory*, Cambridge, UK: Cambridge University Press.

Pasinetti, L.L. (1980–81), 'The rate of interest and the distribution of income in a pure labor economy', *Journal of Post Keynesian Economics*, **3**(2), 170–182.

Pasinetti, L.L. (1981), *Structural Change and Economic Growth*, Cambridge, UK: Cambridge University Press.

Pasinetti, L.L. (2007), *Keynes and the Cambridge Keynesians: A 'Revolution in Economics' to be Accomplished*, Cambridge, UK: Cambridge University Press.

Patinkin, D. (1949), 'Involuntary unemployment and the Keynesian supply function', *The Economic Journal*, **59**(235), 360–383.

Perez Caldentey, E. (2019), *Roy Harrod*, Basingstoke, UK: Palgrave Macmillan.

Perez-Montiel, J.A. and Manera, C. (2020), 'Autonomous expenditures and induced investment: a panel test of the Sraffian supermultiplier model in European countries', *Review of Keynesian Economics*, **8**(2), 220–239.

Perez-Montiel, J.A. and Pariboni, R. (2022), 'Housing is not only the business cycle: a Luxemburg-Kalecki external market empirical investigation for the United States', *Review of Political Economy*, **34**(1), 1–22.

Phillips, A.W. (1958), 'The relationship between unemployment and the rate of change of money wage rates in the United Kingdom, 1861–1957', *Economica*, **25**(100), 283–299.

Piore, M.J. (2016), 'Varieties of capitalism theory: its considerable limits', *Politics & Society*, **44**(2), 237–241.

Pivetti, M. (1987), 'Interest and profit in Smith, Ricardo and Marx', *Political Economy*, **3**(1), 63–74.

Pivetti, M. (1991), *An Essay on Money and Distribution*, Basingstoke, UK: Palgrave Macmillan.

Pivetti, M. (2015), 'Marx and the development of critical political economy', *Review of Political Economy*, **27**(2), 134–153.

Pollin, R. (1991), 'Two theories of money supply endogeneity: some empirical evidence', *Journal of Post Keynesian Economics*, **13**(3), 366–396.

Pollin, R. (1994), 'Marxian and post-Keynesian developments in the sphere of money, credit and finance: building alternative perspectives in monetary macroeconomics', in M. Glick (ed.), *Competition, Technology and Money*, Aldershot, UK and Brookfield, VT: Edward Elgar Publishing.

Pollin, R. (2010), 'Building the Green New Deal in the United States', in S. Dullien, E. Hein, A. Truger and T. van Treeck (eds.), *The World Economy in Crisis – The Return of Keynesianism?*, Marburg: Metropolis.

Pollin, R. (2018), 'De-growth vs. a Green New Deal', *New Left Review*, **112**, 5–25.

Pollin, R. (2020), 'Green recovery: Europe and the world', *Intereconomics*, **55**(6), 360–363.

Pollin, R. (2021), 'The industrial policy requirements for a global climate stabilization project', *International Review of Applied Economics*, **35**(3–4), 389–406.

Prante, F.J. (2018), 'Macroeconomic effects of personal and functional income inequality: theory and empirical evidence for the US and Germany', *Panoeconomicus*, **65**(3), 289–318.

Prante, F.J. (2019), 'Income distribution and the multiplier – an exploration of non-linear distribution effects in linear Kaleckian distribution and growth models', Working Paper No. 121/2019, Institute for International Political Economy (IPE), Berlin School of Economics and Law.

Prante, F.J., Bramucci, A., Hein, E. and Truger, A. (2020), 'Pluralist macroeconomics – an interactive simulator', *International Journal of Pluralism and Economics Education*, **11**(1), 55–78, with Online Scenarios and Simulations, https://projekt.mgwk.de/articles.html.

Prante, F.J., Hein, E. and Bramucci, A. (2022a), 'Varieties and interdependencies of demand and growth regimes in finance-dominated capitalism: a post-Keynesian two-country stock-flow consistent simulation approach', *Review of Keynesian Economics*, **10**(2), 262–288.

Prante, F.J., Bramucci, A., Hein, E. and Truger, A. (2022b), *Introduction to Macroeconomics: Pluralist and Interactive*, Berlin: HWR Berlin, https://eng.mgwk.de/.

Prates, A. (2020), 'Beyond modern money theory: a post-Keynesian approach to the currency hierarchy, monetary sovereignty, and policy space', *Review of Keynesian Economics*, **8**(4), 495–511.

Priewe, J. (2008), 'Capital account management or laissez-faire of capital flows in developing countries', in P. Arestis and L.F. de Paula (eds.), *Financial Liberalization and Economic Performance in Emerging Countries*, Basingstoke, UK: Palgrave Macmillan.

Priewe, J. (2022), 'Growth in the ecological transition – green, zero or de-growth?', *European Journal of Economics and Economic Policies: Intervention*, **19**(1), 19–40.

Priewe, J. and Herr, H. (2005), *The Macroeconomics of Development and Poverty Reduction – Strategies beyond the Washington Consensus*, Baden-Baden: NOMOS.

Qazizada, W. and Stockhammer, E. (2015), 'Government spending multipliers in contraction and expansion', *International Review of Applied Economics*, **29**(2), 238–258.

Radosevic, D. and Cvijanovic, V. (eds.) (2015), *Financialisation and the Financial Crisis in South-Eastern European Countries*, Frankfurt et al.: Peter Lang.

Renaud, J.-F. (2000), 'The problem of the monetary realisation of profits in a Post Keynesian sequential financing model: two solutions of the Kaleckian option', *Review of Political Economy*, **12**(3), 285–303.

Reuten, G. (1988), 'The money expression of value and the credit system: a value-form theoretic outline', *Capital & Class*, **12**(2), 121–141.

Reynolds, P.J. (1987), *Political Economy: A Synthesis of Kaleckian and Post Keynesian Economics*, Sussex and New York: Wheatsheaf Books and St. Martin's Press.

Rezai, A. (2015), 'Demand and distribution in integrated economies', *Cambridge Journal of Economics*, **39**(5), 1399–1414.

Rezai, A. and Stagl, S. (2016), 'Ecological macroeconomics: introduction and review', *Ecological Economics*, **121**, 181–185.

Rezai, A., Taylor, L. and Mechler, R. (2013), 'Ecological macroeconomics: an application to climate change', *Ecological Economics*, **85**, 69–75.

Ricardo, D. (1817), *On the Principles of Political Economy and Taxation, The Works and Correspondence of David Ricardo, Vol. I.*, edited by P. Sraffa, Cambridge, UK: Cambridge University Press, 1951.

Richardson, D.R. (1986), 'Asimakopulos on Kalecki and Keynes on finance, investment and saving', *Cambridge Journal of Economics*, **10**(2), 191–198.

Richters, O. and Siemoneit, A. (2017), 'Consistency and stability analysis of models of a monetary growth imperative', *Ecological Economics*, **136**, 114–125.

Richters, O. and Siemoneit, A. (2019), 'Growth imperatives: substantiating a contested concept', *Structural Change and Economic Dynamics*, **51**(C), 126–137.

Robertson, D.H. (1937), 'Alternative theories of the rate of interest: three rejoinders', *The Economic Journal*, **47**(187), 428–436.

Robertson, D.H. (1938a), 'Mr. Keynes and finance', *The Economic Journal*, **48**(190), 314–318.

Robertson, D.H. (1938b), 'Mr. Keynes and finance: a comment', *The Economic Journal*, **48**(191), 555–556.

Robertson, D.H. (1940), 'Effective demand and the multiplier', in D.H. Robertson, *Essays in Monetary Theory*, London: P.S. King.

Robinson, J. (1953/54), 'The production function and the theory of capital', *Review of Economic Studies*, **21**(2), 81–106.

Robinson, J. (1956), *The Accumulation of Capital*, London: Macmillan.

Robinson, J. (1962), *Essays in the Theory of Economic Growth*, London: Macmillan.

Robinson, J. (1972), 'The second crisis of economic theory', *American Economic Review*, **62**(2), 1–10.

Robinson, J. (1977), 'Michal Kalecki on the economics of capitalism', *Oxford Bulletin of Economics and Statistics*, **39**(1), 7–17.

Robinson, J. and Eatwell, J. (1973), *An Introduction to Modern Economics*, London: McGraw-Hill.

Rochon, L.-P. (1999), *Credit, Money and Production: An Alternative Post-Keynesian Approach*, Cheltenham, UK: Edward Elgar Publishing.

Rochon, L.-P. (2003), 'On money and endogenous money: post-Keynesian and circulation approaches', in L.-P. Rochon and S. Rossi (eds.), *Modern Theories of Money*, Cheltenham, UK: Edward Elgar Publishing.

Rochon, L.-P. (2005), 'The existence of monetary profits within the monetary circuit', in G. Fontana and R. Realfonzo (eds.), *The Monetary Theory of Production. Tradition and Perspectives*, Basingstoke, UK: Palgrave Macmillan.

Rochon, L.-P. and Rossi, S. (2006a), 'Inflation targeting, economic performance, and income distribution: a monetary macroeconomics analysis', *Journal of Post Keynesian Economics*, **28**(4), 615–638.

Rochon, L.-P. and Rossi, S. (2006b), 'The monetary policy of the European Central Bank: does inflation targeting lead to a successful stabilisation policy?', in E. Hein, A. Heise and A. Truger (eds.), *European Economic Policies: Alternatives to Orthodox Analysis and Policy Concepts*, Marburg: Metropolis.

Rochon, L.-P. and Rossi, S. (eds.) (2016), *An Introduction to Macroeconomics: A Heterodox Approach to Economic Analysis*, 2nd edition, Cheltenham, UK: Edward Elgar Publishing, 2021.

Rochon, L.-P. and Rossi, S. (eds.) (2017a), *Advances in Endogenous Money Analysis*, Cheltenham, UK: Edward Elgar Publishing.

Rochon, L.-P. and Rossi, S. (eds.) (2017b), *A Modern Guide to Rethinking Economics*, Cheltenham, UK: Edward Elgar Publishing.

Rochon, L.-P. and Setterfield, M. (2007), 'Interest rates, income distribution and monetary dominance: post-Keynesians and the "fair rate" of interest', *Journal of Post Keynesian Economics*, **30**(1), 13–42.

Rochon, L.-P. and Vernengo, M. (2003), 'State money and the real world or: chartalism and its discontents', *Journal of Post Keynesian Economics*, **26**(1), 57–67.

Rogers, C. (2014), 'Why "state of the art" monetary theory was unable to anticipate the global financial crisis: a child's guide', *European Journal of Economics and Economic Policies: Intervention*, **11**(3), 300–314.

Rogers, C. (2018), 'The new macroeconomics has no clothes', *Review of Keynesian Economics*, **6**(1), 22–33.

Rolim, L.N. (2019), 'Overhead labour and feedback effects between capacity utilization and income distribution: estimations for the USA economy', *International Review of Applied Economics*, **33**(6), 756–773.

Romer, D. (2000), 'Keynesian macroeconomics without the LM curve', *Journal of Economic Perspectives*, **14**(2), 149–169.

Romer, P.M. (1986), 'Increasing returns and long-run growth', *Journal of Political Economy*, **94**(5), 1002–1037.

Roncaglia, A. (2009), *Piero Sraffa*, Basingstoke, UK: Palgrave Macmillan.

Rosenbaum, E. (2015), 'Zero growth and structural change in a Post Keynesian growth model', *Journal of Post Keynesian Economics,* **37**(4), 623–647.

Rowthorn, R.E. (1977), 'Conflict, inflation and money', *Cambridge Journal of Economics*, **1**(3), 215–239.

Rowthorn, R.E. (1981), 'Demand, real wages and economic growth', *Thames Papers in Political Economy*, Autumn, 1–39.

Rowthorn, R.E. (1995), 'Capital formation and unemployment', *Oxford Review of Economic Policy*, **11**(1), 26–39.

Rowthorn, R.E. (1999), 'Unemployment, wage bargaining and capital-labour substitution', *Cambridge Journal of Economics*, **23**(4), 413–425.

Ryoo, S. (2013a), 'The paradox of debt and Minsky's financial instability hypothesis', *Metroeconomica*, **64**(1), 1–24.

Ryoo, S. (2013b), 'Minsky cycles in Keynesian models of growth and distribution', *Review of Keynesian Economics*, **1**(1), 37–60.

Ryoo, S. (2016), 'Household debt and housing bubble: a Minskian approach to boom-bust cycles', *Journal of Evolutionary Economics*, **26**(5), 971–1006.

Ryoo, S. and Kim, Y.K. (2014), 'Income distribution, consumer debt and keeping up with the Joneses', *Metroeconomica*, **65**(4), 585–618.

Ryoo, S. and Skott, P. (2008), 'Financialization in Kaleckian economics with and without labor constraints', *European Journal of Economics and Economic Policies: Intervention*, **5**(2), 357–386.

Samuelson, P.A. (1939), 'Interactions between the multiplier analysis and the principle of acceleration', *Review of Economic Statistics*, **21**(2), 75–78.

Samuelson, P.A. and Solow, R.M. (1960), 'Analytical aspects of anti-inflation policy', *American Economic Review*, **50**(2), 177–194.

Sardoni, C. (1997), 'Keynes and Marx', in G.C. Harcourt and P. Riach (eds.), *A 'Second Edition' of the General Theory, Vol. II*, London: Routledge.

Sardoni, C. (2011), *Unemployment, Recession and Effective Demand: The Contributions of Marx, Keynes and Kalecki*, Cheltenham, UK: Edward Elgar Publishing.

Sawyer, M. (1985), *The Economics of Michal Kalecki*, Armonk, NY: M.E. Sharpe.

Sawyer, M. (2001a), 'Kalecki on money and finance', *European Journal of the History of Economic Thought*, **8**(4), 487–508.

Sawyer, M. (2001b), 'Kalecki on imperfect competition, inflation and money', *Cambridge Journal of Economics*, **25**(2), 245–261.

Sawyer, M. (2002), 'The NAIRU, aggregate demand and investment', *Metroeconomica*, **53**(1), 66–94.

Sawyer, M. (2003), 'Employer of last resort: could it deliver full employment and price stability?', *Journal of Economic Issues*, **37**(4), 881–907.

Sawyer, M. (2004), 'Employer of last resort: a response to my critics', *Journal of Economic Issues*, **38**(1), 256–264.

Sawyer, M. (2009a), 'Teaching macroeconomics when the endogeneity of money is taken seriously', in G. Fontana and M. Setterfield (eds.), *Macroeconomics and Macroeconomic Pedagogy*, Basingstoke, UK: Palgrave Macmillan.

Sawyer, M. (2009b), 'Fiscal and interest rate policies in the "new consensus" framework: a different perspective', *Journal of Post Keynesian Economics*, **31**(4), 549–565.

Sawyer, M. (2013), 'Alternative economic policies for the Economic and Monetary Union', *Contributions to Political Economy*, **32**(1), 11–27.

Sawyer, M (2013/14), 'What is financialization?', *International Journal of Political Economy*, **42**(4), 5–18.

Sawyer, M. (2016), 'Graziani's analysis of the circuit: does it extend to the era of financialisation?', *Review of Keynesian Economics*, **4**(3), 303–315.

Sawyer, M. (2017), 'Lessons on fiscal policy after the Global Financial Crisis', in P. Arestis and M. Sawyer (eds.), *Economic Policies since the Global Financial Crisis. International Papers in Political Economy*, Basingstoke, UK: Palgrave Macmillan.

Sawyer, M. (2020), 'Kalecki on budget deficits and the possibilities for full employment', *Review of Political Economy*, **32**(4), 548–562.

Sawyer, M. and Veronese Passarella, M. (2017), 'The monetary circuit in the age of financialisation: a stock-flow consistent model with a twofold banking sector', *Metroeconomcia*, **68**(2), 321–353.

Schefold, B. (1985), 'Ecological problems as a challenge to classical and Keynesian economics', *Metroeconomica,* **37**(1), 21–61.

Schulten, T. (2002), 'A European solidaristic wage policy?', *European Journal of Industrial Relations*, **8**(2), 173–196.

Schumpeter, J.A. (1954), *History of Economic Analysis*, New York: Oxford University Press.

Sebastiani, M. (1991), 'Observations on Marx's and Kalecki's approaches to the theory of effective demand', in G.A. Caravale (ed.), *Marx and Modern Economic Analysis, Vol. II,* Aldershot, UK: Edward Elgar Publishing.

Seccareccia, M. (1996), 'Post Keynesian fundism and monetary circulation', in G. Deleplace and E. Nell (eds.), *Money in Motion*, London: Macmillan.

Seccareccia, M. (2003), 'Pricing, investment and the financing of production within the framework of the monetary circuit: some preliminary evidence', in L.-P. Rochon and S. Rossi (eds.), *Modern Theories of Money*, Cheltenham, UK: Edward Elgar Publishing.

Seccareccia, M. and Lavoie, M. (2016), 'Income distribution, rentiers, and their role in a capitalist economy: a Keynes–Pasinetti perspective', *International Journal of Political Economy*, **45**(3), 200–223.

Seguino, S. (2010), 'Gender, distribution, and balance of payments constrained growth in developing countries', *Review of Political Economy*, **22**(3), 373–404.

Seguino, S. (2012), 'Macroeconomics, human development, and distribution', *Journal of Human Development and Capabilities: A Multi-Disciplinary Journal for People-Centered Development*, **13**(1), 59–81.

Seguino, S. (2019), 'Feminist and stratification theories' lessons from the crisis and their relevance for post-Keynesian theory', *European Journal of Economics and Economic Policies: Intervention*, **16**(2), 193–207.

Seguino, S. (2020), 'Engendering macroeconomic theory and policy', *Feminist Economics*, **26**(2), 27–61.

Seguino, S. and Braunstein, E. (2019), 'The cost of exclusion: gender job segregation, structural change and the labour share of income', *Development and Change*, **50**(4), 976–1008.

Seguino, S. and Sagrario Floro, M. (2003), 'Does gender have an effect on aggregate saving? An empirical analysis', *International Review of Applied Economics*, **17**(2), 147–166.

Sen, A. (1963), 'Neo-classical and neo-Keynesian theories of distribution', *Economic Record*, **39**(85), 53–64.

Serrano, F. (1995a), *The Sraffian Supermultiplier*, PhD thesis, University of Cambridge, UK, https://sites.google.com/site/biblioeconomicus/Serrano-Sraffiansupermultiplier.pdf.

Serrano, F. (1995b), 'Long-period effective demand and the Sraffian supermultiplier', *Contributions to Political Economy*, **14**(1), 67–90.

Setterfield, M. (2006), 'Is inflation targeting compatible with Post Keynesian economics?', *Journal of Post Keynesian Economics*, **28**(4), 653–671.

Setterfield, M. (2007a), 'The rise, decline and rise of incomes policies in the US during the post-war era: an institutional-analytical explanation of inflation and the functional distribution of income', *Journal of Institutional Economics*, **3**(2), 127–146.

Setterfield, M. (2007b), 'Is there a stabilizing role for fiscal policy in the new consensus?', *Review of Political Economy*, **19**(3), 405–418.

Setterfield, M. (2009a), 'Macroeconomics without the LM curve: an alternative view', *Cambridge Journal of Economics*, **33**(2), 273–293.

Setterfield, M. (2009b), 'Fiscal and monetary policy interactions: lessons for revising the EU Stability and Growth Pact', *Journal of Post Keynesian Economics*, **31**(4), 623–643.

Setterfield, M. (2011), 'The remarkable durability of Thirlwall's Law', *PSL Quarterly Review*, **64**(259), 393–427.

Setterfield, M. (2019), 'Time variation in the size of the multiplier: a Kalecki-Harrod approach', *Review of Keynesian Economics*, **7**(1), 28–42.

Setterfield, M. (2021), 'Whatever happened to the 'Goodwin Pattern'? Profit squeeze dynamics in the modern american labour market', *Review of Political Economy*, advance access, 1–24. doi:10.1080/09538259.2021.1921357.

Setterfield, M. and Kim, Y.K. (2016), 'Debt servicing, aggregate consumption, and growth', *Structural Change and Economic Dynamics*, **36**(1), 22–33.

Setterfield, M. and Kim, Y.K. (2017), 'Household borrowing and the possibility of "consumption-driven, profit-led growth"', *Review of Keynesian Economics*, **5**(1), 43–60.

Setterfield, M. and Lovejoy, T. (2006), 'Aspiration, bargaining power, and macroeconomic performance', *Journal of Post Keynesian Economics*, **29**(1), 117–148.

Setterfield, M., Kim, Y.K. and Rees, J. (2016), 'Inequality, debt servicing and the sustainability of steady state growth', *Review of Political Economy*, **28**(1), 45–63.

Shaikh, A. (1978a), 'An introduction to the history of crisis theories', in Union for Radical Political Economics (ed.), *US Capitalism in Crisis,* New York: Union for Radical Political Economics.

Shaikh, A. (1978b), 'Political economy and capitalism: notes on Dobb's theory of crisis', *Cambridge Journal of Economics*, **2**(2), 233–251.

Shaikh, A. (1987), 'The falling rate of profit and the economic crisis in the U.S.', in Union for Radical Political Economics (ed.), *The Imperiled Economy, Book I: Macroeconomics from a Left Perspective,* New York: Union for Radical Political Economics.

Shaikh, A. (2009), 'Economic policy in a growth context: a classical synthesis of Keynes and Harrod', *Metroeconomica*, **60**(3), 455–494.

Shaikh, A. (2011), 'The first great depression of the 21st century', *Socialist Register*, **47**, 44–63.

Shaikh, A. (2016), *Capitalism: Competition, Conflict, Crises*, Oxford: Oxford University Press.

Skidelsky, R. (1983), *John Maynard Keynes: Hopes Betrayed, 1883–1920, Vol. 1*, London: Macmillan.

Skidelsky, R. (1992), *John Maynard Keynes: The Economist as Saviour, 1920–1937, Vol. 2*, London: Macmillan.

Skidelsky, R. (2000), *John Maynard Keynes. Fighting for Britain, 1937–1946, Vol. 3*, London: Macmillan.

Skidelsky, R. (2003), *John Maynard Keynes, 1883–1946, Economist, Philosopher, Statesman*, London: Macmillan.

Skidelsky, R. (2009), *Keynes: The Return of the Master*, New York: Public Affairs Books.

Skott, P. (2005), 'Fairness as a source of hysteresis in employment and relative wages', *Journal of Economic Behavior and Organization*, **57**(3), 305–331.

Skott, P. (2010), 'Growth, instability and cycles: Harrodian and Kaleckian models of accumulation and income distribution', in M. Setterfield (ed.), *Handbook of Alternative Theories of Economic Growth*, Cheltenham, UK: Edward Elgar Publishing.

Skott, P. (2012), 'Theoretical and empirical shortcomings of the Kaleckian investment function', *Metroeconomica*, **63**(1), 109–138.

Skott, P. (2017), 'Autonomous demand and the Harrodian criticisms of Kaleckian models', *Metroeconomica*, **68**(1), 185–193.

Skott, P. (2019), 'Autonomous demand, Harrodian instability and the supply side', *Metroeconomica*, **70**(2), 233–246.

Skott, P. and Ryoo, S. (2008), 'Macroeconomic implications of financialization', *Cambridge Journal of Economics*, **32**(6), 827–862.

Smith, A. (1776), *An Inquiry into the Nature and Causes of the Wealth of Nations*, The Glasgow Edition of the Works and Correspondence of Adam Smith, edited by R.H. Campbell, A.S. Skinner and W.B. Todd, Oxford: Oxford University Press, 1976.

Smithin, J. (2002/3), 'Interest parity, purchasing power parity, "risk premia", and Post Keynesian economic analysis', *Journal of Post Keynesian Economics*, **25**(2), 219–235.

Smithin, J. (2004), 'Interest rate operating procedures and income distribution', in M. Lavoie and M. Seccareccia (eds.), *Central Banking in the Modern World: Alternative Perspectives*, Cheltenham, UK: Edward Elgar Publishing.

Smithin, J. (2007), 'A real interest rate rule for monetary policy?', *Journal of Post Keynesian Economics*, **30**(1), 101–118.

Smithin, J. (2009), 'Teaching the new consensus model of "modern monetary economics" from a critical perspective: pedagogical issues', in G. Fontana and M. Setterfield (eds.), *Macroeconomics and Macroeconomic Pedagogy*, Basingstoke, UK: Palgrave Macmillan.

Snippe, J. (1985), 'Finance, savings and investment in Keynes's economics', *Cambridge Journal of Economics*, **9**(3), 257–269.

Snowdon, B. and Vane, H. (2005), *Modern Macroeconomics: Its Origins, Development and Current State*, Cheltenham, UK: Edward Elgar Publishing.

Solow, R.M. (1956), 'A contribution to the theory of economic growth', *Quarterly Journal of Economics*, **70**(1), 65–94.

Soskice, D. (1990), 'Wage determination: the changing role of institutions in advanced industrialized countries', *Oxford Review of Economic Policy*, **6**(4), 36–61.

Sowell, T. (1972), *Say's Law: An Historical Analysis*, Princeton: Princeton University Press.

Sraffa, P. (1960), *Production of Commodities by Means of Commodities*, Cambridge, UK: Cambridge University Press.

Stanley, T.D. (2004), 'Does unemployment hysteresis falsify the natural rate hypothesis? A meta-regression analysis', *Journal of Economic Surveys*, **18**(4), 589–612.

Steindl, J. (1952), *Maturity and Stagnation in American Capitalism*, Oxford: Blackwell, second edition, New York and London: Monthly Review Press, 1976.

Steindl, J. (1976), 'Introduction', in J. Steindl (ed.), *Maturity and Stagnation in American Capitalism*, 2nd edition, New York, London: Monthly Review Press.

Steindl, J. (1979), 'Stagnation theory and stagnation policy', *Cambridge Journal of Economics*, **3**(1), 1–14.

Steindl, J. (1981), 'Some comments on the three versions of Kalecki's theory of the trade cycle', in J. Los et al. (eds.), *Studies in Economic Theory and Practice. Essays in Honour of Edward Lipinski*, Amsterdam: North-Holland, reprinted in J. Steindl (1990), *Economic Papers, 1941–1988*, Basingstoke, UK: Palgrave Macmillan.

Steindl, J. (1989), 'From stagnation in the 30s to slow growth in the 70s', in M. Berg (ed.), *Political Economy in the Twentieth Century*, Oxford: Philip Allan, reprinted in J. Steindl (1990), *Economic Papers, 1941–1988*, Basingstoke, UK: Palgrave Macmillan.

Stockhammer, E. (2004a), 'Explaining European unemployment: testing the NAIRU hypothesis and a Keynesian approach', *International Review of Applied Economics*, **18**(1), 3–24.

Stockhammer, E. (2004b), 'Is there an equilibrium rate of unemployment in the long run?', *Review of Political Economy*, **16**(1), 59–77.

Stockhammer, E. (2004c), 'Financialisation and the slowdown of accumulation', *Cambridge Journal of Economics*, **28**(5), 719–741.

Stockhammer, E. (2005/6), 'Shareholder value orientation and the investment-profit puzzle', *Journal of Post Keynesian Economics*, **28**(2), 193–215.

Stockhammer, E. (2008), 'Is the NAIRU a monetarist, new Keynesian, post Keynesian or Marxist theory?', *Metroeconomica*, **59**(4), 479–510.

Stockhammer, E. (2010), 'Income distribution, the finance-dominated accumulation regime, and the present crisis', in S. Dullien, E. Hein, A. Truger and T. van Treeck (eds.), *The World Economy in Crisis – the Return of Keynesianism?*, Marburg: Metropolis.

Stockhammer, E. (2011), 'The macroeconomics of unemployment', in E. Hein and E. Stockhammer (eds.), *A Modern Guide to Keynesian Macroeconomics and Economic Policies*, Cheltenham, UK: Edward Elgar Publishing.

Stockhammer, E. (2012), 'Financialization, income distribution and the crisis', *Investigación Económica*, **71**(279), 39–70.

Stockhammer, E. (2015), 'Rising inequality as a cause of the present crisis', *Cambridge Journal of Economics*, **39**(3), 935–958.

Stockhammer, E. (2017a), 'Wage-led versus profit-led demand: what have we learned? A Kaleckian-Minskyan view', *Review of Keynesian Economics*, **5**(1), 25–42.

Stockhammer, E. (2017b), 'Determinants of the wage share: a panel analysis of advanced and developing economies', *British Journal of Industrial Relations*, **55**(1), 3–33.

Stockhammer, E. (2022), 'Post-Keynesian macroeconomic foundations for comparative political economy', *Politics & Society*, **50**(1), 156–187.

Stockhammer, E. and Ali, S.M. (2018), 'Varieties of capitalism and post-Keynesian economics on Euro crisis', *Wirtschaft und Gesellschaft*, **44**(3), 349–370.

Stockhammer, E. and Klär, E. (2010), 'Capital accumulation, labour market institutions and unemployment in the medium run', *Cambridge Journal of Economics*, **35**(2), 437–457.

Stockhammer, E. and Michell, J. (2017), 'Pseudo-Goodwin cycles in a Minsky model', *Cambridge Journal of Economics*, **41**(1), 105–125.

Stockhammer, E. and Onaran, Ö. (2013), 'Wage-led growth: theory, evidence, policy', *Review of Keynesian Economics*, **1**(1), 61–78.

Stockhammer, E. and Ramskogler, P. (2009), 'Post-Keynesian economics – how to move forward', *European Journal of Economics and Economic Policies: Intervention*, **6**(2), 227–246.

Stockhammer, E. and Sturn, S. (2012), 'The impact of monetary policy on unemployment hysteresis', *Applied Economics*, **44**(21), 2743–2756.

Stockhammer, E. and Wildauer, R. (2016), 'Debt-driven growth? Wealth, distribution and demand in OECD countries', *Cambridge Journal of Economics*, **40**(6), 1609–1634.

Stockhammer, E. and Wildauer, R. (2018), 'Expenditure cascades, low interest rates or property booms? Determinants of household debt in OECD countries', *Review of Behavioural Economics*, **5**(2), 85–121.

Stockhammer, E., Onaran, Ö. and Ederer, S. (2009), 'Functional income distribution and aggregate demand in the Euro Area', *Cambridge Journal of Economics*, **33**(1), 139–159.

Stockhammer, E., Hein, E. and Grafl, L. (2011), 'Globalization and the effects of changes in functional income distribution on aggregate demand in Germany', *International Review of Applied Economics*, **25**(1), 1–23.

Stockhammer, E., Guschanski, A. and Köhler, K. (2014), 'Unemployment, capital accumulation and labour market institutions in the Great Recession', *European Journal of Economics and Economic Policies: Intervention*, **11**(2), 182–194.

Stockhammer, E., Durand, C. and List, L. (2016), 'European growth models and working class restructuring: an international post-Keynesian political economy perspective', *Environment and Planning A*, **48**(9), 1804–1828.

Stockhammer, E., Qazizada, W. and Gechert, S. (2019), 'Demand effects of fiscal policy since 2008', *Review of Keynesian Economics*, **7**(1), 57–74.

Storm, S. (2021), 'Cordon of conformity: why DSGE models are not the future of macroeconomics', *International Journal of Political Economy*, **50**(2), 77–98.

Storm, S. and Naastepad, C.W.M. (2011), 'The productivity and investment effects of wage-led growth', *International Journal of Labour Research*, **3**(2), 197–218.

Storm, S. and Naastepad, C.W.M. (2012), *Macroeconomics beyond the NAIRU*, Cambridge, MA, and London: Harvard University Press.

Storm, S. and Naastepad, C.W.M. (2015), 'Crisis and recovery in the German economy: the real lessons', *Structural Change and Economic Dynamics*, **32**(1), 11–24.

Streeck, W. (2016), 'Varieties of varieties: "VoC" and the growth models', *Politics & Society*, **44**(2), 243–247.

Strunk, B., Ederer, S. and Rezai, A. (2022), 'The role of labor in a socio-ecological transition: combining post-Keynesian and ecological economics perspectives', *European Journal of Economics and Economic Policies: Intervention*, **19**(1), 103–118.

Summers, L.A. (2014), 'U.S. economic prospects: secular stagnation, hysteresis, and the zero lower bound', *Business Economics*, **49**(2), 65–73.

Summers, L.A. (2015), 'Demand side secular stagnation', *American Economic Review: Papers and Proceedings*, **105**(5), 60–65.

Swan, T. (1956), 'Economic growth and capital accumulation', *Economic Record*, **32**(2), 334–361.

Sylos-Labini, P. (1979), 'Prices and income distribution in manufacturing industry', *Journal of Post Keynesian Economics*, **2**(1), 3–25.

Targetti, F. (1992), *Nicholas Kaldor: The Economics and Politics of Capitalism as a Dynamic System*, Oxford: Clarendon Press.

Taylor, L. (1991), *Income Distribution, Inflation, and Growth: Lectures on Structuralist Macroeconomic Theory*, Cambridge, MA, and London: MIT Press.

Taylor, L., Rezai, A. and Foley, D.K. (2016), 'An integrated approach to climate change, income distribution, employment, and economic growth', *Ecological Economics*, **121**, 196–205.

Tcherneva, P.R. (2006), 'Chartalism and the tax-driven approach', in P. Arestis and M. Sawyer (eds.), *A Handbook of Alternative Monetary Economics*, Cheltenham, UK: Edward Elgar Publishing.

Terzi, A. (1986), 'Finance, investment and saving: a comment on Asimakopulos', *Cambridge Journal of Economics*, **10**(1), 77–80.

Terzi, A. (1986/87), 'The independence of finance from saving: a flow-of-funds interpretation', *Journal of Post Keynesian Economics*, **9**(2), 188–197.

Teulings, C. and Baldwin, R. (eds.) (2014a), *Secular Stagnation: Facts, Causes and Cures. A VoxEU. org eBook*, London: Centre for Economic Policy Research (CEPR).

Teulings, C. and Baldwin, R. (2014b), 'Introduction', in C. Teulings and R. Baldwin (eds.), *Secular Stagnation: Facts, Causes and Cures. A VoxEU.org eBook*, London: Centre for Economic Policy Research (CEPR).

Theurl, S. and Tamesberger, D. (2021), 'Does a job guarantee pay off? The fiscal costs of fighting long-term unemployment in Austria', *European Journal of Economics and Economic Policies: Intervention*, **18**(3), 364–378.

Thirlwall, A.P. (1979), 'The balance of payments constraint as an explanation for international growth rate differences', *BNL Quarterly Review*, **32**(128), 45–53.

Thirlwall, A.P. (1987), *Nicholas Kaldor*, New York: New York University Press.

Thirlwall, A.P. (2002), *The Nature of Economic Growth*, Cheltenham, UK: Edward Elgar Publishing.

Thirlwall, A.P. (2011), 'Balance of payments constrained growth models: history and overview', *PSL Quarterly Review*, **64**(259), 307–351.

Thirlwall, A.P. (2013), *Economic Growth in an Open Economy: The Role of Structure and Demand*, Cheltenham, UK: Edward Elgar Publishing.

Thirlwall, A.P. (2019), 'Thoughts on balance-of-payments constrained growth after 40 years', *Review of Keynesian Economics*, **7**(4), 554–567.

Tily, G. (2007), *Keynes's General Theory, the Rate of Interest, and 'Keynesian Economics'*, Basingstoke, UK: Palgrave Mamillan.

Toporowski, J. (2013), *Michal Kalecki: An Intellectual Biography, Volume I: Rendezvous in Cambridge, 1899–1939*, Basingstoke, UK: Palgrave Macmillan.

Toporowski, J. (2018), *Michal Kalecki: An Intellectual Biography, Volume II: By Intellect Alone, 1939–1970*, Basingstoke, UK: Palgrave Macmillan.

Tori, D. and Onaran, Ö. (2017), 'The effects of financialisation and financial development on investment: evidence from firm-level data for Europe', Greenwich Papers in Political Economy, 16089, University of Greenwich: Greenwich Political Economy Research Centre.

Tori, D. and Onaran, Ö. (2018), 'The effects of financialisation on investment: evidence from firm-level data for the UK', *Cambridge Journal of Economics*, **42**(5), 1393–1416.

Traxler, F. (1999), 'Wage-setting institution and European Monetary Union', in G. Huemer, M. Mesch and F. Traxler (eds.), *The Role of Employer Associations and Labour Unions in the EMU*, Aldershot: Ashgate.

Traxler, F. and Kittel, B. (2000), 'The bargaining system and performance: a comparison of 18 OECD countries', *Comparative Political Studies*, **33**(9), 1154–1190.

Tridico, P. (2017), *Inequality in Financial Capitalism*, Abingdon, UK, and New York: Routledge.

Tymoigne, E. and Wray, L.R. (2014), *The Rise and Fall of Money Manager Capitalism: Minsky's Half Century from World War Two to the Great Recession*, London and New York: Routledge.

Tymoigne, E. and Wray, L.R. (2015), 'Modern money theory: a reply to Palley', *Review of Political Economy*, **27**(1), 24–44.

UN (2015), United Nations Climate Change: The Paris Agreement, https://unfccc.int/process-and -meetings/the-paris-agreement/the-paris-agreement.

UNCTAD (2009), *The Global Economic Crisis: Systemic Failures and Multilateral Remedies*, New York and Geneva: UNCTAD.

van der Zwan, N. (2014), 'Making sense of financialization', *Socio-Economic Review*, **12**(1), 99–129.

van Klaveren, M., Gregory, D. and Schulten, T. (eds.) (2015), *Minimum Wages, Collective Bargaining and Economic Development in Asia and Europe: A Labour Perspective*, Basingstoke, UK and New York: Palgrave Macmillan.

van Treeck, T. (2008), 'Reconsidering the investment-profit nexus in finance-led economies: an ARDL-based approach', *Metroeconomica*, **59**(3), 371–404.

van Treeck, T. (2009a), 'A synthetic stock-flow consistent macroeconomic model of financialisation', *Cambridge Journal of Economics*, **33**(3), 467–493.

van Treeck, T. (2009b), 'The political economy debate on "financialisation" – a macroeconomic perspective', *Review of International Political Economy*, **16**(5), 907–944.

van Treeck, T. (2014), 'Did inequality cause the US financial crisis?', *Journal of Economic Surveys*, **28**(3), 421–448.

van Treeck, T. (2015), 'Inequality, the crisis, and stagnation', *European Journal of Economics and Economic Policies: Intervention*, **12**(2), 158–169.

van Treeck, T. and Sturn, S. (2013), 'The role of income inequality as a cause of the Great Recession and global imbalances', in M. Lavoie and E. Stockhammer (eds.), *Wage-Led Growth: An Equitable Strategy for Economic Recovery*, London and Basingstoke, UK: Palgrave Macmillan.

van Treeck, T. and Sturn, S. (2012), 'Income inequality as a cause of the Great Recession? A survey of current debates', Conditions of Work and Employment Series No. 39, Geneva: ILO.

Vasudevan, R. (2017), 'Finance and distribution', *Review of Keynesian Economics*, **5**(1), 78–93.

Veblen, T. (1899), *The Theory of the Leisure Class*, London: Allen and Unwin, 1970.

Vera, L. (2014), 'The simple post-Keynesian monetary policy model: an open economy approach', *Review of Political Economy*, **26**(4), 526–548.

Vergeer, R. and Kleinknecht, A. (2010/11), 'The impact of labor market deregulation on productivity: a panel data analysis of 19 OECD countries (1960–2004)', *Journal of Post Keynesian Economics*, **33**(2), 369–405.

Vergeer, R. and Kleinknecht, A. (2012), 'Do flexible labor markets indeed reduce unemployment? A robustness check', *Review of Social Economy*, **70**(4), 451–467.

Vergeer, R. and Kleinknecht, A. (2014), 'Do labour market reforms reduce productivity growth? A panel analysis of 20 OECD countries (1960–2014)', *International Labour Review*, **153**(3), 365–393.

Vernengo, M. and Pérez Caldentey, E. (2020), 'Modern money theory (MMT) in the tropics: functional finance in developing countries', *Challenge: The Magazine of Economic Affairs*, **63**(6), 332–348.

Victor, P. (2008), *Managing without Growth: Slower by Design, Not Disaster*, Cheltenham, UK: Edward Elgar Publishing.

Victor, P. (2012), 'Growth, degrowth and climate change: a scenario analysis', *Ecological Economics*, **84**, 206–212.

Vieira Mandarino, G., Dos Santos, C.H. and Macedo e Silva, A.C. (2020), 'Workers' debt-financed consumption: a supermultiplier stock-flow consistent model', *Review of Keynesian Economics*, **8**(3), 339–364.

von Weizsäcker, C.C. and Krämer, H. (2021a), *Saving and Investment in the 21st Century: The Great Divergence*, Cham, Switzerland: Springer.

von Weizsäcker, C.C. and Krämer, H. (2021b), 'On capital, saving, and investment in the twenty-first century: a reply to Hein', *European Journal of Economics and Economic Policies: Intervention*, **18**(3), 303–309.

Walras, L. (1874/1954), *Elements of Pure Economics*, London: Allen and Unwin. English translation of the definitive French edition of Walras (1874) by W. Jaffe.

Walsh, C. (2002), 'Teaching inflation targeting: an analysis for intermediate macro', *Journal of Economic Education*, **33**(4), 333–346.

Westphal, U. (1994), *Makroökonomik: Theorie, Empirie und Politikanalyse*, 2nd edition, Berlin et al.: Springer.

Wicksell, K. (1893), *Über Wert, Kapital und Rente nach den neueren nationalökonomischen Theorien*, Jena: Gustav Fischer.

Wolfson, M.H. (1996), 'A post-Keynesian theory of credit rationing', *Journal of Post Keynesian Economics*, **18**(3), 443–470.

Wood, A. (1975), *A Theory of Profits*, Cambridge, UK: Cambridge University Press.

Woodford, M. (2003), *Interest and Prices: Foundations for a Theory of Monetary Policy*, Princeton and Oxford: Princeton University Press.

Woodford, M. (2009), 'Convergence in macroeconomics: elements of the new synthesis', *American Economic Journal: Macroeconomics*, **1**(1), 267–279.

Woodford, M. (2010), 'Financial intermediation and macroeconomic analysis', *Journal of Economic Perspectives*, **24**(4), 21–44.

Wray, L.R. (1988), 'Profit expectations and the investment-saving relation', *Journal of Post Keynesian Economics*, **11**(1), 131–147.

Wray, L.R. (1990), *Money and Credit in Capitalist Economies: The Endogenous Money Approach*, Aldershot, UK: Edward Elgar Publishing

Wray, L.R. (1992a), 'Alternative approaches to money and interest rates', *Journal of Economic Issues*, **26**(4), 1145–1178.

Wray, L.R. (1992b), 'Alternative theories of the rate of interest', *Cambridge Journal of Economics*, **16**(1), 69–89.

Wray, L.R. (1995), 'Keynesian monetary theory: liquidity preference or black box horizontalism', *Journal of Economic Issues*, **29**(1) 273–282.

Wray, L.R. (1998), *Understanding Modern Money: The Key to Full Employment and Price Stability*, Cheltenham, UK: Edward Elgar Publishing.

Wray, L.R. (2002), 'State money', *International Journal of Political Economy*, **32**(3), 23–40.

Wray, L.R. (2006), 'When are interest rates endogenous?', in M. Setterfield (ed.), *Complexity, Endogenous Money and Macroeconomic Theory*, Cheltenham, UK: Edward Elgar Publishing.

Wray, L.R. (2007), 'A Post Keynesian view of central bank independence, policy targets, and the rules versus discretion debate', *Journal of Post Keynesian Economics*, **30**(1), 119–141.

Wray, L.R. (2012), *Modern Money Theory: A Primer on Macroeconomics for Sovereign Monetary Systems*, Basingstoke, UK: Palgrave Macmillan.

Zezza, G. (2008), 'US growth, the housing market, and the distribution of income', *Journal of Post Keynesian Economics*, **30**(3), 375–401.

Zezza, G. and Zezza, F. (2019), 'On the design of empirical stock-flow consistent models', *European Journal of Economics and Economic Policies: Intervention*, **16**(1), 134–158.

Index

Note: Italic page numbers refer to figures and bold page numbers refer to tables; page numbers followed by "n" denote endnotes.